THE McGRAW-HILL
Dictionary
of
Misspelled
and
Easily
Confused
Words

CHOOSE THE RIGHT WORD AND SPELL IT CORRECTLY!

DAVID DOWNING AND DEBORAH K. WILLIAⱮ

McGraw·Hill

New York   Chicago   San Francisco   Lisbon   London   Madrid   Mexico (
Milan   New Delhi   San Juan   Seoul   Singapore   Sydney   Toronto

The McGraw·Hill Companies

Library of Congress Cataloging-in-Publication Data

The McGraw-Hill dictionary of misspelled and easily confused words / David Downing and
    Deborah K. Williams.
            p.   cm.
        "Originally published in two separate volumes as NTC's dictionary of American
    spelling and NTC's dictionary of easily confused words"—T.p. verso.
        ISBN 0-07-145985-5
        1. English language—United States—Orthography and spelling—Dictionaries.
    2. Spelling errors.   3. Americanisms—Dictionaries.   4. English language—
    Homonyms—Dictionaries.   5. English language—Paronyms—Dictionaries.
    I. Downing. David C.   II. Williams, Deborah K.   III. Downing, David C. NTC's
    dictionary of American spelling.   IV. Williams, Deborah K. NTC's dictionary of easily
    confused words.

    PE2817.M38   2006
    423'.1—dc22   2005057696

Originally published in two separate volumes as NTC's *Dictionary of American Spelling*
and NTC's *Dictionary of Easily Confused Words*.

1 2 3 4 5 6 7 8 9 0   FGR/FGR   0 9 8 7 6

ISBN 0-07-145985-5

McGraw-Hill books are available at special quantity discounts to use as premiums and
sales promotions, or for use in corporate training programs. For more information, please
write to the Director of Special Sales, Professional Publishing, McGraw-Hill, Two Penn
Plaza, New York, NY 10121-2298. Or contact your local bookstore.

This book is printed on acid-free paper.

Contents

Dictionary of
Easily Confused Words

Introduction

English is generously endowed with several types of easily confused words. Some of these words are homophones (*homo* 'same,' *phone* 'sound')—words that are pronounced alike but are different in spelling, meaning, or both. Examples of common homophones include *sail* and *sale; their, there,* and *they're;* and *knight* and *night.* Other easily confused words are troublesome because of the grammatical rules that govern their use. Unless one knows the rules that dictate which word should be used in a particular context, it is easy to misuse such pairs as *can* and *may; among* and *between;* and *shall* and *will.* Finally, some words are easily confused simply because they are easy to mix up. Such word pairs as *infer* and *imply; disinterested* and *uninterested;* and *flounder* and *founder* are often used incorrectly because they are similar in meaning and form yet have subtle differences in definition.

This book is an easy-to-use reference guide that will help the user understand confusing words and their usage and to then choose the correct spelling or meaning of a word for any given situation. The dictionary consists of word groups arranged alphabetically by the first word of each set. All sets of words are alphabetized internally as well. For example, *aisle—I'll—isle* is the full entry preceding *all—awl.* Cross-referencing permits the user to locate every word quickly and easily. Each word is followed by a pronunciation key in brackets, a concise definition, and a sentence example demonstrating how the word is used in everyday English. Hence, this dictionary enables the reader not only to find sets of easily confused words, but also to discover how the words are pronounced, what they mean, and how to use them in the written or spoken language.

This dictionary is designed to help speakers and writers master the confusing words in the English language. It will also pique (or is it *peak?*) interest in learning more about these pesky problem words.

Acknowledgments

I wish to thank all of my students—past, present, and future—not only for their contributions to this book, but also for making teaching the rewarding profession that it is.

I am also grateful to Jeanne Breaugh, Trudy Carpenter, John McAlear, and Linda Peckham for the support, enthusiasm, and expertise they offered me during this project.

A special thanks to Dr. Larry Standridge who piqued my interest in adult education and gave me yet another homophone.

And finally, I will always be grateful to my family for allowing me to make a dream come true.

Deborah K. Williams

Pronunciation Guide

Each word in the dictionary is followed by a phonetic transcription in the symbols of the International Phonetic Alphabet (IPA). The style of pronunciation reflected here is conversational or informal and is intended to help users *recognize* the word. The transcriptions distinguish between [a] and [ɔ] and between [w] and [ʍ] even though not all Americans do so. In strict IPA fashion, [j] rather than the [y] substitute is used for the initial sound in "yellow." The most prominent syllable in a multisyllabic word is *preceded* by a [ˈ].

The following chart shows the American English values for each of the IPA symbols used in the phonetic transcriptions. To use the chart, first find the large phonetic symbol whose value you want to determine. The three, simple English words to the right of the symbol contain examples of the sound for which the phonetic symbol stands. The letters in boldface type indicate where the sound in question is found in the English word.

Pronunciation Guide

[ɑ] { stop / top	[ɚ] { bird / turtle	[ŋ] { bring / thing	[u] { food / blue
[æ] { sat / track	[f] { feel / if	[o] { coat / wrote	[ʊ] { put / look
[ɑʊ] { cow / now	[g] { get / frog	[oɪ] { spoil / boy	[v] { save / van
[ɑɪ] { bite / my	[h] { hat / who	[ɔ] { caught / yawn	[w] { well / wind
[b] { beet / bubble	[i] { feet / leak	[p] { tip / pat	[ʌ] { wheel / while
[d] { dead / body	[ɪ] { bit / hiss	[r] { rat / berry	[z] { fuzzy / zoo
[ð] { that / those	[j] { yellow / you	[s] { sun / fast	[ʒ] { pleasure / treasure
[dʒ] { jail / judge	[k] { can / keep	[ʃ] { fish / sure	['] { 'water / ho'tel
[e] { date / sail	[l] { lawn / yellow	[t] { top / pot	
[ɛ] { get / set	[m] { family / slam	[tʃ] { cheese / pitcher	
[ə] { but / nut	[n] { new / funny	[θ] { thin / faith	

xii

A

a while—awhile

- **a while** [əˈʍɑɪl]   a short time. □ *It might be a while before he returns from his errand.*
- **awhile** [əʍɑɪl]   for a short time. □ *We will rest awhile before continuing our hike.*

acts—axe

- **acts** [ækts]   the plural of *act* 'a deed or an action.' □ *In the military, acts of heroism are recognized by the presentation of ribbons and medals.*
- **acts** [ækts]   the plural of *act* 'one of the main divisions of a musical comedy or a play.' □ *Each of the play's three acts ended with a dimming of the stage lights.*
- **acts** [ækts]   the present tense, third person singular of *act* 'to behave.' □ *Gregory acts quite differently at school than he does at home.*
- **ax(e)** [æks]   a hand-held chopping tool, similar to a hatchet. □ *One swing of the axe splintered the logs.*
- **ax(e)** [æks]   to ask something of someone. (An older, now dialect, form of *ask*. Not considered standard English. Spelling may vary.) □ *I want to axe you a question.* □ *Did you axe her yet?*

ad—add

- **ad** [æd]   an abbreviation of *advertisement* 'a notice of some type, usually published or broadcast.' □ *The ad for a part-time farmhand attracted several interested people.*
- **add** [æd]   to increase something in amount, number, or size. □ *Each year, I add several stamps to my collection.* □ *As a child, I found it easier to add than to subtract.*

add See the main entry beginning with *ad.*

addition—edition
- **addition** [ə'dɪʃn] a room or rooms built onto a house or other building. □ *Mr. Smith is building an addition on the back of his house.*
- **addition** [ə'dɪʃn] an increase. □ *The addition of two clerks in the office will lighten everyone's workload.*
- **edition** [ə'dɪʃn] a version of a published book or other document. □ *A later edition of a textbook usually contains some changes to the original.* □ *The morning edition of the newspaper reaches the newsstands very early in the day.*

adds—adze
- **adds** [ædz] the present tense, third person singular of *add* 'to increase the number, size, or amount of something.' □ *Tom usually adds too much salt to the soup.*
- **adze** [ædz] a sharp cutting tool with a curved blade. □ *An adze is one of the tools used by a ship's carpenter.*

adherence—adherents
- **adherence** [ədˈhɛɚ-ənts] a steadfast attachment to something. □ *Joe's strict adherence to high moral principles made him an excellent role model.*
- **adherents** [ədˈhɛɚ-ənts] the plural of *adherent* 'a person who follows or believes a certain doctrine, person, or plan.' □ *The adherents of the religious leader numbered in the tens of thousands.*

adherents See the main entry beginning with *adherence.*

adze See the main entry beginning with *adds.*

affect—effect
- **affect** [əˈfɛkt] to have an impression, influence, or effect on something. □ *Offers of athletic scholarships could affect Jim's decision on which college to attend.*
- **effect** [əˈfɛkt, ɛˈfɛkt] a result or consequence. □ *Some drugs have the effect of causing sleepiness.*

aid—aide
- **aid** [ed] assistance or help. □ *Several nations sent medical and financial aid to the war-torn country.*
- **aide** [ed] a person who acts as a helper or assistant. □ *A general's personal aide must be completely trustworthy.*

aide See the main entry beginning with *aid.*

ail—ale

- **ail** [el]   to be in ill health. ☐ *Many townspeople continued to ail long after the plague swept through their village.*
- **ale** [el]   an alcoholic beverage brewed from malt and hops. ☐ *The members of the wedding party raised their steins filled with ale and sang in unison.*

air—err—heir

- **air** [ɛɚ]   the compound of various gases and oxygen that we breathe. ☐ *On hot, still days the air above large cities is often filled with smog.*
- **air** [ɛɚ]   to broadcast or transmit something. ☐ *The network will air the television special on three consecutive evenings.*
- **air** [ɛɚ]   to expose something to the open air. ☐ *I need to air the sleeping bags before we use them again.*
- **air** [ɛɚ]   the demeanor or manner of a person. ☐ *He has an aristocratic air about him.*
- **err** [ɛɚ]   to make a mistake. ☐ *Sandy did not want to err on her first day on the job.*
- **heir** [ɛɚ]   a person who inherits something. ☐ *Charlie is the heir to his father's dry-cleaning business.*

aired—erred

- **aired** [ɛɚd]   the past tense and past participle of *air* 'to broadcast or transmit something.' ☐ *One of the news channels aired the conference.*
- **aired** [ɛɚd]   the past tense and past participle of *air* 'to expose something to the open air.' ☐ *After Susan aired the house, she closed all of the windows.*
- **erred** [ɚd, ɛɚd]   the past tense and past participle of *err* 'to make a mistake.' ☐ *Our accountant erred on a number of points when he figured our taxes last year.*

aisle—I'll—isle

- **aisle** [aɪl]   a passage or corridor, usually between rows of seats. ☐ *The wedding guests stood when the bride appeared at the head of the aisle.*
- **I'll** [aɪl]   the contraction of *I will* or *I shall.* ☐ *"I'll never pass this exam if I don't learn these equations," moaned Jane.*
- **isle** [aɪl]   a small island. ☐ *The author's dream is to live alone on a beautiful tropical isle.*

ale   See the main entry beginning with *ail.*

all—awl

- **all** [ɔl]   the whole of a number or quantity. ☐ *When making a* *difficult decision, try to consider all aspects of the problem.*

- **awl** [ɔl]   a sharp, pointed tool used to puncture or etch. □ *To create the fine details in her work, the artist used an awl.*

all ready—already

- **all ready** [ɔlˈrɛdi]   completely prepared. □ *When the runners were all ready, the starter fired his gun to begin the race.*
- **already** [ɔlˈrɛdi]   previously; beforehand. □ *Volunteer firemen were already at the scene of the blaze when the police and ambulances arrived.*

all together—altogether

- **all together** [ɔltəˈgɛðɚ]   united; gathered. □ *When I had my fabric all together, I began the tedious task of sewing.*
- **altogether** [ˈɔltəgɛðɚ]   thoroughly; totally. □ *We were altogether surprised when James showed up uninvited.*

all ways—always

- **all ways** [ˈɔlˈwez]   all of the ways. □ *We used a guidebook to study all ways of traveling across the country.*
- **always** [ˈɔwɪz]   without exception; at all times. □ *"Always check for traffic before crossing the street," Aunt Jane reminded him.*

allowed—aloud

- **allowed** [əˈlaʊd]   the past tense and past participle of *allow* 'to permit someone to do something.' □ *The child was never allowed to go outside of his fenced yard without one of his parents.*
- **aloud** [əˈlaʊd]   [speaking] audibly. □ *To help memorize his speech, the candidate rehearsed his message aloud in front of a mirror.*

allusion—elusion—illusion

- **allusion** [əˈluʒn]   an indirect reference to someone or something. □ *I caught the speaker's allusion to waste in government, but the rest of the speech was completely confusing to me.*
- **elusion** [əˈluʒn]   an evasion or escape. □ *His elusion of the uncomfortable situation was obvious.*
- **illusion** [ɪˈluʒn]   a misleading image; a mistaken assumption. □ *The magician is a master of illusion.* □ *I was under the illusion that the doctor was a licensed practitioner, but he was not.*
- **illusion** [ɪˈluʒn]   a fine, filmy transparent fabric. □ *The model's gown was made of ivory satin with an overlay of illusion.*

aloud　See the main entry beginning with *allowed.*

already　See the main entry beginning with *all ready.*

altar—alter
- **altar** [ˈɔltɚ]　a raised platform used in worship or ritual. □ *Each Sunday, vases of fresh flowers grace the altar of the church.*
- **alter** [ˈɔltɚ]　to change something; to make something different. □ *Pilots must sometimes alter their flight plans to avoid severe weather.*

alter　See the main entry beginning with *altar.*

altogether　See the main entry beginning with *all together.*

always　See the main entry beginning with *all ways.*

among—between
- **among** [əˈməŋ]　situated amidst more than two persons or things; in a grouping of more than two persons or things. □ *Among those three poets, Robert Frost is my favorite.*
- **between** [bɪˈtʍin]　adjacent to and separating two persons or things. □ *Mary stood between Tim and Paul.*
- **between** [bɪˈtʍin]　involving two persons, groups, or things. □ *A fight erupted between the two rival gangs.*

ant—aunt
- **ant** [ænt]　a type of tiny insect that lives in a colony and has a complex social system. □ *An ant crawled across my plate at the picnic.*
- **aunt** [ænt, ɑnt]　the sister of one's mother or father; the wife of one's uncle. (Black English and Boston English. The pronunciation [ɑnt] is Southern American English.) □ *My aunt is very proud of the roses in her garden.*

ante—anti—auntie
- **ante** [ˈænti]　a poker stake made to increase the pot. □ *The highest allowable ante in John's poker games is a nickel.*
- **ante** [ˈænti]　before something; in front of something. (A prefix.) □ *The anteroom of the convention hall serves as a foyer.*
- **anti** [ˈænti]　opposed to someone or something. (A prefix.) □ *Anti-war activists protested in front of the memorial all week.*
- **auntie** [ˈænti, ˈɑnti]　a diminutive of *aunt* 'the sister of one's mother or father.' (The pronunciation [ˈɑnti] is Southern American English.) □ *In the movie "The Wizard of Oz," Dorothy lived with her Auntie Em and Uncle Henry.*

anti   See the main entry beginning with *ante.*

any more—anymore
- **any more** [ɛni'mɔɚ]   some more. □ *Do you have any more time to donate?*
- **anymore** [ɛni'mɔɚ]   at the present time; nowadays. (Often viewed as incorrect if used in the affirmative.) □ *The girls do not sit next to each other in class anymore.*

anymore   See the main entry beginning with *any more.*

appraise—apprise
- **appraise** [ə'prez]   to establish the value of something. □ *We let a jeweler appraise the ruby.*
- **apprise [of]** [ə'praɪz]   to inform someone of something. □ *In the future, please apprise me of the problem earlier.*

apprise   See the main entry beginning with *appraise.*

arc—ark
- **arc** [aɚk]   an arch; a curve. □ *One seldom sees a rainbow's arc touching the horizon at both ends.*
- **ark** [aɚk]   a type of ship; the ship built by Noah in the biblical story found in Genesis. □ *According to the Bible, Noah led the animals aboard his ark two by two.*

ark   See the main entry beginning with *arc.*

ascent—assent
- **ascent** [ə'sɛnt]   the act of going up. □ *The ascent of a mountain is no less dangerous than the descent.*
- **ascent** [ə'sɛnt]   the amount of upward slope. □ *The angle of ascent was extremely steep.*
- **assent** [ə'sɛnt]   to agree with someone. □ *Judge Smith will assent with the other justices on all points except one.*

assent   See the main entry beginning with *ascent.*

assistance—assistants
- **assistance** [ə'sɪstɪnts]   help; support; aid. □ *Following World War II, the Civilian Conservation Corps (CCC) was a form of public assistance.*
- **assistants** [ə'sɪstɪnts]   the plural of *assistant* 'a helper; an aide.' □ *Although the office manager has several assistants, she prefers to do all of the typing herself.*

assistants   See the main entry beginning with *assistance.*

ate—eight

- **ate** [et]   the past tense of *eat* 'to take in food.' □ *After a very difficult practice, the rugby team ate ten large pizzas.*
- **ate** [et]   the past tense of *eat* 'to harrass someone; to bother someone.' □ *His intense feelings of guilt ate at his conscience.*
- **eight** [et]   the number between seven and nine. □ *A stop sign has eight sides.*

aught—ought

- **aught** [ɔt]   zero; nothing. □ *Phil always says aught when he reads a zero.* □ *John says his telephone number is two-two-three, aught-aught-four-one.*
- **ought** [ɔt]   to be obliged to do something. □ *"You ought to decline Bob's invitation before you accept Bill's," Mrs. Smith cautioned her daughter.*

aunt   See the main entry beginning with *ant.*

auntie   See the main entry beginning with *ante.*

awhile   See the main entry beginning with *a while.*

awl   See the main entry beginning with *all.*

axe   See the main entry beginning with *acts.*

aye—eye—I

- **aye** [aɪ]   yes. □ *"Aye, aye, captain," responded the ship's first mate.* □ *When the legislative vote was finally taken, the aye votes outnumbered the nays.*
- **eye** [aɪ]   the organ of sight. □ *The sight in her left eye was lost in an accident.*
- **eye** [aɪ]   the center of something. □ *Compared to the turbulent outer edges of a hurricane, the eye of the storm is calm.*
- **I** [aɪ]   the first person, singular pronoun. □ *"I can't find my favorite teddy bear," whined the sleepy child.*

B

bail—bale

- **bail** ['bel] the security money paid to ensure the appearance of a prisoner in court. ☐ *Generally, a higher bail is set for more serious crimes than for minor ones.*
- **bail** ['bel] to remove water from a vessel. ☐ *Before we can go fishing, we must bail out the boat.*
- **bale** ['bel] a large, closely pressed package of material. ☐ *For clean, comfortable dog bedding, nothing beats a fresh, dry bale of straw.*
- **bale** ['bel] evil or sorrow. ☐ *The poet often composed verses of intense bale when she was in a dark mood.*

bait—bate

- **bait** [bet] something used to entice or lure an animal or fish. ☐ *Fisherman often use minnows as bait.*
- **bait** [bet] to nag or tease someone. ☐ *Joan's brother is forever trying to bait her into an argument.*
- **bate** [bet] to decrease the intensity or force of something. ☐ *When angered, Fred always tries to bate his temper by counting to ten.*

bald—balled—bawled

- **bald** [bɔld] having no hair. ☐ *During the winter, the bald man wore a hat to keep his head warm.*
- **bald** [bɔld] bare or unadorned. ☐ *The Christmas tree appeared bald after we removed all the ornaments.*
- **bald** [bɔld] undisguised. ☐ *Her bald lie was immediately noted by everyone present.*
- **balled [up]** [bɔld] the past tense and past participle of *ball [up]* 'to form something into a tightly bound mass.' ☐ *Yards of*

bailer twine balled up inside the jammed machinery.
- **bawled** [bɔld] the past tense and past participle of *bawl* 'to cry out or wail loudly.' □ *During the weaning process, the young calf bawled mournfully for its mother.*

bale See the main entry beginning with *bail.*

balled See the main entry beginning with *bald.*

band—banned
- **band** [bænd] something that binds or restricts something. □ *A tight rubber band kept John's clock from falling apart.*
- **band** [bænd] a musical group. □ *The rock band has a contract to appear nightly at the club for an entire month.*
- **banned** [bænd] the past tense and past participle of *ban* 'to prohibit something.' □ *Some cities have banned smoking in public places due to a rising concern over the use and effects of tobacco products.*

banned See the main entry beginning with *band.*

bard—barred
- **bard** [baɚd] a composer, singer, or poet who related tales of heroes and their heroic deeds. □ *William Shakespeare is considered a bard of unsurpassed talents in English literature.*
- **barred** [baɚd] the past tense and past participle of *bar* 'to place something off limits.' □ *The public was barred from the courtroom proceedings for security reasons.*
- **barred** [baɚd] the past tense and past participle of *bar* 'to fasten with a bar so as to obstruct an entrance or exit.' □ *The doors of the abandoned house were barred and the windows boarded to prevent trespassing.*

bare—bear
- **bare** [bɛɚ] plain; unadorned; lacking covering. □ *Except for some cacti, the desert landscape was bare.*
- **bare** [bɛɚ] to reveal or uncover something. □ *"I swear I will never bare your secrets to a single soul!" exclaimed his confidante.*
- **bear** [bɛɚ] a large mammal belonging to the family Ursidae. □ *A bear may seem like an awkward animal, but it can move quickly when alarmed.*
- **bear** [bɛɚ] to carry someone or something; to support someone or something. □ *Mike is unable to bear much weight on his injured foot.*
- **bear** [bɛɚ] to endure someone or something. □ *I cannot bear to see violent movies.*

baron—barren
- **baron** ['bæɚən] a low-ranking nobleman in various European countries. □ *The woman hoped to marry a baron in order to gain some social standing.*
- **baron** ['bæɚən] a person of powerful influence in some field. □ *The oil baron invested a great deal of money in the project.*
- **barren** ['bæɚən] infertile. □ *Because his wife was barren and could give him no heirs, the king dismissed her.*
- **barren** ['bæɚən] bare. □ *The barren environment of the desert startled Mary, who grew up in the mountains.*

baroness—barrenness
- **baroness** ['bæɚənɛs] the wife or widow of a baron. □ *Contrary to her husband's naive nature, the baroness was a shrewd and cunning woman.*
- **barrenness** ['bæɚənɛs] the lack of productivity. □ *John was fired due to the barrenness of his work.*

barred See the main entry beginning with *bard.*

barren See the main entry beginning with *baron.*

barrenness See the main entry beginning with *baroness.*

base—bass
- **base** [bes] the lower part of something; the bottom and supporting part of something. □ *Standing at the base of the Statue of Liberty, one cannot help but be in awe of its immense size.*
- **base** [bes] a center of operations. □ *The army set up a temporary communications base in the empty warehouse.*
- **base [on]** [bes] to establish a foundation for an idea. □ *I will base my decision on many factors.*
- **bass** [bes] a musical instrument or a person's voice with a low pitch. □ *Debbie plays the bass in the school orchestra.* □ *The small chorus is composed of six sopranos, four altos, two tenors, and a single bass.*

bases—basis
- **bases** ['besɪz] the plural of *base* 'the bottom and supporting part of something.' □ *The bases of the fruit trees were wrapped in tape to prevent damage by small animals and insects.* □ *The bases of all of the stemmed goblets were broken in the dishwasher.*
- **bases** ['besɪz] the plural of *base* 'a center of operations.' □ *Military bases are located all around the country's borders.*
- **bases [on]** ['besɪz] the present tense, third person singular

of *base [on]* 'to establish a foundation for an idea.' □ *She almost always bases her opinions on hearsay.*

- **basis** ['besɪs] a concept on which a reasoned conclusion is based. (The plural is pronounced ['besiz].) □ *Three people will be indicted for the crime on the basis of the woman's testimony.*

basis See the main entry beginning with *bases.*

bass See the main entry beginning with *base.*

bate See the main entry beginning with *bait.*

bawled See the main entry beginning with *bald.*

bazaar—bizarre
- **bazaar** [bə'zɑɹ] a marketplace or fair for the sale of goods. □ *Multitudes of sights, sounds, and smells filled the bazaar in the village square.*
- **bizarre** [bɪ'zɑɹ] odd; eccentric; out of the ordinary. □ *The detective had a bizarre habit of inviting suspects to dinner.*

be—bee
- **be** [bi] to exist; to live; to occupy space or time. □ *We'll be grateful when winter ends and spring arrives.*
- **bee** [bi] an insect that feeds on pollen and produces honey. □ *A hive can have only one queen bee at a time.*
- **bee** [bi] a gathering for a specific purpose. (Typically a *spelling bee, quilting bee,* or a *[corn] husking bee.*) □ *The entire town turned out to watch the day-long spelling bee.*

beach—beech
- **beach** [bitʃ] a stretch of sandy or rocky area along a water's edge. □ *Such interesting creatures as hermit crabs, brittle stars, and jellyfish can be found on the beach after the tide recedes.*
- **beach** [bitʃ] to run a boat or ship onto the shore. □ *The sailors tried to beach their small vessel during the violent storm.*
- **beech** [bitʃ] a type of hardwood tree characterized by smooth gray bark. □ *The beech in our backyard produces an ample supply of nuts for the deer in winter.*

bear See the main entry beginning with *bare.*

beat—beet
- **beat** [bit] to hit someone or something. □ *I beat the rug in an effort to remove as much dust and dirt from it as possible.*
- **beat** [bit] to overcome someone or something; to defeat someone or something. □ *Our hometown football team is not likely*

to beat its arch rival.

- **beat** [bit]   an audible pulsation. ☐ *The drumbeat accompanied tribal members in their ceremonial dance.*
- **beet** [bit]   a garden vegetable with edible leaves and roots. ☐ *Mom's enormous beet won first prize at the state fair.*

beau—bow

(See also *bough—bow*.)

- **beau** [bo]   a boyfriend; a suitor. ☐ *The attention of each new beau only added to Rita's vanity.*
- **bow** [bo]   a ribbon tied in a decorative knot. ☐ *On his first birthday, the child was interested only in the bow on each present given to him.*
- **bow** [bo]   a stick equipped with stretched horsehairs, used to play stringed musical instruments. ☐ *While his violin is an antique, the bow used to play it is new.*
- **bow** [bo]   a curved piece of strong material strung with a cord and used to shoot arrows. ☐ *The bow and arrows were presented to the young hunter as a gift on his sixteenth birthday.*

beaut—butte

- **beaut** [bjut]   an abbreviation of *beauty* 'a beautiful person or thing.' (Slang. Used as an expression of admiration. Often used sarcastically.) ☐ *Your new car is a real beaut.* ☐ *"That black eye you have is a real beaut!" exclaimed Jeff.*
- **butte** [bjut]   a large, solitary hill with steep sides and a small, flat top. ☐ *From a distance, the butte appeared to be a rectangular box sitting on the horizon.*

bee   See the main entry beginning with *be*.

beech   See the main entry beginning with *beach*.

been—bin

- **been** [bɪn]   the past participle of *be* 'to exist.' ☐ *To have been able to sail around the world was, he felt, his greatest opportunity in life.*
- **bin** [bɪn]   a storage container. ☐ *At the end of the harvest, each bin was filled to capacity with corn.*

beer—bier

- **beer** [bɪɚ]   a fermented alcoholic beverage. ☐ *Brewers spend thousands of dollars each year advertising beer on T.V.*
- **bier** [bɪɚ]   a platform on which a corpse or a coffin is placed. ☐ *The body of the chief was set high on a bier in the wilderness.*

beet   See the main entry beginning with *beat*.

bell—belle

- **bell** [bɛl]   a hollow instrument that produces a ringing sound when struck. □ *Kathleen has a tiny glass bell and a huge antique school bell in her collection.*
- **belle** [bɛl]   an attractive, popular woman or girl. □ *Amy felt like the belle of the ball when she was asked to dance five times.*

belle   See the main entry beginning with *bell.*

berry—bury

- **berry** [ˈbɛɚi]   the small, sometimes edible fruit of various plants and shrubs. □ *The berry of the currant bush makes a tasty, tart jam.*
- **bury** [ˈbɛɚi]   to conceal something some place; to cover someone or something with earth. □ *To bury one's face in one's hands can be a sign of joy, grief, or disbelief.* □ *We were not permitted to bury our dog in the backyard.*

berth—birth

- **berth** [bɚθ]   a platform or bed on a train or ship. □ *My berth in the train's sleeping car was extremely small.*
- **berth** [bɚθ]   a place where a ship docks or anchors. □ *Huge oceangoing vessels require a large berth when in port.*
- **berth** [bɚθ]   a job. (Figurative.) □ *Although he had hoped to play in the major leagues, James eagerly accepted a berth in an amateur baseball club.*
- **birth** [bɚθ]   the process by which an offspring emerges from its mother. □ *The birth of a rare white tiger cub caused quite a stir at the zoo.*
- **birth** [bɚθ]   the beginning of something. □ *The birth of the space age spawned a flurry of activity among the world's highly developed nations.*

better—bettor

- **better** [ˈbɛtɚ]   superior, but not the best. □ *While Aaron was an excellent math student, his twin brother Alex was better in science.*
- **bettor** [ˈbɛtɚ]   a person who bets or gambles. □ *The bettor placed his chips nervously on the roulette table.*

bettor   See the main entry beginning with *better.*

between   See the main entry beginning with *among.*

bier   See the main entry beginning with *beer.*

billed—build

- **billed** [bɪld]   the past tense and past participle of *bill* 'to present a statement of charges.' □ *The telephone company incorporectly billed us for several long distance calls.*

- **build** [bɪld] to construct something. □ *In order to build a house on that piece of property, a building permit is required.*
- **build** [bɪld] to establish or increase something. □ *The seminar is designed to help people build self-esteem.*

bin See the main entry beginning with *been.*

birth See the main entry beginning with *berth.*

bizarre See the main entry beginning with *bazaar.*

blew—blue
- **blew** [blu] the past tense of *blow* 'to move something about with air.' □ *A warm, southerly wind gently blew the windsocks in the breeze.*
- **blew [about]** [blu] the past tense of *blow [about]* 'to boast or brag about someone or something.' □ *Jeff blew about even his minor accomplishments to anyone who would listen.*
- **blue** [blu] the color of a clear sky. □ *The clear, sparkling water surrounding the atoll was an amazing shade of deep blue.*
- **blue** [blu] depressed; low in spirit. □ *The death of her cat made Mary blue.*

bloc—block
- **bloc** [blɑk] a united group of people or countries acting together for a common purpose. □ *The bloc of coffee-producing nations opposed the trade embargo levied against one of its members.*
- **block** [blɑk] a solid piece of material with one or more flat surfaces. □ *Tim used a large block of wood to prop up the truck.*
- **block** [blɑk] to obstruct someone or something. □ *The iron gate serves to block any unwanted visitors.*
- **block** [blɑk] an obstacle. □ *The school board's refusal to give teachers dental insurance created a block in the negotiations.*
- **block** [blɑk] one of the parcels of land delineated by a grid of streets. (This refers to the square or rectangular parcels of land as well as the distance of one of the sides of the parcels.) □ *New sidewalks were installed around the entire block of our neighborhood.*

block See the main entry beginning with *bloc.*

blue See the main entry beginning with *blew.*

boar—boor—bore—Boer
- **boar** [bɔɚ] a male mammal of some species, usually the swine

family. ☐ *The hunters captured a wild boar in the woods.*
- **boor** [bʊɚ, bɔɚ] a rude, discourteous person. ☐ *The boor continually disrupted the meeting with his bad behavior.*
- **bore** [bɔɚ] to drill a hole in something. ☐ *Special metal drill bits are needed to bore through granite.*
- **bore** [bɔɚ] the hollow space in a gun barrel or an engine cylinder. ☐ *A bullet passes through the bore of a gun when the gun is fired.*
- **bore** [bɔɚ] to make someone uncomfortable or weary through inactivity or by something tedious. ☐ *Please do not bore us with all of the small details.*
- **Boer** [bɔɚ] a South African of Dutch or Huguenot descent. ☐ *No one but a Boer had been elected to office in many years.*

board—bored
- **board** [bɔɚd] a plank of wood. ☐ *Bill had some difficulty rounding a corner while carrying the long board beneath his arm.*
- **board** [bɔɚd] a game table. ☐ *The board used to play checkers can also be used to play chess.*
- **board** [bɔɚd] a group of governing officers. ☐ *The board of directors meets once a month on Tuesday evenings.*
- **board** [bɔɚd] to go onto a vessel. ☐ *No one is allowed to board the ship without first going through a security check.*
- **bored** [bɔɚd] the past tense and past participle of *bore* 'to make someone uncomfortable or weary through inactivity or by something tedious.' ☐ *After just five minutes with her new doll, the child was utterly bored.*

boarder—border
- **boarder** ['bɔɚdɚ] a person who rents a room, usually in a house or inn. ☐ *A private entrance is available for the boarder who lives in the upstairs apartment.*
- **border** ['bɔɚdɚ] a boundary; an edge. ☐ *The border of the natural bird sanctuary is posted with warning signs that read "Please Do Not Feed The Birds."*

Boer See the main entry beginning with *boar.*

bold—bowled
- **bold** [bold] unafraid in the face of danger. ☐ *Risk-takers tend to be bold in spirit.*
- **bold** [bold] impudent; presumptuous. ☐ *The girl rejected the advances of the bold young man.*
- **bold** [bold] standing out; prominent. ☐ *The new vocabulary words in each chapter are printed in bold type.*

- **bowled** [bold]   the past tense and past participle of *bowl* 'to roll a ball down a lane in the sport of bowling.' □ *Although an amateur, Rachel bowled three perfect games in the tournament.*
- **bowled [over]** [bold]   the past tense and past participle of *bowl [over]* 'to overwhelm someone with surprise.' □ *I was completely bowled over by his extreme generosity.*

bolder—boulder

- **bolder** ['boldɚ]   more fearless than someone or something else. □ *Sam's tiny chihuahua has always been bolder than his timid cat.*
- **boulder** ['boldɚ]   a large rock, usually detached from surrounding rocky masses. □ *The massive boulder that perched above the rustic cabin seemed threatening.*

boll—bowl

- **boll** [bol]   the pod of a cotton plant. □ *Not a single cotton plant showed signs of its boll being infested with weevils.*
- **bowl** [bol]   a rounded dish used for holding liquids and other food. □ *A festive bowl of fresh fruit served as the centerpiece on the table.*

boor   See the main entry beginning with *boar.*

border   See the main entry beginning with *boarder.*

bore   See the main entry beginning with *boar.*

bored   See the main entry beginning with *board.*

born—borne

- **born** [bɔɚn]   the past participle of *bear* 'to give birth to someone or some creature.' □ *Migratory animals have often born offspring under difficult conditions.*
- **borne** [bɔɚn]   the past participle of *bear* 'to carry or support someone or something.' □ *Our pack animals have borne heavy loads of materials on their backs.*
- **borne** [bɔɚn]   the past participle of *bear* 'to accept or assume something.' □ *Throughout history, great leaders have borne responsibility for their decisions and actions.*
- **borne** [bɔɚn]   the past participle of *bear* 'to produce or yield something.' □ *The newly developed plants have borne larger yields of fruits in shorter periods of time.*

borne   See the main entry beginning with *born.*

borough—burro—burrow

- **borough** ['bɝo]   a political division in an urban area. (Particularly in New York City, which has five boroughs.) □ *Mr.*

O'Leary was once a police officer in the borough of Queens in New York City.

- **burro** [ˈbɚo]   a donkey. □ *When one pictures a gold prospector in the western United States, one almost always imagines a burro as his trusty companion.*
- **burrow** [ˈbɚo]   a hole dug in the ground by an animal for living or hiding. □ *The burrow of a groundhog has at least two tunnels for entrance and escape.*
- **burrow** [ˈbɚo]   to excavate a hole or tunnel. □ *Many animals that hibernate for the winter burrow under woodpiles or rocks.*

bough—bow

(See also *beau—bow*.)

- **bough** [baʊ]   the limb of a tree. □ *During the violent thunderstorm, a large bough of the maple tree bent to the ground and snapped.*
- **bow** [baʊ]   to bend forward at the waist, usually as a sign of greeting or deference. □ *Gentlemen should always bow when introduced to Britain's queen, and ladies should always curtsey.*
- **bow** [baʊ]   the forward part of a ship. □ *The huge waves washed over the bow of the boat during the violent windstorm.*

bouillon—bullion

- **bouillon** [ˈbuljən]   a broth made from beef or chicken stock. □ *A cup of hot bouillon tastes good on a cold, wintry evening.*
- **bullion** [ˈbuljɑn]   gold or silver that has been formed into bars. □ *The buried pirate's chest was stuffed with gold bullion and precious gems.*

boulder   See the main entry beginning with *bolder*.

bow   See the main entry beginning with *beau* and the main entry beginning with *bough*.

bowl   See the main entry beginning with *boll*.

bowled   See the main entry beginning with *bold*.

boy—buoy

- **boy** [bɔɪ]   a male child. □ *In some cultures, boys are preferred over girls.*
- **buoy** [ˈbui]   a floating marker in a lake, river, or ocean. □ *When snorkeling or skin diving, a buoy should be anchored near the dive site to alert boaters to divers in the area.*
- **buoy** [ˈbui]   to support someone. □ *We tried to buoy his spirits by telling jokes.*

braid—brayed

- **braid** [bred]   a type of weaving using three or more strands of something, usually hair. □ *The French braid has gained popularity as both a casual and elegant hair fashion.*
- **braid** [bred]   to weave something into a braided pattern. □ *I do not have the patience to braid my daughter's hair every morning.*
- **brayed** [bred]   the past tense and past participle of *bray* 'to utter the loud, harsh sound of a donkey or mule.' □ *Each time visitors came near the donkey, it brayed loudly hoping for a carrot or sugar cube.*

braise—brays—braze

- **braise** [brez]   to prepare food in its own juices with very little water in a covered pot. □ *I prefer to braise my pot roasts in the oven rather than fix them in a pressure cooker.*
- **brays** [brez]   the plural of *bray* 'a loud, harsh sound, as that made by a donkey.' □ *The brays of discordant notes played by the unpracticed band was hardly music to the ears.*
- **brays** [brez]   the present tense, third person singular of *bray* 'to utter a loud, harsh sound, like that made by a donkey.' □ *The mule brays loudly each day around feeding time.*
- **braze** [brez]   to unite metal objects with solder. □ *Tom used solder to braze the broken hitch together.*

brake—break

- **brake** [brek]   to stop a vehicle. □ *He was not able to brake the car in time to avoid hitting the branch in the road.*
- **brake** [brek]   a device used to lock the wheels of a vehicle. □ *Do you always set the emergency brake on your car when parking on a hill?*
- **break** [brek]   to smash something; to separate something into parts, often by force. □ *If you step on that toy, it will surely break.*
- **break** [brek]   an intermission or recess from something. □ *We will take a break halfway through the class.*
- **break** [brek]   to violate or disregard a law, rule, or tradition. □ *If you break the law, you must pay the penalty for your wrongdoing.*

brayed   See the main entry beginning with *braid.*

brays   See the main entry beginning with *braise.*

braze   See the main entry beginning with *braise.*

breach—breech

- **breach** [britʃ] a violation or infraction of a law, norm, or obligation. ☐ *When he failed to live up to the terms of the agreement, the contractor was sued for breach of contract by his employees.*
- **breach** [britʃ] a break, hole, or gap in a structure. ☐ *The breach in the dam posed a serious threat to the safety of the village.*
- **breach** [britʃ] to leap out of the water. ☐ *No one knows for certain the reason whales breach.*
- **breech** [britʃ] the part of a firearm nearest the rear of the barrel. ☐ *The breech of the rifle was damaged when it fell against a rock.*

bread—bred

- **bread** [brɛd] a leavened food made of flour, liquid, and shortening. ☐ *Some bakeries sell only bread made with all natural ingredients and no preservatives.*
- **bread** [brɛd] money. (Slang.) ☐ *"I need some bread so I can take my girl to the movies," said Rusty.*
- **bred** [brɛd] the past tense and past participle of *breed* 'to mate so as to produce offspring.' ☐ *Mares are usually bred on a yearly basis to prevent barrenness.*

break See the main entry beginning with *brake.*

bred See the main entry beginning with *bread.*

breech See the main entry beginning with *breach.*

brewed—brood

- **brewed** [brud] the past tense and past participle of *brew* 'to create a beverage through steeping or fermentation.' ☐ *Mary always brewed a fresh pot of coffee first thing each morning.*
- **brewed [up]** [brud] the past tense and past participle of *brew [up]* 'to plot or contrive something.' ☐ *The thieves brewed up a plan to steal the valuable paintings.*
- **brood** [brud] the young offspring of an animal, particularly fowl. ☐ *The mother hen attentively hovered over her brood of chicks.*
- **brood** [brud] to worry. ☐ *Don't brood over past mistakes; try to avoid future ones.*

brews—bruise

- **brews** [bruz] the present tense, third person singular of *brew* 'to make a beverage by steeping or fermentation.' ☐ *Grandma always brews her herbal tea for exactly four minutes.*

- **brews** [bruz]   the present tense, third person singular of *brew* 'to form or develop.' ☐ *Trouble often brews when those two mischievous children get together.*
- **bruise** [bruz]   a discoloration of the skin. ☐ *The bruise on his arm changed colors before it healed completely.*
- **bruise** [bruz]   to inflict an injury or wound on someone. ☐ *Please do not bruise my ego further by criticizing my work.*

bridal—bridle

- **bridal** ['braɪdl]   having to do with a bride or a wedding. ☐ *Elaborate bridal shows seem to offer everything for the future bride except the groom.* ☐ *The bridal bouquet had roses and tulips in it.*
- **bridle** ['braɪdl]   the headgear worn by a horse by which the rider controls the animal. ☐ *Just before the race began, the jockey noticed his horse's bridle was broken.*
- **bridle** ['braɪdl]   to put headgear on a horse. ☐ *After you saddle and bridle the horse, lead it out to the paddock.*
- **bridle** ['braɪdl]   to curb or restrain someone or something. ☐ *"I wish I could bridle that child's energy," moaned the weary mother.*

bridle   See the main entry beginning with *bridal.*

broach—brooch

- **broach** [brotʃ]   a sharp, pointed tool. ☐ *When the whiskey is fully mature, a broach is used to tap the casks.*
- **broach** [brotʃ]   to open up a topic for discussion. ☐ *It is difficult to broach the subject of his deceased wife without Mr. Jones becoming upset.*
- **brooch** [brotʃ]   a large, decorative pin usually worn by women. ☐ *In old photographs, women are often seen wearing a brooch at the throat of their blouse.*

brooch   See the main entry beginning with *broach.*

brood   See the main entry beginning with *brewed.*

brows—browse

- **brows** [braʊz]   the plural of *brow* 'the forehead, eyebrow, or browridge.' ☐ *The brows of the committee members wrinkled in anger at the unexpected news.*
- **browse** [braʊz]   the young, tender plants or trees on which certain animals like to graze. ☐ *Deer browse often consists of acorns, beechnuts, and the young leaves of various plants.*
- **browse** [braʊz]   to leisurely gaze through, look over, or inspect something. ☐ *To browse casually through a large bookstore is*

one of life's small pleasures.

browse   See the main entry beginning with *brows.*

bruise   See the main entry beginning with *brews.*

build   See the main entry beginning with *billed.*

bullion   See the main entry beginning with *bouillon.*

buoy   See the main entry beginning with *boy.*

burley—burly
- **burley** ['bɚli]   a mild, air-cured tobacco grown primarily in Kentucky. ☐ *When traveling through the Kentucky countryside in late summer, one can see the open-sided sheds where burley ripens to its peak.*
- **burly** ['bɚli]   solidly and strongly built. ☐ *Despite his burly physique, Kent is extremely mild-mannered.*

burly   See the main entry beginning with *burley.*

burro   See the main entry beginning with *borough.*

burrow   See the main entry beginning with *borough.*

bury   See the main entry beginning with *berry.*

bus—buss
- **bus** [bəs]   a large, motorized vehicle usually used for public transportation. ☐ *Group travel by bus or motorcoach is extremely popular today.*
- **bus** [bəs]   to transport someone or something by bus. ☐ *In an effort to integrate their school district, the school board voted to bus students across town.*
- **bus** [bəs]   to tidy tables in a restaurant by clearing away dirty dishes and replacing them with clean ones. ☐ *When he learned that he would have to bus tables as well as wash dishes, Todd decided not to take the restaurant job.*
- **buss** [bəs]   a kiss. ☐ *The tourists were greeted at the airport in Hawaii with a flower lei and a buss on the cheek.*
- **buss** [bəs]   to kiss someone or something. ☐ *Bobby always squirms away from his great-aunt when she tries to buss him.*

buss   See the main entry beginning with *bus.*

bussed—bust
- **bussed** [bəst]   the past tense and past participle of *bus* 'to transport someone or something by bus.' ☐ *The stranded travelers were bussed to nearby motels to spend the evening.*

- **bussed** [bəst]   the past tense and past participle of *bus* 'to clear away dirty dishes and then replace them with clean ones in a restaurant.' □ *Cheryl collected the tips for the waiters as she bussed the tables.*
- **bussed** [bəst]   the past tense and past participle of *buss* 'to kiss someone.' (Slang or colloquial.) □ *The hostess bussed each of the departing dinner guests on the cheek.*
- **bust** [bəst]   a sculpture of the upper part of a human body. □ *A bust of William Shakespeare rests on a pedestal in a public garden in Stratford, Ontario.*
- **bust** [bəst]   the upper portion of a woman's body or the part of a woman's garment between the neck and waist. □ *While the rest of Sheila's gown fit perfectly, the bust was much too tight.*
- **bust** [bəst]   to break someone or something; to ruin someone or something. (Colloquial for *break*. Considered slang or non-standard for *burst*.) □ *Those poor management policies will eventually bust the corporation.*
- **bust** [bəst]   an arrest by the police; police intervention of a criminal activity. (Slang.) □ *The late-night bust of the night-club resulted in the arrest of several gambling suspects.*
- **bust** [bəst]   to hit or punch someone or something. (Slang.) □ *Stop making those ugly remarks or I'll bust you in the mouth.*

bust   See the main entry beginning with *bussed.*

but—butt
- **but** [bət]   except for someone or something; without someone or something. (A conjunction.) □ *The motorist knew the stretch of highway was heavily patrolled, but she continued to exceed the speed limit anyway.*
- **butt** [bət]   the buttocks of a person or animal. (Colloquial and sometimes considered rude.) □ *That type of injection is always given in the butt.*
- **butt** [bət]   to push or strike someone or something with the head or horns. □ *If you step into the pasture, the ornery ram might butt you.*
- **butt** [bət]   to fit or press something end to end; to fit tightly against something. □ *The pieces of wood must butt tightly in order to get a good fit.*

butt   See the main entry beginning with *but.*

butte   See the main entry beginning with *beaut.*

buy—by—bye
- **buy** [baɪ]   to purchase something; to hire or bribe someone,

usually by a payment of money. □ *I want to buy a new computer in the near future.* □ *My money will buy three hours of the plumber's time.*

- **buy** [baɪ]   a bargain; the purchase of something at a good price. □ *The lawn-care tools were priced so low that the gardener couldn't pass up such a good buy.*
- **by** [baɪ]   by means of someone or something; by way of something. □ *We will have to do it by hand.* □ *Ms. Smith seldom travels by highway if she can take a more scenic route.*
- **by** [baɪ]   past something. □ *My father drove right by me and didn't see me.*
- **by** [baɪ]   near or close to someone or something. □ *I left my glasses sitting by the telephone book.*
- **bye** [baɪ]   an abbreviation of good-bye. □ *Mary always says "bye" before hanging up the phone.*
- **bye** [baɪ]   a situation in a tournament or contest where a player or team has no opponent and advances to the next stage without playing. □ *Drawing a bye in the early rounds of the play-offs allowed the team more time to practice.*

by   See the main entry beginning with *buy.*

bye   See the main entry beginning with *buy.*

C

cache—cash

- **cache** [kæʃ]   a hiding place, often for food, fuel, or money; the contents of a hiding place. □ *Few people knew the location of the cache where the excess foodstuffs were stored.* □ *The cache of stolen money was hidden deep inside the cave.*
- **cash** [kæʃ]   bills or coins; money ready at hand. □ *Since I did not have enough cash to pay for my purchase, I had to charge it on my credit card.* □ *John paid cash for his groceries because there was not much money in his checking account.*
- **cash** [kæʃ]   to exchange a check or bill for cash. □ *You may cash your paycheck at the grocery store if it doesn't exceed $300.00.*

caddie—caddy

- **caddie** ['kædi]   a wheeled cart used to transport objects. □ *The movers used a caddie to take the refrigerator from the house to the moving van.*
- **caddie** AND **caddy** ['kædi]   a person who carries clubs and balls for a golfer. □ *Tom has spent the past three summers working as a caddie at the local golf course.* □ *The caddy could not find Bill's ball.*
- **caddy** ['kædi]   a small box or container for storing things. □ *Tea bags remain fresh longer if kept in an airtight caddy.*

caddy   See the main entry beginning with *caddie.*

callous—callus

- **callous** ['kæləs]   hardened. □ *Bill developed a callous growth of skin on his thumb from many years of sorting mail.*
- **callous** ['kæləs]   devoid of feelings; not caring. □ *While the*

tough-minded businesswoman appears to be very callous toward her employees, she is actually kind and considerate.
- **callus** ['kæləs]   a hardened or thickened part of the skin. □ *Mary developed a callus on each heel.*

callus   See the main entry beginning with *callous.*

can—may
- **can** [kæn]   to be capable of or know how to do something. □ *I can find my way around New York City without trouble.*
- **may** [me]   to have permission to do something. □ *You may go to a movie after your chores are done.*

cannon—canon
- **cannon** ['kænən]   a large artillery gun that shoots lead balls or explosive shells. □ *The large cannon on the courthouse lawn gives a certain ambiance to the village square.*
- **canon** ['kænən]   a rule or law of a church or religion. □ *The priest explained the purpose of each canon of the Catholic church to the children.*
- **canon** ['kænən]   a generally accepted standard or principle. □ *An unspoken canon in retail business is that the customer is always right.*
- **canon** ['kænən]   a musical piece of several parts in which the melody is precisely imitated by successive voices or instruments. □ *The group of children sang the old canon "Row, Row, Row Your Boat" with much enthusiasm.*

canon   See the main entry beginning with *cannon.*

cant—can't
- **cant** [kænt]   the angle or slant of something. □ *The cant of the new roof is not steep enough to shed rainwater.*
- **cant** [kænt]   to lean or slope to the side. □ *That sculpture was designed to cant to one side to give it an unusual appearance.*
- **cant** [kænt]   words spoken in a sing-song manner. □ *The beggar's cant was almost unintelligible.*
- **can't** [kænt]   a contraction of *cannot* 'unable to do something.' □ *If you can't finish your term paper on time, ask your instructor for an extension.*

can't   See the main entry beginning with *cant.*

canter—cantor
- **canter** ['kæntɚ]   a horse's gait somewhere between a trot and a gallop. □ *Some riders prefer the smooth movement of a canter to a jerky trot.*

- **cantor** ['kæntɚ] an official of a synagogue who sings or chants prayer. □ *The cantor at our synagogue has a wonderful voice.*

cantor See the main entry beginning with *canter.*

canvas—canvass

- **canvas** ['kænvɪs] a closely woven cloth made of cotton or linen, often used for clothing, ships' sails, and oil paintings. □ *Nowadays racing boats use a lightweight fabric for their sails instead of canvas.*
- **canvass** ['kænvɪs] to travel through voting districts in an effort to gain information or support for political candidates and issues. □ *We will canvass our neighborhood to gain support for our candidate.*

canvass See the main entry beginning with *canvas.*

capital—capitol—Capitol

- **capital** ['kæpɪtl] punishable by death. □ *Murder in the first degree is a capital offense in several states.*
- **capital** ['kæpɪtl] principal; main. □ *Our capital concern was the welfare of the children.*
- **capital** ['kæpɪtl] a city that serves as a seat of government. □ *The capital of a state is not necessarily the state's largest city.*
- **capital** ['kæpɪtl] accumulated money or property. □ *Before he could start a business, Martin had to raise capital to finance the venture.*
- **capitol** ['kæpɪtl] the building in which the legislature of a state meets. □ *The capitol of Michigan was designed by the same architect who designed the Texas capitol.*
- **Capitol** ['kæpɪtl] the building in Washington, D.C., where the United States Congress meets. □ *The U.S. Capitol is located on First Street between Constitution and Independence avenues.*

capitol See the main entry beginning with *capital.*

Capitol See the main entry beginning with *capital.*

carat—caret—carrot—karat

- **carat** AND **karat** ['kæɚət, 'kɛɚət] a measurement of weight for precious stones. (*Carat* is the most common form.) □ *Her diamond engagement ring contained a single marquise-shaped stone weighing less than a carat.*
- **caret** ['kæɚət, 'kɛɚət] a V-like symbol pointing to where something is to be inserted into a line of writing or print. □ *The proofreader used a caret to show where Pamela had omitted a word in the sentence.*

- **carrot** [ˈkæɚ-ət, ˈkɛɚ-ət]   a common garden vegetable having an edible orange root. ☐ *Put a carrot or two in the stew to add both flavor and color.*
- **carrot** [ˈkæɚ-ət, ˈkɛɚ-ət]   a promised but often deceptive reward or advantage. (From the image of a carrot tied to the end of a stick and held out in front of a horse, causing it to move forward in hopes of getting to eat the carrot.) ☐ *To inspire Austin to earn all A's on his report card, his parents coaxed him with a carrot of box seats to the Pirate's opening day game.*
- **karat** [ˈkæɚ-ət, ˈkɛɚ-ət]   a unit of pureness of gold in an alloy. ☐ *What karat is the gold in your wedding ring?*

caret   See the main entry beginning with *carat.*

carol—carrel

- **carol** [ˈkæɚ-əl, ˈkɛɚ-əl]   a song usually associated with the Christmas season. ☐ *Their favorite holiday carol is* "God Rest Ye Merry Gentlemen."
- **carrel** [ˈkæɚ-əl, ˈkɛɚ-əl]   a small, three-sided, desklike enclosure usually found in libraries and other study areas. ☐ *Food, drink, and portable radios are not permitted in any study carrel.*

carrel   See the main entry beginning with *carol.*

carrot   See the main entry beginning with *carat.*

cash   See the main entry beginning with *cache.*

cast—caste

- **cast** [kæst]   to throw someone or something. (Usually with an adverb, such as *away, out,* or *off.*) ☐ *The sailor cast the rope around the piling on the dock.*
- **cast** [kæst]   to assign roles or parts in a production. ☐ *The director cast an unknown actress in the movie's lead role.*
- **cast** [kæst]   to form something in a mold. ☐ *The sculptor cast the statue in bronze.*
- **cast** [kæst]   to direct one's sight onto something. ☐ *As Tommy cast his eyes on his new birthday pony, he became very excited.*
- **caste** [kæst]   a social rank usually based on birth, wealth, or occupation. ☐ *In some societies, individuals are prohibited from moving out of the caste into which they were born.*

caste   See the main entry beginning with *cast.*

cedar—seeder

- **cedar** [ˈsidɚ]   a type of coniferous tree known for its sturdy, aromatic wood. ☐ *The craftsman carefully lined the drawers of the chest with fragrant cedar.*

- **seeder** ['sidɚ] a farm or garden implement used to plant seeds. □ *Planting corn is much easier with the help of a seeder.*

cede—seed

- **cede** [sid] to yield, withdraw, or grant something, usually by a formal treaty. □ *The terms of the cease-fire included an agreement by the defeated country to cede the disputed strip of land to the victors.*
- **seed** [sid] the ripened germ of a plant. □ *The seed sent up a tiny shoot only a week after it was planted.*
- **seed** [sid] to plant or sow seeds. □ *If we seed the lawn just before a rain, the grass has a better chance of taking hold.*

ceiling—sealing

- **ceiling** ['silŋ] the top of a room. □ *A vast mural covers the ceiling of the art room.* □ *Her ceiling consists of a swirled plaster stucco.*
- **ceiling** ['silŋ] the above-ground height of the lowest layer of cloud cover. □ *We delayed our flying lesson yesterday due to the extremely low ceiling.*
- **sealing** ['silŋ] the present participle of *seal* 'to fasten something with something that must be broken to gain access.' □ *After sealing the envelope, Mary placed it in the mailbox.*

cell—sell

- **cell** [sɛl] a small, lockable room or compartment. □ *The prisoner's cell had none of the comforts of home.*
- **cell** [sɛl] a small, microscopic unit of living matter. □ *Each student looked at his or her own skin cell under the microscope.*
- **cell** [sɛl] the smallest basic unit of an organization. □ *The cell of the secret underground group consisted of only four members.*
- **sell** [sɛl] to offer something for sale; to exchange something for money. □ *Tom hopes to sell his old car some day soon.* □ *The spy was willing to sell government security secrets in exchange for a large sum of money.*

cellar—seller

- **cellar** ['sɛlɚ] a basement or underground storeroom. □ *The cellar is nothing but a cold, damp, and unused area of the house.*
- **seller** ['sɛlɚ] a person who offers something for sale. □ *The young seller of the baseball card collection was reluctant to part with his treasures.*

censer—censor—censure—sensor

- **censer** ['sɛnsɚ] a container used to burn incense. □ *A pleasant fragrance floated from the censer.*
- **censor** ['sɛnsɚ] a person who examines published or distributed material and makes recommendations for the deletion of objectionable matter. □ *The censor suggested that some of the dialogue be removed from the author's latest novel.*
- **censor** ['sɛnsɚ] to examine published or distributed material with a view to removing objectionable material. □ *The director of the film knew that the commission would censor her work mercilessly.*
- **censure** ['sɛnʃɚ] [for a legislative body] to reprimand one of its members. □ *The legislature voted to censure its most notorious member.*
- **sensor** ['sɛnsɚ] a device that senses movement, light, or heat and reacts to it in some way. □ *A smoke detector contains a sensor that reacts quickly and noisily to both smoke and heat.*

censor See the main entry beginning with *censer.*

censure See the main entry beginning with *censer.*

census—senses

- **census** ['sɛnsəs] a periodic counting of the population by the government. (This is done every ten years in the United States.) □ *The most recent census showed a sizable shift of people from the Midwestern states to the coastal regions.*
- **senses** ['sɛnsəz] the plural of *sense* 'an ability to perceive sound, sight, touch, smell, and taste.' □ *The senses of sight and hearing usually diminish with age.*
- **senses** ['sɛnsəz] a mental state where one is logical or reasonable. □ *I hope Elaine comes to her senses before she does something she'll regret later.*
- **senses** ['sɛnsəz] the present tense, third person singular of *sense* 'to have a feeling or sensation.' □ *Doug often senses when his daughter is upset.*

cent—scent—sent

- **cent** [sɛnt] one penny; one-hundredth of a dollar. □ *"You won't get a cent from me," yelled the angry customer.*
- **scent** [sɛnt] a smell; an odor. □ *The wonderful scent of lilacs was everywhere.* □ *Our dog easily picked up the scent of the quail on the damp ground.*

- **sent** [sɛnt]   the past tense and past participle of *send* 'to cause someone or something to go somewhere.' □ *We sent the courier to deliver the message.* □ *The fast-breaking news story was sent through the wire services.*

cents—scents—sense
- **cents** [sɛnts]   the plural of *cent* 'one penny; one one-hundredth of a dollar.' □ *Items that once cost a few cents now cost a few dollars.*
- **scents** [sɛnts]   the plural of *scent* 'a smell; an odor.' □ *The combination of scents from the different foods was almost sickening.*
- **sense** [sɛnts]   a feeling or sensation. □ *We had a definite sense of uneasiness as we approached the dimly lit house.*

cereal—serial
- **cereal** ['sɪɚ·iəl]   a food made of grain and eaten for breakfast. □ *The price of cereal in the supermarket has risen dramatically in the past two years.*
- **serial** ['sɪɚ·iəl]   in or of a series, rank, or order. □ *A new automobile is stamped with a serial number to aid in identification.*
- **serial** ['sɪɚ·iəl]   a publication or program offered in segments at intervals. □ *The new book will appear, in part, as a monthly serial in that magazine.*

cession—session
- **cession** ['sɛʃn]   a concession, withdrawal, or yielding to something else. □ *The large cession of land was welcomed by the county that received it.*
- **session** ['sɛʃn]   a meeting for the purpose of transacting business. □ *The collective bargaining session lasted into the wee hours of the night.*
- **session** ['sɛʃn]   the set period of time in which a legislative body meets before adjournment. □ *Congress will not be in session again until after the holidays.*

chance—chants
- **chance** [tʃænts]   a possibility. □ *There is a chance that it will rain tomorrow.*
- **chance** [tʃænts]   an opportunity. □ *Next summer, the Boy Scout troop will have the chance to camp on a very remote island.*
- **chance** [tʃænts]   by coincidence or accident. □ *Quite by chance I saw a former classmate at the bus depot.*
- **chants** [tʃænts]   the plural of *chant* 'a song or statement, sung or spoken in a monotonous tone of voice.' □ *The loud*

chants of the protestors could be heard for several city blocks.

chants See the main entry beginning with *chance.*

chased—chaste

- **chased** [tʃest] the past tense and past participle of *chase* 'to pursue or follow someone or something quickly.' □ *The hounds and hunters chased the fox over miles of countryside.*
- **chaste** [tʃest] pure; virginal; unblemished. □ *Monks are expected to be chaste in thought, word, and deed.*

chaste See the main entry beginning with *chased.*

cheap—cheep

- **cheap** [tʃip] inexpensive; not costly. □ *The garment is made of cheap fabric.*
- **cheap** [tʃip] contemptible or unworthy. □ *The unkind remark was a cheap attempt to embarrass him.*
- **cheep** [tʃip] a faint, shrill sound, often associated with birds and fowl. □ *The cheep of the newly hatched robin brought its parents to its side immediately.*

cheep See the main entry beginning with *cheap.*

chews—choose

- **chews** [tʃuz] the present tense, third person singular of *chew* 'to grind or crush something with the teeth.' □ *Because she chews gum in her classroom, the business teacher allows her students to chew it also.*
- **choose** [tʃuz] to select; to prefer something from among alternatives. □ *I usually choose fish or chicken when dining at restaurants.*

chic—sheik

- **chic** [ʃik] elegant; stylish. (Fashion.) □ *Why don't ordinary people look as chic wearing the latest styles as fashion models do?*
- **sheik** [ʃik, ʃek] an Arab chief. □ *A sheik owns the three new luxury car dealerships in Phoenix.*

Chile—chili—chilly

- **Chile** ['tʃɪle, 'tʃɪli] a country in South America. □ *Chile is right next to Argentina.*
- **chili** ['tʃɪli] a hot, spicy traditional Mexican dish consisting of meat, beans, tomatoes, peppers, and spices. □ *If you're going to eat spicy chili, be prepared for the results.*
- **chili** ['tʃɪli] a hot, sweet pepper. □ *I added a chili to the nachos to give them more flavor.*

- **chilly** ['tʃɪli]   cool; cold. □ *The damp, chilly weather made us shiver.*
- **chilly** ['tʃɪli]   lacking warmth of feeling. □ *Each political opponent gave the other a chilly stare.*

chili   See the main entry beginning with *Chile.*

chilly   See the main entry beginning with *Chile.*

choler—collar

- **choler** ['kɑlɚ]   anger; temper. □ *She was a woman of high choler.*
- **collar** ['kɑlɚ]   a chain or strap worn about the neck. □ *The dog's license, rabies tag, and I.D. are attached to its collar.*
- **collar** ['kɑlɚ]   the neckpiece of a garment. □ *The collar on his shirt was frayed from wear.*
- **collar** ['kɑlɚ]   to capture someone or something. (Slang.) □ *The policemen hope to collar the suspect as soon as possible.*

choose   See the main entry beginning with *chews.*

chorale—coral—corral

- **chorale** [kɔɚˈæl]   a chorus. □ *Joe belongs to the university men's chorale.*
- **coral** ['kɔrəl]   deep pink. □ *Her flowers were red and coral and complemented her gown perfectly.*
- **coral** ['kɔrəl]   the limestone skeletal structures that support various species of marine polyps. □ *They love to go to the warm waters and snorkel amidst the coral reefs.*
- **corral** [kɔɚˈæl]   a fenced enclosure for keeping livestock. □ *Those horses in the corral belong to a riding stable.*
- **corral** [kɔɚˈæl]   to gather, capture, or confine. □ *I tried to corral the escaped geese by shooing them into a corner of the yard.*

chord—cord

- **chord** [kɔɚd]   a harmonious blend of tones. □ *That chord is a difficult one to play on a twelve-string guitar.*
- **chord** [kɔɚd]   a straight line connecting two points on a curve. □ *The geometery instructor asked his class to accurately measure the chord of the circle.*
- **cord** [kɔɚd]   a strong string or rope woven of several strands. □ *Sam's puppy is tied to the clothesline with a cord.*
- **cord** [kɔɚd]   a tubular or ropelike structure. □ *The baby's umbilical cord was wrapped around its neck at birth.*
- **cord** [kɔɚd]   a stack of firewood measuring 4' × 4' × 8'. □ *I was tired and thirsty after stacking the cord of wood in the barn.*

- **cord** [kɔɚd]   a fabric with raised rows of material. □ *Our home economics teacher suggested using a sturdy fabric such as twill, cord, or denim for our project.*

chute—shoot

- **chute** [ʃut]   a sloped passageway through which things may be sent. □ *A clothes chute leading from the bathroom to the basement is very convenient.*
- **chute** [ʃut]   a parachute. (Slang or colloquial.) □ *Tom has to pack his own chute when he goes skydiving.*
- **shoot** [ʃut]   to discharge a gun or other weapon at someone or something. □ *Before you shoot the rifle, make certain you have a clear line of fire.*
- **shoot** [ʃut]   to discharge a gun at someone; to release an arrow at someone. □ *"Please do not shoot me!" begged the clerk.*
- **shoot** [ʃut]   to photograph someone or something. □ *The film company making the movie will shoot some scenes along the waterfront.*
- **shoot** [ʃut]   a small sprout of new plant growth. □ *Warm sunshine and plenty of water will enable the shoot to grow quickly.*

cite—sight—site

- **cite** [saɪt]   to order someone to appear in court. □ *If you get caught speeding, the officer may cite you for a moving violation.*
- **cite** [saɪt]   to quote something from a published source. □ *Her attorney will cite a little-known law when presenting her defense.*
- **cite** [saɪt]   to recognize someone in commendation. □ *During his speech, the speaker will cite the award winner's many accomplishments.*
- **sight** [saɪt]   the ability to see. □ *The child's sight improved greatly following eye surgery.*
- **sight** [saɪt]   a view or glimpse. □ *The Grand Canyon is a magnificent sight.*
- **site** [saɪt]   a position, place, or scene of something such as a town or building. □ *The site for the new veterans memorial has not been decided.*

clause—claws

- **clause** [klɔz]   a group of words containing a subject and a verb, used in either a compound or complex sentence. □ *'While he tinkered in his workshop all morning' is a dependent clause.*
- **clause** [klɔz]   a specific section of a written document. □ *The contract contained an escape clause to protect both parties.*

- **claws** [klɔz]   the plural of *claw* 'a sharp, curved nail on the toe of an animal.' □ *When he decided to keep his cat indoors, Mario had its claws removed.*
- **claws** [klɔz]   the plural of *claw* 'the pincherlike appendage like that of a lobster or crab.' □ *Some fishmarkets offer crab claws for sale.*

claws   See the main entry beginning with *clause.*

click—clique

- **click** [klɪk]   a sharp, taplike sound. □ *Tom knew someone picked up the extension phone when he heard a click on the line.*
- **click** [klɪk]   to make a taplike sound. □ *I dislike hearing people click their tongues in disapproval.*
- **click** [klɪk]   to fit together or agree. □ *Since they both enjoyed classical music, the new roommates knew immediately that they would click.*
- **clique** [klik, klɪk]   an exclusive, closely knit group sharing some similar interest, purpose, or view. □ *There always seems to be a particular clique to which many high-school students want to belong.*

climb—clime

- **climb** [klɑɪm]   to go or move up something. □ *Be careful when you climb the ladder.* □ *The song's climb to the top of the record charts was quick.*
- **clime** [klɑɪm]   a climate. □ *Bonnie prefers a warm clime to a cold one.*

clime   See the main entry beginning with *climb.*

clique   See the main entry beginning with *click.*

close—clothes

- **close** [kloz]   to shut something. □ *Please close the door before leaving.*
- **close** [kloz]   a conclusion; an ending. □ *At the close of the speech, the drowsy audience began to stir.*
- **clothes** [kloz, kloðz]   garments. □ *His clothes always look as if he slept in them.*

clothes   See the main entry beginning with *close.*

coarse—course

- **coarse** [kɔɚs]   rough or harsh. □ *The coarse texture of the garment was irritating to the skin.*

- **coarse** [kɔɚs]   of poor quality. □ *The cabin's coarse furnishings were almost unusable.*
- **coarse** [kɔɚs]   lacking refinement in skills or manners. □ *His behavior is sometimes coarse and offensive.*
- **course** [kɔɚs]   a path of action. □ *The new college students were encouraged to stay on course and not get distracted from their studies.*
- **course** [kɔɚs]   a series of lectures or other materials dealing with a given subject. □ *The most difficult course in the curriculum is entitled "Ethics and Issues."*
- **course** [kɔɚs]   a pathway over which something moves. □ *The sailboat was blown off its course by strong winds.*

collar   See the main entry beginning with *choler.*

collard—collared

- **collard** [ˈkɑlɚd]   a vegetable with smooth leaves belonging to the cabbage family. □ *A pesky rabbit has nibbled every collard in my vegetable garden.*
- **collared** [ˈkɑlɚd]   the past tense and past participle of *collar* 'to fit someone or something with a collar.' □ *High, stiff-collared shirts were a popular men's fashion in the 1800's.*
- **collared** [ˈkɑlɚd]   the past tense and past participle of *collar* 'to catch someone or something; to arrest someone.' (Slang.) □ *I collared the dog and tied it to a tree.* □ *The cops collared the crooks just after the robbery.*

collared   See the main entry beginning with *collard.*

colonel—kernel

- **colonel** [ˈkɚnl]   a rank of commissioned military officer higher than lieutenant colonel but lower than brigadier general. □ *Even a colonel must answer to a higher authority.*
- **kernel** [ˈkɚnl]   the soft, inner part of a fruit stone, nut, or seed. □ *The small child planted a kernel of corn in each tiny hole in the earth.*

complement—compliment

- **complement** [ˈkɑmplɪmənt]   something that enhances or completes someone or something. □ *A fine red wine is a nice complement for a meal including red meat.*
- **complement** [ˈkɑmplɪmənt]   the number or quantity needed to make something complete. □ *When the final complement of troops arrived, the unit moved out.*
- **compliment** [ˈkɑmplɪmənt]   to express admiration or respect for something. □ *"I'd like to compliment you on your fine*

achievements," began the speaker.
- **compliment** ['kɑmplɪmənt]   an expression of praise or recognition. □ *Some people become very embarrassed when paid a compliment.*

compliment   See the main entry beginning with *complement.*

confidant—confident
- **confidant** ['kɑnfɪdɑnt]   a person in whom one confides or trusts. □ *The frightened youngster chose an understanding police officer as a confidant.*
- **confident** ['kɑnfɪdənt]   full of assurance and self-reliance. □ *As the ball game progressed, the pitcher grew more confident of herself.*

confident   See the main entry beginning with *confidant.*

continence—continents
- **continence** ['kɑntɪnənts]   self-restraint. □ *Tom's continence dissolved as the badgering and ridicule of his friends continued.*
- **continence** ['kɑntɪnənts]   the ability to control excretory functions. □ *The stroke victim no longer had continence.*
- **continents** ['kɑntɪnənts]   the plural of *continent* 'one of the seven major land masses on the earth.' □ *Australia is the smallest of the world's continents.*

continents   See the main entry beginning with *continence.*

continual—continuous
- **continual** [kən'tɪnjuəl]   on a regular or frequent basis. □ *Her continual complaints are annoying.*
- **continuous** [kən'tɪnjuəs]   constantly; without an end. □ *That machine's continuous knocking sound must be fixed.*

continuous   See the main entry beginning with *continual.*

coo—coup
- **coo** [ku]   a happy, gurgling sound made by an infant. □ *New parents are often thrilled by the first coo made by their offspring.*
- **coo** [ku]   the low, soft sound of a pigeon or dove. □ *On hot summer mornings the coo of a mourning dove is easily recognizable.*
- **coo** [ku]   to utter a soft cooing sound. □ *To coo like a baby is usually a sign of contentment.*
- **coup** [ku]   a sudden, unexpected, and usually successful action. □ *The unseasoned athlete staged a coup against the champion and eventually won the title.*

coop—coupe

- **coop** [kup] a small shed or enclosure, usually used to keep poultry. □ *That pesky raccoon raids the chicken coop almost every night.*
- **coop [up]** [kup] to confine someone or something in close, restricted quarters. □ *"If you don't behave," threatened the baby-sitter, "I'll coop you up in your room for an hour."*
- **coupe** AND **coupé** [kup, ku'pe] a two-door car with a hard roof. □ *While my brother prefers a convertible, I much prefer a sporty coupe.*

cops—copse

- **cops** [kɑps] the plural of *cop* 'a law enforcement officer.' (Slang.) □ *Cops patrol New York City's streets on horseback.*
- **copse** [kɑps] a small, thick growth of trees or bushes. □ *The copse at the back of the farm is a haven for many birds and small animals.*

copse See the main entry beginning with *cops*.

coral See the main entry beginning with *chorale*.

cord See the main entry beginning with *chord*.

core—corps

- **core** [kɔɚ] the center or foundation of something. □ *At the core of the curriculum are eight required courses.*
- **core** [kɔɚ] the center, inedible part of many fruits. □ *Be sure to remove the core of the apple when slicing it for the salad.*
- **core** [kɔɚ] the central meaning of something. □ *The core of the telephone solicitor's pitch was a request for donations.*
- **corps** [kɔɚ] a group of individuals organized and acting together under common direction; an organized subdivision of a military unit. (The pronunciation [kɔrps] is viewed as an error.) □ *While enlisted in the army, Josh was a clerk in the Army Corps of Engineers.* □ *The city's youth corps provides jobs for many disadvantaged young people.*

corps See the main entry beginning with *core*.

corral See the main entry beginning with *chorale*.

correspondence—correspondents

- **correspondence** [kɔɚə'spɑndənts] a relationship of one thing with another. □ *There is a direct correspondence between diet and the general health of a person.*
- **correspondence** [kɔɚə'spɑndənts] an exchange of written communication. □ *Mrs. Smith has carried on a correspondence*

with her French pen pal for more than forty years.

- **correspondents** [kɔɚə'spandənts]   people who communicate regularly in writing with one another. □ *As correspondents, Kathy and I have enjoyed keeping in touch though we are separated by thousands of miles.*
- **correspondents** [kɔɚə'spandənts]   people who serve as news reporters from a distant location. □ *During the Persian Gulf War, news correspondents reported events as they happened.*

correspondents   See the main entry beginning with *correspondence*.

council—counsel
- **council** ['kaʊnsl]   a body of people that meets to consult or make policy. □ *Our city council meets once a month.*
- **council** ['kaʊnsl]   a federation made up of small, local chapters. □ *The council on physical fitness has established guidelines for school-age children's fitness levels.*
- **counsel** ['kaʊnsl]   to offer someone advice or consultation. □ *Clergymen often counsel young couples preparing for marriage.*
- **counsel** ['kaʊnsl]   an attorney hired to advise or represent someone in legal matters. □ *"Counsel will refrain from badgering the witness," roared the angry judge.*

counsel   See the main entry beginning with *council*.

coup   See the main entry beginning with *coo*.

coupe   See the main entry beginning with *coop*.

course   See the main entry beginning with *coarse*.

coward—cowered
- **coward** ['kaʊɚd]   a person who demonstrates fear. □ *Susan is a real coward when it comes to flying.*
- **cowered** ['kaʊɚd]   the past tense and past participle of *cower* 'to draw away from someone or something in fear.' □ *When the dog heard the bathwater running, it cowered in a corner of the bedroom.*

cowered   See the main entry beginning with *coward*.

creak—creek
- **creak** [krik]   a squeaking or grating noise. □ *The creak of the swing on the front porch annoys me.*
- **creak** [krik]   to produce a creaking sound. □ *That door will creak if you open it slowly.*
- **creek** [krik, krɪk]   a natural stream of water usually smaller

than a river. □ *The homesteaders searched for some land with a creek running through it.*

cream—creme

- **cream** [krim]   the fatty part of whole milk that rises to the top when milk is left standing. □ *Grandma always adds cream to her tea.*
- **cream** [krim]   the best of something or some group. □ *Only the cream of the contestants will go on to the final competition.*
- **cream** [krim]   to whip or beat a substance until it becomes smooth. □ *You should cream the sugar and shortening before adding the other ingredients.*
- **creme** AND **crème** [krim, krɛm]   a sweet, creamy liqueur. □ *He occasionally likes a splash of crème de menthe over ice for a summer beverage.*

creek   See the main entry beginning with *creak.*

creme   See the main entry beginning with *cream.*

crewel—cruel

- **crewel** [krul]   a loosely twisted yarn used in embroidery. □ *The wall hanging in the foyer was done in crewel by her aunt.*
- **cruel** [krul]   causing pain, grief, or injury. □ *Children often utter cruel words to one another in anger.*

crews—cruise

- **crews** [kruz]   the plural of *crew* 'a group of people working together in cooperation.' □ *Each of the work crews was assigned a task to be completed by the day's end.*
- **cruise** [kruz]   to sail through a geographical location. □ *I would someday like to cruise Alaska's inland passage.*
- **cruise** [kruz]   to wander streets randomly. □ *Gangs of youths cruise the streets of the city day and night.*
- **cruise** [kruz]   to travel at the most efficient speed. □ *The pilot announced that the aircraft would cruise at an altitude of 33,000 feet.*

cruel   See the main entry beginning with *crewel.*

cruise   See the main entry beginning with *crews.*

cue—queue

- **cue** [kju]   a signal given to someone for a specific purpose. □ *When the director gave him the cue, Ken strutted onto the stage.*
- **cue** [kju]   to prompt someone. □ *If you forget your lines in the play, a prompter will cue you from behind the curtain.*
- **cue** [kju]   a stick used to strike the balls in pool or billiards.

    □ *For better contact with the ball, put chalk on the end of your cue.*
- **queue [up]** [kju]   to line up in a row. □ *Concert fans began to queue up for tickets at midnight.*
- **queue** [kju]   a line; a row. □ *The queue of antique cars at the fair attracted many admirers.*
- **queue** [kju]   a braid of hair worn dangling at the back of the neck. □ *Mary wore her hair in a queue interwoven with colorful ribbons.*

currant—current
- **currant** ['kɚ-ənt]   the small, berrylike fruit of several shrubs. □ *I ate almost every currant I picked!*
- **current** ['kɚ-ənt]   up-to-date; presently acceptable or practiced. □ *The man prides himself on his knowledge of current world events.* □ *The current medical procedure for curing that ailment is really quite simple.*
- **current** ['kɚ-ənt]   the flow of something in a specific direction. □ *Be careful of the strong current in that river.*

current   See the main entry beginning with *currant*.

cymbal—symbol
- **cymbal** ['sɪmbl]   a percussion instrument made of brass that produces a loud, crashing sound when struck with a stick or another cymbal. □ *To play the cymbal well, one must have perfect timing.*
- **symbol** ['sɪmbl]   something that stands for something else by reason of association or resemblance. □ *The dictator's face became a symbol of hatred to the oppressed people.*

D

dam—damn

- **dam** [dæm]   a structure in a river or a stream preventing the flow of water. □ *The beavers built a dam at the narrowest part of the river.*
- **dam** [dæm]   to place a barrier in a river or a stream to restrict the flow of water. □ *If we dam the flow of water upstream, we can slow the current here.*
- **dam** [dæm]   the female parent of a horse. □ *The filly's dam has a strong racing background.*
- **damn** [dæm]   to condemn someone to punishment. □ *The court chose to damn the traitor to a lifetime of banishment.*
- **damn** [dæm]   to bring ruin upon someone or something. □ *The defeat of that issue will damn any chance of further school improvements.*
- **damn** [dæm]   to condemn someone or something through a curse. □ *"Damn the day my curiosity got the best of me!" wailed the woman.*

damn   See the main entry beginning with *dam.*

days—daze

- **days** [dez]   the plural of *day* 'the period between sunrise and sunset.' □ *During the summertime, days are much longer than during the winter.*
- **days** [dez]   the plural of *day* 'a twenty-four hour period.' □ *You will feel better in a couple of days.*
- **daze** [dez]   to stun or disorient someone or some creature. □ *Repeated blows to the head began to daze the tired but determined boxer.*
- **daze** [dez]   a state of disorientation. □ *Severe jet lag seems to*

put some travelers in a daze.

daze   See the main entry beginning with *days.*

dear—deer
- **dear** [dɪɚ]   highly valued; precious. □ *My grandmother's antique locket is very dear to me.*
- **dear** [dɪɚ]   costly; expensive. □ *For some people, the price paid for personal freedom is dear indeed.*
- **dear** [dɪɚ]   a loved one. (A term of address.) □ *Now, my dear, what may I do for you?*
- **deer** [dɪɚ]   a wild, swift-running animal having hooves and antlers in all males and the females of some species. □ *Each year, the same deer munches on my father's garden.*

deer   See the main entry beginning with *dear.*

demur—demure
- **demur** [dɪˈmjɚ]   to object; to make an objection. □ *I appreciate your suggestion but I must demur. That is the wrong approach.*
- **demure** [dɪˈmjur]   modest; coyly decorous. □ *The demure young priest was very precise in his homily.*

demure   See the main entry beginning with *demur.*

dense—dents
- **dense** [dɛnts]   thick; closely grown. □ *Although Harold has a dense head of hair, his brother Hank is nearly bald.*
- **dense** [dɛnts]   dull; stupid. □ *In the movie, that character is a dense, bumbling door-to-door salesman.*
- **dents** [dɛnts]   the plural of *dent* 'an indentation or hollow made by a blow.' □ *The autobody shop was able to repair all of the dents in the car's bumper.*

dental—dentil
- **dental** [ˈdɛntəl]   having to do with teeth or dentistry. □ *One of the fringe benefits of that job is a complete dental insurance plan.*
- **dental** [ˈdɛntəl]   pronounced with the tip of the tongue against the back of the upper front teeth. □ *The sounds* d *and* t *are said to be dental because of the way they are spoken.*
- **dentil** [ˈdɛntəl]   a small, rectangular decorative block projecting below a cornice or overhang on a building. (Architectural.) □ *A dentil had fallen here and there, but the look of the old building was still pleasant.*

dentil   See the main entry beginning with *dental.*

dents See the main entry beginning with *dense.*

dependence—dependents
- **dependence** [dəˈpɛndənts] the state or quality of relying on someone or something else. □ *Children remain in a state of complete dependence on their parents for many years.*
- **dependents** [dəˈpɛndənts] the plural of *dependent* 'someone who relies upon someone else for support.' □ *How many dependents do you claim on your federal and state income tax?*

dependents See the main entry beginning with *dependence.*

depravation—deprivation
- **depravation** [dɛprəˈveʃn] corruption or downfall. □ *Association with the wrong people seemingly caused the depravation of the innocent woman.*
- **deprivation** [dɛprəˈveʃn] losing or removing something. □ *Deprivation of food and clothing made their existence miserable.*

deprivation See the main entry beginning with *depravation.*

descension—dissension
- **descension** [dəˈsɛnʃn] the process of going from a higher rank, status, or altitude to a lower one. □ *The wrestler's sudden descension in the tournament's ranking was a shock to his teammates.*
- **dissension** [dəˈsɛnʃn, dɪˈsɛnʃn] quarreling; disagreement of opinion. □ *The issue of promotion and seniority caused much dissension among the office workers.* □ *There was little dissension among the Supreme Court justices regarding that case.*

descent—dissent
- **descent** [dəˈsɛnt] a movement downward. □ *The hikers' descent of the mountainside was slow and tedious.*
- **descent** [dəˈsɛnt] birth; lineage. □ *Otis MacFarland can trace his descent back many centuries to some very old Scottish families.*
- **dissent** [dɪˈsɛnt] to withhold agreement from someone or something. □ *I will exercise my right to dissent on that particular issue.*
- **dissent** [dɪˈsɛnt] a difference of opinion. □ *The representative's dissent was noted in the minutes.*

desert—dessert
- **desert** [ˈdɛzɚt] a hot, dry area of land, usually covered with sand. □ *There is hardly any life in the sands of the desert.*
- **desert** [dəˈzɚt] to leave or abandon someone or something

on purpose. □ *Rather than stay and fight, the soldiers chose instead to desert their units.*

- **dessert** [dəˈzɚt]   the last course of a meal, usually something sweet. □ *His favorite dessert is black walnut cake.*

dessert   See the main entry beginning with *desert.*

dew—do—due

- **dew** [du, dju]   the moisture that condenses on a cool surface, usually during the night. □ *As temperatures continue to drop, the dew on the grass will soon become frost.*
- **do** [du]   to perform something; to carry something out. □ *Do your chores first, and then you'll have plenty of time for other activities.*
- **due** [du, dju]   owed or owing as a debt, moral obligation, or right. □ *The electric bill is due on the 15th of each month.* □ *My final paper is due on the last day of class.*

die—dye

- **die** [daɪ]   to cease to live. □ *Certain insects die a day or so after hatching.*
- **die** [daɪ]   to expire. □ *If not acted upon, the bill will die in committee.*
- **die [down]** [daɪ]   to decrease gradually; to stop. □ *I wish the wind would die down so I can rake these leaves.*
- **die** [daɪ]   a six-sided cube with varying numbers of dots on each side that is used in games. □ *With each roll of the die the man's luck seemed to increase.*
- **die** [daɪ]   a tool or device needed to make shapes, forms, or surfaces. □ *The die used for casting that part has cracked and can no longer be used.*
- **dye** [daɪ]   to change the color of something. □ *Everyone will notice if you dye your blond hair black.*
- **dye** [daɪ]   an agent used to change the color of something. □ *The purple dye would not wash off his hands.*

disburse—disperse

- **disburse** [dɪsˈbɚs, dɪˈspɚs]   to pay out money from a fund. □ *Our company will disburse bonus checks at the end of the year.*
- **disburse** [dɪsˈbɚs, dɪˈspɚs]   to distribute something. □ *She requested that her attorney disburse her estate's assets according to her will.*
- **disperse** [dɪˈspɚs]   to scatter or break up something. □ *Police officers tried in vain to disperse the unruly mob.*
- **disperse** [dɪˈspɚs]   to spread or distribute something evenly from a fixed source. □ *Prisms disperse sunlight in unusual*

and beautiful patterns.

discreet—discrete
- **discreet** [dɪˈskrit]   having the ability to show good judgment, especially in conduct and speech. □ *A job that involves handling confidential information requires a discreet employee.*
- **discrete** [dɪˈskrit]   distinct or separate. □ *Though quite similar in appearance, the twins each have a discrete personality.*

discrete   See the main entry beginning with *discreet.*

disinterested—uninterested
- **disinterested** [dɪsˈɪntrɪstɪd]   free from personal motive or interest. □ *Let's ask a disinterested third party to help settle this dispute.*
- **uninterested** [ənˈɪntrɪstɪd]   not interested. □ *The bored audience was obviously uninterested in what the speaker was saying.*

disperse   See the main entry beginning with *disburse.*

dissension   See the main entry beginning with *descension.*

dissent   See the main entry beginning with *descent.*

do   See the main entry beginning with *dew.*

doe—dough
- **doe** [do]   a female deer. □ *The doe flicked her ears and tail nervously while her fawns ate nearby.*
- **doe** [do]   a female of most species where the male is called a buck. □ *Ginny won first prize in the rabbit competition at the fair with her pet doe, Flopsy.*
- **dough** [do]   a mixture of flour, liquid, and other ingredients, usually used for breads, cookies, and pie crusts. □ *My sister's recipe for homemade bread dough is easy to make.*
- **dough** [do]   money. (Slang.) □ *"Hey, man, can you give me some dough?" asked the beggar.*

does—doze
- **does** [doz]   the plural of *doe* 'a female deer or other female animal where the male is called a buck.' □ *In the wild, the number of does outweighs the number of bucks.*
- **does** [dəz]   the third person singular of *do* 'to perform an act.' □ *He does what he is told.*
- **doze** [dəz]   to fall into a light, unintentional sleep. □ *I doze in front of the television set each night during the news.*
- **doze** [doz]   to bulldoze something. □ *A work crew will doze the site of the demolished building.*

done—dun

- **done** [dən] the past participle of *do* 'to perform an act.' □ *After you have done the filing, please type this letter.*
- **done** [dən] completed; finished. □ *When the candy thermometer reads 250 degrees, you'll know that the mixture is done simmering.*
- **dun** [dən] a horse of a neutral light brown color. □ *At the riding stable, Jane was given a dun mare to ride.*
- **dun** [dən] marked by drabness or dullness. □ *The dun color of the room wasn't very attractive.*
- **dun** [dən] to hound someone for the payment of a debt. □ *If you do not pay your bills, they will dun you until you do.*

dough See the main entry beginning with *doe.*

doze See the main entry beginning with *does.*

draft—draught

- **draft** [dræft] to draw up or design something. □ *We were asked to draft a document listing our goals for the projects.*
- **draft** [dræft] capable of pulling a load or doing heavy labor. (Usually said of horses.) □ *The team of draft horses strained under the heavy weight of the load.*
- **draft** [dræft] to inhale or swallow something. □ *Henry can draft an entire stein of beer in one long gulp.*
- **draft** [dræft] to selectively choose someone or something for a particular purpose. □ *The college football coach is hoping to draft some of the top prep players for his team.*
- **draft** [dræft] a current of air entering a closed space. □ *The cold draft coming under the door made sitting in the room most uncomfortable.*
- **draught** [dræft] a move in a chess or checkers game. □ *As usual, Terry defeated me in chess by a clever draught that I missed.*

draught See the main entry beginning with *draft.*

dual—duel

- **dual** [dul, djul] two; double. □ *The hot-rod car has dual exhaust pipes.* □ *Psychiatrists spend a good deal of time studying patients with dual personalities.*
- **duel** [dul, djul] a confrontation between two armed combatants, usually to settle an argument. (*Duels* are now illegal.) □ *A well-known duel in American history involved Alexander Hamilton and Aaron Burr.*
- **duel** [dul, djul] a conflict of interest, persons, forces, or ideas.

☐ *The two courtroom attorneys were locked in a duel of minds.*

ducked—duct

- **ducked** [dəkt]   the past tense and past participle of *duck* 'to push someone or something under water.' ☐ *The children ducked one another during a game in the pool.*
- **ducked** [dəkt]   the past tense and past participle of *duck* 'to hide from or avoid someone or something.' ☐ *He ducked before the intended blow landed on his head.*
- **duct** [dəkt]   a passageway through which something travels. ☐ *The air duct carries warm air in the winter and cool air in the summer.* ☐ *Julie had to go to the doctor because she had an infection in her left tear duct.*

duct   See the main entry beginning with *ducked.*

due   See the main entry beginning with *dew.*

duel   See the main entry beginning with *dual.*

dun   See the main entry beginning with *done.*

dye   See the main entry beginning with *die.*

E

earn—urn

- **earn** [ɚn] to receive payment or reward in return for work that one has done. □ *Jenny hopes to earn enough money to pay her own way through college.* □ *Three young men in that scout pack will soon earn the rank of Eagle Scout.*
- **urn** [ɚn] a vessel with a pedestal used for planting flowers or preserving ashes following cremation. □ *The urn on the patio contains geraniums and marigolds.* □ *The urn on the mantle contains the remains of Uncle Herman.*

eave—eve

- **eave** [iv] a low, usually separate border of a roof that overhangs a wall and is designed to funnel off water. □ *When the antenna blew off the roof, it badly dented an eave.*
- **eve** [iv] the evening or day before a special event. □ *On the eve of her wedding, Jane was nervous and jittery.*
- **eve** [iv] the period immediately preceding something. □ *During the eve of the American Civil War, tensions between the North and South steadily increased.*

edition See the main entry beginning with *addition*.

effect See the main entry beginning with *affect*.

eight See the main entry beginning with *ate*.

elicit—illicit

- **elicit** [əˈlɪsɪt] to bring something out; to draw something forth. □ *Will you help me elicit support among your friends for this cause?*
- **illicit** [ɪˈlɪsɪt] illegal; unlawful. □ *The illicit sale of drugs is a*

major problem in many cities.

elusion   See the main entry beginning with *allusion.*

eminent—imminent
- **eminent** ['ɛmɪnənt]   noted for position, rank, or achievement. □ *The eminent author won many Newbery Awards for his children's books.*
- **eminent** ['ɛmɪnənt]   conspicuous; readily noticeable. □ *The comedian ridiculed the politician's eminent nose.*
- **imminent** ['ɪmɪnənt]   soon to happen or take place. □ *The prisoner on death row knew his execution was imminent.*

ensure—insure
- **ensure** [ɛnˈʃuɚ]   to guarantee something; to make certain of something. □ *I will ensure your safe arrival at your destination.*
- **insure** [ɪnˈʃuɚ]   to acquire or give insurance for; to make certain. □ *Be sure to insure your new motorcycle before driving it.* □ *I will send the letter first class to insure that it arrives as soon as possible.*

epic—epoch
- **epic** ['ɛpɪk]   long in length or scope. □ *The epic novel gave several viewpoints of the conquest of the American West.*
- **epoch** ['ɛpək]   an event or period of time noted as the beginning of a new period or development. □ *With Eli Whitney's invention of interchangeable parts, the epoch of industrialization began in earnest.*
- **epoch** ['ɛpək]   a geological time span. □ *We studied the Miocene epoch in great depth in my geology class.*

epoch   See the main entry beginning with *epic.*

err   See the main entry beginning with *air.*

erred   See the main entry beginning with *aired.*

eve   See the main entry beginning with *eave.*

ewe—yew—you
- **ewe** [ju]   a female sheep or related animal. □ *It is not at all unusual for a ewe to bear triplets or even quadruplets.*
- **yew** [ju]   a type of evergreen tree or shrub that has stiff needles and is often used in landscaping. □ *The tiny yew he planted many years ago has grown into a beautiful tree.*
- **you** [ju]   the second person pronoun that refers to the person or persons being addressed. □ *Would you care to join me for a cup of coffee?*

ewes—use—yews

- **ewes** [juz]   the plural of *ewe* 'a female sheep or related animal.' □ *After lambing, the ewes stay close to their young.*
- **use** [juz]   to utilize or employ someone or something. □ *That contracting business does not use unskilled laborers.*
- **use** [juz]   to expend or consume something. □ *Jeff uses as much solar energy as possible to heat his home.*
- **yews** [juz]   the plural of *yew* 'a type of evergreen tree or shrub that has stiff needles.' □ *Don lined the borders of his property with yews to serve as a windbreak.*

eye   See the main entry beginning with *aye.*

eyed—I'd

- **eyed** [aɪd]   the past tense and past participle of *eye* 'to look or glance at someone or something.' □ *The little girl eyed the colorful hair ribbons longingly.*
- **eyed** [aɪd]   the condition of having eyes. □ *Most of the Dutch children in that community are blue-eyed blondes.*
- **I'd** [aɪd]   a contraction of *I had, I would,* or *I should.* □ *If I'd known you were coming, I'd have tidied up the house a bit.*

F

facts—fax

- **facts** [fækts]   the plural of *fact* 'a piece of information that can be proven.' □ *After we examine all the facts, we'll make a decision.*
- **fax** [fæks]   an electronic facsimile transmission. □ *The realtor agreed to accept the fax of the offer as legal and binding.*
- **fax** [fæks]   to transmit a facsimile by wire. □ *George's business is much more efficient now that he is able to fax information to his clients.*
- **fax** [fæks]   a machine used for electronic facsimile transmissions. □ *I decided to buy a fax when they went on sale.*

faint—feint

- **faint** [fent]   to lose consciousness. □ *Sally will faint at the mere sight of blood.*
- **faint** [fent]   feeling weak, dizzy, or lightheaded. □ *He felt faint for days after suffering the head injury.*
- **faint** [fent]   lacking courage or spirit. □ *Skydiving is no hobby for a faint individual.*
- **feint** [fent]   a trick; a deception. □ *The player's double feint completely caught her opponent off guard.*
- **feint** [fent]   to pretend to do something, usually attack, as a means of distraction. □ *The battalion will feint at the enemy's left flank but then attack the right.*

fair—fare

- **fair** [fɛɚ]   attractive; beautiful. □ *The fair maiden caught the eye of the knight in shining armor.*
- **fair** [fɛɚ]   honest and impartial. □ *That judge is known for his fair decisions.*

- **fair** [fɛɚ] blond or light complexioned. □ *Many Scandinavians are fair and have blue eyes.*
- **fair** [fɛɚ] clear. □ *The weather during our week-long vacation was fair and warm.*
- **fair** [fɛɚ] just and equal. □ *It is important that everyone does his or her fair share of the work.*
- **fair** [fɛɚ] a competitive exhibition. □ *Each year Mary's baked goods win blue ribbons at the fair.*
- **fair** [fɛɚ] a gathering of buyers and sellers. □ *The computer fair was attended by people from all around the world.*
- **fare** [fɛɚ] a range of available food. □ *I know a terrific restaurant that specializes in superb Italian fare.*
- **fare** [fɛɚ] the price charged to transport something or someone. □ *The roundtrip fare was less costly than buying two one-way tickets.*
- **fare** [fɛɚ] to get along; to succeed. □ *Mr. Smith hopes that each of his children will fare well in life.*

fairy—ferry

- **fairy** ['fɛɚi] a tiny, mythical being said to possess magical powers. □ *In the movie "Peter Pan," Tinkerbell is a somewhat mischievous fairy.*
- **fairy** ['fɛɚi] a male with effeminate mannerisms. (Slang. Usually derogatory.) □ *While some students at school called Dave a fairy, his friends knew him to be quite masculine.*
- **ferry** ['fɛɚi] a vessel used to transport goods or people over water; a place where people or objects are transported across water. □ *Visitors can reach the island only by the ferry that crosses the bay twice daily.* □ *At the ferry you can catch a boat that will take you on a sightseeing trip.*
- **ferry** ['fɛɚi] to convey or move something or someone from one place to another. □ *Volunteers will ferry the refugees across the border in private vehicles.*

false—faults

- **false** [fɔls] not real or genuine; imitation. □ *Grandpa was always forgetting where he put his false teeth.*
- **false** [fɔls] intentionally misleading or untrue. □ *She purposely made false statements to try to discredit her employer.*
- **false** [fɔls] impermanent. □ *The library contained a false wall that led into a secret room.*
- **faults** [fɔlts] the plural of *fault* 'a weakness, failing, or imperfection.' □ *While Bob's faults may be many, we still think highly of him.*
- **faults** [fɔlts] the plural of *fault* 'a fracture in the earth's

crust.' □ *Most of California's earthquakes occur along one of several faults in the state.*

fare See the main entry beginning with *fair.*

farther—further
- **farther** ['fɑɚðɚ] AND **further** ['fɚðɚ] a greater distance. □ *The trip from the village to the mountain resort was farther than I thought it would be.*
- **further** ['fɚðɚ] additional. □ *I won't bore you with further details.*
- **further** ['fɚðɚ] to help someone or something progress forward. □ *Bill hopes to further his education by attending college.*

faults See the main entry beginning with *false.*

fax See the main entry beginning with *facts.*

faze—phase
- **faze** [fez] to make an impression on or disturb the composure of someone or something. □ *I doubt that a formal reprimand will even faze Thomas.*
- **phase** [fez] a stage or interval in a cycle or development. □ *The next phase of the project involves the approval of the board of commissioners.*
- **phase** [fez] to schedule something to occur or to be performed. □ *The major automobile makers will phase out their poorest selling models.*

feat—feet—fete
- **feat** [fit] a notable deed, especially one involving great skill or courage. □ *The circus elephant accomplished a most difficult feat.*
- **feet** [fit] the plural of *foot* 'the part of the body at the end of the leg.' □ *The wobbly colt was barely able to stay on its feet immediately after being born.*
- **feet** [fit] the plural of *foot* 'the vertical supports of a leg or a chair.' □ *I constantly bump the feet of the chair when I sweep the floor.*
- **feet** [fit] the plural of *foot* 'a unit of length measuring twelve inches.' □ *The board was six feet long.*
- **fete** AND **fête** [fet, fɛt] an elaborate, large party to commemorate or honor someone or something. □ *A fete recognizing his contributions to literature is scheduled for next month.*
- **fete** AND **fête** [fet, fɛt] to honor someone or something. □ *Her co-workers will fete her new sales record at a special luncheon.*

feet See the main entry beginning with *feat.*

feint See the main entry beginning with *faint.*

ferry See the main entry beginning with *fairy.*

fete See the main entry beginning with *feat.*

feudal—futile
- **feudal** ['fjudl] having to do with feudalism, an ancient politi-cal system where land tenure is granted in exchange for loyalty or tribute. □ *In feudal England, serfs did most of the farming.*
- **futile** ['fjutl, 'fjudl] useless; hopeless. □ *His futile attempt to catch the falling vase caused him to sprain his back.*

find—fined
- **find** [faɪnd] to discover someone or something. □ *I hope to find some unusual seashells on the beach.*
- **find** [faɪnd] to arrive at or reach something. □ *Labor and management hope to find solutions to their disagreement.*
- **find** [faɪnd] to determine the judicial guilt or innocence of an accused person. □ *We think the jury will find the accused not guilty.*
- **fined** [faɪnd] the past tense and past participle of *fine* 'to charge a sum of money as punishment for an offense.' □ *John was fined fifty dollars for parking illegally in a handicapped parking space.*

fined See the main entry beginning with *find.*

fir—fur
- **fir** [fɚ] a type of coniferous tree, such as the pine or evergreen. □ *The Christmas tree we bought was a beautifully shaped fir.*
- **fir** [fɚ] the wood of a coniferous tree such as a fir or ever-green. □ *Rick made the table out of some planks of discarded fir.*
- **fur** [fɚ] the hairy coat of an animal. □ *Sable pelts are a very valuable fur.*
- **fur** [fɚ] a clothing article made with fur. □ *Jane hung her fur in the cedar-lined closet.*

fisher—fissure
- **fisher** ['fɪʃɚ] a dark brown carnivorous mammal belonging to the weasel family. □ *The strange animal we saw may have been a fisher.*
- **fissure** ['fɪʃɚ] a crack or narrow opening resulting from break-age or separation. □ *That fissure in the sidewalk was probably caused by frost.*

- **fissure** ['fɪʃɚ] a disagreement in viewpoint. □ *Because of their fissure on that issue, the men argue constantly.*

fissure See the main entry beginning with *fisher.*

flair—flare

- **flair** [flɛɚ] natural aptitude for something. □ *Christy has a real flair for interior design.*
- **flair** [flɛɚ] an odor. □ *The flair of the skunk seemed to be apparent for miles around.*
- **flare** [flɛɚ] a blaze or flame of fire or light used as a signal to attract attention. □ *Mike has never needed to use the emergency flare he carries in his car.*
- **flare** [flɛɚ] to burn or shine with an unsteady flame or sudden light. □ *A fire in the fireplace will sometimes flare up if a sudden draft occurs.*
- **flare** [flɛɚ] to suddenly become angry, excited, or more intense. □ *If you mention that incident, Brad's temper will flare.*

flare See the main entry beginning with *flair.*

flaunt—flout

- **flaunt** [flɔnt] to make a gaudy or defiant display of something. □ *Even though he is extremely rich, Dr. Shear does not flaunt his wealth.*
- **flout** [flaʊt] to mock or show disrespect for someone or something. □ *The poacher continues to flout the "No Trespassing" signs as he hunts on my property.*

flea—flee

- **flea** [fli] a flightless, bloodsucking insect that feeds on warm-blooded animals. □ *The dog wears a special collar to protect it from fleas and other parasites.*
- **flee** [fli] to run away from danger. □ *The refugees had to flee their war-torn nation.*

flee See the main entry beginning with *flea.*

flew—flu—flue

- **flew** [flu] the past tense of *fly* 'to move through the air, often on wings.' □ *The swallows flew swiftly and gracefully in the air.*
- **flew** [flu] the past tense of *fly* 'to move rapidly or swiftly.' □ *The skiers flew down the steep slopes on the new snow.*
- **flew** [flu] the past tense of *fly* 'to operate an airplane.' □ *The pilot flew the airplane skillfully.*
- **flu** [flu] influenza. □ *The school closed because so many*

children were home sick with the flu.

- **flue** [flu]   an enclosed tube, pipe, or passageway used to convey or channel something. □ *The chimney's flue was blocked by a squirrel's nest.*

floe—flow

- **floe** [flo]   a large sheet of floating ice on the surface of water. □ *Polar bears will sometimes swim out to a floe to eat or rest.*
- **flow** [flo]   to circulate or move about easily. □ *Due to the crowded conditions in the building, air does not flow as it should.* □ *Traffic does not flow smoothly during rush hour.*
- **flow** [flo]   to move in a stream or flood, especially water. □ *The river will flow much faster after the snow melts in the mountains.*

flounder—founder

- **flounder** ['flaʊndɚ]   to make awkward attempts to move or gain balance; to move clumsily or in confusion. □ *I hated to see the beached dolphin flounder about on the shore.* □ *Turn on the lights so we don't flounder about in the darkness.*
- **flounder** ['flaʊndɚ]   a flat-bodied fish often used for food. □ *Jack ordered stuffed flounder for dinner.*
- **founder** ['faʊndɚ]   a person who founds or establishes something. □ *Mr. Brown was the founder of the local historical society.*
- **founder** ['faʊndɚ]   to give way, collapse, or become disabled. □ *The weight of its pack caused the mule to founder.*
- **founder** ['faʊndɚ]   to sink beneath the surface of water. □ *Several ships began to founder during the terrible storm.*

flour—flower

- **flour** ['flaʊɚ]   a finely ground grain meal used for baking or cooking. □ *Sarah uses whole wheat flour to make her homemade bread braids.*
- **flour** ['flaʊɚ]   to cover something in flour. □ *Be sure to grease and flour the bottom and sides of the baking dish.*
- **flower** ['flaʊɚ]   a plant usually grown for its blossoms. □ *The flower in his lapel was a red carnation.*
- **flower** ['flaʊɚ]   to produce flowers. □ *Most desert cacti flower in late spring.*
- **flower** ['flaʊɚ]   to flourish or develop. □ *Despite her tomboy appearance, Casey will eventually flower into a young lady.*

flout   See the main entry beginning with *flaunt.*

flow   See the main entry beginning with *floe.*

flower   See the main entry beginning with *flour.*

flu   See the main entry beginning with *flew.*

flue   See the main entry beginning with *flew.*

foaled—fold
- **foaled** [fold]   the past tense and past participle of *foal* 'to give birth to a newborn horse, donkey, or mule.' ☐ *The racehorse foaled last year.*
- **fold** [fold]   a flock of sheep or an enclosure for such. ☐ *The fold has never been attacked by coyotes.*
- **fold** [fold]   one part of something laid over another part. ☐ *The fold of her skirt concealed the torn seam.*
- **fold** [fold]   to intertwine the fingers of both hands. ☐ *Fold your hands and bow your head when saying grace at the dinner table.*
- **fold** [fold]   to bring to an end or to fail. ☐ *Without further financial support, the company will surely fold.*

fold   See the main entry beginning with *foaled.*

for—fore—four
- **for** [fɔɚ]   a preposition indicating purpose or function. ☐ *The outside fork at a place setting is for the meal while the inside fork is for dessert.*
- **for** [fɔɚ]   to be in support of someone or something. ☐ *Uncle Ray is always for any type of law that favors small businesses.*
- **for** [fɔɚ]   representing someone or something. (A preposition.) ☐ *The speaker said, "I am here for Senator Young who was unable to attend this evening."*
- **fore** [fɔɚ]   occupying a front or leading position. (A prefix.) ☐ *The dining car is located in the forepart of the train.*
- **fore** [fɔɚ]   "Look out!" (A golf term used to warn other players that a ball is being struck, possibly in their direction.) ☐ *Marilyn yelled "fore" when she saw that her tee shot was headed toward the golfers ahead of her.*
- **four** [fɔɚ]   the number between three and five. ☐ *"Can we play euchre with more than four people?" asked Pete.*

fore   See the main entry beginning with *for.*

foreword—forward
- **foreword** ['fɔɚwɚd]   the introductory remarks of a writer or speaker. ☐ *In the foreword of the safety manual, the writers explain the purpose of the text.*
- **forward** ['fɔɚwɚd]   being near or at the front of something.

□ *The foot soldiers were forward of the medical and supply units.*

- **forward** ['fɔɚwɚd]   unabashed; brash. □ *He has always been a forward young man.*
- **forward** ['fɔɚwɚd]   to advance or send something along. □ *I hope the post office will forward this letter if the address has changed.*
- **forward** ['fɔɚwɚd]   getting ready for or relating to the future. □ *Matt's forward thinking has saved his company a great deal of money.*
- **forward** ['fɔɚwɚd]   an offensive player on various types of sports teams. □ *The team's forward set a new school point record at last Friday night's basketball game.*

formally—formerly

- **formally** ['fɔɚməli]   carried out in a ceremonial fashion. □ *The pioneering scientist will formally receive her award in three months.*
- **formerly** ['fɔɚmɚli]   in times past. □ *Our neighbors were formerly stationed in Bangkok, Thailand, before being re-assigned to San Diego, California.*

formerly   See the main entry beginning with *formally.*

forth—fourth

- **forth** [fɔɚθ]   onward or outward in time, place, or order. □ *Step forth into the light where I can see you better.*
- **fourth** [fɔɚθ]   the ordinal number between third and fifth. □ *The huge jumbo jet was fourth in line to take off on the runway.*
- **fourth** [fɔɚθ]   one quarter of a whole. □ *Almost a fourth of her newly planted garden was eaten by rabbits.*

forward   See the main entry beginning with *foreword.*

foul—fowl

- **foul** [faʊl]   offensive to the senses. □ *When we entered the room, we detected a foul odor.*
- **foul** [faʊl]   profane; obscene. □ *That coach will not tolerate foul language from his players.*
- **foul** [faʊl]   treacherous. □ *Due to the foul weather, we can-celled the dinner cruise aboard the yacht.*
- **foul** [faʊl]   an infringement of the rules in a game or sport. □ *Neither Donald nor Russell committed a single foul during the basketball game.*
- **fowl** [faʊl]   a member of the bird family, usually used for food. □ *The wild turkey is an interesting fowl to observe.*

- **fowl** [faʊl]   the meat of birds eaten as food. ☐ *While Mr. Smith prefers red meat, his wife would rather eat fowl.*

founder   See the main entry beginning with *flounder.*

four   See the main entry beginning with *for.*

fourth   See the main entry beginning with *forth.*

fowl   See the main entry beginning with *foul.*

frays—phrase
- **frays** [frez]   the plural of *fray* 'a raveled or worn area of fabric.' ☐ *Trim the frays off the edge of that material before mending it.*
- **frays** [frez]   the present tense, third person singular of *fray* 'to cause a strain on something; to wear at something.' ☐ *Helen is such a sensitive person that even an unkind remark frays her self-esteem.*
- **phrase** [frez]   a grammatical sequence of words. ☐ *An overused, trite phrase is called a cliché.* ☐ *The first sentence of the novel began with the phrase, "To dream the dream of kings...."*
- **phrase** [frez]   to form an utterance. ☐ *Be careful how you phrase your questions.*

frees—freeze—frieze
- **frees** [friz]   the present tense, third person singular of *free* 'to liberate someone or something.' ☐ *Not having to work on Saturday frees Sam to spend time on his hobbies.*
- **freeze** [friz]   to use cold to cause a liquid to solidify or a solid to harden. ☐ *You must freeze water to make ice cubes.*
- **freeze** [friz]   to become chilled with cold. ☐ *"Let's hurry inside before we freeze," said Sandy.*
- **freeze** [friz]   to become fixed or motionless. ☐ *When the suspect began running away, the police officer yelled "Freeze!"*
- **freeze** [friz]   a weather condition marked by cold temperatures. ☐ *The late spring freeze ruined the citrus crop.*
- **frieze** [friz]   a coarse, durable fabric made with wool and other fibers. ☐ *A sweater made of frieze may not be attractive, but it certainly is warm.*
- **frieze** [friz]   an ornamental, usually sculptured, trim on a building. ☐ *The frieze around the mansion's entryway was typical of the 1920's.*

freeze   See the main entry beginning with *frees.*

friar—fryer
- **friar** ['fraɪɚ]   a male member of some types of religious orders.

□ *Why do we usually picture a friar wearing a long, dark, hooded cloak?*
- **fryer** [ˈfraɪɚ] a young chicken. □ *While a fryer is usually a young bird, a stewing chicken is normally older and tougher.*
- **fryer** [ˈfraɪɚ] a cooking pot or pan used to fry foods. □ *Pat slowly simmered the meat and vegetables in the fryer.*

frieze See the main entry beginning with *frees.*

fryer See the main entry beginning with *friar.*

fur See the main entry beginning with *fir.*

further See the main entry beginning with *farther.*

futile See the main entry beginning with *feudal.*

G

gait—gate

- **gait** [get] a manner of walking or moving on foot. ☐ *He moves in an easy, natural gait, never hurrying but never dallying either.*
- **gait** [get] one of the four foot movements or strides of a horse. ☐ *I prefer riding a horse whose gait is a canter.*
- **gait** [get] to lead a show dog before a judge to display its form and movement. ☐ *In showmanship classes, each dog handler is asked to gait his animal in front of the judges.*
- **gate** [get] a doorlike closure for an opening in a wall or fence; a place of entrance or exit. ☐ *The rickety fence gate has almost fallen off its hinges.* ☐ *To find the concession stand at the park, go through the front gate and turn left.*
- **gate** [get] the total number of spectators or admission receipts at a sporting event. ☐ *The gate at the final game of the World Series set a new attendance record.*

gamble—gambol

- **gamble** ['gæmbl] to play a game for money or some other stakes. ☐ *Don't gamble away your life's savings at the casino.*
- **gamble** ['gæmbl] to wager or venture that something will or will not happen. ☐ *He was willing to gamble that his ideas would succeed.*
- **gamble** ['gæmbl] something risky or chancy. ☐ *The rescuers knew their daring lifesaving attempt was a gamble.*
- **gambol** ['gæmbl] to play, romp, or move about in a frisky manner. ☐ *It was fun to watch the new calves gambol about in the pasture.*

gambol See the main entry beginning with *gamble*.

gate   See the main entry beginning with *gait*.

gel—jell

- **gel** [dʒɛl]   to congeal in a more solid form but not become solid. □ *As the soup cools, the fat in it will begin to gel.*
- **gel** [dʒɛl]   a substance having a gelatinlike consistency. □ *That medication comes in both a lotion and a gel.*
- **jell** AND **gel** [dʒɛl]   to solidify into jelly or gelatin. □ *The dessert is about to gel.* □ *We put the dessert mix in the refrigerator to jell.*
- **jell** [dʒɛl]   to become established and certain. □ *In order for the plan to work, everything must jell at precisely the right time.*

genes—jeans

- **genes** [dʒinz]   the plural of *gene* 'the part of a chromosome that contains hereditary characteristics.' □ *Genes that determine brown eyes are dominant over genes that determine blue eyes.*
- **jeans** [dʒinz]   blue jeans; denim trousers of any color, constructed to resemble blue jeans. (Originally from *Genoa* 'a cotton denim or twill fabric.') □ *Almost every student wore jeans to the picnic.*

gild—guild

- **gild** [gɪld]   to cover something with a thin layer of gold. □ *The goldsmith thought he should gild the piece of jewelry to make it brighter and more attractive.*
- **gild** [gɪld]   to wrongly give an attractive appearance to something. □ *The crooked politicians tried to gild the poor financial status of their city.*
- **guild** [gɪld]   a group of people with common interests or aims. □ *The potter's guild puts on a show and sale each year.*

gilt—guilt

- **gilt** [gɪlt]   a young female swine. □ *The hog farmer has an especially fine gilt for sale.*
- **gilt** [gɪlt]   a layer of gold or gold paint on something. □ *At the plant, we saw a machine apply gilt to the edges of books.*
- **gilt** [gɪlt]   covered with gold or a goldlike substance. □ *Don bought an unusual gilt picture frame at the antique auction.*
- **guilt** [gɪlt]   a feeling of blame for an offense. □ *She felt both guilt and shame for having lied to her mother.*
- **guilt** [gɪlt]   culpability; the fact of having done something wrong. □ *The defendant's guilt could not be proven beyond a reasonable doubt.*

gnu—knew—new

- **gnu** [nu]   a large African antelope. □ *On her photo safari, Barb took a picture of a huge gnu.*
- **knew** [nu, nju]   the past tense of *know* 'to sense or perceive something; to be aware of the truth or facts.' □ *I knew I should have stayed home during the bad storm.* □ *The students knew almost all of the answers on their test.*
- **knew** [nu, nju]   the past tense of *know* 'to be acquainted with someone or something.' □ *She knew the famous actor when he was still working at a local restaurant.* □ *I knew the taste of bitter almonds and quickly spat out the bite I had taken.*
- **new** [nu, nju]   recently made or completed. □ *I got a new paint job on my car.*
- **new** [nu, nju]   unfamiliar; unaccustomed. □ *We hope to see some new sights on our next visit to the city.* □ *Because he was new to the job, Greg felt a bit uneasy at first.*

golf—gulf

- **golf** [gɔf, gɔlf]   a game played with a ball and clubs on a grassy course. □ *His dream is to one day play golf at St. Andrews in Scotland.*
- **gulf** [gəlf]   a part of an ocean or sea reaching into land. □ *The boats sailing in the gulf sparkled in the sunlight.*
- **gulf** [gəlf]   a gap, hole, or distance. □ *Such a gulf exists between their beliefs that an agreement is not possible.*

gored—gourd

- **gored** [gɔɚd]   the past tense and past participle of *gore* 'to cut or make something into a triangular shape.' □ *The swirl skirt was gored with several large pieces of fabric.*
- **gored** [gɔɚd]   the past tense and past participle of *gore* '[for an animal] to stab someone or something with its horn or tusk.' □ *The bulls sometimes gore spectators during the annual Corrida de Toros in Pamplona, Spain.*
- **gourd** [gɔɚd]   the edible fruit of certain vine families. □ *The Hubbard squash is a type of gourd that can reach huge proportions.*

gorilla—guerrilla

- **gorilla** [gə'rɪlə]   the biggest member of the ape family, found in Africa. □ *The gorilla has a gentle, kind nature despite its huge size.*
- **gorilla** [gə'rɪlə]   a thug; a large-bodied criminal; a criminal's bodyguard. (Slang.) □ *The boss never went anywhere without a gorilla to protect him.*

- **guerrilla** [gɛˈrɪlə] a person who engages in warfare for hire. □ *Each guerrilla carried his own simple weapons.*
- **guerrilla** [gɛˈrɪlə] having to do with irregular warfare by independent bands. □ *Guerrilla fighting between warring clans broke out in Somalia.*

gourd See the main entry beginning with *gored.*

grade—grayed
- **grade** [gred] a level or stage in school. □ *Cindy moved to a different school after completing fifth grade.*
- **grade** [gred] a naval or military rank. □ *An admiral is a naval officer of very high grade.*
- **grade** [gred] a class indicating the size or quality of goods for sale. □ *A recipe may call for a certain grade of eggs.*
- **grade** [gred] the angle or degree of a slope. □ *The steep grade of the mountainside made traveling dangerous in bad weather.*
- **grade** [gred] having to do with an animal of mixed parentage; a purebred animal crossed with an ordinary animal. □ *Stacey wanted a purebred horse but could only afford a grade animal.*
- **grayed** [gred] the past tense and past participle of *gray* 'to become gray.' □ *Although none became bald, all of the men in our family grayed at an early age.*

grate—great
- **grate** [gret] a framework of bars designed to prevent the passage of someone or something. □ *Each hallway was fitted with an iron grate at its entrance.*
- **grate** [gret] an iron cradle used in stoves and fireplaces to hold what is to be burned. □ *Sweep the ashes from under the grate before you build another fire.*
- **grate [on]** [gret] to bother someone; to irritate someone's nerves. □ *Her annoying habits grate on my nerves.* □ *Your loud voice grates on me!*
- **grate** [gret] to make a harsh, scratching, or grinding sound. □ *When the machinery isn't working properly, the moving parts grate noisily.*
- **grate** [gret] to reduce something to pieces by rubbing it with something coarse. □ *Let's grate the cheese before putting it on the pizza.*
- **great** [gret] large; big. □ *The huge emperor shifted his great form with much difficulty.* □ *Great numbers of people appeared at the grand opening ceremony.*
- **great** [gret] remarkable; famous; distinguished. □ *The salesman went to great lengths to please his customers.* □ *Many*

great athletes never become professional players.
- **great** [gret]   a generation removed in a family relationship. □ *My great-grandmother was a Chippewa Indian.*

grayed   See the main entry beginning with *grade.*

grays—graze
- **grays** [grez]   the present tense, third person singular of *gray* 'to become gray; to become dull or colorless.' □ *A white shirt grays if it is not washed regularly in hot water with bleach.*
- **grays** [grez]   the plural of *gray* 'a gray horse.' □ *The pair of grays looked smart pulling the old-fashioned carriage.*
- **graze** [grez]   to feed randomly on grasses. □ *Sheep require a lot of open land on which to graze.*
- **graze** [grez]   to touch something lightly in passing. □ *Do not graze your shirt sleeves on the freshly painted walls.* □ *The bullet did no more than graze the surface of the skin.*

graze   See the main entry beginning with *grays.*

great   See the main entry beginning with *grate.*

greave—grieve
- **greave** [griv]   a piece of armor worn below the knee. □ *The knight lost a greave during the joust.*
- **grieve** [griv]   to feel a sense of sorrow, distress, or suffering. □ *It is normal to grieve over the loss of a loved pet.*

grieve   See the main entry beginning with *greave.*

grill—grille
- **grill** [grɪl]   a cooking surface on which food is exposed to direct heat. □ *Tom cooked our steaks on the grill.*
- **grill** [grɪl]   to cook on a grill. □ *I like to grill hamburgers and hot dogs outside in the summertime.*
- **grill** [grɪl]   a restaurant that serves broiled foods. □ *The gas station that once stood on the corner is now a bar and grill.*
- **grill** [grɪl]   to question someone heatedly. □ *We will grill the suspect until we arrive at the truth.*
- **grille** [grɪl]   a lattice work; a grate that forms a barrier or screen of some type. □ *Ken damaged the grille on the front of his new car when he hit the mailbox post.* □ *An iron grille covers the front door of the mansion.*

grille   See the main entry beginning with *grill.*

grisly—grizzly
- **grisly** ['grɪzli]   gory; horrible. □ *Even the seasoned police officers were sickened at the grisly scene.*

- **grizzly** ['grɪzli] a large, powerful North American bear known for its ferocity. □ *It is wise to use extreme caution when confronted by a grizzly in the wild.*

grizzly See the main entry beginning with *grisly.*

groan—grown
- **groan** [gron] to utter a moaning sound indicating pain, annoyance, or grief. □ *The student let out a groan when the teacher announced yet another quiz.*
- **grown** [gron] the past participle of *grow* 'to develop in maturity, size, or stature.' □ *Sara has grown into a fine young woman.*
- **grown** [gron] the past participle of *grow* 'to become or to cause something to develop or mature.' □ *The economy has grown sluggish in recent years.* □ *Chris is no longer a boy but a grown man.* □ *In order for coffee to be successfully grown, soil and climate conditions must be just right.*

grown See the main entry beginning with *groan.*

guerrilla See the main entry beginning with *gorilla.*

guessed—guest
- **guessed** [gɛst] the past tense and past participle of *guess* 'to form an answer with little or no evidence.' □ *The student guessed the answer and was correct.*
- **guest** [gɛst] a person invited to some place. □ *Our dinner guest should arrive shortly after six.* □ *A well-known celebrity appears as a guest on the popular talk show each evening.*
- **guest** [gɛst] a patron of a hotel or restaurant. □ *Every guest at the inn is personally greeted by the innkeeper herself.*

guest See the main entry beginning with *guessed.*

guild See the main entry beginning with *gild.*

guilt See the main entry beginning with *gilt.*

guise—guys
- **guise** [gɑɪz] a manner or style of dress. □ *The actress's guise is eccentric.*
- **guise** [gɑɪz] [someone's] outward appearance; a disguise. □ *The undercover agent's guise was that of a beggar.*
- **guys** [gɑɪz] the plural of *guy* 'a man or boy; a person.' (*Guys* can refer to persons of either sex when used in the plural.) □ *Those guys always hang around together at the arcade.*

• **guys** [gɑɪz]   the plural of *guy* 'a length of rope, wire, or chain used as a brace or guide.' □ *Be sure to note the location of the guys on the television antenna.*

gulf   See the main entry beginning with *golf.*

guys   See the main entry beginning with *guise.*

H

hail—hale

- **hail** [hel]   rain frozen into balls of ice. □ *Hail the size of golf balls pelted the spectators during the sudden cloudburst.*
- **hail** [hel]   a shower of something. □ *A hail of confetti rained down from the tall buildings during the parade.*
- **hail [(up)on]** [hel]   to pour down like hail. □ *Strong criticism will probably hail upon the coach if his team loses another game.*
- **hail** [hel]   to call for someone or something. □ *You can hail a cab from almost any hotel or restaurant in town.*
- **hail [from]** [hel]   to come from some place. □ *All of my college roommates hail from the Midwest.*
- **hale** [hel]   healthy; sound. □ *Even at age ninety, our next-door neighbor is as hale as he was twenty years ago.*

hair—hare

- **hair** [hɛɚ]   the external body covering of an animal; the threadlike strands that grow out of the human head. □ *Some animals grow thick coats of coarse hair during long, harsh winters.* □ *As a child, Mary had blond, curly hair.*
- **hair** [hɛɚ]   the width of a hair. □ *We defended our bed race championship by winning this year's contest by a hair.*
- **hare** [hɛɚ]   a type of large rabbit known for its long ears and large hind legs. □ *The hare circled around trying to put off the pursuing hounds.*

hale   See the main entry beginning with *hail.*

hall—haul

- **hall** [hɔl]   a lobby or entryway off which other rooms open.

□ *A dimly lit hall can be frightening to a young child.*

- **hall** [hɔl]   a large room used for public meetings. □ *The great hall in the convention center is the site of many formal receptions.*
- **hall** [hɔl]   a building on a university or college campus. □ *A university may name a hall after a famous professor.*
- **haul** [hɔl]   to transport a burden, usually using a vehicle. □ *We haul all of the building supplies in a flatbed truck.* □ *A tractor was used to haul the heavy logs.*
- **haul** [hɔl]   to pull something; to redirect something. □ *The captain ordered the helmsman to haul the bow of the ship into the wind.*

halve—have

- **halve** [hæv]   to divide something into two equal parts; to reduce something by one half. □ *If I halve this submarine sandwich, would you like part of it?* □ *The girls agreed to halve whatever profits they made selling their baked goods.* □ *The business owner is hoping to halve the number of shoplifting incidents in his store next year.*
- **have** [hæv]   to own or possess someone or something. □ *They have a cottage on the smaller of the two lakes.* □ *We have numerous friends living in New England.* □ *Jerry said, "I have some terrific news to share with you."* □ *While my siblings all have dark locks, I have blond hair.*
- **have [to]** [hæv]   to have an obligation or feel a necessity to do something. □ *I have to go to my great-aunt's birthday party next Sunday.*
- **have** [hæv]   to bear offspring. □ *The couple hopes to have a child in the near future.*

handmade—handmaid

- **handmade** ['hænd'med]   made by hand, not machined. □ *As a housewarming gift, she gave the couple a handmade bed quilt.*
- **handmaid** ['hændmed]   a female servant or attendant. □ *The princess has a handmaid to attend to her every whim.*

handmaid   See the main entry beginning with *handmade.*

hangar—hanger

- **hangar** ['hæŋɚ]   a shed or building where aircraft are housed and repaired. □ *Security is tight around the hangar where the president's aircraft are kept.*
- **hangar** ['hæŋɚ]   to put something in a hangar. □ *We'd better hangar the plane before the storm hits.*
- **hanger** ['hæŋɚ]   something that is used to hang or suspend

something else. □ *After locking his keys inside, Fred used a wire coat hanger to open his car door.*

hanged—hung

- **hanged** [hæŋd]   the past tense and past participle of *hang* 'to put a person to death by suspending the person by the neck.' □ *The judge sentenced the convicted murderer to be hanged.*
- **hung** [həŋ]   the past tense of *hang* 'to suspend or fasten something.' □ *Millie hung a portrait of her mother above the fireplace.*

hanger   See the main entry beginning with *hangar.*

hare   See the main entry beginning with *hair.*

hart—heart

- **hart** [haₐt]   a mature male deer, especially of the red deer species. □ *The hart bounded across the meadow.*
- **heart** [haₐt]   the muscular organ that maintains blood circulation. □ *The patient received a new heart during the transplant surgery.*
- **heart** [haₐt]   the center or most important part. □ *Rather than skirt the issue, the council members wanted to get to the heart of the matter.*
- **heart** [haₐt]   a playing card bearing red hearts. □ *I trumped his card with a higher heart.*
- **heart** [haₐt]   the center of feeling and sincerity. □ *She always speaks from the heart.*

haul   See the main entry beginning with *hall.*

have   See the main entry beginning with *halve.*

hay—hey

- **hay** [he]   a mixture of grasses grown for animal feed. □ *The second cutting of hay is always a bit richer than the first.*
- **hay** [he]   to feed an animal with hay. □ *Be sure you hay the horses twice a day.*
- **hay** [he]   a bed. (Slang. Always found in the idiom *hit the hay.*) □ *"Let's all hit the hay early tonight," suggested Dad.*
- **hey** [he]   an expression used to get someone's attention; a greeting. □ *"Hey, wait a minute!" cried Louise.* □ *"Hey, Fred! What's happening?"*

hays—haze

- **hays** [hez]   the plural of *hay* 'a mixture of grasses grown for animal feed.' □ *Many different hays were exhibited at the state fair.*

- **haze** [hez] a cloud of fine particles in the air that reduces visibility. □ *The early morning haze promised that a sultry day lay ahead.*
- **haze** [hez] a vagueness of mental perception. □ *A severe reaction to the prescription left Joe's mind in a haze.*
- **haze** [hez] to harass and humiliate someone deliberately. □ *Many fraternities no longer haze new initiates.*

haze See the main entry beginning with *hays.*

heal—heel—he'll
- **heal** [hil] to cure something; to make something whole. □ *It may take some time for that nasty cut to heal.* □ *One cannot always heal hurt feelings immediately.* □ *Some economists believe the economy should be left alone to heal itself.*
- **heel** [hil] the back of the human foot. □ *Bob bruised his heel playing soccer.*
- **heel** [hil] the bottom, rear, or low part of some structure. □ *Set the heel of the cabinet down and get a better grasp on the sides.*
- **heel** [hil] the crusty end of a loaf of bread. □ *My brother and I always fought over who would get the heel of the bread.*
- **heel** [hil] to follow closely behind or beside someone. □ *The woman made her dog heel before she crossed the busy street.*
- **he'll** [hil] the contraction of *he will.* □ *If Doug waits in front of the shop, he'll see us when we arrive.*

hear—here
- **hear** [hɪɚ] to perceive something by ear; to listen to someone or something. □ *On a summer's night you can hear the croaking of frogs in the distant swamp.* □ *Be sure you hear the teacher's test directions.*
- **hear** [hɪɚ] to gain information by hearing; to learn something by hearing. □ *I hear what you're saying, and I understand the problem you face.*
- **here** [hɪɚ] this place; this location. □ *Here in Michigan, winters can alternately be mild or severe.* □ *"Come here at once," scolded the naughty child's father.*
- **here** [hɪɚ] an affirmative reply in a roll call. □ *Please reply "here" when your name is called.*

heard—herd
- **heard** [hɚd] the past tense and past participle of *hear* 'to perceive something by ear; to listen to someone or something; to learn something by hearing.' □ *I distinctly heard him say he would not be able to attend the seminar.* □ *The group heard the*

speaker as she related her personal safari experiences. □ *We heard that there will be numerous layoffs at the plant before the year's end.*
- **herd** [hɚd]   a group animals of the same species, usually hoofed animals. □ *The cattle herd will soon be driven to market.* □ *The noise made by the thundering herd of wildebeest was almost deafening.*
- **herd** [hɚd]   an unthinking mass of people. (Figurative.) □ *At the moment the stadium gates opened, the herd of spectators swarmed in.*
- **herd** [hɚd]   to assemble things or people into a group. (Literal for animals. Figurative for people.) □ *Try to herd the sheep into a corner of the pen.* □ *The usher herded my friends and me into the first row.*

heart   See the main entry beginning with *hart.*

he'd—heed
- **he'd** [hid]   the contraction of *he had* or *he would.* □ *If he'd studied for the test, he surely would have passed it.* □ *I'm sure he'd do it if you would ask him.*
- **heed** [hid]   to take notice of someone or something. □ *I hope Tom will heed my warning about the drop-off in the lake.*
- **heed** [hid]   caution; care. (Almost always with *give* or *take.*) □ *Take heed when pulling out into a busy intersection.* □ *Give heed to my warning.*

heed   See the main entry beginning with *he'd.*

heel   See the main entry beginning with *heal.*

heir   See the main entry beginning with *air.*

he'll   See the main entry beginning with *heal.*

herd   See the main entry beginning with *heard.*

here   See the main entry beginning with *hear.*

heroin—heroine
- **heroin** ['hɛɚoɪn]   a strongly addictive narcotic. □ *Cocaine is now more widely used than heroin.*
- **heroine** ['hɛɚoɪn]   a female hero. □ *The heroine in that story is a young poverty-stricken girl.* □ *Mother Theresa is a heroine in most parts of the world.*

heroine   See the main entry beginning with *heroin.*

hew—hue

- **hew** [hju] to cut, fell, or give form to something with heavy, cutting blows. □ *To hew a canoe from a single log is no small task.*
- **hue** [hju] a shade of color. □ *Her favorite hue of blue is azure.*
- **hue** [hju] aspect. □ *Most of Poe's poetry is of a somber hue.*

hey See the main entry beginning with *hay.*

hi—high

- **hi** [haɪ] an informal greeting or salutation. □ *"Hi, Grandma. This is Jennifer," whispered the little girl into the telephone.*
- **high** [haɪ] raised; elevated. □ *The high fence kept curiosity seekers from looking in.*
- **high** [haɪ] sharp; shrill. □ *Joan always speaks rapidly and in a high voice when she's irritated or frightened.*
- **high** [haɪ] noble or noteworthy. □ *He is a man of high principles.*
- **high** [haɪ] strong; forceful. □ *High winds and the sea battered the barrier islands.*

high See the main entry beginning with *hi.*

higher—hire

- **higher** [haɪɚ] the comparative form of *high* 'at a greater height.' □ *The higher he climbed on the ladder, the more nervous he became.*
- **hire** [haɪɚ] to take someone into employment; to engage the personal services of someone. □ *Shall we hire a cab to take us home after the play?*

him—hymn

- **him** [hɪm] the third person singular, objective, masculine pronoun. □ *Give him that invoice to check against the shipment.*
- **hymn** [hɪm] a song of joy, praise, or thanksgiving, usually sung in worship services. □ *Mama's favorite hymn was "Rock of Ages."*

hire See the main entry beginning with *higher.*

hoard—horde

- **hoard** [hoɚd] a concealed supply or cache of something. □ *The crow stashed a hoard of small sparkling items in its nest.*
- **hoard** [hoɚd] to hide a supply or cache of something. □ *It is not safe to hoard valuables in likely hiding places.*
- **horde** [hoɚd] a swarm or throng. □ *A horde of people waited in line all night for the concert tickets.*

- **horde** [hoəd] a group of nomadic people, particularly of Mongolian ancestry. □ *The pastoral horde wandered the region for decades.*

hoarse—horse

- **hoarse** [hoəs] harsh, grating, or rough in sound. □ *Following a bout with bronchitis, Tom's voice was very hoarse.*
- **horse** [hoəs] a four-legged animal with a flowing mane and tail. □ *The horse I was given at the riding stable was a gentle mare.*
- **horse** [hoəs] a gymnastic apparatus consisting of a padded framework mounted on legs. □ *One of Steve's strongest events is the horse.*
- **horse** [hoəs] to move something by force. □ *Be careful not to horse that antique desk around when you move it.*

hoes—hose

- **hoes** [hoz] the plural of *hoe* 'a garden tool used to break up the earth.' □ *The hoes are in the shed with the rest of the garden equipment.*
- **hose** [hoz] a flexible, hollow tube used to convey liquids. □ *I need to replace the water hose in my car.*
- **hose** [hoz] socks or stockings. □ *The splintered chair leg caused a run in Sally's hose.*
- **hose [down]** [hoz] to wash or spray something with a hose. □ *You must hose down the tumbler of the cement truck after each delivery.*

hold—holed

- **hold** [hold] to possess something. □ *She holds a degree in economics.*
- **hold** [hold] to contain someone or something; to support someone or something. □ *Will this box hold all the books?* □ *I don't believe this little chair will hold me.*
- **hold** [hold] to maintain a grasp on someone or something. □ *Hold the kite string tightly or the wind will blow the kite away.*
- **holed [up]** [hold] the past tense of *hole [up]* 'to hide; to retire in a place.' □ *The crooks holed up in a deserted building for a week.*

holed See the main entry beginning with *hold.*

hole—whole

- **hole** [hol] a depression or opening. □ *The meteorite left a huge hole in the earth when it hit the ground.*
- **hole** [hol] a fault or flaw. □ *The burglar discovered a hole in*

the security system of the building.

- **hole** [hol] an awkward position. □ *The sudden departure of three valuable employees left the company in a hole.*
- **whole** [hol] entire or unbroken. □ *Let's look at the whole picture.* □ *The vase remained whole even though I dropped it.*
- **whole** [hol] the complete number or sum of something. □ *The whole list had eleven chores on it.*
- **whole** [hol] a system of parts working together as a single unit. □ *As a whole, our fire department provides excellent service.*

holy—wholly

- **holy** ['holi] sacred; godly; that which evokes or merits reverence or respect. □ *The woman devoted her life to the holy service of God.* □ *People of all faiths observe certain days that are considered holy.*
- **holy** ['holi] used to express intensity. (Idiomatic.) □ *That unruly child is a holy terror!*
- **wholly** ['holi] completely. □ *We are wholly in agreement on that issue.*
- **wholly** ['holi] solely, to the exclusion of others. □ *No one person is wholly responsible for what happened.*

hoop—whoop

- **hoop** [hup] a ring. □ *The circus tiger fearlessly jumped through the hoop of fire.*
- **hoop** [hup] a flexible, rounded framework used to expand a skirt. □ *Dresses with hoop skirts are becoming fashionable again for formal wear.*
- **whoop** [ʍup, wup] a sudden, loud sound emitted in enthusiasm or eagerness. □ *With a whoop, the crowd rose to its feet.*
- **whoop** [ʍup, wup] to utter a loud and enthusiastic sound. □ *"I'll whoop for joy if I pass that exam!" exclaimed Carlos.*

horde See the main entry beginning with *hoard.*

horse See the main entry beginning with *hoarse.*

hose See the main entry beginning with *hoes.*

hostel—hostile

- **hostel** ['hɑstl] a supervised lodging provided for young people when traveling. □ *The college students met interesting people at each hostel.*
- **hostile** ['hɑstl, 'hɑstaɪl] antagonistic or unfriendly; relating to the enemy. □ *Joan is such a hostile person that none of her co-workers like her.* □ *The troops encountered hostile snipers*

on the far side of the river.

hostile   See the main entry beginning with *hostel.*

hour—our
- **hour** [ɑʊɚ]   a period of sixty minutes. □ *Each swimming lesson lasts an hour.*
- **hour** [ɑʊɚ]   the time of day indicated by a timepiece. □ *"Could you please tell me the hour?" inquired the man at the bus stop.*
- **hour** [ɑʊɚ]   a particular time. □ *At the appointed hour and place, the two intelligence agents met secretly.*
- **our** [ɑʊɚ]   first person, plural possessive pronoun. □ *Yesterday our car got a flat tire.*

hue   See the main entry beginning with *hew.*

humerus—humorous
- **humerus** [ˈhjumɚəs]   the long, heavy bone of the upper arm or forelimb extending from the shoulder to the elbow. □ *The humerus of Jacob's left arm was fractured when the scaffolding fell on him.*
- **humorous** [ˈhjumɚəs]   characterized by humor or wit. □ *Generally there is a humorous side to any embarrassing situation.*

humorous   See the main entry beginning with *humerus.*

hung   See the main entry beginning with *hanged.*

hymn   See the main entry beginning with *him.*

I

I See the main entry beginning with *aye.*

I'd See the main entry beginning with *eyed.*

idle—idol—idyll

- **idle** ['aɪdl] lacking purpose or worth. □ *All that talk about going on strike is just idle rumor.*
- **idle** ['aɪdl] not employed or occupied. □ *The autoworkers were idle due to a shutdown of production lines.*
- **idle** ['aɪdl] not being used appropriately. □ *Mischief often results from idle time.*
- **idol** ['aɪdl] something or someone that is worshipped or idolized. □ *That culture has a sunlike symbol as an idol.*
- **idol** ['aɪdl] a person or object of passionate devotion. □ *The teenager was devoted to the rock-and-roll idol.*
- **idyll** ['aɪdl] a simple, descriptive poem or writing depicting the virtues of the peaceful, rustic out-of-doors. □ *The short idyll painted images of a blissful shepherd's life.*

idol See the main entry beginning with *idle.*

idyll See the main entry beginning with *idle.*

I'll See the main entry beginning with *aisle.*

illicit See the main entry beginning with *elicit.*

illusion See the main entry beginning with *allusion.*

imminent See the main entry beginning with *eminent.*

imply—infer

- **imply** [ɪm'plaɪ] to suggest something without saying it specifically. □ *Do you mean to imply that I made a mistake?*

- **infer** [ɪnˈfɚ] to come to a conclusion about something. □ *Since the jury is deadlocked, we can infer that no decision will be reached.*

in—inn

- **in** [ɪn] inside; within; into. (A preposition.) □ *Someday I would like to fly in the Concorde SST.* □ *Please come in out of the rain.*
- **inn** [ɪn] a public lodging for travelers that usually provides food and drink. □ *The inn just outside the village provides comfortable beds and good food.* □ *The men stop each night for a beer at the inn.*

incite—insight

- **incite** [ɪnˈsaɪt] to stir up or move someone or something to action. □ *The speaker failed to incite the crowd to action.*
- **insight** [ˈɪnsaɪt] the ability to see or understand something intuitively. □ *Our physics teacher has great insight into how to motivate uninterested students.*

infer See the main entry beginning with *imply.*

inn See the main entry beginning with *in.*

innocence—innocents

- **innocence** [ˈɪnəsənts] guiltlessness or purity. □ *Throughout the trial, the accused proclaimed her innocence.*
- **innocents** [ˈɪnəsənts] the plural of *innocent* 'a person who is blameless or without fault.' □ *In any war it seems the innocents pay the dearest price.*

innocents See the main entry beginning with *innocence.*

insight See the main entry beginning with *incite.*

instance—instants

- **instance** [ˈɪnstənts] circumstance, example, or case. □ *In that particular instance, you probably should have kept quiet.*
- **instants** [ˈɪnstənts] the plural of *instant* 'a moment; a second; a split second.' □ *During those few frightening instants, we didn't know what would happen.*

instants See the main entry beginning with *instance.*

insure See the main entry beginning with *ensure.*

intense—intents

- **intense** [ɪnˈtɛnts] strong; extreme. □ *Tom felt intense relief after his solo performance.*

- **intense** [ɪnˈtɛnts]   deeply feeling, usually by temperament or nature. □ *Sam is an intense person at all times.*
- **intents** [ɪnˈtɛnts]   the plural of *intent* 'a purpose or an intention.' □ *Our intents have always had your best interests in mind.*

intents   See the main entry beginning with *intense.*

isle   See the main entry beginning with *aisle.*

its—it's
- **its** [ɪts]   the possessive form of *it.* □ *The kitten licked its paws after walking through the puddle of water.*
- **it's** [ɪts]   the contraction of *it is* or *it has.* □ *It's always exciting to have a birthday party—no matter how old you are.*

it's   See the main entry beginning with *its.*

J

jam—jamb

- **jam** [dʒæm]   to press or wedge something into a tight position. □ *Do not try to jam too many clothes into the suitcase.*
- **jam** [dʒæm]   an obstruction or congestion. □ *The traffic jam on the highway caused us to miss our plane.*
- **jam** [dʒæm]   a difficult predicament. □ *Whenever Mary gets in a jam, she calls her parents for help.*
- **jam** [dʒæm]   a condiment made with fruit and sugar. □ *Homemade peach jam is my favorite.*
- **jamb** [dʒæm]   an upright structure or piece forming the side of an opening. □ *Not a single door jamb in the building was straight.*

jamb   See the main entry beginning with *jam.*

jeans   See the main entry beginning with *genes.*

jell   See the main entry beginning with *gel.*

jinks—jinx

- **[high] jinks** [dʒɪŋks]   pranks. □ *"I will not put up with any high jinks while you're here," scolded Grandmother.*
- **jinx** [dʒɪŋks]   someone or something that brings bad luck or misfortune. □ *Eddie was a jinx to our team's winning streak.*
- **jinx** [dʒɪŋks]   to bring bad luck to someone. □ *Mary is so superstitious that she believes a passing black cat will jinx her.*

jinx   See the main entry beginning with *jinks.*

K

karat   See the main entry beginning with *carat.*

kernel   See the main entry beginning with *colonel.*

key—quay

- **key** [ki]   a metal piece used to open a lock. □ *I lost my car key and had to call a locksmith.*
- **key** [ki]   the solution to a problem; the explanation for something complicated. □ *The key to the mystery was the fingerprints that the police found on the doorknob.*
- **key** [ki]   a lever used to play a piano or an organ. □ *I pressed one key after another and nothing happened!*
- **key** [ki]   major; principal. □ *Ted is a key figure in the negotiations.*
- **key** [ki]   a particular musical scale. □ *The entire sonata was in the key of C major.*
- **quay** [ki]   a wharf. □ *Our ship docked at the quay and the passengers got off quickly.*

kill—kiln

- **kill** [kɪl]   to deprive someone or something of life; to murder or slay someone or something. □ *My brother will not even kill a mosquito.*
- **kill** [kɪl]   to put an end to something; to stop something. □ *Another loss will kill the team's hopes of post-season play.* □ *Kill the engine so we don't run out of gas.*
- **kill** [kɪl]   to destroy the vitality of something or someone. □ *Don't kill her enthusiasm by being too critical.*
- **kill** [kɪl]   to let something elapse. □ *We have some time to kill before the movie begins.*

- **kill** [kɪl]   to exhaust someone or something. □ *"If we have to run another mile, it will just kill me," complained Gary.*
- **kill** [kɪl]   something killed. □ *The hunter's kill consisted of two rabbits and three squirrels.*
- **kill** [kɪl]   the act of killing something or someone. □ *When the wounded zebra staggered, the lions moved in for the kill.*
- **kiln** [kɪl, kɪln]   a heated enclosure used to dry substances. □ *The owner of the ceramic shop has just purchased a new kiln.*

kiln   See the main entry beginning with *kill.*

knead—kneed—need
- **knead** [nid]   to form or shape something into a mass with the hands; to rub or squeeze something with the hands. □ *It is best to knead and punch the bread dough twice before letting it rise for the final time.* □ *A massage therapist will knead the muscles in your neck.*
- **kneed** [nid]   the past tense and past participle of *knee* 'to strike someone with one's knee.' □ *Sam was upset when the person sitting behind him kneed him in the back.*
- **need** [nid]   to be in want of something or someone. □ *I need more time to think over my options.*
- **need** [nid]   a lack of something necessary, useful, or desirable. □ *His need for steady employment is pressing.*
- **need** [nid]   an obligation or duty. □ *There is no need to arrive early.*

kneed   See the main entry beginning with *knead.*

knew   See the main entry beginning with *gnu.*

knickers—nickers
- **knickers** [ˈnɪkɚz]   short, loose-fitting pants gathered at the knee. □ *Knickers were once the men's fashion rage in golf.*
- **nickers** [ˈnɪkɚz]   the plural of *nicker* 'the neigh or whinny of a horse.' □ *From the barn we could hear the impatient pony's nickers.*

knight—night
- **knight** [nɑɪt]   in feudal society, a man-at-arms serving a superior noble. □ *The knight in shining armor rescued the princess from the castle tower.*
- **knight** [nɑɪt]   to bestow knighthood upon someone. □ *The king will knight the two men who saved his life.*
- **knight** [nɑɪt]   a chess piece, usually in the shape of a horse bust. □ *In chess, a knight is a higher-ranking piece than a pawn.*

- **night** [naɪt]   darkness. □ *Nocturnal animals are able to see at night.* □ *Night covered the campsite and one by one we turned on our flashlights.*
- **night** [naɪt]   evening. □ *Last night I spotted a shooting star in the sky.*

knit—nit

- **knit** [nɪt]   to interlace yarn or thread in a series of connected loops using needles. □ *Mom always liked to knit rather than crochet.*
- **knit** [nɪt]   to form, tie, or link something closely together. □ *The new trade agreement will knit the nations.*
- **knit** [nɪt]   to contract something into wrinkles. □ *Father used to knit his brow when he was upset or worried.*
- **nit** [nɪt]   a young, parasitic insect or the egg of a young, parasitic insect. □ *Head lice are a type of nit.*

knob—nob

- **knob** [nɑb]   a rounded handle. □ *To open the front door, you must twist the knob.*
- **knob** [nɑb]   a small, isolated hill or mountain. □ *The knob would make a perfect ski slope.*
- **knob** [nɑb]   a lump. □ *The sharp blow raised a knob on his head.*
- **nob** [nɑb]   the head. (Slang.) □ *You'll have a bump on your nob from that nasty insect bite.*
- **nob** [nɑb]   in cribbage, a jack of the same suit as the starter that scores a point for the holder. □ *A nob in cribbage is similar to the "right" or "left" in euchre.*

knock—nock

- **knock** [nɑk]   to hit something with a sharp blow. □ *Please knock on the door before entering the office.*
- **knock** [nɑk]   to collide with something or someone. □ *Be careful not to knock over the figurines.*
- **knock** [nɑk]   to wander about. □ *Ken wants just to knock around for awhile after he graduates from high school.*
- **knock** [nɑk]   a setback or misfortune. □ *Losing the game in the final moments was a hard knock.*
- **knock** [nɑk]   to find fault with someone or something. □ *Don't knock my earnest attempts.*
- **knock** [nɑk]   an abnormal noise originating from the engine of a car or truck. □ *Richard detected an engine knock in his new car.*
- **nock** [nɑk]   a notch in a bow used to hold the bowstring or

the arrow. □ *The craftsman carefully cut a nock into each end of the bow.*
- **nock** [nɑk] the rear notched part of the arrow that is fitted to the bowstring and holds it in place. □ *The archer's aluminum arrow is fitted with a plastic nock.*
- **nock** [nɑk] to fit an arrow to a bowstring. □ *Upon seeing the bear, the frightened hunter was able to nock his bow quickly.*

knot—naught—not

- **knot** [nɑt] an interlacing of string, twine, or rope. □ *I was unable to untangle the knot in my fishing line.*
- **knot** [nɑt] a hard-to-solve problem or dilemma. □ *That issue put a knot in the discussion.*
- **knot** [nɑt] a bond of union, especially marriage. (Always in the idiom *tie the knot*.) □ *The couple has finally decided to tie the knot.*
- **knot** [nɑt] one nautical mile per hour. □ *The tugboat chugged out of the harbor at a single knot.*
- **naught** [nɔt, nɑt] nothing. (Typically with *for*.) □ *All his hard work was for naught.*
- **not** [nɑt] a word indicating *no* or negation. □ *We are not hungry at the moment.*

knotty—naughty

- **knotty** ['nɑti] having many knots, as with hair, rope, or string. □ *After a day in the wind, my hair was all knotty.*
- **knotty** ['nɑti] having many knots, as with lumber containing the bases of many branches. □ *I can't use this board because it is too knotty.*
- **naughty** ['nɔti, 'nɑti] ill-behaved; disobedient. □ *If you are naughty, I will have to send you to bed.*

know—no

- **know** [no] to understand or discern something; to be sure of the truth or certainty of something. □ *Charley does not know how to solve that problem.* □ *I know that she is an honest person.*
- **no** [no] none or not any. □ *There is no other way to the top of the tower other than the steep staircase.*
- **no** [no] a negative reply or denial. □ *No, I don't care for any more coffee.*

knows—nose

- **knows** [noz] the present tense, third person singular of *know* 'to understand or perceive something; to be aware of a fact.' □ *The boy knows he will be punished severely for coming home* *late.* □ *Mary knows a surprise party is being planned in honor of her retirement.*

- **knows** [noz]   the present tense, third person singular of *know* 'to be acquainted with someone or something.' □ *She knows the shortest route to that town.* □ *Mary knows Bob very well.*
- **nose** [noz]   the organ of smell. □ *The actress's nose is her most distinguishing feature.*
- **nose** [noz]   to detect or sense something or someone by smell. □ *His dog can nose a rabbit out of any briar patch.*
- **nose** [noz]   to pry or meddle in something. □ *You have no right to nose about in other people's business.*
- **nose** [noz]   the front part of a structure, vehicle, or craft. □ *As it took off, the nose of the jet seemed to be pointed straight up.*

L

lacks—lax

- **lacks** [læks]   the present tense, third person singular of *lack* 'to be in need of something.' □ *That wine lacks a full, fruity flavor.*
- **lax** [læks]   loose; slack. □ *Hoist the sails up fully so they are not lax.*
- **lax** [læks]   not strict or stringent. □ *Fred is very lax about his personal appearance.*

ladder—latter

- **ladder** ['lædɚ]   a structure of two vertical side poles and numerous horizontal rungs that is used for climbing up and down. □ *Jake refuses to walk underneath any ladder.*
- **ladder** ['lædɚ]   something that resembles a ladder or functions like a ladder. □ *A fish ladder was constructed to help the salmon swim upstream to spawn.*
- **latter** ['lædɚ, 'lætɚ]   referring to the second of two things mentioned. □ *Though Lindsay and Marina are both smart, the latter is the better student.*
- **latter** ['lædɚ, 'lætɚ]   the last; the end. □ *In the latter stages of the conflict, the war-weary soldiers wanted to give up.*

lain—lane

- **lain** [len]   the past participle of *lie* 'to rest or recline in a horizontal position.' □ *She has lain on the sofa so often that it sags in some places.*
- **lain** [len]   the past participle of *lie* 'to occupy a place; to be in a place.' □ *The two rusty plows have lain next to each other in the field for years.*
- **lane** [len]   a narrow path or road; a marked path or route; an

ocean route for sea going vessels. □ *The country lane is lined with wildflowers in the spring.* □ *Jessica was disqualified from the race because she stepped out of her lane on the backstretch.* □ *Jane threw her bowling ball so forcefully that it landed in the next lane.*

lam—lamb

- **lam** [læm]   a hurried or sudden flight from the law. □ *Since the prison escape, the convict has been on a lam.*
- **lamb** [læm]   a young sheep. □ *The white, fluffy lamb frolicked in the pasture with its mother.*
- **lamb** [læm]   a person as weak or gentle as a lamb. □ *Despite his huge size, Bob is a real lamb.*
- **lamb** [læm]   the meat of a young sheep. □ *One of the house specialties at this restaurant is lamb chops with mint sauce.*

lamb   See the main entry beginning with *lam.*

lane   See the main entry beginning with *lain.*

laps—lapse

- **laps** [læps]   the plural of *lap* 'the top of the thighs of a seated person.' □ *The baby-sitters held the twins on their laps while reading them bedtime stories.*
- **laps** [læps]   the plural of *lap* 'a loose panel or flap of fabric or skin.' □ *A current style of women's trousers has billowy laps of fabric along the legs.*
- **laps** [læps]   the plural of *lap* 'one circuit, often around a racecourse or swimming pool.' □ *Our gym teacher always makes the losing relay team run laps around the track.*
- **laps** [læps]   the present tense, third person singular of *lap* 'to drink liquid using the tongue.' □ *The kitten always laps its water noisily.*
- **laps** [læps]   the present tense, third person singular of *lap* 'to move in small, gentle waves.' □ *It is peaceful and relaxing to walk along the beach as the water gently laps the shoreline.*
- **lapse** [læps]   a gap or break in some time period or activity; a discontinuance. □ *There was a temporary lapse in the electrical service to the neighborhood.* □ *During a lapse in the flow of customers, Vince ran out for a quick bite to eat.*
- **lapse** [læps]   an error; a slip. □ *During a lapse in manners, Dad talked with his mouth full.*
- **lapse** [læps]   to backslide or fall into error. □ *Now that he has reached his desired weight, Ron hopes that he doesn't lapse into poor eating habits.*

lapse   See the main entry beginning with *laps.*

latter   See the main entry beginning with *ladder.*

lax   See the main entry beginning with *lacks.*

lay—lei
(See also *lay—lie.*)
- **lay** [le]   to place or set someone or something down. □ *Lay the tools on the workbench.*
- **lay** [le]   to wager or bet something. □ *I will not lay odds on the outcome of that football game.*
- **lay** [le]   to impose as an obligation, reproach, burden, or punishment. □ *The government will lay a heavy tax on those imports.*
- **lay** [le]   to plan or conceive something. □ *Let's lay a plan to make the police think we have disappeared.*
- **lay** [le]   a person not of the clergy; a person not belonging to a certain profession. □ *Guenter Schmidt is a lay reader at his church.* □ *Many computer manuals are written for a lay audience.*
- **lay [down]** [le]   the past tense of *lie [down]* 'to rest or recline in a horizontal position.' □ *He lay down to rest and fell asleep.*
- **lay** [le]   the past tense of *lie* 'to occupy a place; to be situated some place.' □ *At one time those two old sheds lay near the main barn.*
- **lei** [le]   a wreath or necklace of flowers or similar material. □ *The flight attendant placed a lei around Mary's neck when her plane arrived in Hawaii.*

lay—lie
- **lay** [le]   to place someone or something onto something. □ *Lay the tools over on the workbench, please.* □ *Now I lay me down to sleep.*
- **lie** [laɪ]   to rest or recline in a horizontal position. □ *I think you should lie here and rest.*

lays—laze—leis
- **lays** [lez]   the present tense, third person singular of *lay* 'to place or set something down.' □ *Peter always lays his shoes right where they will get stepped on.*
- **lays** [lez]   the present tense, third person singular of *lay* 'to place a bet.' □ *Each time she goes to the racecourse, Susan lays a bet on her favorite horse.*
- **lays** [lez]   the present tense, third person singular of *lay* 'to contrive a plan.' □ *When he doesn't feel like going to school,*

Casey lays a plan to pretend he is ill.

- **laze** [lez]   to pass time in relaxation or idleness. □ *Summertime affords some students time to laze the days away.*
- **leis** [lez]   the plural of *lei* 'a wreath or necklace of flowers or similar material.' □ *The prettiest leis are those made of orchid blossoms.*

laze   See the main entry beginning with *lays.*

leach—leech

- **leach** [litʃ]   to pass something through or out of something by percolation. □ *If we first leach this compound, there won't be as much sediment in the liquid that is left.*
- **leech** [litʃ]   a bloodsucking worm usually found in fresh, slow-moving water. □ *We found a leech in the stagnant pond.*
- **leech** [litʃ]   a hanger-on who seeks to gain favor or position by association. □ *The leech hoped he would gain favors from the new mayor.*
- **leech** [litʃ]   to remove blood from patients, as a treatment for various diseases. (Not widely practiced any longer.) □ *Doctors used to leech patients to rid them of disease.*

lead—led

- **lead** [lɛd]   a heavy, soft metal that can be formed into shapes. □ *Fishing sinkers are usually made of lead.*
- **lead** [lɛd]   a thin rod of a marking material found in pencils and pens. □ *Jeff broke his pencil lead twice during the exam.*
- **led** [lɛd]   the past tense and past participle of *lead* 'to guide, direct, or aim someone or something.' □ *The scout led the pioneers into the wilderness.*
- **led** [lɛd]   the past tense and past participle of *lead* 'to serve as a leader; to be ahead of or in front of someone.' □ *The famous scientist led the team of experts.* □ *Scott led his team in rebounds this year.*

leak—leek

- **leak** [lik]   a crack or hole that unintentionally allows an escape of something. □ *A leak in the water pipe caused the basement to flood.*
- **leak** [lik]   to give out information secretly. □ *Let's not leak this material to the newspapers ahead of schedule.*
- **leek** [lik]   an edible garden herb known for its somewhat pungent taste. □ *Since his wife does not like the flavor of leek, Ted leaves it out of his Chinese dishes.*

lean—lien

- **lean** [lin]   having little or no fat. □ *The circus performer was*

lean and wiry. □ *He eats only lean red meat.*
- **lean** [lin] to rely upon someone or something for support. □ *It's nice to have someone to lean on in times of trouble.*
- **lean** [lin] to bend from a vertical position. □ *Since Sally is almost deaf, she must lean forward to listen when someone speaks.*
- **lean** [lin] to incline toward something in opinion, taste, or desire. □ *My taste in clothing tends to lean toward classic styles.*
- **lien** [lin] a legal charge upon personal property to offset or satisfy some debt or duty. □ *The lien on our neighbor's farm must be settled before the bank will approve a new loan.*

leased—least
- **leased** [list] the past tense and past participle of *lease* 'to rent something for one's use, usually real estate or an automobile, for a specified period of time.' □ *Last year more companies leased business vehicles than ever before.*
- **least** [list] the superlative form of *less.* □ *Of Mary's three children, the youngest boy is the least prone to catching colds.*
- **least** [list] the smallest degree, amount, or size possible. □ *I'm not the least bit worried about what he thinks.*

least See the main entry beginning with *leased.*

led See the main entry beginning with *lead.*

leech See the main entry beginning with *leach.*

leek See the main entry beginning with *leak.*

lei See the main entry beginning with *lay.*

leis See the main entry beginning with *lays.*

lend—loan
- **lend** [lɛnd] to give something to someone with an understanding that what was given (or something equal to it) will be returned. □ *I'll lend you some of my water goblets for your dinner party.*
- **loan** [lon] something given to a borrower temporarily. □ *The loan of Peter's wrench was a great help.* □ *Has the loan for your new house been approved?*

lends—lens
- **lends** [lɛn(d)z] the present tense, third person singular of *lend* 'to make a loan of something to someone.' □ *Henri often lends Kip his car repair tools.* □ *My credit union lends money*

just as most banks do.

- **lens** [lɛnz] a glass or other substance used to focus or direct light rays. □ *The lens of that camera was badly scratched.* □ *A piece of metal was imbedded in the lens of her left eye.*

lens See the main entry beginning with *lends.*

lessen—lesson
- **lessen** [ˈlɛsən] to reduce something in size, number, or degree. □ *Aspirin will lessen the pain of your toothache.*
- **lesson** [ˈlɛsən] a piece of instruction or something to be learned, especially by a student. □ *Today's lesson dealt with right triangles.*
- **lesson** [ˈlɛsən] a rebuke. □ *That incident taught us an important lesson about honesty.*
- **lesson** [ˈlɛsən] a portion of sacred writing read during a worship service. □ *"Our lesson for this day is from the book of Acts," announced the minister.*

lesson See the main entry beginning with *lessen.*

lets—let's
- **lets** [lɛts] the third person singular of *let* 'to permit someone to do something.' □ *She lets the children stay up late on weekends.*
- **let's** [lɛts] the contraction of *let us.* □ *Let's go now.*

let's See the main entry beginning with *lets.*

levee—levy
- **levee** [ˈlɛvi] a dike or embankment of some type used to prevent flooding. □ *The levee was under much stress due to the heavy rainfall.*
- **levee** [ˈlɛvi] a reception for a particular or important person. □ *An afternoon levee was held in honor of the visiting poet.*
- **levy** [ˈlɛvi] to impose or collect an assessment, tax, or something else by legal means. □ *In the future, the court will levy stiffer fines for traffic offenses.*
- **levy** [ˈlɛvi] to wage or carry something on, as if in war. □ *Those two countries continue to levy war on one another.*
- **levy** [ˈlɛvi] to conscript or draft persons into the military. □ *The army needs to levy more troops to increase its numbers.*

levy See the main entry beginning with *levee.*

liar—lyre
- **liar** [ˈlaɪɚ] a person who does not tell the truth. □ *Though*

she has trouble telling the truth, Liz does not consider herself a liar.

- **lyre** [ˈlaɪɚ]   a stringed musical instrument similar to a harp. □ *In the ancient drawing a lyre appears in the hands of a servant girl.*

lie—lye

- **lie** [laɪ]   an untruth that is told deliberately. (See also the entry beginning with *lay.*) □ *The child told a lie to avoid punishment.*
- **lie** [laɪ]   to tell something that is not true in order to deceive someone. □ *Please do not lie to me.*
- **lie** [laɪ]   to rest or recline in a horizontal position. □ *I think you should lie down here and rest.*
- **lie** [laɪ]   to hide. □ *The burglars will lie in wait in the shadows before entering the house.*
- **lie** [laɪ]   to occupy a position in relation to something else. □ *The villages lie on opposite sides of the valley.*
- **lye** [laɪ]   a strong, alkaline solution that comes from wood and is used to make soap. □ *Lye can burn your skin if it is too concentrated.*

lien   See the main entry beginning with *lean.*

light—lite

- **light** [laɪt]   something that illuminates to make vision possible. □ *Turn on the porch light before you leave.* □ *We need some light to be able to see what we are doing.*
- **light** [laɪt]   truth or enlightenment. □ *Casey finally saw the light about the importance of studying hard.*
- **light** [laɪt]   having little pigment. □ *Many red-haired people have light complexions.*
- **light** [laɪt]   easy. □ *Mary is carrying a light class load this term.*
- **light** [laɪt]   cheerful; jovial. □ *The quartet played a light, classical piece of music.*
- **light** [laɪt]   dizzy; giddy. □ *I felt a bit light after hitting my head on the door.*
- **lite** [laɪt]   containing fewer calories; containing less of some ingredient. □ *My wife insists on buying lite bread, margarine, and cottage cheese.*

lightening—lightning

- **lightening** [ˈlaɪtnɪŋ]   the present participle of *lighten* 'to make someone or something lighter.' □ *After lightening the load in my backpack, I was able to keep up with the other hikers.*

☐ *His lightening of my bad mood made me feel much better.*

- **lightening** [ˈlaɪtnɪŋ] the present participle of *lighten* 'to make something brighter.' ☐ *After the storm we saw a lightening of the sky almost immediately.*
- **lightning** [ˈlaɪtnɪŋ] a sudden, bright electrical charge from one cloud to another or from a cloud to earth. ☐ *The thunder clapped and the lightning lit up the sky as if it were daytime.*
- **lightning** [ˈlaɪtnɪŋ] sudden; very fast; having great speed. ☐ *Carl was well-known on the track team for his lightning sprint.*

lightning See the main entry beginning with *lightening.*

links—lynx

- **links** [lɪŋks] the plural of *link* 'a segment of a chain.' ☐ *Because her new watchband was too big, Stella had two links taken out of the band.*
- **links** [lɪŋks] the plural of *link* 'a connection.' ☐ *The police could find no links between the suspects and the crime.*
- **links** [lɪŋks] the plural of *link* 'a piece of jewelry used to fasten the cuffs on a long-sleeved shirt or blouse.' ☐ *Orlando lost one of his cuff links at the dance.*
- **links** [lɪŋks] the plural of *link* 'a tubular segment of sausage.' ☐ *They ate pancakes, eggs, and sausage links for breakfast.*
- **links** [lɪŋks] the present tense, third person singular of *link* 'to join people or things together.' ☐ *The evidence strongly links her to the rumor.*
- **links** [lɪŋks] a golf course. ☐ *Every Saturday morning you can find Mary on the links at the country club.*
- **lynx** [lɪŋks] a wildcat resembling a bobcat but with tufted ears and larger, padded feet. ☐ *Some trappers hunt lynx for their valuable fur.*

lite See the main entry beginning with *light.*

load—lode—lowed

- **load** [lod] something carried by a person or animal. ☐ *The heavy load was too much for the young child to carry.*
- **load** [lod] a mass or weight borne by something. ☐ *There are load limit restrictions on these roads during the springtime.*
- **load** [lod] the amount of work a person is expected to do. ☐ *As a new employee, Stella will carry a lighter load for the first two weeks.*
- **load** [lod] the full sight or story about someone or something; an earful or an eyeful. ☐ *"Wait until you get a load of this!" exclaimed Chuck.*
- **load** [lod] to put someone or something in or on something.

$\square$ *You load the groceries into the car and I'll drive home.* $\square$
Let's load the trailer before it gets dark.
- **load** [lod]   to increase the weight of something. $\square$ *The salt
bags will load down the back of the car.*
- **lode** [lod]   an abundant store of something. $\square$ *Jerry received
a lode of money when he won the lottery.*
- **lode** [lod]   a mineral deposit within certain boundaries. $\square$
*The old prospector bragged about the size of the silver lode he
had discovered.*
- **lowed** [lod]   the past tense and past participle of *low* '[for
cattle] to make a soft, moaning sound.' $\square$ *The restless cows
lowed softly in the pasture.*

loan—lone
(See also the main entry beginning with *lend.*)
- **loan** [lon]   something given for a borrower's temporary use.
$\square$ *The buyer decided not to apply for a loan to buy the new
lawn tractor.* $\square$ *I was grateful for the loan of Joe's computer.*
- **lone** [lon]   alone, sole, only, isolated. $\square$ *The lone Canada
goose flew across the darkening sky.*

loath—loathe
- **loath** [loθ]   reluctant; unwilling. $\square$ *I am loath to sit next to
that obnoxious person for even one more minute!*
- **loathe** [loð]   to hate someone or something. $\square$ *Not only does
he loathe the sight of cooked spinach, he also refuses to eat it.*

loathe   See the main entry beginning with *loath.*

loch—lock
- **loch** [lɔh, lɔk]   a bay or arm of a sea nearly surrounded by land,
especially in Scotland. $\square$ *There is a famous loch in Scotland
where a monster presumably lives.*
- **lock** [lɑk]   a security device operated by a key, combination,
or electrical circuit and used to restrict entrance to or exit
from a place. $\square$ *My new key did not fit the lock properly.*
- **lock** [lɑk]   a tress of hair; a group of human hairs. $\square$ *Mother
keeps a lock of our hair in each of our baby books.*
- **lock** [lɑk]   an enclosure used for raising and lowering vessels
from one water level to another. $\square$ *The ship must pass through
the lock to enter Lake Superior.*
- **lock** [lɑk]   to fasten, join, or hold something together. $\square$ *The
wrestlers must lock hands before beginning a match.*
- **lock** [lɑk]   to secure something with a lock. $\square$ *Be sure to lock
the door when you leave.*

lock   See the main entry beginning with *loch.*

locks—lox
- **locks** [lɑks]   the plural of *lock* 'a security device operated by a key, combination, or electrical circuit and used to restrict entrance to or exit from a place.' □ *As a safety measure, Sam had the locks on all of the doors changed.*
- **locks** [lɑks]   the plural of *lock* 'a tress of hair; a group of human hairs.' □ *Her golden locks were the envy of all of her friends.*
- **locks** [lɑks]   the plural of *lock* 'an enclosure used for raising and lowering vessels from one water level to another.' □ *Most locks do not operate in the winter.*
- **locks** [lɑks]   the present tense, third person singular of *lock* 'to fasten, join, or hold something together.' □ *A computer automatically locks the gates in the prison.* □ *Grandpa never locks his house at night.*
- **lox** [lɑks]   smoked salmon. □ *Her favorite items on the buffet table are the lox and bagels.*

lode   See the main entry beginning with *load.*

lone   See the main entry beginning with *loan.*

loot—lute
- **loot** [lut]   something taken illegally, often by force, especially in war; spoils of war. □ *The soldiers carried the loot into their camp.*
- **loot** [lut]   money. (Slang.) □ *"Where should we hide the loot?" asked one of the bank robbers.*
- **loot** [lut]   illegal gains by public officials. □ *No one was aware of the loot skimmed out of the public treasury by top city officials.*
- **loot** [lut]   to take something illegally by force or violence. □ *Rioters continued to loot the ravaged city day after day.*
- **lute** [lut]   a pear-shaped, stringed musical instrument resembling and played like a guitar. □ *The wandering minstrel played a lute.*

lowed   See the main entry beginning with *load.*

lox   See the main entry beginning with *locks.*

lute   See the main entry beginning with *loot.*

lye   See the main entry beginning with *lie.*

lynx   See the main entry beginning with *links.*

lyre   See the main entry beginning with *liar.*

M

made—maid

- **made** [med]   the past tense and past participle of *make* 'to create something; to manufacture something.' □ *Those lanterns were made in Hong Kong.* □ *Timothy made a cage for his gerbils.*
- **made [up]** [med]   the past tense and past participle of *make [up]* 'to invent a story.' □ *She made up a story that was too silly to believe.*
- **made** [med]   the past tense and past participle of *make* 'to complete something; to succeed at something.' □ *Bill has made his career in politics.*
- **maid** [med]   a female servant. □ *Mrs. Smith's maid gets every other weekend off.*
- **maid** [med]   a young, unmarried girl or woman. (Used only in older stories and fairy tales.) □ *A lovely maid captured the young king's heart.*

maid   See the main entry beginning with *made.*

mail—male

- **mail** [mel]   letters, packages, and other postal material. □ *A former roommate of mine was once a mail carrier in California.*
- **mail** [mel]   to send something by post or mail. □ *Ruth promised to mail the letter in the morning.*
- **mail** [mel]   armor made from metal links or plates. □ *The knight wore heavy mail during the battle.*
- **mail** [mel]   the hard, protective covering of some animals. □ *Such animals as the armadillo are covered with mail.*
- **male** [mel]   a human, plant, or animal of the masculine gender. □ *The test determined that at least one of the unborn twins*

is a male.
- **male** [mel]   bearing masculine characteristics. □ *A male apple tree is needed to pollinate the female trees.*

main—mane
- **main** [men]   chief; essential. □ *The main idea of the poem was hard to figure out.*
- **main** [men]   physical force or strength. (Always in the idiom *might and main.*) □ *Julio pushed the stalled car with all of his might and main.*
- **main** [men]   a major duct, pipe, or circuit responsible for feeding lesser branches of a utility system. □ *A bulldozer accidently hit a water main while digging at the site.*
- **mane** [men]   long, heavy hair growing from the neck of some mammals, especially horses and lions. □ *When I lost my grip on the bridle rein, I grabbed a handful of the horse's mane.*
- **mane** [men]   the heavy tresses of a person's head. □ *Susan has the most beautiful mane of shiny black hair.*

maize—maze
- **maize** [mez]   a type of corn. □ *Maize was one of the food staples for many North American Indian tribes.*
- **maze** [mez]   a complex, confusing network of passageways; a confused or bewildered state. □ *The mouse was able to find its way out of the maze.* □ *My mind was in a maze after the long study session.*

male   See the main entry beginning with *mail.*

mall—maul
- **mall** [mɔl]   a mallet. □ *He hit the sheet of steel with a rubber mall.*
- **mall** [mɔl]   a large, enclosed shopping center. □ *A popular place for teenagers to hang out is at the mall.*
- **mall** [mɔl]   a public walkway often lined with shade trees. □ *Many couples stroll along the mall in the evening.*
- **maul** [mɔl]   to molest, mangle, or handle roughly. □ *Do not allow that young child to maul those tiny kittens.*
- **maul** [mɔl]   a heavy hammer used to drive wedges. □ *We'll need a maul to split the wood.*

mane   See the main entry beginning with *main.*

manner—manor
- **manner** ['mænɚ]   a characteristic way of acting or behaving. □ *His manner has always been kind and gentle.*
- **manner** ['mænɚ]   sort or kind. □ *What manner of person*

would do such a thing?

- **manor** ['mænɚ]   the house or mansion of an estate. □ *The manor sits at the end of a long, winding drive.*
- **manor** ['mænɚ]   a piece of land in which the tenants pay a user's fee either in money or in goods produced on that land. □ *The serfs worked the manor in exchange for a portion of their crop.*
- **manor** ['mænɚ]   in England, a rural territorial unit or organization. □ *That manor is made up mostly of small villages.*

manor   See the main entry beginning with *manner.*

mantel—mantle

- **mantel** ['mæntl]   a shelf above a fireplace. □ *The couple chose an antique barn beam for the mantel in their new home.*
- **mantel** ['mæntl]   a structure that supports the masonry above a fireplace. □ *The bricklayer first built the mantel and then laid up the fireplace facial brick.*
- **mantle** ['mæntl]   a cloak. □ *The actor wore a black mantle throughout the play.*
- **mantle** ['mæntl]   something that encloses or covers something. □ *The captives escaped under a mantle of darkness.*
- **mantle** ['mæntl]   the back, shoulders, and wings of a bird. □ *The feathers on the mantle of the exotic bird were orange and green.*
- **mantle** ['mæntl]   part of the shell of a mollusk. □ *We found an oyster mantle that had washed up on the shore.*
- **mantle** ['mæntl]   part of the earth's surface just above the central core. □ *Do scientists know the depth of the earth's mantle?*
- **mantle** ['mæntl]   to cover or spread over something as with a mantle. □ *Birds of prey will often mantle their kill with their wings.*

mantle   See the main entry beginning with *mantel.*

mare—mayor

- **mare** [mɛɚ]   a female horse, donkey, or mule, especially one of breeding age. □ *The horse that caught the judges' eyes was a flashy mare with spirit.*
- **mare** [mɛɚ]   a supernatural being that causes nightmares. □ *She dreamed that an evil mare flew into her bedroom.*
- **mare** [mɛɚ]   a large, dark patch on the surface of Mars or the moon. □ *The mare on the full moon's surface was visible with the naked eye.*

- **mayor** [mɛɚ, meɚ] the elected chief officer of a city or borough. □ *Our city's mayor is very active in local activities.*

marquee—marquis—marquise

- **marquee** [mɑrˈki] a canopy or signboard that projects over the entrance of a theater or other building and consists of metal, lights, and glass. □ *The bright yellow lights around the border of the marquee flashed on and off.*
- **marquee** [mɑrˈki] a large tent set up for an outdoor gathering. □ *The band will perform under a marquee at the wedding reception.*
- **marquis** [mɑrˈki] a nobleman of inherited rank in some countries. □ *The heroine in that romance novel refused to marry the evil marquis.*
- **marquise** [mɑrˈkis] a gemstone or ring setting in the shape of a long oval with pointed ends. □ *Donna's diamond engagement ring is a brilliant marquise.*

marquis See the main entry beginning with *marquee.*

marquise See the main entry beginning with *marquee.*

marry—merry

- **marry** [ˈmæɚi, ˈmɛɚi] to join two people in matrimony as husband and wife. □ *The rabbi will marry the couple on Friday evening.*
- **marry** [ˈmæɚi, ˈmɛɚi] to take someone as a spouse. □ *John will marry Ellen when he finishes college.*
- **marry** [ˈmæɚi, ˈmɛɚi] to unite two things in a close relationship. □ *The merger will marry two of the largest airlines in the world.*
- **merry** [ˈmɛɚi] jovial, lighthearted, or festive. □ *Everyone attending the festival had a merry time.*

marshal—martial

- **marshal** [ˈmɑrʃl] a person who directs and oversees ceremonial gatherings. □ *A celebrity is usually chosen to act as the grand marshal of the annual parade.*
- **marshal** [ˈmɑrʃl] a federal official in charge of prisoners or having certain judicial duties. □ *The fugitive surrendered to the marshal.*
- **marshal** [ˈmɑrʃl] an administrative head of a city's fire or police department. □ *The local fire marshal inspected the house that was destroyed in the blaze.*
- **martial** [ˈmɑrʃl] pertaining or relating to war, combat, or army or military life. □ *She is taking a course in the martial*

arts as a hobby.

marten—martin

- **marten** ['martn]   any of several small, meat-eating mammals belonging to the weasel family that live in semi-forested areas. □ *The pine marten is making a comeback in some areas of Michigan.*
- **martin** ['martn]   a shiny, blue-black bird belonging to the swallow family known for its ability to eat large numbers of insects. □ *The students put up a birdhouse in the school's nature area in hopes of attracting a martin or two.*

martial   See the main entry beginning with *marshal.*

martin   See the main entry beginning with *marten.*

massed—mast

- **massed** [mæst]   the past tense and past participle of *mass* 'to form or collect something into a body.' □ *The shoreline was littered with debris massed in clumps.*
- **mast** [mæst]   a long, vertical pole in a ship's deck, used to support rigging, sails, and booms. □ *Strong winds threatened to rip apart both the sails and the mast of the ship.*
- **mast** [mæst]   edible nuts accumulated on the forest floor and eaten by animals. □ *Acorns and beechnuts are a favorite mast of whitetail deer.*
- **mast** [mæst]   a naval disciplinary hearing in which the commanding officer listens to and decides cases or charges against his men. □ *Following the mast, the charges against the two enlisted sailors were dropped.*

mast   See the main entry beginning with *massed.*

mat—matte

- **mat** [mæt]   a border around a picture but inside a frame. □ *A large mat around a small picture is overwhelming.*
- **mat** [mæt]   to make or provide a picture with a mat. □ *I would like to mat his portrait in a bright color.*
- **mat** [mæt]   to become entangled. □ *The cat's fur tends to mat easily.*
- **mat** [mæt]   a piece of closely woven coarse fabric used as a covering for a table or floor. □ *In some places, a mat instead of a bed is used for sleeping.*
- **mat** [mæt]   a small rug used at a door for cleaning shoes. □ *Be sure to wipe your feet on the mat before going into the house.*
- **mat** [mæt]   a thick, padded cushion used in such sports as wrestling, gymnastics, and tumbling. □ *The gymnast fell off*

the balance beam and onto the mat beneath it.
- **matte** [mæt]   having a nonglossy or rough, grainy surface. □ *Ellen decided to use a paint that gives a matte finish.*

matte   See the main entry beginning with *mat.*

maul   See the main entry beginning with *mall.*

may   See the main entry beginning with *can.*

mayor   See the main entry beginning with *mare.*

maze   See the main entry beginning with *maize.*

meat—meet—mete
- **meat** [mit]   the flesh of an animal used as food. □ *Grandfather always liked meat and potatoes for Sunday dinner.*
- **meat** [mit]   the edible part of a fruit, nut, or vegetable. □ *We'll only use the meat of ripe nuts for the pecan pie.*
- **meet** [mit]   to approach or come into contact or the presence of someone or something. □ *They agreed to meet for lunch at noon.* □ *I often meet defeat when I try to program the VCR.*
- **meet** [mit]   to settle with or pay something in full. □ *John cannot meet this month's bills because of his recent illness.*
- **meet** [mit]   a gathering for some specific activity or competition. □ *Chris won the two-mile event in last week's track meet.*
- **mete** [mit]   to assign or allot something by measure. □ *Her mother does not like to mete out punishment for the children's misbehavior.*

meatier—meteor
- **meatier** ['mitijɚ]   the comparative form of *meaty* 'having more meat or substance than something else.' □ *I hope the next novel I read has a meatier plot than the last.*
- **meteor** ['mitijɚ, 'mitiɔr]   a piece of falling matter from the solar system that becomes visible when it enters the earth's atmosphere. □ *The meteor shower was visible only for an instant.*

medal—meddle
- **medal** ['mɛdl]   an ornamental metal disk bearing a picture or engraving that remembers a person or event or is rewarded for achievement or excellence. □ *It was a great honor to be awarded a medal by the President of the United States.*
- **meddle** ['mɛdl]   to interfere in something without permission or right. □ *I wish Carl would not meddle in other people's affairs.*

meddle   See the main entry beginning with *medal.*

meet   See the main entry beginning with *meat.*

merry   See the main entry beginning with *marry.*

metal—mettle
- **metal** ['mɛtl, 'mɛdl]   a chemical element that is lustrous, opaque, and fusible. □ *Copper is a soft, easily handled metal.*
- **mettle** ['mɛtl, 'mɛdl]   spirit or stamina. □ *The Boston Marathon is enough to test the mettle of any serious long-distance runner.*

mete   See the main entry beginning with *meat.*

meteor   See the main entry beginning with *meatier.*

mettle   See the main entry beginning with *metal.*

mews—muse
- **mews** [mjuz]   the plural of *mew* 'a soft sound usually associated with cats.' □ *The mournful mews of the trapped kitten brought everyone running to the tree.*
- **mews** [mjuz]   the plural of *mew* 'a gull.' □ *Mews swooped above the harbor docks, hoping for a handout of fresh fish.*
- **muse** [mjuz]   a state of distraction or deep thought. □ *He was in a muse for days trying to decide what to do.*
- **muse [over]** [mjuz]   to think about something reflectively. □ *Grandma likes to muse over times past.*
- **muse** [mjuz]   one of a group of nine goddesses in Greek mythology. □ *A muse was believed to bring inspiration to an artist.*

might—mite
- **might** [maɪt]   a word used to express possibility or probability. □ *The current officeholder might be reelected next year.*
- **might** [maɪt]   strength, power, or authority wielded by someone or something. □ *Despite his great might, the weight lifter was unable to lift the barbell.*
- **mite** [maɪt]   a kind of tiny insect known to infest plants, animals, and foods. □ *The dog was pestered by a mite in its ear.*
- **mite** [maɪt]   a very tiny creature or object. □ *"Mike learned to fish when he was just a little mite," reflected his mother.*
- **mite** [maɪt]   a small bit of something. □ *I'm so hungry that I want to taste a mite of everything on the buffet table.*

mil—mill
- **mil** [mɪl]   a unit of length equal to 1/1000 of an inch. □ *The*

wire required for that circuit was so tiny that it had to be measured to the exact mil.

- **mill** [mɪl] a unit of monetary value equal to 1/1000 of a United States dollar. □ *The school board is requesting an additional mill for operating costs in the special election.*
- **mill** [mɪl] a building used to house cutting or grinding machinery. □ *The old lumber mill has shut down.*
- **mill** [mɪl] to grind grain into a powder, meal, or flour. □ *People in many cultures still mill their grains using primitive equipment.*
- **mill** [mɪl] to move about in a collective mass. □ *The crowd of curious people continued to mill around the accident scene.*

mill See the main entry beginning with *mil.*

mince—mints
- **mince** [mɪnts] to chop or cut something into very tiny pieces. □ *Mince the onion and garlic finely when you make that recipe.*
- **mince** [mɪnts] to speak in a restrained manner within boundaries of decorum. □ *Bob is very straightforward and does not like to mince words.*
- **mints** [mɪnts] the plural of *mint* 'a place where coins are manufactured.' □ *One of the six United States mints is located at Fort Knox, Kentucky.*
- **mints** [mɪnts] the plural of *mint* 'a huge sum of money.' (Colloquial.) □ *Those antique cars are worth mints.*
- **mints** [mɪnts] the plural of *mint* 'an aromatic plant used in flavoring and cooking.' □ *The leaves of two different types of mints are used to make that tea.*
- **mints** [mɪnts] candy flavored with mint. □ *The hostess had dishes filled with nuts and mints sitting on the tables.*
- **mints** [mɪnts] the present tense, third person singular of *mint* 'to stamp coins or money out of metal.' □ *Darlene operates a machine that mints new pennies.*

minds—mines
- **minds** [maɪndz] the plural of *mind* 'the brain's memory and consciousness; that with which people think and reason.' □ *Our minds went blank when we were asked to recall something that happened a long time ago.* □ *The top students in the class have excellent academic minds.*
- **minds** [maɪndz] the plural of *mind* 'a highly intellectual or scientific person.' □ *Some of the best medical minds in the world are searching for a cure for cancer.*
- **minds** [maɪndz] the present tense, third person singular of

mind 'to obey someone.' □ *That child always minds her parents.*

- **minds** [maɪndz]   the present tense, third person singular of *mind* 'to be careful of something.' □ *Jimmy always minds the traffic before crossing the street.*
- **minds** [maɪndz]   the present tense, third person singular of *mind* 'to take charge of someone or something.' □ *The oldest child minds the younger ones when their parents are away.*
- **minds** [maɪndz]   the present tense, third person singular of *mind* 'to be concerned with something; to object to something.' □ *Dave minds the fact that some people call him by a nickname.*
- **mines** [maɪnz]   the plural of *mine* 'a place in the earth from which mineral deposits are taken.' □ *Most of the mines in West Virginia contain coal.*
- **mines** [maɪnz]   the plural of *mine* 'an explosive device; a stationary bomb.' □ *Specially trained experts removed all unexploded mines in the area.*
- **mines** [maɪnz]   the present tense, third person singular of *mine* 'to dig for metal or ore.' □ *The company mines both silver and copper in several western states.*
- **mines** [maɪnz]   the present tense, third person singular of *mine* 'to place explosive mines in strategic positions.' □ *In times of war, a country sometimes mines harbors and other important waterways to discourage enemy use.*

miner—minor

- **miner** ['maɪnɚ]   a person who mines. □ *Like his father and grandfather before him, Dave is a miner in the Pennsylvania coal mines.*
- **minor** ['maɪnɚ]   a person who is under legal age. □ *It is illegal to sell alcohol and tobacco products to a minor.*
- **minor** ['maɪnɚ]   unimportant; inferior in degree, status, number, or size. □ *Linda was disappointed that she received only a minor part in the play.*
- **minor** ['maɪnɚ]   not involving risk to health or life. □ *The man sustained a minor cut to his hand.*
- **minor** ['maɪnɚ]   an academic subject requiring fewer courses to earn a degree than a major. □ *Peter has a major in American literature and a minor in social studies.*
- **minor** ['maɪnɚ]   a musical key. □ *Play the recital piece in D minor.*

mines   See the main entry beginning with *minds*.

minor   See the main entry beginning with *miner*.

mints   See the main entry beginning with *mince.*

missed—mist
- **missed** [mɪst]   the past tense and past participle of *miss* 'to feel the absence of someone or something.' □ *Lori missed her parents while she was away at summer camp.*
- **missed** [mɪst]   the past tense and past participle of *miss* 'to fail to obtain, hit, reach, or make contact with someone or something.' □ *The batter swung at the ball but missed.*
- **missed** [mɪst]   the past tense and past participle of *miss* 'to fail to attend something.' □ *Larry missed his first class because he overslept.*
- **missed** [mɪst]   the past tense and past participle of *miss* 'to fail to experience, sense, or understand something.' □ *I think I missed the point he was trying to make.*
- **mist** [mɪst]   very light, falling, or floating water particles, not as heavy as drizzle or rain. □ *The morning mist covered everything with moisture.* □ *We were unable to see the far side of the pond due to the mist of steam rising from the water.*
- **mist** [mɪst]   to spray or cover something with fine water particles. □ *Mist the fern plants every day rather than watering them once a week.*

mist   See the main entry beginning with *missed.*

mite   See the main entry beginning with *might.*

moan—mown
- **moan** [mon]   a wail; a groan. □ *The accident victim uttered a moan when the rescue workers lifted her onto the stretcher.*
- **moan** [mon]   to utter a wail or groan. □ *The winds seem to moan down in the valley on breezy nights.*
- **mown** [mon]   the past participle of *mow* 'to cut down standing grass or weeds.' (Also *mowed.*) □ *Even after I had mown the grass, dandelions appeared everywhere.*
- **mown [down]** [mon]   the past participle of *mow [down]* 'to kill or destroy people in large numbers without mercy; to cut down standing grass or weeds.' □ *The artillery had mown down all opposition in a matter of minutes.* □ *After the grass had been mown down, I raked it up.*

mode—mowed
- **mode** [mod]   a specific form, style, or variety of something. □ *The bicycle is a popular mode of transportation in Japan.*
- **mode** [mod]   a manner of doing something. □ *The burglar repeatedly used the same mode of operation to gain entry into houses.*

- **mode** [mod]   the most frequent value in a frequency distribution. □ *The instructor asked her students to find the mode in the data she provided.*
- **mowed** [mod]   the past tense of *mow* 'to cut down standing grass or weeds.' □ *The farmer mowed his hay field four times last year.*
- **mowed [down]** [mod]   the past tense of *mow [down]* 'to kill or destroy large numbers of something without mercy.' □ *The ruthless soldiers mowed down every living thing in sight.*

moor—more
- **moor** [mɔɚ, muɚ]   a wasteland of low, boggy ground. □ *Peggy often found it peaceful to walk along the moor at night.*
- **moor** [mɔɚ, muɚ]   to secure something with anchors or lines, particularly a boat. □ *We had better moor the boat in the cove until this storm passes.*
- **more** [mɔɚ]   a greater number, amount, or degree. □ *Nowadays more people live in urban areas than in rural ones.*

moose—mousse
- **moose** [mus]   a large grass-eating mammal that belongs to the deer family and lives in forested parts of North America. □ *While driving along a Canadian highway, we spotted a cow moose and her calf drinking from a lake.*
- **mousse** [mus]   an airy, sweet dessert made of gelatin and whipped cream. □ *Our hostess served raspberry mousse for dessert.*

more   See the main entry beginning with *moor.*

morning—mourning
- **morning** ['mɔɚnɪŋ]   the part of the day from midnight or dawn until noon. □ *He prefers to jog early in the morning when it's cooler.*
- **mourning** ['mɔɚnɪŋ]   the present participle of *mourn* 'to express grief and sorrow about something, such as a person's death.' □ *Mourning clothes are traditionally black.* □ *The players are still mourning the death of their beloved coach.*
- **mourning** ['mɔɚnɪŋ]   a period of grief following a death. □ *The widow continues to wear black to show that she is still in mourning.*

mourning   See the main entry beginning with *morning.*

mousse   See the main entry beginning with *moose.*

mowed   See the main entry beginning with *mode.*

mown   See the main entry beginning with *moan.*

muscle—mussel
- **muscle** ['məsl]   a body tissue that controls motion. □ *The long jumper pulled a muscle in her lower leg.*
- **muscle** ['məsl]   brawn; muscular strength. □ *It will take a lot of muscle to move that large piece of equipment.*
- **mussel** ['məsl]   a marine or freshwater bivalve mollusk. □ *While walking along the shoreline, we found a mussel that had washed up on the beach.*

muse   See the main entry beginning with *mews.*

mussed—must
- **mussed** [məst]   the past tense and past participle of *muss* 'to mess up or make someone or something untidy.' □ *The ride in the convertible certainly mussed her hairdo.*
- **must** [məst]   to be compelled to do something by a person, circumstance, or law. □ *We must try to obey the law at all times.*
- **must** [məst]   an essential item. □ *A small, compact camera is a must when vacationing.*
- **must** [məst]   an imperative need. □ *Complete confidentiality is a must when dealing with private matters.*

mussel   See the main entry beginning with *muscle.*

must   See the main entry beginning with *mussed.*

mustard—mustered
- **mustard** ['məstəd]   a condiment made of powdered mustard seed and other ingredients. □ *Do you like mustard on your hot dogs?*
- **mustard** ['məstəd]   a pungent yellow powder from the mustard plant used in medicine and chemicals. □ *Grandma used to recommend a mustard plaster for chest colds.*
- **mustard** ['məstəd]   zest; vigor. (Slang.) □ *Though in his eighties, that man still has a great deal of mustard.*
- **mustered** ['məstəd]   the past tense and past participle of *muster* 'to collect, gather, or call something forth.' □ *Todd mustered all of his courage before stepping up to the podium to speak.*
- **mustered** ['məstəd]   the past tense and past participle of *muster* 'to enlist or rouse someone.' □ *Troops were mustered from all over the colonial countryside.*

mustered   See the main entry beginning with *mustard.*

N

naught   See the main entry beginning with *knot*.

naughty   See the main entry beginning with *knotty*.

naval—navel

- **naval** ['nevl]   involving or relating to ships, shipping, or a navy. □ *While on vacation, we visited the naval facility at Pearl Harbor on Oahu, Hawaii.*
- **navel** ['nevl]   a depression or scar in the center of the abdomen where the umbilical cord was once attached. □ *The belly dancer wore a gemstone in her navel as part of her costume.*
- **navel** ['nevl]   a particular variety of orange. □ *There is no orange sweeter than a large, juicy navel.*

navel   See the main entry beginning with *naval*.

nay—neigh

- **nay** [ne]   a negative reply or vote; a person who votes no. □ *When the vote was tallied, there were four yeas and one nay.*
- **nay** [ne]   not only this but also. (Formal, stilted, or jocular.) □ *"Nay, there were other misdeeds committed by this individual,"* continued the speaker.
- **neigh** [ne]   the loud, long utterance of a horse, donkey, or mule. □ *We could hear the wild horse's neigh across the wide valley.*
- **neigh** [ne]   to make the utterance of a donkey, horse, or mule. □ *Our donkey will neigh if he hears a loud, piercing noise.*

need   See the main entry beginning with *knead*.

neigh   See the main entry beginning with *nay*.

new See the main entry beginning with *gnu.*

nickers See the main entry beginning with *knickers.*

night See the main entry beginning with *knight.*

nit See the main entry beginning with *knit.*

no See the main entry beginning with *know.*

nob See the main entry beginning with *knob.*

nock See the main entry beginning with *knock.*

none—nun
- **none** [nən]   not any; not a single one. □ *I looked for some ripe avocados at the grocery store, but there were none.*
- **none** [nən]   not at all; by no means. □ *Our band director was none too happy with our recent performance.*
- **nun** [nən]   a woman of a religious order, especially one who vows poverty, chastity, and obedience. □ *The young Catholic girl thought that one day she might become a nun.*

nose See the main entry beginning with *knows.*

not See the main entry beginning with *knot.*

nun See the main entry beginning with *none.*

O

oar—o'er—or—ore

- **oar** [ɔɚ] a long-handled paddle with a flat, broad blade at one end used to propel a boat through water. □ *In his excitement to land the great bass, the fisherman accidentally knocked an oar into the water.*
- **o'er** [ɔɚ] over. □ *The rugged pioneers pushed o'er the mountains, valleys, plains, and deserts in their quest for a better life.*
- **or** [ɔɚ] a word suggesting an alternative. □ *We can leave now to beat the rush, or we can wait and watch the final minutes of the game.*
- **ore** [ɔɚ] a mineral containing a valuable metallic or other element for which it is mined. □ *The discovery of iron ore reshaped many aspects of human existence.*

ode—owed

- **ode** [od] a lyrical song or poem of varying length and complexity, usually addressing a person or event. □ *The haunting song "Ode to Billy Joe" was once very popular.*
- **owed** [od] the past tense and past participle of *owe* 'to be indebted to someone or something.' □ *Sally finally paid me the ten dollars she owed me.*

o'er See the main entry beginning with *oar*.

oh—owe

- **oh** [o] an expression of various emotions, including surprise, pain, and fear. □ *"Oh, my goodness! I've won the lotto jackpot!" exclaimed Andy.*
- **oh** [o] an introductory word used in a direct address. □ *"Oh, Marie, I really don't care to see that movie," said Jill in disgust.*

- **oh** [o]   zero.   □ *Both his house address and his telephone number end in "oh."*
- **owe** [o]   to be indebted to someone or something.   □ *Since I am as much at fault as you, you do not owe me an apology.*

one—won

- **one** [wən]   the number between zero and two.   □ *Connie's jersey for the relay team has the number one on it.*
- **one** [wən]   a single unit or thing.   □ *He doesn't have one item that he can call his own.* □ *One type of woodwind instrument is the clarinet.*
- **one** [wən]   any individual indicated in a vague sense.   □ *I was the first one to misspell a word in the spelling bee.* □ *One really should not do that!*
- **one** [wən]   united; acting or thinking in union.   □ *We are one in our belief that we should preserve our environment.*
- **won** [wən]   the past tense and past participle of *win* 'to gain the highest honor or best prize in a contest.'   □ *Rita won the fudge-making contest.*
- **won** [wən]   the past tense and past participle of *win* 'to earn or obtain something.'   □ *Her kind ways and sense of fairness won his respect.*

or   See the main entry beginning with *oar.*

ordinance—ordnance

- **ordinance** ['ɔɚd(n)nənts]   a municipal law or order.   □ *A public ordinance prohibits loitering on city streets.*
- **ordnance** ['ɔɚd(n)nənts]   military supplies.   □ *The ordnance supply included guns and ammunition.*

ordnance   See the main entry beginning with *ordinance.*

ore   See the main entry beginning with *oar.*

ought   See the main entry beginning with *aught.*

our   See the main entry beginning with *hour.*

overdo—overdue

- **overdo** [ovɚ'du]   to do or use something to excess.   □ *Don't try to overdo things on your first day home from the hospital.* □ *I tend to overdo the pot roasts I prepare.* □ *Don't overdo it with those painkillers.*
- **overdue** [ovɚ'du, ovɚ'dju]   delayed beyond an appointed time.   □ *Carol's baby was three weeks overdue.* □ *My library books are always overdue by the time I return them.*
- **overdue** [ovɚ'du, ovɚ'dju]   remaining unpaid when due to be

paid. □ *Last month's mortgage payment is overdue.*
- **overdue** [ovɚˈdu, ovɚˈdju]   more than ready. □ *James felt he was long overdue for a pay raise.*

overdue   See the main entry beginning with *overdo.*

overseas—oversees
- **overseas** [ovɚˈsiz]   across or beyond the sea. □ *The journalist's next assignment will be somewhere overseas.*
- **oversees** [ovɚˈsiz]   the present tense, third person singular of *oversee* 'to supervise someone or something.' □ *The office manager oversees the work of all of the clerical and support staff.*

oversees   See the main entry beginning with *overseas.*

owe   See the main entry beginning with *oh.*

owed   See the main entry beginning with *ode.*

P

paced—paste

- **paced** [pest]   the past tense and past participle of *pace* 'to establish a reasonable rate of movement or progress.' □ *We paced ourselves to work at a steady rate so we wouldn't tire before the job was done.*
- **paced [off]** [pest]   the past tense and past participle of *pace [off]* 'to mark off a unit of distance based on the length of a human stride.' □ *The umpire paced off the distance between the pitcher's mound and the batter's box.*
- **paced** [pest]   the past tense and past participle of *pace* '[for a horse] to travel so that the legs on the same side of its body move alternately back and forth at the same time.' □ *The horse paced around the track in record time.*
- **paste** [pest]   a wet, sticky mixture used as glue. □ *The preschoolers like to use colored paste on their art projects.*
- **paste** [pest]   to cause something to stick to someone or something. □ *Let's paste these drawings up on the walls all around the room.*
- **paste** [pest]   to hit someone hard. (Slang.) □ *If you say something to anger Terry, he is likely to paste you.*

packed—pact

- **packed** [pækt]   the past tense and past participle of *pack* 'to gather something into a compact form and place it in a container.' □ *The children packed their own suitcases before leaving for camp.*
- **packed** [pækt]   the past tense and past participle of *pack* 'to carry a gun.' (Slang.) □ *The police officer always packed his .357 magnum while on duty.*

113

- **packed** [pækt]   the past tense and past participle of *pack* '[for one] to arrange a deck of cards in such a way as to give one a fraudulent advantage.' □ *Carl liked to win at cards, so he packed the deck in his favor whenever possible.*
- **packed** [pækt]   full of something. □ *Our favorite restaurant is always packed with people on Saturday night.*
- **pact** [pækt]   a contract; an agreement. □ *The neighborhood children formed a pact to meet every day after lunch.*
- **pact** [pækt]   a treaty; a contract. □ *Six countries signed the pact declaring peace.*

pail—pale

- **pail** [pel]   a bucket or other container equipped with a handle and used to carry liquids. □ *Our cow kicked over a full pail of milk.*
- **pale** [pel]   pallid. □ *We knew Henry didn't feel well when he suddenly became very pale.*
- **pale** [pel]   not bright or brilliant. □ *She painted the room a pale shade of yellow.*
- **pale** [pel]   to become less important. □ *All of the other girls pale in comparison to Rosa's great beauty.*
- **pale** [pel]   one of the stakes or pickets of a fence. □ *One pale in the stockade fence is broken and should be replaced.*

pain—pane

- **pain** [pen]   distress; suffering; discomfort. □ *The pain became so unbearable that Emily finally agreed to see a doctor.*
- **pain** [pen]   to cause someone or something to feel pain. □ *It will pain us to see you move so far away.*
- **pain** [pen]   to cause oneself or another trouble or exertion. □ *Do not pain yourself to stand up when you feel so ill.*
- **pane** [pen]   a framed piece of glass found in windows and doors. □ *During the furious storm, a pane of glass blew out of the large picture window.*

pair—pare—pear

- **pair** [pɛɚ]   two corresponding things designed to be used together; two associated or similar things. □ *Now what have I done with that pair of socks?* □ *Jim needs to buy a pair of shirts to take on his trip.*
- **pair** [pɛɚ]   two sweethearts. □ *That young pair will probably marry someday.*
- **pair** [pɛɚ]   two playing cards of the same value or denomination. □ *All she had was a pair of kings in her hand.*
- **pair** [pɛɚ]   a matched set. □ *The buggy was pulled by a pair*

of matched bays.

- **pair** [pɛɚ] to set or arrange something in groups of two. □ *The graduates will pair up to march into the auditorium.*
- **pare** [pɛɚ] to peel or remove the skin or covering from something; to cut something away. □ *Will you please pare the potatoes for dinner?* □ *We need to pare our budget by several thousand dollars.*
- **pear** [pɛɚ] a fleshy, somewhat gritty fruit of a tree belonging to the rose family. □ *The pear was juicy and tasty.*

palate—pallet

- **palate** ['pælət] the roof of the mouth. □ *The dentist had to numb his patient's palate before he could remove the front tooth.*
- **palate** ['pælət] an intellectual taste or enjoyment. □ *That author's writing style does not suit my palate.*
- **pallet** ['pælət] a lightweight, portable framework on which materials in factories and warehouses can be stored or transported. □ *The bags of cement were stacked on a pallet while awaiting shipment.*
- **pallet** ['pælət] a sleeping tick or mattress. □ *A pallet, though not very comfortable, makes an adequate sleeping surface.*
- **pallet** ['pælət] an instrument used for forming or mixing clay or colors. □ *The artist used a pallet to combine several different colors for the portrait.*

pale See the main entry beginning with *pail.*

pallet See the main entry beginning with *palate.*

pane See the main entry beginning with *pain.*

pare See the main entry beginning with *pair.*

passed—past

- **passed** [pæst] the past tense and past participle of *pass* 'to move by and beyond someone or something.' □ *We passed many vacationing families on the highway.*
- **passed [away]** [pæst] the past tense and past participle of *pass [away]* 'to die.' □ *Her great-aunt passed away recently.*
- **passed** [pæst] the past tense and past participle of *pass* 'to hand or transfer someone or something from one person to another person.' □ *The relay team members passed the baton smoothly from one to another.* □ *After her parents died, Tess was passed from relative to relative.*
- **passed** [pæst] the past tense and past participle of *pass* '[for a vote] to win approval from a legislative body.' □ *The bill narrowly passed both houses of the state congress.*

- **past** [pæst]   in a previous time period; ago. □ *In years past, life seemed so much simpler.* □ *Grandpa was a spritely, spirited man a long time past.*
- **past** [pæst]   after. □ *The clock chimed at half past midnight.*
- **past** [pæst]   beyond. □ *Go past the entrance and turn left at the second door.*

past   See the main entry beginning with *passed.*

paste   See the main entry beginning with *paced.*

patience—patients
- **patience** ['peʃənts]   having the capacity to be steadfast, calm, or uncomplaining. □ *Kindergarten teachers must have a great deal of patience.*
- **patients** ['peʃənts]   the plural of *patient* 'a person undergoing medical treatment.' □ *The doctor treats all of her patients with care and interest.*

patients   See the main entry beginning with *patience.*

pause—paws
- **pause** [pɔz]   a temporary break or stop. □ *After a brief pause, the speaker continued.*
- **pause** [pɔz]   to stop or linger for a time. □ *Let's pause at the fountain and toss in a coin.*
- **paws** [pɔz]   the plural of *paw* 'the foot of some warm-blooded terrestrial animal having claws.' □ *A lynx has huge paws.*
- **paws** [pɔz]   the plural of *paw* 'a large, clumsy human hand.' (A figurative use of the previous sense.) □ *"Get your paws off me!" shouted the boy.*
- **paws** [pɔz]   the present tense, third person singular of *paw* 'to touch someone rudely or amorously.' □ *Henry, it seems, paws every girl who goes out with him.*
- **paws** [pɔz]   the present tense, third person singular of *paw* 'to grab at something repeatedly.' □ *The inexperienced mountain climber paws the air wildly each time he loses his footing.*
- **paws** [pɔz]   the present tense, third person singular of *paw* 'to bat or hit at something with a paw.' □ *Each time the cat catches a mouse, it paws its victim pitilessly.* □ *When restless, the stallion paws the stall floor.*

paws   See the main entry beginning with *pause.*

peace—piece
- **peace** [pis]   a state of security, tranquility, or order between individuals, groups, or countries. □ *A war-torn nation knows*

no peace. □ *The feuding brothers have finally made peace.*
- **peace** [pis]   a freedom from mental or emotional upheaval. □ *His cabin in the woods offers him a haven of peace.*
- **peace** [pis]   quiet; silence. □ *With five children in the house, the harried housewife has no peace.*
- **piece** [pis]   a portion of a whole. □ *May I please have the last piece of pie?*
- **piece** [pis]   an artistic or literary composition. □ *The composer's piece for the piano won the competition.* □ *That piece of artwork was the first ever to be sold by the artist.*
- **piece** [pis]   something regarded as an example of a unit of a kind or class. □ *Mary does a piece of work at a time at the garment factory.*
- **piece** [pis]   to patch someone or something together; to complete something by adding pieces. □ *We might be able to piece together a quilt from these scraps.* □ *It was difficult to piece together the jigsaw puzzle.*
- **piece** [pis]   a handgun; a revolver. (Police and underworld slang.) □ *The robber carried his piece in a shoulder holster.*

peak—peek—pique
- **peak** [pik]   a prominent, pointed top or end of something. □ *The mountain peak was covered with snow.*
- **peak** [pik]   the highest level; the greatest degree. □ *He reached the peak of his music career at age thirty.*
- **peak** [pik]   to reach a summit or maximum of something. □ *The physical condition of the racehorse should peak around the date of the race.*
- **peek** [pik]   to glance secretly at something or someone. □ *Children are sometimes tempted to peek at their birthday presents.*
- **peek** [pik]   to take a brief look at someone or something. □ *Out of curiosity she wanted to peek at every room in the house.*
- **pique** [pik]   a fit of irritation or resentment. □ *In a pique of anger, the child broke her favorite toy.*
- **pique** [pik]   to arouse anger or resentment. □ *Try not to pique his wrath by upsetting him.*
- **pique** [pik]   to provoke someone or something by a challenge or rebuff. □ *The coach's pep talk served to pique his team's desire to win.*

peal—peel
- **peal** [pil]   a loud ringing of bells, especially church bells. □ *Every Sunday morning the peal of the church bell summons people to worship.*

- **peal** [pil] a loud sound or succession of sounds. ☐ *Her peal of laughter was heard throughout the house.*
- **peel** [pil] to remove or strip off an outer layer of something. ☐ *I had to peel the apples before I could make the cobbler.*
- **peel** [pil] to remove clothing from a body. ☐ *Let's peel off those wet clothes before you get a chill.*
- **peel** [pil] the skin or rind of a fruit. ☐ *The orange peel was easy to remove.*

pear See the main entry beginning with *pair*.

pearl—purl

- **pearl** [pɚl] the lustrous round growth found in the shell of some mollusks and used as a gem in jewelry. ☐ *The diver found a small pearl in the oyster.*
- **pearl** [pɚl] something resembling a pearl in color, value, or physical qualities. ☐ *Dad always said he got a real pearl when he married Mom.*
- **pearl** [pɚl] to form in tiny droplets. ☐ *The light rain began to pearl on the newly waxed surface.*
- **purl** [pɚl] gold or silver thread. ☐ *Her gown was sewn with silvery purl.*
- **purl** [pɚl] to embroider with gold or silver thread. ☐ *My aunt taught me to purl delicate handmade doilies.*
- **purl** [pɚl the looped stitch on the edge of lace. ☐ *The purl on Jane's lace collar caught on her necklace and ripped.*
- **purl** [pɚl] the soft murmur of a gentle, swirling stream. ☐ *The purl of the slowly flowing brook was barely audible.*
- **purl** [pɚl] to make a murmur. ☐ *The two streams purl quietly where they meet.*

pedal—peddle—petal

- **pedal** ['pɛdl] a foot-operated lever. ☐ *The gas pedal on her car got stuck.*
- **pedal** ['pɛdl] to move or propel something by foot, especially a bicycle. ☐ *Let's pedal up to the corner drugstore for an ice-cream cone.* ☐ *The tiny toddler was not able to pedal his new tricycle.*
- **pedal** ['pɛdl] relating to or involving a pedal. ☐ *That antique sewing machine is pedal-driven.*
- **peddle** ['pɛdl] to sell wares from place to place or door to door. ☐ *The vagrant tried to peddle small items to earn money.*
- **peddle** ['pɛdl] to seek to distribute something; to deal out something. ☐ *Since you can't go to the football game, why don't you try to peddle your tickets at work?*

- **petal** ['pɛdl, 'pɛtl]   a colorful segment of a flower's blossom. □ *The petal of the orchid is an unusual color.*

peddle   See the main entry beginning with *pedal.*

peek   See the main entry beginning with *peak.*

peel   See the main entry beginning with *peal.*

peer—pier

- **peer** [pɪɚ]   of equal standing with another. □ *A peer jury will decide the fate of the accused woman.*
- **peer** [pɪɚ]   one of the ranks of the British peerage system. □ *Sir Arthur George is a peer of high rank.*
- **peer** [pɪɚ]   a companion, friend, or age-mate. □ *The students will join their peer after school for a game of soccer.*
- **peer** [pɪɚ]   to look carefully or curiously at something not easily discernible. □ *If you peer through a beach telescope in Key West, you might be able to see Cuba.*
- **pier** [pɪɚ]   a vertical support between two openings. □ *To enlarge the room, we'll remove the center pier.*
- **pier** [pɪɚ]   a structural landing place extending into water. □ *Fishermen can be seen fishing off the pier at any time of day.*
- **pier** [pɪɚ]   a structure used to form or protect a harbor for vessels. □ *The long rock pier has a lighthouse on its point.*

petal   See the main entry beginning with *pedal.*

phase   See the main entry beginning with *faze.*

phrase   See the main entry beginning with *frays.*

pi—pie

- **pi** [pɑɪ]   the ratio of the circumference of a circle to its diameter. □ *The students were asked to memorize the formula for figuring pi.*
- **pi** [pɑɪ]   the symbol denoting the ratio of a circumference of a circle to its diameter. □ *Helen correctly wrote the pi symbol on her math homework.*
- **pi** [pɑɪ]   the sixteenth letter of the Greek alphabet. □ *Greek letters, such as pi, look so much different than English letters.*
- **pie** [pɑɪ]   a food dish made up of a crust and such filling as fruit or meat. □ *The topping on the banana cream pie was stiff.*
- **pie** [pɑɪ]   a cake layer sliced horizontally and filled with custard, fruit, or cream. □ *Tommy wanted a Boston cream pie for dessert.*
- **pie** [pɑɪ]   a multi-colored animal, usually with irregular markings. □ *The unusually marked horse was a pie.*

pidgin—pigeon

- **pidgin** ['pɪdʒən]   a simplified manner of speech used to communicate between people of different languages. □ *Where more than one language is commonly used, people often choose to speak in pidgin.*
- **pigeon** ['pɪdʒən]   a fairly stout, usually domesticated bird resembling, but larger than, a dove. □ *A fake owl was set on the rooftop to discourage the local pigeon population from landing there.*
- **pigeon** ['pɪdʒən]   a dupe; an easy mark. □ *The con artists thought they could find a pigeon to help carry out their scheme.*
- **pigeon** ['pɪdʒən]   a spherical, molded shape of clay used for target shooting. □ *The young shooter hit every clay pigeon that was thrown into the air.*

pie   See the main entry beginning with *pi.*

piece   See the main entry beginning with *peace.*

pier   See the main entry beginning with *peer.*

pigeon   See the main entry beginning with *pidgin.*

pique   See the main entry beginning with *peak.*

pistil—pistol

- **pistil** ['pɪstl]   the part of a seed plant that bears the ovule needed for reproduction. □ *On some flowers the pistil is more noticeable than on others.*
- **pistol** ['pɪstl]   a small, hand-held firearm. □ *She keeps a licensed pistol for personal protection.*

pistol   See the main entry beginning with *pistil.*

plain—plane

- **plain** [plen]   simple; unadorned. □ *The house is very plain both inside and out.*
- **plain** [plen]   common; ordinary. □ *She has rather plain features.*
- **plain** [plen]   evident. □ *It was plain that Kevin would not change his mind.*
- **plain** [plen]   unobstructed. □ *The hotel on the hill was in plain view of the surrounding area.*
- **plain** [plen]   an extensive, unbroken expanse of flat or rolling treeless countryside. □ *The empty plain looks bare and unwelcoming.*
- **plane** [plen]   a tool used for smoothing or shaving a wood surface. □ *The craftsman used a small plane for his detail work.*

- **plane** [plen] to make something even, level, or smooth. □ *I'll plane the tabletop before sanding and restaining it.*
- **plane** [plen] a flat or level surface. □ *That piece of equipment must rest on a plane so it doesn't tip over.*
- **plane** [plen] an airplane. □ *Passengers should board the plane through gate six.*
- **plane** [plen] to skim across the water or soar on the wind. □ *The sailboats plane across the bay easily on windy days.*

plait—plate

- **plait** [plet] a braid made of hair, straw, or some other material. □ *Her long hair was arranged in an elaborate plait for the celebration.*
- **plait** [plet] to interweave or braid something. □ *If we plait these bundles of straw, they'll be easier to carry.*
- **plate** [plet] a flat, smooth, thin piece of material. □ *The surgeon placed a small steel plate in his patient's head during the operation.*
- **plate** [plet] a piece of table service. □ *Please do not use the cracked plate when we have guests for dinner.*
- **plate** [plet] a thin layer of a precious metal, usually gold or silver. □ *The serving tray had a silver plate.*
- **plate** [plet] a printing surface of some type. □ *Carefully arrange the items to be copied on the plate.*
- **plate** [plet] to cover or coat something with some kind of metal. □ *The jeweler will plate the inexpensive metal ring with gold to make it look shiny.*
- **plate** [plet] the slab of rubber behind which a baseball or softball catcher squats and next to which the batter stands. □ *The umpire cleaned off the plate after the runner slid in.*
- **plate** [plet] a partial denture fitting. □ *He wears a small upper plate.*

plane See the main entry beginning with *plain.*

plate See the main entry beginning with *plait.*

pleas—please

- **pleas** [pliz] the plural of *plea* 'in a hearing or trial, the defendant's answer to the plaintiff's charges.' □ *Since the defendants stood mute, pleas of "not guilty" were entered for them.*
- **pleas** [pliz] the plural of *plea* 'an appeal or entreaty.' □ *Nobody heeded the woman's pleas for help.*
- **please** [pliz] to give pleasure, satisfaction, or gratification to someone. □ *It is not hard to please Jack.*

- **please** [pliz]   to be willing to do something. □ *If you would please be quiet, we can begin.*
- **please** [pliz]   an expression that makes a request or command more polite. □ *Please be seated.*

please   See the main entry beginning with *pleas.*

plum—plumb
- **plum** [pləm]   a purplish-red, smooth-skinned fruit. □ *Mom packed a sandwich, a plum, and some cheese and crackers in my lunch.*
- **plum** [pləm]   any of several trees or shrubs bearing such fruit. □ *Our trees did not bear a single plum last summer.*
- **plum** [pləm]   something superior or excellent. □ *Jill's upbeat solo performance was quite the plum.*
- **plum** [pləm]   the color of plums. □ *The designer suggested accenting her plum decor with forest green.*
- **plumb** [pləm]   a lead weight attached to a line used to indicate vertical position. □ *The plumb showed that the window opening was slightly crooked.*
- **plumb** [pləm]   straight up and down. □ *The walls need to be plumb with the ceiling.*
- **plumb** [pləm]   to measure depth with a lead weight attached to a line. □ *The students are required to plumb the depths of the different soil levels.*
- **plumb** [pləm]   to supply or install plumbing in something. □ *The workers will plumb the new house next week.*

plumb   See the main entry beginning with *plum.*

pole—Pole—poll
- **pole** [pol]   a long, slender shaft. □ *A pole is used to reach the apples in the tops of the trees.*
- **pole** [pol]   the inside position on a racecourse. □ *The fastest qualifying time wins the racecar driver the pole.*
- **pole** [pol]   either extremity of an axis of a sphere. □ *Neither pole of the planet Earth is inhabited by people.*
- **pole** [pol]   either of two opposites. □ *His opinion on the subject takes the opposite pole from his best friend's.*
- **Pole** [pol]   a person of the Polish nationality. □ *Edgar's father was a Pole and his mother a Swede.*
- **poll** [pol]   the casting and recording of votes by a body of persons. □ *The final results of the poll show that neither candidate won a majority of the votes.*
- **poll** [pol]   to question or canvass people randomly. □ *Some voters do not admit in an exit poll how they really voted.*

- **poll** [pol]   to shear or cut hair, wool, treetops, or cattle horns.
  □ *As a safety precaution, the farmers poll all of their cattle's horns.*

poll   See the main entry beginning with *pole*.

poor—pore—pour
- **poor** [pɔɚ, puɚ]   having few material possessions. □ *As a child, he was very poor.*
- **poor** [pɔɚ, puɚ]   inferior in value or quality. □ *An old pickup truck is a poor substitute for a luxury car when it comes to driving comfort.*
- **poor** [pɔɚ, puɚ]   eliciting pity or sympathy. □ *I feel sorry for poor Betsy with all of her troubles.*
- **poor** [pɔɚ, puɚ]   unproductive; fruitless. □ *This year's corn crop was very poor.*
- **pore** [poɚ]   a tiny opening in the surface of a membrane through which materials pass. □ *An infected skin pore can be painful.*
- **pore** [poɚ]   to read or study something attentively. □ *Mark used to pore over any book dealing with jets.*
- **pore** [poɚ]   to reflect on or ponder something. □ *Let me pore over your suggestion before making a decision.*
- **pour** [poɚ, puɚ]   to cause something to flow steadily. □ *Pour the milk slowly so you don't spill it.*
- **pour** [poɚ, puɚ]   to produce something freely in large supply or quantity. □ *Most parents pour love and affection onto their children.*
- **pour** [poɚ, puɚ]   to rain hard. □ *The weatherman said it will pour for the next three days.*

populace—populous
- **populace** ['pɑpjələs]   the general population of a given locale. □ *The populace of any large city is in a constant state of flux.*
- **populace** ['pɑpjələs]   masses of people. □ *A huge populace showed up to support their leader.*
- **populous** ['pɑpjələs]   crowded; densely populated. □ *Tokyo is an excellent example of a populous city.*

populous   See the main entry beginning with *populace*.

pore   See the main entry beginning with *poor*.

pour   See the main entry beginning with *poor*.

praise—prays—preys
- **praise** [prez]   to commend, glorify, or worship someone or

something. □ *"Let us praise the Lord for our blessings,"* began *the minister.*

- **praise** [prez] to express a favorable opinion or evaluation of someone or something. □ *My boss is not afraid to praise a job well done.*
- **praise** [prez] an act of praise. □ *A little praise goes a long way.*
- **prays** [prez] the present tense, third person singular of *pray* 'to speak to God or a deity.' □ *The little girl prays every night before going to sleep.* □ *The couple prays that their lost son will soon be found.*
- **preys** [prez] the plural of *prey* 'an animal hunted by another for food.' □ *The favorite preys of wolves are deer and moose.*
- **preys** [prez] the plural of *prey* 'a target of evil; someone or something that is helpless or unable to fend off attack.' □ *The preys of child molesters are often young, isolated children.*
- **preys [on]** [prez] third person singular of *prey* '[for an animal] to feed on another animal as a matter of preference or habit.' □ *Our snake preys on mice.*
- **preys [(up)on]** [prez] third person singular of *prey* 'to take advantage of someone or something; to have an ill effect on someone or something.' □ *Mary always preys on my kindness.* □ *Pneumonia preys on people who are already weak from other illnesses.*

prays See the main entry beginning with *praise.*

precedent—president
- **precedent** ['prɛsədənt] an example, rule, or judgment that may later serve as a basis for decisions in similar cases. □ *In this judicial case, there is no precedent indicating how the problem might be handled.*
- **precedent** ['prɛsədənt] a prior occurrence of a similar type that provides an example. □ *The teacher's behavior set a precedent for her student's behavior.*
- **president** ['prɛzədənt] any presiding officer of an organization; a chief official or executive; a chief of state. □ *As president of the art guild, Lois has many duties and responsibilities.* □ *In the United States, a president is elected every four years.*

presence—presents
- **presence** ['prɛzənts] attendance. □ *Your presence at the hearing is required.*
- **presence** ['prɛzənts] an individual's immediate space or vicinity. □ *Don't talk like that in the presence of children.*

- **presence** ['prɛzənts]   the bearing or air of a person, usually involving poise and rapport with others. □ *The queen has an unmistakable presence about her.*
- **presents** ['prɛzənts]   the plural of *present* 'a gift.' □ *All of the presents given to him were gag gifts.*

presents   See the main entry beginning with *presence.*

president   See the main entry beginning with *precedent.*

preys   See the main entry beginning with *praise.*

pride—pried

- **pride** [praɪd]   the feeling, quality, or state of being proud. □ *Bob's parents felt a great deal of pride in his accomplishments.*
- **pride** [praɪd]   extreme self-esteem; conceit. □ *Do not let foolish pride keep you from making an apology.*
- **pride** [praɪd]   acceptable or reasonable self-respect. □ *She takes pride in doing her job well.*
- **pride** [praɪd]   to indulge in the feeling, quality, or state of being proud. □ *They pride themselves on having the nicest lawn on the street.*
- **pride** [praɪd]   a group [of lions]. □ *In a pride of lions, the females are the hunters.*
- **pried [into]** [praɪd]   the past tense and past participle of *pry [into]* 'to delve or inquire into something.' □ *She always pried into other people's business.*
- **pried** [praɪd]   the past tense and past participle of *pry* 'to open or move something with a tool.' □ *The thieves pried the window open with a crowbar.*
- **pried [apart]** [praɪd]   the past tense and past participle of *pry [apart]* 'to separate people or things, usually with some difficulty.' □ *The principal pried the fighting boys apart.*

pried   See the main entry beginning with *pride.*

pries—prize

- **pries [into]** [praɪz]   the present tense, third person singular of *pry [into]* 'to inquire into something; to try to find out information about something.' □ *Jane thinks her mother pries into her personal affairs too much.* □ *If he pries too closely into the material, he may discover the truth.*
- **pries [open]** [praɪz]   the present tense, third person singular of *pry [open]* 'to use a tool to open something.' □ *Each morning, he pries open the stuck drawer to get to his socks.*
- **prize** [praɪz]   a reward offered to the winner of a contest or

game. □ *His prize in the hot dog-eating contest was a watermelon.*

- **prize** [prɑɪz]   something very desirable. □ *The girl he has decided to marry is quite a prize.*
- **prize** [prɑɪz]   to value something or someone highly. □ *Employers prize honesty as an important quality.*
- **prize** [prɑɪz]   wartime bounty or booty. □ *The soldiers captured an important airstrip as a prize following the fierce fighting.*

prince—prints

- **prince** [prɪnts]   a male member of a royal family, especially the son of a king or queen. □ *The prince is tutored privately at the castle.* □ *The heir to the king's throne is the eldest prince.*
- **prince** [prɪnts]   a male of high esteem or regard in his profession or class. □ *Jerry is a prince of a boss.*
- **prints** [prɪnts]   the plural of *print* 'a copy of a photograph or piece of artwork.' □ *The prints are ready to be picked up at the store.*
- **prints** [prɪnts]   the plural of *print* 'a fingerprint.' □ *The police found Bill's prints on the doorknob.*
- **prints** [prɪnts]   the present tense, third person singular of *print* 'to press inked type on paper or a similar surface; to publish in type.' □ *The newspaper only prints an early edition of the paper.* □ *His business prints facsimiles of government materials.*
- **prints** [prɪnts]   the present tense, third person singular of *print* 'to write using the letters of Roman type rather than script.' □ *She never prints her name; she always writes in script.*

princes—princess

- **princes** ['prɪnsəz]   the plural of *prince* 'a male member of a royal family, especially the son of a king or queen.' □ *The princes are vacationing with the queen at an exclusive resort.*
- **princes** ['prɪnsəz]   the plural of *prince* 'a male who is held in high esteem by his peers.' □ *Both gentlemen were princes of kindness in the eyes of their friends.*
- **princess** ['prɪnsɛs]   a female member of a royal family; the wife of a prince. □ *The princess was expected to marry nobly.* □ *The princess accompanies the prince on official state business.*
- **princess** ['prɪnsɛs]   a woman known for her outstanding qualities. □ *Ann has always been a princess of graciousness.*
- **princess** ['prɪnsɛs]   high-waisted. (A style of dress, gown, or blouse.) □ *The wedding gown featured a princess waistline.*

princess   See the main entry beginning with *princes.*

principal—principle
- **principal** ['prɪnsəpl]   most important or influential. □ *One of the principal characters in the story is a stray dog.*
- **principal** ['prɪnsəpl]   the authoritative person in control, usually of a school. □ *Ms. Brown will be the new principal of the school.*
- **principal** ['prɪnsəpl]   a sum of money that is loaned and upon which interest is paid and repayment is due; the main part of an estate. □ *The couple made monthly payments on the principal of their car loan.* □ *The elderly man lives on the interest of his estate and does not use the principal.*
- **principle** ['prɪnsəpl]   a fundamental rule, law, or code of conduct. □ *Our system of justice is based on the principle of equality.*
- **principle** ['prɪnsəpl]   the underlying facts of operation of nature. □ *This new invention is based on the principle of gravity.*

principle   See the main entry beginning with *principal.*

prints   See the main entry beginning with *prince.*

prize   See the main entry beginning with *pries.*

profit—prophet
- **profit** ['prɑfət]   a gain or return over and above an expenditure. □ *If you buy those stocks now, you stand to earn a nice profit in the future.*
- **profit** ['prɑfət]   to benefit or gain from something. □ *We will all profit from our hard work.*
- **prophet** ['prɑfət]   a person who tells of divinely inspired revelations or predicts the future. □ *Isaiah was a prophet in biblical times.*
- **prophet** ['prɑfət]   a person gifted with uncommon moral and spiritual insights. □ *The minister was both a prophet and a great leader.*
- **prophet** ['prɑfət]   a spokesperson for a cause or group. □ *In order for any progress to be made, a strong prophet for the cause needs to emerge.*

prophet   See the main entry beginning with *profit.*

pros—prose
- **pros** [proz]   the plural of *pro* 'professional.' □ *Two pros are available at the golf course to give you tips on your game.*
- **prose** [proz]   the common, nonpoetic language of people,

either in the spoken or written form. □ *The author's prose was quite eloquent.*

- **prose** [proz]   a literary style resembling that of common speech. □ *Our homework assignment included reading a selection of prose from our literature book.*

prose   See the main entry beginning with *pros.*

purl   See the main entry beginning with *pearl.*

Q

quarts—quartz

- **quarts** [kʌɔɚts] the plural of *quart* 'a measurement equalling one quarter of a gallon.' □ *Boil the pasta in two quarts of water.*
- **quarts** [kʌɔɚts] the plural of *quart* 'a container with the capacity of one quart.' □ *Please pick up a couple of quarts of milk at the grocery store when you come home.*
- **quartz** [kʌɔɚts] a mineral that occurs in transparent crystals and in natural crystalline masses. □ *The geology instructor brought in several samples of quartz for his class to examine.*

quartz See the main entry beginning with *quarts.*

quay See the main entry beginning with *key.*

queue See the main entry beginning with *cue.*

R

rabbet—rabbit

- **rabbet** ['ræbɪt]   a groove cut into a surface and designed to be fitted with a corresponding member to form a joint. □ *Carpenters will often use a rabbet to join two pieces of wood neatly.*
- **rabbet** ['ræbɪt]   to cut or fit a groove. □ *We need to rabbet this surface in order to get a good fit.*
- **rabbit** ['ræbɪt]   a small, long-eared mammal belonging to the hare family. □ *Sally plans to show her rabbit at the fair this summer.*
- **rabbit** ['ræbɪt]   the fur or pelt of a rabbit. □ *The jacket Mary bought is made of rabbit.*

rabbit   See the main entry beginning with *rabbet.*

rack—wrack

- **rack** [ræk]   a framework on or in which articles are placed, hung, or stored. □ *Lay that wet sweater on the rack rather than hanging it on the clothesline.*
- **rack** [ræk]   an instrument of torture. □ *The guard used the rack to torture the prisoner.*
- **rack** [ræk]   to cause acute pain, suffering, or anguish to someone or something. □ *The disease will continue to rack her weakening body.*
- **rack** [ræk]   to stretch or strain something violently. □ *His violent coughs continued to rack his sore ribs.*
- **rack** [ræk]   a horse's fast-moving, artificial pace. □ *The show horse must perform a series of gaits, including the rack.*
- **rack** [ræk]   a cut of meat from the rib section of an animal. □ *The king served a rack of lamb at the feast.*
- **wrack** [ræk]   to ruin something completely. □ *The hurricane*

will wrack the tiny island village.

- **wrack** [ræk]   a shipwreck. □ *Scuba divers continued to search for the wrack on the reef.*
- **wrack** [ræk]   a type of seaweed or other marine vegetation. □ *Much wrack washed up onto the shore after the storm.*
- **wrack** [ræk]   the violent destruction of a vehicle, structure, or machine. □ *The wrack of the beautiful city by the typhoon was devastating.*

rail—rale

- **rail** [rel]   a bar extending from one support to another that serves as a barrier or guard. □ *Use the rail along the stairs for extra support.*
- **rail** [rel]   the fence that borders a racecourse. □ *The horse on the rail won the race.*
- **rail** [rel]   a railroad or track. □ *Sue prefers to travel by rail rather than by air.*
- **rail** [rel]   a small, marshland bird belonging to the crane family. □ *If we're lucky, we may spot a rail in the swamp.*
- **rail** [rel]   to rant at or scold someone in harsh or abusive language. □ *Even after an apology, the angry man continued to rail at the sales clerk.*
- **rale** [rel]   an abnormal breathing sound. □ *The doctor detected a rale in her patient's chest.*

rain—reign—rein

- **rain** [ren]   falling precipitation in the form of droplets. □ *The cool, refreshing rain was a relief after the hot, windy day.*
- **rain** [ren]   to fall or pour down on someone or something like rain. □ *Insult after insult continued to rain down on the unpopular speaker.*
- **rain** [ren]   to deposit or bestow something abundantly. □ *Parents rain love and affection on their children.*
- **reign** [ren]   to possess or exercise power or authority over someone or something. □ *Our bosses reign over everyone in the company.*
- **reign** [ren]   to predominate or rule over someone or something. □ *Sometimes monarchs reign over their subjects for decades.*
- **reign** [ren]   the period of influence of a monarch or sovereign. □ *The queen's reign was marred by much violence.*
- **rein** [ren]   a check line on either side of a bridle or halter that is used to control an animal. □ *Pull back on the bridle rein to get control of the horse.*
- **rein** [ren]   complete freedom. □ *Some parents give free rein*

to their children at an early age.
- **rein** [ren]   a restraining influence. □ *A parent's control of the car keys will put a rein on any teenager's behavior.*

raise—rays—raze
- **raise** [rez]   to lift or move someone or something upward. □ *Raise the hood of the car, please.*
- **raise** [rez]   an increase in amount, usually in wages, salaries, bets, or bids. □ *After just six months on the job, Kurt received a raise.*
- **raise** [rez]   to rouse or incite someone or something, usually to promote action. □ *If we raise a loud protest, perhaps they will listen to us.*
- **raise** [rez]   to grow or cultivate someone or something. □ *Most parents raise their children carefully.* □ *The Joneses only raise cash crops.*
- **raise** [rez]   to collect something. □ *Our goal is to raise $300 for a new park sign.*
- **raise** [rez]   to bring something up for consideration. □ *Why does no one raise the obvious question?*
- **rays** [rez]   the plural of *ray* 'a beam of light or some other radiant energy.' □ *Warm rays of sunlight shone through the forest canopy.*
- **rays** [rez]   the plural of *ray* 'any line, such as a division or vein.' □ *The rays in those green leaves are dark purple.*
- **raze** [rez]   to destroy or demolish something to ground level. □ *The work crew will raze the condemned building tomorrow.*
- **raze** [rez]   to shave, cut, or scrape something off of something. □ *The young boy tried to raze the peach fuzz from his face.*

rale   See the main entry beginning with *rail.*

rancor—ranker
- **rancor** ['ræŋkɚ, 'ræŋkɔɚ]   hatred. □ *Evil thoughts and rancor seethed within the man.*
- **ranker** ['ræŋkɚ]   an individual who serves or has served in the ranks, usually a commissioned officer who has been promoted. □ *As a ranker, she can identify with troops as well as officers.*

ranker   See the main entry beginning with *rancor.*

rap—wrap
- **rap** [ræp]   a sharp knock or blow. □ *I heard a rap on the door.*
- **rap** [ræp]   a criticism; a rebuke. □ *The man offered a stinging rap to his opponent's comments.*
- **rap [on]** [ræp]   to strike something suddenly or sharply. □

Rap that jar on the table to loosen the lid.

- **rap** [ræp] to arrest, retain, or charge with criminal action. (Police or underworld slang.) □ *The police plan to rap the suspect with the recent crimes.*
- **rap** [ræp] to perform in a rhythmic, musical style by the same name in which lyrics are spoken to a steady background beat rather than sung. □ *Many high school students learn to rap after school.*
- **wrap** [ræp] to enclose or bundle something or someone by enfolding or covering; to embrace someone or something. □ *Let's wrap ourselves in these warm blankets.* □ *The little boy likes to wrap his arms around his favorite stuffed bear when he goes to sleep.*
- **wrap [up]** [ræp] to completely immerse or involve someone in something. □ *Some people wrap themselves up completely in their work.*
- **wrap** [ræp] an outer garment, similar to a cloak, that wraps around the body. □ *Her wrap was a simple woolen shawl.*

rapped—rapt—wrapped

- **rapped [on]** [ræpt] the past tense and past participle of *rap [on]* 'to strike something suddenly or sharply.' □ *I rapped on the window until someone saw me.*
- **rapped** [ræpt] the past tense and past participle of *rap* 'to charge someone with a criminal action.' (Police or underworld slang.) □ *The cops rapped the vagabond with trespassing and vagrancy.*
- **rapped** [ræpt] the past tense and past participle of *rap* 'to perform in a rhythmic, musical style in which lyrics are spoken to a steady background beat.' □ *The musicians rapped until the wee hours of the night.*
- **rapt** [ræpt] wholly absorbed or engrossed in something or someone. □ *We listened to the speaker with rapt attention.*
- **wrapped** [ræpt] the past tense and past participle of *wrap* 'to enclose or bundle someone or something up by enfolding.' □ *I wrapped all of the gifts by myself.*
- **wrapped [around]** [ræpt] the past tense and past participle of *wrap [around]* 'to embrace or surround someone or something.' □ *The friends wrapped their arms around each other.*
- **wrapped [up]** [ræpt] the past tense and past participle of *wrap [up]* 'to completely immerse oneself in or involve oneself in someone or something.' □ *She got so wrapped up in the novel that she couldn't put it down.*

rapt See the main entry beginning with *rapped.*

rays   See the main entry beginning with *raise*.

raze   See the main entry beginning with *raise*.

read—red
(See also *read—reed*.)
- **read** [rɛd]   the past tense and past participle of *read* 'to look at and comprehend written or printed matter.' □ *The child read at an early age.* □ *He read aloud from the morning newspaper.*
- **red** [rɛd]   a color that resembles the color of blood. □ *Jackie wants to buy a red sports car.*
- **red** [rɛd]   something resembling the color red. □ *His face turned red with embarrassment.*
- **red** [rɛd]   a Communist. □ *The artist was once accused of being a red.*
- **red** [rɛd]   a person advocating the overthrow of an existing political or social order. □ *The conservatives hoped to rid the government of every red who threatened the political system.*

read—reed
- **read** [rid]   to understand or utter aloud written or printed matter. □ *Most children learn to read in first or second grade.* □ *Would you please read that part of the article again?*
- **read** [rid]   to interpret the meaning of someone or something. □ *How do you read the sudden change in John's behavior?* □ *How do you read John on this matter?*
- **read** [rid]   to predict or foretell something. □ *Astrologers claim to read the future by studying the stars.*
- **reed** [rid]   a tall, slender grass, usually found growing in marshy areas. □ *The stem of a reed is hollow.*
- **reed** [rid]   a thin, flexible slat of wood or cane fixed to the end of the mouthpiece of some musical instruments. □ *The saxophone and clarinet are two instruments that require a reed to produce sound.*
- **reed** [rid]   a comblike device used to separate the yarns on a loom. □ *You must straighten the fibers using a reed before you begin weaving.*

real—reel
- **real** [ril]   actual; true; authentic. □ *I saw a real giraffe at the zoo.*
- **real** [ril]   something stationary, fixed, or permanent, usually land or buildings. □ *My sister deals in real estate management.*
- **real** [ril]   measured by purchasing power. □ *His real income is fairly substantial.*

- **real** [ril]   very. (Informal.) □ *The students were real happy when they finished their exams.*
- **reel** [ril]   a device around which something is wound. □ *The reel on my fishing pole jammed when I dropped it.*
- **reel** [ril]   a quantity of something wound on a reel. □ *I need a reel of cable to complete the job.*
- **reel** [ril]   to wind something in or upon as if on a reel. □ *Reel the fish in close to the side of the boat so we can see it.*
- **reel** [ril]   to fall or teeter backward as if from a blow. □ *The lack of oxygen made my head reel.*
- **reel** [ril]   a Scottish Highland dance or the music to which it is performed. □ *The dancers kicked and stomped their feet during the lively reel.*

recede—reseed

- **recede** [rə'sid]   to draw or pull back or away from something. □ *After two days at flood level, the river began to recede.*
- **recede** [rə'sid]   to decrease. □ *His financial debt finally began to recede.*
- **recede** [ri'sid]   to cede something back to someone. □ *The landowner decided not to recede his property to his previous tenants.*
- **reseed** ['ri'sid]   to sow seed again. □ *After the heavy rain, we had to reseed the garden.* □ *Each year they reseed their winter wheat field.* □ *Some fields naturally reseed themselves.*

receipt—reseat

- **receipt** [rɪ'sit]   the act of receiving. □ *You will be paid upon the receipt of the signed contract.*
- **receipt** [rɪ'sit]   a written acknowledgement of items or goods received. □ *Bring your receipt if you must return an item to the store.*
- **receipt** [rɪ'sit]   to mark something as paid. □ *I will receipt the invoice when I receive the payment.*
- **reseat** ['ri'sit]   to seat someone again. □ *The ushers were asked to reseat the audience following the false fire alarm.*
- **reseat** ['ri'sit]   to reinstall someone in an office or seat of dignity. □ *The council will reseat its chairperson following his long illness.*
- **reseat** ['ri'sit]   to repair or replace the seat of something. □ *It will be necessary to reseat four of the antique chairs we purchased at the auction.*

red   See the main entry beginning with *read.*

reed   See the main entry beginning with *read.*

reel   See the main entry beginning with *real.*

reign   See the main entry beginning with *rain.*

rein   See the main entry beginning with *rain.*

reseat   See the main entry beginning with *receipt.*

reseed   See the main entry beginning with *recede.*

residence—residents

- **residence** ['rɛzədənts]   the place where a person resides or lives. □ *You must list your permanent residence on the application form.*
- **residence** ['rɛzədənts]   a dwelling. □ *The police discovered the residence of the suspect was empty.*
- **residence** ['rɛzədənts]   the period of time one dwells in a location for the fulfillment of duty or to receive a benefit. □ *Members of Congress must establish residence in their home districts.*
- **residence** ['rɛzədənts]   a period for study, research, practice, or teaching of medicine. □ *The doctor will serve her residence at a local hospital.*
- **residents** ['rɛzədənts]   the plural of *resident* 'someone who lives in a place.' □ *The residents of that house are rarely at home.*
- **residents** ['rɛzədənts]   the plural of *resident* 'a doctor who is going through a period for study, research, practice, or teaching.' □ *The young residents correctly diagnosed the patient's illness.*

residents   See the main entry beginning with *residence.*

rest—wrest

- **rest** [rɛst]   to repose in sleep or relaxation. □ *I think I'll rest after that vigorous walk.*
- **rest** [rɛst]   a place for resting or lodging. □ *My aunt's cat uses her mantle as a rest.*
- **rest** [rɛst]   peace of mind or spirit. □ *He won't have any rest until he knows whether he passed his exams.*
- **rest** [rɛst]   to bring something to an end. □ *Let's just let that unlikely idea rest.*
- **rest** [rɛst]   remains; leftovers. □ *Put the rest of the food in the refrigerator.*
- **rest** [rɛst]   a rhythmic silence in music. □ *The drummer ignored the rest and continued playing.*
- **wrest** [rɛst]   to take something or someone forcibly; to gain something with difficulty. □ *The prince was unable to wrest*

power from the king. □ *The officers had to wrest the gun from the attacker.*

- **wrest** [rɛst] to change the significance or truth of something. □ *Joan tends to wrest the truth when making excuses for herself.*

retch—wretch

- **retch** [rɛtʃ] to vomit; to try to vomit. □ *The grisly sight made me retch.*
- **wretch** [rɛtʃ] a miserable, unfortunate person; an outcast or vile individual. □ *The poor wretch had no job or means of support.* □ *In the movie, the villian was a terrible wretch.*

review—revue

- **review** [rɪ'vju] to look over, inspect, or survey something. □ *Let's review the results of the questionnaire.*
- **review** [rɪ'vju] to examine something again. □ *Be sure to review all of the course material before taking the final exam.*
- **review** [rɪ'vju] a critical evaluation of a movie, book, or play. □ *The off-Broadway play did not receive a very favorable review.*
- **review** [rɪ'vju] a judicial examination. □ *The appeals court has agreed to a review of that particular case.*
- **review** [rɪ'vju] a magazine devoted chiefly to reviews. □ *The monthly business review has increased its readership recently.*
- **revue** [rɪ'vju] a theater production comprised of short songs, dances, and comic sketches. □ *Audiences were excited about the rollicking revue.*

revue See the main entry beginning with *review.*

rigger—rigor

- **rigger** ['rɪgɚ] a specialized, sable brush used in painting portraits or pictures. □ *As a portrait artist, Maggie must periodically replace her rigger with a new one.*
- **rigger** ['rɪgɚ] a ship with a specific rig setup. □ *The square-rigger sailed serenely in the calm seas.*
- **rigger** ['rɪgɚ] a person who fits, arranges, or sets up something. □ *The house alarm is so complicated that the company sends a rigger to install it for the customer.*
- **rigor** ['rɪgɚ] strictness; severity. □ *The father of that family rules with rigor.*
- **rigor** ['rɪgɚ] stiffness; rigidity. □ *The rigor of the old woman's muscles makes stairs difficult to climb.*
- **rigor** ['rɪgɚ] inflexibility of judgment, opinion, or temperament. □ *All of the rigor of his younger days disappeared as he mellowed with age.*

- **rigor** ['rɪgɚ]   a situation or condition that makes life difficult. □ *The rigor of Marie's lifestyle finally took its toll on her health.*

right—rite—wright—write

- **right** [raɪt]   correct; appropriate. □ *Please wear the right type of clothing on the camping trip.* □ *I finally had to admit that you were right.*
- **right** [raɪt]   righteous. □ *He is a right and honorable man.*
- **right** [raɪt]   genuine. □ *Make sure the antiques you purchase are right and are not reproductions.*
- **right** [raɪt]   to justify or change something that is wrong. □ *It is too late to right the damage that has been done.*
- **right** [raɪt]   a direction that is opposite of left. □ *Turn right at the next traffic light.*
- **rite** [raɪt]   ceremony; a precise manner of carrying out a cere-monial tradition. □ *The priest will perform the rite of baptism at the church this morning.*
- **wright** [raɪt]   someone who makes or repairs certain things. (Usually seen in compounds such as *wheelwright* and *ship-wright*.) □ *Grandpa looked all over the county for a wheelwright who could fix up the old buggy.*
- **write** [raɪt]   to draw up, author, or compose something in writing. □ *The author hopes to write a biography about that famous sculptor.* □ *Sue can write very poetic phrases.*

rigor   See the main entry beginning with *rigger*.

ring—wring

- **ring** [rɪŋ]   a circular band used to pull, hold, or hang some-thing. □ *I keep my keys on a big ring so I don't lose any of them.*
- **ring** [rɪŋ]   a piece of jewelry worn on the finger. □ *Tom gave Ann an engagement ring on Thanksgiving Day.*
- **ring** [rɪŋ]   a circular form or shape. □ *The glass of iced tea left a water ring on the tabletop.*
- **ring** [rɪŋ]   an arena where boxing matches take place. □ *The audience applauded as the two boxers entered the ring.*
- **ring** [rɪŋ]   to form or place a ring around something. □ *We'll ring the base of the tree with flowers.*
- **ring** [rɪŋ]   a clear, resonant sound. □ *The teenager ran quickly to the phone when she heard a ring.*
- **ring** [rɪŋ]   to make a clear, resonant sound. □ *When I tried to ring the doorbell, I discovered it didn't work.*
- **ring** [rɪŋ]   a telephone call. □ *I'll give you a ring as soon as I get home.*

- **wring** [rɪŋ]   to twist or squeeze something in order to extract moisture or liquid. □ *Wring the water from your socks after you take them off.*
- **wring** [rɪŋ]   to obtain or acquire something by coercion or violence. □ *The nasty cop tried to wring a confession from the innocent man.*
- **wring** [rɪŋ]   to twist the hands together in an expression of grief or anguish. □ *Her mother used to wring her hands whenever she was upset.*
- **wring** [rɪŋ]   to shake hands vigorously. □ *Why must he always wring everyone's hands so hard?*
- **wring** [rɪŋ]   to contort something by twisting. □ *Did your mother ever tell you that she would wring your neck if you misbehaved?*

rite   See the main entry beginning with *right.*

road—rode—rowed
- **road** [rod]   an open pathway for vehicles, people, and animals. □ *The rural road is a very scenic drive.*
- **road** [rod]   a somewhat protected anchorage place for ships and boats. □ *Lahaina road was a favorite port for early visitors to the island of Maui.*
- **rode** [rod]   the past tense of *ride* 'to travel in or on something.' □ *Jane rode the bus to work for years.*
- **rode** [rod]   the past tense of *ride* 'to be sustained by something; to continue something without interference.' □ *The candidate rode a wave of popularity during his campaign.* □ *The team rode all the way to the championship.*
- **rode** [rod]   the past tense of *ride* 'to nag, tease, or harass someone.' □ *Jane continually rode her husband about his poor golf game.*
- **rowed** [rod]   the past tense and past participle of *row* 'to propel a boat by using oars.' □ *We rowed across the lake against the wind.*
- **rowed** [rod]   the past tense and past participle of *row* 'to form someone's hair into rows.' □ *The hair stylist rowed her client's hair.*

rode   See the main entry beginning with *road.*

roe—row
- **roe** [ro]   the eggs of fish. □ *The roe of sturgeon is known as caviar.*
- **roe** [ro]   a speckled figure sometimes seen in sawn lumber. □ *The lumber buyer would not buy any wood containing a roe.*

- **row** [ro]   to propel a boat by using oars. □ *If you don't want to row, we can use the outboard motor.*
- **row** [ro]   to form something into rows. □ *Be careful how you row the vegetable plants in the garden.*
- **row** [ro]   a number of objects in a sequence or series. □ *Each row of desks was neatly aligned in the classroom.*
- **row** [ro]   a street occupied by a specific kind of enterprise. □ *They live in a row of homes in the new development area.*

roes—rose—rows

(See also *rouse—rows.*)

- **roes** [roz]   the plural of *roe* 'the eggs of fish.' □ *Roes are usually either red, yellow, or black and are often eaten in Japanese restaurants.*
- **roes** [roz]   the plural of *roe* 'a speckled figure sometimes seen in sawn lumber.' □ *Because of so many roes in that wood, the sawmill decided to discount its price.*
- **rose** [roz]   the fragrant blossom of a shrub with thorny stems by the same name. □ *Be sure to cover the rose during the winter.* □ *On her birthday, Katie's husband gave her a single sweetheart rose.*
- **rose** [roz]   a cut of gemstone that resembles a rose. □ *The ring contained a single rose garnet.*
- **rose** [roz]   resembling a rose in shape, fragrance, or color. □ *Mother always wears rose perfume.* □ *She wore a rose dress to the party.*
- **rose** [roz]   the past tense of *rise* 'to elevate oneself or itself; to ascend.' □ *He rose slowly from his comfortable chair.*
- **rows** [roz]   the plural of *row* 'a number of objects in a straight line.' □ *The new cars stood in long rows on the factory lot.* □ *Rows of commercial buildings make up the business district.*
- **rows** [roz]   the present tense, third person singular of *row* 'to propel a boat by using oars.' □ *The avid fisherman rows around the entire pond every afternoon.*

roil—royal

- **roil** [roɪl]   to disturb or rile someone. □ *Don't roil your brother by nagging at him.*
- **roil** [roɪl]   to stir up or move something about violently. □ *The floodwaters will no doubt roil the sediment at the mouth of the river.*
- **royal** [roɪl]   of noble ancestry; relating to the crown. □ *Mark comes from a royal family.* □ *The royal couple will attend the parade.*
- **royal** [roɪl]   of great magnitude, quality, or size. (Colloquial.)

☐ *"I have a royal headache," moaned Liz.*

- **royal** [roɪl]   a male deer of at least eight years that has an antler configuration of at least twelve points. ☐ *We saw a magnificent royal on the mountainside.*
- **royal** [roɪl]   a shade of bright purplish-blue. ☐ *His royal shirt was very handsome.*

role—roll

- **role** [rol]   a part played by a singer or actor. ☐ *Her role in the play was a minor one.*
- **role** [rol]   a function. ☐ *We'll never know for sure what role he played in the discovery.*
- **roll** [rol]   a scroll. ☐ *The messenger handed the roll to the king.*
- **roll** [rol]   a list of names. ☐ *Before we begin, let me call roll.*
- **roll** [rol]   something formed into the shape of a roll. ☐ *Jessie had a roll of dollar bills in his pocket.*
- **roll** [rol]   to cause someone or something to move forward by turning over and over. ☐ *It is easier to roll an object down a hill than to carry it.*
- **roll** [rol]   to rob a person by pilfering his or her pockets. ☐ *Someone entered the dormitory room and tried to roll the occupants while they slept.*
- **roll** [rol]   to travel along something. ☐ *I like the sound of trains as they roll along the tracks.*
- **roll** [rol]   a sound of sustained, rapid drumbeats. ☐ *The drummer was required to perform a long roll during the march.*

roll   See the main entry beginning with *role.*

rose   See the main entry beginning with *roes.*

rote—wrote

- **rote** [rot]   the use of memory with little understanding or intelligence. ☐ *Learning by rote is not the best way to learn.*
- **rote** [rot]   an automatic or mechanical repetition or routine involving little thought. ☐ *Through shear rote Daniel was able to clean his apartment even though he had the flu.*
- **wrote** [rot]   the past tense of *write* 'to spell out words, usually on paper.' ☐ *Mike wrote the alphabet on the blackboard.* ☐ *Dad wrote us a letter to tell us the time his plane would arrive.*

rough—ruff

- **rough** [rəf]   coarse or irregular. ☐ *The dog has a rough coat.*
- **rough** [rəf]   wild; turbulent. ☐ *We had a rough flight over the mountains.*

- **rough** [rəf]   taxing; difficult. □ *The orphan had a rough childhood.*
- **rough** [rəf]   crude; unrefined; something in a preliminary or unfinished state. □ *Jane's manners are a little rough.* □ *A rough copy of that report is due by noon.*
- **rough** [rəf]   the brushy, uneven area bordering a golf fairway. □ *Bob hit the ball into the rough between the sand traps.*
- **rough** [rəf]   to maul or manhandle someone or something. □ *The thug tried to rough up and frighten the old man.*
- **rough** [rəf]   a freshwater perch found in Europe. □ *The restaurant serves a tasty rough every Wednesday night.*
- **ruff** [rəf]   the hair or feathers around the neck of an animal. □ *The dark red dog has a ruff of thick golden hair.*
- **ruff** [rəf]   a stiff, pleated collar worn by women and men in the 1500's and 1600's. □ *The Elizabethan actor looked uncomfortable in the starched ruff.*

rouse—rows

(See also *roes—rose—rows.*)

- **rouse** [raʊz]   to wake someone or something from slumber or repose. □ *It is very difficult to rouse someone from a deep sleep.*
- **rouse** [raʊz]   to stir up or excite someone or something. □ *The mob's leader tried to rouse his followers into action.*
- **rows** [raʊz]   the plural of *row* 'a loud quarrel or argument.' □ *Police were called to the couple's residence because of the noisy rows.*

rout—route

- **rout** [raʊt]   a disorderly retreat. □ *During the rout, the soldiers fled in all directions.*
- **rout** [raʊt]   a state of wild confusion. □ *There was a rout as both baseball teams cleared the benches.*
- **rout** [raʊt]   a disastrous defeat. □ *The game ended in a rout for the home team.*
- **rout** [raʊt]   a disturbance; a riot. □ *Someone reported a rout in the apartment building late last night.*
- **rout** [raʊt]   to defeat someone or something decisively. □ *The commander told his troops they would surely rout the enemy.*
- **rout** [raʊt]   to cut an edge or groove in a surface. □ *Carpenters often rout decorative edges on furniture.*
- **rout** [raʊt]   to dig up or discover something. □ *Let's see if you can rout the truth about what really happened.*
- **rout** [raʊt]   to search something awkwardly; to rummage something. □ *If we rout the room, we may destroy valuable evidence.* □ *Rout around in the drawer for some scissors.*

- **route** [raʊt, rut]   a course or territory to be covered; an established passage for travel. □ *The girl's paper route covers several neighborhoods.* □ *The route I take to work is always busy in the morning.*
- **route** [raʊt, rut]   to cause something or someone to take a specific direction or path. □ *The detour will route traffic away from the road repair area.*

route   See the main entry beginning with *rout*.

row   See the main entry beginning with *roe*.

rowed   See the main entry beginning with *road*.

rows   See the main entry beginning with *roes* and the main entry beginning with *rouse*.

royal   See the main entry beginning with *roil*.

rude—rued

- **rude** [rud]   lacking refinement or tact; offensive in action or manner. □ *His supervisor is a rude person.* □ *The supervisor's rude comments offended many employees.*
- **rued** [rud]   the past tense and past participle of *rue* 'to feel sorrow or regret about something.' (Almost always in the expression *rue the day*.) □ *As a lonely millionaire, John rued the day he wished for fame and fortune.*

rued   See the main entry beginning with *rude*.

ruff   See the main entry beginning with *rough*.

rung—wrung

- **rung** [rəŋ]   a crosspiece of a ladder. □ *Don't use that ladder until the cracked rung is replaced.*
- **rung** [rəŋ]   a stage or degree of ascent. □ *He eventually reached the top rung in the corporation.*
- **rung** [rəŋ]   a spoke of a wheel. □ *A rung in the front wheel is bent.*
- **rung** [rəŋ]   a connecting support in the legs of a chair. □ *Is it possible to replace a broken rung in a chair?*
- **rung** [rəŋ]   the past participle of *ring* 'to make a clear, musical sound, by striking metal or glass.' □ *The alarm had rung loudly for many minutes before Bill turned it off.*
- **rung** [rəŋ]   the past participle of *ring* 'to place a telephone call.' □ *The telephone operator has rung the number repeatedly.*
- **wrung [out]** [rəŋ]   the past participle of *wring [out]* 'to twist or squeeze something to extract moisture.' □ *I had wrung the*

wet clothing out before hanging it on the clothesline.

- **wrung** [rəŋ]   the past participle of *wring* 'to twist one's hands together in grief or anguish.' □ *When first confronted with the bad news, he had wrung his hands, but now he is calmer.*
- **wrung** [rəŋ]   the past participle of *wring* 'to grasp and shake someone's hand vigorously.' □ *It seems the politician had wrung the hands of everyone in town.*
- **wrung** [rəŋ]   the past participle of *wring* 'to twist.' □ *He had wrung the necks of the three chickens in preparation for the big chicken dinner.*

rye—wry

- **rye** [raɪ]   a hardy grain used for cereal or grown for cover. □ *Most of the farmland is planted in barley and rye.*
- **wry** [raɪ]   cleverly humorous, often with a grim or ironic twist. □ *Tom has a wry sense of humor.*
- **wry** [raɪ]   made with facial contortions. □ *His wry smile made me suspicious.*
- **wry** [raɪ]   marked by impropriety. □ *None of us appreciated her pointed, wry comments.*

S

sac—sack

- **sac** [sæk]   a pouch containing fluid inside a plant or animal. □ *Among seahorses, the male carries the egg sac containing the young.*
- **sack** [sæk]   a container made of paper or other material that is used to carry items. □ *I carried my groceries home in a sack.*
- **sack** [sæk]   a loose-fitting style of coat or dress. □ *The sack was once a very popular dress style.*
- **sack** [sæk]   dismissal. □ *After working for the company for ten years, his sack was totally unexpected.*
- **sack** [sæk]   to plunder or loot something after capture. □ *The soldiers continued to sack the city for days.*
- **sack** [sæk]   to put something into a sack. □ *Will you help me sack these groceries?*
- **sack** [sæk]   to fire or let someone go. □ *Most employers don't like to sack faithful workers in bad times.*

sack   See the main entry beginning with *sac*.

sacks—sax

- **sacks** [sæks]   the plural of *sack* 'a container made of paper or other material.' □ *Put all of the empty sacks in the cupboard.*
- **sacks** [sæks]   the plural of *sack* 'a loose-fitting style of coat or dress.' □ *The models wore sacks of various colors over their dresses.*
- **sacks** [sæks]   the present tense, third person singular of *sack* 'to plunder or loot something after capture.' □ *The platoon sacks each city that it conquers.*
- **sacks** [sæks]   the present tense, third person singular of *sack* 'to pack things into a sack.' □ *Bob sacks groceries after school*

and on weekends.

- **sacks** [sæks]   the present tense, third person singular of *sack* 'to dismiss someone from employment.' □ *If your company sacks you, file a complaint immediately.*
- **sax** [sæks]   a saxophone. □ *A sax is an essential part of a jazz band.*

sail—sale

- **sail** [sel]   an expanse of fabric hoisted above sailing vessels to catch the wind and propel the ships through water. □ *Due to the heavy seas and high winds, the main sail tore.*
- **sail** [sel]   to travel aboard a vessel propelled by the wind. □ *The couple wanted to sail from Florida to Bermuda.*
- **sail** [sel]   to glide through something without much effort. □ *Henry hoped to sail through his interview and get the job without any problems.*
- **sale** [sel]   the act of selling something or transferring ownership of something from one person to another. □ *The sale of our home was completed quickly.*
- **sale** [sel]   the disposal of items at bargain prices. □ *The department store sale will last through the weekend.*
- **sale** [sel]   the availability of something for purchase. □ *His tractor is not for sale.*
- **sale** [sel]   gross receipts. □ *The total month's sale was above average.*

sale   See the main entry beginning with *sail.*

sane—seine

- **sane** [sen]   mentally sound or stable. □ *The accused man was declared sane and capable of standing trial.*
- **seine** [sen]   a large, weighted net with floats on one side designed to drag through water and catch fish. □ *We tried to catch minnows in the stream by using a large seine.*
- **seine** [sen]   to fish or catch something with a seine. □ *Terry wanted to seine the pond in hopes of catching the big bass.*

saver—savor

- **saver** ['sevɚ]   a person who collects and keeps something. □ *Bernice is a compulsive saver of food coupons.*
- **saver** ['sevɚ]   a person who rescues someone or something from harm. □ *Mr. Smith is known as a saver of lost or injured animals.*
- **savor** ['sevɚ]   to relish or delight in something. □ *The smell of the first campfire of the season is an odor to savor.*
- **savor** ['sevɚ]   to smell or taste something with great pleasure.

□ *Mary likes to savor her first cup of coffee of the morning.*
- **savor** ['sevɚ]   a distinctive smell or flavor. □ *Vintage wine has a unique savor all its own.*

savor   See the main entry beginning with *saver.*

sax   See the main entry beginning with *sacks.*

scene—seen
- **scene** [sin]   the site of an action or occurrence. □ *The scene of the accident was secured by police.*
- **scene** [sin]   a stage setting. □ *During the play, the scene was darkened to create a feeling of the unknown.*
- **scene** [sin]   a division of a theatrical performance. □ *She does not appear in the play until the third scene.*
- **scene** [sin]   a display of inappropriate behavior or anger. □ *The angry customer made quite a scene.*
- **seen** [sin]   the past participle of *see* 'to visualize someone or something.' □ *In her mind she has seen the man of her dreams.*
- **seen** [sin]   the past participle of *see* 'to understand something.' □ *We have seen the value of saving money.*
- **seen** [sin]   the past participle of *see* 'to perceive someone or something with the eye.' □ *I have never seen him look so happy in his whole life.*
- **seen** [sin]   the past participle of *see* 'to examine or watch someone or something.' □ *The investigators have seen all of the evidence.*
- **seen [to]** [sin]   the past participle of *see [to]* 'to escort or accompany someone to a place.' □ *The volunteers have seen each of the patients safely to his room.*

scent   See the main entry beginning with *cent.*

scents   See the main entry beginning with *cents.*

scull—skull
- **scull** [skəl]   a type of oar used at the stern or back of a boat to move it forward. □ *The scull accidentally fell into the water.*
- **scull** [skəl]   a racing boat propelled by sculls. □ *A great deal of strength is needed to man a racing scull.*
- **scull** [skəl]   to propel a boat using a scull or large oar. □ *The plan was to scull the vessel rather than use its motor.*
- **skull** [skəl]   the skeleton of the head of a vertebrate that encloses and protects the brain. □ *Workmen uncovered the skull of a large mammal at the building site.*
- **skull** [skəl]   a mind. □ *Try to get this message into your skull.*

sea—see

- **sea** [si]   the body of saltwater covering most of the earth's surface; a large body of saltwater that is not quite landlocked. □ *Not all fish can live in the sea.* □ *The sea is surrounded on three sides by land.*
- **sea** [si]   a motion or rough disturbance on the surface of a large body of water. □ *The brisk wind and fairly calm sea made for ideal sailing conditions.*
- **see** [si]   to visualize something or someone. □ *I can see trouble brewing.*
- **see** [si]   to understand something. □ *Susan did not see the point he was trying to make.*
- **see** [si]   to perceive someone or something. □ *We could see storm clouds forming on the horizon.*
- **see** [si]   to examine or watch someone or something. □ *Wait and see what develops.*
- **see** [si]   to escort or accompany someone or something to some place. □ *The boys promised to see their dates home.*

sealing   See the main entry beginning with *ceiling.*

seam—seem

- **seam** [sim]   a joint where two pieces of fabric are sewn together. □ *A seam on my new blouse came apart.*
- **seam** [sim]   to stitch two pieces of fabric together. □ *He will seam the torn tent flap.*
- **seam** [sim]   a ridge, line, or groove formed by the joining of edges. □ *I felt every seam in the bumpy road.*
- **seam** [sim]   a thin layer of mineral between two distinctive layers of earth. □ *A seam of silver runs through the bedrock.*
- **seem** [sim]   to appear; to give evidence of the existence or presence of someone or something. □ *The new nurses seem to enjoy their hard work.* □ *There doesn't seem to be anyone here.*

seas—sees—seize

- **seas** [siz]   the plural of *sea* 'a body of saltwater.' □ *The seas near the arctic are cold and rough.* □ *Three different seas surround the country of Greece.*
- **seas** [siz]   the plural of *sea* 'the surface conditions of a large body of water.' □ *The ship's captain alerted the crew to the rough seas ahead.*
- **sees** [siz]   the present tense, third person singular of *see* 'to visualize something.' □ *Jane sees her future goals as being attainable.*
- **sees** [siz]   the present tense, third person singular of *see* 'to

understand something.' □ *Mother sees the value of teaching her children to be independent.*

- **sees** [siz]   the present tense, third person singular of *see* 'to perceive someone or something with the eye.' □ *Larry awakens early and sees the sun rise each day.*
- **sees** [siz]   the present tense, third person singular of *see* 'to make sure that something is done.' □ *The bus driver sees that the children get off the bus safely.*
- **sees [to]** [siz]   the present tense, third person singular of *see [to]* 'to escort someone to some place.' □ *The butler sees all visitors to the door when they leave.*
- **seize** [siz]   to grasp someone or something; to take something by force. □ *The military will someday try to seize control of the government.* □ *I wanted to seize her arm so we could talk.*
- **seize** [siz]   to capture someone or something. □ *The troops tried without success to seize a truck convoy.*
- **seize** [siz]   to take over one's mind completely. □ *Try not to let jealousy seize your mind.*

sects—sex

- **sects** [sɛkts]   the plural of *sect* 'a religious denomination.' □ *Many different sects were represented at the religious conference.*
- **sects** [sɛkts]   the plural of *sect* 'a party, cult, or faction.' □ *The leaders of those sects demand total obedience from their followers.*
- **sex** [sɛks]   either of the two sexual divisions of organisms, male or female. □ *The expectant parents did not wish to know the sex of their unborn child.*
- **sex** [sɛks]   pertaining to sexual phenomena or behavior. □ *The sex offender was sent to prison.*
- **sex** [sɛks]   to determine the sex of some creature. □ *His job at the chicken hatchery is to sex newly hatched chicks.*

see   See the main entry beginning with *sea.*

seed   See the main entry beginning with *cede.*

seeder   See the main entry beginning with *cedar.*

seem   See the main entry beginning with *seam.*

seen   See the main entry beginning with *scene.*

sees   See the main entry beginning with *seas.*

seine   See the main entry beginning with *sane.*

seize   See the main entry beginning with *seas.*

sell   See the main entry beginning with *cell.*

seller   See the main entry beginning with *cellar.*

sense   See the main entry beginning with *cents.*

senses   See the main entry beginning with *census.*

sensor   See the main entry beginning with *censer.*

sensual—sensuous
- **sensual** ['sɛnʃul]   having to do with physical or sexual satisfaction. □ *The exotic dance was very sensual in nature.*
- **sensuous** ['sɛnʃuəs]   having to do with the senses. □ *Walking through the field of wildflowers was a sensuous delight.*

sensuous   See the main entry beginning with *sensual.*

sent   See the main entry beginning with *cent.*

serf—surf
- **serf** [sɚf]   a member of the peasant class bound to the land and subject to the will of the owner or overseer in a feudal society. □ *Each serf was allowed to keep a portion of the crops he grew.*
- **surf** [sɚf]   the swell, foam, splash, or sound of breaking waves upon a shore. □ *The sound of the surf lulled me to sleep.*
- **surf** [sɚf]   to ride the waves. □ *Curt learned to surf while visiting relatives in California.*

serial   See the main entry beginning with *cereal.*

session   See the main entry beginning with *cession.*

set—sit
- **set** [sɛt]   to place something onto something. □ *Would you please set this vase on the mantel?*
- **sit** [sɪt]   to rest on one's buttocks, as in a chair. □ *Please sit over there.*

sew—so—sow
- **sew** [so]   to stitch or hold something together using needle and thread. □ *Sew that loose button on the shirt before it falls off.*
- **so** [so]   as indicated or suggested. □ *Dad gave us an idea about how to handle the problem, and we agreed to do so.*
- **so** [so]   therefore. □ *That is a silly plan, so let's forget about it.*
- **so** [so]   conforming to actual facts. □ *Lisa said certain things that were not so.*

- **so** [so]   very; to a great degree. □ *Jeff's job promotion made him so happy that he took his family out to dinner.*
- **sow** [so]   to plant with seed. □ *Farmers sow winter wheat in the fall.*
- **sow** [so]   to set something into motion. □ *Mike will try to sow the plans needed to get the project underway.*

sex   See the main entry beginning with *sects.*

shall—will
- **shall** [ʃæl]   in the future. (A form used with the first person, *I* or *we* in formal speech or writing.) □ *I shall consider your idea carefully.* □ *We shall try not to be late.*
- **will** [wɪl]   in the future. (A form used with all three persons *I, we; you;* or *he, she, it, they* except in formal speech or writing.) □ *I will have your report finished by noon.* □ *You will be reimbursed for the lost article.* □ *They will no longer work here after June.*
- **will** [wɪl]   determination; resolve. □ *Where there's a will there's a way.*
- **will** [wɪl]   a legal document that specifies how one's property is disposed of after one's death. □ *My grandfather mentioned me in his will, but there was nothing left of the estate after the lawyers and the tax people took what was theirs.*

shear—sheer
- **shear** [ʃiɚ]   to cut, shave, or clip something, usually hair or wool. □ *Many farmers must shear their own lambs and sheep.*
- **shear** [ʃiɚ]   to cut something with something sharp. □ *A good knife can shear even the toughest pieces of meat.*
- **shear** [ʃiɚ]   a scissors or cutting tool. □ *I need to have my sewing shear sharpened.*
- **sheer** [ʃiɚ]   pure, complete, or utter. □ *People bungee jump for sheer excitement.* □ *It was sheer luck that they met after so many years.*
- **sheer** [ʃiɚ]   transparent; filmy. □ *The costume was made from a sheer fabric.*
- **sheer** [ʃiɚ]   to swerve suddenly or change course. □ *The sudden appearance of the mountaintop caused the pilot to sheer to his left.*

sheer   See the main entry beginning with *shear.*

sheik   See the main entry beginning with *chic.*

shoe—shoo
- **shoe** [ʃu]   an article of footwear. □ *The toddler put his shoe*

on the wrong foot.
- **shoe** [ʃu] something resembling a shoe. □ *The shoe on the sled runner is rusted.*
- **shoe** [ʃu] a device that controls, slows, or stops the motion of some object. □ *One brake shoe on the car has gone bad.*
- **shoe** [ʃu] to provide or fit someone or something with a shoe. □ *Those blacksmiths travel around to farms to shoe any horses needing new horseshoes.*
- **shoo** [ʃu] to brush, scare, or send someone or something away. □ *Shoo those flies away from the freshly baked pies.*

shone—shown
- **shone** [ʃon] the past tense and past participle of *shine* 'to give off rays of light.' □ *The sun shone after the rainstorm.*
- **shone** [ʃon] the past tense and past participle of *shine* 'to be bright and luminous.' □ *His eyes shone brightly as he stepped forward to receive his award.*
- **shone** [ʃon] the past tense and past participle of *shine* 'to be distinguished or eminent.' □ *Her career as an educator shone above all of her peers.*
- **shown** [ʃon] the past participle of *show* 'to exhibit something; to demonstrate something.' □ *That house has been shown by several different real estate agents.* □ *Nancy has shown her crafts at various local shows.*

shoo See the main entry beginning with *shoe.*

shoot See the main entry beginning with *chute.*

shown See the main entry beginning with *shone.*

side—sighed
- **side** [saɪd] the left or right edge of the body. □ *The left side of her body was affected by the stroke.* □ *I prefer to sleep on my side.*
- **side** [saɪd] a space or place in relation to the center of something. □ *Put the book on the left side of the shelf.*
- **side** [saɪd] an outer edge or boundary. □ *Players must remain at the side of the field when not in the game.*
- **side** [saɪd] an activity or attitude of one body or persons with regard to another. □ *My mother's side of the family has brown eyes.*
- **side** [saɪd] to support or agree with someone or something. □ *I refuse to side with either of the quarrelers.*
- **side** [saɪd] to furnish something with sides or siding. □ *Our neighbors want to side their house with a bright color.*

- **sighed** [saɪd]   the past tense and past participle of *sigh* 'to emit a drawn-out, audible breath.' □ *The weary woman sighed after a long day's work.*
- **sighed** [saɪd]   the past tense and past participle of *sigh* 'to say something with a drawn-out, audible breath.' □ *"How much farther do we have to go?" sighed the tired child.*

sighed   See the main entry beginning with *side.*

sighs—size
- **sighs** [saɪz]   the plural of *sigh* 'a drawn-out, audible breath.' □ *After the tense situation ended, people gave many sighs of relief.*
- **sighs** [saɪz]   the present tense, third person singular of *sigh* 'to utter a drawn-out, audible breath.' □ *Her father always sighs when puzzled.*
- **size** [saɪz]   a physical measurement or dimension. □ *Because of Tom's immense size, several pro teams were interested in recruiting him as a blocker.*
- **size** [saɪz]   a series of graduated measures. □ *He wears a large size in clothing.*
- **size** [saɪz]   actual state or condition. □ *We cannot alter the size of the circumstances.*
- **size** [saɪz]   to make a judgment of something or someone. □ *"How do you size up this situation?" asked Jim.*
- **size** [saɪz]   to arrange or classify something by size. □ *The grocer has to size all of the oranges before he can price them.*
- **size** [saɪz]   to stiffen something, usually with starch. □ *The dry cleaners will size your shirts if you request it.*

sight   See the main entry beginning with *cite.*

sign—sine
- **sign** [saɪn]   a signal, motion, or gesture indicating some thought. □ *The referee gave the sign for the game to begin.*
- **sign** [saɪn]   a placard or lettered board used to display advertising or information. □ *The highway sign was visible at night.*
- **sign** [saɪn]   one of the twelve divisions of the zodiac. □ *Jerry was born under the sign of Leo.*
- **sign** [saɪn]   to communicate manually with sign language. □ *The deaf woman never learned to sign.*
- **sign** [saɪn]   to place one's signature on formal written matter. □ *Please sign on the bottom line.*
- **sine** [saɪn]   a mathematical function in trigonometry dealing with angles. □ *The math student was unable to figure the sine of the diagram.*

sine   See the main entry beginning with *sign.*

sit   See the main entry beginning with *set.*

site   See the main entry beginning with *cite.*

size   See the main entry beginning with *sighs.*

skull   See the main entry beginning with *scull.*

slay—sleigh
- **slay** [sle]   to kill or murder someone or something violently. □ *It was wrong to slay the deer merely for its antlers.*
- **slay** [sle]   to overwhelm; to impress. (A slang exaggeration.) □ *Gerry thought he could slay the girls with his good looks.*
- **sleigh** [sle]   a sled with runners designed to carry goods or people over ice and snow. □ *That country inn offers rides in an antique sleigh to its guests during the wintertime.*

sleigh   See the main entry beginning with *slay.*

sleight—slight
- **sleight** [slaɪt]   deception; craftiness. □ *The magician's skillful sleight fooled everyone.*
- **slight** [slaɪt]   trivial. □ *His error was so slight that no one even noticed.*
- **slight** [slaɪt]   scanty. □ *Jane's dress was very slight.*
- **slight** [slaɪt]   having a delicate, slim build. □ *The suspect was described as blond and slight.*
- **slight** [slaɪt]   small in amount, number, or kind. □ *Add just a slight amount of salt to the soup.*
- **slight** [slaɪt]   to treat someone or something as unimportant; to ignore or neglect someone. □ *I didn't mean to slight your question.* □ *If you slight the guest of honor, you'll be considered rude.*
- **slight** [slaɪt]   an insult; rude behavior. □ *Mary's obvious slight of her mother-in-law was noted by many people.*

slight   See the main entry beginning with *sleight.*

so   See the main entry beginning with *sew.*

soar—sore
- **soar** [soɚ]   to sail or fly high and unencumbered. □ *I wonder what it is like to soar in a glider plane.*
- **soar** [soɚ]   to move upward in status or position. □ *The actor's popularity began to soar with the release of his first movie.*
- **sore** [soɚ]   an open, often infected wound. □ *You should put some salve on that sore.*

- **sore** [sɔɚ] a source of irritation or pain. □ *Any discussion of his past was a sore for him.*
- **sore** [sɔɚ] to be painfully sensitive. □ *My back is sore today for some reason.*
- **sore** [sɔɚ] vexed or angered. □ *Don't be a sore loser.*

soared—sword

- **soared** [sɔɚd] the past tense and past participle of *soar* 'to sail or fly high and unencumbered.' □ *The gull soared gracefully with the wind.*
- **soared** [sɔɚd] the past tense and past participle of *soar* 'to move upward in status or position.' □ *The singer's hit record soared to the top of the record charts.*
- **sword** [sɔɚd] a long, sharp blade used for stabbing, cutting, or thrusting. □ *The marine's sash and sword are part of his dress uniform.*

sold—soled—souled

- **sold** [sold] the past tense and past participle of *sell* 'to offer something for sale; to exchange something for money.' □ *The store sold only sporting goods.* □ *Jack sold his old lawn mower to his neighbor.*
- **soled** [sold] the past tense and past participle of *sole* 'to equip footwear with a sole.' □ *The cobbler soled Mary's hiking boots twice in one season.*
- **souled** [sold] the past participle of *soul* 'to equip someone with a kind spirit.' (This occurs only as a past participle.) □ *My aunt was always a kind-souled lady.*

sole—soul

- **sole** [sol] the bottom part of a foot or shoe. □ *I have a cut on the sole of my foot.*
- **sole** [sol] the lower part or base of something on which something else rests. □ *The sole of her golf club has been damaged.*
- **sole** [sol] to furnish something with the lower part or base of something. □ *The cobbler will sole a pair of shoes for only eight dollars.*
- **sole** [sol] a tasty, white-fleshed fish. □ *He couldn't decide whether to order the shrimp or the sole on the menu.*
- **sole** [sol] only; lone. □ *A baby girl was the sole survivor of the auto accident.* □ *The sole judge in the case found the defendant not guilty.*
- **soul** [sol] the spiritual part of a human being. □ *Fred felt that his soul would live on after his death.*

- **soul** [sol]   a person's total self. □ *Sara poured her heart and soul into the difficult project.*
- **soul** [sol]   an essential or active part. □ *Mike was the soul behind the business's success.*

soled   See the main entry beginning with *sold.*

some—sum

- **some** [səm]   an unspecified number, amount, part, person, or thing. □ *Tomorrow the company will be forced to lay off some of its workers.*
- **some** [səm]   noteworthy; important. □ *That was some movie!*
- **some** [səm]   somewhat. □ *I was irritated some at her lack of manners.*
- **sum** [səm]   the total or whole amount; the end result of adding numbers or amounts. □ *The sum of money in the cash register is small.* □ *None of the math students came up with the correct sum.*
- **sum** [səm]   the utmost degree; the highest point. □ *The sum of all her happiness was realized on her wedding day.*
- **sum [up]** [səm]   to summarize something. □ *Would you please sum up his comments in a few words?*

son—sun

- **son** [sən]   a male offspring of human beings. □ *In Scotland it is considered lucky to be the seventh son of a seventh son.*
- **son** [sən]   a person closely associated with a formative body, usually a town, school, or country. □ *The newly elected president is a favorite son of the state of Iowa.*
- **sun** [sən]   a warmth-providing celestial body around which the Earth and other planets revolve. □ *I remember seeing a total eclipse of the sun once as a child.*
- **sun** [sən]   the light or heat given off from the sun. □ *The bright sun seemed to lighten our spirits.*
- **sun** [sən]   something resembling the sun's brilliance. □ *The lawyer had her moment in the sun when she won the famous court case.*

sore   See the main entry beginning with *soar.*

soul   See the main entry beginning with *sole.*

souled   See the main entry beginning with *sold.*

sow   See the main entry beginning with *sew.*

spade—spayed

- **spade** [sped]   a digging tool usually pushed into the ground with either the hand or foot. □ *Using a spade in soft, sandy soil is not difficult.*

- **spade** [sped]   a tool resembling a spade in shape or function. □ *A tree spade was used to plant the large evergreen tree.*
- **spade** [sped]   a playing card having the symbol of a spade on it. □ *Tony threw a high spade on my four to win the hand.*
- **spayed** [sped]   the past tense and past participle of *spay* 'to remove the ovaries of a female animal.' □ *After breeding her once, we decided to have our collie spayed.*

spayed   See the main entry beginning with *spade.*

staid—stayed
- **staid** [sted]   serious. □ *The professor's somber expression and staid manner made him seem unapproachable.*
- **stayed** [sted]   the past tense and past participle of *stay* 'to remain in a certain status, position, or place.' □ *The children stayed friends during their entire lives.* □ *The driver stayed in the passing lane for miles.*
- **stayed** [sted]   the past tense and past participle of *stay* 'to take up temporary residence somewhere.' □ *We stayed with my sister and her family while our parents were on vacation.*
- **stayed** [sted]   the past tense and past participle of *stay* '[for a judge] to issue an order preventing something from happening.' □ *The judge stayed the execution of the man on death row.*

stair—stare
- **stair** [stɛɚ]   a flight of steps leading from one level to another. □ *I took the stair rather than the elevator.*
- **stair** [stɛɚ]   a single step in a staircase. □ *He left his shoes on the stair beside the door.*
- **stare** [stɛɚ]   to look fixedly, conspicuously, or searchingly at something or someone. □ *The man taught his children not to stare at other people.* □ *The young man could not help but stare at his beloved whenever she spoke.*

stake—steak
- **stake** [stek]   a sharp, pointed piece of wood or metal driven into the ground as a marker or support. □ *The tent stake was bent.*
- **stake** [stek]   the prize in a contest. □ *A stake of fifty dollars goes to the winner of the race.*
- **stake** [stek]   something to be lost or gained. □ *If this rumor spreads, the senator's reputation is at stake.*
- **stake** [stek]   an interest in a commercial venture. □ *He has very little stake in the new building project.*

- **stake** [stek]   to place stakes or mark with stakes. □ *Let's stake out the dimensions for the new playhouse.*
- **stake** [stek]   to back someone or something financially. □ *I'll stake you in that business venture if you like.*
- **stake** [stek]   to bet something. □ *The cowboys decided to stake their favorite saddles on the horse race.*
- **steak** [stek]   a cut of meat, usually beef. □ *John likes steak and eggs for breakfast on Sunday mornings.*

stare   See the main entry beginning with *stair.*

stationary—stationery

- **stationary** [ˈsteʃənɛɚi]   not moving; unchanging in place or condition. □ *The weatherman said a stationary storm front had settled over the region.*
- **stationery** [ˈsteʃənɛɚi]   letter-writing materials such as ink, pen, paper, and envelopes. □ *Dad went into the store to buy some stationery items.* □ *I have several pretty styles of stationery.*

stationery   See the main entry beginning with *stationary.*

stayed   See the main entry beginning with *staid.*

steak   See the main entry beginning with *stake.*

steal—steel

- **steal** [stil]   to take something illegally. □ *The boys tried to steal a car from the parking lot.*
- **steal** [stil]   to move about in a quiet, secret manner. □ *A cat burglar knows how to steal about in a home without being seen or heard.*
- **steal** [stil]   to gain or win something by daring, skill, or trickery. □ *The actor's dashing manner and rugged good looks were enough to steal away the girl's heart.*
- **steal** [stil]   an act of stealing. □ *The baseball player's steal at home plate won the ball game.*
- **steal** [stil]   a bargain. □ *I really got a steal when I bought that table at the garage sale.*
- **steel** [stil]   commercial iron that comes from ore and is used in manufacturing. □ *Large amounts of steel were once used to make cars.*
- **steel** [stil]   something made from steel or resembling steel. □ *Those stainless steel knives are guaranteed not to rust.*
- **steel** [stil]   to fill someone with resolve or determination. □ *Police officers are taught to steel themselves against the less pleasant aspects of their jobs.*

steel   See the main entry beginning with *steal.*

step—steppe
- **step** [stɛp]   a stair. □ *She twisted her ankle on the slippery step.*
- **step** [stɛp]   a ladder rung. □ *"Go up one more step," called Janet from the bottom of the ladder.*
- **step** [stɛp]   a stride. □ *Mark always walks with a jaunty step.*
- **step** [stɛp]   the amount of space passed over in one step. □ *The runner lost the race by a single step.*
- **step** [stɛp]   a rank, grade, or degree in scale or quality. □ *The houses in this neighborhood are a step above the others we looked at.*
- **step** [stɛp]   an action taken. □ *It is necessary to take this step in order to avoid further trouble.*
- **step** [stɛp]   to move by raising and lowering the foot over some distance. □ *Please step over here.*
- **step** [stɛp]   to press something down with the foot. □ *Step on the brake slowly and carefully.*
- **step** [stɛp]   to move in a spritely manner. □ *The show dogs step around the ring with style.*
- **steppe** [stɛp]   a vast expanse of flat, treeless plain. □ *Only coarse grasses grow on a steppe.*

steppe   See the main entry beginning with *step.*

stile—style
- **stile** [staɪl]   a set of steps leading up to and crossing over a wall or fence. □ *Grandpa built a stile over the pasture fence.*
- **stile** [staɪl]   a vertical piece of a frame or panel into which other pieces are fitted. □ *The stile of the door frame is cracked.*
- **style** [staɪl]   a way to express thought in language, art, or music. □ *His writing style is one of wry humor.*
- **style** [staɪl]   a mode of mannerism, behavior, or conduct. □ *The nurse's style when dealing with her patients is friendly.*
- **style** [staɪl]   a writing instrument. □ *The poet picked up his style to write a few lines of verse.*
- **style** [staɪl]   to design or copy something from an existing mode. □ *The young acting student has tried to style her work after the famous actor.*

straight—strait
- **straight** [stret]   unwavering or direct. □ *The easiest way to the city is straight up the main road.*
- **straight** [stret]   free from curves, angles, or bends. □ *The*

shortest distance between two points is a straight line.

- **straight** [stret]   upright; virtuous. □ *Gene is a straight, up-standing citizen.*
- **straight** [stret]   frank; candid. □ *The mother demanded a straight answer.*
- **straight** [stret]   marked by no deviations, usually with reference to a political party. □ *Her dad always votes a straight Republican ticket.*
- **straight** [stret]   a homestretch. □ *The stock cars were three abreast coming into the straight.*
- **straight** [stret]   an unbroken sequence in a game resulting in a perfect score. □ *The pool player ran the table for a straight in the pool match.*
- **straight** [stret]   in poker, a combination of five sequential cards. □ *Dad's straight beat my pair of kings.*
- **strait** [stret]   a narrow passage where two large bodies of water meet. □ *The ships sailed through the strait during the night.*
- **strait** [stret]   a perplexing or difficult situation. □ *Helen was in a strait and didn't know what to do.*
- **strait** [stret]   tightly or closely. □ *Her gown was very strait fitting.*

strait   See the main entry beginning with *straight.*

style   See the main entry beginning with *stile.*

succor—sucker

- **succor** ['səkɚ, 'səkɔr]   relief or help. □ *The relief workers provided succor to the homeless people just before winter.*
- **succor** ['səkɚ, 'səkɔr]   to go to the aid of someone. □ *It is difficult for parents not to succor their children in times of trouble.*
- **sucker** ['səkɚ]   a device used to produce suction. □ *A type of sucker was used to remove the water from the ditch.*
- **sucker** ['səkɚ]   a lollipop. □ *The corner drugstore sells every flavor of sucker imaginable.*
- **sucker** ['səkɚ]   a type of freshwater fish related to the carp family. □ *The boys caught a sucker yesterday afternoon.*
- **sucker** ['səkɚ]   a person that is easily fooled or cheated. □ *The con artist was constantly on the lookout for a sucker.*
- **sucker** ['səkɚ]   to deceive someone intentionally. □ *The older boy tried to sucker the younger boy out of his lunch money.*

sucker   See the main entry beginning with *succor.*

suede—swayed

- **suede** [swed]   leather with a napped surface. □ *Suede is used to make shoes, purses, and clothing.*
- **suede** [swed]   made of leather with a napped surface. □ *You'll have to take your suede coat to the cleaners to have the stains removed.*
- **swayed** [swed]   the past tense and past participle of *sway* 'to move rhythmically and slowly, usually from side to side.' □ *The dancers swayed to the sounds of the music.*
- **swayed [from]** [swed]   the past tense and past participle of *sway [from]* 'to divert or influence someone or something from something.' □ *The woman swayed her little girl's attention from the candy counter.*
- **swayed** [swed]   the past tense and past participle of *sway* 'to persuade someone to change an opinion.' □ *The testimony could not have swayed the jury's position.*

suite—sweet

- **suite** [swit]   a group of rooms occupied as a single unit. □ *The only vacancy in the hotel was a large suite.*
- **suite** [swit]   the collection of personnel accompanying a dignitary or ruler on official business. □ *The king's entire suite traveled with him wherever he went.*
- **suite** [swit]   a musical composition with a number of movements, usually in the same key. □ *The audience applauded after the orchestra played the suite of ballet music.*
- **sweet** [swit]   pleasing to the taste, mind, or feelings. □ *The child's sweet temperament was the opposite of her twin sister's.*
- **sweet** [swit]   dearest; much beloved. □ *"Marry me, my sweet," implored the suitor to his lady friend.*
- **sweet** [swit]   great; terrific. □ *Winning the tournament was such a sweet experience.*
- **sweet** [swit]   having a high sugar content. □ *This fudge is so sweet!*

sum   See the main entry beginning with *some.*

sun   See the main entry beginning with *son.*

surf   See the main entry beginning with *serf.*

swayed   See the main entry beginning with *suede.*

sweet   See the main entry beginning with *suite.*

sword   See the main entry beginning with *soared.*

symbol   See the main entry beginning with *cymbal.*

T

tacked—tact

- **tacked [down]** [tækt]   the past tense and past participle of *tack [down]* 'to attach or fasten something down with tacks.' □ *The workers tacked the carpet down rather than just laying it on the floor.*
- **tacked [together]** [tækt]   the past tense and past participle of *tack [together]* 'to make or build something rapidly and carelessly.' □ *The old man tacked the shack together in one afternoon.*
- **tacked [onto]** [tækt]   the past tense and past participle of *tack [onto]* 'to add something onto something in haste.' □ *Emily tacked a postscript onto the end of her letter.*
- **tacked** [tækt]   the past tense and past participle of *tack* 'to change the direction of a sailing vessel.' □ *The racing schooner tacked several times during the course of the race.*
- **tacked** [tækt]   the past tense and past participle of *tack* 'to follow after something in a zigzagging course.' □ *The guided missile tacked its target through the sky.*
- **tact** [tækt]   a sense of what to do or say under given circumstances in order to avoid offending others. □ *Joan always handles the delicate subject of money with tact.*

tacks—tax

- **tacks** [tæks]   the plural of *tack* 'a sharp-pointed, flat-headed pin.' □ *I spilled the box of tacks all over the desktop.*
- **tacks** [tæks]   the plural of *tack* 'the direction of a sailing ship in relation to the set of its sails.' □ *The sailors continually changed the tacks of the ship.*

- **tacks [up]** [tæks]   the present tense, third person singular of *tack [up]* 'to fasten onto a surface with tacks.' □ *Henry tacks up notes all over his apartment to remind himself to do things.*
- **tacks [together]** [tæks]   the present tense, third person singular of *tack [together]* 'to put something together hastily and insecurely.' □ *It seems that contractor tacks together houses wherever he finds an empty lot.*
- **tacks [on]** [tæks]   the present tense, third person singular of *tack [on]* 'to add something onto something.' □ *Mary always tacks on the question "Don't you think?" to her statements.*
- **tacks** [tæks]   the present tense, third person singular of *tack* 'to change direction of a sailing vessel in relation to the wind.' □ *The captain tacks each time the wind changes.*
- **tax** [tæks]   a charge placed by a government body on persons or property. □ *Most people think the amount of property tax they pay is too high.*
- **tax** [tæks]   to levy an assessment on something. □ *The government will tax some items more heavily in the future.*
- **tax** [tæks]   to place someone or something under heavy demands or conditions. □ *Such vigorous exercise might tax her heart beyond its limits.*

tact   See the main entry beginning with *tacked.*

tail—tale
- **tail** [tel]   an extension of the spine at the rear end of an animal, usually covered with hair. □ *My dog has a short, stubby tail.*
- **tail** [tel]   something resembling a tail. □ *The tail of the kite is made from old rags.*
- **tail** [tel]   the end or final process of something. □ *We were all glad to see the tail end of the project in sight.*
- **tail** [tel]   to follow behind or trail something or someone. □ *Streams of exhaust tail the jets through the sky.*
- **tail** [tel]   to follow someone in order to conduct surveillance. □ *The detective decided to tail the suspect all night long.*
- **tale** [tel]   an untrue report or piece of gossip. □ *We could not believe her tale.*
- **tale** [tel]   a report of facts or events. □ *Each listener was spellbound by his tale of adventure.*
- **tale** [tel]   a story. □ *She read the tale with much expression.*
- **tale** [tel]   a lie. □ *She fooled no one with her tale of what happened.*

tale See the main entry beginning with *tail.*

taper—tapir
- **taper** ['tepɚ] a candle that is narrower at the top than at the bottom. □ *A single taper burned on the altar during the wedding ceremony.*
- **taper** ['tepɚ] a faint light. □ *A thin taper of light shone through the crack in the door.*
- **taper** ['tepɚ] to make something gradually narrower at one end. □ *The seamstress wants to taper the trousers at the ankles.*
- **taper [off]** ['tepɚ] to diminish gradually. □ *The holiday shopping season usually starts to taper off after the first of the year.*
- **tapir** ['tepɚ] a large, shy mammal related to the rhinoceros and horse that inhabits the equatorial regions of the Far East and the Americas. □ *The tapir is a gentle but unattractive beast.*

tapir See the main entry beginning with *taper.*

tare—tear
(See also *tear—tier.*)
- **tare** [tɛɚ] a weedy plant often used as ground cover. □ *Many gardeners use a tare to keep the soil from eroding.*
- **tare** [tɛɚ] the calculation of the weight of a substance and its container minus the weight of the container. □ *Your cost will be figured by the tare of the liquid.*
- **tear** [tɛɚ] a hole or flaw caused by tearing. □ *Did you know this shirt has a tear in it?*
- **tear** [tɛɚ] to separate or pull something into parts. □ *We need to tear this paper into long strips.*
- **tear** [tɛɚ] to remove or wrench something from someone or something forcibly. □ *He could not tear himself away from the interesting novel.*
- **tear** [tɛɚ] to move or act hastily or violently. □ *The speeding car continued to tear down the street in a dangerous manner.*

tarry—terry
- **tarry** ['tæɚi, 'tɛɚi] to linger or lag behind; to stay in one place or location. □ *Sally liked to tarry after school to talk with her teachers.*
- **terry** ['tɛɚi] an absorbent fabric made up of uncut loops of cotton. □ *Towels made of terry feel nice against the skin.*

taught—taut
- **taught** [tɔt] the past tense and past participle of *teach* 'to educate or train someone or something in a particular subject;

to perform schooling in general.' □ *She taught school for many years.* □ *The owner of that store taught each of his children the basics of sound business management.*
- **taut** [tɔt]   pulled tightly; stretched. □ *The taut rope suddenly snapped.* □ *Her face was lean and taut.*

taut   See the main entry beginning with *taught.*

tax   See the main entry beginning with *tacks.*

tea—tee
- **tea** [ti]   a beverage made from steeping the leaves of various plants, usually the tea plant, in hot water. □ *Diane likes her tea very strong.*
- **tea** [ti]   a plant that is known for its aromatic leaves and is used to make a beverage by the same name. □ *The fortune-teller claims that she can read tea leaves.*
- **tea** [ti]   a light, late afternoon refreshment usually of cookies, cakes, or crackers served with tea. □ *Our bed and breakfast serves tea every day between three and four o'clock.*
- **tea** [ti]   a reception at which light refreshments are served. □ *The ladies attended a tea after the art show.*
- **tee** [ti]   the areas of a golf course in which the ball is put into play at each hole. □ *Because the golf course was crowded, golfers were lined up at each tee to continue play.*
- **tee** [ti]   a small peg with a flat top on which a golf ball is set to begin play. □ *I lost my tee in the deep grass.*
- **tee [off]** [ti]   to begin play by hitting a golf ball off a tee. □ *It's your turn to tee off at this hole.*

team—teem
- **team** [tim]   a group of individuals associated in a work or sport activity. □ *The wrestling team traveled by bus to each meet.*
- **team** [tim]   a pair of harnessed draft animals. □ *His team of Belgians won a blue ribbon at the fair.*
- **team [up]** [tim]   to join together as a team. □ *Let's team up for the wheelbarrow race.*
- **team** [tim]   performed as a team. □ *With some team effort, this task can be quickly accomplished.*
- **teem** [tim]   to overflow with something. □ *Their personalities seem to teem with energy.*
- **teem** [tim]   to be present in large quantity. □ *Our favorite stream begins to teem with spunky rainbow trout each spring.*

tear—tier

(See also *tare—tear*.)

- **tear** [tɪɚ] a clear, salty liquid secreted by a gland in the eye. □ *A single tear rolled down her cheek.*
- **tear** [tɪɚ] a transparent drop of liquid that resembles a tear. □ *There was a tear of some unknown substance on the surface of the material.*
- **tear** [tɪɚ] to produce tears; to weep. □ *The odor of the hot onions caused his eyes to tear.*
- **tier** [tɪɚ] a layer or row of things arranged one above the other. □ *Each tier of the wedding cake was larger than the one above it.*
- **tier** [tɪɚ] to arrange something in layers or rows one above the other. □ *Let's tier this stack of boxes so they don't fall over.*

teas—tease

- **teas** [tiz] the plural of *tea* 'a beverage made from steeping the leaves of various plants, usually the tea plant, in hot water.' □ *The restaurant serves several different teas.*
- **teas** [tiz] the plural of *tea* 'a plant that is known for its aromatic leaves or buds and is used to make a beverage by the same name.' □ *The plantation grows a number of exotic teas.*
- **teas** [tiz] the plural of *tea* 'a light, late afternoon refreshment of cookies, cakes, or crackers served with tea.' □ *The women tried to outdo each other at their afternoon teas.*
- **teas** [tiz] the plural of *tea* 'a reception at which light refreshments are served.' □ *The final campaign week was filled with countless informal teas and meetings.*
- **tease** [tiz] to poke fun at, annoy, or harass someone. □ *It is not nice to tease people who are different from you.*
- **tease** [tiz] to tantalize someone. □ *Those yummy desserts are enough to tease anyone's appetite.*
- **tease** [tiz] to untangle by laying flat and carding or combing. □ *You must tease the raw wool before spinning it.*
- **tease** [tiz] a person who pokes fun at, harasses, or annoys someone. □ *Linda is such a tease!*

tease See the main entry beginning with *teas*.

tee See the main entry beginning with *tea*.

teem See the main entry beginning with *team*.

tense—tents

- **tense** [tɛnts] nervous; anxious. □ *Tom is always tense before an airplane flight.*

- **tense** [tɛnts]   taut; rigid. □ *My neck muscles feel tense when I am under stress.*
- **tense** [tɛnts]   to become taut, rigid, or nervous. □ *My muscles tense when I am getting an injection.*
- **tense** [tɛnts]   a distinction of verbs indicating time variances. □ *The words* shall *and* will *indicate the future tense.*
- **tents** [tɛnts]   the plural of *tent* 'a collapsible structure made of canvas, nylon, or other material, supported by a framework and used for shelter.' □ *The older campers will sleep in tents instead of in the log cabins.*
- **tents** [tɛnts]   the present tense, third person singular of *tent* 'to camp out or stay in a tent.' □ *Mike tents in the mountains for a week each summer.*

tents   See the main entry beginning with *tense.*

tern—turn
- **tern** [tɝn]   a small, compact bird belonging to the sea gull family. □ *As each wave rolled onto the beach, the tern curiously inspected the shoreline.*
- **turn** [tɝn]   a change of direction or course. □ *His condition took a turn for the worse.*
- **turn** [tɝn]   a chance to do something. □ *"When will it be my turn?" asked the small boy.*
- **turn** [tɝn]   to rotate something or someone; to change the direction or course of something or someone. □ *Turn the chicken on the grill every ten minutes.* □ *The plane will turn at the end of the runway.*
- **turn** [tɝn]   to sour; [for food] to go bad. □ *This cider is beginning to turn.*

terry   See the main entry beginning with *tarry.*

their—there—they're
- **their** [ðɛɚ]   the third person plural pronoun indicating possession or relationship by a group of people or things. □ *Their new house is very beautiful.* □ *The trees shed their leaves each fall.*
- **there** [ðɛɚ]   a place that has been pointed out; a place some distance from the speaker. □ *Please put the blueprints there on the drafting table.* □ *Put it there, not here.*
- **there** [ðɛɚ]   a word used to introduce a sentence or clause, usually when the verb has no definite subject. □ *There have been few changes since you left.*
- **there** [ðɛɚ]   an interjection indicating a variety of emotions. □ *"There, I am finally finished with that job," the man sighed*

triumphantly. □ *"There, everything will be all right," the boy's mother said comfortingly.*

- **they're** [ðɛɚ] the contraction of *they* and *are.* □ *I think they're going to meet us at the stadium.*

there See the main entry beginning with *their.*

they're See the main entry beginning with *their.*

threw—through

- **threw** [θru] the past tense of *throw* 'to cast something or someone through the air.' □ *The outfielder threw the ball all the way to home plate.* □ *The unruly horse threw its jockey into the dirt.*
- **threw** [θru] the past tense of *throw* 'to form something on a potter's wheel.' □ *The potter threw some interesting clay vases on his wheel.*
- **threw** [θru] the past tense of *throw* 'to project something.' □ *The moon threw an eery light through the trees.*
- **threw** [θru] the past tense of *throw* 'to make or break a connection with a power source using a lever or switch.' □ *The electrician threw a switch to cut off the source of power.*
- **through** [θru] by means of something. □ *Through sheer will-power, Julie finally reached her goals.*
- **through** [θru] in one way and out another. □ *We will have to travel through the tunnel in the mountain to reach the other side.*
- **through** [θru] over or across something. □ *We sailed through some rough seas.*
- **through** [θru] from one point up to and including another point. □ *That specialty shop is open Monday through Friday.*

throe—throw

- **throe** [θro] a painful spasm. □ *With each throe of giving birth, the dog whined pitifully.*
- **throe** [θro] a difficult or painful struggle. □ *In his throe to achieve stardom, the actor lost sight of his roots.*
- **throw** [θro] to catapult something through the air. □ *How far can you throw a javelin?*
- **throw** [θro] to cause something to fall. □ *Throw down the bat and run to first base.*
- **throw** [θro] to form something on a potter's wheel. □ *Despite my best efforts, I was unable to throw a single piece of pottery on the wheel.*
- **throw** [θro] to project something. □ *Throw a little more light into that dark corner.*

- **throw** [θro]   to produce something. ☐ *Carrie wants to breed her mare to a horse that will throw a lot of color.*
- **throw** [θro]   to make or break a connection with a power source using a lever or switch. ☐ *A switchman will throw the switch to divert the engine from one track to another.*

throne—thrown

- **throne** [θron]   a seat or place of royalty, deity, or authority. ☐ *Queen Elizabeth II now sits on the throne of England.*
- **throne** [θron]   the person who occupies a seat of authority. ☐ *The final say in the matter rests with the throne.*
- **thrown** [θron]   the past participle of *throw* 'to cast or hurl someone or something.' ☐ *He has thrown the frisbee onto the roof of the house.* ☐ *The child had thrown herself on the floor in a fit of temper.*
- **thrown** [θron]   the past participle of *throw* 'to form something on a potter's wheel.' ☐ *The artist has thrown many interesting pieces on her wheel.*
- **thrown** [θron]   the past participle of *throw* 'to project something.' ☐ *The setting sun has thrown long shadows across the lawn.*
- **thrown** [θron]   the past participle of *throw* 'to produce offspring.' ☐ *That stud dog has never thrown an unusual color pattern in any of its offspring.*
- **thrown** [θron]   the past participle of *throw* 'to turn an electrical switch; to make or break a connection with a power source using a lever or switch.' ☐ *He has accidentally thrown a switch and cut off the power to the building.*

through   See the main entry beginning with *threw.*

throw   See the main entry beginning with *throe.*

thrown   See the main entry beginning with *throne.*

thyme—time

- **thyme** [tɑɪm]   an aromatic garden herb that belongs to the mint family and is used in cooking. ☐ *The recipe calls for one-half teaspoon of thyme.*
- **time** [tɑɪm]   the period during which something occurs. ☐ *I never seem to have enough time to do my chores.*
- **time** [tɑɪm]   an appointed moment or hour when something should happen. ☐ *At what time do you expect to be home?*
- **time** [tɑɪm]   a tempo, rhythm, or beat. ☐ *The drummer kept time with the other musicians.*
- **time** [tɑɪm]   a geological or historical age. ☐ *There was a time*

when dinosaurs roamed the earth.
- **time** [taɪm]   an experience. □ *We had a wonderful time on our vacation.*
- **time** [taɪm]   an hourly wage rate. □ *The workers will get time-and-a-half if they work on the weekend.*
- **time** [taɪm]   to keep the time of something or someone. □ *Jody was asked to time the swimmers at the swim meet.*

tic—tick
- **tic** [tɪk]   a frequent, localized twitch, usually involving facial muscles. □ *His awful experiences during the war left the soldier with a nervous tic.*
- **tick** [tɪk]   a bloodsucking insect that is dependent upon a warm-blooded host for survival and often spreads disease. □ *The common deer tick is responsible for spreading Lyme disease.*
- **tick** [tɪk]   a soft, rhythmic beat often associated with time-pieces. □ *The loud tick of the clock kept Joe awake at night.*
- **tick** [tɪk]   a light mark used as an indicator. □ *Put a tick next to each item on the invoice.*
- **tick** [tɪk]   a straw, feather, or fabric-filled case used as a mattress. □ *This sleeping tick is not very comfortable.*
- **tick** [tɪk]   to make a ticking sound. □ *Those clocks all tick in different tones.*

tick   See the main entry beginning with *tic.*

tide—tied
- **tide** [taɪd]   a rising and falling of the surface of an ocean, sea, or gulf, influenced by the gravitational pull of the sun and moon. □ *Do not go swimming at high tide.*
- **tide** [taɪd]   something that fluctuates like the tide. □ *The tide of her mood swings is unpredictable.*
- **tied** [taɪd]   the past tense and past participle of *tie* 'to make a knot or bow.' □ *The child tied his shoelaces all by himself.*
- **tied [together]** [taɪd]   the past tense and past participle of *tie [together]* 'to unite two or more people or things.' □ *The two corporations tied together to form one company.*
- **tied** [taɪd]   the past tense and past participle of *tie* '[for two teams] to have the same score in a competition.' □ *At the end of nine innings, the score was tied twelve to twelve.*

tied   See the main entry beginning with *tide.*

tier   See the main entry beginning with *tear.*

'til—till
- **'til** [tɪl]   until. □ *We won't see you again 'til much later.*

- **till** [tɪl] to plow, cultivate, or sow crops. □ *It is much easier to till soft, moist ground than hard, dry earth.*
- **till** [tɪl] a cash register or money drawer including its receipts. □ *If you're working alone in the store, do not leave the till unattended.*
- **till** [tɪl] a mixture of rocks, sand, clay, and gravel left behind by receding glaciers. □ *The geologists studied the till of the river basins.*

till See the main entry beginning with *'til.*

timber—timbre
- **timber** ['tɪmbɚ] standing trees. □ *The forest fire destroyed many acres of timber.*
- **timber** ['tɪmbɚ] the wood of living trees. □ *The timber on that mountainside is very valuable.*
- **timber** ['tɪmbɚ] wood material used for construction, either in raw or finished form. □ *It will take a lot of timber to build that cedar log lodge.*
- **timber** ['tɪmbɚ] the rib of a ship. □ *A timber on that ship cracked during the violent storm.*
- **timbre** ['tɪmbɚ, 'tæmbr] the tone or quality of a vocal or musical sound as heard by the ear. □ *The timbre of the alto's voice stood out among the other choir members' voices.*

timbre See the main entry beginning with *timber.*

time See the main entry beginning with *thyme.*

to—too—two
- **to** [tu] a preposition indicating movement toward something, purpose or result of, relation in time, extent, or degree, comparison or proportion. □ *After the soccer match we went to the ice-cream parlor for cold drinks.*
- **too** [tu] also. □ *Besides the house, we plan to sell the car and boat, too.*
- **too** [tu] an extensive degree. □ *I am too tired to stay awake any longer.*
- **two** [tu] the cardinal number between one and three. □ *Those two houses have exactly the same floor plan.* □ *The last card she played was the two of hearts.*
- **two** [tu] a pair. □ *The schoolchildren lined up two by two.*

toad—toed—towed
- **toad** [tod] an amphibian related to the frog but darker in color with dry, warty skin. □ *There is a huge toad in the flower garden.*

- **toad** [tod]   a person or object worthy of contempt. □ *I don't understand what Alice sees in that toad, Dave.*
- **toed** [tod]   the past participle of *toe* 'to equip something with toes; to be equipped with toes.' (This occurs only as a past participle.) □ *The three-toed sloth is a homely creature.* □ *The workers are required to wear steel-toed shoes on the job.*
- **toed** [tod]   the past tense and past participle of *toe* 'to touch or move something about with one's toe.' □ *I toed the drowsy snake until it slithered away.*
- **towed** [tod]   the past tense and past participle of *tow* 'to pull something behind something or someone.' □ *Heavy machinery towed the fallen trees out of the roadway.* □ *After the accident, the cars were towed away by the police.*

toe—tow

- **toe** [to]   one of the digits of the foot. □ *I dropped the heavy sack on my big toe.*
- **toe** [to]   the tip of a shoe. □ *The toe of his shoe has a hole in it.*
- **toe** [to]   to equip something with toes. □ *The cobbler can toe these old work boots for me.*
- **toe** [to]   to operate, move, or reach something or someone with a toe. □ *If you toe my foot again, I'll kick you.*
- **toe** [to]   to drive nails in at a slant. □ *Toe that board to the one beneath it.*
- **tow** [to]   to haul or pull something or someone behind something or someone. □ *We'll have to tow the truck to the repair garage.* □ *The baby-sitter towed the screaming child to the car.*

toed   See the main entry beginning with *toad.*

told—tolled

- **told** [told]   the past tense and past participle of *tell* 'to say something; to utter something; to reveal something.' □ *Linda always told the truth.* □ *She never told me the well-kept secret.* □ *The empty candy wrappers told the mother why her son had no appetite for dinner.* □ *I told my boss that I would be late for work.* □ *The clock on the bank told us the time.*
- **told [on]** [told]   to betray someone; to tattle on someone. □ *My older brother always told on me for sneaking cookies.*
- **tolled** [told]   the past tense and past participle of *toll* 'to sound a bell.' □ *The bell in the steeple tolled midnight.*
- **tolled** [told]   the past tense and past participle of *toll* 'to signal or announce something.' □ *The town crier tolled the royal betrothal.*
- **tolled** [told]   the past tense and past participle of *toll* 'to

charge or collect a toll.' □ *The toll collector tolled each of the travelers a dollar to cross the bridge.*

tole—toll

- **tole** [tol]   a decorative, painted metal surface of various colors often found on ornamental wall hangings, curios, and boxes. □ *She made many attractive gifts with her new-found ability to tole paint.*
- **toll** [tol]   a tax, fee, or levy paid for the privilege of using some public facility, usually a bridge or turnpike. □ *Drivers must pay a toll when entering the turnpike.*
- **toll** [tol]   the cost in loss or detriment at which something is gained. □ *His difficult life took a toll on his health.*
- **toll** [tol]   to sound a bell. □ *The church bells toll the hour of the day.*
- **toll** [tol]   to signal or announce. □ *Trumpets and waving flags toll the end of the fighting.*
- **toll** [tol]   to place or take a toll. □ *The state will toll the use of the new stretch of highway.*

toll   See the main entry beginning with *tole.*

tolled   See the main entry beginning with *told.*

too   See the main entry beginning with *to.*

tort—torte

- **tort** [tɔɚt]   a wrongful act against which civil action may be brought. □ *Trespass is an example of a civil tort.*
- **torte** [tɔɚt]   a rich, layered dessert topped with frosting. □ *Mom always serves her famous four-layer torte at Thanksgiving dinner.*

torte   See the main entry beginning with *tort.*

tough—tuff

- **tough** [təf]   strong; firm. □ *These old shoes are tough enough to last many more years.*
- **tough** [təf]   stubborn. □ *Janice has a tough manner about her.*
- **tough** [təf]   capable of enduring stress, difficulty, or hardship. □ *The journey will require tough adventurers.*
- **tough** [təf]   difficult to deal with. □ *Bill is a tough person to work for.*
- **tough** [təf]   a rough, rowdy individual. □ *The boss always sends his tough to do his dirty work for him.*
- **tuff** [təf]   rock or rock deposits made of disintegrating material, usually volcanic in nature. □ *The heavy spring rains*

washed much tuff out of the mountains and into the river and streambeds.

tow   See the main entry beginning with *toe.*

towed   See the main entry beginning with *toad.*

tracked—tract
- **tracked** [trækt]   the past tense and past participle of *track* 'to follow or trail someone or something.' □ *Rescuers tracked the lost hiker through the snow.*
- **tracked** [trækt]   the past tense and past participle of *track* 'to observe the path of something, using specialized equipment.' □ *Scientists tracked the path of the new comet.*
- **tracked** [trækt]   the past tense and past participle of *track* 'to carry soil or other material on one's feet and deposit it on the floor.' □ *The children tracked mud all through the house.*
- **tract** [trækt]   a pamphlet containing religious or political information. □ *I picked up a tract to read in the waiting room.*
- **tract** [trækt]   an area of land; a parcel of land. □ *The couple purchased a small tract of land as an investment.* □ *That vast tract of land in the foothills is ideal for grazing cattle.*
- **tract** [trækt]   a system of the body whose parts collectively perform some function. □ *This week the class is studying the digestive tract.*

tract   See the main entry beginning with *tracked.*

tray—trey
- **tray** [tre]   a flat-surfaced, open receptacle, often without sides or with shallow sides, used for carrying or displaying articles. □ *Grandmother's silver tea service sits on a tray in the china cabinet.*
- **trey** [tre]   a card, die, or domino displaying three symbols or dots. □ *His poker hand revealed two pairs and a trey.*

trey   See the main entry beginning with *tray.*

troop—troupe
- **troop** [trup]   a group of soldiers. □ *The small troop entered the city after dark.*
- **troop** [trup]   a collection of objects or people. □ *An interested troop of listeners heard the speaker talk.*
- **troop** [trup]   a flock of birds; an assembly of mammals. □ *A baboon troop is a highly organized and complex unit.*
- **troop** [trup]   a unit of Girl or Boy Scouts under the direction of a leader. □ *When my brothers were young, my father served*

as leader of their troop.
- **troop** [trup]   to move as a group or crowd. □ *Let's all troop over to the park to play ball after our cookout.*
- **troupe** [trup]   a group of stage or traveling performers. □ *That theatrical troupe has been on the road performing for a long time.*

troupe   See the main entry beginning with *troop.*

trussed—trust
- **trussed** [trəst]   the past tense and past participle of *truss* 'to bind or secure someone or something tightly.' □ *The police found the victim trussed but otherwise unharmed.* □ *After the turkey was stuffed and trussed, I put it into the oven.*
- **trussed [up]** [trəst]   the past tense and past participle of *truss [up]* 'to strengthen or support something with trusses.' □ *We first put up the sidewalls and then trussed them up temporarily.*
- **trust** [trəst]   to have confidence in someone or something. □ *Something about the way she smiled told me not to trust her.*
- **trust** [trəst]   an obligation or charge imposed in faith. □ *She put trust in his ability to invest her money wisely.*
- **trust** [trəst]   a property interest held by one party for the benefit of another. □ *Funds were put in a trust to help the family whose house burned.*
- **trust** [trəst]   to believe in or rely on someone or something. □ *I trust that you will see to all of the details of the contract.*

trust   See the main entry beginning with *trussed.*

tuff   See the main entry beginning with *tough.*

turn   See the main entry beginning with *tern.*

two   See the main entry beginning with *to.*

U

undo—undue

- **undo** [ənˈdu]   to open or unfasten something by releasing. □ *I was unable to undo the padlock on the gate.*
- **undo** [ənˈdu]   to nullify something. □ *He could not undo the damage done to his garden by the heavy rain.*
- **undo** [ənˈdu]   to ruin or reverse the fortunes of someone or something. □ *The athlete tried to undo his competitor's chances of winning.*
- **undue** [ənˈdju, ənˈdu]   unnecessary or inappropriate. □ *The political candidate thought undue attention was being given to his private life.*
- **undue** [ənˈdju, ənˈdu]   not due. □ *The bill is undue until the end of the month.*

undue   See the main entry beginning with *undo*.

uninterested   See the main entry beginning with *disinterested*.

urn   See the main entry beginning with *earn*.

use   See the main entry beginning with *ewes*.

V

vail—vale—veil

- **vail** [vel]   to remove one's hat to show respect. (Archaic English.) □ *The peasant was told to vail his hat in the presence of the noble family.*
- **vale** [vel]   a valley; a dale. □ *From the mountaintop the little hamlet nestled in the vale looked like a miniature village.*
- **veil** [vel]   a covering of cloth worn to conceal the face. □ *Women in some countries are required to wear a veil when in public.* □ *The bride's veil was made of white netting.*
- **veil** [vel]   a covering used to conceal or hide something. □ *A veil was used to cover the sculpture until the dedication ceremony.*
- **veil** [vel]   to conceal something. □ *The man tried to veil his uneasiness by laughing.*

vain—vane—vein

- **vain** [ven]   conceited; self-centered. □ *The movie star is a very vain person.*
- **vain** [ven]   unsuccessful. □ *Her many vain attempts to pass the driver's test left her unhappy.*
- **vane** [ven]   a device used to determine the direction of the wind. □ *The vane on the roof of the barn is pointing north.*
- **vane** [ven]   the wide, flat part of a feather. □ *The vane on the bird's wing is bright red.*
- **vane** [ven]   a group of feathers or a piece of plastic attached to the rear of an arrow to help guide its flight. □ *One vane was torn as the arrow bounced off a tree.*
- **vane** [ven]   a blade of a windmill. □ *Only a single vane remained on the rusted windmill.*
- **vein** [ven]   a layer of minerals in the earth. □ *The prospector*

discovered a vein of silver in the earth.
- **vein** [ven] a blood vessel that carries blood to the heart. □ *The nurse will draw blood from a vein in your arm.*
- **vein** [ven] the part of a leaf that gives it the appearance of containing lines. □ *The vein of that yellow leaf is dark purple.*
- **vein** [ven] a line of thought. □ *The speaker continued his discussion in a serious vein.* □ *The business will continue to operate along the same vein.*

vale See the main entry beginning with *vail.*

vane See the main entry beginning with *vain.*

vary—very
- **vary** ['væɚi, 'vɛɚi] to change something; to cause something to deviate. □ *Each year the firm tries to vary its marketing campaign.*
- **very** ['vɛɚi] to a high degree. □ *Janice has been very successful in her new job.*
- **very** ['vɛɚi] precise. □ *His comments struck my very conscience.* □ *My aunt bought the very dress I liked.*
- **very** ['vɛɚi] mere. □ *The very idea of eating insects sickened him.*

veil See the main entry beginning with *vail.*

vein See the main entry beginning with *vain.*

very See the main entry beginning with *vary.*

vial—vile
- **vial** [vaɪl] a small, usually cylindrical container. □ *The lab technician carefully marked and dated each vial of pills.*
- **vile** [vaɪl] wicked. □ *That man is a vile individual.*
- **vile** [vaɪl] foul. □ *Decaying debris has a vile odor.*

vice—vise
- **vice** [vaɪs] corruption; crime. □ *The gangster was involved in all sorts of vice.*
- **vice** [vaɪs] a moral or physical shortcoming, imperfection, or taint. □ *Her only vice is a weakness for chocolate.*
- **vice** [vaɪs] secondary; serving in the place of someone. (Part of a title.) □ *His father was the vice-president of the poetry society.*
- **vise** [vaɪs] a device used to hold some object in place by means of a clamp. □ *A vise has many uses in carpentry.*

vile See the main entry beginning with *vial.*

vise See the main entry beginning with *vice.*

W

wade—weighed

- **wade** [wed]   to enter or walk about in shallow water. □ *The children wanted to wade in the stream.*
- **wade** [wed]   to proceed or move about with labor or difficulty. □ *It will take me all day to wade through this paperwork.*
- **wade** [wed]   to approach a project with vigor and enthusiasm. □ *Sam likes to wade right into any challenging task.*
- **weighed** [wed]   the past tense and past participle of *weigh* 'to determine the weight or heaviness of someone or something.' □ *As children, we were weighed at each visit to the doctor's office.*
- **weighed** [wed]   the past tense and past participle of *weigh* 'to consider something carefully.' □ *The judge carefully weighed all of the evidence in the case.*
- **weighed** [wed]   the past tense and past participle of *weigh* 'to pull up an anchor in readiness for departure.' □ *After a night in port, the ship weighed anchor at dawn.*
- **weighed** [wed]   the past tense and past participle of *weigh* 'to be a burden on someone or something.' (Figurative.) □ *Their constant financial worries weighed heavily on their minds.*

wail—wale—whale

- **wail** [wel]   a mournful cry. □ *The forlorn wail of the coyote was heard throughout the valley.*
- **wail** [wel]   a prolonged expression of grief, sadness, or pain. □ *The wail of the mourners was terrible to hear.*
- **wail** [wel]   to utter a cry of grief or pain. □ *We heard the woman wail from a distance.*
- **wale** [wel]   a raised rib in a piece of fabric. □ *That corduroy*

fabric comes in both a wide and narrow wale.

- **wale** [wel]   a welt, usually on the surface of the skin. □ *The scratch by the tree branch left a long wale on his arm.*
- **wale** [wel]   the long, thick, wooden plates on the side of a ship. □ *Each wale of the boat was handmade.*
- **wale** [wel]   to raise or mark the skin with welts. □ *"If you don't behave, I'll wale your behind!" threatened the upset mother.*
- **whale** [ʍel]   a large, ocean mammal that bears and suckles live young. □ *The blue whale is the earth's largest living creature.*
- **whale** [ʍel]   a person, event, or object massive or impressive in size or qualities. □ *"Boy, that was a whale of a concert!" commented Todd.*
- **whale** [ʍel]   to fish or hunt whales. □ *Coastal people in many countries whale for a living.*
- **whale** [ʍel]   to thrash someone. □ *The attackers continued to whale the helpless man.*

waist—waste

- **waist** [west]   the mid-section of a human torso between the ribs and the hips. □ *Scarlett O'Hara boasted the tiniest waist in three counties.*
- **waist** [west]   a short garment or part of a garment covering the body from the neck to the waist; a bodice. □ *The waist of her gown was richly detailed.*
- **waste** [west]   debris; garbage. □ *All of this waste must be hauled to the dump.*
- **waste** [west]   scrap. □ *Collect all of the waste metal to be recycled.*
- **waste** [west]   a broad, barren tract of land; a vast body of open water. □ *We could see nothing but the horizon across the waste of land.*
- **waste** [west]   loss of body weight, tissue, or vigor. □ *To see his waste over a long period of time was very sad.*
- **waste** [west]   sewage or excrement. □ *The city's waste is treated at a nearby sewage treatment plant.*
- **waste** [west]   to ravage; to devastate. □ *The war continues to waste the impoverished nation.*
- **waste** [west]   to cause something to diminish in size, strength, or vitality. □ *We watched her enthusiasm slowly waste away.*
- **waste** [west]   to consume something carelessly; to allow something to be lost or discarded unused. □ *We must be careful not to waste our precious natural resources.*

wait—weight

- **wait** [wet]   to remain in place in expectancy. □ *Let's wait and see what happens next.*
- **wait [for]** [wet]   to delay or postpone. □ *He decided to wait for the rain to stop before dashing to the parking lot.*
- **wait** [wet]   to serve as a waitress or waiter. □ *Greg has decided to wait tables at the local pub for a summer job.*
- **weight** [wet]   a heavy object. □ *A weight is needed to keep this drapery hanging straight.*
- **weight** [wet]   a burden or pressure. □ *The weight of the difficult decision was almost unbearable.*
- **weight** [wet]   a unit of mass or measure. □ *Alex put some weight in the back of his car to give added traction.*
- **weight** [wet]   the relative value or importance given to something. □ *The weight of this issue is very apparent to everyone involved.*
- **weight** [wet]   to place heaviness or weight upon someone or something. □ *Weight down those papers so they don't blow away.*
- **weight** [wet]   to impose a burden upon someone. □ *I didn't mean to weight you down with all of my troubles.*

waive—wave

- **waive** [wev]   to voluntarily relinquish something or give up a right to something. □ *The accused decided to waive his right to a jury trial.*
- **waive** [wev]   to temporarily put something aside. □ *Will you waive some of your course electives until next year?*
- **waive** [wev]   to refrain from prosecuting or enforcing something. □ *The policy will no longer waive those restrictions.*
- **wave** [wev]   a hand motion used as a greeting, farewell, or signal. □ *He gave a quick wave before boarding the ship.*
- **wave** [wev]   a swell on the surface of a body of water. □ *A huge wave washed over the bow of the boat.*
- **wave** [wev]   something resembling a wave. □ *A sudden wave of nausea made her dizzy.*
- **wave** [wev]   an energy transmission through some medium from one point to another. □ *The pictures are being transmitted via a complex radio wave.*
- **wave** [wev]   a distinct condition of weather or temperature. □ *An unexpected heat wave settled over the region.*
- **wave** [wev]   to float or move about in an air current. □ *I love to see palm leaves wave about in the tropical breeze.*

wale   See the main entry beginning with *wail*.

war—wore

- **war** [wɔɚ] a state of declared, armed hostilities. □ *The war lasted only a few short months.*
- **war** [wɔɚ] a state or period of conflict or struggle. □ *Those two giant beverage companies have been at war for years.*
- **war** [wɔɚ] to engage in war, conflict, or hostility. □ *The once-feuding nations have agreed not to war any longer.*
- **wore** [wɔɚ] the past tense of *wear* 'to dress in or adorn oneself with an article of clothing.' □ *The groom wore a dark grey tuxedo.*
- **wore** [wɔɚ] the past tense of *wear* 'to display some type of appearance.' □ *Her father always wore a look of dismay on his face.*
- **wore** [wɔɚ] the past tense of *wear [down]* 'to diminish something through persistence.' □ *The persistent child eventually wore down his mother's defense.*

ware—wear—where

- **ware** [wɛɚ] a manufactured commodity or article; merchandise. □ *The only ware that the company produces is transistor radios.* □ *The peddler's best-selling ware was a variety of pots and pans.*
- **ware** [wɛɚ] pottery of fired clay. □ *After painting the ceramic ware, the artist must fire it again.*
- **wear** [wɛɚ] to dress in or adorn oneself with articles of clothing. □ *Many tennis players now choose to wear bright colored clothing.*
- **wear** [wɛɚ] to display or have an appearance of something. □ *Wear a look of confidence at your job interview.*
- **wear** [wɛɚ] to diminish or deteriorate through use. □ *The carpeting by the front door is beginning to wear.*
- **where** [ʌɛɚ] in, at, or to what place, position, or situation. □ *"Where did you find such a deal?" quizzed Ray.*
- **where** [ʌɛɚ] wherever. □ *The cats tend to wander where they like.*
- **where** [ʌɛɚ] locale or place. □ *No one is sure of the where and why of the crime.*

warn—worn

- **warn** [wɔɚn] to alert, notify, or counsel someone. □ *Doctors must warn their patients of the side effects of medication.*
- **warn** [wɔɚn] to tell someone to go or leave. □ *The referees had to warn the disruptive players off the playing field.*
- **worn** [wɔɚn] the past participle of *wear* 'to dress in or adorn

oneself with an article of clothing.' □ *Have you worn that hat before?*

- **worn** [wɔɚn]   the past participle of *wear* 'to display or have an appearance of something.' □ *It seems he hasn't worn a smile in weeks.*
- **worn [away]** [wɔɚn]   the past participle of *wear [away]* 'to cause something to diminish or deteriorate.' □ *Her illness has worn away her energy.*

waste   See the main entry beginning with *waist.*

wave   See the main entry beginning with *waive.*

wax—whacks

- **wax** [wæks]   a substance secreted by bees that is used to make their honeycombs. □ *Those candles are made from the wax of bees.*
- **wax** [wæks]   any of numerous plant or animal secretions resembling a waxy substance. □ *A doctor removed the excess wax from his patient's ears.*
- **wax** [wæks]   paraffin. □ *Use a good wax to coat the bottom of your skis.*
- **wax** [wæks]   to rub or treat something with wax. □ *If you wax the underside of your toboggan, it will travel faster down the hill.*
- **wax** [wæks]   to grow or increase. □ *The profits of the company tend to wax with buyer demand.*
- **wax** [wæks]   the period of the lunar cycle between a new moon and a full moon. □ *At what time this month will the moon wax?*
- **whacks** [ʍæks]   the plural of *whack* 'a resounding blow.' □ *The baby-sitter gave the naughty child three whacks with a paddle.*
- **whacks** [ʍæks]   the plural of *whack* 'an attempt or opportunity to do something.' (Slang.) □ *The coach offered the second-string pitcher a couple of whacks at starting games.*
- **whacks** [ʍæks]   the present tense, third person singular of *whack* 'to strike or bat at something or someone.' □ *That volleyball player really whacks the ball around the court.*

way—weigh—whey

- **way** [we]   a course of passage or travel. □ *The homing pigeon found its way back to its coop.*
- **way** [we]   a condition. □ *The way I felt led me to take a nap.*
- **way** [we]   a manner or style of doing something. □ *"That is*

no way to eat!" scolded the man.

- **way** [we]   a distance. □ _It's a long way from Florida to California._
- **way** [we]   connected with a stage or point along a route. □ _Fresh horses are available at each way station along the trail._
- **weigh** [we]   to determine the weight or heaviness of something; to measure something on a scale. □ _We must weigh the cargo of the truck before it goes on the road._
- **weigh** [we]   to consider something carefully. □ _Weigh the consequences of your actions before you act._
- **weigh** [we]   to make something heavy. □ _Citizens are asked to weigh down anything that might blow away during the hurricane._
- **weigh** [we]   to pull up an anchor in readiness for departure. □ _The ship will weigh anchor at dawn._
- **weigh** [we]   to have a disheartening effect on someone. □ _I hope this sad news will not weigh heavily on you._
- **whey** [ʍe]   the watery part of whole milk as separate from the part containing the butterfat. □ _Whey is a by-product in the cheese-making process._

we—wee

- **we** [wi]   the first person, plural pronoun. □ _"Let's see if we can win the relay race," Mitch urged his teammates._
- **wee** [wi]   very tiny. □ _When born, a bear cub is just a wee thing._
- **wee** [wi]   miniscule. □ _Add only a wee bit of seasoning to the soup._
- **wee** [wi]   very early. □ _Doctors are quite used to getting up in the wee hours of the morning to handle emergencies._

weak—week

- **weak** [wik]   lacking strength, vigor, or stamina. □ _He felt very weak following his long illness._
- **weak** [wik]   deficient in mental or physical capabilities. □ _As she aged, my aunt's eyesight grew weak._
- **weak** [wik]   not based soundly on fact or logic. □ _The evidence supporting that theory is weak._
- **weak** [wik]   lacking required or usual ingredients. □ _This coffee tastes weak and watery._
- **weak** [wik]   lame or ineffective. □ _The boy offered a weak excuse for his tardiness._
- **weak** [wik]   barely sounded. □ _The kitten uttered a weak meow._
- **week** [wik]   a seven-day cycle or period. □ _They will be vacationing out East for a week in July._

wear See the main entry beginning with *ware.*

weather—wether—whether

- **weather** ['wɛðɚ] climatic or atmospheric conditions. □ *The weather in Michigan is very unpredictable.*
- **weather** ['wɛðɚ] the wind. □ *The captain turned his vessel into the weather.*
- **weather** ['wɛðɚ] to expose something to the open air and the elements. □ *The man wanted to weather the lumber before he used it.*
- **weather** ['wɛðɚ] to endure and come safely through some trying experience. □ *Susan seems able to weather almost any misfortune that comes her way.*
- **wether** ['wɛðɚ] a male sheep castrated before reaching sexual maturity. □ *The sheep farmer kept the ewes but sold off each wether.*
- **whether** ['ʍɛðɚ] a word indicating options or alternatives. □ *Whether he'll take the job in Colorado or the one in Idaho is unknown.*

weave—we've

- **weave** [wiv] to interlace strands of materials. □ *She likes to weave old rags into useful rugs.*
- **weave** [wiv] to make cloth on a loom. □ *His mother taught him to weave at a young age.*
- **weave** [wiv] to spin something. □ *We must first weave the raw material into yarn.*
- **weave** [wiv] to create something by elaborately combining elements. □ *That author is able to weave the most compelling stories.*
- **weave** [wiv] to move in an unsteady, zigzag fashion. □ *We noticed a car weave across the divided highway.*
- **weave** [wiv] a pattern or method for interlacing thread into woven fabric. □ *Do you know how to weave that pattern?*
- **we've** [wiv] the contraction of *we have.* □ *We've always enjoyed living in a state with so many outdoor opportunities.*

we'd—weed

- **we'd** [wid] the contraction of *we had, we would,* or *we should.* □ *We'd better leave before dark, or we'll never find our way.*
- **weed** [wid] a useless plant that tends to choke out areas of desirable plant growth. □ *The weed had roots that extended deep into the ground.*
- **weed** [wid] any undesirable or obnoxious person or thing. □ *My uncle used to say that his brother was a weed in a family*

of roses.

- **weed** [wid]   to clean an area of soil by pulling out undesirable plants. □ *The best time to weed the flower bed is right after a rain.*
- **weed [out]** [wid]   to remove someone or something not wanted. □ *The foreman wants to weed out all of the unproductive workers.*
- **weed** [wid]   marijuana. (Slang.) □ *The student bought a special pipe for smoking weed.*

wee   See the main entry beginning with *we.*

weed   See the main entry beginning with *we'd.*

week   See the main entry beginning with *weak.*

weigh   See the main entry beginning with *way.*

weighed   See the main entry beginning with *wade.*

weight   See the main entry beginning with *wait.*

weir—we're
- **weir** [wiɚ]   a fencelike enclosure built in a waterway and used to trap and collect fish. □ *Salmon are trapped and stripped of their eggs at the weir.*
- **weir** [wiɚ]   a dam or diversion in a waterway used to stop or redirect its flow or raise the water level. □ *A weir was used to funnel the excess water away from the main arm of the river.*
- **we're** [wiɚ]   the contraction of *we are.* □ *"Do you know where we're at?" asked Dave.*

weld—welled
- **weld** [wɛld]   to fasten or join metal parts together using a heating process in which the parts melt and run together. □ *Jerry will weld the broken pieces of axle.*
- **weld** [wɛld]   to join intimately or closely. □ *A formal announcement will weld the two business ventures together.*
- **weld** [wɛld]   a welded joint. □ *He did not get a good weld on his first attempt.*
- **welled [up]** [wɛld]   the past tense and past participle of *well [up]* 'to flow up and overflow.' □ *Water welled up in the sink during the flood.* □ *Tears of joy welled up in the bride's father's eyes as he walked his daughter down the aisle.* □ *Oil welled up from the rigs in record amounts.*

we'll—wheal—wheel
- **we'll** [wil]   the contraction of *we will* or *we shall.* □ *I can't*

promise that we'll be there, but we'll try.

- **wheal** [ʍil]   a suddenly raised formation on the skin; a flat itching or burning area on the skin. □ *The bee sting left a wheal on her face.*
- **wheel** [ʍil]   a circular device made of steel, rubber, or wood mounted on an axle and capable of turning. □ *The wheel on the wagon is wobbly.*
- **wheel** [ʍil]   something resembling a wheel. □ *The steering wheel of that automobile contains an airbag.*
- **wheel** [ʍil]   to change direction in a pivotal movement suddenly. □ *If you suddenly stop and wheel about, you may accidently bump into someone.*
- **wheel** [ʍil]   to convey on or as if on wheels. □ *Wheel those building supplies over here.*

welled   See the main entry beginning with *weld.*

we're   See the main entry beginning with *weir.*

were—whir

- **were** [wɚ]   the past subjunctive tense of *be.* □ *The kittens in the pet shop window were adorable.*
- **whir** [ʍɚ]   to revolve, fly, or move very rapidly, creating a whirring sound. □ *The automated turnstile doors at the store's entrance whir constantly.*

wet—whet

- **wet** [wɛt]   moist, damp. □ *His shirt was wet with sweat.*
- **wet** [wɛt]   containing liquid. □ *This towel is soaking wet.*
- **wet** [wɛt]   processed using water or some other liquid. □ *Wet drilling cement requires fewer drill bits than does dry drilling.*
- **wet** [wɛt]   rainy. □ *Yesterday was a wet day.*
- **wet** [wɛt]   permitting the manufacture and sale of alcoholic beverages. □ *Hubbard County is one of the few wet counties in the state.*
- **wet** [wɛt]   all wrong. (Slang.) □ *Harry was all wet in his recollection of the accident.*
- **wet** [wɛt]   to make something wet. □ *Wet down the driveway to keep the dust from blowing around.*
- **wet** [wɛt]   to urinate on or in something. □ *The child got so excited that she wet her trousers.*
- **whet** [ʍɛt]   to sharpen something by rubbing on or with an object. □ *You may whet that knife on this special stone.*
- **whet** [ʍɛt]   to make something sharp or more acute. □ *A glass of wine before dinner will only whet your appetite.*

wether See the main entry beginning with *weather.*

we've See the main entry beginning with *weave.*

whacks See the main entry beginning with *wax.*

whale See the main entry beginning with *wail.*

wheal See the main entry beginning with *we'll.*

wheel See the main entry beginning with *we'll.*

where See the main entry beginning with *ware.*

whet See the main entry beginning with *wet.*

whether See the main entry beginning with *weather.*

whey See the main entry beginning with *way.*

which—witch
- **which** [ʌɪtʃ] what one or ones out of a group. □ *Which picture do you prefer?*
- **which** [ʌɪtʃ] a pronoun that introduces a clause. □ *The stolen items, which were thought to be lost forever, were finally located.*
- **which** [ʌɪtʃ] whichever. □ *You may choose which you like best.*
- **witch** [wɪtʃ] a woman who practices witchcraft. □ *The woman who lived alone down by the creek was thought to be a witch.*
- **witch** [wɪtʃ] to bewitch someone or something. □ *Don't try to witch me with your black magic.*

while—wile
- **while** [ʌɑɪl] during the time of something. □ *Annette was stationed in Germany while she was in the army.*
- **while** [ʌɑɪl] at the same time as something. □ *I sat on a park bench while he jogged.*
- **while** [ʌɑɪl] to pass time in a boring or leisurely manner. □ *The retiree likes to while away his days fishing.*
- **wile** [wɑɪl] a trick or deception. □ *Her clever wile fooled no one.*
- **wile** [wɑɪl] to entice or lure someone as if by a magic spell. □ *The man tried to wile the woman into believing him.*

whine—wine
- **whine** [ʌɑɪn] a plaintive, prolonged cry. □ *The constant whine of the puppy upset the entire household.*
- **whine** [ʌɑɪn] to cry in a forlorn or distressed way. □ *The baby continued to whine after getting an injection.*
- **whine** [ʌɑɪn] to complain in a manner resembling a whine.

☐ *My sister is not one to whine when things don't go her way.*

- **wine** [waɪn]   a fermented, alcoholic beverage made from fruit or plants; something that intoxicates or makes heady. ☐ *The wine has a full, fruity flavor.* ☐ *Sudden success is like wine to the spirit.*
- **wine** [waɪn]   a purplish-red color. ☐ *The new house is decorated in colors of forest green and wine.*
- **wine** [waɪn]   to drink wine. ☐ *The company likes to wine and dine its new executives.*

whir   See the main entry beginning with *were.*

whither—wither
- **whither** [ˈʍɪðɚ]   where. ☐ *"Whither thou goest . . . " is the beginning of a verse from the book of Ruth in the Bible.*
- **wither** [ˈwɪðɚ]   to droop, dry up, or shrivel, usually from lack of moisture. ☐ *Without rain, the crops began to wither.*
- **wither** [ˈwɪðɚ]   to lose vigor, stamina, or spirit. ☐ *The runner began to wither near the end of the race.*
- **wither** [ˈwɪðɚ]   to stun someone or something. ☐ *She threw me a look that would wither anyone.*

whoa—woe
- **whoa** [wo]   a command given to a horse or draft animal to stop or stand still. ☐ *Pulling back on the reins, Nathan called "whoa" to his horse.*
- **woe** [wo]   misfortune, suffering, or grief. (Also in the fixed form *woe is me.*) ☐ *How could so much woe befall one person?* ☐ *"Oh, woe is me," lamented Candy over her misfortune.*

whole   See the main entry beginning with *hole.*

wholly   See the main entry beginning with *holy.*

whoop   See the main entry beginning with *hoop.*

who's—whose
- **who's** [huz]   the contraction of *who is.* ☐ *He is one of the boys who's going to the summer music festival.*
- **whose** [huz]   a pronoun indicating that which belongs to whom. ☐ *Whose watch is this?*

whose   See the main entry beginning with *who's.*

wild—wiled
- **wild** [waɪld]   untamed; uncivilized. ☐ *The wild West appealed to many people living in the 1800's.*
- **wild** [waɪld]   growing of its own accord without help or care

from humans. □ *Wild strawberries grow in the field behind our home.*

- **wild** [waɪld]   uncontrolled. □ *As they grew tired, the children became wild.*
- **wild** [waɪld]   having to do with the wilderness or wildlife. □ *The men enjoy camping in the wild.*
- **wild** [waɪld]   deviating from the expected. (Slang or colloquial.) □ *The movie had a wild ending.*
- **wiled [out of]** [waɪld]   the past tense and past participle of *wile [out of]* 'to trick or deceive someone into giving something up.' □ *The con artists wiled the old man out of his life savings.*
- **wiled [into]** [waɪl]   the past tense and past participle of *wile [into]* 'to entice or lure someone into doing something.' □ *She wiled her husband into buying her a mink stole.*

wile   See the main entry beginning with *while.*

wiled   See the main entry beginning with *wild.*

will   See the main entry beginning with *shall.*

wine   See the main entry beginning with *whine.*

witch   See the main entry beginning with *which.*

wither   See the main entry beginning with *whither.*

woe   See the main entry beginning with *whoa.*

won   See the main entry beginning with *one.*

wood—would
- **wood** [wʊd]   the hard, fibrous interior of a tree or shrub lying beneath the bark. □ *The wood of the cherry tree is reddish in color.*
- **wood** [wʊd]   timber. □ *How much wood does it take to build a log home?*
- **wood** [wʊd]   a stand of trees. □ *The deer disappeared into the wood.*
- **wood** [wʊd]   something made out of wood. □ *The wood box was carved and painted by a skilled carpenter.*
- **would** [wʊd]   a word indicating desire, preference, or intent. □ *The druggist said he would be happy to deliver your prescription.*
- **would** [wʊd]   could or should. □ *A leather pouch would actually hold liquids quite well.*

wore   See the main entry beginning with *war.*

worn   See the main entry beginning with *warn.*

would   See the main entry beginning with *wood.*

wrack   See the main entry beginning with *rack.*

wrap   See the main entry beginning with *rap.*

wrapped   See the main entry beginning with *rapped.*

wrest   See the main entry beginning with *rest.*

wretch   See the main entry beginning with *retch.*

wright   See the main entry beginning with *right.*

wring   See the main entry beginning with *ring.*

write   See the main entry beginning with *right.*

wrote   See the main entry beginning with *rote.*

wrung   See the main entry beginning with *rung.*

wry   See the main entry beginning with *rye.*

Y

yew See the main entry beginning with *ewe*.

yews See the main entry beginning with *ewes*.

yoke—yolk

- **yoke** [jok] a wooden frame worn over the necks of work animals. □ *The team of oxen were joined by a yoke.*
- **yoke** [jok] a pair of yoked draft animals. □ *The yoke of mules was greatly admired by the farmers.*
- **yoke** [jok] some oppressive or restrictive bond, duty, or agency. □ *His impending court appearance was a yoke he did not look forward to.*
- **yoke** [jok] a shaped and fitted piece of fabric that is part of the shoulders of a garment; the top portion of a skirt. □ *The dress had a smocked yoke.*
- **yoke** [jok] to harness something with a yoke. □ *When you yoke the horses, be sure not to tangle the reins.*
- **yolk** [jok] the mass of yellow inside an egg. □ *I cracked open an egg that had a double yolk.*

yolk See the main entry beginning with *yoke*.

yore—your—you're

- **yore** [jɔɚ] days past or distant times. □ *In days of yore, knights in shining armor rescued princesses from castle towers.*
- **your** [juɚ, jɔɚ] the possessive pronoun showing a relationship to you, yourself, or yourselves. □ *Your helpfulness has been greatly appreciated.*
- **your** [juɚ, jɔɚ] relating to oneself. □ *The party store is on your left as you enter the plaza.*

- **you're** [juɚ, jɔɚ]   the contraction of *you are*. □ *If you're hungry, there are some snacks in the refrigerator.*

you   See the main entry beginning with *ewe*.

you'll—yule
- **you'll** [jul, juəl]   the contraction of *you will* or *you shall*. □ *Hurry up or you'll be late for your appointment.*
- **yule** [jul]   Christmastime. □ *The yule season is a time for joy, celebration, and happiness.*

your   See the main entry beginning with *yore*.

you're   See the main entry beginning with *yore*.

yule   See the main entry beginning with *you'll*.

Dictionary of
Misspelled Words

Introduction

If you don't know how to spell a word, you are supposed to look it up in a dictionary. But how can you look it up if you don't know how to spell it?

For example, if you are not sure how to spell the word for a compulsive thief, you might try looking up "cleptomaniac." In a regular dictionary all your searching in the *c*'s would be in vain, because the word you need begins with a *k*: *kleptomaniac*. And if you gave up on the fancy word and started looking for "theif," you would have just as little success: *Thief* is one of those "*i* before *e*" words.

This *Dictionary of Misspelled Words* is designed to help you discover the correct spelling of a word quickly and easily. It includes more than 7,000 commonly misspelled words and more than 17,000 ways in which those words are most likely to be misspelled. It also includes many words that are commonly confused.

The *Dictionary* is easy to use. Simply look up a word under your best guess at its correct spelling. In the alphabetical word list, you will find an entry that

- identifies the spelling as correct:
- identifies the spelling as incorrect and provides the correct spelling; or
- distinguishes between two or more words commonly confused.

English spelling can be quite illogical. Some of the irregularities can be traced to the language's checkered (or is it *chequered*?) past, especially its many borrowings from other languages. Differences between American and British usage add a bit of craziness. The few "rules" that do help make sense of American English spelling are listed in the Appendix at the end of the *Dictionary*.

How to Use This Dictionary

This *Dictionary* is designed to help you quickly resolve questions of spelling and usage. Here's how it works:

1. Correct spellings are printed in **boldface type** and syllabified. For example:

   pre•scrip•tion

2. Incorrect spellings appear in lightface type without syllabication. They are followed by a colon and the correct spelling printed in **boldface type** and syllabified. For example:

   perscription : **pre•scrip•tion**

3. Spellings that are acceptable British variants appear in lightface type without syllabication. They are followed by the designation *Brit.* in parentheses, then by the preferred American spelling printed in **boldface type** and syllabified. For example:

   acknowledgement (*Brit.*) : **ac•knowl•edg•ment**

4. Entries for easily confused words provide additional information so that you can readily identify the word you need. Entries for easily confused words include brief definitions or synonyms and parts of speech in parentheses. If an incorrect spelling might lend itself to more than one correct spelling, all possible words (and their definitions) are offered. For example:

   ad•vice (*noun*); **ad•vise** (*verb*)
   dear (precious); **deer** (animal)
   it's (it is); **its** (belonging to it)
   per•ish (to cease to exist); **par•ish** (church community)
   exept : **ac•cept** (to receive *or* **ex•cept** (to exclude)

5. Because English spelling is so arbitrary, often more than one form (or variant) of a word is in current usage. Variants of a word that are used with essentially the same frequency are listed in alphabetical order in the word list. However, an incorrect spelling refers only to the variant that comes first alphabetically or that is in slightly more frequent use in

American English. Less commonly used variants are listed as incorrect spellings. For example:

levaled : **lev•eled**
lev•eled *or* **lev•elled**
lev•elled *or* **lev•eled**
Ju•go•sla•via *or* **Yu•go•sla•via**
Yugaslovia : **Yu•go•sla•via**
Yu•go•sla•via *or* **Ju•go•sla•via**

A Note on Syllabication

The words listed in this *Dictionary* have dots (•) to indicate where each word may be hyphenated if it is divided at the end of a line. In general, you should follow these guidelines when hyphenating words:

1. Do not divide one-syllable words. If a one-syllable word will not fit at the end of a line, type the whole word on the next line.

2. Do not leave only one letter at the end of one line (*o•ver, i•dea*) or at the beginning of the next (*word•y, Ohi•o*).

3. Avoid hyphenating the last word on a page.

4. If a word already contains a hyphen, divide it at the hyphen (*self-• esteem*, not *self-es•teem*).

5. In general, words with double consonants may be divided between the consonants (*ar•rogant, fal•lible*). However, when a suffix is added to a root word ending in double consonants, the hyphen comes after both consonants (*kiss•ing, stroll•ing*).

Terms and Abbreviations

adj.	adjective	*noun*	
adv.	adverb	*past of*	past tense of verb
Brit.	British variant spelling	*plur.*	plural form of noun
fem.	feminine form of word	*sing.*	singular form of noun
masc.	masculine form of word	*verb*	

A

abait : **abate**
abalish : **abol·ish**
ab·a·lo·ne
abaloney : **ab·a·lo·ne**
abanden : **aban·don**
aban·don
abarigine : **ab·o·rig·i·ne**
abarrance : **ab·er·rance**
abate
abayance : **abey·ance**
abbandon : **aban·don**
abbate : **abate**
abberance : **ab·er·rance**
ab·bess (head of convent);
  abyss (bottomless pit)
abbet : **ab·bot**
ab·bey
abblaze : **ablaze**
abboard : **aboard**
ab·bot
ab·bre·vi·ate
abbrieviate : **ab·bre·vi·ate**
abbuse : **abuse**
abby : **ab·bey**
abcess : **ab·scess**
  (inflammation) *or* **ob·sess** (to
  preoccupy)
abdecate : **ab·di·cate**
ab·di·cate
ab·do·men
abdomenal : **ab·dom·i·nal**
abdomin : **ab·do·men**
ab·dom·i·nal
abducion : **ab·duc·tion**
ab·duc·tion
aberence : **ab·er·rance**
ab·er·rance
ab·er·rant
aberrent : **ab·er·rance**
abey·ance

abeyence : **abey·ance**
abhominable : **abom·i·na·ble**
ab·hor
abhorance : **ab·hor·ence**
ab·hor·ence
abil·i·ty
abillity : **abil·i·ty**
abismal : **abys·mal**
abiss : **abyss**
ab·jure (to renounce); **ad·jure**
  (to ask)
ablaize : **ablaze**
ablaze
abley : **ably**
ablivion : **obliv·i·on**
ably
abnagate : **ab·ne·gate**
ab·ne·gate
abnigate : **ab·ne·gate**
ab·nor·mal
abnormel : **ab·nor·mal**
abnoxious : **ob·nox·ious**
aboard
abol·ish
abolission : **ab·o·li·tion**
ab·o·li·tion
abollish : **abol·ish**
abolone : **ab·a·lo·ne**
abomanable : **abom·i·na·ble**
abom·i·na·ble
abor : **ab·hor**
abord : **aboard**
aborence : **ab·hor·ence**
ab·o·rig·i·ne
aboriginnie : **ab·o·rig·i·ne**
aboriginy : **ab·o·rig·i·ne**
abracive : **abra·sive**
abrade
abraid : **abrade**
abra·sive

abreast
abregate : **ab•ro•gate**
abrest : **abreast**
abreviate : **ab•bre•vi•ate**
abridgement (*Brit.*) :
   abridg•ment
abridg•ment
abrieviate : **ab•bre•vi•ate**
ab•ro•gate
abrubt : **abrupt**
abrupt
absalute : **ab•so•lute**
absalutely : **ab•so•lute•ly**
abscence : **ab•sence**
ab•scess (inflammation) *or*
   ob•sess (to preoccupy)
ab•sence
absensce : **ab•sence**
absense : **ab•sence**
ab•sen•tee
absentie : **ab•sen•tee**
absenty : **ab•sen•tee**
abserd : **ab•surd**
absess : **ab•scess**
   (inflammation) *or* **ob•sess** (to
   preoccupy)
ab•so•lute
ab•so•lute•ly
absolutly : **ab•so•lute•ly**
ab•sorb
absorbant : **ab•sorb•ent**
ab•sorb•ent
absorbtion : **ab•sorp•tion**
ab•sorp•tion
abstainence : **ab•sti•nence**
abstanence : **ab•sti•nence**
abstinance : **ab•sti•nence**
ab•sti•nence
ab•surd
abun•dance
abun•dant
abundence : **abun•dance**

abundent : **abun•dant**
abuse
abut•ment
abuttment : **abut•ment**
abuze : **abuse**
abys•mal
abyss (bottomless pit); **ab•bess**
   (head of convent)
abyssmal : **abys•mal**
abzerd : **ab•surd**
aca•cia
ac•a•dem•ic
ac•a•dem•i•cal•ly
academicly : **ac•a•dem•i•cal•ly**
acasha : **aca•cia**
accademy : **acad•em•y**
accasion : **oc•ca•sion**
ac•cede (to agree reluctantly);
   ex•ceed (to go beyond)
acceed : **ac•cede**
accelarate : **ac•cel•er•ate**
ac•cel•er•ate
accelerater : **ac•cel•er•a•tor**
ac•cel•er•a•tor
ac•cent
ac•cept (to receive); **ex•cept** (to
   exclude)
ac•cept•able
ac•cept•ance
acceptible : **ac•cept•able**
accesory : **ac•ces•so•ry**
ac•cess
accessable : **ac•ces•si•ble**
accessery : **ac•ces•so•ry**
ac•ces•si•ble
ac•ces•sion
ac•ces•so•ry
accidant : **ac•ci•dent**
ac•ci•dent
ac•ci•den•tal•ly
accidently : **ac•ci•den•tal•ly**
ac•claim

ac·cli·ma·tize

accommadate :
  ac·com·mo·date

ac·com·mo·date

accomodate : ac·com·mo·date

ac·com·pa·ni·ment

accompanyment :
  ac·com·pa·ni·ment

ac·com·plice

accomplis : ac·com·plice

ac·com·plish

ac·cord

accordien : ac·cor·di·on

ac·cor·di·on

ac·count·able

ac·count·ant

accountent : ac·count·ant

ac·cou·ter·ment *or*
  ac·cou·tre·ment

accoutrament : ac·cou·tre·ment

ac·cou·tre·ment *or*
  ac·cou·ter·ment

accross : across

accummulate : ac·cu·mu·late

ac·cu·mu·late

ac·cu·mu·la·tion

ac·cu·ra·cy

ac·cu·rate

accurisy : ac·cu·ra·cy

accurite : ac·cu·rate

ac·cu·sa·tion

ac·cuse

ac·cus·tom

ac·cus·tomed

accustommed : ac·cus·tomed

accutrement : ac·cou·tre·ment

acedemic : aca·dem·ic

acelerate : ac·cel·er·ate

acent : ac·cent

acept : ac·cept

acer·bic

acertain : as·cer·tain

acess : ac·cess

acessible : ac·ces·si·ble

acession : ac·ces·sion

acessory : ac·ces·so·ry

acetic : as·cet·ic

acheive : achieve

achieve

achieve·ment

acident : ac·ci·dent

acknowledgement (*Brit.*) :
  ac·knowl·edg·ment

ac·knowl·edg·ment

acknowlege : ac·knowl·edge

ackumen : acu·men

aclaim : ac·claim

aclimatize : ac·cli·ma·tize

acommodate : ac·com·mo·date

acompaniment :
  ac·com·pa·ni·ment

acomplice : ac·com·plice

acomplish : ac·com·plish

acord : ac·cord

acordion : ac·cor·di·on

acountent : ac·count·ant

acousticks : acous·tics

acous·tics

acoutrement : ac·cou·tre·ment

ac·quain·tance

acquaintence : ac·quain·tance

acquaintense : ac·quain·tance

acquatic : aqua·tic

ac·qui·esce

acquiese : ac·qui·esce

acquiesse : ac·qui·esce

ac·quire

ac·qui·si·tion

ac·quit

acquited : ac·quit·ted

ac·quit·tal

ac·quit·ted

acquittel : ac·quit·tal

acrage : acre·age

acre
acre·age
acrebat : acro·bat
acrige : acre·age
across
actavate : ac·ti·vate
acter : ac·tor
acteress : ac·tress
ac·ti·vate
ac·tor
actoress : ac·tress
ac·tress
ac·tu·al
ac·tu·al·ly
actule : ac·tu·al
actully : ac·tu·al·ly
acu·men
acumin : acu·men
acummulation :
   ac·cu·mu·la·tion
acumulate : ac·cu·mu·late
acumulation : ac·cu·mu·la·tion
acuracy : ac·cu·ra·cy
acurate : ac·cu·rate
acusation : ac·cu·sa·tion
acuse : ac·cuse
acustics : acous·tics
acustom : ac·cus·tom
ad (advertisement); add (to
   combine)
ad·age
ad·a·mant
adament : ad·a·mant
adapt (to modify); adept
   (skilled); adopt (to accept)
adapt·able
adapt·er
adaptible : adapt·able
adaptor : adapt·er
adaquacy : ade·qua·cy
adaquate : ade·quate

add (to combine); ad
   (advertisement)
add hoc : ad hoc
add lib : ad lib
addage : ad·age
addative : ad·di·tive
ad·den·da (*plur.*); ad·den·dum
   (*sing.*)
ad·den·dum (*sing.*); ad·den·da
   (*plur.*)
addept : ad·ept
addick : ad·dict
ad·dict
ad·dic·tion
ad·di·tion (adding); e·di·tion
   (book)
ad·di·tive
addopt : adopt
addrenalin : ad·ren·a·line
ad·dress
addulation : ad·u·la·tion
addult : adult
addulterer : adul·ter·er
addulteress : adul·ter·ess
addultery : adul·ter·y
adeau : adieu
adeiu : adieu
adelescence : ad·o·les·cence
adendum : ad·den·dum
adept (skilled); adapt (to
   modify); adopt (to accept)
adequasy : ade·qua·cy
ade·quate
adequit : ade·quate
adhear : ad·here
adherance : ad·her·ence
ad·her·ence (quality of
   adhering); ad·her·ents
   (followers)
ad hoc
adhoc : ad hoc
adhock : ad hoc

adict : **ad•dict**
adiction : **ad•dic•tion**
adieu (good-bye); **ado** (fuss)
adige : **adage**
ad•ja•cent
adjasent : **ad•ja•cent**
ad•jec•tive
ad•join
ad•journ
ad•ju•di•cate
ad•jure (to ask); **ab•jure** (to renounce)
adjurn : **ad•journ**
ad•just
ad•just•able
adjustible : **ad•just•able**
ad•ju•tant
adjutent : **ad•ju•tant**
ad-lib
admaral : **ad•mir•al**
admendment : **amend•ment**
admeration : **ad•mi•ra•tion**
adminester : **ad•min•is•ter**
ad•min•is•ter
administerate : **ad•min•is•trate**
ad•min•is•trate
administrater : **ad•min•is•tra•tor**
adminition : **ad•mo•ni•tion**
adminster : **ad•min•is•ter**
ad•mi•ral
ad•mir•er
admirerer : **ad•mir•er**
admiror : **ad•mir•er**
admision : **ad•mis•sion**
admissable : **ad•mis•si•ble**
ad•mis•si•ble
admitance : **ad•mit•tance**
admited : **ad•mit•ted**
ad•mit•tance
ad•mit•ted
admittence : **ad•mit•tance**

admittense : **ad•mit•tance**
ad•mo•ni•tion
ado (fuss); **adieu** (good-bye)
ado•be
adobie : **ado•be**
adoby : **ado•be**
adolecense : **ado•les•cence**
adolecent : **ado•les•cent**
ado•les•cence
ado•les•cent
adolesence : **ado•les•cence**
adolesense : **ado•les•cence**
adolesent : **ado•les•cent**
adom : **atom**
adoo : **adieu** (good-bye) *or* **ado** (fuss)
adopt (to accept); **adapt** (to modify); **adept** (skilled)
ador•able
adorible : **ador•able**
adorn
adorn•ment
adourn : **adorn**
adournment : **adorn•ment**
adrenalin : **ad•ren•a•line**
ad•ren•a•line
adrenlin : **ad•ren•a•line**
adrenolin : **ad•ren•a•line**
adres : **ad•dress**
adress : **ad•dress**
adrinalin : **ad•ren•a•line**
adsorb : **ab•sorb**
adsorption (*Brit.*) : **ab•sorp•tion**
adu•la•tion
adult
adultarate : **adul•ter•ate**
adul•ter•er
adul•ter•ess
adulteror : **adul•ter•er**
adul•ter•y
adultrer : **adul•ter•er**

adultress : **adul·ter·ess**
adultry : **adul·ter·y**
advacate : **ad·vo·cate**
advacator : **ad·vo·ca·tor**
ad·vance
advanse : **ad·vance**
ad·van·tage
ad·van·ta·geous
advantagious : **ad·van·ta·geous**
advantige : **ad·van·tage**
advenchure : **ad·ven·ture**
ad·ven·ture
ad·ven·tur·er
adventuror : **ad·ven·tur·er**
adventurur : **ad·ven·tur·er**
adversarry : **ad·ver·sary**
ad·ver·sary
ad·verse (unfavorable); **averse** (disinclined)
ad·ver·tise·ment
ad·ver·tis·er
advertisor : **ad·ver·tis·er**
advertize (*Brit.*) : **ad·ver·tise**
advertizer (*Brit.*) : **ad·ver·tis·er**
advertizing (*Brit.*) : **ad·ver·tis·ing**
ad·vice (*noun*); **ad·vise** (*verb*)
ad·vis·able
ad·vise (*verb*); **ad·vice** (*noun*)
ad·vis·ed·ly
ad·vis·er *or* **ad·vis·or**
advisible : **ad·vis·able**
advisidly : **ad·vis·ed·ly**
ad·vis·or *or* **ad·vis·er**
advizable : **ad·vis·able**
advizer : **ad·vis·er**
ad·vo·cate
advocater : **ad·vo·ca·tor**
ad·vo·ca·tor
aeleron : **ai·le·ron**
aer·ate
aer·i·al

ae·rie (nest); airy (relating to air); ee·rie (weird)
aero·dy·na·mic
aerodynamick : **aero·dy·nam·ic**
aeronatic : **aero·nau·tic**
aero·nau·tic
aeronawtic : **aero·nau·tic**
aeronotic : **aero·nau·tic**
aeronottic : **aero·nau·tic**
aero·sol
aes·thet·ic *or* **es·thet·ic**
afability : **af·fa·bil·i·ty**
afable : **af·fa·ble**
afadavit : **af·fi·da·vit**
afair : **af·fair**
afare : **af·fair**
afect : **af·fect**
afection : **af·fec·tion**
af·fa·bil·i·ty
affabillity : **af·fa·bil·i·ty**
af·fa·ble
affadavet : **af·fi·da·vit**
affadavid : **af·fi·da·vit**
affadavit : **af·fi·da·vit**
af·fair
affare : **af·fair**
af·fect (to influence); **ef·fect** (result; to bring about results)
affense : **of·fense**
affibility : **af·fa·bil·i·ty**
affible : **af·fa·ble**
af·fi·da·vit
af·fil·i·ate
affilliate : **af·fil·i·ate**
af·fin·i·ty
af·fir·ma·tive
affirmitive : **af·fir·ma·tive**
affluance : **af·flu·ence**
affluant : **af·flu·ent**
af·flu·ence

af·flu·ent (prosperous);
  ef·flu·ent (flowing out)
affraid : **afraid**
Afgan : **Af·ghan**
Afganistan : **Af·ghan·i·stan**
Af·ghan
Afghanastan : **Af·ghan·i·stan**
Af·ghan·i·stan
afiliate : **af·fil·i·ate**
afinity : **af·fin·i·ty**
afirm : **af·firm**
afirmative : **af·fir·ma·tive**
afluent : **af·flu·ent**
afore·said
aforism : **aph·o·rism**
aforsaid : **afore·said**
afrade : **afraid**
afraid
against
aganize : **ag·o·nize**
agany : **ag·o·ny**
agast : **aghast**
agate
agatt : **agate**
aged
ageing : **aging**
agen·cy
agensy : **agen·cy**
agetate : **ag·i·tate**
agete : **agate**
aggile : **ag·ile**
aggility : **agil·i·ty**
aggitate : **ag·i·tate**
aggnostic : **ag·nos·tic**
aggnosticism : **ag·nos·ti·cism**
aggonize : **ag·o·nize**
aggony : **ag·o·ny**
aggragate : **ag·gre·gate**
aggrandise (*Brit.*) :
  ag·gran·dize
ag·gran·dize
ag·gra·vate

ag·gra·vat·ed
aggreave : **ag·grieve**
aggreeable : **agree·able**
ag·gre·gate
ag·gre·ga·tion
ag·gress (to attack); egress
  (exit)
aggresser : **ag·gres·sor**
ag·gres·sion
ag·gres·sor
aggrevate : **ag·gra·vate**
aggreve : **ag·grieve**
aggriculture : **ag·ri·cul·ture**
ag·grieve
agground : **aground**
aghast
agid : **aged**
agile
agilety : **agil·i·ty**
agil·i·ty
agill : **ag·ile**
agillity : **agil·i·ty**
agincy : **agen·cy**
aging
aginst : **against**
agi·tate
agnastic : **ag·nos·tic**
agnasticism : **ag·nos·ti·cism**
agnaustic : **ag·nos·tic**
agnausticism : **ag·nos·ti·cism**
ag·nos·tic
agnostick : **ag·nos·tic**
agnosticysm : **ag·nos·ti·cism**
agnostischism : **ag·nos·ti·cism**
agnostisism : **ag·nos·ti·cism**
agoanize : **ag·o·nize**
agoany : **ag·o·ny**
agonie : **ag·o·ny**
agonise (*Brit.*) : **ag·o·nize**
ag·o·nize
agonnize : **ag·o·nize**
agonny : **ag·o·ny**

agraculture : **ag•ri•cul•ture**
agrandize : **ag•gran•dize**
agravate : **ag•gra•vate**
agreable : **agree•able**
agreave : **ag•grieve**
agreculture : **ag•ri•cul•ture**
agreeabal : **agree•able**
agreeabel : **agree•able**
agree•able
agreeible : **agree•able**
agregate : **ag•gre•gate**
agress : **ag•gress** (to attack) *or*
   egress (exit)
agression : **ag•gres•sion**
agriculchure : **ag•ri•cul•ture**
agricullture : **ag•ri•cul•ture**
ag•ri•cul•ture
agrieve : **ag•grieve**
agrikulture : **ag•ri•cul•ture**
aground
agrownd : **aground**
aid (to help); **aide** (helper)
aid-de-camp : **aide-de-camp**
aide (helper); **aid** (to help)
aide-de-camp
ailaron : **ai•ler•on**
ai•ler•on
ailerron : **ai•ler•on**
aim•less
aimliss : **aim•less**
airasol : **aero•sol**
airboarn : **air•borne**
airborn : **air•borne**
air•borne
aireate : **aer•ate**
aireborne : **air•borne**
airial : **ae•ri•al**
airiate : **aer•ate**
airodinamic : **aero•dy•nam•ic**
airodynamic : **aero•dy•nam•ic**
airodynammic : **aero•dy•nam•ic**
aironautic : **aero•nau•tic**

aironawtic : **aero•nau•tic**
airosol : **aero•sol**
airplain : **air•plane**
air•plane
airy (relating to air); **ae•rie**
   (nest)
ais•le (walkway); **is•le** (small
   island)
ajacent : **ad•ja•cent**
ajective : **ad•jec•tive**
ajile : **ag•ile**
ajitate : **ag•i•tate**
ajoin : **ad•join**
ajourn : **ad•journ**
ajudicate : **ad•ju•di•cate**
ajust : **ad•just**
akacia : **aca•cia**
aknowledge : **ac•knowl•edge**
aknowledgment :
   ac•knowl•edg•ment
akre : **acre**
akrobat : **ac•ro•bat**
Al•a•ba•ma
Alabamma : **Al•a•ba•ma**
alabasster : **al•a•bas•ter**
al•a•bas•ter
alabi : **al•i•bi**
alacritty : **alac•ri•ty**
alac•ri•ty
alakrity : **alac•ri•ty**
alamony : **al•i•mo•ny**
Alasca : **Alas•ka**
Alas•ka
alay : **al•lay**
albam : **al•bum**
Albanea : **Al•ba•ni•a**
Al•ba•ni•a
Albaquerque : **Al•bu•quer•que**
albatros : **al•ba•tross**
al•ba•tross
albeat : **al•be•it**
al•be•it

albem : **al•bum**
albetross : **al•ba•tross**
albiet : **al•be•it**
albim : **al•bum**
al•bi•no
albinoes : **al•bi•nos**
al•bi•nos
albinow : **al•bi•no**
Albiquerque : **Al•bu•quer•que**
albitross : **al•ba•tross**
alblum : **al•bum**
al•bum
Al•bu•quer•que
Albuquirque : **Al•bu•quer•que**
alcahol : **al•co•hol**
alcali : **al•ka•li**
alcemy : **al•che•my**
al•che•my
alchohol : **al•co•hol**
alcohal : **al•co•hol**
al•co•hol
alebasster : **al•a•bas•ter**
alebaster : **al•a•bas•ter**
alebi : **al•i•bi**
aledge : **al•lege**
alegation : **al•le•ga•tion**
alege : **al•lege**
Aleghenies : **Al•le•ghe•nies**
alegiance : **al•le•giance**
alegory : **al•le•go•ry**
alegro : **al•le•gro**
alein : **alien**
alergy : **al•ler•gy**
aleron : **ai•ler•on**
aleus : **ali•as**
Aleu•tians
aleviate : **al•le•vi•ate**
alfabet: **al•pha•bet**
al•fal•fa
alfallfa : **al•fal•fa**
alfalpha : **al•fal•fa**
al•ga (*sing.*); **al•gae** (*plur.*)

algabra : **al•ge•bra**
al•gae (*plur.*); **al•ga** (*sing.*)
algaebra : **al•ge•bra**
al•ge•bra
algibra : **al•ge•bra**
aliance : **al•li•ance**
alias
Alibama : **Al•a•ba•ma**
al•i•bi
aliby : **al•i•bi**
alien
aliess : **alias**
aligator : **al•li•ga•tor**
align *or* **aline**
alimmony : **al•i•mo•ny**
alimoney : **al•i•mo•ny**
al•i•mo•ny
aline *or* **align**
aliteration : **al•lit•er•a•tion**
alitteration : **al•lit•er•a•tion**
alkahol : **al•co•hol**
al•ka•li
alkalie : **al•ka•li**
alkeli : **al•ka•li**
alkemy : **al•che•my**
alkohol : **al•co•hol**
Allabama : **Al•a•ba•ma**
allabaster : **al•a•bas•ter**
allacate : **al•lo•cate**
allacrity : **alac•ri•ty**
allagation : **al•le•ga•tion**
allagator : **al•li•ga•tor**
Allaghenies : **Al•le•ghe•nies**
allagorry : **al•le•go•ry**
allagory : **al•le•go•ry**
allagro : **al•le•gro**
allamony : **al•i•mo•ny**
Allaska : **Alas•ka**
al•lay
allaygro : **al•le•gro**
Allbania : **Al•ba•ni•a**
allbatross : **al•ba•tross**

allbeit : **al·be·it**
allbino : **al·bi·no**
allbum : **al·bum**
Allbuquerque : **Al·bu·quer·que**
allchemy : **al·che·my**
allcohol : **al·co·hol**
alleaviate : **al·le·vi·ate**
alledge : **al·lege**
alledgedly : **al·leg·ed·ly**
allegance : **al·le·giance**
al·le·ga·tion
allegator : **al·li·ga·tor**
al·lege
allegence : **al·le·giance**
Al·le·ghe·nies
al·le·giance
allegorey : **al·le·go·ry**
allegorry : **al·le·go·ry**
al·le·go·ry
al·le·gro
allegroe : **al·le·gro**
alleiviate : **al·le·vi·ate**
allergie : **al·ler·gy**
al·ler·gy
allerjy : **al·ler·gy**
alleron : **ai·ler·on**
Alleutians : **Aleu·tians**
al·le·vi·ate
al·ley (road); **al·ly** (friend)
allfalfa : **al·fal·fa**
allgebra : **al·ge·bra**
al·li·ance
allias : **alias**
allibi : **al·i·bi**
allience : **al·li·ance**
alligater : **al·li·ga·tor**
alligation : **al·le·ga·tion**
al·li·ga·tor
alligattor : **al·li·ga·tor**
Allighenies : **Al·le·ghe·nies**
allimony : **al·i·mo·ny**
allirgy : **al·ler·gy**

al·lit·er·a·tion
alliterration : **al·lit·er·a·tion**
allitiration : **al·lit·er·a·tion**
allitteration : **al·lit·er·a·tion**
allkali : **al·ka·li**
allmanac : **al·ma·nac**
allmighty : **al·mighty**
allmond : **al·mond**
allmost : **al·most**
al·lo·cate
alloha : **alo·ha**
al·lot (to assign a portion) **a
 lot** (many)
al·lot·ment
al·lot·ted
al·low
al·low·able
al·low·ance
allowence : **al·low·ance**
allowible : **al·low·able**
allpaca : **al·pa·ca**
allphabet : **al·pha·bet**
all ready *or* **already**
allready : **all ready** *or* **al·ready**
all right
alltercation : **al·ter·ca·tion**
allthough : **al·though**
alltimeter : **al·tim·e·ter**
allto : **al·to**
all to·geth·er (all in one place);
 al·to·geth·er (totally, wholly)
alltruism : **al·tru·ism**
al·lude (to refer); **e·lude** (to
 escape)
alluminum : **alu·min·um**
allurgy : **al·ler·gy**
al·lu·sion (reference); **elu·sion**
 (evasion); **il·lu·sion** (false
 idea or image)
al·lu·sive (making references);
 elu·sive (avoiding); **il·lu·sive**
 (deceptive)

allways : **al·ways**
al·ly (friend); **al·ley** (road)
al·ma·nac
almanack : **al·ma·nac**
almenac : **al·ma·nac**
almend : **al·mond**
al·mighty
alminac : **al·ma·nac**
almity : **al·mighty**
al·mond
al·most
almund : **al·mond**
alocate : **al·lo·cate**
alo·ha
aloominum : **alu·min·um**
a lot (many); **al·lot** (to assign a
   portion)
alot : **al·lot** (to assign a
   portion) *or* **a lot** (many)
alotment : **al·lot·ment**
alottment : **al·lot·ment**
aloud
alow : **al·low**
alowable : **al·low·able**
alowd : **aloud**
alowha : **alo·ha**
al·pa·ca
alpacka : **al·pa·ca**
al·pha·bet
alphalfa : **al·fal·fa**
alphebet : **al·pha·bet**
alphibet : **al·pha·bet**
al·ready *or* **all ready**
alright : **all right**
al·tar (table used in worship);
   al·ter (to change)
altarcation : **al·ter·ca·tion**
al·ter (to change); **al·tar** (table
   used in worship)
al·ter·ca·tion
alterkation : **al·ter·ca·tion**
alternater : **al·ter·na·tor**

al·ter·na·tor
altho : **al·though**
al·though
al·tim·e·ter
altimiter : **al·tim·e·ter**
al·to
altoes : **al·tos**
al·to·geth·er (totally); **all
   to·geth·er** (all in one place)
al·tos
altrueism: al·**tru·ism**
altruesm : al·tru·ism
al·tru·ism
alude : **al·lude** (to refer) *or*
   elude (to escape)
Aluetians : **Aleu·tians**
alumanum : **alu·min·um**
alumenem : **alu·min·um**
alumenum : **alu·min·um**
alu·min·um
alusion : **al·lu·sion** (reference)
   or **elu·sion** (evasion) *or*
   il·lu·sion (false idea or
   image)
alusive : **al·lu·sive** (making
   references) *or* **elu·sive**
   (avoiding) *or* **il·lu·sive**
   (deceptive)
al·ways
amal·gam
amalgem : **amal·gam**
amallgam : **amal·gam**
amarous : **amor·ous**
amass
am·a·teur
amathist : **ame·thyst**
amatoor : **am·a·teur**
amatuer : **am·a·teur**
amature : **am·a·teur**
amaze·ment
amazemint : **amaze·ment**
amazment : **amaze·ment**

ambaguity : **am·bi·gu·i·ty**
ambasador : **am·bas·sa·dor**
ambassader : **am·bas·sa·dor**
am·bas·sa·dor
ambassator : **am·bas·sa·dor**
ambedextrous : **am·bi·dex·trous**
ambeguity : **am·bi·gu·i·ty**
ambent : **am·bi·ent**
ambersand : **am·per·sand**
ambiant : **am·bi·ent**
ambideckstrous :
   am·bi·dex·trous
ambidexterous :
   am·bi·dex·trous
am·bi·dex·trous
ambidextrus : **am·bi·dex·trous**
am·bi·ent
ambigooity : **am·bi·gu·i·ty**
ambiguety : **am·bi·gu·i·ty**
am·bi·gu·i·ty
ambint : **am·bi·ent**
ambivalant : **am·biv·a·lent**
am·biv·a·lent
ambivelent : **am·biv·a·lent**
ambivilent : **am·biv·a·lent**
ambroasia : **am·bro·sia**
ambrosa : **am·bro·sia**
ambrosha : **am·bro·sia**
am·bro·sia
am·bu·lance
ambulence : **am·bu·lance**
ambyent : **am·bi·ent**
ameable : **ami·a·ble**
ameago : **ami·go**
amealiorate : **ame·lio·rate**
ameanable : **ame·na·ble**
ameba : **amoe·ba**
ameeba : **amoe·ba**
ameeliorate : **ame·lio·rate**
amego : **ami·go**
ameleorate : **ame·lio·rate**
ameliarate : **ame·lio·rate**

amelierate : **ame·lio·rate**
ameliorait : **ame·lio·rate**
ame·lio·rate
ame·na·ble
amenaty : **amen·i·ty**
amend (to change or add to);
   emend (to correct)
amend·ment
ameneble : **ame·na·ble**
amenety : **amen·i·ty**
amenible : **ame·na·ble**
ame·ni·ty
amennable : **ame·na·ble**
ameoba : **amoe·ba**
amerous : **amor·ous**
ameteur : **am·a·teur**
amethist : **ame·thyst**
ame·thyst
amfibian : **am·phib·ian**
amfitheater : **am·phi·the·a·ter**
amiabal : **ami·a·ble**
amiabel : **ami·a·ble**
ami·a·ble
amicabal : **am·i·ca·ble**
am·i·ca·ble
amiceble : **am·i·ca·ble**
amicible : **am·i·ca·ble**
amickable : **am·i·ca·ble**
amieble : **ami·a·ble**
amiggo : **ami·go**
ami·go
aminable : **ame·na·ble**
Amish
amithyst : **ame·thyst**
ammass : **amass**
ammeba : **amoe·ba**
ammendment : **amend·ment**
ammenity : **amen·i·ty**
ammethyst : **ame·thyst**
ammigo : **ami·go**
Ammish : **Amish**
ammliorate : **ame·lio·rate**

ammonea : **am·mo·nia**
am·mo·nia
ammonition : **am·mu·ni·tion**
ammonnia : **am·mo·nia**
ammonya : **am·mo·nia**
ammoral : **amor·al**
ammorphus : **amor·phous**
ammortize : **amor·tize**
ammount : **amount**
ammulet : **amu·let**
ammulit : **amu·let**
ammunishin : **am·mu·ni·tion**
am·mu·ni·tion
ammusement : **amuse·ment**
amnasty : **am·nes·ty**
amneasia : **am·ne·sia**
amneesia : **am·ne·sia**
amnesha : **am·ne·sia**
am·ne·sia
amnessty : **am·nes·ty**
amnestie : **am·nes·ty**
am·nes·ty
amoarous : **am·o·rous**
amoartize : **amor·tize**
amoe·ba
among
amonia : **am·mon·ia**
amonya : **am·mo·nia**
amoorous : **amor·ous**
amor·al
amorale : **amor·al**
amorfous : **amor·phous**
amorfus : **amor·phous**
amorish : **am·o·rous**
am·o·rous
amorphis : **amor·phous**
amor·phous
amortise (*Brit.*) : **amor·tize**
amor·tize
amorus : **am·o·rous**
amoung : **among**
amount

amourous : **am·o·rous**
amourphous : **amor·phous**
amourtize : **amor·tize**
ampasand : **am·per·sand**
ampeer : **am·pere**
ampeir : **am·pere**
ampeire : **am·pere**
amper : **am·pere**
am·pere
am·per·sand
ampesand : **am·per·sand**
ampezand : **am·per·sand**
amphatheater :
    am·phi·the·a·ter
amphebian : **am·phib·i·an**
amphetheater :
    am·phi·the·a·ter
am·phib·i·an
amphibien : **am·phib·i·an**
amphibyan : **am·phib·i·an**
am·phi·the·a·ter
amphitheatre (*Brit.*) :
    am·phi·the·a·ter
amphithiater : **am·phi·the·a·ter**
amplefy : **am·pli·fy**
am·pli·fy
am·pu·tee
amputiy : **am·pu·tee**
amputy : **am·pu·tee**
am·u·let
amulette : **am·u·let**
amund : **al·mond**
amunition : **am·mu·ni·tion**
amuse·ment
amusemint : **amuse·ment**
amuzement : **amuse·ment**
amyable : **ami·a·ble**
amythist : **ame·thyst**
anach·ro·nism
anachronnism : **anach·ro·nism**
anachronysm : **anach·ro·nism**
anackronism : **anach·ro·nism**

anacronism : **anach·ro·nism**
anagesic : **an·al·ge·sic**
anagraham : **ana·gram**
ana·gram
anagramm : **ana·gram**
analegy : **anal·o·gy**
analgeasic : **an·al·ge·sic**
analgeesic : **an·al·ge·sic**
analgeezic : **an·al·ge·sic**
an·al·ge·sic
analgesick : **an·al·ge·sic**
analgezic : **an·al·ge·sic**
analigy : **anal·o·gy**
analisees : **anal·y·ses**
analises : **anal·y·ses**
analisis : **anal·y·sis**
analisiss : **anal·y·sis**
analisys : **anal·y·sis**
analitic : **an·a·lyt·ic**
analitick : **an·a·lyt·ic**
analityc : **an·a·lyt·ic**
analize : **an·a·lyze**
analjesic : **an·al·ge·sic**
anallogy : **anal·o·gy**
anallyses : **anal·y·ses**
anallysis : **anal·y·sis**
anallytic : **an·a·lyt·ic**
analoge : **anal·o·gy**
analogee : **anal·o·gy**
analoggy : **anal·o·gy**
analogie : **anal·o·gy**
anal·o·gy
analoje : **anal·o·gy**
analyse (*Brit.*) : **an·a·lyze**
anal·y·ses (*plur.*); **anal·y·sis**
  (*sing.*)
anal·y·sis (*sing.*); **anal·y·ses**
  (*plur.*)
an·a·lyt·ic
an·a·lyze
anamosity : **an·i·mos·i·ty**
ananymity : **an·o·nym·i·ty**

Anapolis : **An·nap·o·lis**
anarchie : **an·ar·chy**
an·ar·chy
anarcky : **an·ar·chy**
anasthesia : **an·es·the·sia**
anatamy : **anat·o·my**
anatome : **anat·o·my**
anatomie : **anat·o·my**
anat·o·my
ancer : **an·chor**
ancerage : **an·chor·age**
ancesstor : **an·ces·tor**
ancester : **an·ces·tor**
ancesteral : **an·ces·tral**
ancestir : **an·ces·tor**
an·ces·tor
ancestoral : **an·ces·tral**
an·ces·tral
ancestrall : **an·ces·tral**
ancestree : **an·ces·try**
ancestrel : **an·ces·tral**
ancestrie : **an·ces·try**
an·ces·try
anchant : **an·cient**
anchar : **an·chor**
ancharage : **an·chor·age**
anchent : **an·cient**
ancher : **an·chor**
ancherage : **an·chor·age**
anchint : **an·cient**
an·chor
an·chor·age
anchoredge : **an·chor·age**
anchorege : **an·chor·age**
anchorige : **an·chor·age**
an·cient
anciety : **an·xi·ety**
ancilary : **an·cil·lary**
an·cil·lary
ancillery : **an·cil·lary**
ancilliary : **an·cil·lary**
ancilliery : **an·cil·lary**

anckor : **an•chor**
anckorage : **an•chor•age**
andiran : **and•iron**
andiren : **and•iron**
andirn : **and•iron**
and•iron
anecdoat : **an•ec•dote**
an•ec•dote (story); **an•ti•dote**
   (remedy)
aneckdote : **an•ec•dote**
aneemia : **ane•mia**
anegesic : **an•al•ge•sic**
anegram : **ana•gram**
anekdote : **an•ec•dote**
anelgesic : **an•al•ge•sic**
anemea : **ane•mia**
ane•mia
anem•o•ne
anemoney : **anem•o•ne**
anemonne : **anem•o•ne**
anemony : **anem•o•ne**
anemosity : **an•i•mos•i•ty**
an•es•the•sia
anesthessia : **an•es•the•sia**
anesthisia : **an•es•the•sia**
anesthsya : **an•es•the•sia**
an•gel (spiritual being); **an•gle**
   (figure in geometry)
an•gel•ic
angelick : **an•gel•ic**
angellic : **an•gel•ic**
an•gle (figure in geometry);
   an•gel (spiritual being)
An•go•ra
Angorra : **An•go•ra**
angxiety : **an•xi•ety**
anhemia : **ane•mia**
anihilate : **an•ni•hi•late**
an•i•mal
animall : **an•i•mal**
animel : **an•i•mal**
animocity : **an•i•mos•i•ty**

animone : **anem•o•ne**
animony : **anem•o•ne**
animositty : **an•i•mos•i•ty**
an•i•mos•i•ty
animossity : **an•i•mos•i•ty**
animul : **an•i•mal**
aniversary : **an•ni•ver•sa•ry**
aniversery : **an•ni•ver•sa•ry**
anjelic : **an•gel•ic**
ankel : **an•kle**
anker : **an•chor**
ankerage : **an•chor•age**
an•kle
annachronism : **anach•ro•nism**
annagram : **ana•gram**
annalogy : **anal•o•gy**
annalyses : **anal•y•ses**
annalysis : **anal•y•sis**
annalytic : **an•a•lyt•ic**
annalyze : **an•a•lyze**
An•nap•o•lis
annarchy : **an•ar•chy**
annatation : **an•no•ta•tion**
annatomy : **anat•o•my**
annaversary : **an•ni•ver•sa•ry**
annaversery : **an•ni•ver•sa•ry**
annesthesia : **an•es•the•sia**
anneversary : **an•ni•ver•sa•ry**
annihalate : **an•ni•hi•late**
an•ni•hi•late
annilate : **an•ni•hi•late**
an•ni•ver•sa•ry
anniversery : **an•ni•ver•sa•ry**
annivursery : **an•ni•ver•sa•ry**
annoint : **anoint**
annomaly : **anom•a•ly**
an•no•ta•tion
announser : **an•nounc•er**
an•noy•ance
annoyence : **an•noy•ance**
an•nu•al
anoint

anomale : **anom·a·ly**
anomally : **anom·a·ly**
anom·a·ly
anommaly : **anom·a·ly**
anonimity : **an·o·nym·i·ty**
anonimous : **anon·y·mous**
an·o·nym·i·ty
anon·y·mous
anonymus : **anon·y·mous**
anotation : **an·no·ta·tion**
anounce : **an·nounce**
anouncer : **an·nounc·er**
anounse : **an·nounce**
anoyance : **an·noy·ance**
anser : **an·swer**
ansestor : **an·ces·tor**
ansestral : **an·ces·tral**
ansestry : **an·ces·try**
anshent : **an·cient**
ansiety : **an·xi·ety**
ansilary : **an·cil·lary**
ansillary : **an·cil·lary**
ansor : **an·swer**
an·swer
ant (insect); **aunt** (female relative)
antaganist : **an·tag·o·nist**
antaggonist : **an·tag·o·nist**
antaginist : **an·tag·o·nist**
an·tag·o·nist
antamology : **en·to·mol·o·gy** (study of insects) *or* **et·y·mol·o·gy** (study of words)
ant·arc·tic
antartic : **ant·arc·tic**
antecedant : **an·te·ced·ent**
an·te·ced·ent
anteceedent : **an·te·ced·ent**
antemology : **en·to·mol·o·gy** (study of insects) *or*

et·y·mol·o·gy (study of words)
antena : **an·ten·na**
an·ten·na
antesedent : **an·te·ced·ent**
antham : **an·them**
an·them
anthim : **an·them**
antholagy : **an·thol·o·gy**
anthollogy : **an·thol·o·gy**
an·thol·o·gy
anthum : **an·them**
antic (clownish); **an·tique** (old)
anticedent : **an·te·ced·ent**
anticepate : **an·ti·ci·pate**
anticipait : **an·ti·ci·pate**
an·ti·ci·pate
an·ti·dote (remedy); **an·ec·dote** (story)
an·tique (old); **an·tic** (clownish)
antisipate : **an·ti·ci·pate**
antissipate : **an·ti·ci·pate**
antomology : **en·to·mol·o·gy** (study of insects) *or* **et·y·mol·o·gy** (study of words)
anual : **an·nu·al**
anxiaty : **an·xi·ety**
an·xi·ety
anxioty : **an·xi·ety**
any·body (any person); **any body** (any body at all)
any·one (any person); **any one** (any item)
Apache
Apachee : **Apache**
apachure : **ap·er·ture**
Apalachian : **Ap·pa·la·chian**
apalogize : **apol·o·gize**
Apamattox : **Ap·po·mat·tox**
aparatus : **ap·pa·ra·tus**
aparel : **ap·par·el**

aparent : **ap•par•ent**
aparint : **ap•par•ent**
apart
aparteid : **apart•heid**
apart•heid
aparthide : **apart•heid**
aparthied : **apart•heid**
apartide : **apart•heid**
apastasy : **apos•ta•sy**
Apatche : **Apache**
ap•a•thet•ic
apathetick : **ap•a•thet•ic**
apa•thy
apatite : **ap•pe•tite**
apature : **ap•er•ture**
apeace : **apiece**
apeal : **ap•peal**
apease : **ap•pease**
apeice : **apiece**
Apelachian : **Ap•pa•la•chian**
apendage : **ap•pend•age**
apendectomy :
   ap•pen•dec•to•my
apendege : **ap•pend•age**
apera : **op•era**
aperchure : **ap•er•ture**
ap•er•ture
apethetic : **ap•a•thet•ic**
apethy : **apa•thy**
apetite : **ap•pe•tite**
apeture : **ap•er•ture**
aphasea : **apha•sia**
aphasha : **apha•sia**
apha•sia
apherism : **aph•o•rism**
aphirism : **aph•o•rism**
aph•o•rism
apiece
apindectomy :
   ap•pen•dec•to•my
apithy : **apa•thy**
apitite : **ap•pe•tite**

aplaud : **ap•plaud**
apliance : **ap•pli•ance**
apocalips : **apoc•a•lypse**
apocalipse : **apoc•a•lypse**
apoc•a•lypse
apocelypse : **apoc•a•lypse**
apockalypse : **apoc•a•lypse**
apockriphal : **apoc•ry•phal**
apockryphal : **apoc•ry•phal**
apocrifal : **apoc•ry•phal**
apocriphal : **apoc•ry•phal**
apocryfal : **apoc•ry•phal**
apoc•ry•phal
apointe : **ap•poin•tee**
apolagise : **apol•o•gize**
apolagize : **apol•o•gize**
apolegize : **apol•o•gize**
apologise (*Brit.*) : **apol•o•gize**
apol•o•gize
apolojize : **apol•o•gize**
Apomattox : **Ap•po•mat•tox**
aposle : **apos•tle**
apossel : **apos•tle**
apossle : **apos•tle**
aposstasy : **apos•ta•sy**
aposstle : **apos•tle**
apostacy : **apos•ta•sy**
apos•ta•sy
aposticy : **apos•ta•sy**
apostisy : **apos•ta•sy**
apos•tle
apos•tro•phe
appairel : **ap•par•el**
appairent : **ap•par•ent**
Appalachan : **Ap•pa•la•chian**
Appalachen : **Ap•pa•la•chian**
Ap•pa•la•chian
Appalachin : **Ap•pa•la•chian**
Appamattox : **Ap•po•mattox**
apparal : **ap•par•el**
apparant : **ap•par•ent**
apparatis : **ap•pa•ra•tus**

ap·pa·ra·tus
ap·par·el
ap·par·ent
apparil : ap·par·el
appart : apart
appartheid : apart·heid
appathetic : ap·a·thet·ic
appatite : ap·pe·tite
appatizing : ap·pe·tiz·ing
appeace : ap·pease
ap·peal
ap·pear·ance
appearanse : ap·pear·ance
appearant : ap·par·ent
appearence : ap·pear·ance
appearense : ap·pear·ance
ap·pease
appeerance : ap·pear·ance
appeil : ap·peal
appeirance : ap·pear·ance
appele : ap·peal
ap·pend·age
appendecktomy :
    ap·pen·dec·to·my
appendectome :
    ap·pen·dec·to·my
ap·pen·dec·to·my
appendege : ap·pend·age
appendidge : ap·pend·age
appendige : ap·pend·age
apperture : ap·er·ture
appetight : ap·pe·tite
appetising (*Brit.*) : ap·pe·tiz·ing
ap·pe·tite
ap·pe·tiz·ing
appettite : ap·pe·tite
appettizing : ap·pe·tiz·ing
appiece : apiece
appiese : ap·pease
appindage : ap·pend·age
appindectomie :
    ap·pen·dec·to·my

appindige : ap·pend·age
appitite : ap·pe·tite
appitizing : ap·pe·tiz·ing
ap·plaud
applawd : ap·plaud
ap·pli·ance
applianse : ap·pli·ance
applicabel : ap·pli·ca·ble
ap·pli·ca·ble
applicabul : ap·pli·ca·ble
appliceble : ap·pli·ca·ble
applicible : ap·pli·ca·ble
applickable : ap·pli·ca·ble
applience : ap·pli·ance
appliense : ap·pli·ance
applod : ap·plaud
applodd : ap·plaud
applyance : ap·pli·ance
appocryphal : apoc·ry·phal
ap·point·ee
appointie : ap·poin·tee
appointy : ap·poin·tee
appologize : apol·o·gize
Appomatox : Ap·po·mat·tox
Ap·po·mat·tox
appostasy : apos·ta·sy
appostrophe : apos·tro·phe
ap·praise (to assess); ap·prise
    (to inform); ap·prize (to
    value)
appreceate : ap·pre·ci·ate
ap·pre·ci·ate
ap·pre·ci·a·tion
appreeciate : ap·pre·ci·ate
apprentace : ap·pren·tice
apprentece : ap·pren·tice
ap·pren·tice
apprentiss : ap·pren·tice
appreshiate : ap·pre·ci·ate
appresiate : ap·pre·ci·ate
appricot : apri·cot
Appril : April

apprintice : **ap·pren·tice**
apprintiss : **ap·pren·tice**
ap·prise (to inform); **ap·praise** (to assess); **ap·prize** (to value)
ap·prize (to value); **ap·praise** (to assess); **ap·prise** (to inform)
ap·proach·able
approachibal : **ap·proach·able**
approachible : **ap·proach·able**
approachibul : **ap·proach·able**
approapriate : **ap·pro·pri·ate**
approchabal : **ap·proach·able**
approchable : **ap·proach·able**
approoval : **ap·prov·al**
appropiate : **ap·pro·pri·ate**
appropreate : **ap·pro·pri·ate**
appropreit : **ap·pro·pri·ate**
ap·pro·pri·ate
ap·prov·al
approvel : **ap·prov·al**
approvil : **ap·prov·al**
approxamate : **ap·prox·i·mate**
approxemate : **ap·prox·i·mate**
approximant : **ap·prox·i·mate**
approximat : **ap·prox·i·mate**
ap·prox·i·mate
approximent : **ap·prox·i·mate**
approximet : **ap·prox·i·mate**
apracot : **apri·cot**
apraise : **ap·praise** (to assess) *or* **ap·prise** (to inform) *or* **ap·prize** (to value)
apreciate : **ap·pre·ci·ate**
aprecot : **apri·cot**
aprentice : **ap·pren·tice**
apri·cot
apricott : **apri·cot**
April
Aprill : **April**

aprise : **ap·prise** (to inform) *or* **ap·prize** (to value)
aproachable : **ap·proach·able**
aprochable : **ap·proach·able**
aprooval : **ap·prov·al**
apropriate : **ap·pro·pri·ate**
aproval : **ap·prov·al**
aproxamate : **ap·prox·i·mate**
aproximate : **ap·prox·i·mate**
apsorb : **ab·sorb**
aptatude : **ap·ti·tude**
aptetude : **ap·ti·tude**
ap·ti·tude
aptutood : **ap·ti·tude**
apurture : **ap·er·ture**
aquaduct : **aq·ue·duct**
aquariam : **aquar·i·um**
aquariem : **aquar·i·um**
aquar·i·um
aquarrium : **aquar·i·um**
aqua·tic
aqueduck : **aq·ue·duct**
aq·ue·duct
aquerium : **aquar·i·um**
aquiduct : **aq·ue·duct**
aquiesce : **ac·qui·esce**
aquire : **ac·quire**
aquisition : **ac·qui·si·tion**
aquit : **ac·quit**
aquittel : **ac·quit·tal**
arabesk : **ar·a·besque**
ar·a·besque
araign : **ar·raign**
arange : **ar·range**
arangement : **ar·range·ment**
arber : **ar·bor**
ar·bor
ar·bo·re·al
arborial : **ar·bo·re·al**
arborreal : **ar·bo·re·al**
arborrial : **ar·bo·re·al**

arc (part of a circle); ark (boat or box)
arcaic : **ar·cha·ic**
arcangel : **arch·an·gel**
Arcansas : **Ar·kan·sas**
arceology : **ar·chae·ol·o·gy**
ar·chae·ol·o·gy *or*
   ar·che·ol·o·gy
ar·cha·ic
archake : **ar·cha·ic**
arch·an·gel
archangil : **arch·an·gel**
archangle : **arch·an·gel**
archanjel : **arch·an·gel**
archaque : **ar·cha·ic**
archatect : **ar·chi·tect**
archealogy : **ar·chae·ol·o·gy**
archeologgy : **ar·chae·ol·o·gy**
ar·che·ol·o·gy *or*
   ar·chae·ol·o·gy
archepelago : **ar·chi·pel·a·go**
archetect : **ar·chi·tect**
archiology : **ar·chae·ol·o·gy**
ar·chi·pel·a·go
archipelego : **ar·chi·pel·a·go**
archipellago : **ar·chi·pel·a·go**
ar·chi·tect
arcipelago : **ar·chi·pel·a·go**
arcitect : **ar·chi·tect**
arckaic : **ar·cha·ic**
arc·tic
arder : **ar·dor**
ar·dor
areal : **ae·ri·al**
areate : **aer·ate**
arebesk : **ar·a·besque**
arebesque : **ar·a·besque**
are·na
arenna : **are·na**
arest : **ar·rest**
arestocracy : **ar·is·toc·ra·cy**
Arezona : **Ar·i·zo·na**

argasy : **ar·go·sy**
argesy : **ar·go·sy**
argossy : **ar·go·sy**
ar·go·sy
arguement : **ar·gu·ment**
ar·gu·ment
arial : **ae·ri·al**
arid
arie : **ae·rie** (nest) *or* **airy**
   (relating to air)
arina : **are·na**
arise
aristockracy : **ar·is·toc·ra·cy**
ar·is·toc·ra·cy
aristocrasy : **ar·is·toc·ra·cy**
aristocricy : **ar·is·toc·ra·cy**
aristocrisy : **ar·is·toc·ra·cy**
arithmatic : **arith·me·tic**
arith·me·tic
arival : **ar·riv·al**
arive : **ar·rive**
Ar·i·zo·na
ark (boat or box); arc (part of
   a circle)
arkaic : **ar·cha·ic**
Arkansah : **Ar·kan·sas**
Ar·kan·sas
Arkansaw : **Ar·kan·sas**
arkeology : **ar·chae·ol·o·gy**
arkitect : **ar·chi·tect**
ar·ma·da
armadda : **ar·ma·da**
ar·ma·dil·lo
armadilo : **ar·ma·dil·lo**
armastice : **ar·mi·stice**
Armeania : **Ar·me·nia**
armedillo : **ar·ma·dil·lo**
Armenea : **Ar·me·nia**
Ar·me·nia
armer : **ar·mor**
armestice : **ar·mi·stice**
armidillo : **ar·ma·dil·lo**

Arminia : **Ar•me•nia**
ar•mi•stice
armistise : **ar•mi•stice**
armistiss : **ar•mi•stice**
ar•mor
armorda : **ar•ma•da**
armordillo : **ar•ma•dil•lo**
armour (*Brit.*) : **ar•mor**
arodinamic : **aero•dy•nam•ic**
arodynamic : **aero•dy•nam•ic**
arogant : **ar•ro•gant**
aro•ma
aronautic : **aero•nau•tic**
arose
arosol : **aero•sol**
around
arouse
aroyo : **ar•royo**
arragant : **ar•ro•gant**
arraighn : **ar•raign**
ar•raign
arrain : **ar•raign**
arraingement : **ar•range•ment**
ar•range
ar•range•ment
arrangemint : **ar•range•ment**
arrangment : **ar•range•ment**
arrena : **are•na**
ar•rest
arrid : **arid**
arrie : **ae•rie** (nest) *or* **airy**
   (relating to air)
arrina : **are•na**
arrise : **arise**
ar•ri•val
ar•rive
arrivel : **ar•riv•al**
arrivil : **ar•riv•al**
arrivle : **ar•riv•al**
arrodinamic : **aero•dy•nam•ic**
arrodynamic : **aero•dy•nam•ic**
ar•ro•gant

arrogent : **ar•ro•gant**
arroio : **ar•royo**
arroma : **aro•ma**
arronautic : **aero•nau•tic**
arrose : **arose**
arrosol : **aero•sol**
arround : **around**
arrouse : **arouse**
ar•royo
arsen : **ar•son**
ar•se•nal
arsenel : **ar•se•nal**
arsenle : **ar•se•nal**
arsin : **ar•son**
arsinal : **ar•se•nal**
arsinel : **ar•se•nal**
ar•son
artachoke : **ar•ti•choke**
artacle : **ar•ti•cle**
artafice : **ar•ti•fice**
artaficial : **ar•ti•fi•cial**
artechoke : **ar•ti•choke**
artefice : **ar•ti•fice**
arteficial : **ar•ti•fi•cial**
arterry : **ar•tery**
ar•tery
artharitis : **ar•thri•tis**
arthiritis : **ar•thri•tis**
arthritas : **ar•thri•tis**
ar•thri•tis
arthritus : **ar•thri•tis**
Ar•thur (name); **au•thor**
   (writer)
artic : **arc•tic**
artical : **ar•ti•cle**
articel : **ar•ti•cle**
artichoak : **ar•ti•choke**
ar•ti•choke
ar•ti•cle
ar•ti•fice
ar•ti•fi•cial
artifise : **ar•ti•fice**

artifishal : **ar·ti·fi·cial**
artifisial : **ar·ti·fi·cial**
artifrice : **ar·ti·fice**
artifricial : **ar·ti·fi·cial**
artilary : **ar·til·lery**
artilery : **ar·til·lery**
artillarry : **ar·til·lery**
artillary : **ar·til·lery**
ar·til·lery
artiry : **ar·tery**
ar·tis·ti·cal·ly
artisticly : **ar·tis·ti·cal·ly**
artory : **ar·tery**
asail : **as·sail**
asailant : **as·sail·ant**
asassin : **as·sas·sin**
asault : **as·sault**
as·cend
as·cen·sion
as·cent (act of going upward);
   as·sent (to agree; agreement)
ascerbic : **acer·bic**
ascert : **as·sert**
as·cer·tain
ascertane : **as·cer·tain**
as·cet·ic
asemble : **as·sem·ble**
asend : **as·cend**
aserbic : **acer·bic**
asert : **as·sert**
asertain : **as·cer·tain**
asess : **as·sess**
asessor : **as·ses·sor**
asetic : **as·cet·ic**
asfalt : **as·phalt**
asfault : **as·phalt**
asfixiate : **as·phyx·i·ate**
ashure : **azure**
asign : **as·sign**
asilim : **asy·lum**
asilum : **asy·lum**
asimilate : **as·sim·i·late**

asist : **as·sist**
asistance : **as·sis·tance**
asistant : **as·sis·tant**
asma : **asth·ma**
asociate : **as·so·ciate**
asparagis : **as·par·a·gus**
as·par·a·gus
asparegus : **as·par·a·gus**
asperagus : **as·par·a·gus**
asperin : **as·pi·rin**
asphallt : **as·phalt**
as·phalt
asphault : **as·phalt**
asphixeate : **as·phyx·i·ate**
asphixiate : **as·phyx·i·ate**
asphyxeate : **as·phyx·i·ate**
as·phyx·i·ate
aspicious : **aus·pi·cious**
aspiren : **as·pi·rin**
as·pi·rin
aspren : **as·pi·rin**
asprin : **as·pi·rin**
as·sail
as·sail·ant
assailent : **as·sail·ant**
assalant : **as·sail·ant**
assalent : **as·sail·ant**
assalt : **as·sault**
assasin : **as·sas·sin**
as·sas·sin
as·sas·sin·a·tion
as·sault
as·sem·ble
assend : **as·cend**
as·sent (to agree; agreement);
   as·cent (act of going upward)
as·sert
as·sess
assesser : **as·ses·sor**
assession : **ac·ces·sion**
as·sess·ment
as·ses·sor

as·sign
assimalate : as·sim·i·late
as·sim·i·late
assimmilate : as·sim·i·late
assine : as·sign
as·sist
as·sis·tance
as·sis·tant
assistence : as·sis·tance
assistense : as·sis·tance
assistent : as·sis·tant
assoceate : as·so·ciate
as·so·ciate
assosheate : as·so·ciate
assoshiate : as·so·ciate
asspirin : as·pi·rin
assteroid : as·ter·oid
assthma : asth·ma
asstrology : as·trol·o·gy
asstronomer : as·tron·o·mer
as·sume
as·sump·tion
assumtion : as·sump·tion
as·sur·ance
assurence : as·sur·ance
assylum : asy·lum
astaroid : as·ter·oid
astere : aus·tere
asteresk : as·ter·isk
as·ter·isk
asterix : as·ter·isk
as·ter·oid
asthema : asth·ma
asthetic : aes·thet·ic
asth·ma
Astralia : Aus·tral·ia
astralogy : as·trol·o·gy
astranaut : as·tro·naut
astranomer : as·tron·o·mer
Astria : Aus·tria
astrisk : as·ter·isk
astroid : as·ter·oid

astroknot : as·tro·naut
astrollogy : as·trol·o·gy
astrologgy : as·trol·o·gy
as·trol·o·gy
astronamer : as·tron·o·mer
as·tro·naut
astronemer : as·tron·o·mer
astronnomer : as·tron·o·mer
as·tron·o·mer
astronot : as·tro·naut
astronought : as·tro·naut
asume : as·sume
asumption : as·sump·tion
asurance : as·sur·ance
asylam : asy·lum
asylim : asy·lum
asy·lum
atainable : at·tain·able
atem : at·om
atemology : en·to·mol·o·gy
   (study of insects) *or*
   et·y·mol·o·gy (study of
   words)
atend : at·tend
athalete : ath·lete
athaletic : ath·let·ic
athelete : ath·lete
atheletic : ath·let·ic
athleet : ath·lete
ath·lete
ath·let·ic
athlettic : ath·let·ic
athority : au·thor·i·ty
atitude : at·ti·tude
atmasphere : at·mo·sphere
atmesphere : at·mo·sphere
atmosfere : at·mo·sphere
atmospere : at·mo·sphere
atmosphear : at·mo·sphere
atmospheer : at·mo·sphere
at·mo·sphere
at·om

atonomy : **au•ton•o•my**
atorney : **at•tor•ney**
atrocety : **atroc•i•ty**
atrochious : **atro•cious**
atro•cious
atrocitty : **atroc•i•ty**
atroc•i•ty
atrocius : **atro•cious**
atroshious : **atro•cious**
atrosity : **atroc•i•ty**
attainabal : **at•tain•able**
attainabel : **at•tain•able**
at•tain•able
attaineble : **at•tain•able**
attainible : **at•tain•able**
attanable : **at•tain•able**
attatude : **at•ti•tude**
at•tend
at•tend•ance
at•tend•ant
attendence : **at•tend•ance**
attendent : **at•tend•ant**
atterney : **at•tor•ney**
atterneys : **at•tor•neys**
atternies : **at•tor•neys**
attierney : **at•tor•ney**
at•ti•tude
attom : **at•om**
attornees : **at•tor•neys**
at•tor•ney
at•tor•neys
attornies : **at•tor•neys**
attorny : **at•tor•ney**
atymology : **en•to•mol•o•gy**
(study of insects) *or*
et•y•mol•o•gy (study of
words)
auc•tion•eer
auctioneir : **auc•tion•eer**
auctionier : **auc•tion•eer**
audable : **au•di•ble**
audacety : **au•dac•i•ty**

au•da•cious
audacitty : **au•dac•i•ty**
au•dac•i•ty
audashious : **au•da•cious**
audasious : **au•da•cious**
audasity : **au•dac•i•ty**
audassity : **au•dac•i•ty**
audatious : **au•da•cious**
audiance : **au•di•ence**
aud•i•ble
au•di•ence
auditer : **au•di•tor**
au•di•tor
au•ger (drilling tool); **au•gur**
(to predict)
au•gur (to predict); **au•ger**
(drilling tool)
auktioneer : **auc•tion•eer**
aunt (female relative); **ant**
(insect)
aurthor : **au•thor**
auspichious : **aus•pi•cious**
aus•pi•cious
auspicius : **aus•pi•cious**
auspisious : **aus•pi•cious**
auspitious : **aus•pi•cious**
Ausstralia : **Aus•tral•ia**
Ausstria : **Aus•tria**
austair : **aus•tere**
austare : **aus•tere**
austeer : **aus•tere**
austeir : **aus•tere**
aus•tere
austier : **aus•tere**
Aus•tral•ia (continent);
Aus•tria (European nation)
Aus•tria (European nation);
Aus•tral•ia (continent)
autharize : **au•thor•ize**
authenic : **au•then•tic**
au•then•tic
auther : **au•thor**

autherize : **au·thor·ize**
au·thor (writer); **Ar·thur**
  (name)
authoraty : **au·thor·i·ty**
authorety : **au·thor·i·ty**
authorise (*Brit.*) : **au·thor·ize**
authoritty : **au·thor·i·ty**
au·thor·i·ty
au·thor·ize
autioneer : **auc·tion·eer**
au·to·mat·i·cal·ly
automaticly : **au·to·mat·i·cal·ly**
automn : **au·tumn**
autonnomy : **au·ton·o·my**
autonome : **au·ton·o·my**
autonomie : **au·ton·o·my**
au·ton·o·my
autum : **au·tumn**
autumm : **au·tumn**
au·tumn
auxilary : **aux·il·ia·ry**
aux·il·ia·ry
auxilliary : **aux·il·ia·ry**
avacado : **av·o·ca·do**
availabal : **avail·able**
avail·able
availible : **avail·able**
avalable : **avail·able**
avalanch : **av·a·lanche**
av·a·lanche
avaleable : **avail·able**
avant-garde
avant-guard : **avant-garde**
avanue : **av·e·nue**
av·a·rice
avarise : **av·a·rice**
avariss : **av·a·rice**
avaunt-garde : **avant-garde**
aveator : **avi·a·tor**
avecado : **av·o·ca·do**
avelanche : **av·a·lanche**
avenoo : **av·e·nue**

aventurer : **ad·ven·tur·er**
av·e·nue
av·er·age
averedge : **av·er·age**
averege : **av·er·age**
averice : **av·a·rice**
averige : **av·er·age**
averise : **av·a·rice**
averse (disinclined); **ad·verse**
  (unfavorable)
avertise : **ad·ver·tise**
avertising : **ad·ver·tis·ing**
aviater : **avi·a·tor**
aviatir : **avi·a·tor**
avi·a·tor
avid
avilanche : **av·a·lanche**
avinue : **av·e·nue**
avirage : **av·er·age**
avocaddo : **av·o·ca·do**
av·o·ca·do
avoidabel : **avoid·able**
avoid·able
avoid·ance
avoidanse : **avoid·ance**
avoidence : **avoid·ance**
avoidense : **avoid·ance**
avoidible : **avoid·able**
avrage : **av·er·age**
avvid : **avid**
awaikening : **awak·en·ing**
awairness : **aware·ness**
await
awak·en·ing
awakining : **awak·en·ing**
awakning : **awak·en·ing**
aware·ness
awareniss : **aware·ness**
awarness : **aware·ness**
awate : **await**
awesom : **awe·some**
awe·some

awesume : **awe•some**

awsome : **awe•some**

axcel : **ax•le** (wheel shaft) *or* **ex•cel** (to be superior)

axel : **ax•le** (wheel shaft) *or* **ex•cel** (to be superior)

axelerate : **ac•cel•erate**

ax•le (wheel shaft); **ex•cel** (to be superior)

azailea : **aza•lea**

aza•lea

azalia : **aza•lea**

azhure : **azure**

azma : **asth•ma**

azthetic : **aes•thet•ic**

azthma : **asth•ma**

azure

B

Babalon : **Bab·y·lon**
babbies : **ba·bies**
babboon : **ba·boon**
babby : **ba·by**
Babbylon : **Bab·y·lon**
Babelon : **Bab·y·lon**
Babillon : **Bab·y·lon**
ba·boon
babtise : **bap·tize**
babtism : **bap·tism**
Babtist : **Bap·tist**
ba·by
Bab·y·lon
babys : **ba·bies**
bacalaureate : **bac·ca·lau·re·ate**
bacan : **ba·con**
bac·ca·lau·re·ate
baccalaureit : **bac·ca·lau·re·ate**
baccalauriate : **bac·ca·lau·re·ate**
baccaloreate : **bac·ca·lau·re·ate**
baccelaureate :
    bac·ca·lau·re·ate
bacchelor : **bach·el·or**
baccilli : **ba·cil·li**
baccilly : **ba·cil·li**
baccon : **ba·con**
baceball : **base·ball**
baceless : **base·less**
bacement : **base·ment**
bacen : **ba·con**
bachalor : **bach·e·lor**
bacheler : **bach·e·lor**
bachelir : **bach·e·lor**
bach·e·lor
bachelore : **bach·e·lor**
bachteria : **bac·te·ri·a**
bachterium : **bac·te·ri·um**
bacically : **ba·si·cal·ly**
bacili : **ba·cil·li**
bacilica : **ba·sil·i·ca**

ba·cil·li (*plur.*); **ba·cil·lus** (*sing.*)
ba·cil·lus (*sing.*); **ba·cil·li** (*plur.*)
bacilus : **ba·cil·lus**
bacin : **ba·sin**
bacinet : **bas·si·net**
bacis : **ba·sis**
backalaureate :
    bac·ca·lau·re·ate
backen : **ba·con**
backfeild : **back·field**
back·field
backgamen : **back·gam·mon**
backgamman : **back·gam·mon**
backgammen : **back·gam·mon**
backgammin : **back·gam·mon**
back·gam·mon
back·ground
backround : **back·ground**
backterea : **bac·te·ri·a**
backteria : **bac·te·ri·a**
backteriem : **bac·te·ri·um**
backterium : **bac·te·ri·um**
back·ward
backwerd : **back·ward**
backword : **back·ward**
backwurd : **back·ward**
ba·con
bactearia : **bac·te·ria**
bactearium : **bac·te·ri·um**
bacterea : **bac·te·ria**
bactereum : **bac·te·ri·um**
bac·te·ria (*plur.*); **bac·te·ri·um**
    (*sing.*)
bac·te·ri·um (*sing.*); **bac·te·ria**
    (*plur.*)
bacterrea : **bac·te·ria**
bacterreum : **bac·te·ri·um**
bacterrium : **bac·te·ri·um**
bactiria : **bac·te·ria**
bactirium : **bac·te·ri·um**

baddinage : **ba·di·nage**
baddly : **bad·ly**
baddminton : **bad·min·ton**
badely : **bad·ly**
badenage : **ba·di·nage**
badenoge : **ba·di·nage**
badge
badinadge : **ba·di·nage**
ba·di·nage
badinoge : **ba·di·nage**
badlly : **bad·ly**
bad·ly
bad·min·ton
badmiton : **bad·min·ton**
badmitten : **bad·min·ton**
badmitton : **bad·min·ton**
bafel : **baf·fle**
baffel : **baf·fle**
baf·fle
bafful : **baf·fle**
bafle : **baf·fle**
bagage : **bag·gage**
bagaje : **bag·gage**
bage : **badge**
bagege : **bag·gage**
bager : **bad·ger**
baggadge : **bag·gage**
bag·gage
baggaje : **bag·gage**
baggege : **bag·gage**
baggie : **bag·gy**
bag·gy
bagy : **bag·gy**
bail (to get out of jail; to
    remove water); **bale** (hay)
bailef : **bai·liff**
baileff : **bai·liff**
bailif : **bai·liff**
bai·liff
baist : **baste**
bait (lure); **bate** (to subside)
baje : **badge**

bajer : **bad·ger**
bakary : **bak·ery**
bakeing : **bak·ing**
baken : **ba·con**
bak·er
bakerry : **bak·ery**
bak·ing
bakker : **bak·er**
balad : **bal·lad**
bal·ance
balanse : **bal·ance**
balast : **bal·last**
balck : **balk**
bal·co·nies
balconnies : **bal·co·nies**
balconny : **bal·co·ny**
bal·co·ny
baldnes : **bald·ness**
bald·ness
baldnis : **bald·ness**
baldniss : **bald·ness**
bale (hay); **bail** (to get out of
    jail; to remove water)
baled : **bal·lad**
balence : **bal·ance**
balerena : **bal·le·ri·na**
balerina : **bal·le·ri·na**
balet : **bal·let**
balif : **bai·liff**
baliff : **bai·liff**
balist : **bal·last**
balit : **bal·lot**
balk
balkonies : **bal·co·nies**
balkonnies : **bal·co·nies**
balkonny : **bal·co·ny**
balkony : **bal·co·ny**
balkonys : **bal·co·nies**
bal·lad
ballance : **bal·ance**
ballarena : **bal·le·ri·na**
ballarina : **bal·le·ri·na**

bal·last
ballat : bal·let
ballay : bal·let
balled : bal·lad
ballence : bal·ance
ballerena : bal·le·ri·na
bal·le·ri·na
ballest : bal·last
bal·let (dance); bal·lot (vote)
balley : bal·let
ballid : bal·lad
ballist : bal·last
ballit : bal·lot
bal·loon
bal·lot (vote); bal·let (dance)
ballote : bal·lot
ballsa : bal·sa
ballsah : bal·sa
ballsam : bal·sam
ballsum : bal·sam
Balltimore : Bal·ti·more
ballud : bal·lad
ballune : bal·loon
ballust : bal·last
balmy
baloon : bal·loon
baloone : bal·loon
balot : ball·let (dance) or
    bal·lot (vote)
bal·sa
balsah : bal·sa
bal·sam
balsum : bal·sam
Baltemore : Bal·ti·more
Bal·ti·more
bam·boo
bambu : bam·boo
bambue : bam·boo
bammboo : bam·boo
bammy : balmy
ba·nal
ba·nana

bananah : ba·nana
bananna : ba·nana
banche : ban·shee
banchee : ban·shee
bandadge : ban·dage
ban·dage
bandaje : ban·dage
ban·dana or ban·dan·na
ban·dan·na or ban·dana
bandedge : ban·dage
bandege : ban·dage
bandeje : ban·dage
bandet : ban·dit
bandetry : ban·dit·ry
bandidge : ban·dage
bandige : ban·dage
ban·dit
banditery : ban·dit·ry
banditt : ban·dit
bandittry : ban·dit·ry
bandwagen : band·wag·on
bandwaggen : band·wag·on
bandwaggon : band·wag·on
band·wag·on
banel : ba·nal
baner : ban·ner
banesh : ban·ish
bangel : ban·gle
ban·gle
bangul : ban·gle
ban·ish
bankrubt : bank·rupt
bankrupcy : bank·rupt·cy
bank·rupt
bank·rupt·cy
bankwet : ban·quet
bankwit : ban·quet
bannal : ba·nal
bannana : ba·nana
bannanna : ba·nana
bannar : ban·ner
bannditry : ban·dit·ry

ban•ner
banngle : ban•gle
bannir : ban•ner
bannish : ban•ish
ban•quet (feast); ban•quette
   (bench)
ban•quette (bench); ban•quet
   (feast)
banquit : ban•quet
banqwit : ban•quet
banshe : ban•shee
ban•shee
banshie : ban•shee
banshy : ban•shee
ban•tam
bantem : ban•tam
bantim : ban•tam
bantum : ban•tam
ban•zai (cheer); bon•sai (dwarf
   tree)
banzi : ban•zai (cheer) or
   bon•sai (dwarf tree)
banzie : ban•zai (cheer) or
   bon•sai (dwarf tree)
baonet : bay•o•net
Baptest : Bap•tist
baptise (Brit.) : bap•tize
baptisim : bap•tism
bap•tism
Bap•tist
baptysm : bap•tism
baracade : bar•ri•cade
baracks : bar•racks
baracuda : bar•ra•cu•da
barage : bar•rage
baratone : bar•i•tone
barbacue : bar•be•cue
barbaque : bar•be•cue
barbarean : bar•bar•i•an
bar•bar•i•an
barbearian : bar•bar•i•an
bar•be•cue

barbequ : bar•be•cue
barbeque : bar•be•cue
barberian : bar•bar•i•an
barbicue : bar•be•cue
barbique : bar•be•cue
bare (uncovered); bear
   (animal); bear (to carry)
bare•back
bare•faced
barefased : bare•faced
bare•foot
bare•hand•ed
barel : bar•rel
bare•ly (just enough); bar•ley
   (grain)
baren : bar•on
bareness : bar•on•ess
   (noblewoman) or
   bar•ren•ness (emptiness)
baretone : bar•i•tone
barette : bar•rette
bar•gain
bargan : bar•gain
barge
bargen : bar•gain
bargin : bar•gain
bargun : bar•gain
barier : bar•ri•er
baritoan : bar•i•tone
bar•i•tone
barje : barge
bar•ley (grain); bare•ly (just
   enough)
barnacel : bar•na•cle
bar•na•cle
barnakel : bar•na•cle
barnakle : bar•na•cle
barnuckle : bar•na•cle
barnukle : bar•na•cle
baroak : ba•roque
baroke : ba•roque
ba•rom•e•ter

baromiter : **ba·rom·e·ter**
bar·on (nobleman); **bar·ren**
   (unproductive)
bar·on·ess (noblewoman);
   bar·ren·ness (emptiness)
baronness : **bar·on·ess**
   (noblewoman) *or*
   bar·ren·ness (emptiness)
baroom : **bar·room**
baroqe : **ba·roque**
ba·roque
barracade : **bar·ri·cade**
barracaid : **bar·ri·cade**
bar·racks
barracooda : **bar·ra·cu·da**
bar·ra·cu·da
bar·rage
barrahge : **bar·rage**
barraks : **bar·racks**
barrakuda : **bar·ra·cu·da**
barratone : **bar·i·tone**
barrbarian : **bar·bar·i·an**
barrecade : **bar·ri·cade**
barrecks : **bar·racks**
barreir : **bar·ri·er**
bar·rel
bar·ren (unproductive); **bar·on**
   (nobleman)
barreness : **bar·on·ess**
   (noblewoman) *or*
   bar·ren·ness (emptiness)
bar·ren·ness (emptiness);
   bar·on·ess (noblewoman)
barret : **bar·rette**
barrete : **bar·rette**
barrett : **bar·rette**
bar·rette
bar·ri·cade
barricaid : **bar·ri·cade**
barricks : **bar·racks**
bar·ri·er
barrikade : **bar·ri·cade**

barril : **bar·rel**
barritone : **bar·i·tone**
barrometer : **ba·rom·e·ter**
barroness : **bar·on·ess**
   (noblewoman) *or*
   bar·ren·ness (emptiness)
barronness : **bar·on·ess**
barron : **bar·on**
bar·room
barry : **ber·ry** (fruit) *or* **bury**
   (to cover with earth)
bary : **ber·ry** (fruit) *or* **bury** (to
   cover with earth)
baryl : **ber·yl**
barytone : **bar·i·tone**
ba·salt
basault : **ba·salt**
basball : **base·ball**
base·ball
base·less
baselica : **ba·sil·i·ca**
baseliss : **base·less**
base·ment
basemint : **base·ment**
basen : **ba·sin**
ba·ses (*plur.*); **ba·sis** (*sing.*)
bash·ful
bashfull : **bash·ful**
ba·si·cal·ly
basicaly : **ba·si·cal·ly**
basicly : **ba·si·cal·ly**
basikally : **ba·si·cal·ly**
basileca : **ba·sil·i·ca**
basili : **ba·cil·li**
ba·sil·i·ca
basilika : **ba·sil·i·ca**
basilli : **ba·cil·li**
basillica : **ba·sil·i·ca**
basillus : **ba·cil·lus**
basilus : **ba·cil·lus**
ba·sin
basinet : **bas·si·net**

ba•sis (*sing.*); ba•ses (*plur.*)
Bask : **Basque**
baskette : **bas•ket**
baskit : **bas•ket**
baskitball : **bas•ket•ball**
basless : **base•less**
basment : **base•ment**
basoon : **bas•soon**
Basque
bassalt : **ba•salt**
bassenet : **bas•si•net**
bassili : **ba•cil•li**
bassilus : **ba•cil•lus**
bassin : **ba•sin**
bas•si•net
bassinette : **bas•si•net**
bassis : **ba•sis**
bassket : **bas•ket**
bassketball : **bas•ket•ball**
bas•soon
basstard : **bas•tard**
Basstille : **Bas•tille**
bast : **baste**
bast•ard
baste
Basteel : **Bas•tille**
Bastele : **Bas•tille**
basterd : **bas•tard**
Bas•tille
bastird : **bas•tard**
basune : **bas•soon**
bata : **be•ta**
bataleon : **bat•tal•ion**
batalion : **bat•tal•ion**
batary : **bat•tery**
batchelor : **bach•el•or**
bate (to subside); **bait** (lure)
Baten Rouge : **Ba•ton Rouge**
baten : **ba•ton**
bater : **bat•ter**
batery : **bat•tery**
bath (*noun*); **bathe** (*verb*)

bathe (*verb*); **bath** (*noun*)
Ba•ton Rouge
Baton Ruge : **Ba•ton Rouge**
ba•ton
battal : **bat•tle**
bat•tal•ion
battallion : **bat•tal•ion**
battary : **bat•tery**
battel : **bat•tle**
battelion : **bat•tal•ion**
bat•ter
batterry : **bat•tery**
bat•tery
bat•tle
battleon : **bat•tal•ion**
Batton Rouge : **Ba•ton Rouge**
batton : **ba•ton**
bauball : **bau•ble**
baubble : **bau•ble**
baubel : **bau•ble**
bau•ble
baucite : **baux•ite**
baudy : **bawdy**
bauk : **balk**
bauxcite : **baux•ite**
baux•ite
bawdie : **bawdy**
bawdy
bayenette : **bay•o•net**
bayinet : **bay•o•net**
bay•o•net
bayonnet : **bay•o•net**
bayoo : **bay•ou**
bay•ou
Bayrut : **Bei•rut**
ba•zaar (a fair); **bi•zarre**
  (strange)
bazar : **ba•zaar** (a fair) *or*
  bi•zarre (strange)
ba•zoo•ka
bazuka : **ba•zoo•ka**
bazzooka : **ba•zoo•ka**

beacan : **bea•con**
beach (shore); **beech** (tree)
beachead : **beach•head**
beach•head
beachnut : **beech•nut**
beacin : **bea•con**
beacker : **beak•er**
bea•con
beaditude : **be•at•i•tude**
beaf : **beef**
beagel : **bea•gle**
bea•gle
beagul : **bea•gle**
bea•ker
beakon : **bea•con**
beam
bear (animal); **bear** (to carry);
   bare (uncovered)
bearacade : **bar•ri•cade**
bearacuda : **bar•ra•cu•da**
bearback : **bare•back**
beard
bearfaced : **bare•faced**
bearfoot : **barefoot**
bearhanded : **bare•hand•ed**
bearly : **bare•ly**
bearometer : **ba•rom•e•ter**
bearrel : **bar•rel**
bearrier : **bar•ri•er**
beast
beastial : **bes•tial**
beat (to strike or to defeat);
   beet (plant)
beatatude : **be•at•i•tude**
beatician : **beau•ti•cian**
beatitood : **be•at•i•tude**
be•at•i•tude
beatle : **bee•tle**
beattitude : **be•at•i•tude**
beau•ti•cian
beautition : **beau•ti•cian**
beautty : **beau•ty**

beautycian : **beau•ti•cian**
bea•ver
becase : **be•cause**
becauze : **be•cause**
becawse : **be•cause**
becuz : **be•cause**
beddlam : **bed•lam**
Beddouin : **Bed•ou•in**
beddspread : **bedspread**
beddstead : **bed•stead**
bed•lam
bedlem : **bed•lam**
bedlum : **bed•lam**
Bedoin : **Bed•ou•in**
Bed•ou•in
Bedowin : **Bed•ou•in**
bed•spread
bedspred : **bed•spread**
bedsted : **bed•stead**
beech (tree); **beach** (shore)
beechhead : **beach•head**
beech•nut
beecon : **bea•con**
beef
beefs *or* **beeves**
beegle : **bea•gle**
beeker : **beak•er**
beekon : **bea•con**
beem : **beam**
beer (brewed drink); **bier**
   (funeral stand)
beerd : **beard**
beest : **beast**
beestial : **bes•tial**
beet (plant); **beat** (to strike or
   to defeat)
beetel : **bee•tle**
beet•le
beever : **bea•ver**
beeves *or* **beefs**
befoar : **be•fore**
befor : **be•fore**

be·foul
befour : be·fore
befowl : be·foul
beger : beg·gar
beg·gar
begger : beg·gar
beggin : be·gin
begginner : be·gin·ner
begginning : be·gin·ning
beggotten : be·got·ten
begguile : be·guile
begial : be·guile
begile : be·guile
be·gin
beginer : be·gin·ner
begining : be·gin·ning
beginn : be·gin
be·go·nia
begonnia : be·go·nia
begonya : be·go·nia
begoten : be·got·ten
begottin : be·got·ten
be·grudge
begrudje : be·grudge
begruge : be·grudge
be·guile
be·hav·ior
behaviour (*Brit.*) : be·hav·ior
beheemoth : be·he·moth
be·he·moth
behemuth : be·he·moth
beig : beige
beige
beighe : beige
beije : beige
beird : beard
Beiroot : Bei·rut
Bei·rut
beish : beige
beknighted : be·night·ed
bekweath : be·queath
beleaf : be·lief

beleager : be·lea·guer
be·lea·guer
beleagur : be·lea·guer
beleavable : be·liev·able
beleave : be·lieve
beleef : be·lief
beleeger : be·lea·guer
beleevable : be·liev·able
beleeve : be·lieve
beleif : be·lief
beleivable : be·liev·able
beleive : be·lieve
Belgem : Bel·gium
Belgim : Bel·gium
Bel·gium
Belgum : Bel·gium
belicose : bel·li·cose
believabel : be·liev·able
be·liev·able
believeble : be·liev·able
beligerent : bel·lig·er·ent
Beljim : Bel·gium
Beljum : Bel·gium
belkonies : bal·co·nies
belkony : bal·co·ny
belleaguer : be·lea·guer
bellegerent : bel·lig·er·ent
Bellgium : Bel·gium
bellicoce : bel·li·cose
bel·li·cose
belligerant : bel·lig·er·ent
bel·lig·er·ent
belligerint : bel·lig·er·ent
bellijerent : bel·lig·er·ent
bellikose : bel·li·cose
bellweather : bell·weth·er
bell·weth·er
beloe : be·low
be·low
belweather : bell·weth·er
belwether : bell·weth·er
bemewsed : be·mused

bemoosed : **be·mused**
be·mused
bemussed : **be·mused**
bemuzed : **be·mused**
benadiction : **ben·e·dic·tion**
benafactor : **ben·e·fac·tor**
benafit : **ben·e·fit**
benal : **ba·nal**
benall : **ba·nal**
benana : **ba·nana**
be·neath
beneathe : **be·neath**
benedicktion : **ben·e·dic·tion**
ben·e·dic·tion
beneeth : **be·neath**
benefacent : **be·nef·i·cent**
ben·e·fac·tor
benefaktor : **ben·e·fac·tor**
benefet : **ben·e·fit**
be·nef·i·cent
benefiscent : **be·nef·i·cent**
benefisent : **be·nef·i·cent**
ben·e·fit
benevolant : **be·nev·o·lent**
be·nev·o·lent
benidiction : **ben·e·dic·tion**
benificent : **be·nef·i·cent**
benifit : **ben·e·fit**
be·night·ed
benightid : **be·night·ed**
benited : **be·night·ed**
bennediction : **ben·e·dic·tion**
bennefactor : **ben·e·fac·tor**
benneficent : **be·nef·i·cent**
bennefit : **ben·e·fit**
bennzene : **ben·zene**
benzean : **ben·zene**
benzeen : **ben·zene**
ben·zene
benzine : **ben·zene**
beqeath : **be·queath**
be·queath

bequeathe : **be·queath**
bequeeth : **be·queath**
beracuda : **bar·ra·cu·da**
beray : **be·ret**
be·reaved
bereeved : **be·reaved**
bereived : **be·reaved**
be·ret
berey : **be·ret**
berieved : **be·reaved**
beril : **ber·yl**
beroque : **ba·roque**
berrage : **bar·rage**
berrel : **bar·rel**
berrier : **bar·ri·er**
berril : **ber·yl**
ber·ry (fruit); **bury** (to cover
    with earth)
ber·serk
bersirk : **ber·serk**
bersurk : **ber·serk**
berth (bed); **birth** (to be born)
Berut : **Bei·rut**
bery : **ber·ry**
ber·yl
beryll : **ber·yl**
berzerk : **ber·serk**
besalt : **ba·salt**
beseach : **be·seech**
be·seech
beseege : **be·siege**
beseich : **be·seech**
beseige : **be·siege**
beserk : **ber·serk**
besiech : **be·seech**
be·siege
besmearch : **be·smirch**
besmerch : **be·smirch**
be·smirch
besmurch : **be·smirch**
bestal : **bes·tial**
bes·tial

bestoe : **be•stow**
be•stow
bestowe : **be•stow**
be•ta
beter : **bet•ter**
Bethlahem : **Beth•le•hem**
Beth•le•hem
Bethlihem : **Beth•le•hem**
betta : **be•ta**
bet•ter
betwean : **be•tween**
be•tween
betwein : **be•tween**
beuaty : **beau•ty**
beutician : **beau•ti•cian**
beuty : **beau•ty**
beval : **bev•el**
bevarage : **bev•er•age**
bev•el
bevelle : **bev•el**
bev•er•age
beveredge : **bev•er•age**
beverege : **bev•er•age**
bevirage : **bev•er•age**
bevvel : **bev•el**
bevvy : **bevy**
bevy
be•wail
bewair : **be•ware**
bewale : **be•wail**
be•ware
bewear : **be•ware**
bewhale : **be•wail**
bewhich : **be•witch**
bewich : **be•witch**
be•witch
bezooka : **ba•zoo•ka**
bi•as
bi•ased
biassed : **bi•ased**
Bibble : **Bi•ble**
bibbliography : **bib•li•og•ra•phy**

Bibel : **Bi•ble**
Bi•ble
bibleography : **bib•li•og•ra•phy**
bibliografy : **bib•li•og•ra•phy**
bib•li•og•ra•phy
bibliogrephy : **bib•li•og•ra•phy**
bibliogrify : **bib•li•og•ra•phy**
bibliogriphy : **bib•li•og•ra•phy**
bi•cy•cle
bi•cy•clist
biege : **beige**
bier (funeral stand); **beer**
  (brewed drink)
Bierut : **Bei•rut**
bieuty : **beau•ty**
bigonia : **be•go•nia**
bi•o•chem•ist
bious : **bi•as**
bioused : **bi•ased**
birth (to be born); **berth** (bed)
bius : **bi•as**
biused : **bi•ased**
biwitch : **be•witch**
Bizantine : **Byz•an•tine**
boalder : **boul•der**
boar (male pig); **boor**
  (ill-mannered person); **bore**
  (to drill a hole; to cause
  boredom; one who bores)
board
Boardeaux : **Bor•deaux**
board•er (renter); **bor•der**
  (boundary)
boarderline : **bor•der•line**
boardom : **bore•dom**
boast
boatanical : **bo•tan•i•cal**
bobble : **bau•ble**
boddy : **bawdy** (lewd) *or* **body**
  (corpus)
body
boemian : **bo•he•mi•an**

bogis : **bo·gus**
bo·gus
boheemian : **bo·he·mi·an**
bo·he·mi·an
boicott : **boy·cott**
Boi·se
Boisee : **Boi·se**
boisenbery : **boy·sen·ber·ry**
boiserus : **bois·ter·ous**
Boisie : **Boi·se**
boisonberry : **boy·sen·ber·ry**
bois·ter·ous
boistrous : **bois·ter·ous**
bokay : **bou·quet**
bol·der (more fearless);
    boul·der (rock)
bollsa : **bal·sa**
bollsam : **bal·sam**
bolsa : **bal·sa**
bolsa : **bal·sam**
bombadeer : **bom·bar·dier**
bombadier : **bom·bar·dier**
bombardeer : **bom·bar·dier**
bombardeir : **bom·bar·dier**
bom·bar·dier
bomb·er
bomberdier : **bom·bar·dier**
bomboo : **bam·boo**
bommer : **bomb·er**
bonannza : **bo·nan·za**
bo·nan·za
bon·dage
bondaje : **bond·age**
bondedge : **bond·age**
bondege : **bond·age**
bondige : **bond·age**
bonet : **bon·net**
boney : **bony**
bonis : **bo·nus**
bonnanza : **bo·nan·za**
bon·net
bonnit : **bon·net**

bonnus : **bo·nus**
bon·sai (dwarf tree); **ban·zai**
    (cheer)
bo·nus
bony
bonzai : **ban·zai** (cheer) *or*
    bon·sai (dwarf tree)
bonzi : **ban·zai** (cheer) *or*
    bon·sai (dwarf tree)
boobonic : **bu·bon·ic**
bookeeper : **book·keep·er**
book·keep·er
boomarang : **boom·er·ang**
boom·er·ang
boor (ill-mannered person);
    boar (male pig); **bore** (to
    drill a hole; to cause
    boredom; one who bores)
boor·ish
boo·tee *or* **boo·tie** (baby shoe);
    boo·ty (spoils of war)
boo·ty (spoils of war); **boo·tee**
    (baby shoe)
booz : **booze**
booze
boquay : **bou·quet**
boquet : **bou·quet**
borbon : **bour·bon**
bord : **board**
borde : **board**
Bor·deaux
bor·der (boundary); **board·er**
    (renter)
bor·der·line
Bordeux : **Bor·deaux**
Bordieux : **Bor·deaux**
Bordoe : **Bor·deaux**
bordom : **bore·dom**
bore (to drill a hole; to cause
    boredom; one who bores);
    boar (male pig); **boor**
    (ill-mannered person)

boredem : **bore·dom**
bore·dom
boredum : **bore·dom**
borgeois : **bour·geois** (*adj.*)
borgeoisie : **bour·geoisie** (*noun*)
borish : **boor·ish**
bor·ough (town); **bur·ro** (pack
  animal); **bur·row** (animal
  hole)
borow : **bor·row**
borro : **bor·row**
bor·row
bos·om
bosoom : **bos·om**
bossom : **bos·om**
botaney : **bot·a·ny**
bo·tan·i·cal
botanicle : **bo·tan·i·cal**
botanikal : **bo·tan·i·cal**
botannical : **bo·tan·i·cal**
botanny : **bot·a·ny**
bot·a·ny
boteny : **bot·a·ny**
botiny : **bot·a·ny**
botle : **bot·tle**
botom : **bot·tom**
bottal : **bot·tle**
bottanical : **bo·tan·i·cal**
bottel : **bot·tle**
bottem : **bot·tom**
bot·tle
bottocks : **but·tocks**
bot·tom
bottoneer : **bou·ton·niere**
bottum : **bot·tom**
bought
bougt : **bought**
bouil·lon (soup); **bul·lion** (gold
  blocks)
boukay : **bou·quet**
boulavard : **boul·e·vard**
boul·der

boul·e·vard
boulevarde : **boul·e·vard**
bounce
bound·ary
boundery : **bound·ary**
boundiry : **bound·ary**
boundry : **bound·ary**
bounse : **bounce**
boun·te·ous
boun·ti·ful
bountifull : **boun·ti·ful**
bountious : **boun·te·ous**
bountius : **boun·te·ous**
bountyful : **boun·ti·ful**
bouquay : **bou·quet**
bou·quet
bourben : **bour·bon**
bour·bon
bourgeis : **bour·geois** (*adj.*)
bourgeisie : **bour·geoisie** (*noun*)
bour·geois (*adj.*); **bour·geoi·sie**
  (*noun*)
bourgeoisee : **bour·geoisie**
  (*noun*)
bour·geoisie (*noun*);
  bour·geois (*adj.*)
bourgois : **bour·geois** (*adj.*)
bourgoisie : **bour·geoisie**
  (*noun*)
bourshois : **bour·geois** (*adj.*)
bourshoisie : **bour·geoisie**
  (*noun*)
bourshwa : **bour·geois** (*adj.*)
bourshwasie : **bour·geoisie**
  (*noun*)
boutoniere : **bou·ton·niere**
bou·ton·niere
bouttoniere : **bou·ton·niere**
bouyancy : **buoy·an·cy**
bouyant : **buoy·ant**
bouyency : **buoy·an·cy**
bouyensy : **buoy·an·cy**

bouyent : **buoy·ant**
bouyint : **buoy·ant**
bownce : **bounce**
bownteous : **boun·te·ous**
boxite : **baux·ite**
boy (lad); **buoy** (sea marker)
boyancy : **buoy·an·cy**
boyant : **buoy·ant**
boycot : **boy·cott**
boy·cott
boyency : **buoy·an·cy**
boyent : **buoy·ant**
boykott : **boy·cott**
Boyse : **Boi·se**
boy·sen·ber·ry
boysonberry : **boy·sen·ber·ry**
boysterous : **bois·ter·ous**
brace·let
bracelett : **brace·let**
bracelit : **brace·let**
bragart : **brag·gart**
brag·gart
braggert : **brag·gart**
braik : **brake** (to slow or stop)
    or **break** (to shatter)
Brail : **Braille**
Braille
brain
brakable : **break·able**
brake (to slow or stop); **break**
    (to shatter)
brakethrough : **break·through**
Brale : **Braille**
Bralle : **Braille**
brane : **brain**
braselet : **brace·let**
braselit : **brace·let**
Brasil : **Bra·zil**
brauny : **brawn·y**
bra·va·do
bravadoe : **bra·va·do**
bravary : **brav·ery**

braverry : **brav·ery**
brav·ery
bravodo : **bra·va·do**
bravry : **brav·ery**
brawny
Bra·zil
Brazill : **Bra·zil**
breach (to break); **breech**
    (hinder or lower part)
breachcloth : **breech·cloth**
breaches (breaks); **breech·es**
    (trousers)
bread (food); **bred** (raised)
breadth
break (to shatter); **brake** (to
    slow or stop)
breakabel : **break·able**
break·able
break·fast
breakfest : **break·fast**
breakfist : **break·fast**
breakible : **break·able**
break·through
breakthru : **break·through**
breakthrugh : **break·through**
breast
breath (*noun*); **breathe** (*verb*)
breathe (*verb*); **breath** (*noun*)
breathren : **breth·ren**
breath·er
breaze : **breeze**
breazily : **breez·i·ly**
breckfast : **break·fast**
bred (raised); **bread** (food)
bredth : **breadth**
breech (hinder or lower part);
    breach (to break)
breech·cloth
breechclothe : **breech·cloth**
breech·es (trousers); **breaches**
    (breaks)
breef : **brief**

breethe : **breathe**
breether : **breath•er**
breezaly : **breez•i•ly**
breeze
breez•i•ly
bregade : **bri•gade**
breif : **brief**
breivity : **brev•i•ty**
brekfast : **break•fast**
brekfest : **break•fast**
brest : **breast**
breth : **breath**
bretheren : **breth•ren**
breth•ren
brevado : **bra•va•do**
brevety : **brev•i•ty**
brev•i•ty
brewary : **brew•ery**
brewerry : **brew•ery**
brew•ery
brewry : **brew•ery**
bribary : **brib•ery**
brib•ery
bribry : **brib•ery**
brid•al (marriage); **brid•le**
  (harness)
bridge
bridje : **bridge**
brid•le (harness); **brid•al**
  (marriage)
brief
brievity : **brev•i•ty**
bri•gade
brigadeer : **brig•a•dier**
brigadeir : **brig•a•dier**
brig•a•dier
brigaid : **bri•gade**
brige : **bridge**
brigedier : **brig•a•dier**
briggade : **bri•gade**
briggadier : **brig•a•dier**
bright•en

brightin : **bright•en**
briliance : **bril•liance**
briliant : **bril•liant**
brillance : **bril•liance**
bril•liance
brillianse : **bril•liance**
bril•liant
brillience : **bril•liance**
brilliense : **bril•liance**
brillient : **bril•liant**
brissle : **bris•tle**
brisstle : **bris•tle**
bristel : **bris•tle**
bris•tle
Brit•ain (nation); **Brit•on**
  (person)
Britan : **Brit•ain** (nation) or
  Brit•on (person)
Britania : **Bri•tan•ni•a**
Bri•tan•ni•a
Britany : **Brit•ta•ny**
Briten : **Brit•ain** (nation) or
  Brit•on (person)
briten : **bright•en**
Britesh : **Brit•ish**
Britian : **Brit•ain** (nation) or
  Brit•on (person)
Brit•ish
britle : **brit•tle**
Britny : **Brit•ta•ny**
Brit•on (person); **Brit•ain**
  (nation)
Brit•ta•ny
brittel : **brit•tle**
Brittish : **Brit•ish**
brit•tle
Britton : **Brit•ain** (nation) or
  Brit•on (person)
broach (to open); **brooch**
  (ornamental pin)
bro•chure
bronny : **brawny**

brooch (ornamental pin);
  broach (to open)
Brooklin : **Brook•lyn**
Brook•lyn
Brooklynn : **Brook•lyn**
broose : **bruise**
broshure : **bro•chure**
brosure : **bro•chure**
broth•er
brouse : **browse**
browse
browze : **browse**
bruise
bruize : **bruise**
bru•net *or* **bru•nette**
bru•nette *or* **bru•net**
brunnette : **bru•net**
bruse : **bruise**
Brusels : **Brus•sels**
brusk : **brusque**
brusqe : **brusque**
brusque
Brussells : **Brus•sels**
Brussels
Brussles : **Brus•sels**
bru•tal
brutel : **bru•tal**
bruther : **broth•er**
brutil : **bru•tal**
brutle : **bru•tal**
Buanos Aires : **Bue•nos Ai•res**
bubbel : **bub•ble**
bub•ble
buble : **bub•ble**
bu•bon•ic
bubonick : **bu•bon•ic**
bubonnic : **bu•bon•ic**
bucanneer : **buc•ca•neer**
buc•ca•neer
buccaneir : **buc•ca•neer**
buccanier : **buc•ca•neer**
buccanneer : **buc•ca•neer**

bucher : **butch•er**
bucholic : **bu•col•ic**
buckaneer : **buc•ca•neer**
buckel : **buc•kle**
buckeneer : **buc•ca•neer**
buc•ket
buckit : **buc•ket**
buc•kle
bucksom : **bux•om**
bu•col•ic
bucolick : **bu•col•ic**
Buda : **Bud•dha**
Budda : **Bud•dha**
Bud•dha
Budd•hist
Buddist : **Budd•hist**
bud•get
budgetarry : **bud•get•ary**
bud•get•ary
budgetery : **bud•get•ary**
budgit : **bud•get**
budgitary : **bud•get•ary**
Budha : **Bud•dha**
Budist : **Budd•hist**
Buenas Aires : **Bue•nos Ai•res**
Bue•nos Ai•res
Buenos Airres : **Bue•nos Ai•res**
Buenos Ires : **Bue•nos Ai•res**
bufalo : **buf•fa•lo**
bufelo : **buf•fa•lo**
bufet : **buf•fet**
buffallo : **buf•fa•lo**
buf•fa•lo
buffat : **buf•fet**
buffay : **buf•fet**
buffelo : **buf•fa•lo**
buf•fet
buffey : **buf•fet**
buf•foon
buffoonary : **buf•foon•ery**
buf•foon•ery
buffune : **buf•foon**

buffunery : **buf·foon·ery**
bufoon : **buf·foon**
bufoonery : **buf·foon·ery**
bugal : **bu·gle**
bugel : **bu·gle**
buget : **bud·get**
bugetary : **bud·get·ary**
buggler : **bu·gler**
buglar : **bu·gler**
bu·gle
bu·gler
build
bukle : **buc·kle**
bukolic : **bu·col·ic**
bulet : **bul·let**
buletin : **bul·le·tin**
bulevard : **boul·e·vard**
bulk·i·er
bulkyer : **bulk·i·er**
bullack : **bul·lock**
bullavard : **boul·e·vard**
bulldoser : **bull·doz·er**
bull·doz·er
bulleck : **bul·lock**
bul·let
bulleten : **bul·le·tin**
bullevard : **boul·e·vard**
bul·le·tin
bul·lion (gold blocks);
    bouil·lon (soup)
bullit : **bul·let**
bullitin : **bul·le·tin**
bul·lock
bullrush : **bul·rush**
bullwark : **bul·wark**
bullwerk : **bul·wark**
bullwork : **bul·wark**
bulock : **bul·lock**
bul·rush
bul·wark
bulwerk : **bul·wark**
bulwork : **bul·wark**

bundal : **bun·dle**
bundel : **bun·dle**
bun·dle
bungaloe : **bun·ga·low**
bun·ga·low
bungelow : **bun·ga·low**
bungolow : **bun·ga·low**
bun·ion
bunnion : **bun·ion**
bunyan : **bun·ion**
bunyen : **bun·ion**
bunyon : **bun·ion**
buoy (sea marker); **boy** (lad)
buoy·an·cy
buoyansy : **buoy·an·cy**
buoy·ant
buquet : **bou·quet**
buray : **be·ret**
burben : **bour·bon**
burbon : **bour·bon**
burch : **birch**
burdansom : **bur·den·some**
bur·den
bur·den·some
burdensum : **bur·den·some**
burdonsome : **bur·den·some**
bureacrisy : **bu·reau·cra·cy**
bu·reau
bu·reau·cra·cy
bureaucrasy : **bu·reau·cra·cy**
burgen : **bur·geon**
burgeois : **bour·geois**
burgeoisie : **bour·geoisie**
bur·geon
bur·glar
bur·glary
burgler : **bur·glar**
burglery : **bur·glary**
burglir : **bur·glar**
burglury : **bur·glary**
buri·al
buriel : **buri·al**

burieu : **bu·reau**
burieucracy : **bu·reau·cra·cy**
bur·lap
burlesk : **bur·lesque**
bur·lesque
bur·ley (tobacco); **bur·ly**
  (muscular)
bur·ly
burreau : **bu·reau**
burreaucracy : **bu·reau·cra·cy**
burret : **bar·rette**
burrette : **bar·rette**
burrey : **bury**
bur·ro (pack animal);
  bor·ough (town); **bur·row**
  (animal hole)
bur·row (animal hole);
  bor·ough (town); **bur·ro**
  (pack animal)
bur·sar
burser : **bur·sar**
burserk : **ber·serk**
bur·si·tis
bursitus : **bur·si·tis**
burthday : **birth·day**
burthmark : **birth·mark**
burthplace : **birth·place**
bury (to cover with earth);
  ber·ry (fruit)
buryal : **buri·al**
bus·es *or* **bus·ses**
bushal : **bush·el**
bush·el
bushell : **bush·el**
busi·er
busi·ness (economic activity);
  busy·ness (being busy)
busom : **bos·om**
bus·ses *or* **bus·es**
bussier : **busi·er**

bussle : **bus·tle**
busstle : **bus·tle**
bustel : **bus·tle**
bus·tle
busyier : **busi·er**
busy·ness (being busy);
  busi·ness (economic activity)
butain : **bu·tane**
bu·tane
butchary : **butch·ery**
butch·er
butch·ery
bute : **butte**
buter : **but·ter**
butition : **beau·ti·cian**
butlar : **but·ler**
butocks : **but·tocks**
butress : **but·tress**
butte
but·ter
buttler : **but·ler**
but·tocks
buttonier : **bou·ton·niere**
buttox : **but·tocks**
but·tress
buttriss : **but·tress**
buty : **beau·ty**
bux·om
buxum : **bux·om**
buzard : **buz·zard**
buze : **booze**
buz·zard
buzzerd : **buz·zard**
bycicle : **bi·cy·cle**
byciclist : **bi·cy·clist**
byochemist : **bi·o·chem·ist**
byou : **bay·ou**
Byzanteen : **Byz·an·tine**
Byz·an·tine
Byzentine : **Byz·an·tine**

C

cabage : **cab•bage**
ca•bana
cabanna : **ca•bana**
cabaray : **cab•a•ret**
cab•a•ret
cab•bage
cabbana : **ca•bana**
cabbedge : **cab•bage**
cabbege : **cab•bage**
cabbin : **cab•in**
caben : **cab•in**
cabenet : **cab•i•net**
caberet : **cab•a•ret**
cab•in
cab•i•net
cabinnet : **cab•i•net**
cabnet : **cab•i•net**
cacafony : **ca•coph•o•ny**
cacaphony : **ca•coph•o•ny**
cacheir : **cash•ier**
cachew : **cash•ew**
cachoo : **cash•ew**
cack•le
cacktus : **cac•tus**
cacle : **cack•le**
cacofony : **ca•coph•o•ny**
ca•coph•o•ny
cactos : **cac•tus**
cac•tus
cacus : **cau•cus**
cadance : **ca•dence**
cadanse : **ca•dence**
ca•dav•er
cadavir : **ca•dav•er**
cadavver : **ca•dav•er**
caddet : **ca•det**
ca•dence
cadense : **ca•dence**
ca•det
cadett : **ca•det**

cadette : **ca•det**
cae•sar•e•an
caesarian : **cae•sar•e•an**
cafaterea : **caf•e•te•ria**
cafateria : **caf•e•te•ria**
cafaterria : **caf•e•te•ria**
cafee : **cof•fee**
cafeen : **caf•feine**
cafeine : **caf•feine**
cafene : **caf•feine**
cafetearia : **caf•e•te•ria**
cafeterea : **caf•e•te•ria**
caf•e•te•ria
cafeterria : **caf•e•te•ria**
caff : **cough**
caffateria : **caf•e•te•ria**
caffee : **cof•fee**
caffeen : **caf•feine**
caf•feine
caffene : **caf•feine**
caffeteria : **caf•e•te•ria**
caffiene : **caf•feine**
caffine : **caf•feine**
cagole : **ca•jole**
caidence : **ca•dence**
cainine : **ca•nine**
cairamel : **car•a•mel**
cairful : **care•ful**
cairless : **care•less**
Cai•ro
cairopractor : **chi•ro•prac•tor**
Cairro : **Cai•ro**
cajoal : **ca•jole**
ca•jole
cajolle : **ca•jole**
cakophony : **ca•coph•o•ny**
caktos : **cac•tus**
caktus : **cac•tus**
calaber : **cal•i•ber**
calacko : **cal•i•co**

Calafornia : **Cal·i·for·nia**
calamety : **ca·lam·i·ty**
calamitty : **ca·lam·i·ty**
ca·lam·i·ty
calammity : **ca·lam·i·ty**
calamny : **cal·um·ny**
calander : **cal·en·dar** (chart of
    dates) *or* **cal·en·der** (pressing
    machine) *or* **col·an·der**
    (drainer)
calaper : **cal·i·per**
calarie : **cal·o·rie** (energy unit)
    or **cel·ery** (vegetable)
calary : **cal·o·rie** (energy unit)
    or **cel·ery** (vegetable)
calasthenics : **cal·is·then·ics**
calceim : **cal·ci·um**
calceum : **cal·ci·um**
cal·ci·um
calcuelate : **cal·cu·late**
cal·cu·late
calculis : **cal·cu·lus**
calcullate : **cal·cu·late**
calcullus : **cal·cu·lus**
calculous : **cal·cu·lus**
cal·cu·lus
caleber : **cal·i·ber**
caleco : **cal·i·co**
Calefornia : **Cal·i·for·nia**
caleidascope : **ka·lei·do·scope**
caleko : **cal·i·co**
cal·en·dar (chart of dates);
    cal·en·der (pressing
    machine);**col·an·der** (drainer)
cal·en·der (pressing machine);
    cal·en·dar (chart of dates);
    col·an·der (drainer)
calenndar : **cal·en·dar** (chart of
    dates) *or* **cal·en·der** (pressing
    machine) *or* **col·an·der**
    (drainer)
caleper : **cal·i·per**

calepso : **ca·lyp·so**
calery : **cal·o·rie** (energy unit)
    or **cel·ery** (vegetable)
cal·i·ber
calibir : **cal·i·ber**
calibre (*Brit.*) : **cal·i·ber**
calicco : **cal·i·co**
calicko : **cal·i·co**
cal·i·co
caliedoscope : **ka·lei·do·scope**
Californea : **Cal·i·for·nia**
Cal·i·for·nia
caliko : **cal·i·co**
calindar : **cal·en·dar** (chart of
    dates) *or* **cal·en·der** (pressing
    machine) *or* **col·an·der**
    (drainer)
calinder : **cal·en·dar** (chart of
    dates) *or* **cal·en·der** (pressing
    machine) *or* **col·an·der**
    (drainer)
cal·i·per
calipper : **cal·i·per**
calipso : **ca·lyp·so**
calis : **cal·lous** (lack of feeling)
    or **cal·lus** (hardened skin)
calissthenics : **cal·is·then·ics**
calissthintics : **cal·is·then·ics**
cal·is·then·ics
calisthinics : **cal·is·then·ics**
callaflower : **cau·li·flow·er**
callamity : **ca·lam·i·ty**
callasthenics : **cal·is·then·ics**
callcium : **cal·ci·um**
callculate : **cal·cu·late**
callculus : **cal·cu·lus**
calldran : **caul·dron**
calldren : **caul·dron**
calldron : **caul·dron**
callendar : **cal·en·dar** (chart of
    dates) *or* **cal·en·der** (pressing

machine) *or* col•an•der
(drainer)

callery : cal•o•rie (energy unit)
or cel•ery (vegetable)

callesthenics : cal•is•then•ics

calliber : cal•i•ber

callico : cal•i•co

callidoscope : ka•lei•do•scope

calliflour : cau•li•flow•er

calliflower : cau•li•flow•er

Callifornia : Cal•i•for•nia

calliper : cal•i•per

callipso : ca•lyp•so

callis : cal•lous (lack of feeling)
or cal•lus (hardened skin)

calliss : cal•lous (lack of
feeling) *or* cal•lus (hardened
skin)

callisthenics : cal•is•then•ics

callisthinicks : cal•is•then•ics

callisthinics : cal•is•then•ics

callorie : cal•o•rie

callory : cal•o•rie

cal•lous (lack of feeling);
cal•lus (hardened skin)

callumny : cal•um•ny

cal•lus (hardened skin);
cal•lous (lack of feeling)

callvary : Cal•va•ry (site of the
Crucifixion) *or* cav•al•ry
(horse troops)

Callvinist : Cal•vin•ist

callypso : ca•lyp•so

calocko : cal•i•co

caloco : cal•i•co

calomny : cal•um•ny

calorey : cal•o•rie

cal•o•rie

calorrey : cal•o•rie

calorrie : cal•o•rie

calory : cal•o•rie

calous : cal•lous (lack of
feeling) *or* cal•lus (hardened
skin)

calqulate : cal•cu•late

calqulus : cal•cu•lus

calseum : cal•ci•um

calsium : cal•ci•um

caluclate : cal•cu•late

calummny : cal•um•ny

calumney : cal•um•ny

calumnie : cal•um•ny

cal•um•ny

calus : cal•lous (lack of feeling)
or cal•lus (hardened skin)

Cal•va•ry (site of the
Crucifixion); cav•al•ry (horse
troops)

calvelry : Cal•va•ry (site of the
Crucifixion) *or* cav•al•ry
(horse troops)

Calvenist : Cal•vin•ist

calvery : Cal•va•ry (site of the
Crucifixion) *or* cav•al•ry
(horse troops)

Cal•vin•ist

Calvinnist : Cal•vin•ist

ca•lyp•so

calypsoe : ca•lyp•so

camal : cam•el

camara : cam•era

ca•ma•ra•de•rie *or* com•rad•ery

camarodery : ca•ma•ra•de•rie

camealia : ca•mel•lia

cameilia : ca•mel•lia

cam•el

camelia : ca•mel•lia

ca•mel•lia

camelya : ca•mel•lia

cam•eo

cam•era

cameraderie : ca•ma•ra•de•rie

camerra : cam•era

camfor : **cam·phor**
camielia : **ca·mel·lia**
camil : **cam·el**
camill : **cam·el**
camillia : **ca·mel·lia**
camio : **cam·eo**
camioe : **cam·eo**
camira : **cam·era**
cammal : **cam·el**
cammara : **cam·era**
cammel : **cam·el**
cammelia : **ca·mel·lia**
cammeo : **cam·eo**
cammera : **cam·era**
cammerra : **cam·era**
cammillia : **ca·mel·lia**
cammio : **cam·eo**
cammira : **cam·era**
cammirra : **cam·era**
cammouflage : **cam·ou·flage**
cammuflauge : **cam·ou·flage**
camoflage : **cam·ou·flage**
camoflauge : **cam·ou·flage**
camofloge : **cam·ou·flage**
cam·ou·flage
campagne : **cam·paign**
cam·paign
campaigne : **cam·paign**
campain : **cam·paign**
campane : **cam·paign**
campes : **cam·pus**
campfor : **cam·phor**
campher : **cam·phor**
cam·phor
camphur : **cam·phor**
campis : **cam·pus**
camppus : **cam·pus**
cam·pus
campuss : **cam·pus**
camra : **cam·era**
camraderie : **ca·ma·ra·de·rie**
camuflague : **cam·ou·flage**

camuflauge : **cam·ou·flage**
camufloge : **cam·ou·flage**
canabal : **can·ni·bal**
canabel : **can·ni·bal**
canable : **can·ni·bal**
Can·a·da
Canadean : **Ca·na·di·an**
Ca·na·di·an
Canadien : **Ca·na·di·an**
Canaidian : **Ca·na·di·an**
canarry : **ca·nary** (bird) *or*
   can·nery (factory)
ca·nary (bird); **can·nery**
   (factory)
canaster : **can·is·ter**
can·cel
cancelation : **can·cel·la·tion**
can·celed *or* **can·celled**
cancell : **can·cel**
cancellaition : **can·cel·la·tion**
can·cel·la·tion
can·celled *or* **can·celed**
can·cer
cancil : **can·cel**
cancillation : **can·cel·la·tion**
cancilled : **can·celed**
cancor : **can·cer**
cancur : **can·cer**
candal : **can·dle**
candalabra : **can·de·la·bra**
candalstick : **can·dle·stick**
canded : **can·did**
candedacy : **can·di·da·cy**
candedasy : **can·di·da·cy**
candel : **can·dle**
can·de·la·bra
candellabra : **can·de·la·bra**
candelstick : **can·dle·stick**
cander : **can·dor**
can·did
can·di·da·cy
candidasy : **can·di·da·cy**

candidcy : **can•di•da•cy**
candidecy : **can•di•da•cy**
candidicy : **can•di•da•cy**
candidisy : **can•di•da•cy**
candil : **can•dle**
candilabra : **can•de•la•bra**
candilstick : **can•dle•stick**
can•dle
candleabra : **can•de•la•bra**
can•dle•stick
can•dor
candur : **can•dor**
Canecticut : **Con•nect•i•cut**
Caneda : **Can•a•da**
canen : **can•non** (artillery) *or*
  can•on (list of books; clergy;
  church law)
canery : **ca•nary** (bird) *or*
  can•nery (factory)
canester : **can•is•ter**
canibal : **can•ni•bal**
Canida : **Can•a•da**
canien : **ca•nine**
canin : **can•non** (artillery) *or*
  can•on (list of books; clergy;
  church law)
ca•nine
canion : **can•yon**
can•is•ter
cannabal : **can•ni•bal**
cannabel : **can•ni•bal**
cannable : **can•ni•bal**
Cannada : **Can•a•da**
Cannadian : **Ca•na•di•an**
cannary : **ca•nary** (bird) *or*
  can•nery (factory)
cannaster : **can•is•ter**
cannebal : **can•ni•bal**
canneble : **can•ni•bal**
cannen : **can•non** (artillery) *or*
  can•on (list of books; clergy;
  church law)

can•nery (factory); **ca•nary**
  (bird)
cannester : **can•is•ter**
Canneticut : **Con•nect•i•cut**
can•ni•bal
cannibel : **can•ni•bal**
cannible : **can•ni•bal**
cannin : **can•non** (artillery) *or*
  can•on (list of books; clergy;
  church law)
cannine : **ca•nine**
cannister : **can•is•ter**
cannoe : **ca•noe**
can•non (artillery); **can•on** (list
  of books; clergy; church law)
cannu : **ca•noe**
cannue : **ca•noe**
cannun : **can•non** (artillery) *or*
  can•on (list of books; clergy;
  church law)
cannuster : **can•is•ter**
cannyon : **can•yon**
ca•noe
can•on (list of books; clergy;
  church law); **can•non**
  (artillery)
canoo : **ca•noe**
Cansas : **Kan•sas**
cansel : **can•cel**
cansellation : **can•cel•la•tion**
canselled : **can•celed**
canser : **can•cer**
cansillation : **can•cel•la•tion**
cant (slope; hypocrisy); **can't**
  (cannot)
can't (cannot); **cant** (slope;
  hypocrisy)
cantakerous : **can•tan•ker•ous**
cantaloape : **can•ta•loupe**
cantalope : **can•ta•loupe**
can•ta•loupe
cantankarous : **can•tan•ker•ous**

can·tan·ker·ous
cantankerus : **can·tan·ker·ous**
can·ta·ta
cantatta : **can·ta·ta**
cantean : **can·teen**
can·teen
canteloape : **can·ta·loupe**
cantelope : **can·ta·loupe**
canteloupe : **can·ta·loupe**
cantene : **can·teen**
can·ter (horse trot); **can·tor**
 (chanter)
cantilope : **can·ta·loupe**
cantiloupe : **can·ta·loupe**
cantine : **can·teen**
can·tor (chanter); **can·ter** (horse
 trot)
cantota : **can·ta·ta**
cantotta : **can·ta·ta**
canue : **ca·noe**
canun : **can·non** (artillery) *or*
 can·on (list of books; clergy;
 church law)
canuster : **can·is·ter**
can·vas (cloth); **can·vass** (to
 survey)
can·vass (to survey); **can·vas**
 (cloth)
canves : **can·vas** (cloth) *or*
 can·vass (to survey)
canvess : **can·vas** (cloth) *or*
 can·vass (to survey)
canvis : **can·vas** (cloth) *or*
 can·vass (to survey)
canviss : **can·vas** (cloth) *or*
 can·vass (to survey)
canvus : **can·vas** (cloth) *or*
 can·vass (to survey)
canvuss : **can·vas** (cloth) *or*
 can·vass (to survey)
canyen : **can·yon**
canyin : **can·yon**

can·yon
capabal : **ca·pa·ble**
capabel : **ca·pa·ble**
ca·pa·bil·i·ty
capabillity : **ca·pa·bil·i·ty**
ca·pa·ble
capablety : **ca·pa·bil·i·ty**
capaccity : **ca·pac·i·ty**
capacety : **ca·pac·i·ty**
capachious : **ca·pa·cious**
ca·pa·cious
capacitty : **ca·pac·i·ty**
ca·pac·i·ty
capallary : **cap·il·lary**
capashious : **ca·pa·cious**
capasious : **ca·pa·cious**
capasitty : **ca·pac·i·ty**
capasity : **ca·pac·i·ty**
capatious : **ca·pa·cious**
capchure : **cap·ture**
capcion : **cap·tion**
capcise : **cap·size**
capcize : **cap·size**
capebility : **ca·pa·bil·i·ty**
capeble : **ca·pa·ble**
capellary : **cap·il·lary**
capibility : **ca·pa·bil·i·ty**
capible : **ca·pa·ble**
capilary : **cap·il·lary**
cap·il·lary
capillerry : **cap·il·lary**
capillery : **cap·il·lary**
cap·i·tal (city; property);
 cap·i·tol (statehouse)
cap·i·tal·ism
capitel : **cap·i·tal** (city;
 property) *or* **cap·i·tol**
 (statehouse)
capitelism : **cap·i·tal·ism**
capitle : **cap·i·tal** (city;
 property) *or* **cap·i·tol**
 (statehouse)

cap·i·tol (statehouse); cap·i·tal
  (city; property)
capitolism : cap·i·tal·ism
capittal : cap·i·tal (city;
  property) *or* cap·i·tol
  (statehouse)
capitul: cap·i·tal (city;
  property) *or* cap·i·tol
  (statehouse)
cappellary : cap·il·lary
cappillary : cap·il·lary
cappital : cap·i·tal (city;
  property) *or* cap·i·tol
  (statehouse)
cappitalism : cap·i·tal·ism
capsel : cap·sule
capsell : cap·sule
capshen : cap·tion
capshun : cap·tion
capshure : cap·ture
capsil : cap·sule
capsill : cap·sule
capsise : cap·size
cap·size
capsool : cap·sule
capsul : cap·sule
cap·sule
cap·tain
captan : cap·tain
capten : cap·tain
capter : cap·tor
captian : cap·tain
captin : cap·tain
cap·tion
captoin : cap·tion
cap·tor (*noun*); cap·ture (*verb*)
captur : cap·tor (*noun*) *or*
  cap·ture (*verb*)
cap·ture (*verb*); cap·tor (*noun*)
Carabean : Car·ib·be·an
caraboo : car·i·bou
carabou : car·i·bou

ca·rafe
caraffe : ca·rafe
caramal : car·a·mel
car·a·mel
caramul : car·a·mel
car·at *or* kar·at (weight of
  gems); car·et (^); car·rot
  (vegetable)
carature : car·i·ca·ture
car·a·van
carbahydrate : car·bo·hy·drate
carban : car·bon
carbean : car·bine
carbeen : car·bine
carbehidrate : car·bo·hy·drate
carbehydrate : car·bo·hy·drate
carben : car·bon
carbene : car·bine
carberater : car·bu·re·tor
carberator : car·bu·re·tor
carberetor : car·bu·re·tor
carbihydrate : car·bo·hy·drate
carbin : car·bon
car·bine
carbohidrait : car·bo·hy·drate
carbohidrate : car·bo·hy·drate
car·bo·hy·drate
car·bon
carborater : car·bu·re·tor
carborator : car·bu·re·tor
carboretor : car·bu·re·tor
carburator : car·bu·re·tor
carbureter : car·bu·re·tor
car·bu·re·tor
car·cass
carcus : car·cass
carcuss : car·cass
cardanal : car·di·nal
cardeac : car·di·ac
cardegan : car·di·gan
cardenal : car·di·nal
cardenel : car·di·nal

car•di•ac
cardiack : car•di•ac
cardiak : car•di•ac
car•di•gan
cardiggan : car•di•gan
cardiggin : car•di•gan
cardigin : car•di•gan
car•di•nal
cardinall : car•di•nal
cardinel : car•di•nal
cardinnal : car•di•nal
carear : ca•reer
carebou : car•i•bou
carecature : car•i•ca•ture
ca•reer
care•ful (cautious); car•ful (full car)
carefull : care•ful
carel : car•ol (song) *or* car•rel (study table)
care•less
careliss : care•less
caremel : car•a•mel
carere : ca•reer
ca•ress
car•et (^); car•rot (vegetable); kar•at (weight of gems)
carevan : car•a•van
car•ful (full car); care•ful (cautious)
cariage : car•riage
Ca•rib•be•an
Caribean : Ca•rib•be•an
Caribian : Ca•rib•be•an
cariboo : car•i•bou
car•i•bou
car•i•ca•ture
caricture : car•i•ca•ture
carisma : char•is•ma
cariture : car•i•ca•ture
carkas : car•cass
carkass : car•cass

carkess : car•cass
carmel : car•a•mel
carnadge : car•nage
car•nage
car•nal
carnavore : car•ni•vore
carnedge : car•nage
carnege : car•nage
carnel : car•nal
carnevore : car•ni•vore
carnidge : car•nage
carnige : car•nage
carnil : car•nal
carnivor : car•ni•vore
car•ni•vore
car•ol (song); car•rel (study table)
carosell : car•ou•sel
ca•rouse
car•ou•sel
carpat : car•pet
car•pen•ter
car•pet
carpinter : car•pen•ter
carpit : car•pet
Carrabean : Ca•rib•be•an
Carrabian : Ca•rib•be•an
carradge : car•riage
carrafe : ca•rafe
carrage : car•riage
carramel : car•a•mel
carrasel : car•ou•sel
carravan : car•a•van
carreer : ca•reer
car•rel (study table); car•ol (song)
carremel : car•a•mel
carresel : car•ou•sel
carress : ca•ress
carrevan : car•a•van
car•riage
Carribean : Ca•rib•be•an

Carribian : **Ca·rib·be·an**
carribou : **car·i·bou**
carridge : **car·riage**
carrige : **car·riage**
carrivan : **car·a·van**
carrol : **car·rel** (study table) *or*
  car·ol (song)
carrosel : **car·ou·sel**
car·rot (vegetable); **car·et** (^);
  kar·at (weight of gems)
carrouse : **ca·rouse**
carrousel : **car·ou·sel**
carryvan : **car·a·van**
cartalage : **car·ti·lage**
cartalege : **car·ti·lage**
cartalige : **car·ti·lage**
cartan : **car·ton**
cartelage : **car·ti·lage**
cartelige : **car·ti·lage**
carten : **car·ton**
car·ti·lage
cartilege : **car·ti·lage**
cartin : **car·ton**
car·ton
car·toon
cartradge : **car·tridge**
cartrage : **car·tridge**
cartredge : **car·tridge**
car·tridge
cartrige : **car·tridge**
cartune : **car·toon**
caseeno : **ca·si·no**
casel : **cas·tle**
caseno : **ca·si·no**
caserole : **cas·se·role**
casheer : **cash·ier**
casheir : **cash·ier**
cashere : **cash·ier**
cash·ew
cash·ier
cashmear : **cash·mere**
cashmeer : **cash·mere**

cashmeir : **cash·mere**
cash·mere
cashmier : **cash·mere**
cashoo : **cash·ew**
cashou : **cash·ew**
ca·si·no
casock : **cas·sock** (robe) *or*
  cos·sack (Russian cavalry)
cassack : **cas·sock** (robe) *or*
  cos·sack (Russian cavalry)
cassarole : **cas·se·role**
cassaroll : **cas·se·role**
cassel : **cas·tle**
casseno : **ca·si·no**
cas·se·role
casseroll : **cas·se·role**
cassick : **cas·sock** (robe) *or*
  cos·sack (Russian cavalry)
cassino : **ca·si·no**
cassirole : **cas·se·role**
cassoc : **cas·sock** (robe) *or*
  cos·sack (Russian cavalry)
cas·sock (robe); **cos·sack**
  (Russian cavalry)
casstle : **cas·tle**
cast (to throw off); **caste** (social
  system)
cas·ta·net
castanette : **cas·ta·net**
caste (social system); **cast** (to
  throw off)
castel : **cas·tle**
castenette : **cas·ta·net**
castinet : **cas·ta·net**
castinette : **cas·ta·net**
cas·tle
catachism : **cat·e·chism**
cataclism : **cat·a·clysm**
cat·a·clysm
cat·a·comb
catacome : **cat·a·comb**
catagory : **cat·e·go·ry**

catakism : **cat•e•chism**
catalist : **cat•a•lyst**
cat•a•log *or* **cat•a•logue**
cat•a•logue *or* **cat•a•log**
cat•a•lyst
catarpillar : **cat•er•pil•lar**
catasstrophe : **ca•tas•tro•phe**
catastrofe : **ca•tas•tro•phe**
ca•tas•tro•phe
catastrophy : **ca•tas•tro•phe**
catchup : **cat•sup**
cat•e•chism
catechysm : **cat•e•chism**
cateclism : **cat•a•clysm**
cateclysm : **cat•a•clysm**
catecomb : **cat•a•comb**
categorey : **cat•e•go•ry**
cat•e•go•ry
catekism : **cat•e•chism**
catelist : **cat•a•lyst**
catelog : **cat•a•log**
caterpilar : **cat•er•pil•lar**
caterpiler : **cat•er•pil•lar**
cat•er•pil•lar
caterpiller : **cat•er•pil•lar**
cathalic : **cath•o•lic**
cathelic : **cath•o•lic**
cathilic : **cath•o•lic**
catholec : **cath•o•lic**
cath•o•lic
Ca•thol•i•cism
Catholisism : **Ca•thol•i•cism**
Cathollicism : **Ca•thol•i•cism**
catilog : **cat•a•log**
catle : **cat•tle**
catsap : **cat•sup**
catsep : **cat•sup**
catshup : **cat•sup**
catsip : **cat•sup**
cat•sup *or* **ketch•up**
cattagory : **cat•e•go•ry**

cattal : **cat•tle**
cattalist : **cat•a•lyst**
cattalog : **cat•a•log**
cattalyst : **cat•a•lyst**
cattasrophe : **ca•tas•tro•phe**
cattegory : **cat•e•go•ry**
cattel : **cat•tle**
catterpillar : **cat•er•pil•lar**
cat•tle
caucas : **cau•cus**
cauchious : **cau•tious**
cau•cus
cauldran : **caul•dron**
cauldren : **caul•dron**
cauldrin : **caul•dron**
caul•dron
cau•li•flow•er
causalitty : **cau•sal•i•ty**
cau•sal•i•ty
causallety : **cau•sal•i•ty**
causallity : **cau•sal•i•ty**
causeous : **cau•tious**
caushion : **cau•tion**
caushious : **cau•tious**
causion : **cau•tion**
causstic : **caus•tic**
caus•tic
caustick : **caus•tic**
cau•tion
cau•tious
cav•al•cade
cavalcaid : **cav•al•cade**
cavaleer : **cav•a•lier**
cavaleir : **cav•a•lier**
cavalere : **cav•a•lier**
cavalery : **Cal•va•ry** (site of the
    Crucifixion) *or* **cav•al•ry**
    (horse troops)
cav•a•lier
cavalkade : **cav•al•cade**
cavallcade : **cav•al•cade**

cav•al•ry (horse troops);
　Cal•va•ry (site of the
　Crucifixion)
cavelcade : cav•al•cade
cavelier : cav•a•lier
cavellry : Cal•va•ry (site of the
　Crucifixion) or cav•al•ry
　(horse troops)
cavelry : Cal•va•ry (site of the
　Crucifixion) or cav•al•ry
　(horse troops)
cavernis : cav•ern•ous
cav•ern•ous
cavernus : cav•ern•ous
cavilcade : cav•al•cade
cavilere : cav•a•lier
cavilier : cav•a•lier
cavilry : Cal•va•ry (site of the
　Crucifixion) or cav•al•ry
　(horse troops)
cavurnous : cav•ern•ous
cawcus : cau•cus
cawldren : caul•dron
cawldron : caul•dron
cawtion : cau•tion
ceadar : ce•dar (tree) or se•der
　(Passover meal)
ce•dar (tree); se•der (Passover
　meal)
cedaver : ca•dav•er
ceder : ce•dar (tree) or se•der
　(Passover meal)
cedir : ce•dar (tree) or se•der
　(Passover meal)
ceesarean : cae•sar•e•an
cegar : ci•gar
cegarette : cig•a•rette
ceil•ing
cejole : ca•jole
celabate : cel•i•bate
celabrant : cel•e•brant
celabration : cel•e•brate

celabrent : cel•e•brant
celabrity : ce•leb•ri•ty
celar : cel•lar
celary : cel•ery (vegetable) or
　sal•a•ry (wages)
celebet : cel•i•bate
celebit : cel•i•bate
celebrait : cel•e•brate
cel•e•brant
cel•e•brate
celebrent : cel•e•brant
celebrety : ce•leb•ri•ty
celebritty : ce•leb•ri•ty
ce•leb•ri•ty
celerry : cel•ery (vegetable) or
　sal•a•ry (wages)
cel•ery (vegetable); sal•a•ry
　(wages)
celesteal : ce•les•tial
ce•les•tial
cel•i•bate
cellabrate : cel•e•brate
cel•lar (basement); sell•er (one
　who sells)
cellary : cel•ery (vegetable) or
　sal•a•ry (wages)
cellebrant : cel•e•brant
cellebrity : ce•leb•ri•ty
celler : cel•lar (basement) or
　sell•er (one who sells)
cellery : cel•ery (vegetable) or
　sal•a•ry (wages)
cellestial : ce•les•tial
cellibate : cel•i•bate
cel•lo
cellouloid : cel•lu•loid
Celltic : Cel•tic
cel•lu•loid
celo : cel•lo
Celon : Cey•lon
Cel•tic
celuloid : cel•lu•loid

cematary : **cem·e·tery**
cematery : **cem·e·tery**
cemeleon : **cha·me·leon**
cemelion : **cha·me·leon**
cemetarry : **cem·e·tery**
cemetary : **cem·e·tery**
cemeterry : **cem·e·tery**
cem·e·tery
cemettery : **cem·e·tery**
cemical : **chem·i·cal**
cemistry : **chem·is·try**
cencership : **cen·sor·ship**
cenchurion : **cen·tu·ri·on**
cenchury : **cen·tu·ry**
cencus : **cen·sus**
cenema : **cin·e·ma**
cen·ser (incense container);
   cen·sor (to remove
   objectionable material);
   cen·sure (to condemn);
   sen·sor (that which senses)
censership : **cen·sor·ship**
censes : **cen·sus**
cen·sor (to remove
   objectionable material);
   cen·ser (incense container);
   censure (to condemn);
   sen·sor (that which senses)
cen·sor·ship
cen·sure (to condemn); **cen·ser**
   (incense container); **cen·sor**
   (to remove objectionable
   material); **sen·sor** (that
   which senses)
cen·sus
censuss : **cen·sus**
centar : **cen·taur**
cen·taur
centerian : **cen·tu·ri·on**
centerion : **cen·tu·ri·on**
centeripetal : **cen·trip·e·tal**
centermeter : **cen·ti·me·ter**

centerpeace : **cen·ter·piece**
centerpece : **cen·ter·piece**
centerpeice : **cen·ter·piece**
cen·ter·piece
centery : **cen·tu·ry**
cen·ti·me·ter
centimetre (*Brit.*) :
   cen·ti·me·ter
centoorion : **cen·tu·ri·on**
centor : **cen·taur**
centour : **cen·taur**
centrepetal : **cen·trip·e·tal**
centrifecal : **cen·trif·u·gal**
centrifegal : **cen·trif·u·gal**
centriffugal : **cen·trif·u·gal**
centrifical : **cen·trif·u·gal**
centrifigal : **cen·trif·u·gal**
centrifucal : **cen·trif·u·gal**
cen·trif·u·gal
centrifugle : **cen·trif·u·gal**
centrimeter : **cen·ti·me·ter**
cen·trip·e·tal
centripetle : **cen·trip·e·tal**
centripidal : **cen·trip·e·tal**
centripital : **cen·trip·e·tal**
centripittal : **cen·trip·e·tal**
cents (money); **sense**
   (intelligence)
centur : **cen·taur**
centurian : **cen·tu·ri·on**
centurien : **cen·tu·ri·on**
cen·tu·ri·on
centurry : **cen·tu·ry**
cen·tu·ry
cerabellum : **cer·e·bel·lum**
ceramec : **ce·ram·ic**
ce·ram·ic
cerammic : **ce·ram·ic**
ceramony : **cer·e·mo·ny**
cerca : **cir·ca**
cerculate : **cir·cu·late**
cercus : **cir·cus**

ce·re·al (grain); se·ri·al (in a series)
cerebellam : cer·e·bel·lum
cerebellem : cer·e·bel·lum
cer·e·bel·lum
cerebelum : cer·e·bel·lum
ce·re·bral
cerebrel : ce·re·bral
ce·re·brum
cereebral : ce·re·bral
ceremoney : cer·e·mo·ny
cer·e·mo·ny
cerial : ce·re·al (grain) or se·ri·al (in a series)
ceribral : ce·re·bral
ceribrum : ce·re·brum
cerimony : cer·e·mo·ny
cerramic : ce·ram·ic
cerrebellum : cer·e·bel·lum
cerremony : cer·e·mo·ny
cerrhosis : cir·rho·sis
cerrosis : cir·rho·sis
cer·tain
certan : cer·tain
certian : cer·tain
certifecate : cer·tif·i·cate
certifficate : cer·tif·i·cate
certificant : cer·tif·i·cate
certificat : cer·tif·i·cate
cer·tif·i·cate
certin : cer·tain
cesairean : cae·sar·e·an
cesarean : cae·sar·e·an
cesarian : cae·sar·e·an
cessarian : cae·sar·e·an
cess·pool
cestern : cis·tern
Cey·lon
chafeur : chauf·feur
chaffer : chauf·feur
chaffuer : chauf·feur
chaffure : chauf·feur

chafure : chauf·feur
chaimberlain : cham·ber·lain
chaimberlin : cham·ber·lain
chairopractor : chi·ro·prac·tor
chaist : chaste
chalera : chol·era
chal·ice
chalise : chal·ice
chaliss : chal·ice
challice : chal·ice
challise : chal·ice
cham·ber·lain
chamberlan : cham·ber·lain
chamberlin : cham·ber·lain
chamealeon : cha·me·leon
chamealion : cha·me·leon
chameeleon : cha·me·leon
chameelion : cha·me·leon
cha·me·leon
chamise : che·mise
cham·pagne
champaigne : cham·pagne
champain : cham·pagne
champaine : cham·pagne
champane : cham·pagne
chanceller : chan·cel·lor
chan·cel·lor
chancelor : chan·cel·lor
chancillor : chan·cel·lor
chandaleer : chan·de·lier
chandalier : chan·de·lier
chandelear : chan·de·lier
chandeleer : chan·de·lier
chandelere : chan·de·lier
chan·de·lier
chandileer : chan·de·lier
chaneled : chan·neled
chanelled : chan·neled
changable : change·able
change·able
changebal : change·able
changeble : change·able

change•ling
changible : change•able
changling : change•ling
chan•neled *or* chan•nelled
chan•nelled *or* chan•neled
chanseller : chan•cel•lor
chansellor : chan•cel•lor
chansillor : chan•cel•lor
cha•os
chaoss : cha•os
chaparone : chap•er•on
chap•el
chapelen : chap•lain
chapelin : chap•lain
chap•er•on *or* chap•er•one
chap•er•one *or* chap•er•on
chaperown : chap•er•on
chapil : chap•el
chap•lain
chaplan : chap•lain
chaplin : chap•lain
chappel : chap•el
char•ac•ter
charactor : char•ac•ter
cha•rade
charaid : cha•rade
charatable : char•i•ta•ble
charaty : char•i•ty
char•coal
charcole : char•coal
charecter : char•ac•ter
charector : char•ac•ter
chareot : char•i•ot
chareoteer : char•i•o•teer
charetable : char•i•ta•ble
charety : char•i•ty
chargable : charge•able
chargeabel : charge•able
charge•able
chargible : charge•able
charicter : char•ac•ter
chariet : char•i•ot

charieteer : char•i•o•teer
char•i•ot
char•i•o•teer
chariotere : char•i•o•teer
chariotier : char•i•o•teer
charish : cher•ish
char•is•ma
char•i•ta•ble
chariteble : char•i•ta•ble
charitible : char•i•ta•ble
char•i•ty
charkcole : char•coal
char•la•tan
charlaten : char•la•tan
charlatin : char•la•tan
charletan : char•la•tan
charleten : char•la•tan
charlitan : char•la•tan
charrade : cha•rade
charrcoal : char•coal
charriot : char•i•ot
charrioteer : char•i•o•teer
charrish : cher•ish
charry : cher•ry
char•treuse
chartroose : char•treuse
chartruese : char•treuse
chartruse : char•treuse
charub : cher•ub
chasiss : chas•sis
chasm
chasses : chas•sis
chassey : chas•sis
chas•sis
chassiss : chas•sis
chasstise : chas•tise
chassy : chas•sis
chast : chaste
chaste
chastety : chas•ti•ty
chas•tise
chastitty : chas•ti•ty

chas•ti•ty
chastize : chas•tise
Chatannooga : Chat•ta•noo•ga
Chatanooga : Chat•ta•noo•ga
cha•teau
chatel : chat•tel
chatieu : cha•teau
chatle : chat•tel
chatoe : cha•teau
Chat•ta•noo•ga
Chattanuga : Chat•ta•noo•ga
chatteau : cha•teau
chat•tel
Chattenooga : Chat•ta•noo•ga
Chattinooga : Chat•ta•noo•ga
chattle : chat•tel
chattow : cha•teau
chauder : chow•der
chauffer : chauf•feur
chauf•feur
chauffuer : chauf•feur
chauvanism : chau•vin•ism
chauvenism : chau•vin•ism
chau•vin•ism
chavinism : chau•vin•ism
cheaky : cheeky
cheap•en
cheapin : cheap•en
chearful : cheer•ful
cheary : cheery
cheatah : chee•tah
cheat•er
Checago : Chi•ca•go
Chechoslovakia :
    Czech•o•slo•va•kia
check•er
cheeftain : chief•tain
cheekey : cheeky
cheeky
cheepen : cheap•en
cheer•ful
cheerfull : cheer•ful

cheery
cheeta : chee•tah
chee•tah
cheeter : cheat•er
cheiftain : chief•tain
cheipen : cheap•en
chekey : cheeky
Chele : Chile
chello : cel•lo
chemacal : chem•i•cal
chemastry : chem•is•try
chemecal : chem•i•cal
chemeese : che•mise
chemeleon : cha•me•leon
chemelion : cha•me•leon
chemese : che•mise
chemestry : chem•is•try
chem•i•cal
chemicle : chem•i•cal
che•mise
chemistery : chem•is•try
chem•is•try
chentz : chintz
chequer (Brit.) : check•er
cherade : cha•rade
Cherakee : Cher•o•kee
cherib : cher•ub
cheriot : char•i•ot
cherioteer : char•i•o•teer
cher•ish
cherlish : churl•ish
Cher•o•kee
Cherokey : Cher•o•kee
cherrish : cher•ish
cherrub : cher•ub
cher•ry
cher•ub
chery : cher•ry
Ches•a•peake
Chesapeeke : Ches•a•peake
Chesipeake : Ches•a•peake
Chesipeeke : Ches•a•peake

chesnut : **chest·nut**
Chessapeake : **Ches·a·peake**
chessnut : **chest·nut**
chest·nut
chetah : **chee·tah**
Cheyanne : **Chey·enne**
Chey·enne
Chicaggo : **Chi·ca·go**
Chi·ca·go
chicainery : **chi·ca·nery**
chicanary : **chi·ca·nery**
chicanerry : **chi·ca·nery**
chi·ca·nery
chickery : **chic·o·ry**
chickory : **chic·o·ry**
chic·o·ry
chief·tain
chieftan : **chief·tain**
chieftin : **chief·tain**
chikanery : **chi·ca·nery**
chikery : **chic·o·ry**
childern : **chil·dren**
chil·dren
Chile
Chille : **Chile**
chimese : **che·mise**
chimnee : **chim·ney**
chim·ney
chimny : **chim·ney**
chimpansey : **chim·pan·zee**
chimpansie : **chim·pan·zee**
chimpansy : **chim·pan·zee**
chim·pan·zee
chimpanzy : **chim·pan·zee**
Chinease : **Chi·nese**
Chineese : **Chi·nese**
Chi·nese
Chineze : **Chi·nese**
chints : **chintz**
chintz
chior : **choir**
chipmonck : **chip·munk**

chipmonk : **chip·munk**
chip·munk
chirapractor : **chi·ro·prac·tor**
chire : **choir**
chiropracktor : **chi·ro·prac·tor**
chiropracter : **chi·ro·prac·tor**
chi·ro·prac·tor
chisal : **chis·el**
chis·el
chisle : **chis·el**
chissel : **chis·el**
chitah : **chee·tah**
chivalery : **chiv·al·ry**
chivalrey : **chiv·al·ry**
chiv·al·ry ˙
chivelry : **chiv·al·ry**
chivilry : **chiv·al·ry**
Chiyenne : **Chey·enne**
chizel : **chis·el**
chizzel : **chis·el**
chloesterol : **cho·les·ter·ol**
chloraform : **chlo·ro·form**
chloreen : **chlo·rine**
chloresterol : **cho·les·ter·ol**
chlo·ride
chloriform : **chlo·ro·form**
chlo·rine
chlo·ro·form
chlouride : **chlo·ride**
chlourine : **chlo·rine**
chluoride : **chlo·ride**
chluorine : **chlo·rine**
chluoroform : **chlo·ro·form**
choake : **choke**
choas : **cha·os**
choir
choiral : **cho·ral**
choireographer :
    cho·re·og·ra·pher
choke
chol·era
cholerra : **chol·era**

cholesteral : **cho·les·ter·ol**
cholesteroil : **cho·les·ter·ol**
cho·les·ter·ol
cholestral : **cho·les·ter·ol**
choot : **chute**
chop sooie : **chop su·ey**
chop sooy : **chop su·ey**
chop su·ey
cho·ral (relating to a choir);
   cho·rale (hymn); **cor·al**
   (reef); **cor·ral** (horse pen)
cho·rale (hymn); **cho·ral**
   (relating to a choir); **cor·al**
   (reef); **cor·ral** (horse pen)
chord (music); **cord** (rope)
chorel : **cho·ral** (relating to a
   choir) *or* **cho·rale** (hymn) *or*
   cor·al (reef) *or* **cor·ral** (horse
   pen)
choreografer :
   cho·re·og·ra·pher
cho·re·og·ra·pher
choriographer :
   cho·re·og·ra·pher
choris : **cho·rus**
choriss : **cho·rus**
cho·rus
chouder : **chow·der**
chovinism : **chau·vin·ism**
chow·der
chrisanthamem :
   chry·san·the·mum
chrisanthamum :
   chry·san·the·mum
chrisanthemum :
   chry·san·the·mum
christhanimum :
   chry·san·the·mum
Chris·tian
Christianety : **Chris·tian·i·ty**
Christianitty : **Chris·tian·i·ty**
Chris·tian·i·ty

Christien : **Chris·tian**
Christienity : **Chris·tian·i·ty**
Christion : **Chris·tian**
Christionity : **Chris·tian·i·ty**
chromeum : **chro·mi·um**
chromiem : **chro·mi·um**
chro·mi·um
chronalogy : **chro·nol·o·gy**
chron·ic
chronical : **chron·i·cle**
chronick : **chron·ic**
chronickal : **chron·i·cle**
chron·i·cle
chronikal : **chron·i·cle**
chronnic : **chron·ic**
chronnicle : **chron·i·cle**
chronnology : **chro·nol·o·gy**
chronollogy : **chro·nol·o·gy**
chronologgy : **chro·nol·o·gy**
chro·nol·o·gy
chrysanthamum :
   chry·san·the·mum
chrysanthemem :
   chry·san·the·mum
chry·san·the·mum
chuckal : **chuck·le**
chuckel : **chuck·le**
chuck·le
chukle : **chuck·le**
churl·ish
churllish : **churl·ish**
chute
cianide : **cy·a·nide**
Ciaro : **Cai·ro**
cibernetics : **cy·ber·net·ics**
cicle : **cy·cle**
ciclone : **cy·clone**
cieling : **ceil·ing**
ciello : **cel·lo**
cifer : **ci·pher**
ci·gar
cigarete : **cig·a·rette**

cig·a·rette
ciger : ci·gar
cigerette : cig·a·rette
ciggar : ci·gar
ciggarette : cig·a·rette
cignet : cyg·net (swan) or
   sig·net (ring)
Ciltic : Cel·tic
cilynder : cyl·in·der
cimbal : cym·bal (brass plate)
   or sym·bol (meaningful
   image)
cimball : cym·bal (brass plate)
   or sym·bol (meaningful
   image)
cimbol : cym·bal (brass plate)
   or sym·bol (meaningful
   image)
cinama : cin·e·ma
cinamin : cin·na·mon
cinamon : cin·na·mon
Cincanati : Cin·cin·nati
Cincenati : Cin·cin·nati
Cincennati : Cin·cin·nati
Cincinati : Cin·cin·nati
Cin·cin·nati
Cincinnatti : Cin·cin·nati
Cincinnaty : Cin·cin·nati
cin·e·ma
cineman : cin·na·mon
cinemon : cin·na·mon
cinicism : cyn·i·cism
cinnama : cin·e·ma
cinnamen : cin·na·mon
cinnamin : cin·na·mon
cin·na·mon
Cinncinati : Cin·cin·nati
Cinncinnati : Cin·cin·nati
cinnema : cin·e·ma
cinneman : cin·na·mon
cinnemon : cin·na·mon
Cinsanati : Cin·cin·nati

Cinsinnati : Cin·cin·nati
ci·pher
cipress : cy·press
cir·ca
circamspect : cir·cum·spect
circemspect : cir·cum·spect
circemstance : cir·cum·stance
circis : cir·cus
circka : cir·ca
cir·cu·late
cir·cum·spect
circumstanse : cir·cum·stance
cir·cus
circuss : cir·cus
cirhosis : cir·rho·sis
cirka : cir·ca
cirkus : cir·cus
Ciro : Cai·ro
ciropractor : chi·ro·prac·tor
cirosis : cir·rho·sis
cirqulate : cir·cu·late
circus : cir·cus
cir·rho·ses (plur.); cir·rho·sis
   (sing.)
cir·rho·sis (sing.); cir·rho·ses
   (plur.)
cirrhosiss : cir·rho·sis
cirrosis : cir·rho·sis
cisstern : cis·tern
cisstirn : cis·tern
cissturn : cis·tern
cis·tern
cistirn : cis·tern
cisturn : cis·tern
cit·a·del
citadell : cit·a·del
citazen : cit·i·zen
citecen : cit·i·zen
citedel : cit·a·del
citezen : cit·i·zen
citicen : cit·i·zen
citicin : cit·i·zen

citidel : **cit·a·del**
cit·ies
cit·i·zen
citrous : **cit·rus**
cit·rus
citties : **cit·ies**
cittizen : **cit·i·zen**
citys : **cit·ies**
cityzen : **cit·i·zen**
civalization : **civ·i·li·za·tion**
civec : **civ·ic**
civelization : **civ·i·li·za·tion**
civ·ic
civick : **civ·ic**
civilisation (*Brit.*) :
  civ·i·li·za·tion
civ·i·li·za·tion
civillization : **civ·i·li·za·tion**
clairet : **clar·et**
clairity : **clar·i·ty**
clair·voy·ance
clairvoyanse : **clair·voy·ance**
clairvoyence : **clair·voy·ance**
clairvoyince : **clair·voy·ance**
clamer : **clam·or**
clamity : **ca·lam·i·ty**
clammer : **clam·or**
clammor : **clam·or**
clam·or
clamour (*Brit.*) : **clam·or**
clarafication : **clar·i·fi·ca·tion**
claranet : **clar·i·net**
clarat : **clar·et**
clarefication : **clar·i·fi·ca·tion**
clarenet : **clar·i·net**
clareon : **clar·i·on**
clar·et
clarety : **clar·i·ty**
clarifacation : **clar·i·fi·ca·tion**
clarifecation : **clar·i·fi·ca·tion**
clarificasion : **clar·i·fi·ca·tion**
clar·i·fi·ca·tion

clar·i·fy
clar·i·net
clar·i·on
clarit : **clar·et**
claritty : **clar·i·ty**
clar·i·ty
clarrion : **clar·i·on**
clarrity : **clar·i·ty**
clarvoyance : **clair·voy·ance**
clasefy : **clas·si·fy**
clasic : **clas·sic**
clasify : **clas·si·fy**
classec : **clas·sic**
classefy : **clas·si·fy**
clas·sic
classick : **clas·sic**
classiffy : **clas·si·fy**
clas·si·fy
clastrophobia :
  claus·tro·pho·bia
Claus (Santa); **clause** (sentence
  part); **claws** (talons)
clause (sentence part); **Claus**
  (Santa); **claws** (talons)
claustraphobia :
  claus·tro·pho·bia
claustrephobia :
  claus·tro·pho·bia
claustrofobia :
  claus·tro·pho·bia
claustrophobea :
  claus·tro·pho·bia
claus·tro·pho·bia
claws (talons); **Claus** (Santa);
  clause (sentence part)
clawstrophobia :
  claus·tro·pho·bia
clean·li·ness
cleanliniss : **clean·li·ness**
cleanlyness : **clean·li·ness**
cleansed
clear·ance

clearanse : **clear·ance**
clearence : **clear·ance**
clearense : **clear·ance**
clearify : **clar·i·fy**
clearrance : **clear·ance**
clearvoyance : **clair·voy·ance**
cleav·age
cleave
cleav·er
cleavidge : **cleav·age**
cleavige : **cleav·age**
cleche : **cli·ché**
cleeche : **cli·ché**
cleerance : **clear·ance**
cleeranse : **clear·ance**
cleerence : **clear·ance**
cleerense : **clear·ance**
cleevage : **cleav·age**
cleeve : **cleave**
cleeveage : **cleav·age**
cleever : **cleav·er**
cleint : **cli·ent**
cleive : **cleave**
cleiver : **cleav·er**
clem·en·cy
clemensy : **clem·en·cy**
clemincy : **clem·en·cy**
cleminsy : **clem·en·cy**
clemmency : **clem·en·cy**
clenliness : **clean·li·ness**
clensed : **cleansed**
cleptomaniac : **klep·to·ma·ni·ac**
cliant : **cli·ent**
cliantele : **cli·en·tele**
cliantell : **cli·en·tele**
clichay : **cli·ché**
cli·ché
click (sound); **clique** (group)
cli·ent
cli·en·tele
clientell : **cli·en·tele**
clientelle : **cli·en·tele**

clieve : **cleave**
cli·mac·tic (of a climax);
　　cli·ma·tic (of a climate)
climat : **cli·mate**
cli·mate
cli·ma·tic (of a climate);
　　cli·mac·tic (of a climax)
climency : **clem·en·cy**
climet : **cli·mate**
climite : **cli·mate**
climmat : **cli·mate**
climmate : **cli·mate**
climmit : **cli·mate**
clinec : **clin·ic**
clin·ic
clinick : **clin·ic**
clinliness : **clean·li·ness**
clinnic : **clin·ic**
clinsed : **cleansed**
clique (group); **click** (sound)
clishay : **cli·ché**
clishee : **cli·ché**
cloak·room
cloasure : **clo·sure**
cloathing : **cloth·ing**
cloisster : **clois·ter**
clois·ter
clokeroom : **cloak·room**
clokroom : **cloak·room**
cloride : **chlo·ride**
clorine : **chlo·rine**
cloroform : **chlo·ro·form**
close (to shut); **clothes**
　　(apparel)
closhure : **clo·sure**
clostrophobia :
　　claus·tro·pho·bi·a
clo·sure
clothes (apparel); **close** (to
　　shut); **cloths** (fabrics)
cloth·ing

cloths (fabrics); clothes
  (apparel)
clouride : chlo•ride
clourine : chlo•rine
cloyster : clois•ter
coaco : co•coa
coaficcient : co•ef•fi•cient
coalece : co•alesce
co•alesce
coalese : co•alesce
coaless : co•alesce
coalicion : co•ali•tion
coalishion : co•ali•tion
co•ali•tion
coalittion : co•ali•tion
coarse (rough); course
  (direction)
coaterie : co•te•rie
cocaign : co•caine
cocain : co•caine
co•caine
cocane : co•caine
cocanut : co•co•nut
cocaonut : co•co•nut
coccaine : co•caine
cochroach : cock•roach
cock•ney
cocknie : cock•ney
cockny : cock•ney
cock•roach
cockroch : cock•roach
cocney : cock•ney
cocny : cock•ney
co•co (palm); co•coa
  (beverage)
co•coa
cocoanut : co•co•nut
co•co•nut
co•coon
cocune : co•coon
codafy : cod•i•fy
coddafy : cod•i•fy

coddefy : cod•i•fy
coddify : cod•i•fy
codeen : co•deine
codefy : cod•i•fy
co•deine
codene : co•deine
cod•ger
codiene : co•deine
cod•i•fy
codine : co•deine
coefficiant : co•ef•fi•cient
co•ef•fi•cient
coeffisient : co•ef•fi•cient
coeffitiant : co•ef•fi•cient
coeffitient : co•ef•fi•cient
coeficient : co•ef•fi•cient
coefisient : co•ef•fi•cient
coelesce : co•alesce
coelition : co•ali•tion
co•erce
coercian : co•er•cion
coercien : co•er•cion
co•er•cion
coerse : co•erce
coersion : co•er•cion
coertion : co•er•cion
cofee : cof•fee
coff : cough
cof•fee
coffen : cof•fin
cofficient : co•ef•fi•cient
cof•fin
cofin : cof•fin
co•gen•cy
cogensy : co•gen•cy
cogentcy : co•gen•cy
cogentsy : co•gen•cy
coger : cod•ger
co•gnac
cognezant : cog•ni•zant
cognisant : cog•ni•zant
cog•ni•zant

coharence : **co•her•ence**
coharent : **co•her•ent**
cohecion : **co•he•sion**
coheerence : **co•her•ence**
coheerent : **co•her•ent**
coheesion : **co•he•sion**
coheirence : **co•her•ence**
coheirent : **co•her•ent**
coherance : **co•her•ence**
coheranse : **co•her•ence**
coherant : **co•her•ent**
coherce : **co•erce**
co•her•ence
coherense : **co•her•ence**
co•her•ent
coherse : **co•erce**
co•he•sion
cohhession : **co•he•sion**
cohision : **co•he•sion**
coin•age
coincedence : **co•in•ci•dence**
co•in•cide
co•in•ci•dence
coincidense : **co•in•ci•dence**
coincidince : **co•in•ci•dence**
coincied : **co•in•cide**
coinege : **coin•age**
coinige : **coin•age**
coinsedence : **co•in•ci•dence**
coinside : **co•in•cide**
coinsidence : **co•in•ci•dence**
cokaine : **co•caine**
cokney : **cock•ney**
cokny : **cock•ney**
cokonut : **co•co•nut**
colaborate : **col•lab•o•rate**
colaborator : **col•lab•o•ra•tor**
colan : **col•on**
col•an•der (drainer); **cal•en•dar**
  (chart of dates); **cal•en•der**
  (pressing machine)
colapse : **col•lapse**

colapsible : **col•laps•ible**
colar : **col•lar**
Colarado : **Col•o•ra•do**
colassal : **co•los•sal**
colateral : **col•lat•er•al**
coldslaw : **cole•slaw**
coleague : **col•league**
colection : **col•lec•tion**
colector : **col•lec•tor**
colege : **col•lege**
colen : **col•on**
colender : **col•an•der**
colera : **chol•era**
cole•slaw
colesterol : **cho•les•ter•ol**
col•ic
coliceum : **col•i•se•um**
colicion : **co•ali•tion**
colick : **col•ic**
col•icky
colicy : **col•icky**
colide : **col•lide**
col•i•se•um (amphitheater);
  Col•os•se•um (amphitheater
  in Rome)
colision : **col•li•sion**
colisium : **col•i•se•um**
colisseum : **col•i•se•um**
colission : **co•a•lition**
colition : **co•a•lition**
collabborate : **col•lab•o•rate**
collabborator : **col•lab•o•ra•tor**
collaberate : **col•lab•o•rate**
collaberator : **col•lab•o•ra•tor**
collabirate : **col•lab•o•rate**
collabirator : **col•lab•o•ra•tor**
col•lab•o•rate
collaborater : **col•lab•o•ra•tor**
col•lab•o•ra•tor
col•lage (composite work);
  col•league (associate);
  col•lege (school)

collander : **col·an·der**
collapce : **col·lapse**
collapsable : **col·laps·ible**
col·lapse
col·laps·ible
col·lar
col·lat·er·al
collaterel : **col·lat·er·al**
colleage : **col·lage** (composite
    work) *or* **col·league**
    (associate) *or* **col·lege**
    (school)
col·league (associate); **col·lage**
    (composite work); **col·lege**
    (school)
collecion : **col·lec·tion**
collecktion : **col·lec·tion**
collecter : **col·lec·tor**
col·lec·tion
col·lec·tor
colledge : **col·lage** (composite
    work) *or* **col·lege** (school)
colleegue : **col·league**
col·lege (school); **col·lage**
    (composite work); **col·league**
    (associate)
collegue : **col·league**
colleigue : **col·league**
collender : **col·an·der**
coller : **col·lar**
collerteral : **col·lat·er·al**
collesterol : **cho·les·ter·ol**
collic : **col·ic**
collicky : **col·icky**
col·lide
col·lie
collied : **col·lide**
colliflauer : **cau·li·flow·er**
colliflour : **cau·li·flow·er**
colliflower : **cau·li·flow·er**
collige : **col·lege**
colliseum : **col·i·se·um**

col·li·sion
collisium : **col·i·se·um**
collisseum : **col·i·se·um**
collission : **col·li·sion**
collizion : **col·li·sion**
collocial : **col·lo·qui·al**
collon : **col·on**
collonade : **col·on·nade**
collonel : **col·o·nel**
collonial : **co·lo·nial**
colloqial : **col·lo·qui·al**
colloqueal : **col·lo·qui·al**
col·lo·qui·al
colloquiel : **col·lo·qui·al**
Collorado : **Col·o·ra·do**
collossal : **co·los·sal**
collslaw : **cole·slaw**
collucion : **col·lu·sion**
collumbine : **col·um·bine**
Collumbus : **Co·lum·bus**
collumn : **col·umn**
col·lu·sion
colly : **col·lie**
Co·lom·bia (South American
    nation); **Co·lum·bia** (federal
    district)
colombine : **col·um·bine**
Colombus : **Co·lum·bus**
co·lon
colonade : **col·on·nade**
coloneal : **co·lo·nial**
col·o·nel (military officer);
    ker·nel (seed)
co·lo·nial
col·on·nade
colonnaid : **col·on·nade**
colonnel : **col·o·nel**
colonnial : **co·lo·nial**
coloquial : **col·lo·qui·al**
Coloraddo : **Col·o·ra·do**
Col·o·ra·do
coloride : **chlo·ride**

colorine : **chlo·rine**
Colorrado : **Col·o·ra·do**
colosal : **co·los·sal**
co·los·sal
Col·os·se·um (amphitheater in Rome); **col·i·se·um** (amphitheater)
colum : **col·umn**
Co·lum·bia (federal district); **Co·lom·bia** (South American nation)
col·um·bine
Co·lum·bus
Columbuss : **Co·lum·bus**
col·umn
columnade : **col·on·nade**
colusion : **col·lu·sion**
co·ma (unconscious state); **com·ma** (,)
comady : **com·e·dy**
comandant : **com·man·dant**
combenation : **com·bi·na·tion**
com·bi·na·tion
combinnation : **com·bi·na·tion**
combonation : **com·bi·na·tion**
combustable : **com·bus·ti·ble**
com·bus·ti·ble
comecal : **com·i·cal**
comeddy : **com·e·dy**
comedean : **co·me·di·an**
co·me·di·an
com·e·dy
comeedian : **co·me·di·an**
come·ly
comememorate : **com·mem·o·rate**
comemmorate : **com·mem·o·rate**
comemorate : **com·mem·o·rate**
comence : **com·mence**
comendable : **com·mend·able**
coment : **com·ment**

comentary : **com·men·tary**
comerce : **com·merce**
comercial : **com·mer·cial**
comersial : **com·mer·cial**
com·et (celestial body); **com·mit** (to entrust)
comfert : **com·fort**
comfertable : **com·fort·able**
com·fort
com·fort·able
comforteble : **com·fort·able**
comfortible : **com·fort·able**
com·ic
com·i·cal
comick : **com·ic**
comince : **com·mence**
comint : **com·ment**
comintary : **com·men·tary**
comiserate : **com·mis·er·ate**
comissar : **com·mis·sar**
comissary : **com·mis·sary**
comit : **com·et** (celestial body) *or* **com·mit** (to entrust)
comite : **com·mit·tee**
comittee : **com·mit·tee**
com·it·y (civility); **com·mit·tee** (task force)
comly : **come·ly**
com·ma (,); **co·ma** (unconscious state)
commady : **com·e·dy**
com·man·dant
commandaunt : **com·man·dant**
com·man·deer (to take by force); **com·mand·er** (leader)
com·mand·er (leader); **com·man·deer** (to take by force)
commant : **com·ment**
commantary : **com·men·tary**
commedian : **co·me·di·an**
commedy : **com·e·dy**

commeidian : **co•me•di•an**
commemerate :
  com•mem•o•rate
com•mem•o•rate
com•mence
com•mend•able
commendeble : **com•mend•able**
commendible : **com•mend•able**
commense : **com•mence**
com•ment
com•men•tary
commenterry : **com•men•tary**
commentery : **com•men•tary**
com•merce
com•mer•cial
commerse : **com•merce**
commershal : **com•mer•cial**
commersial : **com•mer•cial**
commet : **com•et** (celestial
  body) *or* **com•mit** (to
  entrust)
commic : **com•ic**
commical : **com•i•cal**
commince : **com•mence**
commindable : **com•mend•able**
comminse : **com•mence**
commint : **com•ment**
commintary : **com•men•tary**
commisar : **com•mis•sar**
commisary : **com•mis•sary**
com•mis•er•ate
commisirate : **com•mis•er•ate**
com•mis•sar
commissare : **com•mis•sar**
com•mis•sary
commisserate : **com•mis•er•ate**
commisserry : **com•mis•sary**
commissery : **com•mis•sary**
commisurate : **com•mis•er•ate**
commiszar : **com•mis•sar**
com•mit (to entrust); **com•et**
  (celestial body)

commite : **com•mit•tee**
com•mit•tee
committy : **com•mit•tee**
commoddity : **com•mod•i•ty**
commoddore : **com•mo•dore**
com•mode
commodety : **com•mod•i•ty**
commoditty : **com•mod•i•ty**
com•mod•i•ty
commodoar : **com•mo•dore**
commodoor : **com•mo•dore**
commodor : **com•mo•dore**
com•mo•dore
com•mon•er
com•mon•place
commonplaise : **com•mon•place**
commonplase : **com•mon•place**
com•mon•weal
com•mon•wealth
commonweel : **com•mon•weal**
commonweil : **com•mon•weal**
commonwellth :
  com•mon•wealth
commonwelth :
  com•mon•wealth
commoon : **com•mune**
commoonicable :
  com•mu•ni•ca•ble
commoonion : **com•mu•nion**
commoot : **com•mute**
com•mo•tion
com•mune
communety : **com•mu•ni•ty**
communian : **com•mu•nion**
com•mu•ni•ca•ble
com•mu•ni•cate
communiceble :
  com•mu•ni•ca•ble
communickable :
  com•mu•ni•ca•ble
communikate : **com•mu•ni•cate**
com•mu•nion

com·mu·nism
communitty : **com·mu·ni·ty**
com·mu·ni·ty
communiun : **com·mu·nion**
communnity : **com·mu·ni·ty**
communplace : **com·mon·place**
communyon : **com·mu·nion**
commurce : **com·merce**
commurse : **com·merce**
com·mute
comoddity : **com·mod·i·ty**
comode : **com·mode**
comodore : **com·mo·dore**
comoner : **com·mon·er**
comonplace : **com·mon·place**
comotion : **com·mo·tion**
compair : **com·pare**
compairable : **com·pa·ra·ble**
compairative : **com·par·a·tive**
compairison : **com·par·i·son**
com·pan·ion
companiun : **com·pan·ion**
compannion : **com·pan·ion**
companyon : **com·pan·ion**
com·pa·ra·ble
comparason : **com·par·i·son**
com·par·a·tive
com·pare
compareable : **com·pa·ra·ble**
compareble : **com·pa·ra·ble**
compareson : **com·par·i·son**
comparetive : **com·par·a·tive**
comparible : **com·pa·ra·ble**
comparisen : **com·par·i·son**
com·par·i·son
comparisun : **com·par·i·son**
comparitive : **com·par·a·tive**
compas : **com·pass**
compashion : **com·pas·sion**
compasion : **com·pas·sion**
com·pass
com·pas·sion

compatable : **com·pat·i·ble**
compateble : **com·pat·i·ble**
com·pat·i·ble
compeet : **com·pete**
compeit : **com·pete**
com·pel
compell : **com·pel**
compelsory : **com·pul·so·ry**
compencate : **com·pen·sate**
compendeum : **com·pen·di·um**
compendiom : **com·pen·di·um**
com·pen·di·um
com·pen·sate
compesition : **com·po·si·tion**
compess : **com·pass**
competator : **com·pet·i·tor**
com·pete
com·pe·tence
competense : **com·pe·tence**
competicion : **com·pe·ti·tion**
competince : **com·pe·tence**
competirer : **com·pet·i·tor**
competision : **com·pe·ti·tion**
com·pe·ti·tion
com·pet·i·tor
compindium : **com·pen·di·um**
compinsate : **com·pen·sate**
compis : **com·pass**
compisition : **com·po·si·tion**
compitence : **com·pe·tence**
compitition : **com·pe·ti·tion**
com·pla·cen·cy
complacensy : **com·pla·cen·cy**
com·pla·cent (self-satisfied);
    com·plai·sant (eager to
    please)
complacincy : **com·pla·cen·cy**
complaicency : **com·pla·cen·cy**
complaicent : **com·pla·cent**
    (self-satisfied) *or*
    com·plai·sant (eager to
    please)

com·plain
com·plai·sant (eager to please);
   com·pla·cent (self-satisfied)
complaisency : **com·pla·cen·cy**
complane : **com·plain**
complasency : **com·pla·cen·cy**
complasent : **com·pla·cent**
   (self-satisfied) *or*
   com·plai·sant (eager to
   please)
compleat : **com·plete**
complection : **com·plex·ion**
compleet : **com·plete**
compleetion : **com·ple·tion**
com·ple·ment (that which
   completes); **com·pli·ment**
   (flattering remark)
complesion : **com·ple·tion**
com·plete
completian : **com·ple·tion**
com·ple·tion
complexian : **com·plex·ion**
com·plex·ion
com·pli·ance
complianse : **com·pli·ance**
com·pli·ant
complicitty : **com·plic·i·ty**
com·plic·i·ty
complience : **com·pli·ance**
compliense : **com·pli·ance**
complient : **com·pli·ant**
com·pli·ment (flattering
   remark); **com·ple·ment** (that
   which completes)
complisitty : **com·plic·i·ty**
complisity : **com·plic·i·ty**
complition : **com·ple·tion**
compoanent : **com·po·nent**
componant : **com·po·nent**
com·po·nent
composate : **com·pos·ite**
composet : **com·pos·ite**

composhure : **com·po·sure**
composicion : **com·po·si·tion**
composit : **com·pos·ite**
com·pos·ite
com·po·si·tion
compossite : **com·pos·ite**
com·po·sure
compozure : **com·po·sure**
comprahend : **com·pre·hend**
comprahensible :
   com·pre·hen·si·ble
compramise : **com·pro·mise**
compramize : **com·pro·mise**
comprehenceble :
   com·pre·hen·si·ble
comprehencible :
   com·pre·hen·si·ble
com·pre·hend
comprehensable :
   com·pre·hen·si·ble
comprehenseble :
   com·pre·hen·si·ble
com·pre·hen·si·ble
compremise : **com·pro·mise**
compremize : **com·pro·mise**
compreshion : **com·pres·sion**
compresible : **com·press·ible**
compresion : **com·pres·sion**
compresor : **com·pres·sor**
compressable : **com·press·ible**
compresser : **com·pres·sor**
com·press·ible
com·pres·sion
com·pres·sor
comprimise : **com·pro·mise**
comprimize : **com·pro·mise**
com·prise
comprize : **com·prise**
com·pro·mise
compromize : **com·pro·mise**
comp·trol·ler *or* **con·trol·ler**
compulcery : **com·pul·so·ry**

compulsery : **com·pul·so·ry**
com·pul·so·ry
compuss : **com·pass**
comraderie : **ca·ma·ra·de·rie**
comradry : **ca·ma·ra·de·rie**
comroderie : **ca·ma·ra·de·rie**
comune : **com·mune**
comunicable :
   com·mu·ni·ca·ble
comunicate : **com·mu·ni·cate**
comunion : **com·mu·nion**
comunism : **com·mu·nism**
comunity : **com·mu·ni·ty**
comute : **com·mute**
conafer : **co·ni·fer**
concard : **con·cord**
con·ceal
conceave : **con·ceive**
con·cede
conceed : **con·cede**
conceel : **con·ceal**
conceeve : **con·ceive**
conceil : **con·ceal**
con·ceit
con·ceiv·able
con·ceive
conceiveable : **con·ceiv·able**
concensus : **con·sen·sus**
concentrait : **con·cen·trate**
con·cen·trate
con·cen·tric
concentrick : **con·cen·tric**
con·cept
con·cep·tu·al
conceptuel : **con·cep·tu·al**
conceptule : **con·cep·tu·al**
con·cern
con·cert
con·ces·sion
conciderable : **con·sid·er·able**
conciel : **con·ceal**
conciet : **con·ceit**

concieve : **con·ceive**
con·cil·i·ate
conciliatorry : **con·cil·ia·to·ry**
con·cil·ia·to·ry
concillatory : **con·cil·ia·to·ry**
concilleate : **con·cil·i·ate**
concilliate : **con·cil·i·ate**
concilliatory : **con·cil·ia·to·ry**
concillitory : **con·cil·ia·to·ry**
concintrate : **con·cen·trate**
concirt : **con·cert**
con·cise
concomatant : **con·com·i·tant**
concometent : **con·com·i·tant**
con·com·i·tant
concomitent : **con·com·i·tant**
concommitant : **con·com·i·tant**
concommitent : **con·com·i·tant**
con·cord
concreet : **con·crete**
concreit : **con·crete**
con·crete
con·cur
concure : **con·cur**
concurent : **con·cur·rent**
concurn : **con·cern**
concurr : **con·cur**
concurrant : **con·cur·rent**
con·cur·rent
concushion : **con·cus·sion**
concusion : **con·cus·sion**
concussien : **con·cus·sion**
con·cus·sion
concution : **con·cus·sion**
condament : **con·di·ment**
condaminium :
   con·do·min·i·um
condamint : **con·di·ment**
condascend : **con·de·scend**
condascension :
   con·de·scen·sion
condement : **con·di·ment**

condeminium :
con·do·min·i·um
condemm : con·demn
con·demn
condence : con·dense
con·dense
con·de·scend
con·de·scen·sion
condescinsion :
con·de·scen·sion
condesend : con·de·scend
condesension : con·de·scen·sion
condessend : con·de·scend
condicion : con·di·tion
con·di·ment
condiscend : con·de·scend
condission : con·di·tion
con·di·tion
condolance : con·do·lence
condolanse : con·do·lence
con·do·lence
condolense : con·do·lence
condomenium :
con·do·min·i·um
condominiem :
con·do·min·i·um
con·do·min·i·um
condominnium :
con·do·min·i·um
conduceve : con·du·cive
con·du·cive
conducter : con·duc·tor
con·duc·tor
conduet : con·duit
con·duit
condusive : con·du·cive
condute : con·duit
coneac : co·gnac
confadence : con·fi·dence
confadential : con·fi·den·tial
confedaracy : con·fed·er·a·cy
confedence : con·fi·dence

confedential : con·fi·den·tial
con·fed·er·a·cy
confederasy : con·fed·er·a·cy
con·fed·er·ate
confederet : con·fed·er·ate
confederissy : con·fed·er·a·cy
confederisy : con·fed·er·a·cy
confedirate : con·fed·er·ate
conferance : con·fer·ence
conferanse : con·fer·ence
confered : con·ferred
con·fer·ee
con·fer·ence
conferense : con·fer·ence
conferie : con·fer·ee
con·ferred
conferree : con·fer·ee
conferrence : con·fer·ence
confery : con·fer·ee
confesion : con·fes·sion
confessian : con·fes·sion
con·fes·sion
confeti : con·fet·ti
con·fet·ti
con·fi·dant or con·fi·dante (one
confided in); con·fi·dent
(assured)
con·fi·dante or con·fi·dant (one
confided in); con·fi·dent
(assured)
con·fi·dence
confidense : con·fi·dence
confidenshial : con·fi·den·tial
confidensial : con·fi·den·tial
confident (assured);
con·fi·dant (one confided in)
con·fi·den·tial
confidintial : con·fi·den·tial
configeration :
con·fig·u·ra·tion
configguration :
con·fig·u·ra·tion

con•fig•u•ra•tion
con•fla•gra•tion
conflagretion : con•fla•gra•tion
conflegration : con•fla•gra•tion
confligration : con•fla•gra•tion
confuree : con•fer•ee
confurred : con•ferred
con•fused
confuzed : con•fused
con•geal
congeel : con•geal
congeenial : con•ge•nial
congeil : con•geal
con•ge•nial
conginial : con•ge•nial
congizant : cog•ni•zant
congnac : co•gnac
congradulate : con•grat•u•late
congragate : con•gre•gate
congragration : con•gre•ga•tion
congratalate : con•grat•u•late
con•grat•u•late
congregacion : con•gre•ga•tion
con•gre•gate
con•gre•ga•tion
congres : con•gress
con•gress
congrigate : con•gre•gate
congrigation : con•gre•ga•tion
congriss : con•gress
congruance : con•gru•ence
congruanse : con•gru•ence
con•gru•ence
congruense : con•gru•ence
congugal : con•ju•gal
coniac : co•gnac
con•ic
con•i•fer
conivance : con•niv•ance
conjagle : con•ju•gal
conjigal : con•ju•gal
con•ju•gal

conker : con•quer
conkeror : con•quer•or
connatation : con•no•ta•tion
Connectacutt : Con•nect•i•cut
Connectecut : Con•nect•i•cut
Con•nect•i•cut
Connetacut : Con•nect•i•cut
Conneticut : Con•nect•i•cut
connic : con•ic
connifer : co•ni•fer
con•niv•ance
connivanse : con•niv•ance
connivence : con•niv•ance
con•nois•seur
connoser : con•nois•seur
connossure : con•nois•seur
con•no•ta•tion
con•note
conosseur : con•nois•seur
conotation : con•no•ta•tion
conote : con•note
conpare : com•pare
con•quer
conquerer : con•quer•or
con•quer•or
conquor : con•quer
conqur : con•quer
conqurer : con•quer•or
consacrate : con•se•crate
consalate : con•sul•ate
consalation : con•so•la•tion
consarn : con•cern
con•science (moral sense);
    con•scious (awake)
con•scious (awake);
    con•science (moral sense)
conseal : con•ceal
con•se•crate
consede : con•cede
conseed : con•cede
conseel : con•ceal
conseeve : con•ceive

conseil : **con·ceal**
conseit : **con·ceit**
conseive : **con·ceive**
consensis : **con·sen·sus**
con·sen·sus
consentrate : **con·cen·trate**
consentric : **con·cen·tric**
consept : **con·cept**
conseptual : **con·cep·tu·al**
con·se·quence
consequense : **con·se·quence**
consequince : **con·se·quence**
consern : **con·cern**
consert : **con·cert**
conservatian : **con·ser·va·tion**
con·ser·va·tion
con·ser·va·tive
conservatorry : **con·ser·va·to·ry**
con·ser·va·to·ry
conservetive : **con·ser·va·tive**
conservetory : **con·ser·va·to·ry**
conservitive : **con·ser·va·tive**
conseshion : **con·ces·sion**
consesion : **con·ces·sion**
consession : **con·ces·sion**
consice : **con·cise**
consicrate : **con·se·crate**
con·sid·er·able
considerible : **con·sid·er·able**
consieve : **con·ceive**
consilate : **con·sul·ate**
consilation : **con·so·la·tion**
consilatory : **con·cil·ia·to·ry**
consiliate : **con·cil·i·ate**
consiliatory : **con·cil·ia·to·ry**
consilitory : **con·cil·ia·to·ry**
consillatory : **con·cil·ia·to·ry**
consilliate : **con·cil·i·ate**
consilliatory : **con·cil·ia·to·ry**
consillitory : **con·cil·ia·to·ry**
consintrate : **con·cen·trate**
consise : **con·cise**

consistancy : **con·sis·ten·cy**
consistansy : **con·sis·ten·cy**
consistant : **con·sis·tent**
con·sis·ten·cy
consistensy : **con·sis·ten·cy**
con·sis·tent
consoladate : **con·sol·i·date**
con·so·la·tion
consoledate : **con·sol·i·date**
con·sol·i·date
consoomer : **con·sum·er**
conspeeracy : **con·spir·a·cy**
consperacy : **con·spir·a·cy**
con·spir·a·cy
conspirasy : **con·spir·a·cy**
conspirater : **con·spir·a·tor**
con·spir·a·tor
conspirisy : **con·spir·a·cy**
constabble : **con·sta·ble**
con·sta·ble
constallation : **con·stel·la·tion**
con·stan·cy
constapate : **con·sti·pate**
constatute : **con·sti·tute**
consteble : **con·sta·ble**
constelation : **con·stel·la·tion**
con·stel·la·tion
constency : **con·stan·cy**
constensy : **con·stan·cy**
constepate : **con·sti·pate**
constetue : **con·sti·tute**
con·sti·pate
constituancy : **con·stit·u·en·cy**
con·stit·u·en·cy
constituensy : **con·stit·u·en·cy**
con·sti·tute
con·sul (diplomat); **coun·cil**
    (assembly); **coun·sel** (advice;
    lawyer)
con·sul·ate
consulltane: **con·sul·tant**
con·sul·tant

consultent : **con·sul·tant**
con·sum·er
consumor : **con·sum·er**
consurn : **con·cern**
consurvation : **con·ser·va·tion**
contageous : **con·ta·gious**
con·ta·gious
containence : **con·ti·nence**
  (self-restraint) *or*
  coun·te·nance (face)
contajious : **con·ta·gious**
contamenate : **con·tam·i·nate**
con·tam·i·nate
contemperary :
  con·tem·po·rary
contempirary : **con·tem·po·rary**
contemporarry :
  con·tem·po·rary
con·tem·po·rary
contemporery :
  con·tem·po·rary
contenence : **con·ti·nence**
  (self-restraint) *or*
  coun·te·nance (face)
contenent : **con·ti·nent**
contenentel : **con·ti·nen·tal**
contengent : **con·tin·gent**
con·tes·tant
contestent : **con·tes·tant**
contestint : **con·tes·tant**
contimporary :
  con·tem·po·rary
continance : **con·ti·nence**
  (self-restraint) *or*
  coun·te·nance (face)
con·ti·nence (self-restraint);
  coun·te·nance (face)
con·ti·nent
con·ti·nen·tal
continentle : **con·ti·nen·tal**
con·tin·gent
contingint : **con·tin·gent**

con·tin·u·al
continuel : **con·tin·u·al**
continule : **con·tin·u·al**
con·tour
con·tra·band
con·tra·cep·tive
contracter : **con·trac·tor**
con·trac·tor
con·tra·dict
contradictery : **con·tra·dic·to·ry**
contradictorry :
  con·tra·dic·to·ry
con·tra·dic·to·ry
contrarry : **con·trary**
con·trary
contraseptive : **con·tra·cep·tive**
contravercial : **con·tro·ver·sial**
contravercy : **con·tro·ver·sy**
contraverseal : **con·tro·ver·sial**
contraversial : **con·tro·ver·sial**
contraversy : **con·tro·ver·sy**
contreband : **con·tra·band**
contreceptive : **con·tra·cep·tive**
contredict : **con·tra·dict**
contredictory : **con·tra·dic·to·ry**
contrery : **con·trary**
contreversial : **con·tro·ver·sial**
contreversy : **con·tro·ver·sy**
contriband : **con·tra·band**
contridict : **con·tra·dict**
contridictory : **con·tra·dic·to·ry**
con·triv·ance
contrivence : **con·triv·ance**
contrivense : **con·triv·ance**
con·trol
controll : **con·trol**
con·trol·ler *or* **comp·trol·ler**
con·tro·ver·sial
con·tro·ver·sy
contry : **coun·try**
contur : **con·tour**
conture : **con·tour**

convacation : **con•vo•ca•tion**
con•va•les•cence
convalescense : **con•va•les•cence**
convalesence : **con•va•les•cence**
convalessence : **con•va•les•cence**
convay : **con•vey**
convayance : **con•vey•ance**
convean : **con•vene**
conveen : **con•vene**
conveenience : **con•ve•nience**
convelescence : **con•va•les•cence**
con•vene
conveneance : **con•ve•nience**
con•ve•nience
conveniense : **con•ve•nience**
con•ve•nient
con•ver•gence
convergince : **con•ver•gence**
convertable : **con•vert•ible**
con•vert•er (one that converts);
  con•vert•or (electrical device)
con•vert•ible
con•vert•or (electrical device);
  con•vert•er (one that
  converts)
convexety : **con•vex•i•ty**
convexitty : **con•vex•i•ty**
con•vex•i•ty
con•vey
con•vey•ance
conveyence : **con•vey•ance**
convication : **con•vo•ca•tion**
convience : **con•ve•nience**
convient : **con•ve•nient**
convilescence : **con•va•les•cence**
convine : **con•vene**
convinience : **con•ve•nience**
convinient : **con•ve•nient**
con•vo•ca•tion
convurgence : **con•ver•gence**
conyac : **co•gnac**
coocumber : **cu•cum•ber**

coogar : **cou•gar**
cooger : **cou•gar**
cookoo : **cuck•oo**
coo•lie (laborer); **cool•ly** (in a
  cool manner)
cool•ly (in a cool manner);
  coo•lie (laborer)
co•op•er•ate
coopon : **cou•pon**
co•or•di•nate
corage : **cour•age**
corageous : **cou•ra•geous**
cor•al (reef); **cho•ral** (relating
  to a choir); **cho•rale** (hymn);
  cor•ral (horse pen)
corale : **cho•ral** (relating to a
  choir) *or* **cho•rale** (hymn) *or*
  cor•al (reef) *or* **cor•ral** (horse
  pen)
coralle : **cho•ral** (relating to a
  choir) *or* **cho•rale** (hymn) *or*
  cor•al (reef) *or* **cor•ral** (horse
  pen)
coranation : **cor•o•na•tion**
cord (rope); **chord** (music)
cordaroy : **cor•du•roy**
cordeal : **cor•dial**
cordeality : **cor•dial•i•ty**
corderoy : **cor•du•roy**
cordialety : **cor•dial•i•ty**
cor•dial•i•ty
cordiallity : **cor•dial•i•ty**
cordiroy : **cor•du•roy**
cor•du•roy
corect : **cor•rect**
corel : **cho•ral** (relating to a
  choir) *or* **cho•rale** (hymn) *or*
  cor•al (reef) *or* **cor•ral** (horse
  pen)
corelate : **cor•re•late**
coreographer :
  cho•re•og•ra•pher

corespondence :
  cor·re·spon·dence
corgeality : cor·dial·i·ty
corgial : cor·dial
coridor : cor·ri·dor
coriographer :
  cho·re·og·ra·pher
cornace : cor·nice
cornation : cor·o·na·tion
cor·nea
cornia : cor·nea
cor·nice
cornise : cor·nice
corobarate : cor·rob·o·rate
corode : cor·rode
corolary : cor·ol·lary
cor·ol·lary
cor·o·na·tion
cor·o·ner
cororoborate : cor·rob·o·rate
corparate : cor·po·rate
corperal : cor·po·ral
corperate : cor·po·rate
cor·po·ral
cor·po·rate
corporel : cor·po·ral
corps (military unit); corpse
  (dead body)
corpse (dead body); corps
  (military unit)
corrador : cor·ri·dor
corragation : cor·ru·ga·tion
cor·ral (horse pen); cho·ral
  (relating to a choir);
  cho·rale (hymn); cor·al (reef)
corralate : cor·re·late
corrallary : cor·ol·lary
cor·rect
correl : cho·ral (relating to a
  choir) or cho·rale (hymn) or
  cor·al (reef) or cor·ral (horse
  pen)

cor·re·late
corresponanse :
  cor·re·spon·dence
correspondance :
  cor·re·spon·dence
cor·re·spon·dence
corridoor : cor·ri·dor
cor·ri·dor
corrobborate : cor·rob·o·rate
corroberate : cor·rob·o·rate
cor·rob·o·rate
cor·rode
corroll : cho·ral (relating to a
  choir) or cho·rale (hymn) or
  cor·al (reef) or cor·ral (horse
  pen)
corrollary : cor·ol·lary
corrollery : cor·ol·lary
corroner : cor·o·ner
cor·ru·ga·tion
cor·rupt
corrus : cho·rus
corteous : cour·te·ous
cortesy : cour·te·sy
corugation : cor·ru·ga·tion
corupt : cor·rupt
corus : cho·rus
corvet : cor·vette
cor·vette
cosmapolitan :
  cos·mo·pol·i·tan
cosmepolitan : cos·mo·pol·i·tan
cos·met·ic
cosmettic : cos·met·ic
cos·mo·pol·i·tan
cosmopoliten :
  cos·mo·pol·i·tan
cosmopollitan :
  cos·mo·pol·i·tan
cotarie : co·te·rie
coteree : co·te·rie
co·te·rie

cotery : **co•te•rie**
cot•tage
cottege : **cot•tage**
cotten : **cot•ton**
cottige : **cot•tage**
cot•ton
cou•gar
couger : **cou•gar**
cough
coun•cil (assembly); **con•sul**
　　(diplomat); **coun•sel** (advice;
　　lawyer)
coun•sel (advice; lawyer);
　　con•sul (diplomat); **coun•cil**
　　(assembly)
counseler : **coun•sel•or**
counsellor : **coun•sel•or**
coun•sel•or
counsillor : **coun•sel•or**
coun•te•nance (face);
　　con•ti•nence (self-restraint)
countenanse : **con•ti•nence**
　　(self-restraint) *or*
　　coun•te•nance (face)
countenence : **con•ti•nence**
　　(self-restraint) *or*
　　coun•te•nance (face)
coun•ter•feit
counterfet : **coun•ter•feit**
counterfiet : **coun•ter•feit**
counterfit : **coun•ter•feit**
count•ess
countinance : **con•ti•nence**
　　(self-restraint) *or*
　　coun•te•nance (face)
countiss : **count•ess**
coun•try
coupan : **cou•pon**
coupelet : **coup•let**
coupeling : **coup•ling**
coupleing : **coup•ling**
coup•let

coup•ling
cou•pon
couponn : **cou•pon**
cour•age
cou•ra•geous
couragious : **cou•ra•geous**
courege : **cour•age**
cou•ri•er
courige : **cour•age**
courrier : **cou•ri•er**
course (direction); **coarse**
　　(rough)
courtasy : **cour•te•sy**
　　(politeness) *or* **curt•sy** (bow)
cour•te•ous
courtessy : **cour•te•sy**
　　(politeness) *or* **curt•sy** (bow)
cour•te•sy (politeness); **curt•sy**
　　(bow)
courtious : **cour•te•ous**
courtisy : **cour•te•sy**
　　(politeness) *or* **curt•sy** (bow)
courtmarshall : **court-mar•tial**
court-mar•tial
cousen : **cous•in**
cous•in
cov•e•nant
covenent : **cov•e•nant**
covennant : **cov•e•nant**
cov•er•age
coverege : **cov•er•age**
coverige : **cov•er•age**
covrage : **cov•er•age**
cowardace : **cow•ard•ice**
cow•ard•ice
cowardise : **cow•ard•ice**
cowardiss : **cow•ard•ice**
cowerdice : **cow•ard•ice**
coy•ote
coyotee : **coy•ote**
coyotie : **coy•ote**
crainium : **cra•ni•um**

cranbary : **cran·ber·ry**
cran·ber·ry
cranbery : **cran·ber·ry**
craniem : **cra·ni·um**
cra·ni·um
cra·ter
crator : **cra·ter**
cra·vat
cravatt : **cra·vat**
creak (noise); **creek** (stream)
creamary : **cream·ery**
creamerry : **cream·ery**
cream·ery
creamory : **cream·ery**
crease
creater : **cre·ator**
cre·ator
crea·ture
crecent : **cres·cent**
credability : **cred·i·bil·i·ty**
credable : **cred·i·ble**
cre·dence
credense : **cre·dence**
credibilety : **cred·i·bil·i·ty**
cred·i·bil·i·ty
credibillity : **cred·i·bil·i·ty**
cred·i·ble
credince : **cre·dence**
cre·do
creedence : **cre·dence**
creedo : **cre·do**
creek (stream); **creak** (noise);
   crick (pain in neck)
creemery : **cream·ery**
creep
creese : **crease**
creeture : **crea·ture**
cre·scen·do
cres·cent
creshendo : **cre·scen·do**
cressant : **cres·cent**
cressendo : **cre·scen·do**

cressent : **cres·cent**
creture : **crea·ture**
crev·asse (crack in ice);
   crev·ice (narrow crack)
crevat : **cra·vat**
crevatte : **cra·vat**
·**crev·ice** (narrow crack);
   crev·asse (crack in ice)
crevisse : **crev·asse** (crack in
   ice) *or* **crev·ice** (narrow
   crack)
criator : **cre·ator**
crick (pain in neck); **creek**
   (stream)
crimenal : **crim·i·nal**
crim·i·nal
crimminal : **crim·i·nal**
crimsen : **crim·son**
crim·son
criptic : **cryp·tic**
crisanthamum :
   chry·san·the·mum
crisanthemum :
   chry·san·the·mum
cri·ses (*plur.*); **cri·sis** (*sing.*)
cri·sis (*sing.*); **cri·ses** (*plur.*)
crissis : **cri·sis**
cristal : **crys·tal**
Cristian : **Chris·tian**
Cristianity : **Chris·tian·i·ty**
critacism : **crit·i·cism**
critearia : **cri·te·ria**
critearion : **cri·te·ri·on**
criteek : **cri·tique**
criteeque : **cri·tique**
criteeria : **cri·te·ria**
criteerion : **cri·te·ri·on**
cri·te·ria (*plur.*); **cri·te·ri·on**
   (*sing.*)
cri·te·ri·on (*sing.*); **cri·te·ria**
   (*plur.*)
crit·ic

criticise (*Brit.*) : **crit·i·cize**
crit·i·cism
crit·i·cize
cri·tique
critiria : **cri·te·ria**
critirion : **cri·te·ri·on**
critisism : **crit·i·cism**
critisize : **crit·i·cize**
crittacize : **crit·i·cize**
crittic : **crit·ic**
critticism : **crit·i·cism**
critticize : **crit·i·cize**
crocadial : **croc·o·dile**
crocadile : **croc·o·dile**
crockodile : **croc·o·dile**
croc·o·dile
cromeum : **chro·mi·um**
cromiem : **chro·mi·um**
cromium : **chro·mi·um**
cronic : **chron·ic**
cronicle : **chron·i·cle**
cronollogy : **chro·nol·o·gy**
cronologgy : **chro·nol·o·gy**
cronology : **chro·nol·o·gy**
croose : **cruise**
croud : **crowd**
crowd
crucefy : **cru·ci·fy**
cru·cial
crucibal : **cru·ci·ble**
cru·ci·ble
cruciffy : **cru·ci·fy**
cru·ci·fy
cruise
cruse : **cruise**
crushall : **cru·cial**
crusial : **cru·cial**
crusible : **cru·ci·ble**
crusify : **cru·ci·fy**
crus·ta·cean
crustacion : **crus·ta·cean**
crustashean : **crus·ta·cean**

cruze : **cruise**
cryp·tic
cryptick : **cryp·tic**
crysanthamum :
    chry·san·the·mum
crysanthemum :
    chry·san·the·mum
crys·tal
crystall : **crys·tal**
crystell : **crys·tal**
csar : **czar**
cuadrant : **quad·rant**
cuarto : **quar·to**
cubbard : **cup·board**
cub·i·cal (cube-shaped);
    cub·i·cle (compartment)
cub·i·cle (compartment);
    cub·i·cal (cube-shaped)
cuck·oo
cucomber : **cu·cum·ber**
cucoo : **cuck·oo**
cu·cum·ber
cud·gel
cudgle : **cud·gel**
cue (signal; poolstick); **queue**
    (pigtail; line)
Cuebec : **Que·bec**
cujel : **cud·gel**
culenery : **cu·li·nary**
cu·li·nary
cullenery : **cu·li·nary**
cullinary : **cu·li·nary**
cullmination : **cul·mi·na·tion**
cullprit : **cul·prit**
culltivate : **cul·ti·vate**
culmanation : **cul·mi·na·tion**
culmenation : **cul·mi·na·tion**
cul·mi·na·tion
culpabal : **cul·pa·ble**
cul·pa·ble
culpible : **cul·pa·ble**
culpret : **cul·prit**

cul·prit
cultavate : **cul·ti·vate**
cul·ti·vate
cummercial : **com·mer·cial**
cumpass : **com·pass**
cup·board
cupbord : **cup·board**
cup·ful
cupfull : **cup·ful**
cuplet : **coup·let**
cupling : **coup·ling**
cupon : **cou·pon**
curafe : **ca·rafe**
curage : **cour·age**
curdal : **cur·dle**
curdel : **cur·dle**
cur·dle
cureo : **cu·rio**
curiculum : **cur·ric·u·lum**
cu·rio
curios : **cu·ri·ous**
curiosety : **cu·ri·os·i·ty**
cu·ri·os·i·ty
curiossity : **cu·ri·os·i·ty**
cu·ri·ous
curnel : **col·o·nel** (military
    officer) *or* **ker·nel** (seed)
cur·rant (berry); **cur·rent**
    (*noun,* flow; *adj.,*
    contemporary)
cur·rent (*noun,* flow; *adj.,*
    contemporary); **cur·rant**
    (berry)
cur·ric·u·lum
currier : **cou·ri·er**
cursary : **cur·so·ry**
curserry : **cur·so·ry**
cursery : **cur·so·ry**
cur·so·ry
curteous : **cour·te·ous**
curt·sey *or* **curt·sy** (bow);
    cour·te·sy (politeness)

curt·sy *or* **curt·sey** (bow);
    cour·te·sy (politeness)
cusin : **cous·in**
cus·tard
custerd : **cus·tard**
custodean : **cus·to·di·an**
cus·to·di·an
cus·tom·er
custommer : **cus·tom·er**
cut·lass
cutless : **cut·lass**
cutliss : **cut·lass**
cuzzin : **cous·in**
cwire : **choir**
cy·a·nide
cyanied : **cy·a·nide**
cy·ber·net·ics
cybernettics : **cy·ber·net·ics**
cycal : **cy·cle**
cy·cle (rotation); **sick·le** (knife)
cycloan : **cy·clone**
cy·clone
cyg·net (swan); **sig·net** (ring)
cyl·in·der
cyllinder : **cyl·in·der**
cym·bal (brass plate); **sym·bol**
    (meaningful image)
cymbol : **cym·bal** (brass plate)
    or **sym·bol** (meaningful
    image)
cyn·i·cism
cynisism : **cyn·i·cism**
cyote : **coy·ote**
cy·press
cypriss : **cy·press**
czar *or* **tsar**
Czechoslavokia :
    Czecho·slo·va·kia
Czecho·slo·va·kia
Czeckoslovakia :
    Czecho·slo·va·kia

D

dachshound : **dachs•hund**
dachs•hund
dackshund : **dachs•hund**
dad•dy
dady : **dad•dy**
daery : **dairy** (milk farm) *or*
  di•a•ry (daybook)
daffadil : **daf•fo•dil**
daffault : **de•fault**
daf•fo•dil
daffodill : **daf•fo•dil**
dafodil : **daf•fo•dil**
daggerotype : **da•guerre•o•type**
da•guerre•o•type
daguerrotype :
  da•guerre•o•type
dahl•ia
dai•ly
dai•qui•ri
daiquiry : **dai•qui•ri**
dairdevil : **dare•dev•il**
dairy (milk farm); **di•a•ry**
  (daybook)
Dalas : **Dal•las**
daley : **dai•ly**
dalinquent : **de•lin•quent**
Dal•las
Dalles : **Dal•las**
dallia : **dahl•ia**
dal•li•ance
dallianse : **dal•li•ance**
dallience : **dal•li•ance**
Dallis : **Dal•las**
Dallmatian : **Dal•ma•tian**
dallyance : **dal•li•ance**
Dalmashin : **Dal•ma•tian**
Dal•ma•tian
Dalmation : **Dal•ma•tian**
daly : **dai•ly**
damadge : **dam•age**

dam•age
damidge : **dam•age**
damige : **dam•age**
dammed (blocked); **damned**
  (condemned)
damned (condemned);
  dammed (blocked)
damozel : **dam•sel**
dam•sel
damsill : **dam•sel**
damsul : **dam•sel**
damzel : **dam•sel**
danc•er
dandalion : **dan•de•li•on**
dan•de•li•on
dandilion : **dan•de•li•on**
dandreff : **dan•druff**
dandriff : **dan•druff**
dan•druff
dandylion : **dan•de•li•on**
Danemark : **Den•mark**
Danesh : **Dan•ish**
dangeriss : **dan•ger•ous**
dan•ger•ous
Dan•ish
Dannish : **Dan•ish**
Dannube : **Dan•ube**
danser : **danc•er**
Dan•ube
dapravity : **de•prav•i•ty**
daquerri : **dai•qui•ri**
daquiri : **dai•qui•ri**
daralict : **der•e•lict**
daredevel : **dare•dev•il**
dare•dev•il
dary : **dairy** (milk farm) *or*
  di•a•ry (daybook)
da•ta (*plur.*); **da•tum** (*sing.*)
da•tum (*sing.*); **da•ta** (*plur.*)
daugh•ter

dauter : **daugh•ter**
dautter : **daugh•ter**
dazle : **daz•zle**
dazzal : **daz•zle**
dazzel : **daz•zle**
daz•zle
deacan : **dea•con**
dea•con
deadicate : **ded•i•cate**
dead•li•er
deadlyer : **dead•li•er**
deaf•en
deaf•ness
deafniss : **deaf•ness**
deakon : **dea•con**
dealt
deapth : **depth**
dear (precious); **deer** (animal)
dearth
death
deaty : **de•i•ty**
debachery : **de•bauch•ery**
de•ba•cle
debait : **de•bate**
debakle : **de•ba•cle**
debanair : **deb•o•nair**
de•bate
debauchary : **de•bauch•ery**
de•bauch•ery
debawchery : **de•bauch•ery**
debbacle : **de•ba•cle**
debbate : **de•bate**
debbonair : **deb•o•nair**
debbonare : **deb•o•nair**
debbris : **de•bris**
debecal : **de•ba•cle**
debinair : **deb•o•nair**
deb•o•nair
debonare : **deb•o•nair**
debree : **de•bris**
debres : **de•bris**

de•bris
debter : **debt•or**
debt•or (one who owes); **de•ter**
  (to prevent)
debue : **de•but**
de•but
decadance : **de•ca•dence**
decadanse : **de•ca•dence**
de•cade
de•ca•dence
decadense : **de•ca•dence**
decaid : **de•cade**
decapatate : **de•cap•i•tate**
decapetate : **de•cap•i•tate**
decapitait : **de•cap•i•tate**
de•cap•i•tate
decappitate : **de•cap•i•tate**
decarate : **dec•o•rate**
decathalon : **de•cath•lon**
decathelon : **de•cath•lon**
de•cath•lon
deccade : **de•cade**
deccadence : **de•ca•dence**
deccorate : **dec•o•rate**
de•ceased
deceatful : **de•ceit•ful**
deceave : **de•ceive**
decebel : **dec•i•bel**
deceble : **dec•i•bel**
decedence : **de•ca•dence**
deceesed : **de•ceased**
deceised : **de•ceased**
de•ceit•ful
deceitfull : **de•ceit•ful**
de•ceive
decemal : **dec•i•mal**
De•cem•ber
de•cen•cy
decendant : **de•scen•dant**
decendent : **de•scen•dant**
decensy : **de•cen•cy**

de·cent (respectable); de·scent
(act of going down);
dis·sent (disagreement)
decesed : de·ceased
decetful : de·ceit·ful
deceve : de·ceive
decibal : dec·i·bel
dec·i·bel
decibell : dec·i·bel
de·cide
decidewous : de·cid·u·ous
deciduiss : de·cid·u·ous
de·cid·u·ous
decietful : de·ceit·ful
decietfull : de·ceit·ful
decieve : de·ceive
decifer : de·ci·pher
dec·i·mal
decimel : dec·i·mal
decimmal : dec·i·mal
decincy : de·cen·cy
de·ci·pher
deciphur : de·ci·pher
deciple : dis·ci·ple
decisian : de·ci·sion
de·ci·sion
decission : de·ci·sion
decizion : de·ci·sion
deckade : de·cade
decklaration : dec·la·ra·tion
deckorate : dec·o·rate
declair : de·clare
declaratian : dec·la·ra·tion
dec·la·ra·tion
de·clare
decleration : dec·la·ra·tion
decliration : dec·la·ra·tion
decontamanate :
de·con·tam·i·nate
decontamenate :
de·con·tam·i·nate
de·con·tam·i·nate

decontamminate :
de·con·tam·i·nate
de·cor
decoram : de·co·rum
dec·o·rate
decore : de·cor
decorem : de·co·rum
decorr : de·cor
decorrum : de·co·rum
de·co·rum
decreace : de·crease
de·crease
decreece : de·crease
decreese : de·crease
decreise : de·crease
decrepatude : de·crep·i·tude
decrepet : de·crep·it
decrepid : de·crep·it
de·crep·it
de·crep·i·tude
decreppit : de·crep·it
decreppitude : de·crep·i·tude
decrese : de·crease
dedacate : ded·i·cate
deddicate : ded·i·cate
dedduce : de·duce
dedduction : de·duc·tion
dedecate : ded·i·cate
ded·i·cate
dedlier : dead·li·er
dedoose : de·duce
de·duce
deducktion : de·duc·tion
de·duc·tion
deduse : de·duce
deecon : dea·con
deer (animal); dear (precious)
deesall : die·sel
deesel : die·sel
deeth : death
de·face
defacit : def·i·cit

defallt : **de·fault**
defalt : **de·fault**
def·a·ma·tion
defammation : **def·a·ma·tion**
defanitely : **def·i·nite·ly**
defanition : **def·i·ni·tion**
defase : **de·face**
defaullt : **de·fault**
de·fault
de·feat
defeet : **de·feat**
defeit : **de·feat**
defemation : **def·a·ma·tion**
defence (*Brit.*) : **de·fense**
defencible : **de·fen·si·ble**
de·fen·dant
defendent : **de·fen·dant**
defendint : **de·fen·dant**
defensable : **de·fen·si·ble**
de·fense
defenseble : **de·fen·si·ble**
defensibal : **de·fen·si·ble**
de·fen·si·ble
defered : **de·ferred**
de·ferred
defete : **de·feat**
defface : **de·face**
deffamation : **def·a·ma·tion**
deffeat : **de·feat**
deffen : **deaf·en**
deffenatly : **def·i·nite·ly**
deffendent : **de·fen·dant**
deffense : **de·fense**
deffered : **de·ferred**
defferred : **de·ferred**
defficit : **def·i·cit**
deffinitely : **def·i·nite·ly**
deffinition : **def·i·ni·tion**
deffness : **deaf·ness**
de·fi·ance
defianse : **de·fi·ance**
de·fi·cient

def·i·cit
defience : **de·fi·ance**
defiense : **de·fi·ance**
defimation : **def·a·ma·tion**
de·fin·able
definately : **def·i·nite·ly**
definatly : **def·i·nite·ly**
defineable : **de·fin·able**
defineble : **de·fin·able**
definetion : **def·i·ni·tion**
definetly : **def·i·nite·ly**
definibal : **de·fin·able**
definible : **de·fin·able**
def·i·nite·ly
def·i·ni·tion
definitly : **def·i·nite·ly**
defiset : **def·i·cit**
defisient : **de·fi·cient**
defisit : **def·i·cit**
defrad : **de·fraud**
de·fraud
defrod : **de·fraud**
defth : **depth**
defyance : **de·fi·ance**
degenarate : **de·gen·er·ate**
de·gen·er·ate
degennerate : **de·gen·er·ate**
deginerate : **de·gen·er·ate**
deginnerate : **de·gen·er·ate**
deg·ra·da·tion
degradeation : **deg·ra·da·tion**
degredation : **deg·ra·da·tion**
dehidrate : **de·hy·drate**
dehli : **Del·hi** (city) *or* **deli**
  (delicatessen)
dehydrait : **de·hy·drate**
de·hy·drate
deiffy : **de·i·fy**
de·i·fy
deisel : **die·sel**
deitary : **di·etary**
de·i·ty

dekathalon : **de·cath·lon**
dekathlon : **de·cath·lon**
delacacy : **del·i·ca·cy**
delacate : **del·i·cate**
delagate : **del·e·gate**
delaget : **del·e·gate**
delapidated : **di·lap·i·dat·ed**
delaterious : **del·e·te·ri·ous**
Delawair : **Del·a·ware**
Del·a·ware
Delawear : **Del·a·ware**
delearious : **de·lir·i·ous**
deleat : **de·lete**
delecacy : **del·i·ca·cy**
delecktable : **de·lec·ta·ble**
de·lec·ta·ble
delectibal : **de·lec·ta·ble**
delectible : **de·lec·ta·ble**
deleerious : **de·lir·i·ous**
deleet : **de·lete**
del·e·gate
delerious : **de·lir·i·ous**
de·lete
del·e·te·ri·ous
Deleware : **Del·a·ware**
Del·hi (city); **deli** (delicatessen)
deli (delicatessen); **Del·hi** (city)
delibberate : **de·lib·er·ate**
de·lib·er·ate
deliberet : **de·lib·er·ate**
del·i·ca·cy
delicasy : **del·i·ca·cy**
del·i·cate
delicatessan : **del·i·ca·tes·sen**
del·i·ca·tes·sen
deliceous : **de·li·cious**
delicet : **del·i·cate**
delicetessen : **del·i·ca·tes·sen**
de·li·cious
delinguent : **de·lin·quent**
delinquant : **de·lin·quent**
de·lin·quent

de·lir·i·ous
delishous : **de·li·cious**
deliterious : **del·e·te·ri·ous**
de·liv·er·ance
deliveranse : **de·liv·er·ance**
deliverence : **de·liv·er·ance**
dellaterious : **del·e·te·ri·ous**
Dellaware : **Del·a·ware**
dellegate : **del·e·gate**
Delleware : **Del·a·ware**
dellhi : **Del·hi** (city) *or* deli
  (delicatessen)
delli : **Del·hi** (city) *or* deli
  (delicatessen)
dellicacy : **del·i·ca·cy**
dellicate : **del·i·cate**
dellicatessen : **del·i·ca·tes·sen**
delliverence : **de·liv·er·ance**
delt : **dealt**
demacracy : **de·moc·ra·cy**
demagod : **demi·god**
dem·a·gog *or* **dem·a·gogue**
dem·a·gogue *or* **dem·a·gog**
demalition : **dem·o·li·tion**
demanstrate : **dem·on·strate**
de·mean
demeen : **de·mean**
demenshia : **de·men·tia**
demension : **di·men·sion**
de·men·tia
demeret : **de·mer·it**
de·mer·it
demerrit : **de·mer·it**
demi·god
demigogue : **dem·a·gogue**
demilition : **de·mo·li·tion**
de·mise
demize : **de·mise**
demmagogue : **dem·a·gogue**
demmigod : **demi·god**
demmise : **de·mise**
demmocracy : **de·moc·ra·cy**

demmolition : **de·mo·li·tion**
demmonstrate : **dem·on·strate**
de·moc·ra·cy
democrasy : **de·moc·ra·cy**
democricy : **de·moc·ra·cy**
democrisy : **de·moc·ra·cy**
demogod : **demi·god**
demogogue : **dem·a·gogue**
demolission : **de·mo·li·tion**
demolitian : **de·mo·li·tion**
de·mo·li·tion
demolizion : **de·mo·li·tion**
demonstrait : **dem·on·strate**
dem·on·strate
demuir : **de·mur** (to disagree)
    or **de·mure** (modest)
de·mur (to disagree); **de·mure**
    (modest)
de·mure (modest); **de·mur** (to
    disagree)
denam : **den·im**
denazen : **den·i·zen**
dence : **dense**
dencity : **den·si·ty**
denezen : **den·i·zen**
den·im
denisen : **den·i·zen**
den·i·zen
Denmarck : **Den·mark**
Den·mark
dennim : **den·im**
dennizen : **den·i·zen**
dennotation : **de·no·ta·tion**
dennote : **de·note**
dennounce : **de·nounce**
denntal : **den·tal**
dennum : **den·im**
denomanation :
    de·nom·i·na·tion
denomenation :
    de·nom·i·na·tion
de·nom·i·na·tion

denommination :
    de·nom·i·na·tion
de·no·ta·tion
de·note
denottation : **de·no·ta·tion**
de·nounce
denounciation :
    de·nun·ci·a·tion
denounse : **de·nounce**
denownce : **de·nounce**
densaty : **den·si·ty**
dense
densety : **den·si·ty**
densitty : **den·si·ty**
den·si·ty
den·tal
dentel : **den·tal**
dentestry : **den·tist·ry**
dentistery : **den·tist·ry**
den·tist·ry
denum : **den·im**
de·nun·ci·a·tion
denunsiation : **de·nun·ci·a·tion**
deoderant : **de·odor·ant**
deodirant : **de·odor·ant**
de·odor·ant
deodorent : **de·odor·ant**
depaty : **dep·u·ty**
dependabal : **de·pend·able**
de·pend·able
dependant : **de·pen·dent**
dependible : **de·pend·able**
depety : **dep·u·ty**
depewty : **dep·u·ty**
dephth : **depth**
de·plor·able
deploreble : **de·plor·able**
deplorible : **de·plor·able**
depopalate : **de·pop·u·late**
depoppulate : **de·pop·u·late**
de·pop·u·late
deposet : **de·pos·it**

de·pos·it
depossit : de·pos·it
depozit : de·pos·it
depposit : de·pos·it
depprivation : de·pri·va·tion
depravety : de·prav·i·ty
depravitty : de·prav·i·ty
de·prav·i·ty
depresent : de·pres·sant
de·pres·sant
depressent : de·pres·sant
deprevation : de·pri·va·tion
deprivatian : de·pri·va·tion
de·pri·va·tion
depth
deputty : dep·u·ty
dep·u·ty
deralict : der·e·lict
derelect : der·e·lict
derelick : der·e·lict
der·e·lict
derick : der·rick
derilict : der·e·lict
derishion : de·ri·sion
de·ri·sion
derission : de·ri·sion
derizion : de·ri·sion
dermatoligist : der·ma·tol·o·gist
dermatollogist :
   der·ma·tol·o·gist
der·ma·tol·o·gist
dermetologist :
   der·ma·tol·o·gist
dermitologist :
   der·ma·tol·o·gist
derreck : der·rick
derrelict : der·e·lict
der·rick
derrik : der·rick
derth : dearth
desacrate : des·e·crate
de·scen·dant or de·scen·dent

de·scen·dent or de·scen·dant
de·scent (act of going down);
   de·cent (respectable);
   dis·sent (disagreement)
describtion : de·scrip·tion
descriptian : de·scrip·tion
de·scrip·tion
deseased : de·ceased
des·e·crate
deseive : de·ceive
Desember : De·cem·ber
de·sert (arid land); des·sert
   (sweet dish)
desibel : dec·i·bel
desible : dec·i·bel
deside : de·cide
desiduous : de·cid·u·ous
desifer : de·ci·pher
de·sign
de·sign·er
designor : de·sign·er
desimal : dec·i·mal
desimel : dec·i·mal
desine : de·sign
desiner : de·sign·er
desipher : de·ci·pher
desirabal : de·sir·able
de·sir·able
desireble : de·sir·able
de·spair
desparado : des·per·a·do
desparate : des·per·ate
despare : de·spair
des·per·a·do
des·per·ate
desperato : des·per·a·do
despirate : des·per·ate
de·spise
despize : de·spise
des·pot
dessecrate : des·e·crate
dessect : dis·sect

dessendant : **de·scen·dant**
des·sert (sweet dish); **de·sert**
  (arid land)
dessign : **de·sign**
dessirable : **de·sir·able**
destanation : **des·ti·na·tion**
destany : **des·ti·ny**
destatute : **des·ti·tute**
desteny : **des·ti·ny**
destetute : **des·ti·tute**
des·ti·na·tion
destinct : **dis·tinct**
destinnation : **des·ti·na·tion**
destinny : **des·ti·ny**
des·ti·ny
des·ti·tute
destructable : **de·struc·ti·ble**
de·struc·ti·ble
de·tach
de·tain
detaintion : **de·ten·tion**
detanate : **det·o·nate**
detane : **de·tain**
detatch : **de·tach**
deteariorate : **de·te·ri·o·rate**
de·ten·tion
de·ter (to prevent); **debt·or** (one
  who owes)
deterent : **de·ter·rent**
detereorate : **de·te·ri·o·rate**
de·te·ri·o·rate
determen : **de·ter·mine**
determin : **de·ter·mine**
de·ter·mine
deterr : **debt·or** (one who owes)
  or **de·ter** (to prevent)
deterrant : **de·ter·rent**
de·test·able
detestible : **de·test·able**
deth : **death**
detinate : **det·o·nate**
detiriorate : **de·te·ri·o·rate**

det·o·nate
detramental : **det·ri·men·tal**
detremental : **det·ri·men·tal**
det·ri·men·tal
dettain : **de·tain**
detter : **debt·or** (one who owes)
  or **de·ter** (to prevent)
dettermine : **de·ter·mine**
dettonate : **det·o·nate**
dettor : **debt·or** (one who
  owes) or **de·ter** (to prevent)
devan : **di·van**
dev·as·tate
deveate : **de·vi·ate**
devel : **dev·il**
devellop : **de·vel·op**
de·vel·op
de·vel·oped
developped : **de·vel·oped**
deveous : **de·vi·ous**
devest : **di·vest**
devestate : **dev·as·tate**
de·vi·ate
de·vice (*noun*); **de·vise** (*verb*)
devide : **di·vide**
dev·il
devine : **di·vine**
devinity : **di·vin·i·ty**
de·vi·ous
de·vise (*verb*); **de·vice** (*noun*)
devision : **di·vi·sion**
devistate : **dev·as·tate**
devorce : **di·vorce**
devorse : **di·vorce**
dev·o·tee
devotie : **dev·o·tee**
devoty : **dev·o·tee**
de·vour
devowr : **de·vour**
devulge : **di·vulge**
devvil : **dev·il**
dexteriss : **dex·ter·ous**

dex·ter·ous
dexterus : **dex·ter·ous**
dextrous : **dex·ter·ous**
dezine : **de·sign**
diabalical : **di·a·bol·i·cal**
diabeates : **di·a·be·tes**
diabeetes : **di·a·be·tes**
di·a·be·tes
diabetese : **di·a·be·tes**
di·a·bet·ic
diabetis : **di·a·be·tes**
di·a·bol·i·cal
diabollical : **di·a·bol·i·cal**
di·ag·no·sis
di·a·gram
dialate : **di·late**
di·a·log *or* **di·a·logue**
di·a·logue *or* **di·a·log**
diamater : **di·am·e·ter**
diameater : **di·am·e·ter**
diameeter : **di·am·e·ter**
diameiter : **di·am·e·ter**
diamend : **di·a·mond**
di·am·e·ter
diamiter : **di·am·e·ter**
di·a·mond
diamund : **di·a·mond**
di·a·per
diarea : **di·ar·rhea**
diarhea : **di·ar·rhea**
di·ar·rhea
diarrhia : **di·ar·rhea**
di·a·ry (daybook); **dairy** (milk farm)
diaty : **de·i·ty**
dibetes : **di·a·be·tes**
dibetic : **di·a·bet·ic**
dibolical : **di·a·bol·i·cal**
Dicksie : **Dix·ie**
dicktator : **dic·ta·tor**
dictater : **dic·ta·tor**
dic·ta·tor

dic·tio·nary
dictionery : **dic·tio·nary**
die (perish); **dye** (color)
diefy : **de·i·fy**
diery : **dairy** (milk farm) *or* **di·a·ry** (daybook)
die·sel
diesell : **die·sel**
dietarry : **di·etary**
di·etary
dieterry : **di·etary**
dietery : **di·etary**
diety : **de·i·ty**
diferent : **dif·fer·ent**
diffacult : **dif·fi·cult**
diffecult : **dif·fi·cult**
differant : **dif·fer·ent**
dif·fer·ent
dif·fi·cult
diffrent : **dif·fer·ent**
dificult : **dif·fi·cult**
digestable : **di·gest·ible**
digesteble : **di·gest·ible**
di·gest·ible
dig·i·tal
digitel : **dig·i·tal**
digittal : **dig·i·tal**
dignafied : **dig·ni·fied**
dignatary : **dig·ni·tary**
dignaty : **dig·ni·ty**
dignefied : **dig·ni·fied**
dignetary : **dig·ni·tary**
dignety : **dig·ni·ty**
dig·ni·fied
dignifyed : **dig·ni·fied**
dignitarry : **dig·ni·tary**
dig·ni·tary
dignitery : **dig·ni·tary**
dignitty : **dig·ni·ty**
dig·ni·ty
dignosis : **di·ag·no·sis**
digram : **di·a·gram**

dijestible : **di·gest·ible**
dike
dilapedated : **di·lap·i·dat·ed**
di·lap·i·dat·ed
dilappidated : **di·lap·i·dat·ed**
di·late
dilectable : **de·lec·ta·ble**
dilema : **di·lem·ma**
di·lem·ma
dilemna : **di·lem·ma**
dil·i·gence
diligense : **dil·i·gence**
dilimma : **di·lem·ma**
dilirious : **de·lir·i·ous**
dilligence : **dil·i·gence**
dilogue : **di·a·logue**
dimend : **di·a·mond**
dimensian : **di·men·sion**
di·men·sion
dimond : **di·a·mond**
dinamic : **dy·nam·ic**
dinamite : **dy·na·mite**
dinasaur : **di·no·saur**
dinasty : **dy·nas·ty**
dinesaur : **di·no·saur**
di·no·saur
dinosore : **di·no·saur**
diodorant : **de·odor·ant**
diper : **di·a·per**
diplamat : **dip·lo·mat**
diplimat : **dip·lo·mat**
dip·lo·mat
directer : **di·rec·tor**
di·rec·tor
dirrea : **di·ar·rhea**
dirrhea : **di·ar·rhea**
dirth : **dearth**
diry : **di·a·ry**
disapearance : **dis·ap·pear·ance**
disapearence : **dis·ap·pear·ance**
disapoint : **dis·ap·point**
dis·ap·pear·ance

disappearanse :
  dis·ap·pear·ance
dis·ap·point
disasster : **dis·as·ter**
dis·as·ter
disasterous : **di·sas·trous**
di·sas·trous
disatisfy : **dis·sat·is·fy**
disberse : **dis·burse**
disbirse : **dis·burse**
disburce : **dis·burse**
dis·burse
disc or **disk**
discerage : **dis·cour·age**
dis·cern
discipal : **dis·ci·ple**
dis·ci·ple
dis·ci·pline
discloshure : **dis·clo·sure**
dis·clo·sure
dis·cour·age
discourige : **dis·cour·age**
dis·creet (prudent); **dis·crete**
  (separate)
dis·crep·an·cy
discrepency : **dis·crep·an·cy**
dis·crete (separate); **dis·creet**
  (prudent)
discurage : **dis·cour·age**
dis·ease
disect : **dis·sect**
diseese : **dis·ease**
disent : **de·cent** (respectable) or
  de·scent (act of going down)
  or **dis·sent** (disagreement)
disese : **dis·ease**
disgise : **dis·guise**
dis·guise
disguize : **dis·guise**
dis·in·fec·tant
disinfectent : **dis·in·fec·tant**
disintagrate : **dis·in·te·grate**

dis•in•te•grate
disipline : **dis•ci•pline**
disk *or* **disc**
dis•mal
dismel : **dis•mal**
disobediance : **dis•obe•di•ence**
dis•obe•di•ence
disobediense : **dis•obe•di•ence**
disobeedience : **dis•obe•di•ence**
dispair : **de•spair**
dis•par•age
dispare : **de•spair**
disparige : **dis•par•age**
disparrage : **dis•par•age**
dis•pel
dispell : **dis•pel**
dispence : **dis•pense**
dispencible : **dis•pen•sable**
dispensabal : **dis•pen•sable**
dis•pen•sable
dis•pense
dispensible : **dis•pen•sable**
dispise : **de•spise**
dis•pos•al
disposel : **dis•pos•al**
dispot : **des•pot**
dis•put•able
disputible : **dis•put•able**
disqualefy : **dis•qual•i•fy**
dis•qual•i•fy
disrubt : **dis•rupt**
dis•rupt
dis•sat•is•fy
dis•sect
dis•sent (disagreement);
   de•cent (respectable);
   de•scent (act of going down)
dissern : **dis•cern**
dissiple : **dis•ci•ple**
dis•tance
distanse : **dis•tance**
distence : **dis•tance**

distilary : **dis•till•ery**
distilery : **dis•till•ery**
distillary : **dis•till•ery**
dis•till•ery
dis•tinct
distributer : **dis•trib•u•tor**
dis•trib•u•tor
distructible : **de•struc•ti•ble**
diury : **di•a•ry**
di•van
divann : **di•van**
divedend : **div•i•dend**
divergance : **di•ver•gence**
di•ver•gence
divergense : **di•ver•gence**
di•vest
divet : **div•ot**
di•vide
div•i•dend
dividind : **div•i•dend**
divied : **di•vide**
di•vine
divinety : **di•vin•i•ty**
divinitty : **di•vin•i•ty**
di•vin•i•ty
divinnity : **di•vin•i•ty**
divishion : **di•vi•sion**
di•vi•sion
divission : **di•vi•sion**
divit : **div•ot**
divizion : **di•vi•sion**
di•vorce
divorse : **di•vorce**
div•ot
divour : **de•vour**
di•vulge
divurgence : **di•ver•gence**
divvest : **di•vest**
divvide : **di•vide**
divvot : **div•ot**
Dixee : **Dix•ie**
Dix•ie

Dixy : **Dix·ie**
diziness : **diz·zi·ness**
dizmal : **dis·mal**
diz·zi·ness
dizziniss : **diz·zi·ness**
dizzyness : **diz·zi·ness**
docell : **doc·ile**
dochshund : **dachs·hund**
doc·ile
docilitty : **do·cil·i·ty**
do·cil·i·ty
docill : **doc·ile**
docillety : **do·cil·i·ty**
docillity : **do·cil·i·ty**
docksology : **dox·ol·o·gy**
docter : **doc·tor**
docterate : **doc·tor·ate**
doc·tor
doc·tor·ate
doctoret : **doc·tor·ate**
doctorit : **doc·tor·ate**
doctren : **doc·trine**
doctrenaire : **doc·tri·naire**
doctrin : **doc·trine**
doc·tri·naire
doctrinare : **doc·tri·naire**
doc·trine
doctrinnaire : **doc·tri·naire**
documentarry :
   doc·u·men·ta·ry
doc·u·men·ta·ry
documentery : **doc·u·men·ta·ry**
documentry : **doc·u·men·ta·ry**
documintary : **doc·u·men·ta·ry**
dogerel : **dog·ger·el**
doggarel : **dog·ger·el**
doggeral : **dog·ger·el**
dog·ger·el
doggerle : **dog·ger·el**
doilie : **doi·ly**
doi·ly
dolar : **dol·lar**

doldrams : **dol·drums**
doldrems : **dol·drums**
dol·drums
doledrums : **dol·drums**
doler : **dol·lar**
dolfin : **dol·phin**
dol·lar
dolldrums : **dol·drums**
doller : **dol·lar**
dollphin : **dol·phin**
dolphen : **dol·phin**
dol·phin
do·main
domanant : **dom·i·nant**
domane : **do·main**
domaneering : **dom·i·neer·ing**
domenance : **dom·i·nance**
domeno : **dom·i·no**
domesstic : **do·mes·tic**
domessticity : **do·mes·tic·i·ty**
do·mes·tic
domesticety : **do·mes·tic·i·ty**
domesticitty : **do·mes·tic·i·ty**
do·mes·tic·i·ty
domestick : **do·mes·tic**
domestisity : **do·mes·tic·i·ty**
do·mi·cile
domicill : **do·mi·cile**
dom·i·nance
dominanse : **dom·i·nance**
dom·i·nant
dominearing : **dom·i·neer·ing**
dom·i·neer·ing
domineiring : **dom·i·neer·ing**
dominence : **dom·i·nance**
dominense : **dom·i·nance**
dominent : **dom·i·nant**
dom·i·no
dominoe : **dom·i·no**
domisile : **do·mi·cile**
domminance : **dom·i·nance**
domminant : **dom·i·nant**

dommino : **dom·i·no**
domocile : **do·mi·cile**
domosile : **do·mi·cile**
doner : **do·nor**
donkee : **don·key**
don·key
donkie : **don·key**
do·nor
doormouse : **dor·mouse**
dooty : **du·ty**
dor·mant
dormatory : **dor·mi·to·ry**
dorment : **dor·mant**
dormetory : **dor·mi·to·ry**
dormitorry : **dor·mi·to·ry**
dor·mi·to·ry
dor·mouse
dor·sal
dorsel : **dor·sal**
dorssal : **dor·sal**
dosadge : **dos·age**
dos·age
dosege : **dos·age**
dosier : **dos·sier**
dosige : **dos·age**
dosile : **doc·ile**
dosility : **do·cil·i·ty**
dosill : **doc·ile**
dossage : **dos·age**
dossiay : **dos·sier**
dos·sier
dossiey : **dos·sier**
dot·age
dotege : **dot·age**
dotige : **dot·age**
dottage : **dot·age**
doubal : **dou·ble**
doubel : **dou·ble**
doubious : **du·bi·ous**
dou·ble
doubley : **dou·bly**
dou·bloon

doublune : **dou·bloon**
dou·bly
doubt·ful
doubtfull : **doubt·ful**
doubt·less
doubtliss : **doubt·less**
doughter : **daugh·ter**
doul : **dow·el** (peg) *or* **du·al**
   (double) *or* **du·el** (fight)
douplex : **du·plex**
doutful : **doubt·ful**
doutless : **doubt·less**
dow·a·ger
dowajer : **dow·a·ger**
doweger : **dow·a·ger**
dow·el
dowell : **dow·el**
dowerry : **dow·ry**
dowery : **dow·ry**
dowger : **dow·a·ger**
dowiger : **dow·a·ger**
dowl : **dow·el**
downpore : **down·pour**
down·pour
down·ward
downwerd : **down·ward**
downword : **down·ward**
dow·ry
doxhund : **dachs·hund**
doxolagy : **dox·ol·o·gy**
doxoligy : **dox·ol·o·gy**
doxollogy : **dox·ol·o·gy**
dox·ol·o·gy
doyly : **doi·ly**
doz·en
dozin : **doz·en**
dozzen : **doz·en**
draft
dragen : **drag·on**
draggon : **drag·on**
dragin : **drag·on**
drag·on

dra·ma
dra·mat·i·cal·ly
dramaticaly : **dra·mat·i·cal·ly**
dramaticly : **dra·mat·i·cal·ly**
dramatise (*Brit.*) : **dra·ma·tize**
dra·ma·tize
dramattically : **dra·mat·i·cal·ly**
drametize : **dra·ma·tize**
dramitize : **dra·ma·tize**
dramma : **dra·ma**
drammatically : **dra·mat·i·cal·ly**
drammatize : **dra·ma·tize**
drapary : **drap·ery**
draperry : **drap·ery**
drap·ery
drapry : **drap·ery**
dras·ti·cal·ly
drasticaly : **dras·ti·cal·ly**
drastickally : **dras·ti·cal·ly**
drasticly : **dras·ti·cal·ly**
drastikally : **dras·ti·cal·ly**
draught (*Brit.*) : **draft**
dread·ful
dreadfull : **dread·ful**
dream
drearally : **drea·ri·ly**
drearely : **drea·ri·ly**
drea·ri·ly
drearly : **drea·ri·ly**
drea·ry
dredful : **dread·ful**
dreem : **dream**
dreerily : **drea·ri·ly**
dreery : **drea·ry**
dreiry : **drea·ry**
dreser : **dress·er**
dress·er
dressor : **dress·er**
dri·er (more dry); **dry·er**
  (device for drying)
drily : **dry·ly**
drinkabel : **drink·able**

drink·able
drinkeble : **drink·able**
drinkibal : **drink·able**
drinkible : **drink·able**
drival : **driv·el**
driv·el
drivle : **driv·el**
drivvel : **driv·el**
drizle : **driz·zle**
drizzal : **driz·zle**
driz·zle
drousiness : **drow·si·ness**
drow·si·ness
drowsiniss : **drow·si·ness**
drowsyness : **drow·si·ness**
drowziness : **drow·si·ness**
drudgerry : **drudg·ery**
drudg·ery
drudgiry : **drudg·ery**
drudgry : **drudg·ery**
drudjery : **drudg·ery**
drugery : **drudg·ery**
druggest : **drug·gist**
drug·gist
drugist : **drug·gist**
drunk·ard
drunkerd : **drunk·ard**
dry·er (device for drying);
  dri·er (more dry)
dry·ly
du·al (double); **du·el** (fight)
dubble : **dou·ble**
dubbloon : **dou·bloon**
dubblune : **dou·bloon**
dubbly : **dou·bly**
dubeous : **du·bi·ous**
du·bi·ous
dubloon : **dou·bloon**
dubly : **dou·bly**
Duch : **Dutch**
duch·ess
duchiss : **duch·ess**

duchuss : **duch•ess**
ducktile : **duc•tile**
ductel : **duc•tile**
duc•tile
ductill : **duc•tile**
ductle : **duc•tile**
du•el (fight); **du•al** (double)
dufel : **duf•fel**
duf•fel
duffle : **duf•fel**
dulard : **dull•ard**
dull•ard
dullerd : **dull•ard**
dullird : **dull•ard**
dul•ly (with dullness); **du•ly** (as
   is due)
du•ly (as is due); **dul•ly** (with
   dullness)
dumb•bell
dumbell : **dumb•bell**
dumb•found *or* **dum•found**
dumb•wait•er
dumbwaitor : **dumb•wait•er**
dumby : **dum•my**
dum•found *or* **dumb•found**
dummey : **dum•my**
dummie : **dum•my**
dum•my
dumwaiter : **dumb•wait•er**
dunce
dun•ga•ree
dungarey : **dun•ga•ree**
dungarie : **dun•ga•ree**
dungary : **dun•ga•ree**
dungean : **dun•geon**
dungen : **dun•geon**
dun•geon
dungeree : **dun•ga•ree**
dungin : **dun•geon**
dungiree : **dun•ga•ree**
dunjeon : **dun•geon**
dunse : **dunce**

duplacator : **du•pli•ca•tor**
duplecate : **du•pli•cate**
duplects : **du•plex**
du•plex
du•plic•ate
du•pli•ca•tor
duplicety : **du•plic•i•ty**
duplicitty : **du•plic•i•ty**
du•plic•i•ty
duplisity : **du•plic•i•ty**
durabal : **du•ra•ble**
durabilety : **du•ra•bil•i•ty**
du•ra•bil•i•ty
durabillity : **du•ra•bil•i•ty**
du•ra•ble
durebility : **du•ra•bil•i•ty**
dureble : **du•ra•ble**
du•ress
durible : **du•ra•ble**
durrable : **du•ra•ble**
durress : **du•ress**
durth : **dearth**
dutaful : **du•ti•ful**
Dutch
dutchess : **duch•ess**
du•te•ous
du•ti•ful
dutifull : **du•ti•ful**
dutious : **du•te•ous**
dutius : **du•te•ous**
dutty : **du•ty**
du•ty
dutyful : **du•ti•ful**
dutyous : **du•te•ous**
duzen : **doz•en**
duzzen : **doz•en**
dye (color); **die** (perish)
dye•ing (coloring); **dy•ing**
   (perishing)
dy•ing (perishing); **dye•ing**
   (coloring)
dyke : **dike**

dy·nam·ic
dynamick : **dy·nam·ic**
dynamight : **dy·na·mite**
dy·na·mite
dynammic : **dy·nam·ic**
dynassty : **dy·nas·ty**

dy·nas·ty
dynesty : **dy·nas·ty**
dynimite : **dy·na·mite**
dynisty : **dy·nas·ty**
dynomite : **dy·na·mite**
dyrea : **di·ar·rhea**

E

eagel : **ea·gle**
ea·ger
eagger : **ea·ger**
ea·gle
eaked : **eked**
eaking : **ek·ing**
ear·ache
earacke : **ear·ache**
earaik : **ear·ache**
earake : **ear·ache**
earie : **ae·rie** (nest) *or* **ee·rie** (weird) *or* **Erie** (lake and canal)
earing : **ear·ring** (jewelry) *or* **err·ing** (mistaking)
ear·li·er
ear·ly
earlyier : **ear·li·er**
earn (to work to gain); **urn** (vase)
ear·nest (sincere); **Er·nest** (name)
ear·ring (jewelry); **err·ing** (mistaking)
earth·en·ware
earthenwear : **earth·en·ware**
earth·ly
easal : **ea·sel**
ea·sel
easell : **ea·sel**
easill : **ea·sel**
eas·i·ly
easyly : **eas·i·ly**
eat·able
eather : **ei·ther** (one or the other) *or* **ether** (gas)
eatible : **eat·able**
eaves·drop·ping
ebbony : **eb·o·ny**
eboney : **eb·o·ny**

ebonie : **eb·o·ny**
ebonny : **eb·o·ny**
eb·o·ny
ebulient : **ebul·lient**
ebulliant : **ebul·lient**
ebul·lient
eccede : **ac·cede** (to give in) *or* **ex·ceed** (to surpass)
ecceed : **ac·cede** (to give in) *or* **ex·ceed** (to surpass)
ec·cen·tric
eccentrick : **ec·cen·tric**
eccept : **ac·cept** (to take) *or* **ex·cept** (to leave out)
eccerpt : **ex·cerpt**
eccert : **ex·cerpt** (to extract) *or* **ex·ert** (to put forth)
eccise : **ex·cise**
ecco : **echo**
eccology : **ecol·o·gy**
ecconomy : **econ·o·my**
Eccuador : **Ec·ua·dor**
Eccuadorian : **Ec·ua·do·re·an**
ecentric : **ec·cen·tric**
echalon : **ech·e·lon**
ech·e·lon
echilon : **ech·e·lon**
echo
echoe : **echo**
ecko : **echo**
eclec·tic
eclectick : **eclec·tic**
eclexic : **eclec·tic**
eclips : **eclipse**
eclipse
ecolagy : **ecol·o·gy**
ecollogy : **ecol·o·gy**
ecol·o·gy
econamy : **econ·o·my**
econimy : **econ·o·my**

econnomy : **econ•o•my**
econ•o•my
Ecquador : **Ec•ua•dor**
Ecquadorian : **Ec•ua•dor•ean**
ecsentric : **ec•cen•tric**
ecsort : **es•cort** (to accompany)
  or **ex•hort** (to urge)
ecstacy : **ec•sta•sy**
ecstassy : **ec•sta•sy**
ec•sta•sy
ec•stat•ic
ecstattic : **ec•stat•ic**
ecstesy : **ec•sta•sy**
ecstisy : **ec•sta•sy**
Ec•ua•dor
Ec•ua•dor•ean
Ecudor : **Ec•ua•dor**
Ecudore : **Ec•ua•dor**
Ecudorian : **Ec•ua•dor•ean**
ec•ze•ma
eczemma : **ec•ze•ma**
edable : **ed•i•ble**
edafy : **ed•i•fy**
Edanburgh : **Ed•in•burgh**
edator : **ed•i•tor**
eddible : **ed•i•ble**
eddify : **ed•i•fy**
Eddinburgh : **Ed•in•burgh**
eddit : **ed•it**
edditor : **ed•i•tor**
edditorial : **ed•it•or•i•al**
edducation : **ed•u•ca•tion**
edefy : **ed•i•fy**
ed•i•ble
ed•i•fy
Edinborough : **Ed•in•burgh**
Edinburg : **Ed•in•burgh**
Ed•in•burgh
Edinburo : **Ed•in•burgh**
edit
editer : **ed•i•tor**

edi•tion (book); **ad•di•tion**
  (adding)
ed•i•tor
editoreal : **ed•i•to•ri•al**
ed•i•to•ri•al
educatian : **ed•u•ca•tion**
ed•u•ca•tion
eegle : **ea•gle**
eeked : **eked**
eeking : **ek•ing**
ee•rie *or* **ee•ry** (weird);
  ae•rie(nest); Erie (lake and
  canal)
ee•ry *or* **ee•rie**
eesel : **ea•sel**
eevesdropping : **eaves•drop•ping**
Efel : **Eif•fel**
efemininate : **ef•fem•i•nate**
efervescent : **ef•fer•ves•cent**
efete : **ef•fete**
effeat : **ef•fete**
ef•fect (result); **af•fect** (to
  influence)
effegy : **ef•fi•gy**
effemanate : **ef•fem•i•nate**
ef•fem•i•nate
effeminent : **ef•fem•i•nate**
effemminate : **ef•fem•i•nate**
effervecent : **ef•fer•ves•cent**
effervesant : **ef•fer•ves•cent**
ef•fer•ves•cent
effervessent : **ef•fer•ves•cent**
ef•fete
efficency : **ef•fi•cien•cy**
efficiancy : **ef•fi•cien•cy**
ef•fi•cien•cy
efficiensy : **ef•fi•cien•cy**
ef•fi•gy
effiminant : **ef•fem•i•nate**
effinity : **af•fin•i•ty**
effishiency : **ef•fi•cien•cy**
effite : **ef•fete**

effrontary : **ef·fron·tery**
ef·fron·tery
effrontry : **ef·fron·tery**
eficiency : **ef·fi·cien·cy**
efigy : **ef·fi·gy**
efrontery : **ef·fron·tery**
eger : **ea·ger**
eggress : **egress** (exit) *or*
  ag·gress (to attack)
Egipt : **Egypt**
Egiptian : **Egyp·tian**
Egiypt : **Egypt**
Egiyptian : **Egyp·tian**
egle : **ea·gle**
egreegrious : **egre·grious**
egre·gious
egregous : **egre·grious**
egreigious : **egre·grious**
egrejious : **egre·grious**
egress (exit); **ag·gress** (to
  attack)
Eguador : **Ec·ua·dor**
Eguadorean : **Ec·ua·dor·ean**
eguana : **igua·na**
Egypt
Egyp·tian
Egyption : **Egyp·tian**
egzalt : **ex·alt** (to honor) *or*
  ex·ult (to rejoice)
egzema : **ec·ze·ma**
Eifel : **Eif·fel**
Eif·fel
Eiffle : **Eif·fel**
eightean : **eigh·teen**
eigh·teen
eightteen : **eigh·teen**
eiked : **eked**
eir : **err** (to mistake) *or* **heir**
  (inheritor)
eiress : **heir·ess**
eiriss : **heir·ess**
eirloom : **heir·loom**

eirlume : **heir·loom**
eisel : **ea·sel**
ei·ther (one or the other);
  ether (gas)
ejecktion : **ejec·tion**
ejec·tion
ekcentric : **ec·cen·tric**
eked
ekeing : **ek·ing**
ek·ing
eklectic : **eclec·tic**
ekstasy : **ec·sta·sy**
elabarate : **elab·o·rate**
elaberate : **elab·o·rate**
elab·o·rate
elaboret : **elab·o·rate**
elaborite : **elab·o·rate**
elagance : **el·e·gance**
elagy : **el·e·gy**
elament : **el·e·ment**
elamental : **el·e·men·tal**
elaphant : **el·e·phant**
elaquence : **el·o·quence**
elasstic : **elas·tic**
elastec : **elas·tic**
elas·tic
elastick : **elas·tic**
elavate : **el·e·vate**
elavator : **el·e·va·tor**
El·ba (island); **El·be** (river)
El·be (river); **El·ba** (island)
elbo : **el·bow**
elboe : **el·bow**
el·bow
el·dest
eldist : **el·dest**
elead : **elide**
eleaven : **elev·en**
electefy : **elec·tri·fy**
electokute : **elec·tro·cute**
electracute : **elec·tro·cute**
electrafy : **elec·tri·fy**

electrecute : **elec•tro•cute**
elec•tric
electricety : **elec•tric•i•ty**
elec•tri•cian
electricion : **elec•tri•cian**
electricitty : **elec•tric•i•ty**
elec•tric•i•ty
electricute : **elec•tro•cute**
elec•tri•fy
electrision : **elec•tri•cian**
electrisity : **elec•tric•i•ty**
electrition : **elec•tri•cian**
elec•tro•cute
elede : **elide**
elefant : **el•e•phant**
el•e•gance
eleganse : **el•e•gance**
elegants : **el•e•gance**
elegence : **el•e•gance**
elegible : **el•i•gi•ble** (qualified)
   or **il•leg•i•ble** (unreadable)
el•e•gy
elejy : **el•e•gy**
elektric : **elec•tric**
el•e•ment
el•e•men•tal
elementel : **el•e•men•tal**
elementle : **el•e•men•tal**
elemintal : **el•e•men•tal**
el•e•phant
elephent : **el•e•phant**
elephunt : **el•e•phant**
elete : **elite**
elevait : **el•e•vate**
elevan : **elev•en**
el•e•vate
elevater : **el•e•va•tor**
el•e•va•tor
elev•en
elicet : **elic•it** (to draw out) or
   il•lic•it (unlawful)

elic•it (to draw out); **il•lic•it**
   (unlawful)
elickser : **elix•ir**
elide
eligance : **el•e•gance**
eligeble : **el•i•gi•ble** (qualified)
   or **il•leg•i•ble** (unreadable)
eli•gi•ble (qualified); **il•leg•i•ble**
   (unreadable)
eligy : **el•e•gy**
elijible : **el•i•gi•ble** (qualified)
   or **il•leg•i•ble** (unreadable)
elimental : **el•e•men•tal**
elim•i•nate
eliphant : **el•e•phant**
eliquence : **el•o•quence**
elisit : **elic•it** (to draw out) or
   il•lic•it (unlawful)
elite
elivate : **el•e•vate**
elivator : **el•e•va•tor**
elixer : **elix•ir**
elix•ir
elixor : **elix•ir**
ellagy : **el•e•gy**
ellbow : **el•bow**
ellectrify : **elec•tri•fy**
ellectrocute : **elec•tro•cute**
ellegance : **el•e•gance**
ellegy : **el•e•gy**
ellement : **el•e•ment**
ellemental : **el•e•men•tal**
ellephant : **el•e•phant**
ellevate : **el•e•vate**
ellevator : **el•e•va•tor**
elleven : **elev•en**
ellicit : **elic•it** (to draw out) or
   il•lic•it (unlawful)
ellide : **elide**
elligible : **el•i•gi•ble** (qualified)
   or **il•leg•i•ble** (unreadable)
ellite : **elite**

ellixir : **elix·ir**
elloquence : **el·o·quence**
ellucidate : **elu·ci·date**
ellusive : **elu·sive**
eloapment : **elope·ment**
elope·ment
elopment : **elope·ment**
el·o·quence
eloquense : **el·o·quence**
eloquince : **el·o·quence**
elucedate : **elu·ci·date**
elu·ci·date
elucive : **al·lu·sive** (making
   references) *or* **elu·sive**
   (avoiding) *or* **il·lu·sive**
   (deceptive)
elude (to escape); **al·lude** (to
   refer)
elusidate : **elu·ci·date**
elu·sion (evasion); **al·lu·sion**
   (reference); **il·lu·sion** (false
   idea or image)
elu·sive (avoiding); **al·lu·sive**
   (making references);
   il·lu·sive (deceptive)
emaceated : **ema·ci·at·ed**
ema·ci·at·ed
emagrant : **em·i·grant**
emancepate : **eman·ci·pate**
eman·ci·pate
emanent : **em·i·nent** (famous)
   or **im·ma·nent** (dwelling
   within) *or* **im·mi·nent**
   (impending)
emansipate : **eman·ci·pate**
emarald : **em·er·ald**
emasarry : **em·is·sary**
emas·cu·late
emasiate : **ema·ci·ate**
embacy : **em·bas·sy**
em·balm
embam : **em·balm**

em·bank·ment
embarass : **em·bar·rass**
embaress : **em·bar·rass**
em·bar·go
embariss : **em·bar·rass**
em·bark
em·bar·rass
embarriss : **em·bar·rass**
embasey : **em·bas·sy**
em·bas·sy
embasy : **em·bas·sy**
embelish : **em·bel·lish**
embellash : **em·bel·lish**
embellesh : **em·bel·lish**
em·bel·lish
embezel : **em·bez·zle**
embezle : **em·bez·zle**
embezzal : **em·bez·zle**
embezzel : **em·bez·zle**
em·bez·zle
embibe : **im·bibe**
emblam : **em·blem**
emblazen : **em·bla·zon**
em·bla·zon
em·blem
emblim : **em·blem**
emblum : **em·blem**
em·bodi·ment
embodimint : **em·bodi·ment**
embodyment : **em·bodi·ment**
embom : **em·balm**
embracable : **em·brace·able**
em·brace
em·brace·able
embracible : **em·brace·able**
embraice : **em·brace**
embrase : **em·brace**
embrasible : **em·brace·able**
embreo : **em·bryo**
embrio : **em·bryo**
embroidary : **em·broi·dery**
embroiderry : **em·broi·dery**

em·broi·dery
embroydery : em·broi·dery
em·bryo
embue : im·bue
emcumbrance : en·cum·brance
emegrant : em·i·grant (one
   leaving) *or* im·mi·grant (one
   coming in)
emend (to correct); amend (to
   change or add to)
em·er·ald
emeratus : emer·i·tus
emeretus : emer·i·tus
emer·gen·cy
emergensy : emer·gen·cy
emergincy : emer·gen·cy
emeritas : emer·i·tus
emeritis : emer·i·tus
emer·i·tus
emerold : em·er·ald
emerritus : emer·i·tus
emesarry : em·is·sary
emfeeble : en·fee·ble
emgagement : en·gage·ment
em·i·grant (one leaving);
   im·mi·grant (one coming in)
emind : emend
em·i·nent (famous);
   im·ma·nent (dwelling
   within); im·mi·nent
   (impending)
emisary : em·is·sary
emision : emis·sion
em·is·sary
emisserry : em·is·sary
emissery : em·is·sary
emissian : emis·sion
emis·sion
emition : emis·sion
emity : en·mi·ty
emmaculate : im·mac·u·late
emmancipate : eman·ci·pate

emmasculate : emas·cu·late
emmend : emend
emmerald : em·er·ald
emmergency : emer·gen·cy
emmeritus : emer·i·tus
emmigrant : em·i·grant (one
   leaving) *or* im·mi·grant (one
   coming in)
emminent : em·i·nent (famous)
   or im·ma·nent (dwelling
   within) *or* im·mi·nent
   (impending)
emmissary : em·is·sary
emmity : en·mi·ty
emmusion : emul·sion
emorald : em·er·ald
empact : im·pact
empair : im·pair
empale : im·pale
empanel : im·pan·el
empart : im·part
empassioned : im·pas·sioned
empeach : im·peach
empearian : em·py·re·an
empeccable : im·pec·ca·ble
empede : im·pede
empediment : im·ped·i·ment
emperial : im·pe·ri·al
emperil : im·pe·ri·al (relating
   to empire) *or* im·per·il (to
   endanger)
emphisema : em·phy·se·ma
emphisima : em·phy·se·ma
emphyseama : em·phy·se·ma
em·phy·se·ma
emphysima : em·phy·se·ma
emphyzema : em·phy·se·ma
empier : em·pire
empierian : em·py·re·an
em·pire
empirial : im·pe·ri·al
empirian : em·py·re·an

emplant : **im·plant**
emporeum : **em·po·ri·um**
emporiam : **em·po·ri·um**
em·po·ri·um
emposter : **im·pos·tor**
empouarium : **em·po·ri·um**
empound : **im·pound**
empoureum : **em·po·ri·um**
empoverish : **im·pov·er·ish**
empyre : **em·pire**
em·py·re·an
empyrian : **em·py·re·an**
emullsion : **emul·sion**
emulsian : **emul·sion**
emul·sion
emultion : **emul·sion**
emvironment : **en·vi·ron·ment**
emzyme : **en·zyme**
enamal : **enam·el**
enam·el
enamell : **enam·el**
enamerd : **enam·ored**
enamered : **enam·ored**
enamil : **enam·el**
enammel : **enam·el**
enammored : **enam·ored**
enam·ored
enamoured (*Brit.*) : **enam·ored**
enamy : **en·e·my**
enargy : **en·er·gy**
enbalm : **em·balm**
enbam : **em·balm**
enbankment : **em·bank·ment**
enbargo : **em·bar·go**
enbark : **em·bark**
enbarrass : **em·bar·rass**
enbassy : **em·bas·sy**
enbelish : **em·bel·lish**
enbellish : **em·bel·lish**
enbezzle : **em·bez·zle**
enblazon : **em·bla·zon**
enblem : **em·blem**

enbodiment : **em·bodi·ment**
enbrace : **em·brace**
enbraceable : **em·brace·able**
enbroidery : **em·broi·dery**
enbryo : **em·bryo**
encantation : **in·can·ta·tion**
encendiary : **in·cen·di·ary**
encercle : **en·cir·cle**
encessant : **in·ces·sant**
enciclopedia : **en·cyc·lo·pe·dia**
encinerate : **in·cin·er·ate**
encircel : **en·cir·cle**
en·cir·cle
encirkal : **en·cir·cle**
encirkle : **en·cir·cle**
encite : **in·cite** (to urge on) *or*
  in·sight (discernment)
encouradge : **en·cour·age**
en·cour·age
encourege : **en·cour·age**
encourige : **en·cour·age**
en·cum·brance
encumbranse : **en·cum·brance**
encumbrence : **en·cum·brance**
encumbrince : **en·cum·brance**
encurage : **en·cour·age**
encyclapedia : **en·cy·clo·pe·dia**
encyclepedia : **en·cy·clo·pe·dia**
encyclipedia : **en·cy·clo·pe·dia**
encyclopeadia :
  en·cy·clo·pe·dia
encyclopedea : **en·cy·clo·pe·dia**
en·cy·clo·pe·dia
encyclopeedia : **en·cy·clo·pe·dia**
endeaver : **en·deav·or**
en·deav·or
endevor : **en·deav·or**
endevvor : **en·deav·or**
endite : **in·dict** (to charge with
  a crime) *or* **in·dite** (to write)
endolent : **in·do·lent**
endomitable : **in·dom·i·ta·ble**

endoument : **en·dow·ment**
endowmate : **en·dow·ment**
endowmeant : **en·dow·ment**
en·dow·ment
endowmint : **en·dow·ment**
endulge : **in·dulge**
en·dur·ance
enduranse : **en·dur·ance**
endurence : **en·dur·ance**
endurrance : **en·dur·ance**
endurrence : **en·dur·ance**
endustrial : **in·dus·tri·al**
enebriate : **ine·bri·ate**
enemmy : **en·e·my**
en·e·my
en·er·gy
enerjy : **en·er·gy**
enerrgy : **en·er·gy**
enert : **in·ert**
enertia : **in·er·tia**
enfallible : **in·fal·li·ble**
enfatuate : **in·fat·u·ate**
enfeable : **en·fee·ble**
enfeebal : **en·fee·ble**
en·fee·ble
enfeible : **en·fee·ble**
enferior : **in·fe·ri·or**
enferno : **in·fer·no**
enfidel : **in·fi·del**
enfinite : **in·fi·nite**
enfirmary : **in·fir·ma·ry**
enfirmity : **in·fir·mi·ty**
enflammable : **in·flam·ma·ble**
enflexible : **in·flex·i·ble**
enfluence : **in·flu·ence**
enfuriate : **in·fu·ri·ate**
en·gage·ment
engagment : **en·gage·ment**
engeneer : **en·gi·neer**
engenious : **in·ge·nious**
engenue : **in·ge·nue**
engenuous : **in·gen·u·ous**

engest : **in·gest**
en·gi·neer
enginier : **en·gi·neer**
En·gland
englorious : **in·glo·ri·ous**
Englund : **En·gland**
engredient : **in·gre·di·ent**
enhabit : **in·hab·it**
enhale : **in·hale**
enhancemeant : **en·hance·ment**
en·hance·ment
enhancemint : **en·hance·ment**
enhansement : **en·hance·ment**
enherent : **in·her·ent**
enherit : **in·her·it**
enhibit : **in·hib·it**
eniggma : **enig·ma**
enig·ma
enimical : **in·im·i·cal**
enimy : **en·e·my**
enitial : **ini·tial**
enitiate : **ini·ti·ate**
enjineer : **en·gi·neer**
enmaty : **en·mi·ty**
enmety : **en·mi·ty**
enmitty : **en·mi·ty**
en·mi·ty
ennamel : **enam·el**
ennamored : **enam·ored**
ennate : **in·nate**
ennemy : **en·e·my**
ennigma : **enig·ma**
ennocence : **in·no·cence**
ennovate : **in·no·vate**
ennue : **en·nui**
ennuee : **en·nui**
en·nui
ennumerable : **in·nu·mer·a·ble**
ennumerate : **enu·mer·ate**
enoomerate : **enu·mer·ate**
enoui : **en·nui**
enounciate : **enun·ci·ate**

enperil : **im•pe•ri•al** (relating to empire) *or* **im•per•il** (to endanger)
enphysema : **em•phy•se•ma**
enpire : **em•pire**
enpireal : **im•pe•ri•al**
enporium : **em•po•ri•um**
enpyrean : **em•py•re•an**
enscrutable : **in•scru•ta•ble**
ensiclopedia : **en•cy•clo•pe•dia**
en•sign
ensine : **en•sign**
ensipid : **in•sip•id**
ensircle : **en•cir•cle**
ensolence : **in•so•lence**
ensoluble : **in•sol•u•ble**
ensolvent : **in•sol•vent**
ensomnia : **in•som•nia**
ensouciant : **in•sou•ci•ant**
enstill : **in•still**
ensular : **in•su•lar**
ensulin : **in•su•lin**
ensurance : **in•sur•ance**
ensurgent : **in•sur•gent**
ensyclopedia : **en•cy•clo•pe•dia**
ensyme : **en•zyme**
entegrate : **in•te•grate**
entellect : **in•tel•lect**
entelligent : **in•tel•li•gent**
enteprise : **en•ter•prise**
enterance : **en•trance**
enterence : **en•trance**
enterpreneur : **en•tre•pre•neur**
enterpretation : **in•ter•pre•ta•tion**
en•ter•prise
enterprize : **en•ter•prise**
enterrogate : **in•ter•ro•gate**
en•ter•tain
entertane : **en•ter•tain**
enterval : **in•ter•val**
entervene : **in•ter•vene**

enterview : **in•ter•view**
entestine : **in•tes•tine**
entimacy : **in•ti•ma•cy**
entimate : **in•ti•mate**
entolerable : **in•tol•er•a•ble**
entolerance : **in•tol•er•ance**
entolerant : **in•tol•er•ant**
entouradge : **en•tou•rage**
en•tou•rage
entouraje : **en•tou•rage**
entouroge : **en•tou•rage**
entoxicate : **in•tox•i•cate**
en•trance
entranse : **en•trance**
entransigent : **in•tran•si•gent**
entrapreneur : **en•tre•pre•neur**
entraypreneur : **en•tre•pre•neur**
entrence : **en•trance**
entrense : **en•trance**
entrepeneur : **en•tre•pre•neur**
entrepid : **in•trep•id**
en•tre•pre•neur
entreprenoir : **en•tre•pre•neur**
entreprenoor : **en•tre•pre•neur**
entreprineur : **en•tre•pre•neur**
entricacy : **in•tri•ca•cy**
entricate : **in•tri•cate**
entrigue : **in•trigue**
entrince : **en•trance**
entrinse : **en•trance**
entroduce : **in•tro•duce**
entuition : **in•tu•ition**
enturage : **en•tou•rage**
enui : **en•nui**
enumarate : **enu•mer•ate**
enu•mer•ate
enunceate : **enun•ci•ate**
enun•ci•ate
enundate : **in•un•date**
enunsiate : **enun•ci•ate**
envade : **in•vade**

envalid : **in·va·lid** (sick or
disabled) *or* **in·val·id** (not
valid)
envalope : **en·ve·lope** (*noun*)
envellope : **en·ve·lope** (*noun*)
enveloap : **en·ve·lope** (*noun*)
en·vel·op (*verb*); **en·ve·lope**
(*noun*)
en·ve·lope (*noun*); **en·vel·op**
(*verb*)
enventory : **in·ven·to·ry**
enveous : **en·vi·ous**
envestigate : **in·ves·ti·gate**
enveterate : **in·vet·er·ate**
enviernment : **en·vi·ron·ment**
envigorate : **in·vig·o·rate**
envilope : **en·ve·lope** (*noun*)
envincible : **in·vin·ci·ble**
enviolable : **in·vi·o·la·ble**
enviolate : **in·vi·o·late**
enviornment : **en·vi·ron·ment**
enviorns : **en·vi·rons**
en·vi·ous
enviran : **en·vi·rons**
enviranment : **en·vi·ron·ment**
envirenment : **en·vi·ron·ment**
envirens : **en·vi·rons**
envirnment : **en·vi·ron·ment**
envirns : **en·vi·rons**
en·vi·ron·ment
en·vi·rons
enviruns : **en·vi·rons**
en·vis·age
envisege : **en·vis·age**
envisible : **in·vis·i·ble**
envisige : **en·vis·age**
envissage : **en·vis·age**
envius : **en·vi·ous**
envizage : **en·vis·age**
en·voy
envyous : **en·vi·ous**
enwee : **en·nui**

enzime : **en·zyme**
en·zyme
epacurean : **ep·i·cu·re·an**
epasode : **ep·i·sode**
epataph : **ep·i·taph**
epathet : **ep·i·thet**
epecurean : **ep·i·cu·re·an**
epesode : **ep·i·sode**
ep·ic (narrative); **ep·och** (era)
epick : **ep·ic** (narrative) *or*
ep·och (era)
ep·i·cu·re·an
epicurian : **ep·i·cu·re·an**
ep·i·gram
Episcapalian : **Epis·co·pa·lian**
Episcipalian : **Epis·co·pa·lian**
Epis·co·pa·lian
episoad : **ep·i·sode**
ep·i·sode
epissel : **epis·tle**
epissle : **epis·tle**
epis·tle
epistol : **epis·tle**
epitaff : **ep·i·taph**
ep·i·taph
ep·i·thet
ep·och (era); **ep·ic** (narrative)
eppic : **ep·ic** (narrative) *or*
ep·och (era)
eppicurean : **ep·i·cu·re·an**
eppigram : **ep·i·gram**
Eppiscopalian : **Epis·co·pa·lian**
eppisode : **ep·i·sode**
eppistle : **epis·tle**
eppitaph : **ep·i·taph**
eppithet : **ep·i·thet**
eqal : **equal**
eqity : **eq·ui·ty**
Equador : **Ec·ua·dor**
Equadorian : **Ec·ua·dor·ean**
equal
equall : **equal**

equassion : **equa·tion**
equater : **equa·tor**
equatian : **equa·tion**
equa·tion
equa·tor
equaty : **eq·ui·ty**
equel : **equal**
equetty : **eq·ui·ty**
equety : **eq·ui·ty**
equil : **equal**
equitty : **eq·ui·ty**
eq·ui·ty
erand : **er·rand**
erase
eratic : **er·rat·ic**
eratick : **er·rat·ic**
erb : **herb**
erbage : **herb·age**
erbal : **herb·al**
erbege : **herb·age**
erbel : **herb·al**
erbige : **herb·age**
Erie (lake and canal); **ee·rie**
(weird)
erlier : **ear·li·er**
erly : **ear·ly**
ermen : **er·mine**
ermin : **er·mine**
er·mine
ern : **earn** (to work to gain) *or*
urn (vase)
Er·nest (name); **ear·nest**
(sincere)
eroodite : **er·u·dite**
eror : **er·ror**
erosean : **ero·sion**
erosian : **ero·sion**
erosien : **ero·sion**
ero·sion
erossion : **ero·sion**
er·otic
erotick : **erot·ic**

erotion : **ero·sion**
erottic : **erot·ic**
err (to mistake); **heir** (inheritor)
er·rand
errase : **erase**
er·rat·ic
errattic : **er·rat·ic**
errend : **er·rand**
errer : **er·ror**
errind : **er·rand**
errir : **er·ror**
errlier : **ear·li·er**
er·ror
errosion : **ero·sion**
errotic : **erot·ic**
errudite : **er·u·dite**
erthenware : **earth·en·ware**
erthly : **earth·ly**
er·u·dite
esay : **es·say**
es·cape
eschoir : **es·quire**
es·cort
escuire : **es·quire**
esel : **ea·sel**
esence : **es·sence**
esential : **es·sen·tial**
eshelon : **ech·e·lon**
eshilon : **ech·e·lon**
Eskamo : **Es·ki·mo**
Eskemo : **Es·ki·mo**
Eskimmo : **Es·ki·mo**
Es·ki·mo
Eskimoe : **Es·ki·mo**
eskwire : **es·quire**
esofagus : **esoph·a·gus**
esophagas : **esoph·a·gus**
esophages : **esoph·a·gus**
esophagis : **esoph·a·gus**
esoph·a·gus
esophegus : **esoph·a·gus**
esophigus : **esoph·a·gus**

esophogus : **esoph·a·gus**
especialy : **es·pe·cial·ly**
es·pe·cial·ly
esquier : **es·quire**
es·quire
essance : **es·sence**
es·say
es·sence
essencial : **es·sen·tial**
essense : **es·sence**
essenshial : **es·sen·tial**
es·sen·tial
essintial : **es·sen·tial**
essophagus : **esoph·a·gus**
essquire : **es·quire**
estamate : **es·ti·mate**
estatic : **ec·stat·ic**
es·teem
estemate : **es·ti·mate**
esteme : **es·teem**
es·thet·ic *or* **aes·thet·ic**
estimant : **es·ti·mate**
es·ti·mate
estiment : **es·ti·mate**
etaquette : **et·i·quette**
etequette : **et·i·quette**
eter·nal
eternall : **eter·nal**
eternel : **eter·nal**
eternetty : **eter·ni·ty**
eternety : **eter·ni·ty**
eternitty : **eter·ni·ty**
eter·ni·ty
ethacal : **eth·i·cal**
etheareal : **ethe·re·al**
ethecal : **eth·i·cal**
etheerial : **ethe·re·al**
etheirial : **ethe·re·al**
Etheopia : **Ethi·o·pia**
ether (gas); **ei·ther** (one or the other)
ethe·re·al

etherial : **ethe·re·al**
eth·i·cal
ethicle : **eth·i·cal**
ethikal : **eth·i·cal**
Ethiopea : **Ethi·o·pia**
Ethi·o·pia
ethnec : **eth·nic**
eth·nic
ethnick : **eth·nic**
etikit : **et·i·quette**
etiquet : **et·i·quette**
et·i·quette
etiquit : **et·i·quette**
etiquitte : **et·i·quette**
etternal : **eter·nal**
ettiquette : **et·i·quette**
eturnal : **eter·nal**
Eucarist : **Eu·cha·rist**
Eu·cha·rist
Euchrist : **Eu·cha·rist**
eufemism : **eu·phe·mism**
eufonious : **eu·pho·ni·ous**
euforia : **eu·pho·ria**
eulagy : **eu·lo·gy**
eulegy : **eu·lo·gy**
euligy : **eu·lo·gy**
euloggy : **eu·lo·gy**
eu·lo·gy
eunach : **eu·nuch**
eunech : **eu·nuch**
euneck : **eu·nuch**
eunich : **eu·nuch**
eunick : **eu·nuch**
eu·nuch
euphamism : **eu·phe·mism**
euphemesm : **eu·phe·mism**
eu·phe·mism
euphimism : **eu·phe·mism**
euphoneous : **eu·pho·ni·ous**
eu·pho·ni·ous
euphonius : **eu·pho·ni·ous**
euphorea : **eu·pho·ria**

eu·pho·ria
euphorria : eu·pho·ria
eureaka : eu·re·ka
eureeka : eu·re·ka
eu·re·ka
eurika : eu·re·ka
Euroap : Eu·rope
Europ : Eu·rope
Eu·rope
euthanacia : eu·tha·na·sia
eu·tha·na·sia
euthanazia : eu·tha·na·sia
euthenasia : eu·tha·na·sia
euthinasia : eu·tha·na·sia
evacion : eva·sion
evacive : eva·sive
evacooate : evac·u·ate
evacuait : evac·u·ate
evac·u·ate
evadence : ev·i·dence
evakauate : evac·u·ate
evalution : ev·o·lu·tion
evalutionary : ev·o·lu·tion·ary
ev·a·nes·cence
evanescense : ev·a·nes·cence
evanesense : ev·a·nes·cence
evanessance : ev·a·nes·cence
evanessence : ev·a·nes·cence
evangelesm : evan·ge·lism
evan·ge·lism
evangellism : evan·ge·lism
evanjelism : evan·ge·lism
evaparate : evap·o·rate
evaperate : evap·o·rate
evapirate : evap·o·rate
evaporait : evap·o·rate
evap·o·rate
evapperate : evap·o·rate
evapporate : evap·o·rate
Evarest : Ev·er·est
Evarist : Ev·er·est
evaseve : eva·sive

eva·sion
eva·sive
evassion : eva·sion
evassive : eva·sive
evation : eva·sion
evazion : eva·sion
evedence : ev·i·dence
eveneng : eve·ning
evenescence : ev·a·nes·cence
eve·ning
event·ful
eventfull : event·ful
eventially : even·tu·al·ly
even·tu·al·ly
eventualy : even·tu·al·ly
eventuelly : even·tu·al·ly
eventuilly : even·tu·al·ly
eventuily : even·tu·al·ly
Ev·er·est
Everist : Ev·er·est
evesdropping : eaves·drop·ping
evidanse : ev·i·dence
ev·i·dence
evidense : ev·i·dence
evilution : ev·o·lu·tion
evilutionary : ev·o·lu·tion·ary
evinescence : ev·a·nes·cence
evintful : event·ful
Evirest : Ev·er·est
evning : eve·ning
evolusion : ev·o·lu·tion
evolusionary : ev·o·lu·tion·ary
evolutian : ev·o·lu·tion
evolutianary : ev·o·lu·tion·ary
ev·o·lu·tion
evolutionarry : ev·o·lu·tion·ary
ev·o·lu·tion·ary
evolutionerry : ev·o·lu·tion·ary
evolutionery : ev·o·lu·tion·ary
Evrist : Ev·er·est
ewe (female sheep); yew (tree);
   you (pron.)

exacution : **ex·e·cu·tion**
exacutive : **ex·ec·u·tive**
exadus : **ex·o·dus**
exagerate : **ex·ag·ger·ate**
exaggarate : **ex·ag·ger·ate**
ex·ag·ger·ate
exaggirate : **ex·ag·ger·ate**
exajerate : **ex·ag·ger·ate**
exale : **ex·hale**
ex·alt (to honor); **ex·ult** (to
    rejoice)
examplary : **ex·em·pla·ry**
exaqution : **ex·e·cu·tion**
exasparate : **ex·as·per·ate**
exasperait : **ex·as·per·ate**
ex·as·per·ate
exasperrate : **ex·as·per·ate**
exaspirate : **ex·as·per·ate**
exassperate : **ex·as·per·ate**
exaust : **ex·haust**
excape : **es·cape**
excasperate : **ex·as·per·ate**
excavatian : **ex·ca·va·tion**
ex·ca·va·tion
excede : **ac·cede** (to give in) *or*
    ex·ceed (to surpass)
ex·ceed (to surpass); **ac·cede**
    (to give in)
ex·cel
excelence : **ex·cel·lence**
excell : **ex·cel**
excellance : **ex·cel·lence**
excellanse : **ex·cel·lence**
ex·cel·lence
excellense : **ex·cel·lence**
excemplify : **ex·em·pli·fy**
excempt : **ex·empt**
ex·cept (to leave out); **ac·cept**
    (to take)
excercise : **ex·er·cise**
ex·cerpt
excersise : **ex·er·cise**

excert : **ex·cerpt** (extract) *or*
    ex·ert (to put forth)
excertion : **ex·er·tion**
excevation : **ex·ca·va·tion**
excibition : **ex·hi·bi·tion**
excilarate : **ex·hil·a·rate**
excilaration : **ex·hil·a·ra·tion**
excile : **ex·ile**
excirpt : **ex·cerpt**
ex·cise
excist : **ex·ist**
excistence : **ex·is·tence**
excistentialism :
    ex·is·ten·tial·ism
excitemeant : **ex·cite·ment**
ex·cite·ment
excitment : **ex·cite·ment**
excize : **ex·cise**
ex·claim
exclaimation : **ex·cla·ma·tion**
exclamasion : **ex·cla·ma·tion**
exclamatian : **ex·cla·ma·tion**
ex·cla·ma·tion
exclame : **ex·claim**
exclemation : **ex·cla·ma·tion**
exclimation : **ex·cla·ma·tion**
excloosive : **ex·clu·sive**
exclucive : **ex·clu·sive**
excluseve : **ex·clu·sive**
ex·clu·sive
excort : **es·cort** (to accompany)
    or **ex·hort** (to urge)
excrament : **ex·cre·ment**
excremant : **ex·cre·ment**
ex·cre·ment
excriment : **ex·cre·ment**
excroosiating : **ex·cru·ci·at·ing**
excruceating : **ex·cru·ci·at·ing**
ex·cru·ci·at·ing
excrusiating : **ex·cru·ci·at·ing**
excume : **ex·hume**
exebition : **ex·hi·bi·tion**

execkutive : **ex·ec·u·tive**
execusion : **ex·e·cu·tion**
executeve : **ex·ec·u·tive**
executian : **ex·e·cu·tion**
ex·e·cu·tion
ex·ec·u·tive
exedus : **ex·o·dus**
exeed : **ac·cede** (to give in) *or*
  ex·ceed (to surpass)
exel : **ax·le** (wheel shaft) *or*
  ex·cel (to be superior)
exelence : **ex·cel·lence**
exellence : **ex·cel·lence**
exema : **ec·ze·ma**
exemplafy : **ex·em·pli·fy**
exemplarry : **ex·em·pla·ry**
ex·em·pla·ry
exemplerry : **ex·em·pla·ry**
exemplery : **ex·em·pla·ry**
exempley : **ex·em·pli·fy**
ex·em·pli·fy
exemplury : **ex·em·pla·ry**
ex·empt
exept : **ac·cept** (to take) *or*
  ex·cept (to leave out)
exeqution : **ex·e·cu·tion**
exercion : **ex·er·tion**
ex·er·cise
exercize : **ex·er·cise**
exerpt : **ex·cerpt**
exersion : **ex·er·tion**
exersise : **ex·er·cise**
ex·ert (to put forth); **ex·cerpt**
  (extract)
exertian : **ex·er·tion**
ex·er·tion
exhail : **ex·hale**
exhailation : **ex·ha·la·tion**
ex·ha·la·tion
ex·hale
ex·haust
exhawst : **ex·haust**

exhibbit : **ex·hib·it**
exhibet : **ex·hib·it**
ex·hib·it
ex·hi·bi·tion
ex·hil·a·rate
ex·hil·a·ra·tion
exhile : **ex·ile**
exhilerate : **ex·hil·a·rate**
exhileration : **ex·hil·a·ra·tion**
exhilirate : **ex·hil·a·rate**
exhorbitant : **ex·or·bi·tant**
ex·hort
exhuberance : **ex·u·ber·ance**
ex·hume
exibbet : **ex·hib·it**
exibit : **ex·hib·it**
exibition : **ex·hi·bi·tion**
exicution : **ex·e·cu·tion**
exidus : **ex·o·dus**
exigancy : **ex·i·gen·cy**
ex·i·gen·cy
exigensy : **ex·i·gen·cy**
exilarait : **ex·hil·a·rate**
exilarate : **ex·hil·a·rate**
exilaration : **ex·hil·a·ra·tion**
ex·ile
exileration : **ex·hil·a·ra·tion**
exise : **ex·cise**
exishency : **ex·i·gen·cy**
ex·ist
existance : **ex·is·tence**
existanse : **ex·is·tence**
existantialism :
  ex·is·ten·tial·ism
ex·is·tence
existencialism :
  ex·is·ten·tial·ism
existense : **ex·is·tence**
existensialism :
  ex·is·ten·tial·ism
ex·is·ten·tial·ism

existentiallism :
   ex•is•ten•tial•ism
exitement : **ex•cite•ment**
exize : **ex•cise**
exodas : **ex•o•dus**
exodis : **ex•o•dus**
exodos : **ex•o•dus**
ex•o•dus
ex•or•bi•tant
exort : **ex•hort**
expance : **ex•panse**
ex•panse
expeadient : **ex•pe•di•ent**
expearience : **ex•pe•ri•ence**
expeariment : **ex•per•i•ment**
ex•pec•tant
expectent : **ex•pec•tant**
expeddition : **ex•pe•di•tion**
expediant : **ex•pe•di•ent**
ex•pe•di•ent
expedision : **ex•pe•di•tion**
ex•pe•di•tion
expedittion : **ex•pe•di•tion**
expeedient : **ex•pe•di•ent**
expeerience : **ex•pe•ri•ence**
expeeriment : **ex•per•i•ment**
expeirience : **ex•pe•ri•ence**
expeiriment : **ex•per•i•ment**
expence : **ex•pense**
expencive : **ex•pen•sive**
expendachure : **ex•pen•di•ture**
expendature : **ex•pen•di•ture**
expendeture : **ex•pen•di•ture**
ex•pen•di•ture
ex•pense
expenseve : **ex•pen•sive**
ex•pen•sive
experament : **ex•per•i•ment**
experement : **ex•per•i•ment**
experiance : **ex•pe•ri•ence**
experianse : **ex•pe•ri•ence**
ex•pe•ri•ence

experiense : **ex•pe•ri•ence**
ex•per•i•ment
ex•pert
expier : **ex•pire**
ex•plain
explaination : **ex•pla•na•tion**
ex•pla•na•tion
explane : **ex•plain**
explannation : **ex•pla•na•tion**
explenation : **ex•pla•na•tion**
explination : **ex•pla•na•tion**
expload : **ex•plode**
exploasion : **ex•plo•sion**
ex•plode
explosian : **ex•plo•sion**
ex•plo•sion
explotion : **ex•plo•sion**
explozion : **ex•plo•sion**
expurt : **ex•pert**
exquesite : **ex•qui•site**
exquisate : **ex•qui•site**
exquiset : **ex•qui•site**
ex•qui•site
exquizite : **ex•qui•site**
exsasperate : **ex•as•per•ate**
exsel : **ex•cel**
exsellanse : **ex•cel•lence**
exsellence : **ex•cel•lence**
exsercise : **ex•er•cise**
exsertion : **ex•er•tion**
exsibition : **ex•hi•bi•tion**
exsilaration : **ex•hil•a•ra•tion**
exsile : **ex•ile**
exsileration : **ex•hil•a•ra•tion**
exsise : **ex•cise**
exsist : **ex•ist**
exsistence : **ex•is•tence**
exsistentialism :
   ex•is•ten•tial•ism
exsitement : **ex•cite•ment**
exsize : **ex•cise**
exsort : **ex•hort**

exspire : **ex·pire**
exstol : **ex·tol**
exsume : **ex·hume**
extenguish : **ex·tin·guish**
extermanate : **ex·ter·mi·nate**
extermenate : **ex·ter·mi·nate**
exterminait : **ex·ter·mi·nate**
ex·ter·mi·nate
extinguesh : **ex·tin·guish**
ex·tin·guish
extinquish : **ex·tin·guish**
ex·tol
extoll : **ex·tol**
extraordenary :
   ex·traor·di·nary
extraordinarry :
   ex·traor·di·nary
ex·traor·di·nary
extraordinery : **ex·traor·di·nary**
ex·trav·a·gance
extravaganse : **ex·trav·a·gance**

extravagence : **ex·trav·a·gance**
extravegance : **ex·trav·a·gance**
extravert : **ex·tro·vert**
extravigance : **ex·trav·a·gance**
extravirt : **ex·tro·vert**
extream : **ex·treme**
extreem : **ex·treme**
ex·treme
extrivert : **ex·tro·vert**
extroardinary : **ex·traor·di·nary**
extrordinary : **ex·traor·di·nary**
ex·tro·vert
exubarance : **ex·u·ber·ance**
ex·u·ber·ance
exuberanse : **ex·u·ber·ance**
exuberence : **ex·u·ber·ance**
exuberense : **ex·u·ber·ance**
ex·ult (to rejoice); **ex·alt** (to
  honor)
exume : **ex·hume**
exurpt : **ex·cerpt**

F

fabble : **fa·ble**
fabbric : **fab·ric**
fabel : **fa·ble**
fa·ble
fabrec : **fab·ric**
fab·ric
fabrick : **fab·ric**
fa·cade
facaid : **fa·cade**
facalty : **fa·cil·i·ty** (aptitude;
    building) *or* **fac·ul·ty** (ability;
    teachers)
faceal : **fa·cial** (relating to the
    face) *or* **fac·ile** (superficial)
faceatious : **fa·ce·tious**
faceetious : **fa·ce·tious**
faceitious : **fa·ce·tious**
facelty : **fa·cil·i·ty** (aptitude;
    building) *or* **fac·ul·ty** (ability;
    teachers)
faceshious : **fa·ce·tious**
fac·et
fa·ce·tious
facetius : **fa·ce·tious**
fa·cial (relating to the face);
    fac·ile (superficial)
fac·ile (superficial); **fa·cial**
    (relating to the face)
facilety : **fa·cil·i·ty**
fa·cil·i·ty
facillity : **fa·cil·i·ty**
facimile : **fac·sim·i·le**
facination : **fas·ci·na·tion**
facism : **fas·cism**
facit : **fac·et**
facksimile : **fac·sim·i·le**
fackulty : **fac·ul·ty**
facsimely : **fac·sim·i·le**
fac·sim·i·le
facsimily : **fac·sim·i·le**

facsimmile : **fac·sim·i·le**
factary : **fac·to·ry**
factery : **fac·to·ry**
fac·to·ry
fac·ul·ty
faery : **fairy** (sprite) *or* **fer·ry**
    (boat)
Fahr·en·heit
Fahrenhiet : **Fahr·en·heit**
Fahrenhite : **Fahr·en·heit**
faign : **feign**
faimous : **fa·mous**
fair (equitable; bazaar); **fare**
    (fee)
Fairenheit : **Fahr·en·heit**
fairwell : **fare·well**
fairy (sprite); **fer·ry** (boat)
falacious : **fal·la·cious**
falacy : **fal·la·cy**
falcan : **fal·con**
falcify : **fal·si·fy**
fal·con
falible : **fal·li·ble**
falken : **fal·con**
falkon : **fal·con**
fallable : **fal·li·ble**
fal·la·cious
fallacius : **fal·la·cious**
fal·la·cy
fallashious : **fal·la·cious**
fallasy : **fal·la·cy**
fallatious : **fal·la·cious**
fallcon : **fal·con**
falleble : **fal·li·ble**
fallecy : **fal·la·cy**
fallesy : **fal·la·cy**
fallibal : **fal·li·ble**
fallibel : **fal·li·ble**
fal·li·ble
fallic : **phal·lic**

fallicy : **fal·la·cy**
fallisy : **fal·la·cy**
fallsify : **fal·si·fy**
fallty : **faulty**
falsafy : **fal·si·fy**
falsefy : **fal·si·fy**
falsety : **fal·si·ty**
fal·si·fy
falsitty : **fal·si·ty**
fal·si·ty
famaly : **fam·i·ly**
famely : **fam·i·ly**
famen : **fam·ine**
fameous : **fa·mous**
famesh : **fam·ish**
familar : **fa·mil·iar**
fa·mil·iar
familier : **fa·mil·iar**
familliar : **fa·mil·iar**
familly : **fam·i·ly**
fam·i·ly
famin : **fam·ine**
fam·ine
fam·ish
fammiliar : **fa·mil·iar**
fammily : **fam·i·ly**
fammine : **fam·ine**
fammish : **fam·ish**
fa·mous
fanatec : **fa·nat·ic**
fa·nat·ic
fanatick : **fa·nat·ic**
fanattic : **fa·nat·ic**
fan·ci·ful
fancifull : **fan·ci·ful**
fan·cy
fancyful : **fan·ci·ful**
fane : **feign**
fanfair : .**fan·fare**
fan·fare
fannatic : **fa·nat·ic**
fansiful : **fan·ci·ful**

fansy : **fan·cy**
fantasstic : **fan·tas·tic**
fantassy : **fan·ta·sy**
fantastec : **fan·tas·tic**
fan·tas·tic
fantastick : **fan·tas·tic**
fan·ta·sy or **phan·ta·sy**
fantesy : **fan·ta·sy**
fantissy : **fan·ta·sy**
fantisy : **fan·ta·sy**
fantom : **phan·tom**
farce
farcecal : **far·ci·cal**
far·ci·cal
farcicle : **far·ci·cal**
fare (fee); **fair** (equitable;
   bazaar)
fare·well
farmacy : **phar·ma·cy**
Farrenheit : **Fahr·en·heit**
farry : **fairy** (sprite) or **fer·ry**
   (boat)
farse : **farce**
farsecal : **far·ci·cal**
farsical : **far·ci·cal**
fasade : **fa·cade**
fascenation : **fas·ci·na·tion**
fascesm : **fas·cism**
fascinacion : **fas·ci·na·tion**
fascinatian : **fas·ci·na·tion**
fas·ci·na·tion
fas·cism
faset : **fac·et**
fasetious : **fa·ce·tious**
fashial : **fa·cial**
fashianable : **fash·ion·able**
fashienable : **fash·ion·able**
fash·ion·able
fashionibal : **fash·ion·able**
fashionible : **fash·ion·able**
fasility : **fa·cil·i·ty**
fasination : **fas·ci·na·tion**

fasit : **fac•et**
fasodd : **fa•cade**
fassetious : **fa•ce•tious**
fassination : **fas•ci•na•tion**
fassionable : **fash•ion•able**
fassism : **fas•cism**
fasteadious : **fas•tid•i•ous**
fasteedious : **fas•tid•i•ous**
fastideous : **fas•tid•i•ous**
fas•tid•i•ous
fastidius : **fas•tid•i•ous**
fat•al
fateague : **fa•tigue**
fategue : **fa•tigue**
fatel : **fa•tal**
fatham : **fa•thom**
fathem : **fa•thom**
fa•thom
fatige : **fa•tigue**
fa•tigue
fatique : **fa•tigue**
fatteague : **fa•tigue**
fattigue : **fa•tigue**
fau•cet
faucit : **fau•cet**
faul•ty
faun (mythical being); **fawn**
  (young deer)
fauset : **fau•cet**
favarable : **fa•vor•able**
faverable : **fa•vor•able**
faverite : **fa•vor•ite**
fa•vor•able
favorate : **fa•vor•ite**
favoret : **fa•vor•ite**
favorible : **fa•vor•able**
fa•vor•ite
fawn (young deer); **faun**
  (mythical being)
faze (to disturb); **phase** (step in
  a process)
feable : **fee•ble**

feacundity : **fe•cun•di•ty**
Feaji : **Fi•ji**
feance : **fi•an•cé** (*masc.*) *or*
  fi•an•cée (*fem.*)
fear•ful
fearfull : **fear•ful**
feasable : **fea•si•ble**
feasco : **fi•as•co**
feaseble : **fea•si•ble**
feasibal : **fea•si•ble**
fea•si•ble
feath•er
feazible : **fea•si•ble**
Feb•ru•ary
Februery : **Feb•ru•ary**
Febuarry : **Feb•ru•ary**
Febuery : **Feb•ru•ary**
fecundety : **fe•cun•di•ty**
fecunditty : **fe•cun•di•ty**
fe•cun•di•ty
fedaral : **fed•er•al**
fedderal : **fed•er•al**
fedelity : **fi•del•i•ty**
fed•er•al
federel : **fed•er•al**
federil : **fed•er•al**
fediral : **fed•er•al**
fedrel : **fed•er•al**
feebal : **fee•ble**
fee•ble
Feegee : **Fi•ji**
Feejee : **Fi•ji**
feerful : **fear•ful**
feesible : **fea•si•ble**
feetus : **fe•tus**
feign
feild : **field**
fein : **feign**
feirful : **fear•ful**
felan : **fel•on**
felany : **fel•o•ny**
felen : **fel•on**

feleny : **fel·o·ny**
felicety : **fe·lic·i·ty**
felicitty : **fe·lic·i·ty**
fe·lic·i·ty
felisity : **fe·lic·i·ty**
fellicity : **fe·lic·i·ty**
fellisity : **fe·lic·i·ty**
fellon : **fel·on**
fellony : **fel·o·ny**
fel·on
fel·o·ny
femail : **fe·male**
fe·male
femaminity : **fem·i·nin·i·ty**
femanine : **fem·i·nine**
femenine : **fem·i·nine**
feminen : **fem·i·nine**
feminenity : **fem·i·nin·i·ty**
feminin : **fem·i·nine**
fem·i·nine
femininety : **fem·i·nin·i·ty**
femininitty : **fem·i·nin·i·ty**
fem·i·nin·i·ty
feminity : **fem·i·nin·i·ty**
feminnine : **fem·i·nine**
femminine : **fem·i·nine**
femmininity : **fem·i·nin·i·ty**
fenagle : **fi·na·gle**
fence
Fenix : **Phoe·nix**
fennagle : **fi·na·gle**
fenomenal : **phe·nom·e·nal**
fenomenon : **phe·nom·e·non**
fense : **fence**
ferlough : **fur·lough**
ferlow : **fur·lough**
fernace : **fur·nace**
fe·ro·cious
feroshious : **fe·ro·cious**
ferotious : **fe·ro·cious**
ferrocious : **fe·ro·cious**
fer·ry (boat); **fairy** (sprite)

fertalizer : **fer·til·iz·er**
fer·tile
fertilety : **fer·til·i·ty**
fertiliser : **fer·til·iz·er**
fertilitty : **fer·til·i·ty**
fer·til·i·ty
fer·til·iz·er
fertill : **fer·tile**
fertillity : **fer·til·i·ty**
fertillizer : **fer·til·iz·er**
fervant : **fer·vent**
fer·vent
ferver : **fer·vor**
fer·vor
fesible : **fea·si·ble**
festaval : **fes·ti·val**
festeval : **fes·ti·val**
fes·ti·val
festivall : **fes·ti·val**
festivel : **fes·ti·val**
festivle : **fes·ti·val**
fether : **feath·er**
fetis : **fe·tus**
fetther : **feath·er**
fe·tus
feud
feu·dal (medieval social order);
  fu·tile (without success)
feudel : **feu·dal** (medieval social
  order) *or* **fu·tile** (without
  success)
feushia : **fuch·sia**
Fevruary : **Feb·ru·ary**
fewd : **feud**
fi·an·cé (*masc.*); **fi·an·cée**
  (*fem.*)
fi·an·cée (*fem.*); **fi·an·cé**
  (*masc.*)
fiancey : **fiancé** (*masc.*) *or*
  fi·an·cée (*fem.*)
fianse : **fi·an·cé** (*masc.*) *or*
  fi·an·cée (*fem.*)

fiansey : **fi·an·cé** (*masc.*) *or*
  fi·an·cée (*fem.*)
fiary : **fi·ery**
fi·as·co
fiasko : **fi·as·co**
fickal : **fick·le**
fickel : **fick·le**
fick·le
ficsion : **fis·sion**
fidelety : **fi·del·i·ty**
fidelitty : **fi·del·i·ty**
fi·del·i·ty
fidellity : **fi·del·i·ty**
field
fi·ery
fiftean : **fif·teen**
fif·teen
fiftene : **fif·teen**
fif·ti·eth
fif·ty
fiftyeth : **fif·ti·eth**
Figi : **Fi·ji**
Fi·ji
fikle : **fick·le**
filabuster : **fi·li·bus·ter**
fil·a·ment
filamete : **fil·a·ment**
Filapino : **Fil·i·pi·no**
filay : **fi·let** (filet mignon) *or*
  fil·let (boneless meat or fish)
fileal : **fil·ial**
filement : **fil·a·ment**
Filepino : **Fil·i·pi·no**
fi·let (filet mignon); **fil·let**
  (boneless meat or fish)
filey : **fi·let** (filet mignon) *or*
  fil·let (boneless meat or fish)
fil·ial
fi·li·bus·ter
filiel : **fil·ial**
filiment : **fil·a·ment**
Filipeno : **Fil·i·pi·no**

Fil·i·pi·no
fillabuster : **fi·li·bus·ter**
fillay : **fi·let** (filet mignon) *or*
  fil·let (boneless meat or fish)
fil·let (boneless meat or fish);
  fi·let (filet mignon)
filley : **fi·let** (filet mignon) *or*
  fil·let (boneless meat or fish)
fillial : **fil·ial**
fillibuster : **fi·li·bus·ter**
filliment : **fil·a·ment**
Fillipino : **Fil·i·pi·no**
fimale : **fe·male**
finagal : **fi·na·gle**
fi·na·gle
finaly : **fi·nal·ly**
fi·nal·ly
fi·nance
financeer : **fi·nan·cier**
financeir : **fi·nan·cier**
fi·nan·cial
fi·nan·cier
finanse : **fi·nance**
finanseir : **fi·nan·cier**
finanshial : **fi·nan·cial**
finansier : **fi·nan·cier**
finantial : **fi·nan·cial**
finesce : **fi·nesse**
finess : **fi·nesse**
fi·nesse
fin·icky
finicy : **fin·icky**
fin·ish (to complete); **Finn·ish**
  (from Finland)
Fin·land
finnagle : **fi·na·gle**
finnally : **fi·nal·ly**
finness : **fi·nesse**
finnicky : **fin·icky**
Finn·ish (from Finland);
  fin·ish (to complete)
Finnland : **Fin·land**

fiord *or* fjord
firey : **fi•ery**
firlough : **fur•lough**
firtile : **fer•tile**
firtility : **fer•til•i•ty**
firy : **fi•ery**
fishary : **fish•ery**
fisherry : **fish•ery**
fish•ery
fishion : **fis•sion**
fision : **fis•sion**
fis•sion
fistacuffs : **fist•i•cuffs**
fistecuffs : **fist•i•cuffs**
fist•i•cuffs
fitus : **fe•tus**
fivteen : **fif•teen**
fivtieth : **fif•ti•eth**
fivty : **fif•ty**
fixety : **fix•i•ty**
fixitty : **fix•i•ty**
fix•i•ty
fizion : **fis•sion**
fjord *or* **fiord**
flac•cid
flacid : **flac•cid**
flagan : **flag•on**
flagen : **flag•on**
flaggon : **flag•on**
flag•on
fla•grant
flagrent : **fla•grant**
flair (talent); **flare** (torch)
flamboiant : **flam•boy•ant**
flam•boy•ant
flamboyent : **flam•boy•ant**
flambuoyant : **flam•boy•ant**
flameboyant : **flam•boy•ant**
flanel : **flan•nel**
flannal : **flan•nel**
flan•nel
flare (torch); **flair** (talent)

flasid : **flac•cid**
flassid : **flac•cid**
flautest : **flut•ist**
flaut•ist *or* **flut•ist**
flaver : **fla•vor**
fla•vor
fleacy : **fleecy**
flecksible : **flex•i•ble**
fledgleng : **fledg•ling**
fledg•ling
fleecy
fleesy : **fleecy**
flertatious : **flir•ta•tious**
flexable : **flex•i•ble**
flexeble : **flex•i•ble**
flex•i•ble
flimsey : **flim•sy**
flim•si•ness
flimssness : **flim•si•ness**
flimziness : **flim•si•ness**
flimzy : **flim•sy**
flipant : **flip•pant**
flip•pant
flippent : **flip•pant**
flippint : **flip•pant**
flirtacious : **flir•ta•tious**
flirtashious : **flir•ta•tious**
flir•ta•tious
flirtatius : **flir•ta•tious**
floatsam : **flot•sam**
floora : **flo•ra**
Floorida : **Flor•i•da**
flo•ra
flored : **flor•id** (ornate; ruddy)
    or **flu•o•ride** (dental
    treatment)
Floreda : **Flor•i•da**
flo•res•cent (flowering);
    flu•o•res•cent (emitting light)
floresh : **flour•ish**
florest : **flo•rist**

flor·id (ornate; ruddy);
  flu·o·ride (dental treatment)
Flor·i·da
floridation : flu·o·ri·da·tion
floride : flor·id (ornate; ruddy)
  or flu·o·ride (dental
  treatment)
florish : flour·ish
flo·rist
florra : flo·ra
florrescent : flo·res·cent
  (flowering) or flu·o·res·cent
  (emitting light)
florressent : flo·res·cent
  (flowering) or flu·o·res·cent
  (emitting light)
florrid : flor·id (ornate; ruddy)
  or flu·o·ride (dental
  treatment)
Florrida : Flor·i·da
florridation : flu·o·ri·da·tion
florride : flor·id (ornate;
  ruddy) or flu·o·ride (dental
  treatment)
florrish : flour·ish
florrist : flo·rist
flot·sam
flotsem : flot·sam
flotsum : flot·sam
flottsam : flot·sam
floun·der
flour (grain meal); flow·er
  (plant)
flourescent : flu·o·res·cent
flouresh : flour·ish
flouridation : flu·o·ri·da·tion
flouride : flor·id (ornate;
  ruddy) or flu·o·ride (dental
  treatment)
flour·ish
flourrish : flour·ish
floutest : flut·ist

floutist : flut·ist
flow·er (plant); flour (grain
  meal)
flowera : flo·ra
flowerist : flo·rist
flownder : floun·der
fluancy : flu·en·cy
fluansy : flu·en·cy
fluant : flu·ent
flu·en·cy
fluensy : flu·en·cy
flu·ent
fluoradation : flu·o·ri·da·tion
fluoredation : flu·o·ri·da·tion
flu·o·res·cent (emitting light);
  flo·res·cent (flowering)
fluoresent : flo·res·cent
  (flowering) or flu·o·res·cent
  (emitting light)
fluoressent : flo·res·cent
  (flowering) or flu·o·res·cent
  (emitting light)
fluorid : flor·id (ornate; ruddy)
  or flu·o·ride (dental
  treatment)
flu·o·ri·da·tion
flu·o·ride (dental treatment);
  flor·id (ornate; ruddy)
fluoried : flor·id (ornate;
  ruddy) or flu·o·ride (dental
  treatment)
flutest : flut·ist
flut·ist or flaut·ist
fluttist : flut·ist
foacal : fo·cal
foacused : fo·cused
foam
fobia : pho·bia
fo·cal
focel : fo·cal
fo·cused

fo•cus•ing
focussed : **fo•cused**
focussing : **fo•cus•ing**
Foenix : **Phoe•nix**
foe•tus (*Brit.*) : **fe•tus**
fog•ey (old-fashioned person);
   fog•gy (misty) *or* **fo•gy**
   (old-fashioned person)
fog•gy (misty); **fo•gy**
   (old-fashioned person)
fo•gy *or* **fog•ey** (old-fashioned
   person); **fog•gy** (misty)
foibal : **foi•ble**
foibel : **foi•ble**
foi•ble
foilage : **fo•liage**
foilege : **fo•liage**
foilige : **fo•liage**
fokal : **fo•cal**
fokissed : **fo•cused**
fokle : **fo•cal**
fokused : **fo•cused**
folage : **fo•liage**
foleo : **fo•lio**
fo•liage
folicle : **fol•li•cle**
folige : **fo•liage**
fo•lio
follacle : **fol•li•cle**
follakle : **fol•li•cle**
follecle : **fol•li•cle**
follekle : **fol•li•cle**
folleo : **fo•lio**
follical : **fol•li•cle**
fol•li•cle
follikle : **fol•li•cle**
follio : **fo•lio**
folyage : **fo•liage**
fome : **foam**
fonetic : **pho•net•ic**
foram : **fo•rum**

forarm : **fore•arm**
forbare : **for•bear** (to restrain
   oneself) *or* **fore•bear**
   (ancestor)
forbarence : **for•bear•ance**
for•bear (to restrain oneself);
   fore•bear (ancestor)
for•bear•ance
forbearanse : **for•bear•ance**
forbearence : for•bear•ance
forbearense : **for•bear•ance**
forberance : **for•bear•ance**
for•bid
forbode : **fore•bode**
forcast : **fore•cast**
forcaster : **fore•cast•er**
forceble : **forc•ible**
force•ful
forcefull : **force•ful**
forcibal : **forc•ible**
forcibel : **forc•ible**
forc•ible
fore•arm
forebare : **for•bear** (to restrain
   oneself) *or* **fore•bear**
   (ancestor)
fore•bear (ancestor); **for•bear**
   (to restrain oneself)
forebearance : **for•bear•ance**
forebid : **for•bid**
foreboad : **fore•bode**
fore•bode
fore•cast
fore•cast•er
forecastor : **fore•cast•er**
fore•fa•ther
forefeit : **for•feit**
forefet : **for•feit**
forefit : **for•feit**
foregetful : **for•get•ful**
foregive : **for•give**
foregn : **for•eign**

foregner : **for·eign·er**
fore·go *or* **for·go**
fore·gone
foregotten : **for·got·ten**
fore·head
for·eign
for·eign·er
foreignor : **for·eign·er**
forelorn : **for·lorn**
forem : **fo·rum**
fore·man
foremat : **for·mat**
foremidable : **for·mi·da·ble**
foremula : **for·mu·la**
foren : **for·eign**
forencic : **fo·ren·sic**
forener : **for·eign·er**
forenicate : **for·ni·cate**
forensec : **fo·ren·sic**
fo·ren·sic
forensick : **fo·ren·sic**
fore·see
foreshadoe : **fore·shad·ow**
fore·shad·ow
for·est
fore·stall
forestary : **for·est·ry**
foresterry : **for·est·ry**
forestery : **for·est·ry**
for·est·ry
foreswear : **for·swear**
foresythia : **for·syth·ia**
foreteen : **four·teen**
fore·tell
foretification : **for·ti·fi·ca·tion**
foretress : **for·tress**
foretuitious : **for·tu·itous**
foretunate : **for·tu·nate**
foretune : **for·tune**
foreward : **fore·word** (preface)
   or **for·ward** (ahead)
fore·warn

fore·word (preface); **for·ward**
   (ahead)
forfather : **fore·fa·ther**
for·feit
forfet : **for·feit**
forfiet : **for·feit**
forfit : **for·feit**
forgary : **forg·ery**
forgerry : **forg·ery**
forg·ery
for·get·ful
forgetfull : **for·get·ful**
forgeting : **for·get·ting**
for·get·ting
forgitful : **for·get·ful**
forgiting : **for·get·ting**
forgitting : **for·get·ting**
for·give
for·go *or* **fore·go**
forgone : **fore·gone**
for·got·ten
forgry : **forg·ery**
forhead : **fore·head**
forign : **for·eign**
forigner : **for·eign·er**
forim : **fo·rum**
forin : **for·eign**
foriner : **for·eign·er**
forinsic : **fo·ren·sic**
forist : **for·est**
foristry : **for·est·ry**
forjery : **forg·ery**
for·lorn
formadyhide : **form·al·de·hyde**
formaldehide : **form·al·de·hyde**
formaldehied : **form·al·de·hyde**
form·al·de·hyde
formaldihyde : **form·al·de·hyde**
formalldehyde :
   form·al·de·hyde
forman : **fore·man**
for·mat

formeldehyde : **form·al·de·hyde**
for·mi·da·ble
formiddable : **for·mi·da·ble**
formideble : **for·mi·da·ble**
formidibal : **for·mi·da·ble**
formidibel : **for·mi·da·ble**
formidible : **for·mi·da·ble**
formoola : **for·mu·la**
for·mu·la
formulah : **for·mu·la**
formulla : **for·mu·la**
fornacate : **for·ni·cate**
fornecate : **for·ni·cate**
fornicait : **for·ni·cate**
for·ni·cate
forram : **fo·rum**
forrem : **fo·rum**
forrensic : **fo·ren·sic**
forrest : **for·est**
forrestry : **for·est·ry**
forrim : **fo·rum**
forrist : **for·est**
forristry : **for·est·ry**
forrum : **fo·rum**
forsee : **fore·see**
forseful : **force·ful**
forshadow : **fore·shad·ow**
forsible : **forc·ible**
forsithea : **for·syth·ia**
forsithia : **for·syth·ia**
forstall : **fore·stall**
forsware : **for·swear**
for·swear
forsythea : **for·syth·ia**
for·syth·ia
fort (bulwark); **forte** (strong
  point)
fortafication : **for·ti·fi·ca·tion**
fortafy : **for·ti·fy**
fortatude : **for·ti·tude**
forte (strong point); **fort**
  (bulwark)

forteen : **four·teen**
fortefication : **for·ti·fi·ca·tion**
fortefy : **for·ti·fy**
fortell : **fore·tell**
fortetude : **for·ti·tude**
forth (forward); **fourth** (4th)
fortien : **for·tune**
for·ti·eth
fortifacation : **for·ti·fi·ca·tion**
for·ti·fi·ca·tion
fortifikation : **for·ti·fi·ca·tion**
for·ti·fy
fortifycation : **for·ti·fi·ca·tion**
fortine : **for·tune**
fortitood : **for·ti·tude**
for·ti·tude
fortooitous : **for·tu·itous**
fortoon : **for·tune**
fortoonate : **for·tu·nate**
fortres : **for·tress**
fortrese : **for·tress**
for·tress
fortriss : **for·tress**
fortruss : **for·tress**
fortuatous : **for·tu·itous**
fortuetous : **for·tu·itous**
fortuitious : **for·tu·itous**
for·tu·itous
fortuitus : **for·tu·itous**
for·tu·nate
for·tune
fortunet : **for·tu·nate**
fortunete : **for·tu·nate**
fortunit : **for·tu·nate**
for·ty
fortyeth : **for·ti·eth**
fortyith : **for·ti·eth**
fo·rum
forust : **for·est**
forustry : **for·est·ry**
for·ward (ahead); **fore·word**
  (preface)

forwarn : **fore·warn**
fosell : **fos·sil**
fosil : **fos·sil**
fosile : **fos·sil**
fossel : **fos·sil**
fossell : **fos·sil**
fos·sil
fossile : **fos·sil**
fossill : **fos·sil**
fotagrafy : **pho·tog·ra·phy**
foul (offensive); **fowl** (bird)
foundary : **found·ry**
founderry : **found·ry**
foundery : **found·ry**
foundiry : **found·ry**
found·ry
foun·tain
founten : **foun·tain**
fountian : **foun·tain**
fountin : **foun·tain**
fourarm : **fore·arm**
fourbid : **for·bid**
fourbode : **fore·bode**
fourcast : **fore·cast**
fourcaster : **fore·cast·er**
fourensic : **fo·ren·sic**
fourfather : **fore·fa·ther**
fourtean : **four·teen**
four·teen
fourtene : **four·teen**
fourth (4th); **forth** (forward)
fourtieth : **for·ti·eth**
fourtification : **for·ti·fi·ca·tion**
fourtify : **for·ti·fy**
fourtine : **four·teen**
fourtress : **for·tress**
fourtuitous : **for·tu·itous**
fourtunate : **for·tu·nate**
fourtune : **for·tune**
fourty : **for·ty**
fowl (bird); **foul** (offensive)
foyble : **foi·ble**

fra·cas
frachion : **frac·tion**
frachure : **frac·ture**
fracis : **fra·cas**
frackas : **fra·cas**
fracktion : **frac·tion**
frackture : **frac·ture**
frackus : **fra·cas**
fractian : **frac·tion**
frac·tion
frac·ture
fracus : **fra·cas**
fragell : **frag·ile**
fraggile : **frag·ile**
fragil : **frag·ile**
frag·ile
fragill : **frag·ile**
fra·grance
fragranse : **fra·grance**
fra·grant
fragrence : **fra·grance**
fragrense : **fra·grance**
fragrent : **fra·grant**
fragrince : **fra·grance**
fragrinse : **fra·grance**
fragrint : **fra·grant**
fragrunce : **fra·grance**
fragrunse : **fra·grance**
fragrunt : **fra·grant**
fraighter : **freight·er**
frail
fraiter : **freight·er**
frajile : **frag·ile**
frakas : **fra·cas**
frale : **frail**
franc (money); **frank** (honest)
fran·chise
franchize : **fran·chise**
franetic : **fre·net·ic**
frank (honest); **franc** (money)
franshise : **fran·chise**
frater : **freight·er**

fraternety : **fra·ter·ni·ty**
fraternitty : **fra·ter·ni·ty**
fra·ter·ni·ty
fraturnity : **fra·ter·ni·ty**
fraudulant : **fraud·u·lent**
fraud·u·lent
frawdulent : **fraud·u·lent**
fraxion : **frac·tion**
fraxure : **frac·ture**
freak
freckal : **freck·le**
freckel : **freck·le**
freck·le
freek : **freak**
freight·er
freightor : **freight·er**
freik : **freak**
freind : **friend**
freiter : **freight·er**
freke : **freak**
frekkle : **freck·le**
frend : **friend**
fre·net·ic
frenetick : **fre·net·ic**
frenettic : **fre·net·ic**
frennetic : **fre·net·ic**
frensy : **fren·zy**
fren·zy
frequancy : **fre·quen·cy**
frequansy : **fre·quen·cy**
fre·quen·cy
frequensy : **fre·quen·cy**
fri·ar (monk); **fry·er** (fried
    fowl)
frieghter : **freight·er**
friend
fri·er or **fry·er** (fried fowl);
    fri·ar (monk)
frigat : **frig·ate**
frig·ate
friged : **frig·id**
frigedity : **fri·gid·i·ty**

friget : **frig·ate**
friggate : **frig·ate**
frigget : **frig·ate**
friggid : **frig·id**
friggidity : **fri·gid·i·ty**
friggit : **frig·ate**
frig·id
frigidety : **fri·gid·i·ty**
frigiditty : **fri·gid·i·ty**
fri·gid·i·ty
frigit : **frig·ate** (ship) or **frig·id**
    (cold)
frinetic : **fre·net·ic**
friquency : **fre·quen·cy**
frivalous : **friv·o·lous**
frivalus : **friv·o·lous**
frivelous : **friv·o·lous**
frivilous : **friv·o·lous**
frivilus : **friv·o·lous**
frivolety : **fri·vol·i·ty**
frivolis : **friv·o·lous**
fri·vol·i·ty
frivollity : **fri·vol·i·ty**
friv·o·lous
frol·ic
frolick : **frol·ic**
frollic : **frol·ic**
frontadge : **front·age**
front·age
fron·tal
frontear : **fron·tier**
fronteer : **fron·tier**
frontege : **front·age**
fronteir : **fron·tier**
frontel : **fron·tal**
frontespiece : **fron·tis·piece**
frontidge : **front·age**
fron·tier
frontige : **front·age**
frontispeace : **fron·tis·piece**
frontispeice : **fron·tis·piece**
frontispice : **fron·tis·piece**

fron·tis·piece
frontspiece : **fron·tis·piece**
frovolitty : **fri·vol·i·ty**
fru·gal
frugel : **fru·gal**
fruit·ful
fruitfull : **fruit·ful**
frutful : **fruit·ful**
fry·er *or* **fri·er** (fried fowl);
   fri·ar (monk)
fuchea : **fuch·sia**
fuchia : **fuch·sia**
fuch·sia
fucilage : **fu·se·lage**
fuciloge : **fu·se·lage**
fudal : **feu·dal** (medieval social
   order) *or* **fu·tile** (without
   success)
fued : **feud**
fuedal : **feu·dal** (medieval
   social order) *or* **fu·tile**
   (without success)
fugative : **fu·gi·tive**
fugetive : **fu·gi·tive**
fugiteve : **fu·gi·tive**
fu·gi·tive
fujitive : **fu·gi·tive**
fulcram : **ful·crum**
fulcrem : **ful·crum**
fulcrim : **ful·crum**
ful·crum
ful·fil *or* **ful·fill**
ful·fill *or* **ful·fil**
fullcrem : **ful·crum**
fullcrum : **ful·crum**
fullfil : **ful·fill**
fullfill : **ful·fill**
fullsome : **ful·some**
ful·some
fumagate : **fum·i·gate**
fumegate : **fum·i·gate**
fumigait : **fum·i·gate**

fum·i·gate
fun·da·men·tal
fundamintal : **fun·da·men·tal**
fundemental : **fun·da·men·tal**
fundimental : **fun·da·men·tal**
funel : **fun·nel**
funell : **fun·nel**
funil : **fun·nel**
funill : **fun·nel**
funnal : **fun·nel**
fun·nel
funnell : **fun·nel**
funnil : **fun·nel**
furer : **fu·ror**
fur·lough
furlowe : **fur·lough**
fur·nace
furnature : **fur·ni·ture**
furnece : **fur·nace**
furness : **fur·nace**
furneture : **fur·ni·ture**
furnice : **fur·nace**
furniss : **fur·nace**
fur·ni·ture
furoar : **fu·ror**
fu·ror
furrer : **fu·ror**
furror : **fu·ror**
fusalage : **fu·se·lage**
fu·se·lage
fuselodge : **fu·se·lage**
fuseloge : **fu·se·lage**
fushea : **fuch·sia**
fushia : **fuch·sia**
fusilage : **fu·se·lage**
fusiloge : **fu·se·lage**
fu·sion
fussion : **fu·sion**
futele : **feu·dal** (medieval social
   order) *or* **fu·tile** (without
   success)

futell : **feu·dal** (medieval social order) *or* **fu·tile** (without success)
fu·tile (without success); **feu·dal** (medieval social order)
futilety : **fu·til·i·ty**

futilitty : **fu·til·i·ty**
fu·til·i·ty
futill : **fu·tile**
futillity : **fu·til·i·ty**
fuzion : **fu·sion**
fyord : **fjord**

G

gabardeen : **gab•ar•dine**

gabardene : **gab•ar•dine**

gab•ar•dine *or* **gab•er•dine**

gabbardine : **gab•ar•dine**

gabberdine : **gab•ar•dine**

gab•ble (to babble); **ga•ble**
(roof feature)

gabel : **gab•ble** (to babble) *or*
ga•ble (roof feature)

gab•er•dine *or* **gab•ar•dine**

ga•ble (roof feature); **gab•ble**
(to babble)

gache : **gauche**

gad•get

gadgit : **gad•get**

gadjet : **gad•get**

Gaelec : **Gael•ic**

Gael•ic

gaget : **gad•get**

gai•ety *or* **gay•ety**

Gailic : **Gael•ic**

gai•ly *or* **gay•ly**

gait (way of walking); **gate**
(door)

ga•la

galactec : **ga•lac•tic**

ga•lac•tic

galary : **gal•lery**

gal•axy

galen : **gal•lon**

galery : **gal•lery**

Galic : **Gael•ic**

galion : **gal•le•on** (ship) *or*
gal•lon (measure)

galip : **gal•lop**

galla : **ga•la**

gallacksy : **gal•axy**

gallactic : **ga•lac•tic**

gallantery : **gal•lant•ry**

gal•lant•ry

gallap : **gal•lop**

gallary : **gal•lery**

gallaxy : **gal•axy**

gallen : **gal•le•on** (ship) *or*
gal•lon (measure)

gallentry : **gal•lant•ry**

gal•le•on (ship); **gal•lon**
(measure)

gallep : **gal•lop**

gal•lery

gallexy : **gal•axy**

gal•ley

gallin : **gal•le•on** (ship) *or*
gal•lon (measure)

gallintry : **gal•lant•ry**

gallion : **gal•le•on** (ship) *or*
gal•lon (measure)

gallip : **gal•lop**

gallixy : **gal•axy**

gal•lon (measure); **gal•le•on**
(ship)

gal•lop (canter); **Gal•lup** (poll)

gallosh : **ga•losh** (footwear) *or*
gou•lash (stew)

galluntry : **gal•lant•ry**

Gal•lup (poll); **gal•lop** (canter)

gally : **gal•ley**

galon : **gal•le•on** (ship) *or*
gal•lon (measure)

galop : **gal•lop**

ga•losh (footwear); **gou•lash**
(stew)

galvanise : **gal•va•nize**

gal•va•nize

galvenize : **gal•va•nize**

galvinize : **gal•va•nize**

gambet : **gam•bit**

gam•bit

gam•ble (to risk or bet);
gam•bol (to frolic)

gam·bol (to frolic); **gam·ble** (to risk or bet)

gamet : **gam·ut**

gamit : **gam·ut**

gammet : **gam·ut**

gammit : **gam·ut**

gammut : **gam·ut**

gam·ut

gandola : **gon·do·la**

gangrean : **gan·grene**

gangreen : **gan·grene**

gan·grene

gangrine : **gan·grene**

gaol (*Brit.*) : **jail**

ga·rage

garantee : **guar·an·tee**

garason : **gar·ri·son**

gardeenia : **gar·de·nia**

gar·den

gar·de·nia

gardian : **guard·ian**

gardin : **gar·den**

gardinia : **gar·de·nia**

garentee : **guar·an·tee**

garesh : **gar·ish**

garet : **gar·ret**

gargoil : **gar·goyle**

gargoyl : **gar·goyle**

gar·goyle

garintee : **guar·an·tee**

gar·ish

garison : **gar·ri·son**

garit : **gar·ret**

gar·land

garlec : **gar·lic**

garlend : **gar·land**

gar·lic

garlick : **gar·lic**

garlind : **gar·land**

garlund : **gar·land**

garmant : **gar·ment**

gar·ment

garmet : **gar·ment**

garmint : **gar·ment**

gar·net

garnit : **gar·net**

garodge : **ga·rage**

garoge : **ga·rage**

garrage : **ga·rage**

garrentee : **guar·an·tee**

garreson : **gar·ri·son**

gar·ret

garrisen : **gar·ri·son**

garrish : **gar·ish**

gar·ri·son

garrit : **gar·ret**

gar·ru·lous

garulous : **gar·ru·lous**

gasaleen : **gas·o·line**

gasalene : **gas·o·line**

gasaline : **gas·o·line**

gas·e·ous

gasiline : **gas·o·line**

gasious : **gas·e·ous**

gas·ket

gaskit : **gas·ket**

gasolean : **gas·o·line**

gasoleen : **gas·o·line**

gasolene : **gas·o·line**

gas·o·line

gasseous : **gas·e·ous**

gassoline : **gas·o·line**

gastly : **ghast·ly**

gate (door); **gait** (way of walking)

gauche

gaudy

gauge

gauky : **gawky**

gaurantee : **guar·an·tee**

gaurd : **guard**

gaurdian : **guard·ian**

gause : **gauze**

gauze

gaval : **gav·el**
gav·el
gavell : **gav·el**
gavil : **gav·el**
gavvel : **gav·el**
gavvil : **gav·el**
gawdy : **gaudy**
gawky
gawze : **gauze**
gay·ety *or* **gai·ety**
gay·ly *or* **gai·ly**
gazet : **ga·zette**
gazett : **ga·zette**
ga·zette
gazzette : **ga·zette**
geagraphy : **ge·og·ra·phy**
Gealic : **Gael·ic**
gealogy : **ge·ol·o·gy**
geametry : **ge·om·e·try**
geanology : **ge·ne·al·o·gy**
gear
gearth : **girth**
geer : **gear**
gehad : **ji·had**
geir : **gear**
geiser : **gey·ser**
gel *or* jell
gelaten : **gel·a·tin**
gel·a·tin
gelitin : **gel·a·tin**
gellatin : **gel·a·tin**
Gem·i·ni
Geminie : **Gem·i·ni**
Geminni : **Gem·i·ni**
gemnasium : **gym·na·si·um**
gemnasstics : **gym·nas·tics**
gemnast : **gym·nast**
gemnastecs : **gym·nas·tics**
gemnasticks : **gym·nas·tics**
gemnest : **gym·nast**
gemnist : **gym·nast**
genarator : **gen·er·a·tor**

ge·ne·al·o·gy
Geneava : **Ge·ne·va**
Geneeva : **Ge·ne·va**
geneology : **ge·ne·al·o·gy**
gen·era (*plur.*, class or kind);
    genre (class of literature)
gen·er·al
generater : **gen·er·a·tor**
gen·er·a·tor
generel : **gen·er·al**
ge·ner·ic
generick : **ge·ner·ic**
generil : **gen·er·al**
gen·er·ous
generric : **ge·ner·ic**
generus : **gen·er·ous**
gen·e·sis
geneticks : **ge·net·ics**
ge·net·ics
genettics : **ge·net·ics**
Ge·ne·va
Genieva : **Ge·ne·va**
genious : **gen·ius**
geniral : **gen·er·al**
genirator : **gen·er·a·tor**
genirous : **gen·er·ous**
genisis : **gen·e·sis**
gen·ius (intellectual power);
    ge·nus (*sing.*, class or kind)
Geniva : **Ge·ne·va**
gennerate : **gen·er·ate**
gennerator : **gen·er·a·tor**
genneric : **ge·ner·ic**
gennerous : **gen·er·ous**
gennesis : **gen·e·sis**
gennetics : **ge·net·ics**
gennirate : **gen·er·ate**
genooine : **gen·u·ine**
genre (class of literature);
    gen·era (*plur.*, class or kind)
genteal : **gen·teel**

gen•teel (polite); gen•tile (not Jewish)

gentele : gen•teel (polite) *or* gen•tile (not Jewish)

gen•tile (not Jewish); gen•teel (polite)

genuin : gen•u•ine

gen•u•ine

ge•nus (*sing.,* class or kind); gen•ius (intellectual power)

genuwine : gen•u•ine

geoggrapy : ge•og•ra•phy

geografy : ge•og•ra•phy

ge•og•ra•phy

geogrefy : ge•og•ra•phy

geogrephy : ge•og•ra•phy

geogriphy : ge•og•ra•phy

geolegy : ge•ol•o•gy

geollogy : ge•ol•o•gy

geologgy : ge•ol•o•gy

ge•ol•o•gy

ge•om•e•try

geomettry : ge•om•e•try

geommetry : ge•om•e•try

geonoligy : ge•ne•al•o•gy

geonollogy : ge•ne•al•o•gy

geonre : genre

Georga : Geor•gia

Geor•gia

gerage : ga•rage

gerand : ger•und

geraneum : ge•ra•ni•um

geraniam : ge•ra•ni•um

geraniem : ge•ra•ni•um

ge•ra•ni•um

gerantology : ger•on•tol•o•gy

gerder : gird•er

gerdle : gir•dle

gerend : ger•und

gerkin : gher•kin

Germanny : Ger•ma•ny

Ger•ma•ny

Germeny : Ger•ma•ny

gerontolegy : ger•on•tol•o•gy

gerontoligy : ger•on•tol•o•gy

gerontollogy : ger•on•tol•o•gy

ger•on•tol•o•gy

gerranium : ge•ra•ni•um

gerrund : ger•und

gerth : girth

ger•und

gess : guess

gessture : ges•ture

gest : gist (essence) *or* jest (joke)

gester : ges•ture (movement) *or* jest•er (joker)

ges•ture (movement); jest•er (joker)

gesyr : gey•ser

gettho : ghet•to

Gettisburg : Get•tys•burg

getto : ghet•to

Gettysberg : Get•tys•burg

Get•tys•burg

Gettysburgh : Get•tys•burg

geuss : guess

gey•ser

ghast•ly

gherken : gher•kin

gher•kin

ghet•to

ghoul•ish

ghulish : ghoul•ish

ghurkin : gher•kin

gi•ant

gibe (to taunt); jibe (to change course in boat; to agree)

Gibralltar : Gi•bral•tar

Gi•bral•tar

Gibralter : Gi•bral•tar

gidance : guid•ance

gient : gi•ant

gier : gear

gieser : **gey•ser**

gihad : **ji•had**

gild (to cover with gold); **gilled** (having gills); **guild** (union)

gillatine : **guil•lo•tine**

gilled (having gills); **gild** (to cover with gold); **guild** (union)

gilliteen : **guil•lo•tine**

gillotine : **guil•lo•tine**

gilt (covered with gold); **guilt** (shame)

gimick : **gim•mick**

Gimini : **Gem•i•ni**

gimmeck : **gim•mick**

gimmic : **gim•mick**

gim•mick

gimnasium : **gym•na•si•um**

gimnasstics : **gym•nas•tics**

gimnast : **gym•nast**

gimnastecs : **gym•nas•tics**

gimnasticks : **gym•nas•tics**

gimnest : **gym•nast**

gimnist : **gym•nast**

ginacology : **gy•ne•col•o•gy**

ginasis : **gen•e•sis**

gincolijy : **gy•ne•col•o•gy**

ginecolligy : **gy•ne•col•o•gy**

ginecollogy : **gy•ne•col•o•gy**

gingam : **ging•ham**

ging•ham

ginghem : **ging•ham**

gingum : **ging•ham**

ginicology : **gy•ne•col•o•gy**

ginocology : **gy•ne•col•o•gy**

gipcem : **gyp•sum**

gipcim : **gyp•sum**

gipsam : **gyp•sum**

gipsem : **gyp•sum**

gipsey : **gyp•sy**

gipsim : **gyp•sum**

gipsy : **gyp•sy**

girafe : **gi•raffe**

gi•raffe

girage : **ga•rage**

giraph : **gi•raffe**

girascope : **gy•ro•scope**

girate : **gy•rate**

gird•er

gir•dle

girgle : **gur•gle**

girocompass : **gy•ro•com•pass**

girocompess : **gy•ro•com•pass**

girrate : **gy•rate**

girth

giser : **gey•ser**

gist (essence); **jest** (joke)

gister : **ges•ture** (movement) *or* **jest•er** (joker)

gitar : **gui•tar**

gittar : **gui•tar**

giullotine : **guil•lo•tine**

giutar : **gui•tar**

glaceir : **gla•cier**

glacher : **gla•cier**

gla•cier

gladdiator : **glad•i•a•tor**

gladeator : **glad•i•a•tor**

gladiater : **glad•i•a•tor**

glad•i•a•tor

glamarous : **glam•or•ous**

glamerous : **glam•or•ous**

glammorous : **glam•or•ous**

glam•or *or* **glam•our**

glam•or•ous

glamorus : **glam•or•ous**

glam•our *or* **glam•or**

glamourous : **glam•or•ous**

glance

glanse : **glance**

Glasco : **Glas•gow**

Glascoe : **Glas•gow**

Glascow : **Glas•gow**

Glas•gow

glasher : **gla·cier**
Glasscow : **Glas·gow**
glass·ware
glasswear : **glass·ware**
glasware : **glass·ware**
gleam
gleem : **gleam**
gleim : **gleam**
glemmer : **glim·mer**
glimer : **glim·mer**
glim·mer
glimpce : **glimpse**
glimpse
glimse : **glimpse**
glissen : **glis·ten**
glissten : **glis·ten**
glis·ten
gloabal : **glob·al**
gloat
glob·al
globall : **glob·al**
globel : **glob·al**
glorafication : **glo·ri·fi·ca·tion**
glorafy : **glo·ri·fy**
glorefication : **glo·ri·fi·ca·tion**
glorefy : **glo·ri·fy**
gloreous : **glo·ri·ous**
glorifacation : **glo·ri·fi·ca·tion**
glorifecation : **glo·ri·fi·ca·tion**
glo·ri·fi·ca·tion
glo·ri·fy
glo·ri·ous
glorius : **glo·ri·ous**
glorrification : **glo·ri·fi·ca·tion**
glorrify : **glo·ri·fy**
glorrious : **glo·ri·ous**
glorry : **glo·ry**
glo·ry
glosary : **glos·sa·ry**
glosery : **glos·sa·ry**
glos·sa·ry
glossery : **glos·sa·ry**

glote : **gloat**
gluton : **glut·ton**
glutonny : **glut·tony**
gluttan : **glut·ton**
glutten : **glut·ton**
gluttenny : **glut·tony**
glutteny : **glut·tony**
gluttin : **glut·ton**
gluttiny : **glut·tony**
glut·ton
glut·tony
gnarled
gnarreled : **gnarled**
gnarrled : **gnarled**
gnash
gnat
gnaw
gnoam : **gnome**
gnome (dwarf); **Nome** (city)
gnu (antelope); **knew** (was
    aware); **new** (not old)
goache : **gauche**
goal
goard : **gourd**
goashe : **gauche**
goa·tee
goatey : **goa·tee**
goatie : **goa·tee**
gobblen : **gob·lin**
gobblet : **gob·let**
gobblin : **gob·lin**
gobblit : **gob·let**
goblen : **gob·lin**
gob·let
gob·lin
goblit : **gob·let**
goche : **gauche**
goddes : **god·dess**
god·dess
goddiss : **god·dess**
godess : **god·dess**
god·li·ness

godlyness : **god•li•ness**
gofer : **go•pher**
gole : **goal**
gon•do•la
gondolla : **gon•do•la**
gooce : **goose**
good-by *or* **good-bye**
good-bye *or* **good-by**
goose
go•pher
gophur : **go•pher**
gord : **gourd**
gorey : **gory**
gor•geous
Gorgia : **Geor•gia**
gorgious : **gor•geous**
gorgius : **gor•geous**
gorila : **go•ril•la** (ape) *or*
  guer•ril•la (warrior)
go•ril•la (ape); **guer•ril•la**
  (warrior)
gorjeous : **gor•geous**
gormay : **gour•met**
gormet : **gour•met**
gorry : **gory**
gory
gosamer : **gos•sa•mer**
gosemer : **gos•sa•mer**
gosimer : **gos•sa•mer**
gosip : **gos•sip**
gos•pel
gospell : **gos•pel**
gospil : **gos•pel**
gospul : **gos•pel**
gos•sa•mer
gossamere : **gos•sa•mer**
gossamir : **gos•sa•mer**
gossemer : **gos•sa•mer**
gossep : **gos•sip**
gossimer : **gos•sa•mer**
gos•sip
gosspel : **gos•pel**

gossup : **gos•sip**
gosup : **gos•sip**
gotee : **goa•tee**
gothec : **goth•ic**
goth•ic
gothick : **goth•ic**
gou•lash (stew); **ga•losh**
  (footwear)
goulosh : **ga•losh** (footwear) *or*
  gou•lash (stew)
goun : **gown**
gourd
gourmay : **gour•met**
gour•met
gourmey : **gour•met**
govanor : **gov•er•nor**
govenor : **gov•er•nor**
goverment : **gov•ern•ment**
gov•ern
gov•er•nance
governanse : **gov•er•nance**
governence : **gov•er•nance**
governense : **gov•er•nance**
governer : **gov•er•nor**
governince : **gov•er•nance**
governmant : **gov•ern•ment**
gov•ern•ment
gov•er•nor
govirn : **gov•ern**
govirnance : **gov•er•nance**
govner : **gov•er•nor**
govurn : **gov•ern**
govurnor : **gov•er•nor**
govvern : **gov•ern**
govvernance : **gov•er•nance**
govvernment : **gov•ern•ment**
govvernnor : **gov•er•nor**
gown
grace•ful
gracefull : **grace•ful**
graceous : **gra•cious**
gra•cious

gracius : **gra•cious**
graddual : **grad•u•al**
gradduate : **grad•u•ate**
gradeant : **gra•di•ent**
gradiant : **gra•di•ent**
gra•di•ent
graduait : **grad•u•ate**
grad•u•al
grad•u•ate
graduel : **grad•u•al**
graduill : **grad•u•al**
graduwel : **grad•u•al**
graffec : **graph•ic**
graffete : **graf•fi•ti** (writing) *or*
  graph•ite (carbon)
graffic : **graph•ic**
graffically : **graph•i•cal•ly**
graf•fi•ti (writing); **graph•ite**
  (carbon)
graffitti : **graf•fi•ti**
grafitti : **graf•fi•ti**
gragarious : **gre•gar•i•ous**
graiceful : **grace•ful**
grainarry : **gra•na•ry**
grainary : **gra•na•ry**
grainerry : **gra•na•ry**
grainery : **gra•na•ry**
grainular : **gran•u•lar**
grainule : **gran•ule**
graitful : **grate•ful**
graiven : **grav•en**
graize : **graze**
gramar : **gram•mar**
gramer : **gram•mar**
gram•mar
grammer : **gram•mar**
grammir : **gram•mar**
granade : **gre•nade**
granaid : **gre•nade**
gra•na•ry
grandelaquence :
  gran•dil•o•quence

grandelloquence :
  gran•dil•o•quence
grandeloquance :
  gran•dil•o•quence
grandeloquence :
  gran•dil•o•quence
grandeoce : **gran•di•ose**
grandeose : **gran•di•ose**
gran•deur
grandilaquence :
  gran•dil•o•quence
gran•dil•o•quence
grandiloquense :
  gran•dil•o•quence
grandiloquince :
  gran•dil•o•quence
grandioce : **gran•di•ose**
gran•di•ose
grandoor : **gran•deur**
grandur : **gran•deur**
grandure : **gran•deur**
granerry : **gra•na•ry**
granery : **gra•na•ry**
grannule : **gran•ule**
granool : **gran•ule**
granoolar : **gran•u•lar**
gran•u•lar
gran•ule
granuler : **gran•u•lar**
granulir : **gran•u•lar**
graphec : **graph•ic**
graphecally : **graph•i•cal•ly**
grapheit : **graph•ite**
graph•ic
graph•i•cal•ly
graphick : **graph•ic**
graphickelly : **graph•i•cal•ly**
graphicly : **graph•i•cal•ly**
graph•ite (carbon); **graf•fi•ti**
  (writing)
graple : **grap•ple**
grappal : **grap•ple**

grappel : **grap·ple**
grap·ple
graseful : **grace·ful**
grasious : **grac·ious**
gratafication : **grat·i·fi·ca·tion**
gratafy : **grat·i·fy**
gratatude : **grat·i·tude**
grate (framework); **great** (large)
grate·ful
gratefull : **grate·ful**
gratefy : **grat·i·fy**
gratetude : **grat·i·tude**
gratful : **grate·ful**
gratiffication : **grat·i·fi·ca·tion**
grat·i·fi·ca·tion
grat·i·fy
grat·is
gratitood : **grat·i·tude**
grat·i·tude
gratitued : **grat·i·tude**
gratiutous : **gra·tu·itous**
grattafication : **grat·i·fi·ca·tion**
grattatude : **grat·i·tude**
grattifacation : **grat·i·fi·ca·tion**
grattification : **grat·i·fi·ca·tion**
grattify : **grat·i·fy**
grattis : **grat·is**
grattitude : **grat·i·tude**
grattuitous : **gra·tu·itous**
grattus : **grat·is**
gratuetous : **gra·tu·itous**
gratuitious : **gra·tu·itous**
gra·tu·itous
gratus : **grat·is**
gravatate : **grav·i·tate**
grav·el
gravell : **grav·el**
grav·en
gravetate : **grav·i·tate**
gravety : **grav·i·ty**
gravil : **grav·el**
grav·i·tate

gravitty : **grav·i·ty**
grav·i·ty
gravvel : **grav·el**
gravvitate : **grav·i·tate**
gravvity : **grav·i·ty**
gray *or* **grey**
grayhound : **grey·hound**
graze
gready : **greedy**
greanery : **green·ery**
Greasian : **Gre·cian**
greasy
great (large); **grate** (framework)
greatful : **grate·ful**
greating : **greet·ing**
greavance : **griev·ance**
greave (armored legging);
    grieve (to mourn)
Gre·cian
Greecian : **Gre·cian**
greedy
greenary : **green·ery**
greenerry : **green·ery**
green·ery
Greenich : **Green·wich**
Green·wich
Greenwitch : **Green·wich**
Greesian : **Gre·cian**
greesy : **greasy**
greet·ing
greevance : **griev·ance**
grefitti : **graf·fi·ti**
gregairious : **gre·gar·i·ous**
gregareous : **gre·gar·i·ous**
gre·gar·i·ous
gregarius : **gre·gar·i·ous**
greggarious : **gre·gar·i·ous**
greif : **grief**
greisy : **greasy**
greivance : **griev·ance**
greive : **greave** (armored
    legging) *or* **grieve** (to mourn)

greivence : **griev·ance**
gremlan : **grem·lin**
gremlen : **grem·lin**
grem·lin
gremlun : **grem·lin**
gre·nade
grenaid : **gre·nade**
Grennich : **Green·wich**
Grenwich : **Green·wich**
Grenwitch : **Green·wich**
greve : **greave** (armored
   legging) *or* **grieve** (to mourn)
grey *or* **gray**
grey·hound
gridiern : **grid·iron**
gridiren : **grid·iron**
gridirn : **grid·iron**
grid·iron
grief
griefance : **griev·ance**
griefitti : **graf·fi·ti**
griev·ance
grievanse : **griev·ance**
grieve (to mourn); **greave**
   (armored legging)
grievense : **griev·ance**
grif·fin *or* **grif·fon** *or* **gryph·on**
griffiti : **graf·fi·ti**
grif·fon *or* **grif·fin** *or* **gryph·on**
grigarious : **gre·gar·i·ous**
grill (to broil); **grille** (screen)
grille (screen); **grill** (to broil)
gri·mace
grimece : **gri·mace**
grimice : **gri·mace**
grimise : **gri·mace**
grimlin : **grem·lin**
grimmace : **gri·mace**
grisled : **griz·zled**
gris·ly (gruesome); **griz·zly**
   (grayish, as the bear)
grissel : **gris·tle**

grissle : **gris·tle**
gris·tle
grivance : **griev·ance**
griz·zled
griz·zly (grayish, as the bear);
   gris·ly (gruesome)
groacer : **gro·cer**
groacery : **gro·cery**
groaned
groap : **grope**
groape : **grope**
groatesque : **gro·tesque**
gro·cer
grocerry : **gro·cery**
gro·cery
grociary : **gro·cery**
grociery : **gro·cery**
groned : **groaned**
grooling : **gru·el·ing**
grope
groser : **gro·cer**
grotesk : **gro·tesque**
groteske : **gro·tesque**
gro·tesque
grouchy
grov·eled *or* **grov·elled**
grov·el·ing *or* **grov·el·ling**
grov·elled *or* **grov·eled**
grov·el·ling *or* **grov·el·ing**
groviled : **grov·eled**
grovilling : **grov·el·ing**
grovveled : **grov·eled**
growchy : **grouchy**
gru·el·ing
gruesom : **grue·some**
grue·some
gruling : **gru·el·ing**
grulling : **gru·el·ing**
grusome : **grue·some**
grusum : **grue·some**
gryph·on *or* **grif·fin** *or* **grif·fon**
guage : **gauge**

guar·an·tee
guard
guard·ian
guardien : **guard·ian**
guarintie : **guar·an·tee**
Guatamala : **Gua·te·ma·la**
Gua·te·ma·la
Guatemalla : **Gua·te·ma·la**
Guattemala : **Gua·te·ma·la**
guerila : **go·ril·la** (ape) *or*
 guer·ril·la (warrior)
guer·ril·la (warrior); **go·ril·la**
 (ape)
guess
guetar : **gui·tar**
guid·ance
guidanse : **guid·ance**
guiddance : **guid·ance**
guidence : **guid·ance**
guidense : **guid·ance**
guild (union); **gild** (to cover
 with gold); **gilled** (having
 gills)
guillatine : **guil·lo·tine**
guilletine : **guil·lo·tine**
guillotene : **guil·lo·tine**
guil·lo·tine
guilt (shame); **gilt** (covered with
 gold)
gui·tar
gulash : **ga·losh** (footwear) *or*
 gou·lash (stew)
gulet : **gul·let**
gulible : **gul·li·ble**
gullable : **gul·li·ble**
gullat : **gul·let**
gulleble : **gul·li·ble**
gul·let
gullibal : **gul·li·ble**
gul·li·ble
gullit : **gul·let**

gulosh : **ga·losh** (footwear) *or*
 gou·lash (stew)
gunery : **gun·nery**
gunnary : **gun·nery**
gun·nel *or* gun·wale
gunnerry : **gun·nery**
gun·nery
gun·wale *or* gun·nel
guord : **gourd**
guormet : **gour·met**
gurgal : **gur·gle**
gurgel : **gur·gle**
gur·gle
gurilla : **go·ril·la** (ape) *or*
 guer·ril·la (warrior)
gurkin : **gher·kin**
gurth : **girth**
guse : **goose**
Gwatemala : **Gua·te·ma·la**
gymnaisium : **gym·na·si·um**
gymnaseum : **gym·na·si·um**
gymnasiem : **gym·na·si·um**
gym·na·si·um
gymnasstics : **gym·nas·tics**
gym·nast
gymnastecs : **gym·nas·tics**
gymnasticks : **gym·nas·tics**
gym·nas·tics
gymnest : **gym·nast**
gymnist : **gym·nast**
gynacology : **gy·ne·col·o·gy**
gyncolijy : **gy·ne·col·o·gy**
gynecolligy : **gy·ne·col·o·gy**
gynecollogy : **gy·ne·col·o·gy**
gy·ne·col·o·gy
gynicology : **gy·ne·col·o·gy**
gynocology : **gy·ne·col·o·gy**
gyp
gypcem : **gyp·sum**
gypcim : **gyp·sum**
gyped : **gypped**
gypped

gypsam : **gyp•sum**
gypsem : **gyp•sum**
gypsey : **gyp•sy**
gypsie : **gyp•sy**
gypsim : **gyp•sum**
gyp•sum
gyp•sy
gyracompass : **gy•ro•com•pass**
gyrait : **gy•rate**
gyrascope : **gy•ro•scope**

gy•rate
gyricompass : **gy•ro•com•pass**
gyriscope : **gy•ro•scope**
gy•ro•com•pass
gyrocompess : **gy•ro•com•pass**
gyrocompiss : **gy•ro•com•pass**
gyroscoap : **gy•ro•scope**
gy•ro•scope
gyrrate : **gy•rate**
gyser : **gey•ser**

H

habbet : **hab·it**
habbit : **hab·it**
habbitable : **hab·it·able**
habetable : **hab·it·able**
hab·it
habitabel : **hab·it·able**
hab·it·able
habitibal : **hab·it·able**
habitible : **hab·it·able**
haceinda : **ha·ci·en·da**
hachery : **hatch·ery**
hachet : **hatch·et**
hachit : **hatch·et**
ha·ci·en·da
haciendah : **ha·ci·en·da**
hack·neyed
hacknied : **hack·neyed**
hackny : **hack·neyed**
haddeck : **had·dock**
haddoc : **had·dock**
had·dock
hadj *or* hajj (pilgrimage); **hag**
  (witch); **Hague** (city)
hadock : **had·dock**
Haeti : **Hai·ti**
haf : **half**
hafhazard : **hap·haz·ard**
hag (witch); **Hague** (city); **hajj**
  (pilgrimage)
hagard : **hag·gard**
haggal : **hag·gle**
hag·gard
haggel : **hag·gle**
haggerd : **hag·gard**
haggird : **hag·gard**
hag·gle
Hague (city); **hag** (witch); **hajj**
  (pilgrimage)
hailo : **ha·lo**
hailstoan : **hail·stone**

hail·stone
hair (on head); **heir** (inheritor)
hairbrained : **hare·brained**
hairbraned : **hare·brained**
hairlip : **hare·lip**
haissen : **has·ten**
haisten : **has·ten**
Haitee : **Hai·ti**
Hai·ti
Haity : **Hai·ti**
hajj *or* **hadj** (pilgrimage); **hag**
  (witch); **Hague** (city)
halabut : **hal·i·but**
halatosis : **hal·i·to·sis**
halceon : **hal·cy·on**
halcion : **hal·cy·on**
hal·cy·on
halebut : **hal·i·but**
halestone : **hail·stone**
haletosis : **hal·i·to·sis**
half (*sing.*); **halve** (*verb*);
  halves (*plur.*)
halfhazard : **hap·haz·ard**
halfs : **halves**
haliard : **hal·yard**
halibet : **hal·i·but**
hal·i·but
halitoses : **hal·i·to·sis**
hal·i·to·sis
hallabet : **hal·i·but**
hallalujah : **hal·le·lu·jah**
Hallaween : **Hal·low·een**
hallcyon : **hal·cy·on**
halleloojah : **hal·le·lu·jah**
hal·le·lu·jah
halleluyah : **hal·le·lu·jah**
hal·liard *or* **hal·yard**
hallibut : **hal·i·but**
hallierd : **hal·yard**
hallilujah : **hal·le·lu·jah**

hallitosis : **hal·i·to·sis**
Halloeen : **Hal·low·een**
halloocination :
   hal·lu·ci·na·tion
Hallowean : **Hal·low·een**
Hal·low·een
Hallowene : **Hal·low·een**
hallucenation : **hal·lu·ci·na·tion**
hal·lu·ci·na·tion
hallusination : **hal·lu·ci·na·tion**
hallyard : **hal·yard**
ha·lo
Haloween : **Hal·low·een**
halseon : **hal·cy·on**
halsion : **hal·cy·on**
halucination : **hal·lu·ci·na·tion**
halve (*verb*); **half** (*sing.*);
   halves (*plur.*)
halves (*plur.*); **half** (*sing.*);
   halve (*verb*)
hal·yard *or* **hal·liard**
hamberger : **ham·burg·er**
hambirger : **ham·burg·er**
ham·burg·er
hamburgur : **ham·burg·er**
hamer : **ham·mer**
hammack : **ham·mock**
hammar : **ham·mer**
hammeck : **ham·mock**
ham·mer
ham·mock
hamock : **ham·mock**
handal : **han·dle**
handecap : **hand·i·cap**
handecraft : **hand·i·craft**
Han·del (composer); **han·dle**
   (part for grasping)
handework : **hand·i·work**
hand·ful
handfull : **hand·ful**
hand·i·cap
hand·i·craft

handikraft : **hand·i·craft**
handil : **han·dle**
handiwerk : **hand·i·work**
hand·i·work
handiwurk : **hand·i·work**
handkercheif : **hand·ker·chief**
hand·ker·chief
handkerchiff : **hand·ker·chief**
handkirchief : **hand·ker·chief**
handkurchief : **hand·ker·chief**
han·dle (part for grasping);
   Han·del (composer)
hand·made (made by hand);
   hand·maid (female servant)
hand·maid (female servant);
   hand·made (made by hand)
hand·some (good-looking);
   han·som (cab)
handycap : **hand·i·cap**
handycraft : **hand·i·craft**
handywork : **hand·i·work**
han·gar (airplane shed);
   hang·er (device for hanging)
hang·er (device for hanging);
   han·gar (airplane shed)
hankercheif : **hand·ker·chief**
hankerchief : **hand·ker·chief**
hankerchiff : **hand·ker·chief**
hanndle : **han·dle**
han·som (cab); **hand·some**
   (good-looking)
hant : **haunt**
hanted : **haun·ted**
hap·haz·ard
haphazerd : **hap·haz·ard**
haphazzard : **hap·haz·ard**
haphazzerd : **hap·haz·ard**
hapiness : **hap·pi·ness**
hap·less
hapliss : **hap·less**
hap·pi·ness
happiniss : **hap·pi·ness**

happless : **hap·less**
happyness : **hap·pi·ness**
haram : **har·em**
harasment : **ha·rass·ment**
ha·rass
ha·rass·ment
harbar : **har·bor**
harbenger : **har·bin·ger**
harber : **har·bor**
har·bin·ger
harbinjer : **har·bin·ger**
harboar : **har·bor**
har·bor
har·di·ness
hardiniss : **har·di·ness**
hard·ware
hardwear : **hard·ware**
hardwere : **hard·ware**
hardwhere : **hard·ware**
hardyness : **har·di·ness**
hare·brained
harebraned : **hare·brained**
hare·lip
har·em
haress : **ha·rass** (to annoy) *or*
   heir·ess (inheritor)
haretic : **her·e·tic**
harim : **har·em**
Harlam : **Har·lem**
harlaquin : **har·le·quin**
Har·lem
harlequen : **har·le·quin**
har·le·quin
harlequine : **har·le·quin**
harlet : **har·lot**
harliquin : **har·le·quin**
harlit : **har·lot**
har·lot
Harlum : **Har·lem**
harmoanious : **har·mo·ni·ous**
harmoneous : **har·mo·ni·ous**
har·mon·i·ca

harmonicka : **har·mon·i·ca**
harmonika : **har·mon·i·ca**
har·mo·ni·ous
harmonius : **har·mo·ni·ous**
harmonnica : **har·mon·i·ca**
harnass : **har·ness**
harnes : **har·ness**
har·ness
harniss : **har·ness**
harnuss : **har·ness**
Har·old (name); **her·ald**
   (messenger)
har·poon
harpsachord : **harp·si·chord**
harpsechord : **harp·si·chord**
harp·si·chord
harpsicord : **harp·si·chord**
harpune : **har·poon**
harram : **har·em**
harrasment : **ha·rass·ment**
harrass : **ha·rass** (to annoy) *or*
   heir·ess (inheritor)
harrassment : **ha·rass·ment**
harrbinger : **har·bin·ger**
harrbor : **har·bor**
harrem : **har·em**
harress : **ha·rass** (to annoy) *or*
   heir·ess (inheritor)
harrim : **har·em**
harring : **her·ring**
Harrlem : **Har·lem**
harrlequin : **har·le·quin**
harrlot : **har·lot**
harrum : **har·em**
hart (male deer); **heart** (body
   organ)
hartbeat : **heart·beat**
hartbroken : **heart·bro·ken**
hartburn : **heart·burn**
harten : **heart·en**
harth : **hearth**
harty : **hearty**

harum : **har•em**
har•vest
harvist : **har•vest**
harvust : **har•vest**
hasard : **haz•ard**
hasienda : **ha•ci•en•da**
hasle : **has•sle**
hassal : **has•sle**
hassel : **has•sle**
hassen : **has•ten**
hassienda : **ha•ci•en•da**
has•sle
has•ten
hatchary : **hatch•ery**
hatcherry : **hatch•ery**
hatch•ery
hatch•et
hatchit : **hatch•et**
Hati : **Hai•ti**
haugh•ty
haunt•ed
havec : **hav•oc**
haveck : **hav•oc**
havic : **hav•oc**
havick : **hav•oc**
hav•oc
havock : **hav•oc**
havvoc : **hav•oc**
Hawahi : **Ha•waii**
Hawai : **Ha•waii**
Ha•waii
Hawiei : **Ha•waii**
Hawii : **Ha•waii**
hawnt : **haunt**
haw•thorn (shrub);
  Haw•thorne (author)
Haw•thorne (author);
  haw•thorn (shrub)
hawtty : **haugh•ty**
Hawyii : **Ha•waii**
hayday : **hey•day**
haz•ard

hazellnut : **ha•zel•nut**
ha•zel•nut
hazerd : **haz•ard**
hazilnut : **ha•zel•nut**
hazird : **haz•ard**
hazzard : **haz•ard**
hazzerd : **haz•ard**
heackle : **heck•le**
head•ache
headacke : **head•ache**
headake : **head•ache**
head•dress
head•line
headonism : **he•do•nism**
headress : **head•dress**
heafer : **heif•er**
heal (to cure); **heel** (back of the
  foot)
healix : **he•lix**
healpful : **help•ful**
health
heanous : **hei•nous**
heap
hearce : **hearse**
heard (*past of* to hear); **herd**
  (group of animals)
hear•ing
hear•say (rumor); **her•e•sy**
  (dissent)
hearse (funeral car); **hers**
  (belonging to her)
heart (body organ); **hart** (male
  deer)
heart•beat
heart•bro•ken
heart•burn
hearth
hearty
heath
hea•then
heath•er
heave

heav·en
heavi·ly
heaviweight : heavy·weight
heaviwieght : heavy·weight
heavy
heavyly : heavi·ly
heavywaight : heavy·weight
heavy·weight
heccle : heck·le
heckal : heck·le
heckel : heck·le
heck·le
hecktic : hec·tic
hectec : hec·tic
hec·tic
hectick : hec·tic
hedache : head·ache
heddonism : he·do·nism
hedline : head·line
hedonesm : he·do·nism
he·do·nism
heed·ful
heedfull : heed·ful
heel (back of the foot); heal (to
    cure)
heep : heap
heering : hear·ing
heeth : heath
heethen : hea·then
heffer : heif·er
hegeminny : he·ge·mo·ny
hegemone : he·ge·mo·ny
he·ge·mo·ny
hegimony : he·ge·mo·ny
heif·er
height
hei·nous
heir (inheritor); hair (on head)
heir·ess (inheritor); ha·rass (to
    annoy)
heiriss : heir·ess
heir·loom

heirlume : heir·loom
heirse : hearse
heithen : hea·then
heive : heave
hejemony : he·ge·mo·ny
hejiminy : he·ge·mo·ny
helacopter : hel·i·cop·ter
helecopter : hel·i·cop·ter
heleum : he·li·um
helicks : he·lix
hel·i·cop·ter
heliem : he·li·um
helikopter : hel·i·cop·ter
he·li·um
he·lix
hellacopter : hel·i·cop·ter
hellecopter : hel·i·cop·ter
hellicopter : hel·i·cop·ter
hellium : he·li·um
hellix : he·lix
hellmet : hel·met
hellth : health
hel·met
helmit : hel·met
helmut : hel·met
help·ful
helpfull : help·ful
helth : health
hemasphere : hemi·sphere
hemesphere : hemi·sphere
hemisfere : hemi·sphere
hemispear : hemi·sphere
hemispfere : hemi·sphere
hemisphear : hemi·sphere
hemispheir : hemi·sphere
hemi·sphere
hemmisphere : hemi·sphere
hemmophilia : he·mo·phil·ia
hemmorrhage : hem·or·rhage
hemmorroid : hem·or·rhoid
hemofilia : he·mo·phil·ia
hemophealia : he·mo·phil·ia

hemophelea : **he•mo•phil•ia**
hemophelia : **he•mo•phil•ia**
he•mo•phil•ia
hemophillia : **he•mo•phil•ia**
hemorhoid : **hem•or•rhoid**
hemoridge : **hem•or•rhage**
hemorige : **hem•or•rhage**
hemoroid : **hem•or•rhoid**
hemorredge : **hem•or•rhage**
hemorrege : **hem•or•rhage**
hem•or•rhage
hemorrhige : **hem•or•rhage**
hem•or•rhoid
hemorrige : **hem•or•rhage**
hemorroid : **hem•or•rhoid**
hencefoarth : **hence•forth**
hence•forth
hencefourth : **hence•forth**
henseforth : **hence•forth**
her•ald (messenger); **Har•old**
 (name)
heraldery : **her•ald•ry**
her•ald•ry
herass : **ha•rass** (to annoy) *or*
 heir•ess (inheritor)
herassment : **ha•rass•ment**
herasy : **her•e•sy**
heratage : **her•i•tage**
heratic : **her•e•tic**
herb•age
herb•al
herbedge : **herb•age**
herbege : **herb•age**
herbel : **herb•al**
herbiage : **herb•age**
herbige : **herb•age**
herd (group of animals); **heard**
 (past *of* to hear)
herdle : **hur•dle** (to leap a
 barrier) *or* **hur•tle** (to dash)
heredditary : **he•red•i•tary**
heredetery : **he•red•i•tary**

heredety : **he•red•i•ty**
he•red•i•tary
herediterry : **he•red•i•tary**
hereditery : **he•red•i•tary**
hereditty : **he•red•i•ty**
he•red•i•ty
heresay : **hear•say** (rumor) *or*
 her•e•sy (dissent)
heresey : **hear•say** (rumor) *or*
 her•e•sy (dissent)
her•e•sy (dissent); **hear•say**
 (rumor)
heretage : **her•i•tage**
her•e•tic
heretick : **her•e•tic**
hering : **her•ring**
herissy : **her•e•sy**
her•i•tage
heritedge : **her•i•tage**
heritege : **her•i•tage**
heritige : **her•i•tage**
hermat : **her•mit**
hermatige : **her•mit•age**
hermet : **her•mit**
hermetage : **her•mit•age**
hermett : **her•mit**
her•mit
her•mit•age
hermut : **her•mit**
hernea : **her•nia**
her•nia
hernya : **her•nia**
her•o•in (drug); **her•o•ine** (great
 woman)
her•o•ine (great woman);
 her•o•in (drug)
heroldery : **her•ald•ry**
heroldry : **her•ald•ry**
her•on
Heroshima : **Hi•ro•shi•ma**
herrald : **her•ald**
herraldry : **her•ald•ry**

herreditary : **he•red•i•tary**
herredity : **he•red•i•ty**
herress : **ha•rass** (to annoy) *or*
  heir•ess (inheritor)
herressy : **her•e•sy**
herresy : **her•e•sy**
herretic : **her•e•tic**
herrin : **her•on**
her•ring
herritage : **her•i•tage**
herron : **her•on**
herrse : **hearse**
hers (belonging to her); **hearse**
  (funeral car)
her's : **hers**
herse : **hearse**
herth : **hearth**
hertle : **hur•dle** (to leap a
  barrier) *or* **hur•tle** (to dash)
he's (he is); **his** (belonging to
  him)
hesatant : **hes•i•tant**
hesatate : **hes•i•tate**
hes•i•tant
hes•i•tate
hesitent : **hes•i•tant**
hessitant : **hes•i•tant**
hessitate : **hes•i•tate**
het•er•o•ge•neous *or*
  het•er•og•e•nous
heterogenius :
  het•er•o•ge•neous
het•er•og•e•nous *or*
  het•er•o•ge•neous
hether : **heath•er**
heve : **heave**
heven : **heav•en**
hevven : **heav•en**
hevvy : **heavy**
hevvyweight : **heavy•weight**
hevy : **heavy**
hevywait : **heavy•weight**

hey•day
hezitant : **hes•i•tant**
hiacenth : **hy•a•cinth**
hiacinth : **hy•a•cinth**
hiararchy : **hi•er•ar•chy**
hiasenth : **hy•a•cinth**
hiasinth : **hy•a•cinth**
hiatis : **hi•a•tus**
hi•a•tus
hibernait : **hi•ber•nate**
hi•ber•nate
hibred : **hy•brid**
hibryd : **hy•brid**
hiburnate : **hi•ber•nate**
hiccough (*Brit.*) : **hic•cup**
hic•cup
hickarry : **hick•o•ry**
hickary : **hick•o•ry**
hickerry : **hick•o•ry**
hickery : **hick•o•ry**
hick•o•ry
hiddeous : **hid•eous**
hiddious : **hid•eous**
hid•eous
hidious : **hid•eous**
hidius : **hid•eous**
hidrant : **hy•drant**
hidraulic : **hy•draul•ic**
hidrent : **hy•drant**
hidrint : **hy•drant**
hidrogen : **hy•dro•gen**
hieana : **hy•e•na**
hiefer : **heif•er**
hieght : **height**
hiena : **hy•e•na**
hienous : **hei•nous**
hi•er•ar•chy
hierarky : **hi•er•ar•chy**
hieress : **heir•ess**
hierloom : **heir•loom**
hifen : **hy•phen**
higene : **hy•giene**

highjack : **hi•jack**
high•ness
highniss : **high•ness**
hight : **height**
higiene : **hy•giene**
hi•jack
hilairious : **hi•lar•i•ous**
hilareous : **hi•lar•i•ous**
hi•lar•i•ous
hillarious : **hi•lar•i•ous**
him (that man); **hymn** (song)
himmorroid : **hem•or•rhoid**
himn : **hymn**
himnal : **hym•nal**
himnel : **hym•nal**
himorhoid : **hem•or•rhoid**
himoroid : **hem•or•rhoid**
himorrhage : **hem•or•rhage**
himorroid : **hem•or•rhoid**
hinderance : **hin•drance**
hinderense : **hin•drance**
hin•drance
hindranse : **hin•drance**
hindrence : **hin•drance**
hindrense : **hin•drance**
hiness : **high•ness**
hinotism : **hyp•no•tism**
hipadermic : **hy•po•der•mic**
hiphen : **hy•phen**
hipnatism : **hyp•no•tism**
hipnetism : **hyp•no•tism**
hipnosis : **hyp•no•sis**
hipnotism : **hyp•no•tism**
hipocrisy : **hy•poc•ri•sy**
hipocrite : **hyp•o•crite**
hipodermic : **hy•po•der•mic**
hipothesis : **hy•poth•e•sis**
hirarchy : **hi•er•ar•chy**
Hiroshema : **Hi•ro•shi•ma**
Hi•ro•shi•ma
his (belonging to him); **he's** (he is)

hisstory : **his•to•ry**
histarical : **hys•ter•i•cal**
histeria : **hys•te•ria**
histerical : **hys•ter•i•cal**
histericle : **hys•ter•i•cal**
histerikal : **hys•ter•i•cal**
histery : **his•to•ry**
historey : **his•to•ry**
historry : **his•to•ry**
his•to•ry
histry : **his•to•ry**
hite : **height**
hoard (cache); **horde** (multitude)
hoarmone : **hor•mone**
hoarse (rough-voiced); **horse** (animal)
hoary
hoastess : **hos•tess**
holacaust : **hol•o•caust**
ho•li•ness
hollacaust : **hol•o•caust**
hollocaust : **hol•o•caust**
hollocost : **hol•o•caust**
Holloween : **Hal•low•een**
hol•ly (tree); **ho•ly** (sacred); **whol•ly** (completely)
hol•o•caust
holocost : **hol•o•caust**
ho•ly (sacred); **hol•ly** (tree); **whol•ly** (completely)
holyness : **ho•li•ness**
homacidal : **ho•mi•cid•al**
homacide : **ho•mi•cide**
homadge : **hom•age**
hom•age
homage : **hom•age**
homagenious : **ho•mo•ge•neous**
homaly : **hom•i•ly**
homasidal : **ho•mi•cid•al**
homaside : **ho•mi•cide**
homasidel : **ho•mi•cid•al**

348

homege : **hom•age**
home•ly (plain); **hom•i•ly**
  (sermon)
homesidal : **ho•mi•cid•al**
homeside : **ho•mi•cide**
home•stead
homested : **home•stead**
ho•mi•cid•al
ho•mi•cide
homidge : **hom•age**
homige : **hom•age**
hom•i•ly (sermon); **home•ly**
  (plain)
hommage : **hom•age**
hommige : **hom•age**
hommily : **hom•i•ly**
hommonim : **hom•onym**
hommonym : **hom•onym**
homocidal : **ho•mi•cid•al**
homocide : **hom•i•cide**
ho•mo•ge•neous *or*
  ho•mog•e•nous
homogenious : **ho•mo•ge•neous**
homogenius : **ho•mo•ge•neous**
ho•mog•e•nize
ho•mog•e•nous *or*
  ho•mo•ge•neous
homogonize : **ho•mog•e•nize**
homonim : **hom•onym**
hom•onym
homosidal : **ho•mi•cid•al**
homoside : **ho•mi•cide**
homosidel : **ho•mi•cid•al**
Honalulu : **Ho•no•lu•lu**
honarary : **hon•or•ary**
honasty : **hon•es•ty**
Honelulu : **Ho•no•lu•lu**
honer : **hon•or**
honerary : **hon•or•ary**
hon•est
hon•esty
hon•ey

honie : **hon•ey**
honist : **hon•est**
Honnelulu : **Ho•no•lu•lu**
honnest : **hon•est**
honnesty : **hon•es•ty**
honney : **hon•ey**
honnist : **hon•est**
Honnolulu : **Ho•no•lu•lu**
honnor : **hon•or**
honnorable : **hon•or•able**
honnorary : **hon•or•ary**
Ho•no•lu•lu
hon•or
hon•or•able
hon•or•ary
honorery : **hon•or•ary**
honorible : **hon•or•able**
hoodlam : **hood•lum**
hoodlem : **hood•lum**
hoodlim : **hood•lum**
hood•lum
hoolagan : **hoo•li•gan**
hoolegan : **hoo•li•gan**
hoo•li•gan
horascope : **horo•scope**
horde (multitude); **hoard**
  (cache)
horey : **hoary**
horible : **hor•ri•ble**
horify : **hor•ri•fy**
horizen : **ho•ri•zon**
ho•ri•zon
horizun : **ho•ri•zon**
hormoan : **hor•mone**
hor•mone
hor•net
hornit : **hor•net**
hornut : **hor•net**
horo•scope
horrable : **hor•ri•ble**
horrafy : **hor•ri•fy**
horreble : **hor•ri•ble**

horred : **hor•rid**
horrefy : **hor•ri•fy**
horribal : **hor•ri•ble**
hor•ri•ble
hor•rid
hor•ri•fy
horrizon : **ho•ri•zon**
horroscope : **horo•scope**
horry : **hoary**
horse (animal); **hoarse**
 (rough-voiced)
hortaculture : **hor•ti•cul•ture**
horteculture : **hor•ti•cul•ture**
hor•ti•cul•ture
hosary : **ho•siery**
hoserry : **ho•siery**
hosery : **ho•siery**
ho•siery
hospece : **hos•pice**
hospetal : **hos•pi•tal**
hos•pice
hospise : **hos•pice**
hos•pi•ta•ble
hos•pi•tal
hospiteble : **hos•pi•ta•ble**
hospitibal : **hos•pi•ta•ble**
hospitible : **hos•pi•ta•ble**
hospitle : **hos•pi•tal**
hospittable : **hos•pi•ta•ble**
hospittal : **hos•pi•tal**
hospittle : **hos•pi•tal**
hos•tage
hostege : **hos•tage**
hos•tel (lodging house);
 hos•tile (antagonistic)
hostes : **host•ess**
host•ess
hostige : **hos•tage**
hostil : **hos•tel** (lodging house)
 or **hos•tile** (antagonistic)
hos•tile (antagonistic); **hos•tel**
 (lodging house)

hostilety : **hos•til•i•ty**
hostilitty : **hos•til•i•ty**
hos•til•i•ty
hostill : **hos•tel** (lodging house)
 or **hos•tile** (antagonistic)
hostillity : **hos•til•i•ty**
hostiss : **host•ess**
houghty : **haugh•ty**
hour (60 minutes); **our**
 (belonging to us)
Housten : **Hous•ton**
Hous•ton
hoval : **hov•el**
hov•el
hovil : **hov•el**
hovvel : **hov•el**
huligan : **hoo•li•gan**
humain : **hu•mane**
hu•man (human being);
 hu•mane (compassionate)
hu•mane (compassionate);
 hu•man (human being)
humanety : **hu•man•i•ty**
humanitty : **hu•man•i•ty**
hu•man•i•ty
humannity : **hu•man•i•ty**
humed : **hu•mid**
humer : **hu•mor**
humerous : **hu•mer•us** (arm
 bone) *or* **hu•mor•ous** (funny)
hu•mer•us (arm bone);
 hu•mor•ous (funny)
humess : **hu•mus**
hu•mid
humiddity : **hu•mid•i•ty**
humidefy : **hu•mid•i•fy**
humidetty : **hu•mid•i•ty**
humidety : **hu•mid•i•ty**
humidiffy : **hu•mid•i•fy**
hu•mid•i•fy
humiditty : **hu•mid•i•ty**
hu•mid•i•ty

humileate : **hu•mil•i•ate**
humilety : **hu•mil•i•ty**
hu•mil•i•ate
humilitty : **hu•mil•i•ty**
hu•mil•i•ty
humilliate : **hu•mil•i•ate**
humillity : **hu•mil•i•ty**
humis : **hu•mus**
hummid : **hu•mid**
hummidify : **hu•mid•i•fy**
hummor : **hu•mor**
hu•mor
hu•mor•ous (funny);
    hu•mer•us (arm bone)
humorus : **hu•mer•us** (arm
    bone) *or* **hu•mor•ous** (funny)
humous : **hu•mus**
hu•mus
Hun•ga•ry (nation); **hun•gry**
    (having hunger)
hungery : **Hun•ga•ry** (nation)
    or **hun•gry** (having hunger)
hun•gry (having hunger);
    Hun•ga•ry (nation)
hunta : **jun•ta**
hurdel : **hur•dle** (to leap a
    barrier) *or* **hur•tle** (to dash)
hurdil : **hur•dle** (to leap a
    barrier) *or* **hur•tle** (to dash)
hurdill : **hur•dle** (to leap a
    barrier) *or* **hur•tle** (to dash)
hur•dle (to leap a barrier);
    hur•tle (to dash)
hurecane : **hur•ri•cane**
huricane : **hur•ri•cane**
hurracane : **hur•ri•cane**
hurrecane : **hur•ri•cane**
hurricain : **hur•ri•cane**
hur•ri•cane
hur•tle (to dash); **hur•dle** (to
    leap a barrier)
hus•band

husbandery : **hus•band•ry**
hus•band•ry
husbend : **hus•band**
husbendry : **hus•band•ry**
husbind : **hus•band**
husbindry : **hus•band•ry**
hussband : **hus•band**
hussel : **hus•tle**
hussle : **hus•tle**
husstle : **hus•tle**
Husston : **Hous•ton**
hustal : **hus•tle**
hustel : **hus•tle**
hus•tle
Huston : **Hous•ton**
hy•a•cinth
hyatus : **hi•a•tus**
hybred : **hy•brid**
hy•brid
hydragen : **hy•dro•gen**
hydrallic : **hy•drau•lic**
hy•drant
hydraulec : **hy•drau•lic**
hy•drau•lic
hydraulick : **hy•drau•lic**
hydrawlic : **hy•drau•lic**
hydregen : **hy•dro•gen**
hydrent : **hy•drant**
hydrigen : **hy•dro•gen**
hydrint : **hy•drant**
hy•dro•gen
hydrojen : **hy•dro•gen**
hydrojin : **hy•dro•gen**
hydrollic : **hy•drau•lic**
hyeana : **hy•e•na**
hyeena : **hy•e•na**
hy•e•na
hyfen : **hy•phen**
hyfin : **hy•phen**
hygeine : **hy•giene**
hygene : **hy•giene**
hy•giene

hyicinth : **hy·a·cinth**
hyina : **hy·e·na**
hymn (song); **him** (that man)
hym·nal
hymnel : **hym·nal**
hymnul : **hym·nal**
hypacrite : **hyp·o·crite**
hypedermic : **hy·po·der·mic**
hy·per·bo·la (curved line);
   hy·per·bo·le (exaggeration)
hy·per·bo·le (exaggeration);
   hy·per·bo·la (curved line)
hy·phen
hyphin : **hy·phen**
hypnetism : **hyp·no·tism**
hypnitism : **hyp·no·tism**
hypnoasis : **hyp·no·sis**
hyp·no·sis
hyp·no·tism
hypockrisy : **hy·poc·ri·sy**
hypocracy : **hy·poc·ri·sy**
hypocrassy : **hy·poc·ri·sy**
hypocrasy : **hy·poc·ri·sy**

hypocresy : **hy·poc·ri·sy**
hypocrete : **hyp·o·crite**
hypocricy : **hy·poc·ri·sy**
hy·poc·ri·sy
hypocrit : **hyp·o·crite**
hyp·o·crite
hy·po·der·mic
hypodermick : **hy·po·der·mic**
hypodirmic : **hy·po·der·mic**
hypothasis : **hy·poth·e·sis**
hy·poth·e·ses (*plur.*);
   hy·poth·e·sis (*sing.*)
hy·poth·e·sis (*sing.*);
   hy·poth·e·ses (*plur.*)
hystaria : **hys·te·ria**
hystarical : **hys·ter·i·cal**
hysterea : **hys·te·ria**
hys·te·ria
hys·ter·i·cal
hystericle : **hys·ter·i·cal**
hysterikal : **hys·ter·i·cal**
hysterria : **hys·te·ria**

I

iadine : **io·dine**
Iawa : **Io·wa**
icecle : **ici·cle**
icecycle : **ici·cle**
icical : **ici·cle**
ici·cle
ic·ing
icon *or* **ikon**
iconaclast : **icon·o·clast**
iconiclast : **icon·o·clast**
iconnoclast : **icon·o·clast**
icon·o·clast
iconoklast : **icon·o·clast**
icycle : **ici·cle**
Ida·ho
iddiocy : **id·i·o·cy**
iddiom : **id·i·om**
iddiosyncrasy : **id·io·syn·cra·sy**
iddiot : **id·i·ot**
ide·al
idealise (*Brit.*) : **ide·al·ize**
idealogy : **ide·ol·o·gy**
ideel : **ide·al**
ideelize : **ide·al·ize**
Ideho : **Ida·ho**
idele : **ide·al**
idelize : **ide·al·ize**
ideloigy : **ide·ol·o·gy**
identacal : **iden·ti·cal**
identecal : **iden·ti·cal**
identety : **iden·ti·ty**
iden·ti·cal
identicle : **iden·ti·cal**
identidy : **iden·ti·ty**
identikal : **iden·ti·cal**
identikle : **iden·ti·cal**
identitty : **iden·ti·ty**
iden·ti·ty
ideocy : **id·i·o·cy**
ideolijy : **ide·ol·o·gy**

ideollogy : **ide·ol·o·gy**
ide·ol·o·gy
ideom : **id·i·om**
ideosyncrasy : **id·io·syn·cra·sy**
idiacy : **id·i·o·cy**
idiam : **id·i·om**
idiasy : **id·i·o·cy**
idiasyncrasy : **id·io·syn·cra·sy**
idiel : **ide·al**
idielize : **ide·al·ize**
Idiho : **Ida·ho**
idine : **io·dine**
id·i·o·cy
idiology : **ide·ol·o·gy**
id·i·om
idiosincrasy : **id·io·syn·cra·sy**
idiosincresy : **id·io·syn·cra·sy**
idiosy : **id·i·o·cy**
idiosyncrassy : **id·io·syn·cra·sy**
id·io·syn·cra·sy
idiosyncrissy : **id·io·syn·cra·sy**
id·i·ot
idium : **id·i·om**
idle (inactive); **idol** (image);
  idyll (pastoral)
idol (image); **idle** (inactive);
  idyll (pastoral)
idol·a·ter
idolator : **idol·a·ter**
idoliter : **idol·a·ter**
idyl *or* **idyll** (pastoral); **idle**
  (inactive); **idol** (image)
idyll *or* **idyl** (pastoral); **idle**
  (inactive); **idol** (image)
Ifel : **Eif·fel**
iffete : **ef·fete**
Iffle : **Eif·fel**
ig·loo
iglu : **ig·loo**
ig·ne·ous

ignetion : **ig•ni•tion**
ignight : **ig•nite**
ignious : **ig•ne•ous**
ignishion : **ig•ni•tion**
ignission : **ig•ni•tion**
ig•nite
ignitian : **ig•ni•tion**
ig•ni•tion
ignittion : **ig•ni•tion**
ignius : **ig•ne•ous**
ignobal : **ig•no•ble**
ignobel : **ig•no•ble**
ig•no•ble
ignomenious : **ig•no•min•i•ous**
ignomineous : **ig•no•min•i•ous**
ig•no•min•i•ous
ignominius : **ig•no•min•i•ous**
ignominnious : **ig•no•min•i•ous**
ignoraimus : **ig•no•ra•mus**
ignorammis : **ig•no•ra•mus**
ignorammus : **ig•no•ra•mus**
ig•no•ra•mus
ig•no•rance
ignoranse : **ig•no•rance**
ignoremus : **ig•no•ra•mus**
ignorence : **ig•no•rance**
ignorense : **ig•no•rance**
igua•na
iguanna: **igua•na**
igwana : **igua•na**
ikon *or* **icon**
ikonoclast : **icon•o•clast**
iland : **is•land**
ilastic : **elas•tic**
ilectefy : **elec•tri•fy**
ilectracute : **elec•tro•cute**
ilectrafy : **elec•tri•fy**
ilectrecute : **elec•tro•cute**
ilectric : **elec•tric**
ilectricety : **elec•tric•i•ty**
ilectricion : **elec•tri•cian**
ilectricitty : **elec•tric•i•ty**

ilectricity : **elec•tric•i•ty**
ilectricute : **elec•tro•cute**
ilectrify : **elec•tri•fy**
ilectrision : **elec•tri•cian**
ilectrisity : **elec•tric•i•ty**
ilectrition : **elec•tri•cian**
ilectrocute : **elec•tro•cute**
ilectrokute : **elec•tro•cute**
ilegible : **el•i•gi•ble** (qualified)
    or **il•leg•i•ble** (unreadable)
ilektric : **elec•tric**
ilicit : **elic•it** (to draw out) *or*
    il•lic•it (unlawful)
ilickser : **elix•ir**
iliminate : **elim•i•nate**
Ilinois : **Il•li•nois**
iliterate : **il•lit•er•ate**
ilixer : **elix•ir**
ilixir : **elix•ir**
ilixor : **elix•ir**
Illanois : **Il•li•nois**
illastic : **elas•tic**
illastrate : **il•lus•trate**
illeagal : **il•le•gal**
illectrify : **elec•tri•fy**
illectrocute : **elec•tro•cute**
illeegal : **il•le•gal**
il•le•gal
illegeble : **el•i•gi•ble** (qualified)
    or **il•leg•i•ble** (unreadable)
illegel : **il•le•gal**
illegibal : **el•i•gi•ble** (qualified)
    or **il•leg•i•ble** (unreadable)
il•leg•i•ble (unreadable);
    el•i•gi•ble (qualified)
illegitemant : **il•le•git•i•mate**
illegitemate : **il•le•git•i•mate**
il•le•git•i•mate
illegitimet : **il•le•git•i•mate**
illegle : **il•le•gal**
illejitimate : **il•le•git•i•mate**
illestrate : **il•lus•trate**

il·lic·it (unlawful); elic·it (to draw out)
Il·li·nois
Illinoy : Il·li·nois
illistrate : il·lus·trate
il·lit·er·ate
illixir : elix·ir
illude : elude (to escape) or al·lude (to refer)
illumanate : il·lu·mi·nate
illumenate : il·lu·mi·nate
il·lu·mi·nate
Illunois : Il·li·nois
illusary : il·lu·so·ry
illusery : il·lu·so·ry
il·lu·sion (false idea or image); al·lu·sion (reference); elu·sion (evasion)
il·lu·sive (deceptive); al·lu·sive (making references); elu·sive (avoiding)
il·lu·so·ry
illusry : il·lu·so·ry
illustrait : il·lus·trate
il·lus·trate
iloapment : elope·ment
ilopement : elope·ment
ilopment : elope·ment
ilude : elude (to escape) or al·lude (to refer)
iluminate : il·lu·mi·nate
ilusion : al·lu·sion (reference) or elu·sion (evasion) or il·lu·sion (false idea or image)
ilusive : al·lu·sive (making references) or elu·sive (avoiding) or il·lu·sive (deceptive)
ilusory : il·lu·so·ry
imaculate : im·mac·u·late
imaculet : im·mac·u·late

imagary : im·ag·ery
im·age
imagenation : imag·i·na·tion
imagene : imag·ine
im·ag·ery
imagin : imag·ine
imag·i·na·tion
imagry : im·ag·ery
imancepate : eman·ci·pate
imancipate : eman·ci·pate
imanent : em·i·nent (famous) or im·ma·nent (dwelling within) or im·mi·nent (impending)
imansipate : eman·ci·pate
imarald : em·er·ald
imasarry : em·is·sary
imatate : im·i·tate
imbacile : im·be·cile
imbacy : em·bas·sy
imbalm : em·balm
imbam : em·balm
imbankment : em·bank·ment
imbargo : em·bar·go
imbark : em·bark
imbasey : em·bas·sy
imbassy : em·bas·sy
imbasy : em·bas·sy
im·be·cile
imbecill : im·be·cile
imbelish : em·bel·lish
imbellash : em·bel·lish
imbellesh : em·bel·lish
imbellish : em·bel·lish
imbesill : im·be·cile
imbezel : em·bez·zle
imbezle : em·bez·zle
imbezzal : em·bez·zle
imbezzel : em·bez·zle
imbezzle : em·bez·zle
im·bibe
imbicile : im·be·cile

imblam : **em·blem**
imblazen : **em·bla·zon**
imblazon : **em·bla·zon**
imblem : **em·blem**
imblim : **em·blem**
imblum : **em·blem**
imbodiment : **em·bod·i·ment**
imbodimint : **em·bod·i·ment**
imbodyment : **em·bod·i·ment**
imbom : **em·balm**
imbrace : **em·brace**
imbrase : **em·brace**
imbreo : **em·bryo**
imbrio : **em·bryo**
imbroidary : **em·broi·dery**
imbroiderry : **em·broi·dery**
imbroidery : **em·broi·dery**
imbryo : **em·bryo**
im·bue
imediate : **im·me·di·ate**
imege : **im·age**
imerald : **em·er·ald**
imeratus : **emer·i·tus**
imeritus : **emer·i·tus**
imerold : **em·er·ald**
imerritus : **emer·i·tus**
imesarry : **em·is·sary**
imige : **im·age**
imigery : **im·ag·ery**
iminent : **em·i·nent** (famous) *or*
  im·ma·nent (dwelling within)
  or **im·mi·nent** (impending)
imisary : **em·is·sary**
imissary : **em·is·sary**
im·i·tate
imity : **en·mi·ty**
im·mac·u·late
immaculet : **im·mac·u·late**
immage : **im·age**
immagery : **im·ag·ery**
immagination : **imag·i·na·tion**
immakulate : **im·mac·u·late**

immancipate : **eman·ci·pate**
im·ma·nent (dwelling within);
  em·i·nent (famous);
  im·mi·nent (impending)
immeadiate : **im·me·di·ate**
immedeate : **im·me·di·ate**
im·me·di·ate
immediet : **im·me·di·ate**
immeediate : **im·me·di·ate**
immerald : **em·er·ald**
im·mi·grant (one coming in);
  em·i·grant (one leaving)
im·mi·nent (impending);
  em·i·nent (famous);
  im·ma·nent (dwelling within)
immissary : **em·is·sary**
immitate : **im·i·tate**
immity : **en·mi·ty**
im·mor·al
immorel : **im·mor·al**
im·mor·tal
immortel : **im·mor·tal**
im·mov·able
immovibal : **im·mov·able**
immovible : **im·mov·able**
im·mune
imoral : **im·mor·al**
imorald : **em·er·ald**
imortal : **im·mor·tal**
imovable : **im·mov·able**
impacient : **im·pa·tient**
impail : **im·pale**
im·pair
impairious : **im·pe·ri·ous**
impairitive : **im·per·a·tive**
impaitient : **im·pa·tient**
im·pale
im·pal·pa·ble
impalpeble : **im·pal·pa·ble**
impalpibal : **im·pal·pa·ble**
impalpible : **im·pal·pa·ble**
imparative : **im·per·a·tive**

imparcial : **im·par·tial**
impare : **im·pair**
imparil : **im·per·il**
imparious : **im·pe·ri·ous**
imparshial : **im·par·tial**
im·part
im·par·tial
impashient : **im·pa·tient**
impashioned : **im·pas·sioned**
impass : **im·passe**
im·passe
im·pas·sioned
impatiant : **im·pa·tient**
im·pa·tient
impatus : **im·pe·tus**
im·peach
impead : **im·pede**
impearian : **em·py·re·an**
impecable : **im·pec·ca·ble**
im·pec·ca·ble
impeccibal : **im·pec·ca·ble**
impeccible : **im·pec·ca·ble**
impeckable : **im·pec·ca·ble**
impeckible : **im·pec·ca·ble**
impeddament : **im·ped·i·ment**
impeddement : **im·ped·i·ment**
impeddiment : **im·ped·i·ment**
im·pede
impedimant : **im·ped·i·ment**
im·ped·i·ment
impeech : **im·peach**
impeerial : **im·pe·ri·al**
impeid : **im·pede**
impeirial : **im·pe·ri·al**
impenatent : **im·pen·i·tent**
impenitant : **im·pen·i·tent**
im·pen·i·tent
im·per·a·tive
impereal : **im·pe·ri·al**
imperel : **im·per·il**
im·pe·ri·al
im·per·il

imperill : **im·per·il**
im·pe·ri·ous
imperitive : **im·per·a·tive**
imperril : **im·per·il**
impertenent : **im·per·ti·nent**
impertinant : **im·per·ti·nent**
im·per·ti·nent
imperveous : **im·per·vi·ous**
im·per·vi·ous
impervius : **im·per·vi·ous**
impetis : **im·pe·tus**
impettis : **im·pe·tus**
im·pe·tus
imphisema : **em·phy·se·ma**
imphisima : **em·phy·se·ma**
imphyseama : **em·phy·se·ma**
imphysema : **em·phy·se·ma**
imphysima : **em·phy·se·ma**
impiatty : **im·pi·e·ty**
impier : **em·pire**
impierian : **em·py·re·an**
impietty : **im·pi·e·ty**
im·pi·e·ty
impinitent : **im·pen·i·tent**
impire : **em·pire**
impirian : **em·py·re·an**
impitus : **im·pe·tus**
implament : **im·ple·ment**
im·plant
im·ple·ment
impliment : **im·ple·ment**
imporeum : **em·po·ri·um**
imporiam : **em·po·ri·um**
imporium : **em·po·ri·um**
im·por·tant
importent : **im·por·tant**
im·pos·ter *or* **im·pos·tor**
im·pos·tor *or* **im·pos·ter**
impotance : **im·po·tence**
im·po·tence
impotense : **im·po·tence**
impouarium : **em·po·ri·um**

impoureum : **em•po•ri•um**
impoveresh : **im•pov•er•ish**
im•pov•er•ish
impovrish : **im•pov•er•ish**
impracate : **im•pre•cate**
impractacle : **im•prac•ti•cal**
impractecle : **im•prac•ti•cal**
im•prac•ti•cal
impracticle : **im•prac•ti•cal**
impravise : **im•pro•vise**
im•pre•cate
impreshion : **im•pres•sion**
impresion : **im•pres•sion**
impressian : **im•pres•sion**
im•pres•sion
impricate : **im•pre•cate**
imprisen : **im•pris•on**
im•pris•on
imprisson : **im•pris•on**
imprivise : **im•pro•vise**
imprizen : **im•pris•on**
imprizon : **im•pris•on**
impromptoo : **im•promp•tu**
im•promp•tu
impromptue : **im•promp•tu**
impromtu : **im•promp•tu**
im•pro•vise
improvize : **im•pro•vise**
im•pugn
impune : **im•pugn**
impunety : **im•pu•ni•ty**
impunitty : **im•pu•ni•ty**
im•pu•ni•ty
impurvious : **im•per•vi•ous**
impyre : **em•pire**
impyrean : **em•py•re•an**
inagurate : **in•au•gu•rate**
inain : **inane**
inamerd : **en•am•ored**
inamered : **en•am•ored**
inammored : **en•am•ored**
inamored : **en•am•ored**

inamoured : **en•am•ored**
inamy : **en•e•my**
inane
in•apt (not apt); **in•ept**
  (unskilled)
inargy : **en•er•gy**
inate : **in•nate**
inaugarate : **in•au•gu•rate**
inaugerate : **in•au•gu•rate**
inaugurait : **in•au•gu•rate**
in•au•gu•rate
inawgurate : **in•au•gu•rate**
inbalm : **en•balm**
inbankment : **em•bank•ment**
inbargo : **em•bar•go**
inbark : **em•bark**
inbassy : **em•bas•sy**
inbelish : **em•bel•lish**
inbellish : **em•bel•lish**
inbezzle : **em•bez•zle**
inbibe : **im•bibe**
inblazon : **em•bla•zon**
inblem : **em•blem**
inbodiment : **em•bodi•ment**
inbrace : **em•brace**
inbroidery : **em•broi•dery**
inbryo : **em•bryo**
incandecent : **in•can•des•cent**
incandescant : **in•can•des•cent**
in•can•des•cent
incandessent : **in•can•des•cent**
incapabal : **in•ca•pa•ble**
in•ca•pa•ble
incapeble : **in•ca•pa•ble**
incapibal : **in•ca•pa•ble**
incapible : **in•ca•pa•ble**
in•car•cer•ate
incarcirate : **in•car•cer•ate**
incarserate : **in•car•cer•ate**
in•cen•di•ary
incendierry : **in•cen•di•ary**
incendiery : **in•cen•di•ary**

incenerate : **in·cin·er·ate**
incercle : **en·cir·cle**
incert : **in·sert**
incesant : **in·ces·sant**
in·ces·sant
incessent : **in·ces·sant**
incessint : **in·ces·sant**
in·cest
inciclopedia : **en·cy·clo·pe·dia**
in·ci·dent
incinarate : **in·cin·er·ate**
in·cin·er·ate
incinnerate : **in·cin·er·ate**
incinuate : **in·sin·u·ate**
incipiant : **in·cip·i·ent**
in·cip·i·ent
incippient : **in·cip·i·ent**
incircel : **en·cir·cle**
incircle : **en·cir·cle**
incirkal : **en·cir·cle**
incirkle : **en·cir·cle**
inciser : **in·ci·sor**
in·ci·sion
in·ci·sor
incission : **in·ci·sion**
in·cite (to urge on); **in·sight**
  (discernment)
incizion : **in·ci·sion**
incizor : **in·ci·sor**
inclament : **in·cle·ment**
inclemant : **in·cle·ment**
in·cle·ment
incliment : **in·cle·ment**
incohairent : **in·co·her·ent**
incoharent : **in·co·her·ent**
incoherant : **in·co·her·ent**
in·co·her·ent
incredable : **in·cred·i·ble**
in·cred·i·ble
incumbrance : **en·cum·brance**
incumbranse : **en·cum·brance**
incumbrence : **en·cum·brance**

incumbrince : **en·cum·brance**
incyclapedia : **en·cy·clo·pe·dia**
incyclepedia : **en·cy·clo·pe·dia**
incyclipedia : **en·cy·clo·pe·dia**
incyclopeadia : **en·cy·clo·pe·dia**
incyclopedea : **en·cy·clo·pe·dia**
incyclopedia : **en·cy·clo·pe·dia**
incyclopeedia : **en·cy·clo·pe·dia**
indago : **in·di·go**
indalent : **in·do·lent**
indavidual : **in·di·vid·u·al**
Indeana : **In·di·ana**
indeaver : **en·deav·or**
indeavor : **en·deav·or**
indegent : **in·di·gent**
indego : **in·di·go**
indelable : **in·del·i·ble**
indeleble : **in·del·i·ble**
indelent : **in·do·lent**
in·del·i·ble
indellible : **in·del·i·ble**
independance : **in·de·pen·dence**
independanse : **in·de·pen·dence**
in·de·pen·dence
independense : **in·de·pen·dence**
indepindence : **in·de·pen·dence**
indevidual : **in·di·vid·u·al**
indevor : **en·deav·or**
indevvor : **en·deav·or**
in·dex
in·dex·es *or* **in·di·ces**
In·di·ana
Indianaplis : **In·di·a·nap·o·lis**
In·di·a·nap·o·lis
Indianappolis :
  In·di·a·nap·o·lis
Indianna : **In·di·ana**
Indiannapolis :
  In·di·a·nap·o·lis
in·di·ces *or* **in·dex·es**
in·dict (to charge with a
  crime); **in·dite** (to write)

in·dict·ment
in·di·gent
indiggo : in·di·go
indigint : in·di·gent
in·dig·nant
indignate : in·dig·nant
indignent : in·dig·nant
indignety : in·dig·ni·ty
indignint : in·dig·nant
indignitty : in·dig·ni·ty
in·dig·ni·ty
in·di·go
in·dis·pens·able
indispensible : in·dis·pens·able
in·dite (to write); in·dict (to
    charge with a crime)
inditement : in·dict·ment
inditment : in·dict·ment
in·di·vid·u·al
individuel : in·di·vid·u·al
individule : in·di·vid·u·al
indivvidual : in·di·vid·u·al
indolant : in·do·lent
in·do·lent
indolint : in·do·lent
indomatable : in·dom·i·ta·ble
indometable : in·dom·i·ta·ble
in·dom·i·ta·ble
indomitibal : in·dom·i·ta·ble
indomitible : in·dom·i·ta·ble
indommitable : in·dom·i·ta·ble
indoument : en·dow·ment
indowmate : en·dow·ment
indowmeant : en·dow·ment
indowment : en·dow·ment
indowmint : en·dow·ment
in·dulge
indurance : en·dur·ance
induranse : en·dur·ance
indurence : en·dur·ance
indurrance : en·dur·ance
indurrence : en·dur·ance

industreal : in·dus·tri·al
in·dus·tri·al
industriel : in·dus·tri·al
ineabriate : ine·bri·ate
inebreate : ine·bri·ate
ine·bri·ate
inecksorable : in·ex·o·ra·ble
inedable : in·ed·i·ble
ineddible : in·ed·i·ble
inedeble : in·ed·i·ble
inedibal : in·ed·i·ble
in·ed·i·ble
inefable : in·ef·fa·ble
in·ef·fa·ble
ineffeble : in·ef·fa·ble
ineffibal : in·ef·fa·ble
ineffible : in·ef·fa·ble
inemmy : en·e·my
inemy : en·e·my
in·ept (unskilled); in·apt (not
    apt)
inercia : in·er·tia
inergy : en·er·gy
inerjy : en·er·gy
inerrgy : en·er·gy
inershia : in·er·tia
in·ert
inertea : in·er·tia
in·er·tia
inetible : in·ed·i·ble
inettible : in·ed·i·ble
inevatable : in·ev·i·ta·ble
in·ev·i·ta·ble
ineviteble : in·ev·i·ta·ble
inevitibal : in·ev·i·ta·ble
inevitible : in·ev·i·ta·ble
inexerable : in·ex·o·ra·ble
in·ex·o·ra·ble
inexorible : in·ex·o·ra·ble
infadel : in·fi·del
infalible : in·fal·li·ble
infallable : in·fal·li·ble

infalleble : **in·fal·li·ble**
infallibal : **in·fal·li·ble**
in·fal·li·ble
infammous : **in·fa·mous**
infammus : **in·fa·mous**
in·fa·mous
infamus : **in·fa·mous**
in·fan·cy
infansy : **in·fan·cy**
infantary : **in·fan·try**
infantcy : **in·fan·cy**
infantery : **in·fan·try**
in·fan·try
infantsy : **in·fan·cy**
infattuate : **in·fat·u·ate**
in·fat·u·ate
infeable : **en·fee·ble**
infearior : **in·fe·ri·or**
infechion : **in·fec·tion**
infectian : **in·fec·tion**
in·fec·tion
infedel : **in·fi·del**
infeebal : **en·fee·ble**
infeeble : **en·fee·ble**
infeerior : **in·fe·ri·or**
infeible : **en·fee·ble**
infemous : **in·fa·mous**
infency : **in·fan·cy**
infensy : **in·fan·cy**
infentry : **in·fan·try**
infereor : **in·fe·ri·or**
inferier : **in·fe·ri·or**
in·fe·ri·or
infermary : **in·fir·ma·ry**
infermity : **in·fir·mi·ty**
in·fer·nal
infernel : **in·fer·nal**
in·fer·no
infexion : **in·fec·tion**
in·fi·del
infidelety : **in·fi·del·i·ty**
infidelitty : **in·fi·del·i·ty**

in·fi·del·i·ty
infidell : **in·fi·del**
infidellity : **in·fi·del·i·ty**
infinate : **in·fi·nite**
infincy : **in·fan·cy**
infinet : **in·fi·nite**
infinete : **in·fi·nite**
infinety : **in·fin·i·ty**
in·fi·nite
in·fin·i·ty
infinnite : **in·fi·nite**
infinnity : **in·fin·i·ty**
infinsy : **in·fan·cy**
infintry : **in·fan·try**
in·fir·ma·ry
infirmery : **in·fir·ma·ry**
infirmety : **in·fir·mi·ty**
infirmitty : **in·fir·mi·ty**
in·fir·mi·ty
infirmry : **in·fir·ma·ry**
infirory : **in·fir·ma·ry**
inflaimable : **in·flam·ma·ble**
inflamable : **in·flam·ma·ble**
inflamatory : **in·flam·ma·to·ry**
inflameble : **in·flam·ma·ble**
inflametory : **in·flam·ma·to·ry**
in·flam·ma·ble
inflammatorry :
    in·flam·ma·to·ry
in·flam·ma·to·ry
inflammetory :
    in·flam·ma·to·ry
inflammibal : **in·flam·ma·ble**
inflammible : **in·flam·ma·ble**
inflammitory :
    in·flam·ma·to·ry
inflecksible : **in·flex·i·ble**
inflexable : **in·flex·i·ble**
inflexeble : **in·flex·i·ble**
inflexibal : **in·flex·i·ble**
in·flex·i·ble
inflooence : **in·flu·ence**

influance : **in•flu•ence**
influanse : **in•flu•ence**
in•flu•ence
influense : **in•flu•ence**
infureate : **in•fu•ri•ate**
in•fu•ri•ate
infurnal : **in•fer•nal**
infurno : **in•fer•no**
infurriate : **in•fu•ri•ate**
ingagement : **en•gage•ment**
ingagment : **en•gage•ment**
ingat : **in•got**
ingeanious : **in•ge•nious**
ingeenious : **in•ge•nious**
ingeneer : **en•gi•neer**
ingeneous : **in•ge•nious**
ingenew : **in•ge•nue**
in•ge•nious (intelligent);
　　in•gen•u•ous (simple-minded)
ingenius : **in•ge•nious**
ingenoo : **in•ge•nue**
in•ge•nue
in•gen•u•ous (simple-minded);
　　in•ge•nious (intelligent)
in•gest
inget : **in•got**
ingineer : **en•gi•neer**
inginier : **en•gi•neer**
inginue : **in•ge•nue**
ingloreous : **in•glo•ri•ous**
in•glo•ri•ous
inglorius : **in•glo•ri•ous**
Inglund : **En•gland**
in•got
ingott : **in•got**
ingreadient : **in•gre•di•ent**
ingredeant : **in•gre•di•ent**
ingrediant : **in•gre•di•ent**
in•gre•di•ent
ingreedient : **in•gre•di•ent**
ingridient : **in•gre•di•ent**
ingure : **in•jure**

inhabbet : **in•hab•it**
inhabbit : **in•hab•it**
inhabet : **in•hab•it**
in•hab•it
inhail : **in•hale**
in•hale
inhancement : **en•hance•ment**
inhancemint : **en•hance•ment**
inhansement : **en•hance•ment**
inharent : **in•her•ent**
inharit : **in•her•it**
inharitance : **in•her•i•tance**
inharrit : **in•her•it**
inharritance : **in•her•i•tance**
inhear : **in•here**
inhearent : **in•her•ent**
inherant : **in•her•ent**
in•here
in•her•ent
inheret : **in•her•it**
inheretance : **in•her•i•tance**
inherint : **in•her•ent**
in•her•it
in•her•i•tance
inheritanse : **in•her•i•tance**
inheritence : **in•her•i•tance**
inheritense : **in•her•i•tance**
inherrit : **in•her•it**
inherritance : **in•her•i•tance**
inhibbet : **in•hib•it**
inhibbit : **in•hib•it**
inhibet : **in•hib•it**
in•hib•it
inhirent : **in•her•ent**
inibit : **in•hib•it**
inicial : **ini•tial**
iniciate : **ini•tiate**
iniggma : **enig•ma**
inigma : **enig•ma**
inimacal : **in•im•i•cal**
inimecal : **in•im•i•cal**
in•im•i•cal

inimicle : **in·im·i·cal**
inimikal : **in·im·i·cal**
inimmical : **in·im·i·cal**
inimy : **en·e·my**
inindate : **in·un·date**
iniqiety : **in·iq·ui·ty**
iniquitty : **in·iq·ui·ty**
in·iq·ui·ty
inishall : **ini·tial**
inishiate : **ini·tiate**
initeate : **ini·tiate**
ini·tial
ini·tiate
injere : **in·jure**
injery : **in·ju·ry**
injest : **in·gest**
injineer : **en·gi·neer**
injur : **in·jure**
in·jure
injurry : **in·ju·ry**
in·ju·ry
inmaty : **en·mi·ty**
inmety : **en·mi·ty**
inmitty : **en·mi·ty**
inmity : **en·mi·ty**
innacence : **in·no·cence**
innait : **in·nate**
innamored : **enam·ored**
in·nate
innavate : **in·no·vate**
innemy : **en·e·my**
innert : **in·ert**
innervene : **in·ter·vene**
innerview : **in·ter·view**
innigma : **enig·ma**
innitial : **ini·tial**
innitiate : **ini·tiate**
innivate : **in·no·vate**
in·no·cence
innocense : **in·no·cence**
innocince : **in·no·cence**
innocinse : **in·no·cence**

innovait : **in·no·vate**
in·no·vate
in·nu·en·do
innuindo: **in·nu·en·do**
in·nu·mer·a·ble
innumerible : **in·nu·mer·a·ble**
innumirable : **in·nu·mer·a·ble**
inocence : **in·no·cence**
inovate : **in·no·vate**
inphysema : **em·phy·se·ma**
inpire : **em·pire**
inporium : **em·po·ri·um**
inquisator : **in·quis·i·tor**
inquisiter : **in·quis·i·tor**
in·quis·i·tor
inquissitor : **in·quis·i·tor**
inquizitor : **in·quis·i·tor**
in·road
inrode : **in·road**
insain : **in·sane**
in·sane
in·scru·ta·ble
inscruteble : **in·scru·ta·ble**
inscrutibal : **in·scru·ta·ble**
inscrutible : **in·scru·ta·ble**
inseart : **in·sert**
insectacide : **in·sec·ti·cide**
in·sec·ti·cide
insectiside : **in·sec·ti·cide**
insendiary : **in·cen·di·ary**
insenerate : **in·cin·er·ate**
insenuate : **in·sin·u·ate**
insergent : **in·sur·gent**
in·sert
insessant : **in·ces·sant**
insessent : **in·ces·sant**
insest : **in·cest**
inshurance : **in·sur·ance**
insiclopedia : **en·cy·clo·pe·dia**
insiddious : **in·sid·i·ous**
insident : **in·ci·dent**
insideous : **in·sid·i·ous**

in·sid·i·ous
insidius : in·sid·i·ous
in·sight (discernment); in·cite
  (to urge on)
insign : en·sign
insinarate : in·cin·er·ate
insine : en·sign
insinerate : in·cin·er·ate
insinnuate : in·sin·u·ate
in·sin·u·ate
insiped : in·sip·id
insipiant : in·cip·i·ent
in·sip·id
insipient : in·cip·i·ent
insippid : in·sip·id
insippient : in·cip·i·ent
insircle : en·cir·cle
insision : in·ci·sion
insisor : in·ci·sor
insistance : in·sis·tence
in·sis·tence
insistense : in·sis·tence
insizor : in·ci·sor
insoalence : in·so·lence
in·so·lence
insolense : in·so·lence
insollance : in·so·lence
insollence : in·so·lence
insolluble : in·sol·u·ble
insoluable : in·sol·u·ble
insolubal : in·sol·u·ble
in·sol·u·ble
insolvant : in·sol·vent
in·sol·vent
insomnea : in·som·nia
in·som·nia
insouceant : in·sou·ci·ant
in·sou·ci·ant
insoucient : in·sou·ci·ant
inspecter : in·spec·tor
in·spec·tor
instagate : in·sti·gate

in·stance
instanse : in·stance
instantaineous :
   in·stan·ta·neous
in·stan·ta·neous
instantanious : in·stan·ta·neous
instantanius : in·stan·ta·neous
instatute : in·sti·tute
in·stead
insted : in·stead
instegate : in·sti·gate
instence : in·stance
instetute : in·sti·tute
instigait : in·sti·gate
in·sti·gate
instil : in·still
in·still
in·sti·tute
instructer : in·struc·tor
in·struc·tor
insuciant : in·sou·ci·ant
in·su·lar
insulen : in·su·lin
insuler : in·su·lar
in·su·lin
insullin : in·su·lin
in·sur·ance
insuranse : in·sur·ance
insurence : in·sur·ance
insurense : in·sur·ance
in·sur·gent
insurgient : in·sur·gent
insyclopedia : en·cy·clo·pe·dia
intagrate : in·te·grate
intallect : in·tel·lect
intarogate : in·ter·ro·gate
intarrogate : in·ter·ro·gate
intarrupt : in·ter·rupt
intearior : in·te·ri·or
inteerior : in·te·ri·or
integrait : in·te·grate
in·te·grate

intelect : **in·tel·lect**
inteligent : **in·tel·li·gent**
intellagent : **in·tel·li·gent**
in·tel·lect
intellegent : **in·tel·li·gent**
in·tel·li·gent
intence : **in·tense**
in·tense
inteprise : **en·ter·prise**
interagate : **in·ter·ro·gate**
interance : **en·trance**
in·ter·cede
interceed : **in·ter·cede**
in·ter·cept
interduce : **in·tro·duce**
interem : **in·ter·im**
interence : **en·trance**
in·ter·est
interfear : **in·ter·fere**
interfearence : **in·ter·fer·ence**
interfeer : **in·ter·fere**
interfeerence : **in·ter·fer·ence**
interferance : **in·ter·fer·ence**
interferanse : **in·ter·fer·ence**
in·ter·fere
in·ter·fer·ence
interferense : **in·ter·fer·ence**
interier : **in·te·ri·or**
in·ter·im
in·te·ri·or
interist : **in·ter·est**
interogate : **in·ter·ro·gate**
interpratation :
    in·ter·pre·ta·tion
in·ter·pre·ta·tion
interprise : **en·ter·prise**
interpritation :
    in·ter·pre·ta·tion
interprize : **en·ter·prise**
interragate : **in·ter·ro·gate**
interrigate : **in·ter·ro·gate**
interrim : **in·ter·im**

interrogait : **in·ter·ro·gate**
in·ter·ro·gate
interrum : **in·ter·im**
in·ter·rupt
intersede : **in·ter·cede**
interseed : **in·ter·cede**
intersept : **in·ter·cept**
in·ter·state (between states);
    in·tra·state (within a state)
intertain : **en·ter·tain**
intertane : **en·ter·tain**
interum : **in·ter·im**
interupt : **in·ter·rupt**
in·ter·val
intervean : **in·ter·vene**
interveen : **in·ter·vene**
interveiw : **in·ter·view**
intervel : **in·ter·val**
in·ter·vene
intervenous : **in·tra·ve·nous**
in·ter·view
intervil : **in·ter·val**
intesten : **in·tes·tine**
intestin : **in·tes·tine**
in·tes·tine
intigrate : **in·te·grate**
intillect : **in·tel·lect**
in·ti·ma·cy
intimant : **in·ti·mate**
intimassy : **in·ti·ma·cy**
intimasy : **in·ti·ma·cy**
in·ti·mate
intiment : **in·ti·mate**
intimet : **in·ti·mate**
intimissy : **in·ti·ma·cy**
intimisy : **in·ti·ma·cy**
intimit : **in·ti·mate**
intimmacy : **in·ti·ma·cy**
intirval : **in·ter·val**
intiution : **in·tu·ition**
intocksicate : **in·tox·i·cate**
in·tol·er·a·ble

in·tol·er·ance
intoleranse : in·tol·er·ance
in·tol·er·ant
intolerence : in·tol·er·ance
intolerent : in·tol·er·ant
intolerible : in·tol·er·a·ble
intolirable : in·tol·er·a·ble
intollarent : in·tol·er·ant
intollerable : in·tol·er·a·ble
intollerance : in·tol·er·ance
intollerant : in·tol·er·ant
intoxacate : in·tox·i·cate
intoxecate : in·tox·i·cate
in·tox·i·cate
intracacy : in·tri·ca·cy
intracate : in·tri·cate
intraduce : in·tro·duce
intrance : en·trance
intrancigent : in·tran·si·gent
intransagent : in·tran·si·gent
intranse : en·trance
intransegent : in·tran·si·gent
in·tran·si·gent
in·tra·state (within a state);
   in·ter·state (between states)
intravainous : in·tra·ve·nous
intravanous : in·tra·ve·nous
intraveinous : in·tra·ve·nous
intravenious : in·tra·ve·nous
in·tra·ve·nous
intravienous : in·tra·ve·nous
intreague : in·trigue
intrecacy : in·tri·ca·cy
intreeg : in·trigue
intrence : en·trance
intrense : en·trance
intrensic : in·trin·sic
intreped : in·trep·id
in·trep·id
intreppid : in·trep·id
intrest : in·ter·est
intrevenous : in·tra·ve·nous

in·tri·ca·cy
intricait : in·tri·cate
intricassy : in·tri·ca·cy
intricasy : in·tri·ca·cy
intricat : in·tri·cate
in·tri·cate
intricet : in·tri·cate
intricisy : in·tri·ca·cy
in·trigue
intrince : en·trance
intrinse : en·trance
in·trin·sic
intrinsick : in·trin·sic
in·tro·duce
introduse : in·tro·duce
intrupt : in·ter·rupt
intuishion : in·tu·i·tion
intuission : in·tu·i·tion
in·tu·i·tion
inuendo : in·nu·en·do
inumerable : in·nu·mer·a·ble
inunciate : enun·ci·ate
in·un·date
in·vade
invaid : in·vade
invaigh : in·veigh
invaled : in·va·lid (sick or
   disabled) or in·val·id (not
   valid)
in·va·lid (sick or disabled);
   in·val·id (not valid)
invallid : in·va·lid (sick or
   disabled) or in·val·id (not
   valid)
invalope : en·vel·op (verb) or
   en·ve·lope (noun)
in·va·sion
invassion : in·va·sion
invation : in·va·sion
invay : in·veigh
invazion : in·va·sion
in·veigh

invelid : **in·va·lid** (sick or
disabled) *or* **in·val·id** (not
valid)
invellope : **en·vel·op** (*verb*) *or*
en·ve·lope (*noun*)
inveloap : **en·vel·op** (*verb*) *or*
en·ve·lope (*noun*)
invelop : **en·vel·op** (*verb*) *or*
en·ve·lope (*noun*)
invelope : **en·vel·op** (*verb*) *or*
en·ve·lope (*noun*)
invencible : **in·vin·ci·ble**
inventorry : **in·ven·to·ry**
in·ven·to·ry
inveous : **en·vi·ous**
investagate : **in·ves·ti·gate**
investegate : **in·ves·ti·gate**
investigait : **in·ves·ti·gate**
in·ves·ti·gate
invetarate : **in·vet·er·ate**
inveterat : **in·vet·er·ate**
in·vet·er·ate
inveteret : **in·vet·er·ate**
invetterate : **in·vet·er·ate**
invey : **in·veigh**
invialable : **in·vi·o·la·ble**
invialate : **in·vi·o·late**
inviernment : **en·vi·ron·ment**
invigarate : **in·vig·o·rate**
invigerate : **in·vig·o·rate**
inviggorate : **in·vig·o·rate**
in·vig·o·rate
invilable : **in·vi·o·la·ble**
invilate : **in·vi·o·late**
invilope : **en·vel·op** (*verb*) *or*
en·ve·lope (*noun*)
invinceble : **in·vin·ci·ble**
in·vin·ci·ble
invinsible : **in·vin·ci·ble**
invintory : **in·ven·to·ry**
in·vi·o·la·ble
in·vi·o·late

inviolible : **in·vi·o·la·ble**
inviornment : **en·vi·ron·ment**
invious : **en·vi·ous**
inviranment : **en·vi·ron·ment**
invirenment : **en·vi·ron·ment**
invirirnment : **en·vi·ron·ment**
invirnment : **en·vi·ron·ment**
invironment : **en·vi·ron·ment**
invisable : **in·vis·i·ble**
in·vis·i·ble
invissible : **in·vis·i·ble**
invius : **en·vi·ous**
invizible : **in·vis·i·ble**
invyous : **en·vi·ous**
io·dine
Io·wa
Ioway : **Io·wa**
iracible : **iras·ci·ble**
iragate : **ir·ri·gate**
irasceble : **iras·ci·ble**
iras·ci·ble
irassible : **iras·ci·ble**
iratate : **ir·ri·tate**
irelevant : **ir·rel·e·vant**
irevocable : **ir·re·vo·ca·ble**
irie : **ae·rie** (nest) *or* **ee·rie**
(weird) *or* **Erie** (lake and
canal)
irigate : **ir·ri·gate**
iritate : **ir·ri·tate**
irn : **earn** (to work to gain) *or*
urn (vase)
irragate : **ir·ri·gate**
ir·rel·e·vant
irrelevent : **ir·rel·e·vant**
irretate : **ir·ri·tate**
ir·re·vo·ca·ble
irrevokable : **ir·re·vo·ca·ble**
ir·ri·gate
ir·ri·tate
isalation : **iso·la·tion**
isicle : **ici·cle**

ising : **ic•ing**
is•land
ismis : **isth•mus**
ismiss : **isth•mus**
ismus : **isth•mus**
iso•la•tion
iso•mer
isomere : **iso•mer**
isoscelees : **isos•ce•les**
isos•ce•les
isoseles : **isos•ce•les**
isoselles : **isos•ce•les**
isosseles : **isos•ce•les**
iso•tope
Is•ra•el
Israle : **Is•ra•el**
Isreal : **Is•ra•el**
issotope : **iso•tope**
isthmas : **isth•mus**
isthmis : **isth•mus**
isthmiss : **isth•mus**
isth•mus
italacize : **ital•i•cize**
italasize : **ital•i•cize**
italecize : **ital•i•cize**
ital•ic

italicise : **ital•i•cize**
ital•i•cize
italick : **ital•ic**
italisize : **ital•i•cize**
itallic : **ital•ic**
itallicize : **ital•i•cize**
itemise : **item•ize**
item•ize
itenerant : **itin•er•ant**
itenerent : **itin•er•ant**
ither : **ei•ther** (one or the other) *or* **ether** (gas)
ithsmis : **isth•mus**
itimize : **item•ize**
itinarant : **itin•er•ant**
itin•er•ant
itinerent : **itin•er•ant**
itomize : **item•ize**
its (belonging to it); **it's** (it is)
it's (it is); **its** (belonging to it)
itumize : **item•ize**
ivary : **ivo•ry**
ivery : **ivo•ry**
ivesdropping : **eaves•drop•ping**
ivo•ry
ivvory : **ivo•ry**

J

jack•al
jackel : **jack•al**
jackle : **jack•al**
jagaur : **jag•uar**
jaged : **jag•ged**
jag•ged
jaggid : **jag•ged**
jag•uar
jaguarr : **jag•uar**
jaguire : **jag•uar**
jagwar : **jag•uar**
jagwer : **jag•uar**
jail
jail•er *or* **jail•or**
jail•or *or* **jail•er**
jale : **jail**
jaler : **jail•er**
jallopy : **ja•lopy**
jaloppe : **ja•lopy**
ja•lopy
Jamaca : **Ja•mai•ca**
Jamaeca : **Ja•mai•ca**
Ja•mai•ca
Jamaika : **Ja•mai•ca**
Jamayka : **Ja•mai•ca**
jambaree : **jam•bo•ree**
jambiree : **jam•bo•ree**
jam•bo•ree
jamborie : **jam•bo•ree**
jambory : **jam•bo•ree**
janator : **jan•i•tor**
janatorial : **jan•i•to•ri•al**
jandice : **jaun•dice**
janetor : **jan•i•tor**
janetorial : **jan•i•to•ri•al**
jangal : **jan•gle** (harsh ringing
sound) *or* **jin•gle** (pleasant
ringing sound)

jangel : **jan•gle** (harsh ringing
sound) *or* **jin•gle** (pleasant
ringing sound)
jan•gle (harsh ringing sound);
jin•gle (pleasant ringing
sound)
janiter : **jan•i•tor**
janiterial : **jan•i•to•ri•al**
jan•i•tor
janitoreal : **jan•i•to•ri•al**
jan•i•to•ri•al
jannitor : **jan•i•tor**
jannitorial : **jan•i•to•ri•al**
Jannuary : **Jan•u•ary**
janquil : **jon•quil**
Januarry : **Jan•u•ary**
Jan•u•ary
Januerry : **Jan•u•ary**
Januery : **Jan•u•ary**
Januwary : **Jan•u•ary**
Januwery : **Jan•u•ary**
Ja•pan
Japaneese : **Jap•a•nese**
Jap•a•nese
Japaneze : **Jap•a•nese**
Japannese : **Jap•a•nese**
Jappan : **Ja•pan**
Jappanese : **Jap•a•nese**
jargan : **jar•gon**
jargen : **jar•gon**
jargin : **jar•gon**
jar•gon
jasmen : **jas•mine**
jasmin : **jas•mine**
jas•mine *or* **jes•sa•mine**
jassmine : **jas•mine**
jaudiss : **jaun•dice**
jaundace : **jaun•dice**
jaundase : **jaun•dice**
jaun•dice

jaundish : **jaun•dice**
javalen : **jav•e•lin**
javalin : **jav•e•lin**
javaline : **jav•e•lin**
javelen : **jav•e•lin**
jav•e•lin
javlen : **jav•e•lin**
javlin : **jav•e•lin**
jazmine : **jas•mine**
jazzmine : **jas•mine**
jealis : **jeal•ous**
jeallous : **jeal•ous**
jeal•ous
jealus : **jeal•ous**
jehad : **ji•had**
jejoon : **je•june**
je•june
jell *or* **gel**
jellitan : **gel•a•tin**
jellous : **jeal•ous**
jelopy : **ja•lopy**
jelous : **jeal•ous**
Jemaica : **Ja•mai•ca**
jemnasium : **gym•na•si•um**
jemnasstics : **gym•nas•tics**
jemnast : **gym•nast**
jemnastecs : **gym•nas•tics**
jemnasticks : **gym•nas•tics**
jemnest : **gym•nast**
jemnist : **gym•nast**
jengle : **jan•gle** (harsh ringing
    sound) *or* **jin•gle** (pleasant
    ringing sound)
jenre : **genre**
jeop•ar•dy
jeoprady : **jeop•ar•dy**
jeoprody : **jeop•ar•dy**
jepardy : **jeop•ar•dy**
jepordy : **jeop•ar•dy**
jepperdy : **jeop•ar•dy**
jepprady : **jeop•ar•dy**
jepprody : **jeop•ar•dy**

jeramiad : **jer•e•mi•ad**
jeremaid : **jer•e•mi•ad**
jer•e•mi•ad
jerimiad : **jer•e•mi•ad**
jernalism : **jour•nal•ism**
jerrand : **ger•und**
jerremiad : **jer•e•mi•ad**
jerrund : **ger•und**
Jerrusalem : **Je•ru•sa•lem**
jerrybilt : **jer•ry-built**
jer•ry-built
jersee : **jer•sey**
jer•sey
jersie : **jer•sey**
jerssey : **jer•sey**
jersy : **jer•sey**
jerund : **ger•und**
Je•ru•sa•lem
Jeruselem : **Je•ru•sa•lem**
Jerushalom : **Je•ru•sa•lem**
jerybuilt : **jer•ry-built**
jesamine : **jas•mine**
jessamen : **jas•mine**
jessamin : **jas•mine**
jes•sa•mine *or* **jas•mine**
jesster : **ges•ture** (movement) *or*
    jest•er (joker)
jessymine : **jas•mine**
jest (joke); **gist** (essence)
jest•er (joker); **ges•ture**
    (movement)
jestor : **jest•er** (joker) *or*
    ges•ture (movement)
jesture : **jest•er** (joker) *or*
    ges•ture (movement)
jetison : **jet•ti•son**
jet•sam
jetsem : **jet•sam**
jetsim : **jet•sam**
jetsum : **jet•sam**
jettason : **jet•ti•son**
jettisen : **jet•ti•son**

jet•ti•son
jettsam : jet•sam
jeuel : jew•el
jeueled : jew•eled
jeueler : jew•el•er
jeuelry : jew•el•ry
jewal : jew•el
jewaled : jew•eled
jewaler : jew•el•er
jewalry : jew•el•ry
jewbilee : ju•bi•lee
Jewdism : Ju•da•ism
Jewdyism : Ju•da•ism
jew•el
jew•eled *or* jew•elled
jew•el•er *or* jew•el•ler
jewelery : jew•el•ry
jew•elled *or* jew•eled
jew•el•ler *or* jew•el•er
jewellery (*Brit.*) : jew•el•ry
jewl : jew•el
jewled : jew•eled
jewler : jew•el•er
jewlry : jew•el•ry
jibe (to change course in boat; to agree); gibe (to taunt)
ji•had
jijune : je•june
jilopy : ja•lopy
Jimaica : Ja•mai•ca
Jimaka : Ja•mai•ca
jimnasium : gym•na•si•um
jimnasstics : gym•nas•tics
jimnast : gym•nast
jimnastecs : gym•nas•tics
jimnasticks : gym•nas•tics
jimnest : gym•nast
jimnist : gym•nast
jingal : jan•gle (harsh ringing sound) *or* jin•gle (pleasant ringing sound)

jingel : jan•gle (harsh ringing sound) *or* jin•gle (pleasant ringing sound)
jin•gle (pleasant ringing sound); jan•gle (harsh ringing sound)
jip : gyp
jipcem : gyp•sum
jipcim : gyp•sum
jipped : gypped
jipsam : gyp•sum
jipsem : gyp•sum
jipsey : gyp•sy
jipsim : gyp•sum
jipsy : gyp•sy
jirascope : gy•ro•scope
jirate : gy•rate
jirocompass : gy•ro•com•pass
jirocompess : gy•ro•com•pass
jirrate : gy•rate
jirsey : jer•sey
jist : gist (essence) *or* jest (joke)
jockee : jock•ey
jock•ey
jocky : jock•ey
jo•cose
joc•u•lar
joculer : joc•u•lar
joddper : jodh•pur
jodhper : jodh•pur
jodh•pur
jodper : jodh•pur
jodpur : jodh•pur
johdpur : jodh•pur
johnquil : jon•quil
joiful : joy•ful
joious : joy•ous
joist
jokose : jo•cose
jokular : joc•u•lar
jolity : jol•li•ty
jollety : jol•li•ty

jollitty : **jol·li·ty**
jol·li·ty
joncuil : **jon·quil**
jon·quil
jonquill : **jon·quil**
jonra : **genre**
joocy : **juicy**
joonta : **jun·ta**
jornalism : **jour·nal·ism**
jorneyman : **jour·ney·man**
jossel : **jos·tle**
jostel : **jos·tle**
jos·tle
jour·nal·ism
journelism : **jour·nal·ism**
jour·ney·man
jouryman : **jour·ney·man**
joveal : **jo·vial**
jo·vial
joy·ful
joyfull : **joy·ful**
joy·ous
joyst : **joist**
joyus : **joy·ous**
jubalant : **ju·bi·lant**
jubalee : **ju·bi·lee**
jubalint : **ju·bi·lant**
jubelant : **ju·bi·lant**
ju·bi·lant
ju·bi·lee
jubilent : **ju·bi·lant**
jubillee : **ju·bi·lee**
jubilly : **ju·bi·lee**
jucstapose : **jux·ta·pose**
jucy : **juicy**
Judahism : **Ju·da·ism**
Ju·da·ism
judeciary : **ju·di·cia·ry**
judge
judgement (*Brit.*) : **judg·ment**
judgerry : **ju·di·cia·ry**
judg·ment

judiceal : **ju·di·cial**
ju·di·cial
judiciarry : **ju·di·cia·ry**
ju·di·cia·ry
ju·di·cious
judishall : **ju·di·cial**
judishious : **ju·di·cious**
judisial : **ju·di·cial**
Judism : **Ju·da·ism**
judissiary : **ju·di·ci·ary**
judissious : **ju·di·cious**
juditial : **ju·di·cial**
juditiary : **ju·di·ci·ary**
juditious : **ju·di·cious**
juge : **judge**
jugement : **judg·ment**
jugernaut : **jug·ger·naut**
juggal : **jug·gle**
juggerknot : **jug·ger·naut**
jug·ger·naut
juggernot : **jug·ger·naut**
jugglar : **jug·gler** (one who
    juggles) *or* **jug·u·lar** (vein)
jug·gle
jug·gler (one who juggles);
    jug·u·lar (vein)
juggular : **jug·gler** (one who
    juggles) *or* **jug·u·lar** (vein)
jugguler : **jug·gler** (one who
    juggles) *or* **jug·u·lar** (vein)
jugler : **jug·gler** (one who
    juggles) *or* **jug·u·lar** (vein)
Ju·go·sla·via *or* **Yu·go·sla·via**
jugoular : **jug·gler** (one who
    juggles) *or* **jug·u·lar** (vein)
jug·u·lar (vein); **jug·gler** (one
    who juggles)
juguler : **jug·gler** (one who
    juggles) *or* **jug·u·lar** (vein)
jugulir : **jug·gler** (one who
    juggles) *or* **jug·u·lar** (vein)
juicy

ju•lep
julip : **ju•lep**
jullip : **ju•lep**
junaper : **ju•ni•per**
junchure : **junc•ture**
juncion : **junc•tion**
juncshion : **junc•tion**
juncshure : **junc•ture**
junc•tion
junc•ture
juncure : **junc•ture**
Ju•neau (city); **Ju•no** (goddess)
Juneoh : **Ju•neau**
juneper : **ju•ni•per**
jungal : **jun•gle**
jungel : **jun•gle**
jun•gle
junier : **jun•ior**
Junieu : **Ju•neau**
jun•ior
ju•ni•per
junipper : **ju•ni•per**
jun•ket
junkit : **jun•ket**
junktion : **junc•tion**
junkture : **junc•ture**
junnior : **ju•nior**
Ju•no (goddess); **Ju•neau** (city)
Junoe : **Ju•neau**
junquet : **jun•ket**
jun•ta
juntah : **jun•ta**
juntion : **junc•tion**
jurer : **ju•ror**
juresdiction : **ju•ris•dic•tion**
juressdiction : **ju•ris•dic•tion**
jurisdicion : **ju•ris•dic•tion**
jurisdicktion : **ju•ris•dic•tion**
ju•ris•dic•tion
jurissdiction : **ju•ris•dic•tion**
jurnalism : **jour•nal•ism**
jurneyman : **jour•ney•man**

ju•ror
jurrer : **ju•ror**
jurybuilt : **jer•ry-built**
justace : **jus•tice**
justafiable : **jus•ti•fi•able**
justefiable : **jus•ti•fi•able**
justefy : **jus•ti•fy**
jus•tice
justiffy : **jus•ti•fy**
justifiabel : **jus•ti•fi•able**
jus•ti•fi•able
jus•ti•fy
justifyable : **jus•ti•fi•able**
justis : **jus•tice**
justise : **jus•tice**
justiss : **jus•tice**
juvanile : **ju•ve•nile**
juvenial : **ju•ve•nile**
ju•ve•nile
juvinile : **ju•ve•nile**
jux•ta•pose
jymnaisium : **gym•na•si•um**
jymnaseum : **gym•na•si•um**
jymnasiem : **gym•na•si•um**
jymnasstics : **gym•nas•tics**
jymnastecs : **gym•nas•tics**
jymnasticks : **gym•nas•tics**
jymnest : **gym•nast**
jymnist : **gym•nast**
jyp : **gyp**
jypcem : **gyp•sum**
jypcim : **gyp•sum**
jyped : **gypped**
jypped : **gypped**
jypsam : **gyp•sum**
jypsem : **gyp•sum**
jypsey : **gyp•sy**
jypsie : **gyp•sy**
jypsim : **gyp•sum**
jyracompass : **gy•ro•com•pass**
jyrait : **gy•rate**
jyrascope : **gy•ro•scope**

jyricompass : **gy·ro·com·pass**
jyriscope : **gy·ro·scope**
jyrocompess : **gy·ro·com·pass**

jyrocompiss : **gy·ro·com·pass**
jyroscoap : **gy·ro·scope**
jyrrate : **gy·rate**

K

kacki : **kha·ki**
kactis : **cac·tus**
kactus : **cac·tus**
kadet : **ca·det**
kaffee : **cof·fee**
kahki : **kha·ki**
Kairo : **Cai·ro**
kakhi : **kha·ki**
kaki : **kha·ki**
kakki : **kha·ki**
kakky : **kha·ki**
kaky : **kha·ki**
kaleidascope : **ka·lei·do·scope**
kaleidescope : **ka·lei·do·scope**
ka·lei·do·scope
kalico : **cal·i·co**
kalidoscope : **ka·lei·do·scope**
kaliedoscope : **ka·lei·do·scope**
kalipso : **ca·lyp·so**
kalisthenics : **cal·is·then·ics**
kalisthinics : **cal·is·then·ics**
kalleidoscope : **ka·lei·do·scope**
kallisthenics : **cal·is·then·ics**
kalypso : **ca·lyp·so**
kan·ga·roo
kangarue : **kan·ga·roo**
kangeroo : **kan·ga·roo**
kangiroo : **kan·ga·roo**
kangroo : **kan·ga·roo**
kanguru : **kan·ga·roo**
kanine : **ca·nine**
kaos : **cha·os**
Kan·sas
Kansus : **Kan·sas**
kar·at *or* **car·at** (weight of gems); **car·et** (^); **car·rot** (vegetable)
karet : **kar·at** (weight of gems) *or* car·et (^) *or* **car·rot** (vegetable)

karisma : **char·is·ma**
karosene : **ker·o·sene**
karrat : **kar·at** (weight of gems) *or* car·et (^) *or* **car·rot** (vegetable)
karret : **kar·at** (weight of gems) *or* car·et (^) *or* **car·rot** (vegetable)
kataclism : **cat·a·clysm**
kataclysm : **cat·a·clysm**
katsup : **cat·sup**
kayac : **kay·ak**
kayack : **kay·ak**
kay·ak
keanness : **keen·ness**
keeness : **keen·ness**
keen·ness
keesh : **quiche**
kelogram : **ki·lo·gram**
Keltic : **Celt·ic**
kemono : **ki·mo·no**
ken (to know); **kin** (relatives)
kendal : **kin·dle**
kendengarten : **kin·der·gar·ten**
kendle : **kin·dle**
kendling : **kin·dling**
kendred : **kin·dred**
kenel : **ken·nel**
kenetic : **ki·net·ic**
kennal : **ken·nel**
ken·nel
kennle : **ken·nel**
Kentuckey : **Ken·tucky**
Ken·tucky
Kentuky : **Ken·tucky**
keosk : **ki·osk**
kerasene : **ker·o·sene**
kernal : **col·o·nel** (military officer) *or* **ker·nel** (seed)

ker•nel (seed); col•o•nel
(military officer)
kernele : col•o•nel (military
officer) or ker•nel (seed)
keroseen : ker•o•sene
ker•o•sene
kerosine : ker•o•sene
kerrosene : ker•o•sene
ketchap : cat•sup
ketchep : cat•sup
ketch•up or cat•sup
ketle : ket•tle
ketsup : cat•sup
kettal : ket•tle
kettel : ket•tle
ket•tle
keyosk : ki•osk
kha•ki
khaky : kha•ki
kiask : ki•osk
kibbits : kib•butz (collective
farm) or ki•bitz (to offer
advice)
kibbitz : kib•butz (collective
farm) or ki•bitz (to offer
advice)
kib•butz (collective farm);
ki•bitz (to offer advice)
kibetz : kib•butz (collective
farm) or ki•bitz (to offer
advice)
kibits : kib•butz (collective
farm) or ki•bitz (to offer
advice)
ki•bitz (to offer advice);
kib•butz (collective farm)
kiche : quiche
kichen : kitch•en
kichin : kitch•en
kiddergarden : kin•der•gar•ten
kiddney : kid•ney
kid•nap•er or kid•nap•per

kid•nap•ing or kid•nap•ping
kid•nap•per or kid•nap•er
kid•nap•ping or kid•nap•ing
kid•ney
kidnie : kid•ney
kidny : kid•ney
kilagram : ki•lo•gram
Kilamanjaro : Kil•i•man•ja•ro
kilameter : ki•lo•me•ter
kilegram : ki•lo•gram
Kilemanjaro : Kil•i•man•ja•ro
kiligram : ki•lo•gram
Kil•i•man•ja•ro
killogram : ki•lo•gram
killometer : ki•lo•me•ter
ki•lo•gram
kilomeater : ki•lo•me•ter
kilomeeter : ki•lo•me•ter
ki•lo•me•ter
kilometre (Brit.) : ki•lo•me•ter
kimmono : ki•mo•no
ki•mo•no
kin (relatives); ken (to know)
kindal : kin•dle
kindel : kin•dle
kindergarden : kin•der•gar•ten
kindergardin : kin•der•gar•ten
kin•der•gar•ten
kinderguarden : kin•der•gar•ten
kin•dle
kindleing : kin•dling
kin•dling
kindread : kin•dred
kin•dred
kindrid : kin•dred
kindrud : kin•dred
ki•net•ic
kinetick : ki•net•ic
kinettic : ki•net•ic
kingdam : king•dom
kingdem : king•dom
king•dom

kingdum : **king·dom**
kinnetic : **ki·net·ic**
kintergarden : **kin·der·gar·ten**
kintergarten : **kin·der·gar·ten**
Kintucky : **Ken·tucky**
ki·osk
kishe : **quiche**
kis·met
kismit : **kis·met**
kiss·able
kissible : **kiss·able**
kissmet : **kis·met**
kitch·en
kitchin : **kitch·en**
kitchun : **kitch·en**
kiten : **kit·ten**
kitshen : **kitch·en**
kit·ten
kittin : **kit·ten**
kiyak : **kay·ak**
kizmet : **kis·met**
klepptomaniac :
　klep·to·ma·ni·ac
kleptamaniac : **klep·to·ma·ni·ac**
kleptemaniac : **klep·to·ma·ni·ac**
kleptomainiac :
　klep·to·ma·ni·ac
kleptomaneac :
　klep·to·ma·ni·ac
klep·to·ma·ni·ac
kliptomaniac : **klep·to·ma·ni·ac**
knap·sack
knew (was aware); **gnu**
　(antelope); **new** (not old)
knicht : **knight**
knick·knack
knicknack : **knick·knack**
knife
knifes (verb); knives (*plur.*)
knight (medieval soldier);
　night (not day)
knigt : **knight**

knikknak : **knick·knack**
knite : **knight**
knives (*plur.*); **knifes** (*verb*)
knoal : **knoll**
knole : **knoll**
knoll
knolledge : **knowl·edge**
knollege : **knowl·edge**
knollegible : **knowl·edge·able**
knot (in rope; one nautical
　mile); **not** (negative)
knot·hole
know (to be aware of); **no**
　(negative); **now** (at this time)
knowledgable :
　knowl·edge·able
knowl·edge
knowl·edge·able
knowledgible : **knowl·edge·able**
knowlege : **knowl·edge**
knowlegeable : **knowl·edge·able**
knowlegible : **knowl·edge·able**
knowlidge : **knowl·edge**
knowlige : **knowl·edge**
knuckal : **knuck·le**
knuckel : **knuck·le**
knuck·le
knukkle : **knuck·le**
ko·ala
koalla : **ko·ala**
koff : **cough**
koffee : **cof·fee**
kohlrabbi : **kohl·ra·bi**
kohl·ra·bi
kohlrobbi : **kohl·ra·bi**
kohlrobi : **kohl·ra·bi**
kohlroby : **kohl·ra·bi**
koleidoscope : **ka·lei·do·scope**
kollidoscope : **ka·lei·do·scope**
kollrabi : **kohl·ra·bi**
kolrabi : **kohl·ra·bi**
komquat : **kum·quat**

Ko·rea
Koria : **Ko·rea**
Korrea : **Ko·rea**
kough : **cough**
kowala : **ko·ala**
kowalla : **ko·ala**
kremlen : **krem·lin**
krem·lin
krimlin : **krem·lin**
krimmlin : **krem·lin**
kripton : **kryp·ton**
kryppton : **kryp·ton**

kryp·ton
kumkwat : **kum·quat**
kum·quat
kumquot : **kum·quat**
kurnel : **col·o·nel** (military officer) *or* **ker·nel** (seed)
kwagmire : **quag·mire**
kwick : **quick**
kyack : **kay·ak**
kymono : **ki·mo·no**
kyosk : **ki·osk**

L

labal : **la·bel**
laballed : **la·beled**
labarinth : **lab·y·rinth**
labbel : **la·bel**
labbor : **la·bor**
labbored : **la·bored**
labborious : **la·bo·ri·ous**
la·bel
la·beled *or* **la·belled**
la·belled *or* **la·beled**
laber : **la·bor**
labered : **la·bored**
laberinth : **lab·y·rinth**
laberynth : **lab·y·rinth**
labil : **la·bel**
labirinth : **lab·y·rinth**
labirynth : **lab·y·rinth**
lable : **la·bel**
labled : **la·beled**
la·bor
laboratorry : **lab·o·ra·to·ry**
lab·o·ra·to·ry
la·bored
laboreous : **la·bo·ri·ous**
la·bo·ri·ous
laborratory : **lab·o·ra·to·ry**
laborred : **la·bored**
laborrious : **la·bo·ri·ous**
labortory : **lab·o·ra·to·ry**
Labradoor : **Lab·ra·dor**
Lab·ra·dor
Labradore : **Lab·ra·dor**
labratory : **lab·o·ra·to·ry**
Labredor : **Lab·ra·dor**
labretory : **lab·o·ra·to·ry**
Labridor : **Lab·ra·dor**
labrinth : **lab·y·rinth**
labritory : **lab·o·ra·to·ry**
labrotory : **lab·o·ra·to·ry**
labrynth : **lab·y·rinth**

labul : **la·bel**
lab·y·rinth
lacadaisical : **lack·a·dai·si·cal**
lacerait : **lac·er·ate**
lac·er·ate
lacey : **lacy**
lacivious : **las·civ·i·ous**
lack·a·dai·si·cal
lackadasical : **lack·a·dai·si·cal**
lacker : **lac·quer**
lacksitive : **lax·a·tive**
lacksity : **lax·i·ty**
lackydaisical : **lack·a·dai·si·cal**
lac·quer
lacuer : **lac·quer**
lacy
ladal : **la·dle**
ladel : **la·dle**
ladill : **la·dle**
laditude : **lat·i·tude**
la·dle
laff : **laugh**
laffable : **laugh·able**
laffible : **laugh·able**
laffter : **laugh·ter**
lagard : **lag·gard**
la·ger (beer); **log·ger** (tree
    cutter)
lag·gard
lagger : **la·ger** (beer) *or* **log·ger**
    (tree cutter)
laggerd : **lag·gard**
laggoon : **la·goon**
la·goon
lagune : **la·goon**
lair (nest, burrow); **lay·er** (one
    that lays; one thickness)
laith : **lath** (board) *or* **lathe**
    (machine)

laithe : **lath** (board) *or* **lathe** (machine)
lamanate : **lam·i·nate**
lamenate : **lam·i·nate**
lam·i·nate
laminnate : **lam·i·nate**
lamminate : **lam·i·nate**
lam·poon
lampune : **lam·poon**
lanalen : **lan·o·lin**
lanalin : **lan·o·lin**
lance
lan·cet
lanch : **launch**
lancit : **lan·cet**
landlover : **land·lub·ber**
land·lub·ber
landluvver : **land·lub·ber**
landscaip : **land·scape**
land·scape
landskape : **land·scape**
lannolin : **lan·o·lin**
lanolen : **lan·o·lin**
lan·o·lin
lanse : **lance**
lanset : **lan·cet**
lansit : **lan·cet**
lapal : **la·pel**
la·pel
lapell : **la·pel**
lappel : **la·pel**
laquer : **lac·quer**
lar·ce·ny
larciny : **lar·ce·ny**
larengitis : **lar·yn·gi·tis**
larenx : **lar·ynx**
lar·gess *or* **lar·gesse**
lar·gesse *or* **lar·gess**
lar·i·at
lariet : **lar·i·at**
laringitis : **lar·yn·gi·tis**
larinks : **lar·ynx**

larinx : **lar·ynx**
larrangitis : **lar·yn·gi·tis**
larrengitus : **lar·yn·gi·tis**
larriat : **lar·i·at**
larriet : **lar·i·at**
larrinks : **lar·ynx**
larrinx : **lar·ynx**
larseny : **lar·ce·ny**
larsinny : **lar·ce·ny**
larsiny : **lar·ce·ny**
lar·va (*sing.*); **lar·vae** (*plur.*)
lar·vae (*plur.*); **lar·va** (*sing.*)
lar·yn·gi·tis
laryngitus : **lar·yn·gi·tis**
larynjitis : **lar·yn·gi·tis**
lar·ynx
lasarate : **lac·er·ate**
lasciveous : **las·civ·i·ous**
las·civ·i·ous
laserate : **lac·er·ate**
lasserate : **lac·er·ate**
lassivious : **las·civ·i·ous**
Latan : **Lat·in**
latancy : **la·ten·cy**
latansy : **la·ten·cy**
latant : **la·tent**
latarel : **lat·er·al**
latatude : **lat·i·tude**
Laten : **Lat·in**
la·ten·cy
latensy : **la·ten·cy**
la·tent
lat·er·al
laterel : **lat·er·al**
latetude : **lat·i·tude**
lath (board); **lathe** (machine)
lathe (machine); **lath** (board)
latice : **lat·tice**
Lat·in
latise : **lat·tice**
latiss : **lat·tice**
lat·i·tude

lattece : **lat·tice**
latteral : **lat·er·al**
lat·tice
Lattin : **Lat·in**
lattise : **lat·tice**
lattiss : **lat·tice**
lattiude : **lat·i·tude**
laud·able
laudible : **laud·able**
laugh
laugh·able
laughible : **laugh·able**
laugh·ter
launch
laundary : **laun·dry**
launderry : **laun·dry**
laundery : **laun·dry**
laun·dry
lavalear : **lav·a·liere**
lavaleer : **lav·a·liere**
lav·a·liere
lavander : **lav·en·der**
laveleer : **lav·a·liere**
lavelier : **lav·a·liere**
laveliere : **lav·a·liere**
lavendar : **lav·en·der**
lav·en·der
lavesh : **lav·ish**
lavinder : **lav·en·der**
lav·ish
lavvish : **lav·ish**
lawdable : **laud·able**
lawdible : **laud·able**
law·ful
lawfull : **law·ful**
lawnch : **launch**
lawndry : **laun·dry**
lax·a·tive
laxety : **lax·i·ty**
laxitive : **lax·a·tive**
laxitty : **lax·i·ty**
lax·i·ty

lay (to put down; *past of* to lie); **lie** (to recline)
lay·er (one that lays; one thickness); **lair** (nest, burrow)
lay·ing (act of putting down); **ly·ing** (act of reclining)
leace : **lease**
leach (to dissolve); **leech** (bloodsucker)
lead (to guide; a metal); **led** (*past of* to lead)
lead·en
leaf
leafs : **leaves**
leag : **league**
leagal : **le·gal**
leagality : **le·gal·i·ty**
leagion : **le·gion**
leagle : **le·gal**
league
leak (to let out); **leek** (vegetable)
lean (to incline); **lien** (legal claim)
leanient : **le·nient**
lean-to
leap
leapard : **leop·ard**
leaperd : **leop·ard**
leaque : **league**
learn
lear·y *or* **leer·y**
lease
leasure : **lei·sure**
leater : **li·ter**
leathal : **le·thal**
leath·er
leavel : **lev·el**
leaveled : **lev·eled**
leav·en
leaverage : **lev·er·age**
leaves

leavity : **lev·i·ty**
leaward : **lee·ward**
Lebannon : **Leb·a·non**
Leb·a·non
Lebbanon : **Leb·a·non**
Lebenon : **Leb·a·non**
Lebinon : **Leb·a·non**
lechary : **lech·ery**
lech·ery
led (*past of* to lead); **lead** (to guide; a metal)
ledden : **lead·en**
led·ger
leece : **lease**
leech (bloodsucker); **leach** (to dissolve)
leef : **leaf**
leefs : **leaves**
leegue : **league**
leek (vegetable); **leak** (to let out)
leen : **lean** (to incline) *or* **lien** (legal claim)
leento : **lean-to**
leep : **leap**
leer·y *or* **lear·y**
leese : **lease**
leesure : **lei·sure**
leeter : **li·ter**
leethal : **le·thal**
leeves : **leaves**
lee·ward
leewerd : **lee·ward**
leeword : **lee·ward**
leftenant : **lieu·ten·ant**
legability : **leg·i·bil·i·ty**
leg·a·cy
le·gal
legalety : **le·gal·i·ty**
legalitty : **le·gal·i·ty**
le·gal·i·ty
legallity : **le·gal·i·ty**

legassy : **leg·a·cy**
legasy : **leg·a·cy**
legebility : **leg·i·bil·i·ty**
legeble : **leg·i·ble**
legel : **le·gal**
leg·end
legendarry : **leg·end·ary**
leg·end·ary
legenderry : **leg·end·ary**
legendery : **leg·end·ary**
legeon : **le·gion**
leger : **led·ger**
legeslator : **leg·is·la·tor**
leggend : **leg·end**
leggendery : **leg·end·ary**
legger : **led·ger**
leggion : **le·gion**
leggislator : **leg·is·la·tor**
leggitimate : **le·git·i·mate**
legian : **le·gion**
legibal : **leg·i·ble**
legibel : **leg·i·ble**
legibilety : **leg·i·bil·i·ty**
legibilitty : **leg·i·bil·i·ty**
leg·i·bil·i·ty
legibillity : **leg·i·bil·i·ty**
leg·i·ble
legicy : **leg·a·cy**
legind : **leg·end**
le·gion
legislater : **leg·is·la·tor**
leg·is·la·tor
legissy : **leg·a·cy**
legitamacy : **le·git·i·ma·cy**
legitamet : **le·git·i·mate**
legitemacy : **le·git·i·ma·cy**
legitemate : **le·git·i·mate**
le·git·i·ma·cy
legitimassy : **le·git·i·ma·cy**
legitimasy : **le·git·i·ma·cy**
le·git·i·mate
legitimet : **le·git·i·mate**

legitimisy : **le•git•i•ma•cy**
legittimacy : **le•git•i•ma•cy**
legle : **le•gal**
leip : **leap**
leishure : **lei•sure**
lei•sure
lejend : **leg•end**
lejendary : **leg•end•ary**
lemen : **lem•on**
lemenade : **lem•on•ade**
lemin : **lem•on**
leminade : **lem•on•ade**
lemmon : **lem•on**
lemmonade : **lem•on•ade**
lemmur : **le•mur**
lem•on
lem•on•ade
lemonaid : **lem•on•ade**
le•mur
lemure : **le•mur**
lenghth : **length**
length
leniant : **le•nient**
le•nient
lental : **len•til** (legume) *or*
   lin•tel (door beam)
lenth : **length**
len•til (legume); **lin•tel** (door
   beam)
lentle : **lentil** (legume) *or*
   lin•tel (door beam)
leop•ard
leoperd : **leop•ard**
lepard : **leop•ard**
lep•er
leperd : **leop•ard**
leppard : **leop•ard**
lepper : **lep•er**
lepperd : **leop•ard**
lerch : **lurch**
lerk : **lurk**
lern : **learn**

les•sen (to decrease); **les•son**
   (thing studied)
les•son (thing studied); **les•sen**
   (to decrease)
letchery : **lech•ery**
leter : **li•ter**
le•thal
lethel : **le•thal**
lether : **leath•er**
lettise : **let•tuce**
lettiss : **let•tuce**
let•tuce
lettus : **let•tuce**
lettuse : **let•tuce**
leucimia : **leu•ke•mia**
leukeamia : **leu•ke•mia**
leukemea : **leu•ke•mia**
leu•ke•mia
leukimia : **leu•ke•mia**
leval : **lev•el**
levaled : **lev•eled**
levarage : **lev•er•age**
lev•el
lev•eled
levelled : **lev•eled**
leven : **leav•en**
lev•er•age
leverege : **lev•er•age**
leverige : **lev•er•age**
levety : **lev•i•ty**
le•vi•a•than
leviathen : **le•vi•a•than**
leviethan : **le•vi•a•than**
levirige : **lev•er•age**
levitty : **lev•i•ty**
lev•i•ty
levven : **leav•en**
levvity : **lev•i•ty**
lewdicrous : **lu•di•crous**
liabilety : **li•a•bil•i•ty**
li•a•bil•i•ty
liabillity : **li•a•bil•i•ty**

li•a•ble (responsible or susceptible); li•bel (damaging printed statements)

li•ai•son

li•ar (teller of lies); lyre (stringed instrument)

liason : li•ai•son

libaral : lib•er•al

libartine : lib•er•tine

libary : li•brary

libberal : lib•er•al

libbertine : lib•er•tine

libberty : lib•er•ty

libedo : li•bi•do

li•bel (damaging printed statements); li•a•ble (responsible or susceptible)

libelity : li•a•bil•i•ty

lib•er•al

liberall : lib•er•al

liberel : lib•er•al

libertean : lib•er•tine

liberteen : lib•er•tine

libertene : lib•er•tine

lib•er•tine

lib•er•ty

li•bi•do

librarry : li•brary

li•brary

librery : li•brary

licarish : lic•o•rice

licence : li•cense

li•cense

licenze : li•cense

licerice : lic•o•rice

li•chen (fungus); lik•en (to compare)

licken : li•chen (fungus) or lik•en (to compare)

lickerish : lic•o•rice

lic•o•rice

licorish : lic•o•rice

lie (to recline); lay (to put down)

lieing : lay•ing (act of putting down) or ly•ing (act of reclining)

lien (legal claim); lean (to incline)

lietenent : lieu•ten•ant

lieu•ten•ant

lieutennant : lieu•ten•ant

lifegard : life•guard

lifegaurd : life•guard

life•guard

lik•en (to compare); li•chen (fungus)

li•lac

lilack : li•lac

lilly : lily

lily

limarick : lim•er•ick

lim•er•ick

limet : lim•it

lim•it

limmerick : lim•er•ick

limmit : lim•it

limosine : lim•ou•sine

limouseen : lim•ou•sine

limousene : lim•ou•sine

lim•ou•sine

limozene : lim•ou•sine

limozine : lim•ou•sine

limph : lymph

limrick : lim•er•ick

limur : le•mur

linament : lin•ea•ment (outline) or lin•i•ment (painkiller)

Lin•coln

Lincon : Lin•coln

Linconn : Lin•coln

lin•ea•ment (outline); lin•i•ment (painkiller)

lin•ear

linement : **lin•ea•ment** (outline)
  or **lin•i•ment** (painkiller)
lin•en
lingeray : **lin•ge•rie**
lingerey : **lin•ge•rie**
lin•ge•rie
linght : **length**
liniar : **lin•ear**
linient : **le•nient**
lin•i•ment (painkiller);
  lin•ea•ment (outline)
linnament : **lin•e•a•ment**
  (outline) *or* **lin•i•ment**
  (painkiller)
linnear : **lin•ear**
linnen : **lin•en**
linniar : **lin•ear**
linnoleum : **li•no•leum**
li•no•leum
linoliem : **li•no•leum**
linolium : **li•no•leum**
linon : **lin•en**
linsherie : **lin•ge•rie**
lintal : **len•til** (legume) *or*
  lin•tel (door beam)
lin•tel (door beam); **len•til**
  (legume)
lintle : **len•til** (*legume*)or **lin•tel**
  (door beam)
linx : lynx
li•on•ess
lionness : **li•on•ess**
liquaffy : **liq•ue•fy**
liquafy : **liq•ue•fy**
liqued : **li•quid**
liq•ue•fy
liq•uid
liquiffy : **liq•ue•fy**
liquify : **liq•ue•fy**
liquorice (*Brit.*) : **lic•o•rice**
liquorish : **lic•o•rice**
lirk : **lurk**

lisense : **li•cense**
lissener : **lis•ten•er**
lis•ten•er
lit•a•ny
litaracy : **lit•er•a•cy**
litegate : **lit•i•gate**
liteny : **lit•a•ny**
li•ter
literachure : **lit•er•a•ture**
lit•er•a•cy
literassy : **lit•er•a•cy**
lit•er•a•ture
litergy : **lit•ur•gy**
litericy : **lit•er•a•cy**
literissy : **lit•er•a•cy**
literisy : **lit•er•a•cy**
literture : **lit•er•a•ture**
lit•i•gate
litiny : **lit•a•ny**
litrature : **lit•er•a•ture**
litre (*Brit.*) : **li•ter**
littany : **lit•a•ny**
littature : **lit•er•a•ture**
litteracy : **lit•er•a•cy**
litterature : **lit•er•a•ture**
littigate : **lit•i•gate**
litturgy : **lit•ur•gy**
lit•ur•gy
liturjy : **lit•ur•gy**
live•li•hood
livelyhood : **live•li•hood**
livlihood : **live•li•hood**
liz•ard
lizerd : **liz•ard**
lizzard : **liz•ard**
lizzerd : **liz•ard**
loathesome : **loath•some**
loath•some
lo•cal (regional); **lo•cale**
  (region, setting)
lo•cale (region, setting); **lo•cal**
  (regional)

locamotion : **lo•co•mo•tion**
lo•co•mo•tion
logarhythm : **log•a•rithm**
logarithem : **log•a•rithm**
log•a•rithm
logarythm : **log•a•rithm**
loggarithm : **log•a•rithm**
log•ger (tree cutter); **la•ger**
   (beer)
logorithm : **log•a•rithm**
loial : **loy•al**
Londen : **Lon•don**
Londin : **Lon•don**
Lon•don
lone•li•ness
lone•ly
longatude : **lon•gi•tude**
longerie : **lin•ge•rie**
longetude : **lon•gi•tude**
longevety : **lon•gev•i•ty**
longevitty : **lon•gev•i•ty**
lon•gev•i•ty
longitood : **lon•gi•tude**
lon•gi•tude
longitued : **lon•gi•tude**
longivity : **lon•gev•i•ty**
longue : **lounge**
lonliness : **lone•li•ness**
lonly : **lone•ly**
loobricant : **lu•bri•cant**
loodricrous : **lu•di•crous**
lookemia : **leu•ke•mia**
loominary : **lu•mi•nary**
loonacy : **lu•na•cy**
loonasy : **lu•na•cy**
loonatic : **lu•na•tic**
loose (not attached); **lose** (to
   misplace)
Loosiana : **Lou•i•si•ana**
lootenent : **lieu•ten•ant**
loquaceous : **lo•qua•cious**

lo•qua•cious
loquaicious : **lo•qua•cious**
loquasious : **lo•qua•cious**
loquatious : **lo•qua•cious**
loquecious : **lo•qua•cious**
lose (to misplace); **loose** (not
   attached)
losinge : **loz•enge**
lossinge : **loz•enge**
lotery : **lot•tery**
lothesome : **loath•some**
lothsome : **loath•some**
lotis : **lo•tus**
lottary : **lot•tery**
lotterry : **lot•tery**
lot•tery
lo•tus
Loueesiana : **Lou•i•si•ana**
Louiseana : **Lou•i•si•ana**
Lou•i•si•ana
Louiziana : **Lou•i•si•ana**
Lousiana : **Lou•i•si•ana**
lounge
loungue : **lounge**
lov•able
loveable : **lov•able**
love•li•er
loveloarn : **love•lorn**
love•lorn
lovelyer : **love•li•er**
lovible : **lov•able**
lovlier : **love•li•er**
lovlorn : **love•lorn**
lowngue : **lounge**
loy•al
loyel : **loy•al**
loyil : **loy•al**
loyl : **loy•al**
loz•enge
lozinge : **loz•enge**
lozzinge : **loz•enge**

lubracant : **lu•bri•cant**
lubrecant : **lu•bri•cant**
lu•bri•cant
lubricent : **lu•bri•cant**
luced : **lu•cid**
lucer : **lu•cre**
luchre : **lu•cre**
lu•cid
lucksuriant : **lux•u•ri•ant**
lucksury : **lux•u•ry**
lu•cra•tive
lu•cre
lucretive : **lu•cra•tive**
ludacrous : **lu•di•crous**
ludecrous : **lu•di•crous**
ludicrace : **lu•di•crous**
ludicrass : **lu•di•crous**
ludicris : **lu•di•crous**
lu•di•crous
ludicrus : **lu•di•crous**
luekemia : **leu•ke•mia**
luetenant : **lieu•ten•ant**
lugage : **lug•gage**
lugege : **lug•gage**
lug•gage
luggege : **lug•gage**
luggidge : **lug•gage**
luggige : **lug•gage**
lugguage : **lug•gage**
lugige : **lug•gage**
Luisiana : **Lou•i•si•ana**
lukemia : **leu•ke•mia**
luker : **lu•cre**
lukre : **lu•cre**
lulaby : **lul•la•by**
luliby : **lul•la•by**
lul•la•by
lulleby : **lul•la•by**
lulliby : **lul•la•by**
lum•bar (of the loins); **lum•ber**
 (timber)

lum•ber (timber); **lum•bar** (of
 the loins)
lumenary : **lu•mi•nary**
lumenescent : **lu•mi•nes•cent**
luminarry : **lu•mi•nary**
lu•mi•nary
luminecent : **lu•mi•nes•cent**
luminery : **lu•mi•nary**
lu•mi•nes•cent
luminescint : **lu•mi•nes•cent**
luminessent : **lu•mi•nes•cent**
lu•na•cy
lunasy : **lu•na•cy**
lu•na•tic
lunatick : **lu•na•tic**
lun•cheon
lunchin : **lun•cheon**
lunchion : **lun•cheon**
lunesy : **lu•na•cy**
lunetic : **lu•na•tic**
lunissy : **lu•na•cy**
lunisy : **lu•na•cy**
lunitic : **lu•na•tic**
lurch
lu•rid
lurk
lurn : **learn**
lurrid : **lu•rid**
lurtch : **lurch**
lused : **lu•cid**
lusid : **lu•cid**
lus•ter
lustre (*Brit.*) : **lus•ter**
lutenant : **lieu•ten•ant**
luxeriant : **lux•u•ri•ant**
luxerry : **lux•u•ry**
luxery : **lux•u•ry**
luxiry : **lux•u•ry**
luxureant : **lux•u•ri•ant**
lux•u•ri•ant
luxurient : **lux•u•ri•ant**

lux•u•ry
lying (act of reclining); **lay•ing**
  (act of putting down)
lymph

lynx
lyre (stringed instrument); **li•ar**
  (teller of lies)

M

macab : **ma·ca·bre**
macaber : **ma·ca·bre**
ma·ca·bre
macah : **ma·caw**
macanic : **me·chan·ic**
macanical : **me·chan·i·cal**
macannic : **me·chan·ic**
macannical : **me·chan·i·cal**
macaroney : **mac·a·ro·ni**
mac·a·ro·ni
macarony : **mac·a·ro·ni**
ma·caw
maccaroni : **mac·a·ro·ni**
machanic : **me·chan·ic**
machanical : **me·chan·i·cal**
macharel : **mack·er·el**
macharell : **mack·er·el**
macharil : **mack·er·el**
ma·chete
machetey : **ma·chete**
machetie : **ma·chete**
machette : **ma·chete**
machettie : **ma·chete**
machinary : **ma·chin·ery**
ma·chine
machinerry : **ma·chin·ery**
ma·chin·ery
macironi : **mac·a·ro·ni**
mackarel : **mack·er·el**
mackaroni : **mac·a·ro·ni**
mackeral : **mack·er·el**
mack·er·el
mackiral : **mack·er·el**
macob : **ma·ca·bre**
Mad·a·gas·car
Madagascer : **Mad·a·gas·car**
Madagaskar : **Mad·a·gas·car**
madamoiselle : **mad·e·moi·selle**
madamozel : **mad·e·moi·selle**
Maddagascar : **Mad·a·gas·car**

mademaselle : **ma·de·moi·selle**
mademoisell : **ma·de·moi·selle**
ma·de·moi·selle
mademoizelle : **ma·de·moi·selle**
mademoselle : **ma·de·moi·selle**
madragal : **mad·ri·gal**
madregal : **mad·ri·gal**
mad·ri·gal
madrigall : **mad·ri·gal**
madrigle : **mad·ri·gal**
maelstorm : **mael·strom**
mael·strom
maelstrum : **mael·strom**
mae·stro
magasine : **mag·a·zine**
magazean : **mag·a·zine**
magazene : **mag·a·zine**
mag·a·zine
magec : **mag·ic**
ma·gen·ta
magesstic : **ma·jes·tic**
magestic : **ma·jes·tic**
magestrate : **mag·is·trate**
magesty : **maj·es·ty**
magezine : **mag·a·zine**
maggazine : **mag·a·zine**
magget : **mag·got**
maggistrate : **mag·is·trate**
maggit : **mag·got**
mag·got
maggut : **mag·got**
mag·ic
magichian : **ma·gi·cian**
ma·gi·cian
magicion : **ma·gi·cian**
magick : **mag·ic**
maginta : **ma·gen·ta**
mag·is·trate
magizine : **mag·a·zine**
magnafy : **mag·ni·fy**

magnanamous :
  mag•nan•i•mous
magnanemous :
  mag•nan•i•mous
mag•nan•i•mous
magnanimus : **mag•nan•i•mous**
magnannimous :
  mag•nan•i•mous
mag•nate (important person);
  mag•net (something with
  attractive force)
magnatude : **mag•ni•tude**
magnefy : **mag•ni•fy**
mag•net (something with
  attractive force); **mag•nate**
  (important person)
mag•net•ic
magnettic : **mag•net•ic**
magnetude : **mag•ni•tude**
magniffy : **mag•ni•fy**
mag•ni•fy
magnitood : **mag•ni•tude**
mag•ni•tude
magnoalia : **mag•no•lia**
mag•no•lia
magnollia : **mag•no•lia**
magnolya : **mag•no•lia**
magot : **mag•got**
ma•ha•ra•ja *or* **ma•ha•ra•jah**
ma•ha•ra•jah *or* **ma•ha•ra•ja**
maharasha : **ma•ha•ra•ja**
maharoja : **ma•ha•ra•ja**
mahoganie : **ma•hog•a•ny**
ma•hog•a•ny
mahogeny : **ma•hog•a•ny**
mahoggany : **ma•hog•a•ny**
mahogginy : **ma•hog•a•ny**
mahoginy : **ma•hog•a•ny**
mailstrom : **mael•strom**
main (primary); **Maine** (state);
  mane (hair)

Maine (state); **main** (primary);
  mane (hair)
mainia : **ma•nia**
maintainence : **main•te•nance**
main•te•nance
maintenanse : **main•te•nance**
maintenence : **main•te•nance**
maintenense : **main•te•nance**
maintennance : **main•te•nance**
maintinance : **main•te•nance**
maintinence : **main•te•nance**
maistro : **mae•stro**
maitenance : **main•te•nance**
maize (corn); **maze** (labyrinth)
majaraja : **ma•ha•ra•ja**
majenta : **ma•gen•ta**
majessty : **maj•es•ty**
ma•jes•tic
majestick : **ma•jes•tic**
maj•es•ty
majorety : **ma•jor•i•ty**
majoritty : **ma•jor•i•ty**
ma•jor•i•ty
majorrity : **ma•jor•i•ty**
mal•a•dy
mal•aise
malaize : **mal•aise**
malard : **mal•lard**
malarea : **ma•lar•ia**
ma•lar•ia
malase : **mal•aise**
malaze : **mal•aise**
maleable : **mal•lea•ble**
maledy : **mal•a•dy**
malerd : **mal•lard**
maleria : **ma•lar•ia**
malestrom : **mael•strom**
malet : **mal•let**
malevalent : **ma•lev•o•lent**
malevelent : **ma•lev•o•lent**
ma•lev•o•lent
malevolint : **ma•lev•o•lent**

mal·fea·sance
malfeasanse : **mal·fea·sance**
malfeasence : **mal·fea·sance**
malfeasense : **mal·fea·sance**
malfeasince : **mal·fea·sance**
malfeazance : **mal·fea·sance**
malfeesance : **mal·fea·sance**
malfisance : **mal·fea·sance**
mal·ice
malidy : **mal·a·dy**
ma·lign
ma·lig·nant
malignent : **ma·lig·nant**
malignint : **ma·lig·nant**
malird : **mal·lard**
malise : **mal·ice**
maliss : **mal·ice**
mallady : **mal·a·dy**
mallaise : **mal·aise**
mal·lard
mallaria : **ma·lar·ia**
mallarria : **ma·lar·ia**
mallat : **mal·let**
malleabal : **mal·lea·ble**
mal·lea·ble
mallerd : **mal·lard**
malleria : **ma·lar·ia**
mal·let
malliable : **mal·lea·ble**
mallible : **mal·lea·ble**
mallice : **mal·ice**
mallign : **ma·lign**
mallignant : **ma·lig·nant**
mallird : **mal·lard**
mallit : **mal·let**
mallovolent : **ma·lev·o·lent**
mallyable : **mal·lea·ble**
malody : **mal·a·dy**
malstrom : **mael·strom**
mamal : **mam·mal**
mamel : **mam·mal**

mameth : **mam·moth**
mamil : **mam·mal**
mamith : **mam·moth**
mam·mal
mammel : **mam·mal**
mammeth : **mam·moth**
mammil : **mam·mal**
mammith : **mam·moth**
mam·moth
mamoth : **mam·moth**
man·a·cle
manacure : **man·i·cure**
manafest : **man·i·fest**
manafesto : **man·i·fes·to**
manafold : **man·i·fold**
man·age
manageabal : **man·age·able**
man·age·able
managible : **man·age·able**
manakin : **man·i·kin** (little man) *or* **man·ne·quin** (model)
mandalen : **man·do·lin**
mandalin : **man·do·lin**
mandatorry : **man·da·to·ry**
man·da·to·ry
mandelin : **man·do·lin**
mandetory : **man·da·to·ry**
mandilin : **man·do·lin**
manditory : **man·da·to·ry**
man·do·lin
mane (hair); **main** (primary); **Maine** (state)
manea : **ma·nia**
maneac : **ma·ni·ac**
manecle : **man·a·cle**
manecure : **man·i·cure**
manefest : **man·i·fest**
manefesto : **man·i·fes·to**
manefold : **man·i·fold**
manege : **man·age**

manekin : **man·i·kin** (little man) *or* **man·ne·quin** (model)

manequin : **man·i·kin** (little man) *or* **man·ne·quin** (model)

ma·neu·ver

Manhatan : **Man·hat·tan**

Manhaten : **Man·hat·tan**

Man·hat·tan

Manhatten : **Man·hat·tan**

Manhattin : **Man·hat·tan**

ma·nia

ma·ni·ac

maniack : **ma·ni·ac**

manicle : **man·a·cle**

man·i·cure

man·i·fest

man·i·fes·to

man·i·fold

manige : **man·age**

man·i·kin *or* **man·ni·kin** (little man); **man·ne·quin** (model)

Ma·nila

Manilla : **Ma·nila**

man·li·ness

manlynes : **man·li·ness**

mannacle : **man·a·cle**

mannafest : **man·i·fest**

mannafesto : **man·i·fes·to**

mannage : **man·age**

mannageable : **man·age·able**

mannaquin : **man·i·kin** (little man) *or* **man·ne·quin** (model)

mannefest : **man·i·fest**

mannefesto : **man·i·fes·to**

mannekin : **man·i·kin** (little man) *or* **man·ne·quin** (model)

man·ne·quin (model); **man·i·kin** (little man)

man·ner (a way of doing); **man·or** (estate)

manneuver : **ma·neu·ver**

mannia : **ma·nia**

manniac : **ma·ni·ac**

mannical : **man·a·cle**

mannicure : **man·i·cure**

mannifest : **man·i·fest**

mannifesto : **man·i·fes·to**

man·ni·kin *or* **man·i·kin** (little man); **man·ne·quin** (model)

Mannila : **Ma·nila**

mannual : **man·u·al**

mannure : **ma·nure**

manny : **many**

manoor : **ma·nure**

manoor : **ma·nure**

manoover : **ma·neu·ver**

man·or (estate); **man·ner** (a way of doing)

mantal : **man·tel** (shelf) *or* **man·tle** (cape)

man·tel (shelf); **man·tle** (cape)

mantil : **man·tel** (shelf) *or* **man·tle** (cape)

mantill : **man·tel** (shelf) *or* **man·tle** (cape)

man·tis

man·tle (cape); **man·tel** (shelf)

mantus : **man·tis**

man·u·al

manuer : **ma·nure**

manuever : **ma·neu·ver**

manule : **man·u·al**

ma·nure

manuver : **ma·neu·ver**

many

manyfold : **man·i·fold**

maraner : **mar·i·ner**

maratal : **mar·i·tal**

mar·a·thon

ma·raud·er

marawder : **ma·raud·er**
marbal : **mar·ble**
marbel : **mar·ble**
marbil : **mar·ble**
marbile : **mar·ble**
mar·ble
mareen : **ma·rine**
marene : **ma·rine**
marener : **mar·i·ner**
maretal : **mar·i·tal**
marethon : **mar·a·thon**
margaren : **mar·ga·rine**
margarene : **mar·ga·rine**
margarin : **mar·ga·rine**
mar·ga·rine
margenal : **mar·gin·al**
margeren : **mar·ga·rine**
margerene : **mar·ga·rine**
margerin : **mar·ga·rine**
margerine : **mar·ga·rine**
mar·gin·al
marginel : **mar·gin·al**
marginnal : **mar·gin·al**
mariage : **mar·riage**
marige : **mar·riage**
mari·gold
Mariland : **Mary·land**
ma·rine
mar·i·ner
marinner : **mar·i·ner**
mar·i·tal
maritel : **mar·i·tal**
marithon : **mar·a·thon**
mar·ket·able
marketibal : **mar·ket·able**
marketible : **mar·ket·able**
markitable : **mar·ket·able**
mar·lin (fish); **mar·line** (cord)
mar·line (cord); **mar·lin** (fish)
mar·ma·lade
marmalaid : **mar·ma·lade**
marmelade : **mar·ma·lade**

marmelaid : **mar·ma·lade**
marmilade : **mar·ma·lade**
marmolade : **mar·ma·lade**
marmolaid : **mar·ma·lade**
marodder : **ma·raud·er**
ma·roon
marrage : **mar·riage**
marratal : **mar·i·tal**
marrathon : **mar·a·thon**
marrauder : **ma·raud·er**
marrege : **mar·riage**
mar·riage
marrige : **mar·riage**
marrine : **ma·rine**
marriner : **mar·i·ner**
marrital : **mar·i·tal**
marroon : **ma·roon**
marrune : **ma·roon**
marryage : **mar·riage**
Marryland : **Mary·land**
marrytal : **mar·i·tal**
Marsailles : **Mar·seilles**
Marsay : **Mar·seilles**
Mar·seilles
Marselles : **Mar·seilles**
Marsey : **Mar·seilles**
mar·shal (leader of military or police force); **mar·tial** (pertaining to war or combat)
marshall : **mar·shal** (leader of military or police force) *or* **mar·tial** (pertaining to war or combat)
marsh·mal·low
marshmellow : **marsh·mal·low**
marsoopial : **mar·su·pi·al**
marsupeal : **mar·su·pi·al**
mar·su·pi·al
martar : **mar·tyr**
marteeni : **mar·ti·ni**
marter : **mar·tyr**

mar•tial (pertaining to war or combat); mar•shal (leader of military or police force)
mar•ti•ni
martiny : mar•ti•ni
martir : mar•tyr
martor : mar•tyr
mar•tyr
marune : ma•roon
marvalous : mar•vel•ous
mar•vel
marvell : mar•vel
mar•vel•lous or mar•vel•ous
mar•vel•ous or mar•vel•lous
marvelus : mar•vel•ous
marvle : mar•vel
marygold : mari•gold
Mary•land
marytal : mar•i•tal
Masachusetts : Mas•sa•chu•setts
masacre : mas•sa•cre
mascaline : mas•cu•line
mas•cara
mascarra : mas•cara
masceline : mas•cu•line
mas•cot
mascott : mas•cot
masculen : mas•cu•line
masculin : mas•cu•line
mas•cu•line
mashean : ma•chine
masheenery : ma•chin•ery
mashete : ma•chete
mashette : ma•chete
mashine : ma•chine
mashinery : ma•chin•ery
maskara : mas•cara
maskarade : mas•quer•ade
maskarra : mas•cara
maskerade : mas•quer•ade
maskott : mas•cot

maskulen : mas•cu•line
maskuline : mas•cu•line
mas•och•ism
masokism : mas•och•ism
ma•son
mas•quer•ade
masquirade : mas•quer•ade
massacer : mas•sa•cre
Massachoosetts : Mas•sa•chu•setts
Mas•sa•chu•setts
Massachusitts : Mas•sa•chu•setts
mas•sa•cre
massecre : mas•sa•cre
Massichusetts : Mas•sa•chu•setts
massochism : mas•och•ism
masson : ma•son
masstoddon : mast•odon
mastadon : mast•odon
mastedon : mast•odon
masterpeace : mas•ter•piece
masterpeece : mas•ter•piece
masterpeice : mas•ter•piece
mas•ter•piece
mas•tery
mastidon : mast•odon
mast•odon
mastodont : mast•odon
mastry : mas•tery
matadoor : mat•a•dor
mat•a•dor
matanee : mat•i•nee
matearial : ma•te•ri•al (matter) or ma•té•ri•el (military equipment)
matedor : mat•a•dor
mateirial : ma•te•ri•al (matter) or ma•té•ri•el (military equipment)
matenance : main•te•nance

matenee : **mat•i•nee**
ma•te•ri•al (matter);
　ma•té•ri•el (military
　equipment)
ma•té•ri•el *or* **ma•te•ri•el**
　(military equipment);
　ma•te•ri•al (matter)
ma•ter•nal
maternel : **ma•ter•nal**
maternety : **ma•ter•ni•ty**
maternitty : **ma•ter•ni•ty**
ma•ter•ni•ty
mathamatics : **math•e•mat•ics**
mathematicks : **math•e•mat•ics**
math•e•mat•ics
mathemattics : **math•e•mat•ics**
mathimathics : **math•e•mat•ics**
mathmatics : **math•e•mat•ics**
matidor : **mat•a•dor**
matinay : **mat•i•nee**
mat•i•nee *or* **mat•i•née**
matiney : **mat•i•nee**
matramony : **mat•ri•mo•ny**
matremony : **mat•ri•mo•ny**
matress : **mat•tress**
matriarc : **ma•tri•arch**
ma•tri•arch
matrimoney : **mat•ri•mo•ny**
mat•ri•mo•ny
matriss : **mat•tress**
mattador : **mat•a•dor**
matterial : **ma•te•ri•al** (matter)
　or **ma•té•ri•el** (military
　equipment)
matternal : **ma•ter•nal**
mattinee : **mat•i•nee**
mat•tress
mattriss : **mat•tress**
maturety : **ma•tu•ri•ty**
maturitty : **ma•tu•ri•ty**
ma•tu•ri•ty
maturnal : **ma•ter•nal**

maturnity : **ma•ter•ni•ty**
maudlen : **maud•lin**
maud•lin
mausaleum : **mau•so•le•um**
mau•so•le•um
mausoliem : **mau•so•le•um**
mausolium : **mau•so•le•um**
mauzoleum : **mau•so•le•um**
mavarick : **mav•er•ick**
mav•er•ick
mawdlin : **maud•lin**
maxamum : **max•i•mum**
maxem : **max•im**
maxemum : **max•i•mum**
max•im
maximem : **max•i•mum**
max•i•mum
maxum : **max•im**
mayennaise : **may•on•naise**
mayer : **may•or**
may•hem
mayhim : **may•hem**
mayinnaise : **may•on•naise**
maynaise : **may•on•naise**
mayonaise : **may•on•naise**
mayonaize : **may•on•naise**
may•on•naise
mayonnase : **may•on•naise**
may•or
maze (labyrinth); **maize** (corn)
mazerka : **ma•zur•ka**
mazochism : **mas•och•ism**
ma•zur•ka
meadian : **me•di•an**
meadiate : **me•di•ate**
meadiocre : **me•di•o•cre**
mead•ow
mea•ger
meagre : **mea•ger**
meanial : **me•nial**
meant
measels : **mea•sles**

mea·sles
measley : **mea·sly**
mea·sly
meastro : **mae·stro**
mea·sure
meazels : **mea·sles**
meazles : **mea·sles**
mecabre : **ma·ca·bre**
me·chan·ic
mechanick : **me·chan·ic**
mechannic : **me·chan·ic**
mechannical : **me·chan·i·cal**
medacal : **med·i·cal**
medacate : **med·i·cate**
medaeval : **me·di·eval**
medal (decoration); **med·dle** (to interfere); **met·tle** (spirit)
medalion : **me·dal·lion**
medallian : **me·dal·lion**
me·dal·lion
medatate : **med·i·tate**
medatation : **med·i·ta·tion**
meddeval : **me·di·eval**
meddevil : **me·di·eval**
meddic : **med·ic**
meddical : **med·i·cal**
meddicate : **med·i·cate**
meddicinal : **me·dic·i·nal**
medditate : **med·i·tate**
medditation : **med·i·ta·tion**
Medditerranean :
  Med·i·ter·ra·nean
med·dle (to interfere); **med·al** (decoration); **met·tle** (spirit)
med·dler (one who meddles); **med·lar** (tree)
meddley : **med·ley**
meddow : **mead·ow**
medeate : **me·di·ate**
medecate : **med·i·cate**
medeival : **me·di·eval**
medetate : **med·i·tate**

medetation : **med·i·ta·tion**
Medeterranean :
  Med·i·ter·ra·nean
medeval : **me·di·eval**
mediacrity : **me·di·oc·ri·ty**
me·di·ae·val or **me·di·eval**
mediam : **me·di·um**
me·di·an
me·di·ate
med·ic
med·i·cal
med·i·cate
medicen : **med·i·cine**
medicenal : **me·dic·i·nal**
medicin : **med·i·cine**
me·dic·i·nal
med·i·cine
medicinel : **me·dic·i·nal**
medick : **med·ic**
medicle : **med·i·cal**
mediem : **me·di·um**
medien : **me·di·an**
me·di·eval or **me·di·ae·val**
medievel : **me·di·eval**
mediocer : **me·di·o·cre**
mediocraty : **me·di·oc·ri·ty**
me·di·o·cre
mediocrety : **me·di·oc·ri·ty**
mediocritty : **me·di·oc·ri·ty**
me·di·oc·ri·ty
medioker : **me·di·o·cre**
medisinal : **me·dic·i·nal**
medissinal : **me·dic·i·nal**
meditacion : **med·i·ta·tion**
meditait : **med·i·tate**
meditashion : **med·i·ta·tion**
med·i·tate
meditatian : **med·i·ta·tion**
Mediteranean :
  Med·i·ter·ra·nean
Mediterrainian :
  Med·i·ter·ra·nean

Med·i·ter·ra·nean
Mediterranian :
   Med·i·ter·ra·nean
me·di·um
medival : me·di·eval
med·lar (tree); med·dler (one
   who meddles)
med·ley
medlie : med·ley
medly : med·ley
medow : mead·ow
meedian : me·di·an
meediate : me·di·ate
meediocre : me·di·o·cre
meedium : me·di·um
meeger : mea·ger
meer : mere (nothing more
   than) or mir·ror (glass)
meesles : mea·sles
meesly : mea·sly
meger : mea·ger
meidian : me·di·an
meiger : mea·ger
meinial : me·nial
meladrama : melo·dra·ma
melady : mel·o·dy
melaise : mal·aise
melan : mel·on
melanchaly : mel·an·choly
mel·an·choly
melancolly : mel·an·choly
melancoly : mel·an·choly
mé·lange
melay : me·lee
me·lee
melencholy : mel·an·choly
melidy : mel·o·dy
melincholy : mel·an·choly
mellady : mel·o·dy
mellan : mel·on
mellancholy : mel·an·choly
mellange : mé·lange

mellencholy : mel·an·choly
mellidy : mel·o·dy
mellincholy : mel·an·choly
mellodrama : melo·dra·ma
mellody : mel·o·dy
mellon : mel·on
mel·low
mellowdrama : melo·dra·ma
melo·dra·ma
melodramma : melo·dra·ma
mel·o·dy
mel·on
melonge : mé·lange
melow : mel·low
memarabilia : mem·o·ra·bil·ia
memarable : mem·o·ra·ble
memarize : mem·o·rize
memary : mem·o·ry
membrain : mem·brane
mem·brane
me·men·to
Memfis : Mem·phis
meminto : me·men·to
memior : mem·oir
memiry : mem·o·ry
memmento : me·men·to
memmoir : mem·oir
memmorabilia :
   mem·o·ra·bil·ia
memmorable : mem·o·ra·ble
memmorial : me·mo·ri·al
memmorize : mem·o·rize
memmory : mem·o·ry
mem·oir
memorabeelia : mem·o·ra·bil·ia
mem·o·ra·bil·ia
memorabillia : mem·o·ra·bil·ia
mem·o·ra·ble
memoreal : me·mo·ri·al
memoreble : mem·o·ra·ble
me·mo·ri·al
memoribal : mem·o·ra·ble

memoribilia : **mem•o•ra•bil•ia**
memorible : **mem•o•ra•ble**
memorise (*Brit.*) : **mem•o•rize**
mem•o•rize
memorrial : **me•mo•ri•al**
mem•o•ry
memorybilia : **mem•o•ra•bil•ia**
Mem•phis
Memphiss : **Mem•phis**
Memphus : **Mem•phis**
men•ace
me•nag•er•ie
menagerrie : **me•nag•er•ie**
menagery : **me•nag•er•ie**
menagirie : **me•nag•er•ie**
menajerie : **me•nag•er•ie**
menapause : **men•o•pause**
mendacety : **men•dac•i•ty**
mendacitty : **men•dac•i•ty**
men•dac•i•ty
mendasity : **men•dac•i•ty**
mendassity : **men•dac•i•ty**
meneal : **me•nial**
meneral : **min•er•al**
meneret : **min•a•ret**
me•nial
menice : **men•ace**
meniss : **men•ace**
menistrone : **min•e•stro•ne**
mennace : **men•ace**
mennagerie : **me•nag•er•ie**
menneret : **min•a•ret**
mennice : **men•ace**
mennopause : **men•o•pause**
mennow : **min•now**
men•o•pause
Menphis : **Mem•phis**
ment : **meant**
men•tal
mentalety : **men•tal•i•ty**
mentalitty : **men•tal•i•ty**
men•tal•i•ty

mentallity : **men•tal•i•ty**
mentel : **men•tal**
menter : **men•tor**
menthal : **men•thol**
menthall : **men•thol**
men•thol
mentholl : **men•thol**
men•tor
merage : **mi•rage**
merangue : **me•ringue**
mercary : **mer•cu•ry**
mer•ce•nary
mercenery : **mer•ce•nary**
mercerial : **mer•cu•ri•al**
merchandice : **mer•chan•dise**
mer•chan•dise
mer•chant
merchantdise : **mer•chan•dise**
merchendise : **mer•chan•dise**
merchent : **mer•chant**
merchindise : **mer•chan•dise**
merchint : **mer•chant**
mer•ci•ful
mercifull : **mer•ci•ful**
mercinary : **mer•ce•nary**
mercureal : **mer•cu•ri•al**
mer•cu•ri•al
mer•cu•ry
mer•cy
mercyful : **mer•ci•ful**
mere (nothing more than);
    mir•ror (glass)
merecle : **mir•a•cle**
meremaid : **mer•maid**
meret : **mer•it**
merg•er
meriad : **myr•i•ad**
meriddian : **me•rid•i•an**
me•rid•i•an
meridien : **me•rid•i•an**
meringe : **me•ringue**
me•ringue

mer·it
merky : **murky**
mermade : **mer·maid**
mer·maid
mermer : **mur·mur**
mermur : **mur·mur**
merrangue : **me·ringue**
merridian : **me·rid·i·an**
mer·ri·ly
mer·ri·ment
merringue : **me·ringue**
merrit : **mer·it**
merryment : **mer·ri·ment**
mersenary : **mer·ce·nary**
mersiful : **mer·ci·ful**
mersinary : **mer·ce·nary**
mersy : **mer·cy**
merth : **mirth**
me·sa
mesage : **mes·sage**
mesiah : **mes·si·ah**
meskeet : **mes·quite**
mes·mer·ism
mesmirism : **mes·mer·ism**
mesmurism : **mes·mer·ism**
mesquete : **mes·quite**
mes·quite
messa : **me·sa**
mes·sage
messege : **mes·sage**
messia : **mes·si·ah**
mes·si·ah
messige : **mes·sage**
messmerism : **mes·mer·ism**
messquite : **mes·quite**
messure : **mea·sure**
mesure : **mea·sure**
metabalism : **me·tab·o·lism**
metabelism : **me·tab·o·lism**
metablism : **me·tab·o·lism**
me·tab·o·lism
metafor : **met·a·phor**

metallergy : **me·tal·lur·gy**
me·tal·lur·gy
metalurgy : **me·tal·lur·gy**
metamorfosis :
    meta·mor·pho·sis
metamorphasis :
    meta·mor·pho·sis
metamorphisis :
    meta·mor·pho·sis
meta·mor·pho·sis
met·a·phor
metaphore : **met·a·phor**
me·te·or
meteorallogy : **me·te·o·rol·o·gy**
meteoralogy : **me·te·o·rol·o·gy**
meteorollogy : **me·te·o·rol·o·gy**
me·te·o·rol·o·gy
me·ter
methain : **meth·ane**
methal : **meth·yl**
meth·ane
methel : **meth·yl**
methil : **meth·yl**
meth·yl
metickulous : **me·tic·u·lous**
me·tic·u·lous
meticulus : **me·tic·u·lous**
metifor : **met·a·phor**
metior : **me·te·or**
metiorology : **me·te·o·rol·o·gy**
metiphor : **met·a·phor**
metir : **me·ter**
metre (*Brit.*) : **me·ter**
met·ric
metrick : **met·ric**
metropalis : **me·trop·o·lis**
metropolice : **me·trop·o·lis**
me·trop·o·lis
metropoliss : **me·trop·o·lis**
mettabolism : **me·tab·o·lism**
mettaphor : **met·a·phor**
metticulous : **me·tic·u·lous**

met•tle (spirit); med•al
(decoration); med•dle (to
interfere)
mettric : met•ric
mettropolis : me•trop•o•lis
Mexaco : Mex•i•co
Mex•i•co
mezmerism : mes•mer•ism
Mi•ami
Miammi : Mi•ami
Miamy : Mi•ami
Michagan : Mich•i•gan
Michegan : Mich•i•gan
Mich•i•gan
micraphone : mi•cro•phone
microcosem : mi•cro•cosm
microcosim : mi•cro•cosm
mi•cro•cosm
microcossm : mi•cro•cosm
microcozm : mi•cro•cosm
mi•cro•phone
midaeval : me•di•eval
middal : mid•dle
middel : mid•dle
mid•dle
midg•et
midgit : midg•et
midieval : me•di•eval
Miditerranean :
    Med•i•ter•ra•nean
midle : mid•dle
miestro : mae•stro
mighty
migrain : mi•graine
mi•graine
migrane : mi•graine
mi•grant
migratery : mi•gra•to•ry
migratorry : mi•gra•to•ry
mi•gra•to•ry
migrent : mi•grant
migretory : mi•gra•to•ry

migritory : mi•gra•to•ry
milage : mile•age
milameter : mil•li•met•er
milatant : mil•i•tant
milatary : mil•i•tary
mile•age
mileau : mi•lieu
milege : mile•age
milenium : mil•len•ni•um
milennium : mil•len•ni•um
miletant : mil•i•tant
miletary : mil•i•tary
miliage : mile•age
milicia : mi•li•tia
mi•lieu
milimeter : mil•li•me•ter
milionaire : mil•lion•aire
miliou : mi•lieu
milisha : mi•li•tia
mil•i•tant
militarry : mil•i•tary
mil•i•tary
militent : mil•i•tant
militery : mil•i•tary
mi•li•tia
milleniem : mil•len•ni•um
mil•len•ni•um
millieu : mi•lieu
mil•li•me•ter
millimetre (Brit.) : mil•li•me•ter
millinnium : mil•len•ni•um
millionair : mil•lion•aire
mil•lion•aire
millionare : mil•lion•aire
millionnaire : mil•lion•aire
millitant : mil•i•tant
millitary : mil•i•tary
millitia : mi•li•tia
Millwaukee : Mil•wau•kee
Millwauky : Mil•wau•kee
Milwakee : Mil•wau•kee
Mil•wau•kee

Milwuakee : **Mil·wau·kee**
mim·ic
mimick : **mim·ic**
mimickery : **mim·ic·ry**
mim·ic·ry
mimmic : **mim·ic**
mimmicry : **mim·ic·ry**
mimmosa : **mi·mo·sa**
mi·mo·sa
minace : **men·ace**
minagerie : **me·nag·er·ie**
minamum : **min·i·mum**
minarel : **min·er·al**
min·a·ret
minarette : **min·a·ret**
Minasota : **Min·ne·so·ta**
minastrone : **min·e·stro·ne**
minature : **min·ia·ture**
Mineapolis : **Min·ne·ap·o·lis**
minemum : **min·i·mum**
min·er (mine worker); **min·or**
   (not major)
min·er·al
min·er·al·o·gy
minerel : **min·er·al**
mineret : **min·a·ret**
minerollogy : **min·er·al·o·gy**
minerology : **min·er·al·o·gy**
Minesota : **Min·ne·so·ta**
minester : **min·is·ter**
min·e·stro·ne
minestroni : **min·e·stro·ne**
minestrony : **min·e·stro·ne**
min·ia·ture
minimem : **min·i·mum**
min·i·mum
miniret : **min·a·ret**
min·is·ter
ministrone : **min·e·stro·ne**
miniture : **min·ia·ture**
minnace : **men·ace**
minnaret : **min·a·ret**

Minnasota : **Min·ne·so·ta**
Min·ne·ap·o·lis
Minneapolus : **Min·ne·ap·o·lis**
minneral : **min·er·al**
minneret : **min·a·ret**
Minnesoda : **Min·ne·so·ta**
Min·ne·so·ta
Minniapolis : **Min·ne·ap·o·lis**
minniature : **min·ia·ture**
minnimum : **min·i·mum**
Minnisota : **Min·ne·so·ta**
minnister : **min·is·ter**
min·now
min·or (not major); **min·er**
   (mine worker)
minstral : **min·strel**
min·strel
minstrell : **min·strel**
minstril : **min·strel**
minthol : **men·thol**
miopic : **my·o·pic**
mioppic : **my·o·pic**
mir·a·cle
mir·age
mircenary : **mer·ce·nary**
mirchandise : **mer·chan·dise**
mirchant : **mer·chant**
mirciful : **mer·ci·ful**
mircurial : **mer·cu·ri·al**
mircury : **mer·cu·ry**
mirecle : **mir·a·cle**
mirger : **merg·er**
miriad : **myr·i·ad**
mirical : **mir·a·cle**
miricle : **mir·a·cle**
mirky : **murky**
mirmaid : **mer·maid**
mirmur : **mur·mur**
miror : **mir·ror**
mirracle : **mir·a·cle**
mirrage : **mi·rage**
mirrer : **mir·ror**

mirrh : **mir•ror** (glass) *or*
  myrrh (perfume)
mir•ror
mirth
misanthroape : **mis•an•thrope**
mis•an•thrope
misarable : **mis•er•a•ble**
misary : **mis•ery**
miscelaneous : **mis•cel•la•neous**
mis•cel•la•neous
miscellanious : **mis•cel•la•neous**
mischeff : **mis•chief**
mischeif : **mis•chief**
mischeivous : **mis•chie•vous**
mis•chief
mischiefous : **mis•chie•vous**
mischievious : **mis•chie•vous**
mis•chie•vous
mischiff : **mis•chief**
mischiffous : **mis•chie•vous**
misdameanor : **mis•de•mean•or**
misdemeaner : **mis•de•mean•or**
mis•de•mean•or
misdemeenor : **mis•de•mean•or**
misdemenor : **mis•de•mean•or**
misdimeanor : **mis•de•mean•or**
miselanious : **mis•cel•la•neous**
misellaneous : **mis•cel•la•neous**
misenthrope : **mis•an•thrope**
mis•er•a•ble
miserble : **mis•er•a•ble**
miserible : **mis•er•a•ble**
mis•ery
Mishigan : **Mich•i•gan**
misinanthrope : **mis•an•thrope**
misionary : **mis•sion•ary**
Misissippi : **Mis•sis•sip•pi**
misle : **mis•sal** (prayerbook) *or*
  mis•sile (projectile)
misogenist : **mi•sog•y•nist**
misoginist : **mi•sog•y•nist**
mi•sog•y•nist

misogynnist : **mi•sog•y•nist**
misojinist : **mi•sog•y•nist**
Misouri : **Mis•sou•ri**
mispell : **mis•spell**
mis•sal (prayerbook); **mis•sile**
  (projectile)
missel : **mis•sal** (prayerbook) *or*
  mis•sile (projectile)
misseltoe : **mis•tle•toe**
misserable : **mis•er•a•ble**
missery : **mis•ery**
missiah : **mes•si•ah**
mis•sile (projectile); **mis•sal**
  (prayerbook)
mis•sion•ary
missionery : **mis•sion•ary**
Missisipi : **Mis•sis•sip•pi**
Mississipi : **Mis•sis•sip•pi**
Mis•sis•sip•pi
missle : **mis•sal** (prayerbook) *or*
  mis•sile (projectile)
missletoe : **mis•tle•toe**
mis•spell
Mis•sou•ri
misstress : **mis•tress**
Missuri : **Mis•sou•ri**
mistery : **mys•tery**
mistic : **mys•tic**
misticism : **mys•ti•cism**
mis•tle•toe
mistletow : **mis•tle•toe**
mis•tress
mithical : **myth•i•cal**
mithology : **my•thol•o•gy**
mity : **mighty**
mizery : **mis•ery**
mne•mon•ic
mnemonnic : **mne•mon•ic**
mneumonic : **mne•mon•ic**
mnimonic : **mne•mon•ic**
moaring : **moor•ing**
mobil : **mo•bile**

mo·bile
mobilety : mo·bil·i·ty
mo·bil·i·ty
mobillity : mo·bil·i·ty
moble : mo·bile
moccasen : moc·ca·sin
moc·ca·sin
moccason : moc·ca·sin
mockasin : moc·ca·sin
modafy : mod·i·fy
modarate : mod·er·ate
moddel : mod·el
modderate : mod·er·ate
moddern : mod·ern
moddest : mod·est
moddify : mod·i·fy
moddist : mod·est
moddle : mod·el
modefy : mod·i·fy
mod·el
mod·er·ate
moderet : mod·er·ate
mod·ern
mod·est
modiffy : mod·i·fy
mod·i·fy
modirn : mod·ern
modist : mod·est
modle : mod·el
mogal : mo·gul
mogel : mo·gul
mogle : mo·gul
mo·gul
mogule : mo·gul
molacule : mol·e·cule
molaculer : mo·lec·u·lar
mo·lar
mo·lec·u·lar
mol·e·cule
moleque : mol·e·cule
moler : mo·lar
molify : mol·li·fy

mollafy : mol·li·fy
mollecular : mo·lec·u·lar
mollecule : mol·e·cule
mollefy : mol·li·fy
mollesk : mol·lusk
mol·li·fy
mol·lusk
molusk : mol·lusk
momento : me·men·to
monalog : mon·o·logue
monapoly : mo·nop·o·ly
mon·ar·chy
monarky : mon·ar·chy
monastary : mon·as·tery
monasterry : mon·as·tery
mon·as·tery
monater : mon·i·tor
monatery : mon·e·tary
Mon·day
monestery : mon·as·tery
mon·e·tary
monetery : mon·e·tary
mon·ey
mon·eys or mon·ies
mon·ies or mon·eys
monitary : mon·e·tary
moniter : mon·i·tor
mon·i·tor
monnastery : mon·as·tery
monnitor : mon·i·tor
monnogamy : mo·nog·a·my
monnolith : mon·o·lith
monnolog : mon·o·logue
monnopoly : mo·nop·o·ly
Monntana : Mon·tana
monnument : mon·u·ment
monogammy : mo·nog·a·my
mo·nog·a·my
monogemy : mo·nog·a·my
monoleth : mon·o·lith
mon·o·lith
monolog : mon·o·logue

403

mon·o·logue
monopaly : **mo·nop·o·ly**
monoply : **mo·nop·o·ly**
mo·nop·o·ly
monsterous : **mon·strous**
monstrocity : **mon·stros·i·ty**
mon·stros·i·ty
monstrossity : **mon·stros·i·ty**
mon·strous
monstrousity : **mon·stros·i·ty**
mon·tage
Mon·tana
Montanna : **Mon·tana**
montoge : **mon·tage**
Mon·tre·al
Montreall : **Mon·tre·al**
Montrial : **Mon·tre·al**
montrosety : **mon·stros·i·ty**
mon·u·ment
mony : **mon·ey**
moor·ing
moose (elk); **mousse** (dessert)
morabund : **mor·i·bund**
mor·al (ethical; lesson);
   mo·rale (emotional state)
mo·rale (emotional state);
   mor·al (ethical; lesson)
moralety : **mo·ral·i·ty**
mo·ral·i·ty
morallity : **mo·ral·i·ty**
mo·rass
morcel : **mor·sel**
mor·dant (biting); **mor·dent**
   (Musical)
mor·dent *(Musical)*; **mor·dant**
   (biting)
morfeen : **mor·phine**
morfine : **mor·phine**
morgage : **mort·gage**
morgege : **mort·gage**
mor·i·bund
morings : **moor·ing**

Morman : **Mor·mon**
Mormen : **Mor·mon**
Mor·mon
mornful : **mourn·ful**
Mo·roc·co
Morocko : **Mo·roc·co**
Moroco : **Mo·roc·co**
morpheen : **mor·phine**
morphene : **mor·phine**
mor·phine
morrality : **mo·ral·i·ty**
morrass : **mo·rass**
morribund : **mor·i·bund**
mor·sel
morsil : **mor·sel**
morsle : **mor·sel**
mortafy : **mor·ti·fy**
mor·tal
mor·tar
mortefy : **mor·ti·fy**
mortel : **mor·tal**
morter : **mor·tar**
mort·gage
mortiffy : **mor·ti·fy**
mor·ti·fy
mortor : **mor·tar**
mor·tu·ary
mortuery : **mor·tu·ary**
mosk : **mosque**
moskeeto : **mos·qui·to**
moskito : **mos·qui·to**
Mos·lem *or* **Mus·lim**
Moslim : **Mus·lim**
mosque
mos·qui·to
mossoleum : **mau·so·le·um**
motavate : **mo·ti·vate**
moter : **mo·tor**
mo·ti·vate
mot·ley
mo·tor
mottley : **mot·ley**

moun·tain
mountan : **moun·tain**
Mountana : **Mon·ta·na**
mountian : **moun·tain**
mountin : **moun·tain**
mourn·ful
mournfull : **mourn·ful**
mouse (rodent); **mousse**
(dessert)
mousse (dessert); **moose** (elk);
mouse (rodent)
mov·able *or* **move·able**
move·able *or* **mov·able**
movible : **mov·able**
Mozlem : **Mus·lim**
mu·cous (*adj.*); **mu·cus** (*noun*)
mu·cus (*noun*); **mu·cous** (*adj.*)
muffen : **muf·fin**
muf·fin
multaple : **mul·ti·ple**
multaply : **mul·ti·ply**
multeple : **mul·ti·ple**
multeply : **mul·ti·ply**
multipal : **mul·ti·ple**
mul·ti·ple
mul·ti·ply
multipple : **mul·ti·ple**
mundain : **mun·dane**
mun·dane
Munday : **Mon·day**
municions : **mu·ni·tions**
mu·nic·i·pal
municiple : **mu·nic·i·pal**
munisipal : **mu·nic·i·pal**
mu·ni·tions
mu·ral
murcenary : **mer·ce·nary**
murchandise : **mer·chan·dise**
murchant : **mer·chant**
murcury : **mer·cu·ry**
murger : **merg·er**
murky

murmaid : **mer·maid**
murmer : **mur·mur**
mur·mur
murral : **mu·ral**
murrel : **mu·ral**
mursenary : **mer·ce·nary**
murth : **mirth**
mus·cle (body tissue); **mus·sel**
(bivalve mollusk)
musecal : **mu·si·cal**
mu·se·um
mu·si·cal
mu·si·cian
musicion : **mu·si·cian**
musicle : **mu·si·cal**
musiem : **mu·se·um**
musium : **mu·se·um**
mus·ket
mus·ke·teer
musketere : **mus·ke·teer**
musketier : **mus·ke·teer**
muskit : **mus·ket**
muskiteer : **mus·ke·teer**
muslen : **mus·lin**
Mus·lim *or* **Mos·lem**
mus·lin
mus·sel (bivalve mollusk);
mus·cle (body tissue)
mussle : **mus·cle** (body tissue)
or **mus·sel** (bivalve mollusk)
musstard : **mus·tard**
mus·tard
musterd : **mus·tard**
mustird : **mus·tard**
mu·ta·bil·i·ty
mutabillity : **mu·ta·bil·i·ty**
mutalate : **mu·ti·late**
mutaneer : **mu·ti·neer**
mu·tant
mutany : **mu·ti·ny**
muteneer : **mu·ti·neer**
mutent : **mu·tant**

muteny : **mu•ti•ny**
mutibility : **mu•ta•bil•i•ty**
mu•ti•late
mutillate : **mu•ti•late**
mu•ti•neer
mutinere : **mu•ti•neer**
mutinier : **mu•ti•neer**
mu•ti•ny
mutten : **mut•ton**
muttin : **mut•ton**
mut•ton
muzel : **muz•zle**
muzeum : **mu•se•um**
Muzlim : **Mus•lim**
muzlin : **mus•lin**
muzzel : **muz•zle**
muz•zle
Myami: Mi•**ami**
mygraine : mi•graine

myistisism : **mys•ti•cism**
my•o•pic
myopick : **my•o•pic**
myoppic : **my•o•pic**
myr•i•ad
myrrh
mysterry : **mys•tery**
mys•tery
mys•tic
mys•ti•cism
mystick : **mys•tic**
mythacal : **myth•i•cal**
mythalogy : **my•thol•o•gy**
mythecal : **myth•i•cal**
myth•i•cal
mythicle : **myth•i•cal**
mythollogy : **my•thol•o•gy**
my•thol•o•gy

N

na•bob
nacent : na•scent
nadar : na•dir
nadeer : na•dir
nader : na•dir
na•dir
naevete : na•ive•te
naevety : na•ive•te
naibob : na•bob
naife : na•ive
naighbor : neigh•bor
naipalm : na•palm
naipam : na•palm
naipom : na•palm
Nai•ro•bi
nai•ve *or* na•ïve
naivetay : na•ive•te
na•ive•te *or* na•ive•té
naivety (*Brit.*) : na•ive•te
naivity : na•ive•te
na•ked
nakid : na•ked
nakked : na•ked
na•palm
napken : nap•kin
nap•kin
napom : na•palm
napsack : knap•sack
narate : nar•rate
naration : nar•ra•tion
narator : nar•ra•tor
narcisism : nar•cis•sism
nar•cis•sism
nar•cot•ic
narcotick : nar•cot•ic
narcottic : nar•cot•ic
narled : gnarled
nar•rate
narrater : nar•ra•tor
nar•ra•tion

nar•ra•tor
narrled : gnarled
narsisism : nar•cis•sism
na•sal
nasall : na•sal
na•scent
nascint : na•scent
nasea : nau•sea
nasel : na•sal
nasell : na•sal
nasent : na•scent
nash : gnash
nat : gnat
natiral : nat•u•ral
nativety : na•tiv•i•ty
nativitty : na•tiv•i•ty
na•tiv•i•ty
nattural : nat•u•ral
nat•u•ral
naturel : nat•u•ral
naturral : nat•u•ral
nau•sea
nau•se•ate
nausha : nau•sea
nausheate : nau•se•ate
naushia : nau•sea
nausia : nau•sea
nausiate : nau•se•ate
naut : knot (rope; one nautical mile); not (negative); nought (zero)
nau•ti•cal
nauticle : nau•ti•cal
nautilis : nau•ti•lus
nautillus : nau•ti•lus
nau•ti•lus
navagator : nav•i•ga•tor
Nav•a•ho *or* Nav•a•jo
Nav•a•jo *or* Nav•a•ho

na•val (of the navy); na•vel
  (belly button)
navegator : nav•i•ga•tor
Naveho : Nav•a•ho
na•vel (belly button); na•val (of
  the navy)
navigater : nav•i•ga•tor
nav•i•ga•tor
Naviho : Nav•a•ho
navil : na•val (of the navy) or
  na•vel (belly button)
navvigator : nav•i•ga•tor
naw : gnaw
nawsea : nau•sea
nawseate : nau•se•ate
nawsia : nau•sea
nawtical : nau•ti•cal
nawtilus : nau•ti•lus
naybob : na•bob
nay (no); neigh (whinny)
naypalm : na•palm
naypam : na•palm
naypom : na•palm
nealithic : neo•lith•ic
neap
neaphyte : neo•phyte
near
nearvous : ner•vous
neat
Nebbraska : Ne•bras•ka
nebbula : neb•u•la (sing.)
nebbulous : neb•u•lous
Ne•bras•ka
Nebrasska : Ne•bras•ka
neb•u•la (sing.)
neb•u•lae or neb•u•las (plur.)
neb•u•las or neb•u•lae (plur.)
nebulla : neb•u•la (sing.)
nebullous : neb•u•lous
neb•u•lous
nebulus : neb•u•lous
necesary : ne•ces•sary

necesity : ne•ces•si•ty
nec•es•sary
necessery : nec•es•sary
necessety : ne•ces•si•ty
necessitty : ne•ces•si•ty
ne•ces•si•ty
necissary : nec•es•sary
neck•lace
necklase : neck•lace
necklise : neck•lace
neckliss : neck•lace
necktar : nec•tar
necktarine : nec•tar•ine
nec•tar
nectarean : nec•tar•ine
nectareen : nec•tar•ine
nectarene : nec•tar•ine
nec•tar•ine
necter : nec•tar
necterine : nec•tar•ine
nectir : nec•tar
nectirine : nec•tar•ine
neece : niece
needal : nee•dle
needel : nee•dle
nee•dle
neep : neap
neer : near
neese : niece
neet : neat
nefew : neph•ew
neffew : neph•ew
neg•a•tive
negetive : neg•a•tive
neggative : neg•a•tive
neghbor : neigh•bor
negitive : neg•a•tive
neglagee : neg•li•gee
neglagence : neg•li•gence
neglegee : neg•li•gee
neglegence : neg•li•gence
neglegible : neg•li•gi•ble

negligeble : **neg·li·gi·ble**
negligibal : **neg·li·gi·ble**
neg·li·gee
neg·li·gence
negligense : **neg·li·gence**
negligibel : **neg·li·gi·ble**
neg·li·gi·ble
negligince : **neg·li·gence**
neglishay : **neg·li·gee**
neglishee : **neg·li·gee**
negociate : **ne·go·ti·ate**
negoshiate : **ne·go·ti·ate**
negoteate : **ne·go·ti·ate**
ne·go·ti·ate
neice : **niece**
neigh (whinny); **nay** (no)
neighber : **neigh·bor**
neigh·bor
neise : **niece**
nei·ther
nemesees : **nem·e·ses** (*plur.*)
nem·e·ses (*plur.*)
nem·e·sis (*sing.*)
nemesus : **nem·e·sis** (*sing.*)
nemises : **nem·e·ses** (*plur.*)
nemisis : **nem·e·sis** (*sing.*)
nemmises : **nem·e·ses** (*plur.*)
nemmisis : **nem·e·sis** (*sing.*)
nemonic : **mne·mon·ic**
nemonnic : **mne·mon·ic**
neofite : **neo·phyte**
neofyte : **neo·phyte**
neo·lith·ic
neolithick : **neo·lith·ic**
neolythic : **neo·lith·ic**
neo·phyte
neph·ew
nephiw : **neph·ew**
nephue : **neph·ew**
nervana : **nir·va·na**
nerviss : **ner·vous**
ner·vous

nervus : **ner·vous**
nesessary : **nec·es·sary**
nesessity : **ne·ces·si·ty**
nesissary : **nec·es·sary**
neugat : **nou·gat** (candy) *or*
    nug·get (lump)
neu·ral
neuralogy : **neu·rol·o·gy**
neurel : **neu·ral**
neuroligy : **neu·rol·o·gy**
neurollogy : **neu·rol·o·gy**
neu·rol·o·gy
neu·ron
neurosees : **neu·ro·ses** (*plur.*)
neu·ro·ses (*plur.*)
neu·ro·sis (*sing.*)
neurosus : **neu·ro·sis** (*sing.*)
neu·ter
neuteral : **neu·tral**
neu·tral
neutrel : **neu·tral**
neu·tron
Nev·a·da
Nevadda : **Nev·a·da**
new (not old); **gnu** (antelope);
    knew (was aware)
New·found·land
Newfundland : **New·found·land**
newget : **nou·gat** (candy) *or*
    nug·get (lump)
New Hampshir : **New**
    Hamp·shire
New Hamp·shire
New Hampsure : **New**
    Hamp·shire
New Hamshire : **New**
    Hamp·shire
New Jer·sey
New Jersy : **New Jer·sey**
New Mex·i·co
New Or·leans
New Orlines : **New Or·leans**

newrosis : **neu•ro•sis** (*sing.*)
newsreal : **news•reel**
news•reel
news•stand
newstand : **news•stand**
newter : **neu•ter**
newtron : **neu•tron**
New York
Newyork : **New York**
New Zea•land
New Zealund : **New Zea•land**
New Zeeland : **New Zea•land**
New Zeland : **New Zea•land**
Ni•ag•a•ra
Niagera : **Ni•ag•a•ra**
Niaggara : **Ni•ag•a•ra**
Niagra : **Ni•ag•a•ra**
nialism : **ni•hil•ism**
Niarobi : **Nai•ro•bi**
niave : **na•ive**
niavete : **na•ive•te**
Nibraska : **Ne•bras•ka**
nicatine : **nic•o•tine**
niccotine : **nic•o•tine**
nice•ty
nich : **niche**
niche
nicitty : **nice•ty**
nicity : **nice•ty**
nickal : **nick•el**
nickalodeon : **nick•el•ode•on**
nick•el
nick•el•ode•on
nickelodion : **nick•el•ode•on**
nickle : **nick•el**
nickleodeon : **nick•el•ode•on**
nicknack : **knick•knack**
nickotine : **nic•o•tine**
nicoteen : **nic•o•tine**
nicotene : **nic•o•tine**
nic•o•tine
niece

nieghbor : **neigh•bor**
niese : **niece**
niether : **nei•ther**
nieve : **na•ive**
nievete : **na•ive•te**
nife : **knife**
nifes : **knifes** (stabs) *or* **knives** (*plur.*)
nigardly : **nig•gard•ly**
Nigeeria : **Ni•ge•ria**
Nigerea : **Ni•ge•ria**
Ni•ge•ria
nig•gard•ly
niggerdly : **nig•gard•ly**
night (not day); **knight** (medieval soldier)
nihalism : **ni•hil•ism**
nihelism : **ni•hil•ism**
ni•hil•ism
Nijeria : **Ni•ge•ria**
nilism : **ni•hil•ism**
nilon : **ny•lon**
nimf : **nymph**
nimises : **nem•e•ses** (*plur.*)
nimisis : **nem•e•sis** (*sing.*)
nimmises : **nem•e•ses** (*plur.*)
nimmisis : **nem•e•sis** (*sing.*)
nimmonic : **mne•mon•ic**
nimonic : **mne•mon•ic**
nimph : **nymph**
ninetean : **nine•teen**
nine•teen
ninetene : **nine•teen**
nineth : **ninth**
nine•ti•eth
nine•ty
ninetyeth : **nine•ti•eth**
ninetyith : **nine•ti•eth**
ninteen : **nine•teen**
ninth
nintieth : **nine•ti•eth**
ninty : **nine•ty**

niophyte : **neo·phyte**
Nirobi : **Nai·ro·bi**
nir·va·na
nirvanna : **nir·va·na**
nitch : **niche**
nite : **knight** (medieval soldier)
  or **night** (not day)
nitragen : **ni·tro·gen**
nitregen : **ni·tro·gen**
ni·tro·gen
nitrogin : **ni·tro·gen**
nives : **knives**
no (negative); **know** (to be
  aware of); **now** (at this time)
noam : **gnome** (dwarf) *or*
  Nome (city)
nobilety : **no·bil·i·ty**
no·bil·i·ty
nobillity : **no·bil·i·ty**
noboddy : **no·body**
no·body
nockturnal : **noc·tur·nal**
nocternal : **noc·tur·nal**
noc·tur·nal
nocturnall : **noc·tur·nal**
nocturnel : **noc·tur·nal**
noddule : **nod·ule**
noduel : **nod·ule**
nod·ule
noledge : **knowl·edge**
noll : **knoll**
no·mad
Nome (city); **gnome** (dwarf)
nomenal : **nom·i·nal**
nomenate : **nom·i·nate**
nomenee : **nom·i·nee**
nom·i·nal
nom·i·nate
nom·i·nee
nominy : **nom·i·nee**
nommad : **no·mad**
nomminal : **nom·i·nal**

nomminate : **nom·i·nate**
nomminee : **nom·i·nee**
non·cha·lant
nonchalont : **non·cha·lant**
nonchelant : **non·cha·lant**
nonchilant : **non·cha·lant**
non·de·script
nondiscript : **non·de·script**
nonsence : **non·sense**
non·sense
nonshalant : **non·cha·lant**
nonshillant : **non·cha·lant**
nonsince : **non·sense**
nor·mal
nor·mal·cy
normalsy : **nor·mal·cy**
Normandee : **Nor·man·dy**
Nor·man·dy
normel : **nor·mal**
normelcy : **nor·mal·cy**
Normendy : **Nor·man·dy**
Normindy : **Nor·man·dy**
North Caralina : **North
  Car·o·li·na**
North Carlina : **North
  Car·o·li·na**
North Car·o·li·na
North Carrolina : **North
  Car·o·li·na**
North Dahkota : **North
  Da·ko·ta**
North Da·ko·ta
North Dakotah : **North
  Da·ko·ta**
Norwaygian : **Nor·we·gian**
Norweegian : **Nor·we·gian**
Norwegean : **Nor·we·gian**
Nor·we·gian
Norwejian : **Nor·we·gian**
nosetril : **nos·tril**
nostalgea : **nos·tal·gia**
nos·tal·gia

nostallgia : **nos•tal•gia**
nos•tril
nostrill : **nos•tril**
not (negative); **knot** (rope; one nautical mile); **nought** (zero)
not•a•ble
notafy : **not•i•fy**
notariety : **no•to•ri•ety**
noteble : **no•ta•ble**
notefy : **no•ti•fy**
noteriety : **no•to•ri•ety**
nothole : **knot•hole**
notible : **no•ta•ble**
noticable : **no•tice•able**
no•tice
no•tice•able
noticible : **no•tice•able**
notiffy : **no•ti•fy**
no•ti•fy
notiriety : **no•to•ri•ety**
notise : **no•tice**
notiseable : **no•tice•able**
notiss : **no•tice**
notoreous : **no•to•ri•ous**
notorietty : **no•to•ri•ety**
no•to•ri•ety
no•to•ri•ous
notorrious : **no•to•ri•ous**
notoryity : **no•to•ri•ety**
nottice : **no•tice**
nou•gat (candy); **nug•get** (lump)
nought (zero); **knot** (rope; one nautical mile); **not** (negative)
nour•ish
Nova Scocia : **No•va Sco•tia**
Nova Scosha : **No•va Sco•tia**
No•va Sco•tia
Nova Scotshia : **No•va Sco•tia**
novacaine : **no•vo•caine**
novacane : **no•vo•caine**
nov•ice

novise : **nov•ice**
noviss : **nov•ice**
no•vo•caine
novocane : **no•vo•caine**
novvice : **nov•ice**
now (at this time); **know** (to be aware of); **no** (negative)
now•a•days
nowdays : **now•a•days**
nowledge : **knowl•edge**
nozal : **noz•zle**
nozle : **noz•zle**
nozzal : **noz•zle**
noz•zle
nu : **gnu**
nu•ance
nuanse : **nu•ance**
nuckle : **knuck•le**
nu•cle•ar
nucleer : **nu•cle•ar**
nuclere : **nu•cle•ar**
nu•cle•us
nuclius : **nu•cle•us**
nucular : **nu•cle•ar**
nuculer : **nu•cle•ar**
nuculis : **nu•cle•us**
nuculus : **nu•cle•us**
nudaty : **nu•di•ty**
nudety : **nu•di•ty**
nuditty : **nu•di•ty**
nu•di•ty
nuematic : **pneu•mat•ic**
nuemonia : **pneu•mo•nia**
nueral : **neu•ral**
nuerology : **neu•rol•o•gy**
nueron : **neu•ron**
nueroses : **neu•ro•ses** (*plur.*)
nuerosis : **neu•ro•sis** (*sing.*)
nueter : **neu•ter**
nuetral : **neu•tral**
nuetron : **neu•tron**

nuget : **nougat** (candy) *or*
  nug•get (lump)
nugget (lump); **nou•gat** (candy)
nuggit : **nougat** (candy) *or*
  nug•get (lump)
nui•sance
nuisanse : **nui•sance**
nuisence : **nui•sance**
nuisense : **nui•sance**
nulify : **nul•li•fy**
nullafy : **nul•li•fy**
nullefy : **nul•li•fy**
nul•li•fy
num : **numb**
numaral : **nu•mer•al**
numarical : **nu•mer•i•cal**
numatic : **pneu•mat•ic**
numb
numb•ly
numbskull : **num•skull**
nu•mer•al
numerel : **nu•mer•al**
nu•mer•i•cal
numericle : **nu•mer•i•cal**
numiral : **nu•mer•al**
numly : **numb•ly**
numonia : **pneu•mo•nia**
num•skull
nunery : **nun•nery**
nunnary : **nun•nery**
nun•nery
nup•tial
nuptual : **nup•tial**
nuptuel : **nup•tial**
nuptule : **nup•tial**

nural : **neu•ral**
nurcery : **nurs•ery**
nurish : **nour•ish**
nurology : **neu•rol•o•gy**
nuron : **neu•ron**
nuroses : **neu•ro•ses** (*plur.*)
nurosis : **neu•ro•sis** (*sing.*)
nurral : **neu•ral**
nurralolgy : **neu•rol•o•gy**
nurrish : **nour•ish**
nurron : **neu•ron**
nursary : **nurs•ery**
nurserry : **nurs•ery**
nurs•ery
nursury : **nurs•ery**
nusance : **nui•sance**
nutral : **neu•tral**
nutrative : **nu•tri•tive**
nutreant : **nu•tri•ent**
nutretive : **nu•tri•tive**
nutriant : **nu•tri•ent**
nu•tri•ent
nu•tri•tion
nu•tri•tive
nutrittion : **nu•tri•tion**
nutron : **neu•tron**
nuzle : **nuz•zle**
nuzzal : **nuz•zle**
nuz•zle
nyeve : **na•ive**
nyevete : **na•ive•te**
ny•lon
nymf : **nymph**
nymph
Nyrobi : **Nai•ro•bi**

O

Oahoo : **Oa·hu**
Oa·hu
Oaklahoma : **Okla·ho·ma**
oa·ses (*plur.*)
oa·sis (*sing.*)
obaisance : **obei·sance**
obalisk : **obe·lisk**
obbelisk : **obe·lisk**
obcess : **ab·scess**
    (inflammation) *or* **ob·sess** (to
    preoccupy)
obcession : **ob·ses·sion**
obderate : **ob·du·rate**
ob·du·rate
obdurrate : **ob·du·rate**
obeadience : **obe·di·ence**
obeadient : **obe·di·ent**
obease : **obese**
obeasity : **obe·si·ty**
obecity : **obe·si·ty**
obedeance : **obe·di·ence**
obedianse : **obe·di·ence**
obediant : **obe·di·ent**
obe·di·ence
obediense : **obe·di·ence**
obe·di·ent
obeedience : **obe·di·ence**
obeedient : **obe·di·ent**
obeesity : **obe·si·ty**
obei·sance
obeisence : **obei·sance**
obeisense : **obei·sance**
obelesk : **obe·lisk**
obe·lisk
obellisk : **obe·lisk**
obese
obesety : **obe·si·ty**
obesitty : **obe·si·ty**
obe·si·ty
obeysance : **obei·sance**

obeysense : **obei·sance**
obittuary : **obit·u·ary**
obit·u·ary
obituery : **obit·u·ary**
objectafy : **ob·jec·ti·fy**
objectefy : **ob·jec·ti·fy**
objectiffy : **ob·jec·ti·fy**
ob·jec·ti·fy
obleek : **oblique**
obleeque : **oblique**
oblique
oblivian : **obliv·i·on**
oblivien : **obliv·i·on**
obliv·i·on
obnocksious : **ob·nox·ious**
ob·nox·ious
obo : **oboe**
oboe
obsalescent : **ob·so·les·cent**
ob·scene
obscerity : **ob·scu·ri·ty**
obscurety : **ob·scu·ri·ty**
ob·scu·ri·ty
obsean : **ob·scene**
obsene : **ob·scene**
obsequeous : **ob·se·qui·ous**
ob·se·qui·ous
ob·ser·vance
observanse : **ob·ser·vance**
observence : **ob·ser·vance**
observince : **ob·ser·vance**
obsesion : **ob·ses·sion**
ob·sess (to preoccupy);
    ab·scess (inflammation)
ob·ses·sion
obsiquious : **ob·se·qui·ous**
obsoleat : **ob·so·lete**
obsoleet : **ob·so·lete**
ob·so·les·cent
obsolessant : **ob·so·les·cent**

obsolessent : **ob·so·les·cent**
ob·so·lete
obstacal : **ob·sta·cle**
ob·sta·cle
obstecle : **ob·sta·cle**
obsticle : **ob·sta·cle**
ob·sti·nate
obstinet : **ob·sti·nate**
ob·tain
obtane : **ob·tain**
obthamalogy :
   oph·thal·mol·o·gy
obtical : **op·ti·cal**
obtimal : **op·ti·mal**
obtimism : **op·ti·mism**
obtimist : **op·ti·mist**
obtometrist : **op·tom·e·trist**
obtuce : **ob·tuse**
ob·tuse
obveate : **ob·vi·ate**
ob·vi·ate
obviaus : **ob·vi·ous**
ocaen : **ocean**
ocasion : **oc·ca·sion**
oc·ca·sion
occassion : **oc·ca·sion**
oc·cult
oc·cu·pant
occupent : **oc·cu·pant**
occupint : **oc·cu·pant**
oc·cur
occured : **oc·curred**
occurence : **oc·cur·rence**
occurrance : **oc·cur·rence**
occurranse : **oc·cur·rence**
oc·curred
oc·cur·rence
ocean
ocien : **ocean**
oc·ta·gon
octain : **oc·tane**
oc·tane

octapus : **oc·to·pus**
octegon : **oc·ta·gon**
octigon : **oc·ta·gon**
oc·to·pus
octopuss : **oc·to·pus**
ocult : **oc·cult**
ocupant : **oc·cu·pant**
ocupent : **oc·cu·pant**
ocupint : **oc·cu·pant**
ocur : **oc·cur**
ocured : **oc·curred**
ocurence : **oc·cur·rence**
ocurrance : **oc·cur·rence**
ocurrence : **oc·cur·rence**
oddety : **odd·i·ty**
oddissey : **od·ys·sey**
odd·i·ty
oddysey : **od·ys·sey**
oder : **odor**
odissey : **od·ys·sey**
odor
odysey : **od·ys·sey**
od·ys·sey
odyssie : **od·ys·sey**
ofense : **of·fense**
offacer : **of·fi·cer**
offecer : **of·fi·cer**
offen : **of·ten**
of·fence *or* **of·fense**
of·fense *or* **of·fence**
offeratory : **of·fer·to·ry**
offeritory : **of·fer·to·ry**
of·fer·to·ry
of·fi·cer
of·ten
oftin : **of·ten**
oger : **ogre**
ogre
Ohio
Okla·ho·ma
Oklihoma : **Okla·ho·ma**
ole·an·der

olfactary : **ol·fac·to·ry**
olfactery : **ol·fac·to·ry**
ol·fac·to·ry
oliander : **ole·an·der**
Olimpic : **Olym·pic**
Olym·pic
Olympick : **Olym·pic**
omaga : **ome·ga**
omage : **hom·age**
ome·ga
om·elet *or* **om·elette**
om·elette *or* **om·elet**
omen
omenous : **om·i·nous**
omilet : **om·elet**
omin : **omen**
om·i·nous
omision : **omis·sion**
omis·sion
omit
omlet : **om·elet**
omlette : **om·elet**
ommage : **hom·age**
ommelet : **om·elet**
ommit : **omit**
ommlet : **om·elet**
omnipotance : **om·nip·o·tence**
om·nip·o·tence
omnipotense : **om·nip·o·tence**
onamatopoeia :
    on·o·mato·poe·ia
onarous : **oner·ous**
oner·ous
one·self
onesself : **one·self**
onest : **hon·est**
onix : **on·yx**
onnest : **hon·est**
onnist : **hon·est**
onnix : **on·yx**
onnomatopoeia :
    on·o·mato·poe·ia

onnor : **hon·or**
onnorable : **hon·or·able**
onnorible : **hon·or·able**
onnui : **en·nui**
onnyx : **on·yx**
onomatopia : **on·o·mato·poe·ia**
on·o·mato·poe·ia
onomotapoeia :
    on·o·mato·poe·ia
onor : **hon·or**
onorable : **hon·or·able**
onorarium : **hon·o·rar·i·um**
onoreble : **hon·or·able**
onorible : **hon·or·able**
Ontareo : **On·tar·io**
On·tar·io
Ontarrio : **On·tar·io**
Onterio : **On·tar·io**
ontourage : **en·tou·rage**
ontrepreneur : **en·tre·pre·neur**
on·ward
onwerd : **on·ward**
onword : **on·ward**
on·yx
opacety : **opac·i·ty**
opacitty : **opac·i·ty**
opac·i·ty
opal
opassity : **opac·i·ty**
opel : **opal**
openess : **open·ness**
open·ness
op·era
op·er·a·ble
operible : **op·er·a·ble**
opeum : **opi·um**
oph·thal·mol·o·gy
ophthemalogy :
    oph·thal·mol·o·gy
ophthmalligy :
    oph·thal·mol·o·gy

ophthmallogy :
   oph·thal·mol·o·gy
ophthmollogy :
   oph·thal·mol·o·gy
opiem : **opi·um**
opi·um
oponant : **op·po·nent**
oponent : **op·po·nent**
oportunity : **op·por·tu·ni·ty**
oposite : **op·po·site**
oppal : **opal**
oppasite : **op·po·site**
oppera : **op·era**
opperable : **op·er·a·ble**
oppertunity : **op·por·tu·ni·ty**
oppiset : **op·po·site**
oppisite : **op·po·site**
opponant : **op·po·nent**
op·po·nent
opponint : **op·po·nent**
opportunety : **op·por·tu·ni·ty**
opportunitty : **op·por·tu·ni·ty**
op·por·tu·ni·ty
opposate : **op·po·site**
opposet : **op·po·site**
op·po·site
oppresion : **op·pres·sion**
oppresor : **op·pres·sor**
op·press
oppresser : **op·pres·sor**
op·pres·sion
op·pres·sor
oppulence : **op·u·lence**
opress : **op·press**
opression : **op·pres·sion**
opressor : **op·pres·sor**
optamism : **op·ti·mism**
optemal : **op·ti·mal**
optemism : **op·ti·mism**
opthalmology :
   oph·thal·mol·o·gy

opthamology :
   oph·thal·mol·o·gy
opthemology :
   oph·thal·mol·o·gy
op·tic
optick : **op·tic**
optickal : **op·ti·cal**
opticle : **op·ti·cal**
op·ti·mal
optimel : **op·ti·mal**
optimest : **op·ti·mist**
op·ti·mism
op·ti·mist
optimizm : **op·ti·mism**
optimmism : **op·ti·mism**
optimmist : **op·ti·mist**
optomatrist : **op·tom·e·trist**
op·tom·e·trist
optomitrist : **op·tom·e·trist**
optommetrist : **op·tom·e·trist**
opulance : **op·u·lence**
opulanse : **op·u·lence**
op·u·lence
opulense : **op·u·lence**
opullence : **op·u·lence**
oracion : **ora·tion**
or·a·cle
orafice : **or·i·fice**
oragin : **or·i·gin**
Oragon : **Or·e·gon**
oral
orangatang : **orang·utan**
or·ange
orangootan : **orang·utan**
orang·utan
orashion : **ora·tion**
orater : **or·a·tor**
ora·tion
or·a·tor
orbet : **or·bit**
or·bit
orcestra : **or·ches·tra**

or·chard
orched : **or·chid**
orcherd : **or·chard**
or·ches·tra
or·chid
orchird : **or·chard**
orchistra : **or·ches·tra**
or·dain
ordanary : **or·di·nary**
ordane : **or·dain**
or·deal
ordeel : **or·deal**
ordenance : **or·di·nance** (rule,
   law) *or* **ord·nance**
   (weaponry)
ordenary : **or·di·nary**
ordenince : **or·di·nance** (rule,
   law) *or* **ord·nance**
   (weaponry)
or·di·nance (rule, law);
   ord·nance (weaponry)
ordinarry : **or·di·nary**
or·di·nary
ordinense : **or·di·nance** (rule,
   law) *or* **ord·nance**
   (weaponry)
ordinerry : **or·di·nary**
ordinery : **or·di·nary**
ordnance (weaponry);
   ordinance (rule, law)
ordnanse : **or·di·nance** (rule,
   law) *or* **ord·nance**
   (weaponry)
orecle : **or·a·cle**
orefice : **or·i·fice**
Or·e·gon (state); or·i·gin
   (beginning)
Oregone : **Or·e·gon**
orel : **oral**
orenge : **or·ange**
oreole : **ori·ole**
oretor : **or·a·tor**

orfan : **or·phan**
orfanage : **or·phan·age**
orfin : **or·phan**
orfinage : **or·phan·age**
orfun : **or·phan**
orfunage : **or·phan·age**
or·gan·dy
organesm : **or·gan·ism**
or·gan·ic
organick : **or·gan·ic**
or·gan·ism
organnic : **or·gan·ic**
orgendy : **or·gan·dy**
orgenism : **or·gan·ism**
orgindy : **or·gan·dy**
oriant : **ori·ent**
orical : **or·a·cle**
oricle : **or·a·cle**
ori·ent
ori·en·tal
orientall : **ori·en·tal**
orientel : **ori·en·tal**
or·i·fice
orifise : **or·i·fice**
orifiss : **or·i·fice**
orifrice : **or·i·fice**
origen : **Or·e·gon** (state) *or*
   or·i·gin (beginning)
origenal : **orig·i·nal**
origenate : **orig·i·nate**
or·i·gin (beginning); Or·e·gon
   (state)
originait : **orig·i·nate**
orig·i·nal
orig·i·nate
originel : **orig·i·nal**
originnate : **orig·i·nate**
Origon : **Or·e·gon**
orijen : **or·i·gin**
oringe : **or·ange**
oriol : **ori·ole**
ori·ole

orioll : **ori•ole**
oritor : **or•a•tor**
orkestra : **or•ches•tra**
orkid : **or•chid**
orkistra : **or•ches•tra**
ornait : **or•nate**
ornameant : **or•na•ment**
or•na•ment
ornamint : **or•na•ment**
ornamment : **or•na•ment**
ornary : **or•nery**
or•nate
ornathology : **or•ni•thol•o•gy**
ornement : **or•na•ment**
ornerry : **or•nery**
or•nery
ornethology : **or•ni•thol•o•gy**
orniment : **or•na•ment**
ornithalogy : **or•ni•thol•o•gy**
ornitholigy : **or•ni•thol•o•gy**
ornithollogy : **or•ni•thol•o•gy**
or•ni•thol•o•gy
ornory : **or•nery**
or•phan
or•phan•age
orphanege : **or•phan•age**
orphanige : **or•phan•age**
orphen : **or•phan**
orphenage : **or•phan•age**
orphin : **or•phan**
orphinage : **or•phan•age**
orphun : **or•phan**
orphunage : **or•phan•age**
orral : **oral**
orrange : **or•ange**
orrangutang : **orang•utan**
orrator : **or•a•tor**
orrattion : **ora•tion**
Orregon : **Or•e•gon**
orrient : **ori•ent**
orrifice : **or•i•fice**
orrigin : **or•i•gin**

orriginal : **orig•i•nal**
orringe : **or•ange**
orriole : **ori•ole**
orthadontist : **or•tho•don•tist**
orthadox : **or•tho•dox**
orthedontist : **or•tho•don•tist**
orthedox : **or•tho•dox**
orthodontest : **or•tho•don•tist**
or•tho•don•tist
or•tho•dox
oscellate : **os•cil•late**
oscilate : **os•cil•late**
os•cil•late
osify : **os•si•fy**
osillate : **os•cil•late**
osmoasis : **os•mo•sis**
os•mo•sis
osmossis : **os•mo•sis**
ospray : **os•prey**
ospree : **os•prey**
os•prey
osprie : **os•prey**
ospry : **os•prey**
ossafy : **os•si•fy**
ossefy : **os•si•fy**
ossiffy : **os•si•fy**
os•si•fy
ossillate : **os•cil•late**
ostencible : **os•ten•si•ble**
ostensable : **os•ten•si•ble**
ostensibal : **os•ten•si•ble**
os•ten•si•ble
ostentacious : **os•ten•ta•tious**
ostentashious : **os•ten•ta•tious**
os•ten•ta•tious
os•teo•path
ostinsible : **os•ten•si•ble**
ostintatious : **os•ten•ta•tious**
ostiopath : **os•teo•path**
ostracesm : **os•tra•cism**
ostracise : **os•tra•cize**
os•tra•cism

os•tra•cize
ostrage : os•trich
ostrasism : os•tra•cism
ostrasize : os•tra•cize
ostrech : os•trich
ostrecism : os•tra•cism
ostrecize : os•tra•cize
ostrege : os•trich
ostretch : os•trich
os•trich
ostricism : os•tra•cism
ostricize : os•tra•cize
ostrige : os•trich
ostritch : os•trich
Otawa : Ot•ta•wa
otoman : ot•to•man
Ot•ta•wa
Ottiwa : Ot•ta•wa
Ottoa : Ot•ta•wa
ot•to•man
ottomin : ot•to•man
Ottowa : Ot•ta•wa
ounce
ounse : ounce
our (belonging to us); hour (60
    minutes)
outrageious : out•ra•geous
out•ra•geous
outrageus : out•ra•geous
outragious : out•ra•geous
ova (plur.); ovum (sing.)
ovar•i•an
ovarrian : ovar•i•an

ova•ry
ovaryan : ovar•i•an
overian : ovar•i•an
overrian : ovar•i•an
overry : ova•ry
overwelm : over•whelm
over•whelm
overy : ova•ry
overyan : ovar•i•an
ovum (sing.); ova (plur.)
ovvary : ova•ry
Owahu : Oa•hu
ownce : ounce
ownerous : on•er•ous
oxadation : ox•i•da•tion
oxagen : ox•y•gen
oxedation : ox•i•da•tion
oxegen : ox•y•gen
oxegin : ox•y•gen
Oxferd : Ox•ford
Ox•ford
ox•i•da•tion
oxigen : ox•y•gen
oxigin : ox•y•gen
oxsidation : ox•i•da•tion
ox•y•gen
oys•ter
oystir : oys•ter
Ozark
ozmosis : os•mo•sis
ozoan : ozone
ozone
Ozzark : Ozark
ozzone : ozone

P

pablem : **pab•u•lum**
pablum : **pab•u•lum**
pabulem : **pab•u•lum**
pab•u•lum
pacefy : **pac•i•fy**
pacifec : **pa•cif•ic**
paciffy : **pac•i•fy**
pa•cif•ic
pac•i•fi•er
pac•i•fist
pac•i•fy
pacivist : **pac•i•fist**
pac•ket
Packistan : **Pa•ki•stan**
packit : **pack•et**
pagamas : **pa•ja•mas**
pa•gan
pag•eant
pagen : **pa•gan**
pagent : **pag•eant**
paggan : **pa•gan**
pagiant : **pag•eant**
pagin : **pa•gan**
pagint : **pag•eant**
pa•go•da
pagota : **pa•go•da**
paid
pain (ache); **pane** (glass)
pain•ful
painfull : **pain•ful**
pair (two things); **pare** (to cut
    away); **pear** (fruit)
pais•ley
paizley : **pais•ley**
pa•ja•mas
pajammas : **pa•ja•mas**
Pakastan : **Pa•ki•stan**
paket : **pack•et**
Pa•ki•stan
palacade : **pal•i•sade**

pal•ace
palacial : **pa•la•tial**
palasade : **pal•i•sade**
palasaid : **pal•i•sade**
palase : **pal•ace**
palashial : **pa•la•tial**
pal•at•able
pa•la•tial
palatible : **pal•at•able**
Pal•es•tine
palice : **pal•ace**
palid : **pal•lid**
pal•i•sade
paliss : **pal•ace**
Palistine : **Pal•es•tine**
pallace : **pal•ace**
pallatable : **pal•at•able**
Pallestine : **Pal•es•tine**
pal•lid
pallisade : **pal•i•sade**
pal•lor
palm (tree; hand); **Pam** (name)
palor : **pal•lor**
pal•pa•ble
palpibal : **pal•pa•ble**
palpible : **pal•pa•ble**
Pam (name); **palm** (tree; hand)
pamflet : **pam•phlet**
pam•phlet
pamphlit : **pam•phlet**
pamplet : **pam•phlet**
pan•a•cea
panacia : **pan•a•cea**
Pa•na•ma
Panamma : **Pa•na•ma**
panaply : **pan•o•ply**
panarama : **pan•ora•ma**
panasia : **pan•a•cea**
pan•cre•as
pancreus : **pan•cre•as**

pandamonium :
   pan·de·mo·ni·um
pandemoniem :
   pan·de·mo·ni·um
pan·de·mo·ni·um
pandimonium :
   pan·de·mo·ni·um
pane (glass); **pain** (ache)
paneful : **pain·ful**
pan·el
pan·eled *or* **pan·elled**
panell : **pan·el**
pan·elled *or* **pan·eled**
panerama : **pan·ora·ma**
pan·ic
paniced : **pan·icked**
panick : **pan·ic**
pan·icked
pan·icky
panicy : **pan·icky**
paniked : **pan·icked**
panil : **pan·el**
paniled : **pan·eled**
panisea : **pan·a·cea**
pankreas : **pan·cre·as**
pankrius : **pan·cre·as**
pannacea : **pan·a·cea**
Pannama : **Pa·na·ma**
pannel : **pan·el**
panneled : **pan·eled**
panneply : **pan·o·ply**
pannic : **pan·ic**
panniply : **pan·o·ply**
pannoply : **pan·o·ply**
pan·o·ply
pan·ora·ma
panoramma : **pan·ora·ma**
panphlet : **pam·phlet**
pan·sy
panzy : **pan·sy**
pa·pa·cy
papasy : **pa·pa·cy**

paper mache : **pa·pier-mâ·ché**
papicy : **pa·pa·cy**
pa·pier-mâ·ché
papirus : **pa·py·rus**
papisy : **pa·pa·cy**
pappyrus : **pa·py·rus**
papreeka : **pa·pri·ka**
pa·pri·ka
papyris : **pa·py·rus**
pa·py·rus
paraboala: **pa·rab·o·la**
pa·rab·o·la
parabula : **pa·rab·o·la**
para·chute
paracite : **par·a·site**
pa·rade
paradice : **par·a·dise**
par·a·digm
paradime : **par·a·digm**
par·a·dise
par·a·dox
parafenalia : **par·a·pher·na·lia**
par·af·fin
par·a·gon
para·graph
paraid : **pa·rade**
par·a·keet
paralel : **par·al·lel**
paralesis : **pa·ral·y·sis**
paralisis : **pa·ral·y·sis**
par·al·lel
pa·ral·y·sis
para·noia
paranoya : **para·noia**
paraphenalia :
   par·a·pher·na·lia
par·a·pher·na·lia
paraphinalia : **par·a·pher·na·lia**
paraphrenalia :
   par·a·pher·na·lia
parashute : **para·chute**
par·a·site

para·sol
par·cel
parcell : **par·cel**
parcely : **pars·ley**
parden : **par·don**
pardin : **par·don**
par·don
pare (to cut away); **pair** (two things); **pear** (fruit)
paredigm : **par·a·digm**
paredime : **par·a·digm**
paredise : **par·a·dise**
paregon : **par·a·gon**
paret : **par·rot**
parety : **par·i·ty**
parichute : **para·chute**
paridigm : **par·a·digm**
paridise : **par·a·dise**
paridox : **par·a·dox**
paridy : **par·o·dy**
pariffin : **par·af·fin**
parifin : **par·af·fin**
parigraph : **para·graph**
parikeet : **par·a·keet**
par·ish (church community); **per·ish** (to cease to exist)
parisite : **par·a·site**
parisol : **para·sol**
paritty : **par·i·ty**
par·i·ty
parlament : **par·lia·ment**
par·lance
parlanse : **par·lance**
parlence : **par·lance**
parlense : **par·lance**
parler : **par·lor**
parleyment : **par·lia·ment**
par·lia·ment
parliment : **par·lia·ment**
par·lor
pa·ro·chi·al
par·o·dy

parot : **par·rot**
parrabola : **pa·rab·o·la**
parrade : **pa·rade**
parradise : **par·a·dise**
parradox : **par·a·dox**
parrafin : **par·af·fin**
parralel : **par·al·lel**
parralysis : **pa·ral·y·sis**
parret : **par·rot**
parridy : **par·o·dy**
parrifin : **par·af·fin**
parriket : **par·a·keet**
parrish : **par·ish** (church community) *or* **per·ish** (to cease to exist)
parrit : **par·rot**
parrity : **par·i·ty**
parrochial : **pa·ro·chi·al**
parrody : **par·o·dy**
parrokeet : **par·a·keet**
par·rot
parsel : **par·cel**
parsell : **par·cel**
pars·ley
parsly : **pars·ley**
partacle : **par·ti·cle**
partasan : **par·ti·san**
partesan : **par·ti·san**
partical : **par·ti·cle**
particepant : **par·tic·i·pant**
par·tic·i·pant
particlar : **par·tic·u·lar**
par·ti·cle
particlear : **par·tic·u·lar**
par·tic·u·lar
partikle : **par·ti·cle**
par·ti·san
partisen : **par·ti·san**
partisipant : **par·tic·i·pant**
partredge : **par·tridge**
partrege : **par·tridge**
par·tridge

partrige : **par•tridge**
Pas•a•de•na
Pasadina : **Pas•a•de•na**
pasafier : **pac•i•fi•er**
pasage : **pas•sage**
pashion : **pas•sion**
pasific : **pa•cif•ic**
pasifier : **pac•i•fi•er**
pasifist : **pac•i•fist**
pasify : **pac•i•fy**
pasion : **pas•sion**
pasley : **pais•ley**
Passadena : **Pas•a•de•na**
pas•sage
passege : **pas•sage**
passifier : **pac•i•fi•er**
passige : **pas•sage**
pas•sion
passtime : **pas•time**
pastary : **past•ry**
pas•tel
pastell : **pas•tel**
past•er (one that pastes);
    pas•tor (clergy)
pastery : **past•ry**
pasterize : **pas•teur•ize**
pas•teur•ize
pas•time
pas•tor (clergy); **past•er** (one
    that pastes)
pastorize : **pas•teur•ize**
past•ry
pasttime : **pas•time**
pasturize : **pas•teur•ize**
patchy
pateo : **pa•tio**
paternety : **pa•ter•ni•ty**
paternitty : **pa•ter•ni•ty**
pa•ter•ni•ty
pathalogy : **path•ol•o•gy**
pa•thet•ic
pathetick : **pa•thet•ic**

pathettic : **pa•thet•ic**
patholigy : **path•ol•o•gy**
pathollogy : **path•ol•o•gy**
path•ol•o•gy
pa•tio
patreot : **pa•tri•ot**
pa•tri•ot
pa•trol
patroll : **pa•trol**
pa•tron•age
patronige : **pa•tron•age**
pattio : **pa•tio**
paturnity : **pa•ter•ni•ty**
paucety : **pau•ci•ty**
pau•ci•ty
pause (to hesitate); **paws**
    (animal feet)
pausity : **pau•ci•ty**
pavilian : **pa•vil•ion**
pa•vil•ion
pavillion : **pa•vil•ion**
pawm : **palm**
paws (animal feet); **pause** (to
    hesitate)
payed : **paid**
peace (absence of conflict);
    piece (portion)
peace•ful
peacefull : **peace•ful**
peachy
peal (to ring); **peel** (to strip)
pea•nut
peany : **pe•o•ny**
pear (fruit); **pair** (two things);
    pare (to cut away)
pearl (gem); **purl** (knitting
    stitch)
peas•ant
peaseful : **peace•ful**
peasent : **peas•ant**
peasint : **peas•ant**
peavish : **pee•vish**

pebbal : **peb·ble**
pebbel : **peb·ble**
peb·ble
peble : **peb·ble**
pe·can
peccan : **pe·can**
pe·cu·liar
peculier : **pe·cu·liar**
pedagree : **ped·i·gree**
ped·al (foot lever); **ped·dle** (to sell); **pet·al** (flower part)
ped·ant
peddant : **ped·ant**
peddestal : **ped·es·tal**
peddigree : **ped·i·gree**
ped·dle (to sell); **ped·al** (foot lever); **pet·al** (flower part)
pedent : **ped·ant**
ped·es·tal
pedestill : **ped·es·tal**
ped·i·gree
pedistal : **ped·es·tal**
peeceful : **peace·ful**
peechy : **peachy**
peel (to strip); **peal** (to ring)
peenut : **pea·nut**
peeple : **peo·ple**
peeriod : **pe·ri·od**
pee·vish
peice : **peace** (absence of conflict) *or* **piece** (portion)
peirce : **pierce**
peise : **peace** (absence of conflict) *or* **piece** (portion)
pekan : **pe·can**
pelecan : **pel·i·can**
pelet : **pel·let**
pel·i·can
pelikan : **pel·i·can**
pel·let
pellican : **pel·i·can**
pellit : **pel·let**

pelvice : **pel·vis**
pel·vis
pelviss : **pel·vis**
penacillin : **pen·i·cil·lin**
pe·nal
pen·al·ty
pen·ance
penanse : **pen·ance**
penatrate : **pen·e·trate**
pencel : **pen·cil**
pen·chant
penchent : **pen·chant**
penchint : **pen·chant**
pen·cil
pen·dant (*noun or adj.*); **pen·dent** (*adj. only*)
pen·dent (*adj. only*); **pen·dant** (*noun or adj.*)
pendulam : **pen·du·lum**
pendulem : **pen·du·lum**
pen·du·lum
pen·e·trate
pen·guin
penicilin : **pen·i·cil·lin**
penicillan : **pen·i·cil·lin**
pen·i·cil·lin
penil : **pe·nal**
penilty : **pen·al·ty**
penince : **pen·ance**
penisillin : **pen·i·cil·lin**
pennacle : **pin·na·cle**
pennal : **pe·nal**
pennalty : **pen·al·ty**
pennance : **pen·ance**
pennetrate : **pen·e·trate**
pennicillin : **pen·i·cil·lin**
Pennsilvania : **Penn·syl·va·nia**
Pennsylvanea : **Penn·syl·va·nia**
Penn·syl·va·nia
pensil : **pen·cil**
pentaggon : **pen·ta·gon**
pen·ta·gon

pentegon : **pen·ta·gon**
penulty : **pen·al·ty**
penut : **pea·nut**
peonny : **pe·o·ny**
pe·o·ny
peo·ple
percarious : **pre·car·i·ous**
per·ceive
per·cent·age
percentege : **per·cent·age**
percentige : **per·cent·age**
perceve : **per·ceive**
percieve : **per·ceive**
percintage : **per·cent·age**
percipitation : **pre·cip·i·ta·tion**
peremptary : **pe·remp·to·ry**
peremptery : **pe·remp·to·ry**
pe·remp·to·ry
perfarate : **per·fo·rate**
perfectable : **per·fect·ible**
perfectibal : **per·fect·ible**
per·fect·ible
perfirate : **per·fo·rate**
per·fo·rate
per·for·mance
performanse : **per·for·mance**
performence : **per·for·mance**
performince : **per·for·mance**
perfunctary : **per·func·to·ry**
per·func·to·ry
perfunctry : **per·func·to·ry**
perfunktory : **per·func·to·ry**
perichute : **para·chute**
periferal : **pe·riph·er·al**
perigon : **par·a·gon**
per·il
pe·ri·od
peripharel : **pe·riph·er·al**
pe·riph·er·al
peri·scope
per·ish (to cease to exist);
    par·ish (church community)

perity : **par·i·ty**
perjery : **per·ju·ry**
per·ju·ry
perl : **pearl** (gem) *or* **purl**
    (knitting stitch)
per·ma·nent
per·me·able
per·me·ate
permeible : **per·me·able**
permenant : **per·ma·nent**
permiabel : **per·me·able**
permiable : **per·me·able**
permiate : **per·me·ate**
perminent : **per·ma·nent**
permisible : **per·mis·si·ble**
permissable : **per·mis·si·ble**
per·mis·si·ble
peroose : **pe·ruse**
perouette : **pir·ou·ette**
per·pe·trate
perpettual : **per·pet·u·al**
per·pet·u·al
perpetuel : **per·pet·u·al**
perpitrate : **per·pe·trate**
perril : **per·il**
perriod : **pe·ri·od**
perriscope : **peri·scope**
perruse : **pe·ruse**
persacute : **per·se·cute**
perscription : **pre·scrip·tion**
perseccute : **per·se·cute**
per·se·cute
persentage : **per·cent·age**
perserve : **pre·serve**
perserverance : **per·se·ver·ance**
perseveirance : **per·se·ver·ance**
per·se·ver·ance
perseveranse : **per·se·ver·ance**
perseverence : **per·se·ver·ance**
persicute : **per·se·cute**
per·son·age

per·son·al (private);
  per·son·nel (employees)
personege : **per·son·age**
personige : **per·son·age**
per·son·nel (employees);
  per·son·al (private)
per·suade
persuaid : **per·suade**
persue : **pur·sue**
persume : **pre·sume**
perswade : **per·suade**
pertanent : **per·ti·nent**
pertenant : **per·ti·nent**
perterb : **per·turb**
pertinant : **per·ti·nent**
per·ti·nent
pertinnent : **per·ti·nent**
per·turb
pe·ruse
peruze : **pe·ruse**
pervacive : **per·va·sive**
pervaseve : **per·va·sive**
per·va·sive
pervassive : **per·va·sive**
per·vert
pesimism : **pes·si·mism**
pesimist : **pes·si·mist**
pessamism : **pes·si·mism**
pessamist : **pes·si·mist**
pessant : **peas·ant**
pessemism : **pes·si·mism**
pessemist : **pes·si·mist**
pessent : **peas·ant**
pessimest : **pes·si·mist**
pes·si·mism
pes·si·mist
pessimizm : **pes·si·mism**
pessint : **peas·ant**
pestalence : **pes·ti·lence**
pestelence : **pes·ti·lence**
pestilance : **pes·ti·lence**
pes·ti·lence

pestilense : **pes·ti·lence**
pet·al (flower part); **ped·al**
  (foot lever); **ped·dle** (to sell)
peteet : **pe·tite**
petete : **pe·tite**
pe·tite
petoonia : **pe·tu·nia**
petrafy : **pet·ri·fy**
petrefy : **pet·ri·fy**
petriffy : **pet·ri·fy**
pet·ri·fy
pe·tro·leum
petroliam : **pe·tro·leum**
petrolium : **pe·tro·leum**
petrollium : **pe·tro·leum**
pettete : **pe·tite**
pettite : **pe·tite**
pettrify : **pet·ri·fy**
pettroleum : **pe·tro·leum**
pettulant : **pet·u·lant**
pettunia : **pe·tu·nia**
pet·u·lant
petulent : **pet·u·lant**
pe·tu·nia
petunya : **pe·tu·nia**
peuter : **pew·ter**
pew·ter
phalic : **phal·lic**
phal·lic
phantastic : **fan·tas·tic**
phan·ta·sy *or* **fan·ta·sy**
phan·tom
phar·ma·cy
pharmicy : **phar·ma·cy**
pharmissy : **phar·ma·cy**
pheas·ant
pheasco : **fi·as·co**
pheasent : **pheas·ant**
pheasint : **pheas·ant**
pheeble : **fee·ble**
Phenix : **Phoe·nix**
phe·nom·e·nal

phe·nom·e·non
phenominal : phe·nom·e·nal
phenominnal : phe·nom·e·nal
phenominnon : phe·nom·e·non
phenominon : phe·nom·e·non
phenommenal : phe·nom·e·nal
phenommenon :
   phe·nom·e·non
Pheonix : Phoe·nix
phesant : pheas·ant
phesible : fea·si·ble
phessant : pheas·ant
Philapino : Fil·i·pi·no
philibuster : fi·li·bus·ter
Philipino : Fil·i·pi·no
Phil·ip·pines
phillabuster : fi·li·bus·ter
Phillipines : Phil·ip·pines
Phillipino : Fil·i·pi·no
Phillippines : Phil·ip·pines
philoligy : phi·lol·o·gy
philollogy : phi·lol·o·gy
phi·lol·o·gy
philosiphy : phi·los·o·phy
phi·los·o·phy
philossophy : phi·los·o·phy
phinomenal : phe·nom·e·nal
phinomenon : phe·nom·e·non
phisical : phys·i·cal
phisician : phy·si·cian
phisics : phys·ics
phission : fis·sion
phobea : pho·bia
pho·bia
Phoe·nix
pho·net·ic
phonetick : pho·net·ic
phonettic : pho·net·ic
phosel : fos·sil
phosferris : phos·pho·rous
   (adj.) or phos·pho·rus
   (noun)

phosforus : phos·pho·rous
   (adj.) or phos·phor·us
   (noun)
phos·pho·rous (adj.);
   phos·pho·rus (noun)
phos·pho·rus (noun);
   phos·pho·rous (adj.)
phossil : fos·sil
photografy : pho·tog·ra·phy
pho·tog·ra·phy
physecal : phys·i·cal
phys·i·cal
phy·si·cian
physicion : phy·si·cian
physicks : phys·ics
physicle : phys·i·cal
phys·ics
physikal : phys·i·cal
physission : phy·si·cian
pianeer : pi·o·neer
piatza : pi·az·za (veranda) or
   piz·za (pie)
piaza : pi·az·za (veranda) or
   piz·za (pie)
pi·az·za (veranda); piz·za (pie)
piccalo : pic·co·lo
piccilo : pic·co·lo
pic·co·lo
pickal : pick·le
pickel : pick·le
pick·et
pickilo : pic·co·lo
pickit : pick·et
pick·le
picknic : pic·nic
picknick : pic·nic
picknicked : pic·nicked
pic·nic
picniced : pic·nicked
picnick : pic·nic
pic·nicked
picolo : pic·co·lo

428

pictoreal : **pic•to•ri•al**
pic•to•ri•al
picturial : **pic•to•ri•al**
pid•gin (language); **pi•geon**
 (bird)
piece (portion); **peace** (absence
 of conflict)
pierce
pierouette : **pir•ou•ette**
pietty : **pi•ety**
pi•ety
pi•geon (bird); **pid•gin**
 (language)
piggin : **pid•gin** (language) or
 pi•geon (bird)
pigion : **pid•gin** (language) or
 pi•geon (bird)
pigmy : **pyg•my**
pijamas : **pa•ja•mas**
pilar : **pil•lar**
pilet : **pi•lot**
pilgrem : **pil•grim**
pil•grim
pilgrum : **pil•grim**
pil•lar
pillary : **pil•lo•ry**
piller : **pil•lar**
pillery : **pil•lo•ry**
pillgrim : **pil•grim**
pil•lo•ry
pilory : **pil•lo•ry**
pi•lot
pinacle : **pin•na•cle**
pinchant : **pen•chant**
pindulem : **pen•du•lum**
pineer : **pi•o•neer**
pinguin : **pen•guin**
pin•na•cle
pinnecal : **pin•na•cle**
pinnical : **pin•na•cle**
pintagon : **pen•ta•gon**
pi•o•neer

pioneir : **pi•o•neer**
pionere : **pi•o•neer**
pi•ra•cy
pirassy : **pi•ra•cy**
pi•rate
pirce : **pierce**
piret : **pi•rate**
pirete : **pi•rate**
piricy : **pi•ra•cy**
pirissy : **pi•ra•cy**
pirl : **pearl** (gem) or **purl**
 (knitting stitch)
pirmeate : **per•me•ate**
piroette : **pir•ou•ette**
piromaniac : **py•ro•ma•ni•ac**
pir•ou•ette
pisston : **pis•ton**
pistal : **pis•til** (flower part) or
 pis•tol (handgun)
pistan : **pis•ton**
pisten : **pis•ton**
pis•til (flower part); **pis•tol**
 (handgun)
pis•tol (handgun); **pis•til**
 (flower part)
pis•ton
pitaful : **piti•ful**
pit•e•ous
pithon : **py•thon**
piti•able
piti•ful
pitious : **pit•e•ous**
Pitsburg : **Pitts•burgh**
pittiful : **piti•ful**
Pittsberg : **Pitts•burgh**
Pittsburg : **Pitts•burgh**
Pitts•burgh
pittuitary : **pit•u•itary**
pituetary : **pit•u•itary**
pit•u•itary
pituitery : **pit•u•itary**
pitunia : **pe•tu•nia**

pityable : **piti·able**
pityful : **piti·ful**
pityous : **pit·e·ous**
pivat : **piv·ot**
pivet : **piv·ot**
piv·ot
pivvot : **piv·ot**
piz·za (pie); **pi·az·za** (veranda)
plac·ard
placcid : **plac·id**
placed : **plac·id**
plac·id
plackard : **plac·ard**
plackerd : **plac·ard**
plagerism : **pla·gia·rism**
pla·gia·rism
plagierism : **pla·gia·rism**
plaguerism : **pla·gia·rism**
planed (leveled); **planned**
  (organized)
plan·et
planetariem : **plan·e·tar·i·um**
plan·e·tar·i·um
planetarrium : **plan·e·tar·i·um**
planeterium : **plan·e·tar·i·um**
planit : **plan·et**
planitarium : **plan·e·tar·i·um**
planned (organized); **planed**
  (leveled)
plannet : **plan·et**
plannetarium : **plan·e·tar·i·um**
plasstic : **plas·tic**
plastec : **plas·tic**
plas·tic
plastick : **plas·tic**
platanum : **plat·i·num**
platatude : **plat·i·tude**
pla·teau
platenum : **plat·i·num**
plat·i·num
plat·i·tude
pla·toon

platteau : **pla·teau**
plattinum : **plat·i·num**
plattitude : **plat·i·tude**
plattoon : **pla·toon**
plattow : **pla·teau**
platune : **pla·toon**
plausable : **plau·si·ble**
plauseble : **plau·si·ble**
plau·si·ble
playright : **play·wright**
play·wright
playwrite : **play·wright**
plead
pleas·ant
please
pleasent : **pleas·ant**
pleasint : **pleas·ant**
plea·sure
pleat
plebbisite : **pleb·i·scite**
pleb·i·scite
pledge
pleebiscite : **pleb·i·scite**
pleed : **plead**
pleese : **please**
pleet : **pleat**
pleez : **please**
plege : **pledge**
plenatude : **plen·i·tude**
plen·i·tude *or* **plen·ti·tude**
plentatude : **plen·i·tude**
plen·ti·tude *or* **plen·i·tude**
plentytude : **plen·i·tude**
pleshure : **plea·sure**
plessant : **plea·sant**
plessure : **plea·sure**
plesure : **plea·sure**
pli·able
pli·ant
plibiscite : **pleb·i·scite**
plible : **pli·able**
plient : **pli·ant**

Plimouth : **Plym·outh**
plum·age
plumb·er
plumb·ing
plumeage : **plum·age**
plumer : **plumb·er**
plumige : **plum·age**
plummer : **plumb·er**
plumming : **plumb·ing**
plu·ral
plurel : **plu·ral**
plurral : **plu·ral**
plurrel : **plu·ral**
plyable : **pli·able**
Plymath : **Plym·outh**
Plymeth : **Plym·outh**
Plym·outh
pneu·mat·ic
pneumattic : **pneu·mat·ic**
pneumoania : **pneu·mo·nia**
pneu·mo·nia
pnuematic : **pneu·mat·ic**
pnuemonia : **pneu·mo·nia**
pnumatic : **pneu·mat·ic**
pnumonia : **pneu·mo·nia**
poadium : **po·di·um**
poddium : **po·di·um**
po·di·um
po·em
pogoda : **pa·go·da**
poi·gnant
poignent : **poi·gnant**
poiniant : **poi·gnant**
poinsetta : **poin·set·tia**
poin·set·tia
poisen : **poi·son**
poi·son
poisson : **poi·son**
po·lar
polaritty : **po·lar·i·ty**
po·lar·i·ty
polarrity : **po·lar·i·ty**

polatics : **pol·i·tics**
polece : **po·lice**
po·lem·ic
polemick : **po·lem·ic**
polemmic : **po·lem·ic**
poleo : **po·lio**
poler : **po·lar**
polerity : **po·lar·i·ty**
po·lice
pol·i·cy
polimic : **po·lem·ic**
po·lio
polise : **po·lice**
polissy : **pol·i·cy**
polisy : **pol·i·cy**
politicks : **pol·i·tics**
pol·i·tics
pollanate : **pol·li·nate**
pollarity : **po·lar·i·ty**
pol·len
pollenate : **pol·li·nate**
pollice : **po·lice**
pollicy : **pol·i·cy**
pollin : **pol·len**
pol·li·nate
pollitics : **pol·i·tics**
pome : **po·em**
pomp·ous
pompus : **pomp·ous**
ponteff : **pon·tiff**
pon·tiff
pontive : **pon·tiff**
poodel : **poo·dle**
poo·dle
poperrie : **pot·pour·ri**
pop·lar (tree); **pop·u·lar**
  (accepted)
popler : **pop·lar** (tree) *or*
  pop·u·lar (accepted)
poporry : **pot·pour·ri**
poppulace : **pop·u·lace** (*noun*)
  or **pop·u·lous** (*adj.*)

poppulous : **pop•u•lace** (*noun*) or **pop•u•lous** (*adj.*)
populace (*noun*); **pop•u•lous** (*adj.*)
pop•u•lar (*accepted*); **pop•lar** (*tree*)
populise : **pop•u•lace** (*noun*) or **pop•u•lous** (*adj.*)
pop•u•lous (*adj.*); **pop•u•lace** (*noun*)
popurrie : **pot•pour•ri**
por•ce•lain
porcelin : **por•ce•lain**
porcilain : **por•ce•lain**
poreous : **po•rous**
poridge : **por•ridge**
po•rous
porrage : **por•ridge**
porrege : **por•ridge**
por•ridge
porrige : **por•ridge**
porrous : **po•rous**
porselin : **por•ce•lain**
por•ta•ble
portaco : **por•ti•co**
por•tal
portel : **por•tal**
portfoleo : **port•fo•lio**
port•fo•lio
portfollio : **port•fo•lio**
portible : **por•ta•ble**
porticko : **por•ti•co**
por•ti•co
Porto Rico : **Puer•to Ri•co**
por•trait
portrate : **por•trait**
portrayt : **por•trait**
portret : **por•trait**
Portugeese : **Por•tu•guese**
Portugese : **Por•tu•guese**
Portugeze : **Por•tu•guese**
Por•tu•guese

posative : **pos•i•tive**
posess : **pos•sess**
posible : **pos•si•ble**
pos•i•tive
possable : **pos•si•ble**
pos•se
pos•sess
pos•si•ble
possitive : **pos•i•tive**
possy : **pos•se**
post•age
post•al
postarity : **pos•ter•i•ty**
postege : **post•age**
postel : **post•al**
posteritty : **pos•ter•i•ty**
pos•ter•i•ty
posterrity : **pos•ter•i•ty**
postige : **post•age**
po•ta•ble
po•ta•to
potatoe : **po•ta•to**
po•ta•toes
potatos : **po•ta•toes**
potible : **po•ta•ble**
potperrie : **pot•pour•ri**
pot•pour•ri
potpurrie : **pot•pour•ri**
pottable : **po•ta•ble**
povarty : **pov•er•ty**
pov•er•ty
povirty : **pov•er•ty**
poyson : **poi•son**
pracktical : **prac•ti•cal**
practacal : **prac•ti•cal**
prac•ti•cal
practicle : **prac•ti•cal**
prafer : **pre•fer**
prai•rie
prarie : **prai•rie**
preach

precareous : **pre·car·i·ous**
pre·car·i·ous
pre·cede (to go before);
   pro·ceed (to continue)
prec·e·dent (that which comes
   before); **pres·i·dent** (one who
   presides)
precepice : **prec·i·pice**
pre·cious
precipace : **prec·i·pice**
precipatation : **pre·cip·i·ta·tion**
prec·i·pice
pre·cip·i·ta·tion
precippation : **pre·cip·i·ta·tion**
predater : **pred·a·tor**
pred·a·tor
preditor : **pred·a·tor**
predjudice : **prej·u·dice**
preech : **preach**
pre-empt
preemptory : **pe·remp·to·ry**
preest : **priest**
pref·ace
pre·fer
prefface : **pref·ace**
preffer : **pre·fer**
prefice : **pref·ace**
prefiss : **pref·ace**
prefundity : **pro·fun·di·ty**
preg·nant
pregnent : **preg·nant**
pregnint : **preg·nant**
preimpt : **pre-empt**
preist : **priest**
prejewdice : **prej·u·dice**
prejudace : **prej·u·dice**
prej·u·dice
prejudiss : **prej·u·dice**
premeer : **pre·mier** (prime
   minister) *or* **pre·miere** (first
   performance)

premeir : **pre·mier** (prime
   minister) *or* **pre·miere** (first
   performance)
premere : **pre·mier** (prime
   minister) *or* **pre·miere** (first
   performance)
pre·mier (prime minister);
   pre·miere (first performance)
pre·miere (first performance);
   pre·mier (prime minister)
prepair : **pre·pare**
pre·pare
prescious : **pre·cious**
pre·scrip·tion
pres·ence (*noun*, being
   present); **pre·sents** (*verb*,
   introduces); **pres·ents** (*noun*,
   gifts)
pre·serve
pres·i·dent (one who presides);
   pre·ce·dent (that which
   comes before)
presious : **pre·cious**
presipice : **prec·i·pice**
presipitation : **pre·cip·i·ta·tion**
pressipice : **prec·i·pice**
presstige : **pres·tige**
prestege : **pres·tige**
presteze : **pres·tige**
pres·tige
pre·sume
presumetuous :
   pre·sump·tu·ous
pre·sump·tu·ous
presumtuous : **pre·sump·tu·ous**
pretence : **pre·tense**
pre·tense
pretsel : **pret·zel**
pret·zel
pretzell : **pret·zel**
pretzil : **pret·zel**
pre·vail

prevailent : **prev·a·lent**
prevale : **pre·vail**
prev·a·lent
prevelant : **prev·a·lent**
prevert : **per·vert**
previlent : **prev·a·lent**
priempt : **pre-empt**
prier : **pri·or**
priest
primative : **prim·i·tive**
prim·i·tive
primmitive : **prim·i·tive**
principal (*noun,* one in charge;
  adj., most important);
  prin·ci·ple (rule, standard)
principle (rule, standard);
  prin·ci·pal (*noun,* one in
  charge; *adj.,* most important)
pri·or
priorety : **pri·or·i·ty**
pri·or·i·ty
priorrity : **pri·or·i·ty**
prisen : **pris·on**
prism
pris·on
prisson : **pris·on**
pri·va·cy
privalege : **priv·i·lege**
pri·vate
privelege : **priv·i·lege**
privet (bush); **pri·vate** (personal)
privicy : **pri·va·cy**
priviledge : **priv·i·lege**
priv·i·lege
privilige : **priv·i·lege**
privissy : **pri·va·cy**
prizm : **prism**
prizzen : **pris·on**
prob·a·ble
probible : **prob·a·ble**
prob·lem
problim : **prob·lem**

problum : **prob·lem**
pro·ce·dure
pro·ceed (to continue);
  pre·cede (to go before)
proceedure : **pro·ce·dure**
procidure : **pro·ce·dure**
procktor : **proc·tor**
pro·claim
proclaimation : **proc·la·ma·tion**
proc·la·ma·tion
proclame : **pro·claim**
proclemation : **proc·la·ma·tion**
proclimation : **proc·la·ma·tion**
procrasstinate : **pro·cras·ti·nate**
procrastentate : **pro·cras·ti·nate**
pro·cras·ti·nate
procter : **proc·tor**
proc·tor
proddigal : **prod·i·gal**
prodegy : **prod·i·gy**
prodicle : **prod·i·gal**
prod·i·gal
prodigle : **prod·i·gal**
prod·i·gy
prodogy : **prod·i·gy**
pro·duce
produse : **pro·duce**
profacy : **proph·e·cy** (*noun*) *or*
  proph·e·sy (*verb*)
profain : **pro·fane**
pro·fane
profanety : **pro·fan·i·ty**
pro·fan·i·ty
profannity : **pro·fan·i·ty**
profesor : **pro·fes·sor**
professer : **pro·fes·sor**
pro·fes·sor
profet : **prof·it**
proffit : **prof·it**
prof·it
profoundity : **pro·fun·di·ty**
profundety : **pro·fun·di·ty**

pro·fun·di·ty
prohibbit : pro·hib·it
prohibet : pro·hib·it
pro·hib·it
proliffic : pro·lif·ic
pro·lif·ic
promanent : prom·i·nent
prom·e·nade
promice : prom·ise
prominade : prom·e·nade
prominant : prom·i·nent
prom·i·nent
prom·ise
promisory : prom·is·so·ry
promiss : prom·ise
prom·is·so·ry
prommenade : prom·e·nade
promminent : prom·i·nent
prommise : prom·ise
pronounciation :
    pro·nun·ci·a·tion
pro·nun·ci·a·tion
pro·pa·gan·da
propeganda : pro·pa·gan·da
propencity : pro·pen·si·ty
pro·pen·si·ty
prophacy : proph·e·cy (*noun*)
    or proph·e·sy (verb)
proph·e·cy (*noun*); proph·e·sy
    (*verb*)
proph·e·sy (*verb*); proph·e·cy
    (*noun*)
prophissy : proph·e·cy (*noun*)
    or proph·e·sy (*verb*)
propiganda : pro·pa·gan·da
propinsity : pro·pen·si·ty
proppaganda : pro·pa·gan·da
pros·e·cute
prosicute : pros·e·cute
pros·per·ous
prospirous : pros·per·ous
prossicute : pros·e·cute

protacol : pro·to·col
Prot·es·tant
Protestint : Prot·es·tant
Protistant : Prot·es·tant
protocall : pro·to·col
pro·to·col
prowace : prow·ess
prow·ess
prowice : prow·ess
prowiss : prow·ess
proximety : prox·im·i·ty
prox·im·i·ty
proximmity : prox·im·i·ty
psalm
psam : psalm
pseudanym : pseu·do·nym
pseudonim : pseu·do·nym
pseu·do·nym
psiche : psy·che
psichiatrist : psy·chi·a·trist
psichic : psy·chic
psichologist : psy·chol·o·gist
psichology : psy·chol·o·gy
psudonym : pseu·do·nym
psuedonym : pseu·do·nym
psychalogist : psy·chol·o·gist
psychalogy : psy·chol·o·gy
psy·che
psy·chi·a·trist
psy·chic
psycholagist : psy·chol·o·gist
psycholagy : psy·chol·o·gy
psychollogist : psy·chol·o·gist
psychollogy : psy·chol·o·gy
psy·chol·o·gist
psy·chol·o·gy
psychyatrist : psy·chi·a·trist
psycologist : psy·chol·o·gist
psycology : psy·chol·o·gy
ptarodactyl : ptero·dac·tyl
pteradactyl : ptero·dac·tyl
pteridactyl : ptero·dac·tyl

pterodactile : **ptero•dac•tyl**
pterodactill : **ptero•dac•tyl**
ptero•dac•tyl
ptomain : **pto•maine**
pto•maine
ptomane : **pto•maine**
Puarto Rico : **Puer•to Ri•co**
publacize : **pub•li•cize**
publicety : **pub•lic•i•ty**
publicise : **pub•li•cize**
pub•li•cist
publicitty : **pub•lic•i•ty**
pub•lic•i•ty
pub•li•cize
publisist : **pub•li•cist**
publisity : **pub•lic•i•ty**
puddel : **pud•dle**
pud•dle
pudle : **poo•dle** (dog) *or*
  pud•dle (water)
Puer•to Ri•co
pueter : **pew•ter**
pullmonary : **pul•mo•nary**
pulmanary : **pul•mo•nary**
pul•mo•nary
pulmonery : **pul•mo•nary**
pulpet : **pul•pit**
pul•pit
pumace : **pum•ice**
pum•ice
pumiss : **pum•ice**
pumkin : **pump•kin**
pummice : **pum•ice**
pumpken : **pump•kin**
pump•kin
pundet : **pun•dit**
pun•dit
punesh : **pun•ish**
pun•gent

pungint : **pun•gent**
pun•ish
punken : **pump•kin**
punkin : **pump•kin**
punnish : **pun•ish**
pupel : **pu•pil**
pu•pil
pup•pet
puppil : **pu•pil**
puppit : **pup•pet**
purety : **pu•ri•ty**
puriffy : **pu•ri•fy**
pu•ri•fy
pu•ri•tan
puriten : **pu•ri•tan**
puritty : **pu•ri•ty**
pu•ri•ty
purjury : **per•ju•ry**
purl (knitting stitch); **pearl**
  (gem)
purpetrate : **per•pe•trate**
purrify : **pu•ri•fy**
purritan : **pu•ri•tan**
purrity : **pu•ri•ty**
pursacute : **per•se•cute**
pursuade : **per•suade**
pur•sue
purterb : **per•turb**
putrafy : **pu•tre•fy**
pu•tre•fy
putriffy : **pu•tre•fy**
putrify : **pu•tre•fy**
puzle : **puz•zle**
puzzal : **puz•zle**
puzzel : **puz•zle**
puz•zle
pyg•my
py•ro•ma•ni•ac
py•thon

Q

Quabec : **Que·bec**
quack
quackary : **quack·ery**
quack·ery
quackry : **quack·ery**
quadrain : **qua·train**
quadrangel : **quad·ran·gle**
quad·ran·gle
quad·rant
quadrill : **qua·drille**
qua·drille
quadruble : **qua·dru·ple**
quadrublet : **qua·dru·plet**
qua·dru·ple
quaf : **quaff**
quafe : **quaff**
quaff
quaggmire : **quag·mire**
quagmier : **quag·mire**
quag·mire
quagmyre : **quag·mire**
quaik : **quake**
quail
quaint
quaisar : **qua·sar**
quaiver : **qua·ver**
quak : **quack**
quake
qualafication : **qual·i·fi·ca·tion**
qualafied : **qual·i·fied**
qualafy : **qual·i·fy**
qualaty : **qual·i·ty**
quale : **quail**
qualefy : **qual·i·fy**
qualifacation : **qual·i·fi·ca·tion**
qual·i·fi·ca·tion
qual·i·fied
qual·i·fy
qual·i·ty
quallification : **qual·i·fi·ca·tion**

quallified : **qual·i·fied**
quallify : **qual·i·fy**
quallity : **qual·i·ty**
qualm
quam : **qualm**
quan·da·ry
quandery : **quan·da·ry**
quandrent : **quad·rant**
quandry : **quan·da·ry**
quanity : **quan·ti·ty**
quantafy : **quan·ti·fy**
quante : **quaint**
quantety : **quan·ti·ty**
quan·ti·fy
quan·ti·ty
quantom : **quan·tum**
quan·tum
quaranteen : **quar·an·tine**
quar·an·tine
quarel : **quar·rel**
quareled : **quar·reled**
quareling : **quar·rel·ing**
quarentine : **quar·an·tine**
quarintine : **quar·an·tine**
quarl : **quar·rel**
quar·rel
quar·reled or **quar·relled**
quar·rel·ing or **quar·rel·ling**
quar·relled or **quar·reled**
quar·rel·ling or **quar·rel·ing**
quarrey : **quar·ry**
quar·ry
quart
quar·ter
quarts (*plur.*); **quartz** (mineral)
quartz (mineral); **quarts** (*plur.*)
quary : **quar·ry**
qua·sar
quasarre : **qua·sar**
quaser : **qua·sar**

437

quater : **quar·ter**
qua·train
quatrane : **qua·train**
quatrangle : **quad·ran·gle**
qua·ver
quawlified : **qual·i·fied**
quawlify : **qual·i·fy**
quay (wharf); **key** (for a lock)
quazar : **qua·sar**
Qubec : **Que·bec**
que : **queue** (pigtail; line) *or*
  cue (signal; poolstick)
quean : **queen**
quear : **queer**
queary : **que·ry**
queasaly : **quea·si·ly**
quea·si·ly
queasly : **quea·si·ly**
quea·sy
queazy : **quea·sy**
Que·bec
Quebeck : **Que·bec**
queeche : **quiche**
queen
queer
queery : **que·ry**
queesh : **quiche**
queesly : **quea·si·ly**
queesy : **quea·sy**
queezy : **quea·sy**
queishe : **quiche**
quene : **queen**
quere : **queer**
querie : **que·ry**
querry : **que·ry**
que·ry
questin : **ques·tion**
ques·tion
questionaire : **ques·tion·naire**
questionnair : **ques·tion·naire**
ques·tion·naire

queue (pigtail; line); **cue**
  (signal; poolstick)
quey : **quay**
quiche
quick
quicksotic : **quix·o·tic**
quiescant : **qui·es·cent**
qui·es·cent
quiesent : **qui·es·cent**
quiessent : **qui·es·cent**
qui·et (silent); **quite** (entirely)
quik : **quick**
quillt : **quilt**
quilt
quinntet : **quin·tet**
quintecence : **quin·tes·sence**
quintescence : **quin·tes·sence**
quintesence : **quin·tes·sence**
quin·tes·sence
quintessense : **quin·tes·sence**
quin·tet
quintette : **quin·tet**
quior : **choir**
quire : **choir**
quiseen : **cui·sine**
quisine : **cui·sine**
quis·ling
quite (entirely); **qui·et** (silent)
quivver : **quiv·er**
quix·ot·ic
quixottic : **quix·ot·ic**
quizacal : **quiz·zi·cal**
quizes : **quiz·zes**
quizical : **quiz·zi·cal**
quizine : **cui·sine**
quizling : **quis·ling**
quizotic : **quix·ot·ic**
quizzacal : **quiz·zi·cal**
quiz·zi·cal
quoat : **quote**
quoatable : **quot·able**
quoatient : **quo·tient**

quoff : **quaff**
quoram : **quo•rum**
quorom : **quo•rum**
quorrey : **quar•ry**
quorrum : **quo•rum**
quort : **quart**
quo•rum
quoshent : **quo•tient**
quotabile : **quot•able**
quot•able
quoteable : **quot•able**
quotent : **quo•tient**
quo•tient
qwack : **quack**
qwackery : **quack•ery**
qwadrangle : **quad•ran•gle**
qwadrant : **quad•rant**
qwadruple : **qua•dru•ple**
qwadruplet : **qua•dru•plet**
qwaff : **quaff**
qwagmire : **quag•mire**

qwaint : **quaint**
qwake : **quake**
qwalified : **qual•i•fied**
qwalify : **qual•i•fy**
qwality : **qual•i•ty**
qwandary : **quan•da•ry**
qwantify : **quan•ti•fy**
qwantity : **quan•ti•ty**
qwarantine : **quar•an•tine**
qwarrel : **quar•rel**
qwarreling : **quar•rel•ing**
qwarry : **quar•ry**
qwart : **quart**
qwarter : **quar•ter**
qwartz : **quartz**
qwasar : **qua•sar**
qwaver : **qua•ver**
qweasily : **quea•si•ly**
qweasy : **quea•sy**
Qwebec : **Que•bec**
qwote : **quote**

R

rabbed : **ra•bid**
rab•bi
rabbid : **ra•bid**
rabi : **rab•bi**
ra•bid
rac•coon
raccune : **rac•coon**
rac•ism
rack•et
rackit : **rack•et**
rackonteur : **ra•con•teur**
ra•con•teur
racontoor : **ra•con•teur**
racontuer : **ra•con•teur**
racoon : **rac•coon**
racunteur : **ra•con•teur**
raddish : **rad•ish**
radeator : **ra•di•a•tor**
radesh : **rad•ish**
radiam : **ra•di•um**
ra•di•ance
radianse : **ra•di•ance**
radiater : **ra•di•a•tor**
ra•di•a•tor
radience : **ra•di•ance**
radiense : **ra•di•ance**
rad•ish
ra•di•um
rag•ged
raggid : **rag•ged**
raign : **reign**
rai•ment
raindeer : **rein•deer**
rainment : **rai•ment**
raisen : **rai•sin**
rai•sin
rament : **rai•ment**
ram•pant
rampent : **ram•pant**
rampint : **ram•pant**

ranced : **ran•cid**
rancer : **ran•cor**
ran•cid
ran•cor
rancore : **ran•cor**
randam : **ran•dom**
randem : **ran•dom**
randim : **ran•dom**
ran•dom
randum : **ran•dom**
rangler : **wran•gler**
rankor : **ran•cor**
ransid : **ran•cid**
raon : **ray•on**
rap•id
raport : **rap•port**
rappid : **rap•id**
rappore : **rap•port**
rap•port
rappsody : **rhap•so•dy**
rapsady : **rhap•so•dy**
rapsody : **rhap•so•dy**
rarafied : **rar•efied**
rar•efied
rarety : **rar•i•ty**
rarified : **rar•efied**
raritty : **rar•i•ty**
rar•i•ty
rarrity : **rar•i•ty**
rasberry : **rasp•ber•ry**
ras•cal
rasen : **rai•sin**
rasin : **rai•sin**
rasism : **rac•ism**
raskal : **ras•cal**
raskel : **ras•cal**
rasor : **ra•zor**
raspbarry : **rasp•ber•ry**
rasp•ber•ry
raspbery : **rasp•ber•ry**

rasscal : **ras·cal**
rassel : **wres·tle**
rassle : **wres·tle**
ratafy : **rat·i·fy**
ratefy : **rat·i·fy**
ratiffy : **rat·i·fy**
rat·i·fy
ratler : **rat·tler**
rattify : **rat·i·fy**
rattlar : **rat·tler**
rat·tler
raught : **wrought**
rav·age
raveen : **ra·vine**
ravege : **rav·age**
ravene : **ra·vine**
raveoli : **rav·i·o·li**
ravesh : **rav·ish**
ravige : **rav·age**
ra·vine
raviole : **rav·i·o·li**
rav·i·o·li
ravioly : **rav·i·o·li**
rav·ish
ravvage : **rav·age**
ravvish : **rav·ish**
ray·on
razer : **ra·zor**
ra·zor
razzberry : **rasp·ber·ry**
razzor : **ra·zor**
reacter : **re·ac·tor**
re·ac·tor
read (book); **red** (color); **reed** (grass)
read·able
readible : **read·able**
readolent : **red·o·lent**
ready
reak : **reek** (to stink) *or* **wreak** (to inflict)
realise (*Brit.*) : **re·al·ize**

re·al·ize
realm
realter : **re·al·tor**
re·al·tor
reap
reasin : **rea·son**
rea·son
reath : **wreath** (*noun*) *or* **wreathe** (*verb*)
reathe : **wreath** (*noun*) *or* **wreathe** (*verb*)
rebelion : **re·bel·lion**
rebellian : **re·bel·lion**
re·bel·lion
re·but·tal
rebuttel : **re·but·tal**
rebuttle : **re·but·tal**
recalcetrant : **re·cal·ci·trant**
re·cal·ci·trant
recalcitrent : **re·cal·ci·trant**
recalsitrant : **re·cal·ci·trant**
reccognize : **re·cog·nize**
reccommend : **rec·om·mend**
recead : **re·cede**
re·cede
receed : **re·cede**
re·ceipt
receit : **re·ceipt**
re·ceive
recepe : **rec·i·pe**
re·cep·ta·cle
receptecle : **re·cep·ta·cle**
receptical : **re·cep·ta·cle**
recepticle : **re·cep·ta·cle**
recete : **re·ceipt**
receve : **re·ceive**
rech : **retch** (to vomit) *or* **wretch** (miserable one)
reciept : **re·ceipt**
recieve : **re·ceive**
rec·i·pe
recipiant : **re·cip·i·ent**

re·cip·i·ent
recippy : rec·i·pe
reciprical : re·cip·ro·cal
re·cip·ro·cal
reciprocitty : re·ci·proc·i·ty
re·ci·proc·i·ty
reciproety : re·ci·proc·i·ty
reciprosity : re·ci·proc·i·ty
reciprossity : re·ci·proc·i·ty
re·cit·al
re·cite
recitel : re·cit·al
recitle : re·cit·al
reck : wreak (to inflict) *or*
   wreck (to destroy)
reckage : wreck·age
reckondite : re·con·dite
reckonize : rec·og·nize
recognise (*Brit.*) : rec·og·nize
rec·og·nize
recomend : rec·om·mend
rec·om·mend
recompence : rec·om·pense
rec·om·pense
recompince : rec·om·pense
recompinse : rec·om·pense
rec·on·cile
recondight : re·con·dite
re·con·dite
reconsile : re·con·cile
recorse : re·course
recource : re·course
re·course
recovary : re·cov·ery
re·cov·ery
re·cruit
recrut : re·cruit
recrute : re·cruit
rectafy : rec·ti·fy
rectatude : rec·ti·tude
rectefy : rec·ti·fy
rectetude : rec·ti·tude

rectiffy : rec·ti·fy
rec·ti·fy
rectitood : rec·ti·tude
rec·ti·tude
recumpense : rec·om·pense
recurence : re·cur·rence
recurrance : re·cur·rence
re·cur·rence
red (color); read (book)
redalent : red·o·lent
reddolent : red·o·lent
reddress : re·dress
redduce : re·duce
reddy : ready
redeam : re·deem
re·deem
redeme : re·deem
rediculous : ri·dic·u·lous
red·o·lent
redolint : red·o·lent
re·dress
re·duce
re·dun·dant
redundent : re·dun·dant
reduse : re·duce
reed (grass); read (book)
reek (to stink); wreak (to
   inflict)
reelize : re·al·ize
reeltor : re·al·tor
reep : reap
reeson : rea·son
referance : ref·er·ence
ref·er·ee
ref·er·ence
referense : ref·er·ence
ref·er·ent
referie : ref·er·ee
referint : ref·er·ent
referrence : ref·er·ence
referrent : ref·er·ent
refery : ref·er·ee

refferee : **ref•er•ee**
refference : **ref•er•ence**
refirent : **ref•er•ent**
refrigarator : **re•frig•er•a•tor**
refrigerater : **re•frig•er•a•tor**
re•frig•er•a•tor
refriggerator : **re•frig•er•a•tor**
refrijerator : **re•frig•er•a•tor**
re•fus•al
re•fuse (*verb*); **ref•use** (*noun*)
refusel : **re•fus•al**
refussal : **re•fus•al**
regada : **re•gat•ta**
regadda : **re•gat•ta**
regail : **re•gale**
re•gal
re•gale
regamen : **reg•i•men**
re•gard
re•gat•ta
regaurd : **re•gard**
regeme : **re•gime**
regemen : **reg•i•men**
re•gen•cy
regensy : **re•gen•cy**
regergitate : **re•gur•gi•tate**
regester : **reg•is•ter**
reggale : **re•gale**
reggimen : **reg•i•men**
reggister : **reg•is•ter**
reggular : **reg•u•lar**
regiman : **reg•i•men**
re•gime
reg•i•men
regirgitate : **re•gur•gi•tate**
reg•is•ter
regle : **re•gal**
regotta : **re•gat•ta**
reguard : **re•gard**
reg•u•lar
reguler : **reg•u•lar**
regulir : **reg•u•lar**

regurgetate : **re•gur•gi•tate**
re•gur•gi•tate
regurjitate : **re•gur•gi•tate**
rehabilatate : **re•ha•bil•i•tate**
re•ha•bil•i•tate
rehabillitate : **re•ha•bil•i•tate**
rehearcel : **re•hears•al**
re•hears•al
re•hearse
rehearsel : **re•hears•al**
reherce : **re•hearse**
rehercil : **re•hears•al**
rehersal : **re•hears•al**
reherse : **re•hearse**
reign
reimberse : **re•im•burse**
reimburce : **re•im•burse**
re•im•burse
rein•deer
reitarate : **re•it•er•ate**
re•it•er•ate
reiterrate : **re•it•er•ate**
re•joice
rejoise : **re•joice**
rejoyce : **re•joice**
rejuvanate : **re•ju•ve•nate**
re•ju•ve•nate
rejuvinate : **re•ju•ve•nate**
reknown : **re•nown**
relagate : **rel•e•gate**
rel•a•tive
relavent : **rel•e•vant**
releace : **re•lease**
re•lease
releave : **re•lieve**
rel•e•gate
releive : **re•lieve**
relenquish : **re•lin•quish**
relese : **re•lease**
relesh : **rel•ish**
rel•e•vant
releve : **re•lieve**

relevent : **rel•e•vant**
reliabal : **re•li•able**
re•li•able
re•li•ance
relianse : **re•li•ance**
re•li•ant
relible : **re•li•able**
rel•ic
relick : **rel•ic**
relieble : **re•li•able**
relience : **re•li•ance**
reliense : **re•li•ance**
relient : **re•li•ant**
re•lieve
religate : **rel•e•gate**
relinquesh : **re•lin•quish**
re•lin•quish
rel•ish
relitive : **rel•a•tive**
relize : **re•al•ize**
rellative : **rel•a•tive**
rellavent : **rel•e•vant**
rellegate : **rel•e•gate**
rellevant : **rel•e•vant**
relliable : **re•li•able**
rellic : **rel•ic**
relligate : **rel•e•gate**
rellish : **rel•ish**
relm : **realm**
re•luc•tance
reluctanse : **re•luc•tance**
re•luc•tant
reluctense : **re•luc•tance**
reluctent : **re•luc•tant**
reluctince : **re•luc•tance**
reluctint : **re•luc•tant**
relyance : **re•li•ance**
remady : **rem•e•dy**
re•main
remane : **re•main**
remanisce : **rem•i•nisce**
re•mark•able

remarkible : **re•mark•able**
remeadial : **re•me•di•al**
remeddy : **rem•e•dy**
remedeal : **re•me•di•al**
re•me•di•al
rem•e•dy
remedyal : **re•me•di•al**
remeedial : **re•me•di•al**
remeidial : **re•me•di•al**
re•mem•brance
remembranse : **re•mem•brance**
remembrence : **re•mem•brance**
remembrense : **re•mem•brance**
remembrince : **re•mem•brance**
remiddy : **rem•e•dy**
remidy : **rem•e•dy**
reminice : **rem•i•nisce**
rem•i•nisce
reminiss : **rem•i•nisce**
remitance : **re•mit•tance**
re•mit•tance
remittanse : **re•mit•tance**
remittence : **re•mit•tance**
remittense : **re•mit•tance**
remittince : **re•mit•tance**
remminisce : **rem•i•nisce**
remmittance : **re•mit•tance**
remmoval : **re•mov•al**
rem•nant
remnent : **rem•nant**
remnint : **rem•nant**
re•mov•al
removel : **re•mov•al**
remunarate : **re•mu•ner•ate**
re•mu•ner•ate
remunnerate : **re•mu•ner•ate**
renagade : **ren•e•gade**
renavate : **ren•o•vate**
rench : **wrench**
rendavous : **ren•dez•vous**
rendevoo : **ren•dez•vous**
ren•dez•vous

ren·e·gade
re·new·al
renewel : **re·new·al**
renigade : **ren·e·gade**
rennagade : **ren·e·gade**
rennovate : **ren·o·vate**
renoun : **re·nown**
re·nounce
renounse : **re·nounce**
ren·o·vate
re·nown
renownce : **re·nounce**
renumerate : **re·mu·ner·ate**
reoccurrence : **re·cur·rence**
Reo de Janeiro : **Rio de Ja·nei·ro**
reostat : **rheo·stat**
re·pair
repare : **re·pair**
re·peal
re·peat
repeel : **re·peal**
repeet : **re·peat**
repele : **re·peal**
repelent : **re·pel·lent**
repellant : **re·pel·lent**
re·pel·lent
re·pen·tance
repentanse : **re·pen·tance**
repentence : **re·pen·tance**
rep·e·ti·tion
repintance : **re·pen·tance**
repitition : **rep·e·ti·tion**
repleat : **re·plete**
repleca : **rep·li·ca**
repleet : **re·plete**
re·plen·ish
replennish : **re·plen·ish**
re·plete
rep·li·ca
replicka : **rep·li·ca**
replinish : **re·plen·ish**

repplica : **rep·li·ca**
repprobate : **rep·ro·bate**
repramand : **rep·ri·mand**
repreave : **re·prieve**
reprehencible : **rep·re·hen·si·ble**
reprehensable : **rep·re·hen·si·ble**
rep·re·hen·si·ble
repreive : **re·prieve**
repremand : **rep·ri·mand**
repreve : **re·prieve**
repribate : **rep·ro·bate**
re·prieve
reprihensible : **rep·re·hen·si·ble**
rep·ri·mand
re·pri·sal
reprisel : **re·pri·sal**
reprissal : **re·pri·sal**
reprizal : **re·pri·sal**
re·proach
rep·ro·bate
reproch : **re·proach**
re·proof (*noun*); re·prove (*verb*)
reproove : **re·proof** (*noun*) *or* **re·prove** (*verb*)
re·prove (*verb*); re·proof (*noun*)
reptial : **rep·tile**
rep·tile
republec : **re·pub·lic**
re·pub·lic
republick : **re·pub·lic**
repudeate : **re·pu·di·ate**
re·pu·di·ate
rep·u·ta·ble
reputible : **rep·u·ta·ble**
requiam : **re·qui·em**
re·qui·em
requiset : **req·ui·site**
req·ui·site
requissite : **req·ui·site**
requium : **re·qui·em**
requizite : **req·ui·site**

resarrect : **res·ur·rect**
resavoir : **res·er·voir**
rescend : **re·scind**
re·scind
re·search
reseptacle : **re·cep·ta·cle**
reserch : **re·search**
resergence : **re·sur·gence**
res·er·voir
residdence : **res·i·dence**
res·i·dence
residense : **res·i·dence**
re·sign
resiliant : **re·sil·ient**
re·sil·ient
resillient : **re·sil·ient**
res·in
resine : **re·sign**
resipe : **rec·i·pe**
resipient : **re·cip·i·ent**
resiprocal : **re·cip·ro·cal**
resiprocity : **rec·i·proc·i·ty**
resipy : **rec·i·pe**
resirgence : **re·sur·gence**
re·sis·tance
resistence : **re·sis·tance**
resistense : **re·sis·tance**
resital : **re·cit·al**
resite : **re·cite**
resivoir : **res·er·voir**
reson : **rea·son**
resorce : **re·source**
resorse : **re·source**
re·source
resourse : **re·source**
re·spect·able
respectible : **re·spect·able**
resperator : **res·pi·ra·tor**
respirater : **res·pi·ra·tor**
res·pi·ra·tor
respit : **res·pite**
res·pite

responcible : **re·spon·si·ble**
responsable : **re·spon·si·ble**
responseble : **re·spon·si·ble**
re·spon·si·ble
ressel : **wres·tle**
ressend : **re·scind**
ressidence : **res·i·dence**
ressin : **res·in**
ressind : **re·scind**
ressle : **wres·tle**
restarant : **res·tau·rant**
restatution : **res·ti·tu·tion**
res·tau·rant
restetution : **res·ti·tu·tion**
res·ti·tu·tion
restle : **wres·tle**
restorant : **res·tau·rant**
resurect : **res·ur·rect**
re·sur·gence
resurgince : **re·sur·gence**
res·ur·rect
retacence : **ret·i·cence**
re·tail
retale : **re·tail**
retaleate : **re·tal·i·ate**
re·tal·i·ate
retalliate : **re·tal·i·ate**
retch (to vomit); wretch
  (miserable one)
ret·i·cence
reticense : **ret·i·cence**
ret·i·na
ret·i·nue
retisense : **ret·i·cence**
retreave : **re·trieve**
retreive : **re·trieve**
retreve : **re·trieve**
re·trieve
rettail : **re·tail**
retticence : **ret·i·cence**
rettina : **ret·i·na**
rettinue : **ret·i·nue**

revalation : **rev•e•la•tion**
revalry : **rev•el•ry**
revanue : **rev•e•nue**
revarence : **rev•er•ence**
revarent : **rev•er•ent**
revarie : **rev•er•ie**
re•veal
revecable : **re•vo•ca•ble**
reveel : **re•veal**
rev•eil•le
reveilly : **rev•eil•le**
rev•el
rev•e•la•tion
revele : **re•veal**
revell : **rev•el**
revellie : **rev•eil•le**
rev•el•ry
revennue : **rev•e•nue**
rev•e•nue
reverance : **rev•er•ence**
revercil : **re•ver•sal**
reveree : **rev•er•ie**
rev•er•ence
reverense : **rev•er•ence**
rev•e•rent
rev•er•ie
re•ver•sal
reversel : **re•ver•sal**
revery : **rev•er•ie**
revil : **rev•el**
revilation : **rev•e•la•tion**
reville : **rev•eil•le**
revinue : **rev•e•nue**
revirence : **rev•er•ence**
revirie : **rev•er•ie**
revirsal : **re•ver•sal**
re•vise
re•vi•sion
revission : **re•vi•sion**
re•viv•al
revivel : **re•viv•al**
revize : **re•vise**

revizion : **re•vi•sion**
re•vo•ca•ble
revoceble : **re•vo•ca•ble**
revocibal : **re•vo•ca•ble**
revokable : **re•vo•ca•ble**
revokeble : **re•vo•ca•ble**
rezervoir : **res•er•voir**
rezin : **res•in**
rhapsady : **rhap•so•dy**
rhapsiddy : **rhap•so•dy**
rhapsidy : **rhap•so•dy**
rhap•so•dy
rheo•stat
rhetaric : **rhet•o•ric**
rhet•o•ric
rhetorick : **rhet•o•ric**
rhettoric : **rhet•o•ric**
rhine•stone
rhi•noc•er•os
rhinocirus : **rhi•noc•er•os**
rhinoseros : **rhi•noc•er•os**
rhinosserus : **rhi•noc•er•os**
rhithm : **rhythm**
Rhode Is•land
rhu•barb
rhyme (poetry); **rime** (frost)
rhythem : **rhythm**
rhythm
rhythum : **rhythm**
rib•ald
ribbald : **rib•ald**
ribben : **rib•bon**
ribbin : **rib•bon**
rib•bon
ribon : **rib•bon**
ricachay : **ric•o•chet**
rickachet : **ric•o•chet**
rickashay : **ric•o•chet**
rick•ety
rickitty : **rick•ety**
rickity : **rick•ety**
ric•o•chet

ricoshay : **ric•o•chet**
ridacule : **rid•i•cule**
riddecule : **rid•i•cule**
riddicule : **rid•i•cule**
riddiculous : **ri•dic•u•lous**
rid•i•cule
ri•dic•u•lous
ridiculus : **ri•dic•u•lous**
rie : **rye** (grain) *or* **wry** (ironic)
riegn : **reign**
riendeer : **rein•deer**
rifal : **rif•fle** (to thumb
    through) *or* **ri•fle** (gun)
rifel : **rif•fle** (to thumb
    through) *or* **ri•fle** (gun)
rif•fle (to thumb through);
    ri•fle (gun)
ri•fle (gun); **rif•fle** (to thumb
    through)
rig•a•ma•role *or* **rig•ma•role**
riged : **rig•id**
riger : **rig•or**
riggamarole : **rig•ma•role**
riggid : **rig•id**
riggle : **wrig•gle**
riggor : **rig•or**
righ•teous
rightious : **righ•teous**
rightius : **righ•teous**
rig•id
rig•ma•role *or* **rig•a•ma•role**
rigmaroll : **rig•ma•role**
rigmerole : **rig•ma•role**
rig•or
rijid : **rig•id**
rime (frost); **rhyme** (poetry)
rimedial : **re•me•di•al**
rinagade : **ren•e•gade**
rinestone : **rhine•stone**
rinkle : **wrin•kle**
rinoceros : **rhi•noc•er•os**
rinovate : **ren•o•vate**

Rio de Ja•nei•ro
Rio de Janerro : **Rio de
    Ja•nei•ro**
Rio de Janiero : **Rio de
    Ja•nei•ro**
riostat : **rheo•stat**
riskay : **ris•qué**
risquay : **ris•qué**
ris•qué
rist : **wrist**
riter : **writ•er**
rithe : **writhe**
rithm : **rhythm**
rithum : **rhythm**
riting : **writ•ing**
rittual : **rit•u•al**
rit•u•al
rituel : **rit•u•al**
ri•val
rivel : **ri•val**
roadeo : **ro•deo**
Road Island : **Rhode Is•land**
robbot : **ro•bot**
ro•bot
robott : **ro•bot**
rock•et
rocketery : **rock•et•ry**
rock•et•ry
rockit : **rock•et**
rockitry : **rock•et•ry**
rodant : **ro•dent**
roddent : **ro•dent**
Rode Island : **Rhode Is•land**
ro•dent
ro•deo
rodio : **ro•deo**
roial : **roy•al**
roiel : **roy•al**
rollette : **rou•lette**
ro•mance
romanntic : **ro•man•tic**
romanse : **ro•mance**

ro·man·tic
romantick : **ro·man·tic**
rondavoo : **ren·dez·vous**
rondezvous : **ren·dez·vous**
roomate : **room·mate**
room·mate
rootabaga : **ru·ta·ba·ga**
rosarry : **ro·sa·ry**
ro·sa·ry
roserry : **ro·sa·ry**
rosery : **ro·sa·ry**
rotarry : **ro·ta·ry**
ro·ta·ry
roterry : **ro·ta·ry**
rotery : **ro·ta·ry**
rotory : **ro·ta·ry**
rough·age
roughege : **rough·age**
roughian : **ruf·fi·an**
roughige : **rough·age**
rought : **wrought**
rou·lette
routean : **rou·tine**
routeen : **rou·tine**
routene : **rou·tine**
rou·tine
roy·al
royel : **roy·al**
rubarb : **rhu·barb**
rubrec : **ru·bric**
ru·bric
rubrick : **ru·bric**
ruckas : **ruck·us**
ruckis : **ruck·us**

ruck·us
rudament : **ru·di·ment**
rudement : **ru·di·ment**
ru·di·ment
ruff : **rough**
ruffein : **ruf·fi·an**
ruf·fi·an
ruffien : **ruf·fi·an**
rufian : **ruf·fi·an**
rulette : **rou·lette**
rumage : **rum·mage**
rumanante : **ru·mi·nate**
rumer : **ru·mor**
ru·mi·nate
rum·mage
rummege : **rum·mage**
rummige : **rum·mage**
rumminnate : **ru·mi·nate**
rummor : **ru·mor**
ru·mor
rumpace : **rum·pus**
rumpis : **rum·pus**
rum·pus
Rushia : **Rus·sia**
Rusia : **Rus·sia**
Rus·sia
rus·tic
rustick : **rus·tic**
ru·ta·ba·ga
rutabaiga : **ru·ta·ba·ga**
rutabega : **ru·ta·ba·ga**
rutebaga : **ru·ta·ba·ga**
rutine : **rou·tine**
rye (grain); **wry** (ironic)
ryly : **wry·ly**

S

sabateur : **sab•o•teur**
Sabath : **Sab•bath**
sabatical : **sab•bat•i•cal**
sabatoor : **sab•o•teur**
Sab•bath
sab•bat•i•cal
sabbaticle : **sab•bat•i•cal**
Sabbeth : **Sab•bath**
Sabbith : **Sab•bath**
sabbotage : **sab•o•tage**
sabboteur : **sab•o•teur**
sa•ber or **sa•bre**
sabitage : **sab•o•tage**
sab•o•tage
sab•o•teur
saboture : **sab•o•teur**
sa•bre or **sa•ber**
sachel : **satch•el**
sacksiphone : **sax•o•phone**
sacrafice : **sac•ri•fice**
sac•ra•ment
sa•cred
sacrefice : **sac•ri•fice**
sacrement : **sac•ra•ment**
sacrid : **sa•cred**
sac•ri•fice
sacriment : **sac•ra•ment**
saddal : **sad•dle**
saddel : **sad•dle**
sad•dle
sa•fa•ri
safarri : **sa•fa•ri**
safe•ty
saffari : **sa•fa•ri**
saffire : **sap•phire**
safire : **sap•phire**
safty : **safe•ty**
Sahaira : **Sa•ha•ra**
Sa•ha•ra
Saharra : **Sa•ha•ra**

sail•er (ship); **sail•or** (one who sails)
sail•or (one who sails); **sail•er** (ship)
sal•able or **sale•able**
sal•ad
sal•a•man•der
sal•a•ry (wages); **cel•ery** (vegetable)
sale•able or **sal•able**
saleble : **sal•able**
salery : **cel•ery** (vegetable) or **sal•a•ry** (wages)
saliant : **sa•lient**
salible : **sal•able**
salid : **sal•ad**
sa•lient
salimander : **sal•a•man•der**
saliry : **cel•ery** (vegetable) or **sal•a•ry** (wages)
sa•li•va
sallable : **sal•able**
sallad : **sal•ad**
sallamander : **sal•a•man•der**
sallary : **cel•ery** (vegetable) or **sal•a•ry** (wages)
salled : **sal•ad**
sallid : **sal•ad**
sallient : **sa•lient**
salliva : **sa•li•va**
sallmon : **salm•on**
sallon : **sa•lon**
salloon : **sa•loon**
sallune : **sa•loon**
sallute : **sa•lute**
sallvage : **sal•vage**
salman : **salm•on**
salmin : **salm•on**
salm•on
sa•lon

sa·loon
salor : **sail·or**
sa·lute
sal·vage
salve (ointment); **save** (to rescue); **solve** (to find a solution)
salvege : **sal·vage**
salvige : **sal·vage**
Sambeezi : **Zam·be·zi**
Sambezi : **Zam·be·zi**
sammon : **salm·on**
sammurai : **sam·u·rai**
samon : **salm·on**
samouri : **sam·u·rai**
sampel : **sam·ple**
sam·ple
sampul : **sam·ple**
sam·u·rai
samuri : **sam·u·rai**
sanatarium : **san·a·to·ri·um**
sanatary : **san·i·tary**
san·a·to·ri·um *or* **san·i·tar·i·um**
san·dal
sandel : **san·dal**
sandle : **san·dal**
sandwhich : **sand·wich**
sand·wich
sandwitch : **sand·wich**
sanety : **san·i·ty**
San Fran·cis·co
San Francisko : **San Fran·cis·co**
San Fransisco : **San Fran·cis·co**
san·i·tar·i·um *or* **san·a·to·ri·um**
san·i·tary
saniterium : **san·a·to·ri·um**
sanitery : **san·i·tary**
sanitty : **san·i·ty**
san·i·ty
sannatarium : **san·a·to·ri·um**
sannatary : **san·i·tary**
sannity : **san·i·ty**

Sansibar : **Zan·zi·bar**
santer : **saun·ter**
Sanzibar : **Zan·zi·bar**
saphire : **sap·phire**
sap·phire
sarcasem : **sar·casm**
sarcasim : **sar·casm**
sar·casm
sarcasstic : **sar·cas·tic**
sar·cas·tic
sarcazm : **sar·casm**
sardeen : **sar·dine**
sardene : **sar·dine**
sar·dine
sarene : **se·rene**
sargent : **ser·geant**
sargient : **ser·geant**
sarrate : **ser·rate**
sassage : **sau·sage**
satalite : **sat·el·lite**
sa·tan·ic
satanick : **sa·tan·ic**
satannic : **sa·tan·ic**
satarize : **sat·i·rize**
satasfy : **sat·is·fy**
satch·el
satelite : **sat·el·lite**
sat·el·lite
Saterday : **Sat·ur·day**
saterize : **sat·i·rize**
Satern : **Sat·urn**
satesfactory : **sat·is·fac·to·ry**
satesfy : **sat·is·fy**
sat·in
sat·i·rize
satisfactery : **sat·is·fac·to·ry**
sat·is·fac·to·ry
sat·is·fy
sattelite : **sat·el·lite**
sattellite : **sat·el·lite**
satten : **sat·in**
sattin : **sat·in**

sattirize : **sat·i·rize**
sattisfactory : **sat·is·fac·to·ry**
sattisfy : **sat·is·fy**
Satturday : **Sat·ur·day**
Satturn : **Sat·urn**
Sat·ur·day
Sat·urn
saucege : **sau·sage**
sau·cer
saun·ter
sau·sage
sausege : **sau·sage**
sauser : **sau·cer**
sausige : **sau·sage**
sav : **salve** (ointment) *or* **save**
  (to rescue)
sav·age
save (to rescue); **salve**
  (ointment)
savege : **sav·age**
saveor : **sav·ior**
sav·ior *or* **sav·iour**
sav·iour *or* **sav·ior**
sa·vor
savour (*Brit.*) : **sa·vor**
sawcer : **sau·cer**
saxaphone : **sax·o·phone**
saxiphone : **sax·o·phone**
sax·o·phone
Saylon : **Cey·lon**
scabard : **scab·bard**
scab·bard
scabboard : **scab·bard**
scabbord : **scab·bard**
scaf·fold
scafold : **scaf·fold**
scairy : **scary**
scald
scalpal : **scal·pel**
scal·pel
scalple : **scal·pel**
scan·dal

scandel : **scan·dal**
Scandenavia : **Scan·di·na·via**
Scandinavea : **Scan·di·na·via**
Scan·di·na·via
Scandinnavia : **Scan·di·na·via**
scandle : **scan·dal**
scar·ab
scareb : **scar·ab**
scared (frightened); **scarred**
  (having a scar)
scarey : **scary**
scarib : **scar·ab**
scar·let
scarlit : **scar·let**
scarred (having a scar); **scared**
  (frightened)
scary
scauld : **scald**
scedule : **sched·ule**
sceme : **scheme**
sce·nar·io
scenarrio : **sce·nar·io**
scenary : **scen·ery**
sceneario : **sce·nar·io**
scenec : **sce·nic**
scenerry : **scen·ery**
scen·ery
sce·nic
scenick : **sce·nic**
scent·ed
sceptacism : **skep·ti·cism**
sceptecism : **skep·ti·cism**
scep·ter
scep·tic *or* **skep·tic**
scep·ti·cism *or* **skep·ti·cism**
sceptick : **skep·tic**
sceptisism : **skep·ti·cism**
sceptor : **scep·ter**
sceptre (*Brit.*) : **scep·ter**
scervy : **scur·vy**
scheam : **scheme**
scheddule : **sched·ule**

scheduel : **sched•ule**
sched•ule
scheme
schism
schissors : **scis•sors**
schisum : **schism**
schitxophrenia : **schizo•phre•nia**
schizm : **schism**
schizofrenai : **schizo•phre•nia**
schizophreania :
  schizo•phre•nia
schizo•phre•nia
schizzophrenia :
  schizo•phre•nia
scho•lar
scholasstic : **scho•las•tic**
scho•las•tic
scholer : **scho•lar**
schollar : **scho•lar**
schollastic : **scho•las•tic**
school
schoon•er
schuner : **schoon•er**
sciance : **sci•ence**
sci•ence
sciense : **sci•ence**
scientiffic : **sci•en•tif•ic**
sci•en•tif•ic
scimatar : **scim•i•tar**
scim•i•tar
scinted : **scent•ed**
scirry : **scur•ry**
scism : **schism**
scisors : **scis•sors**
scissers : **scis•sors**
scissophrania : **schizo•phre•nia**
scis•sors
scithe : **scythe**
scizzors : **scis•sors**
scolar : **scho•lar**
scolastic : **scho•las•tic**
scooner : **schoon•er**

scorpian : **scor•pi•on**
scorpien : **scor•pi•on**
scor•pi•on
scoundral : **scoun•drel**
scoun•drel
scoundril : **scoun•drel**
scourge
scrach : **scratch**
scral : **scroll**
scraped (rubbed); **scrapped**
  (discarded)
scrapped (discarded); **scraped**
  (rubbed)
scratch
screach : **screech**
scream
screan : **screen**
screech
screem : **scream**
screen
screne : **screen**
scrimage : **scrim•mage**
scrim•mage
scrimmege : **scrim•mage**
scroll
scrutanize : **scru•ti•nize**
scru•ti•nize
sculpter : **sculp•tor** (artist) *or*
  sculp•ture (work of art)
sculp•tor (artist); **sculp•ture**
  (work of art)
sculp•ture (work of art);
  sculp•tor (artist)
scurge : **scourge**
scur•ry
scur•vy
scythe (blade); **sigh** (deep
  breath)
seafairer : **sea•far•er**
sea•far•er
seafaror : **sea•far•er**
seamy

sé·ance

seap : seep

search

seasen : sea·son

seasin : sea·son

sea·son

seathe : seethe

Seattal : Se·at·tle

Seattel : Se·at·tle

Se·at·tle

secand : sec·ond

se·cede

seceed : se·cede

seceshion : se·ces·sion

se·ces·sion

secide : se·cede

seckular : sec·u·lar

sec·ond

secracy : se·cre·cy

secratary : sec·re·tary

se·cre·cy

secresy : se·cre·cy

se·cret

sec·re·tary

secretery : sec·re·tary

secrisy : se·cre·cy

secrit : se·cret

secritary : sec·re·tary

secter : sec·tor

sec·tor

sec·u·lar

seculer : sec·u·lar

secund : sec·ond

securety : se·cu·ri·ty

securitty : se·cu·ri·ty

se·cu·ri·ty

securrity : se·cu·ri·ty

sedament : sed·i·ment

se·dan

sedar : ce·dar (tree) or se·der
   (Passover meal)

sed·a·tive

seddan : se·dan

seddative : sed·a·tive

seddiment : sed·i·ment

seddition : se·di·tion

se·der (Passover meal); ce·dar
   (tree)

sedetive : sed·a·tive

sed·i·ment

se·di·tion

seditive : sed·a·tive

seefarer : sea·far·er

seege : siege

seemy : seamy

seep

seeson : sea·son

seethe

seeze : seize

segragate : seg·re·gate

seg·re·gate

segrigate : seg·re·gate

seige : siege

seis·mic

seismollogy : seis·mol·o·gy

seis·mol·o·gy

seive : sieve

seize

seizh : siege

seizmic : seis·mic

seizmology : seis·mol·o·gy

selary : cel·ery (vegetable) or
   sal·a·ry (wages)

seldem : sel·dom

sel·dom

selebrate : cel·e·brate

selebrity : ce·leb·ri·ty

se·lect

selery : cel·ery (vegetable) or
   sal·a·ry (wages)

selestial : ce·les·tial

selldom : sel·dom

sellect : se·lect

sellestial : ce·les·tial

selluloid : **cel·lu·loid**
Seltic : **Cel·tic**
sematary : **cem·e·tery**
sematery : **cem·e·tery**
sem·blance
semblanse : **sem·blance**
semblence : **sem·blance**
semenar : **sem·i·nar**
semenary : **sem·i·nary**
semesster : **se·mes·ter**
se·mes·ter
semeterry : **cem·e·tery**
semetery : **cem·e·tery**
sem·i·nar
sem·i·nary
seminerry : **sem·i·nary**
seminery : **sem·i·nary**
semmester : **se·mes·ter**
semminar : **sem·i·nar**
semminary : **sem·i·nary**
senario : **sce·nar·io**
sen·ate
senater : **sen·a·tor**
sen·a·tor
sence : **sense** (intelligence) *or*
  since (from that time)
sencery : **sen·so·ry**
sencible : **sen·si·ble**
senery : **scen·ery**
senet : **sen·ate**
senic : **sce·nic**
se·nile
senilety : **se·nil·i·ty**
se·nil·i·ty
senillity : **se·nil·i·ty**
senitor : **sen·a·tor**
sennate : **sen·ate**
sennator : **sen·a·tor**
sennile : **se·nile**
sensable : **sen·si·ble**
sensary : **sen·so·ry**
sensative : **sen·si·tive**

sense (intelligence); **cents**
  (money); **since** (from that
  time)
senseble : **sen·si·ble**
senser : **cen·ser** (incense
  container) *or* **cen·sor** (to
  remove objectionable
  material) *or* **cen·sure** (to
  condemn) *or* **sen·sor** (that
  which senses)
sensery : **sen·so·ry**
sensetive : **sen·si·tive**
sensibal : **sen·si·ble**
sen·si·ble
sensis : **cen·sus**
sen·si·tive
sen·sor (that which senses);
  cen·ser (incense container);
  cen·sor (to remove
  objectionable material);
  cen·sure (to condemn)
sen·so·ry
sen·su·al
sensuel : **sen·su·al**
sensus : **cen·sus**
sentament : **sen·ti·ment**
sentaur : **cen·taur**
sented : **scent·ed**
sentenal : **sen·ti·nel**
sen·ti·ment
sentimeter : **cen·ti·me·ter**
sentinal : **sen·ti·nel**
sen·ti·nel
sentinle : **sen·ti·nel**
sentrifugal : **cen·trif·u·gal**
sentripetal : **cen·trip·e·tal**
sentury : **cen·tu·ry**
sep·a·rate
sepea : **se·pia**
seperate : **sep·a·rate**
se·pia
sepirate : **sep·a·rate**

seppalcre : **sep•ul•cher**
seppalker : **sep•ul•cher**
sepparate : **sep•a•rate**
sepperate : **sep•a•rate**
seppia : **se•pia**
seppulchre : **sep•ul•cher**
Sep•tem•ber
Septembre : **Sep•tem•ber**
septer : **scep•ter**
Septimber : **Sep•tem•ber**
septor : **scep•ter**
sep•ul•cher or **sep•ul•chre**
sepulcre : **sep•ul•cher**
se•quence
sequense : **se•quence**
sequince : **se•quence**
sequinse : **se•quence**
Seracuse : **Syr•a•cuse**
seram : **se•rum**
seramic : **ce•ram•ic**
serate : **ser•rate**
serch : **search**
serean : **se•rene**
serebellum : **cer•e•bel•lum**
serebral : **cer•e•bral**
sereen : **se•rene**
seremony : **cer•e•mo•ny**
se•rene
serf (peasant); **surf** (waves)
serge (cloth); **surge** (to rise up)
ser•geant
sergent : **ser•geant**
sergeon : **sur•geon**
sergery : **sur•gery**
sergient : **ser•geant**
se•ri•al (in a series); **ce•re•al** (grain)
serine : **se•rene**
serman : **ser•mon**
sermin : **ser•mon**
ser•mon
ser•pent

serpint : **ser•pent**
serplus : **sur•plice** (vestment) or **sur•plus** (excess)
ser•rate
sertain : **cer•tain**
sertificate : **cer•tif•i•cate**
se•rum
servace : **ser•vice**
servaceable : **ser•vice•able**
ser•vant
servent : **ser•vant**
ser•vice
ser•vice•able
serviceble : **ser•vice•able**
servicible : **ser•vice•able**
servint : **ser•vant**
servise : **ser•vice**
servisible : **ser•vice•able**
serviss : **ser•vice**
servissible : **ser•vice•able**
ses•a•me
sesede : **se•cede**
seseed : **se•cede**
sesession : **se•ces•sion**
sesime : **ses•a•me**
sessame : **ses•a•me**
sessimy : **ses•a•me**
sesspool : **cess•pool**
sevarity : **se•ver•i•ty**
seveer : **se•vere**
sev•er•al
se•vere
severel : **sev•er•al**
severety : **se•ver•i•ty**
severitty : **se•ver•i•ty**
se•ver•i•ty
sevier : **se•vere**
seviral : **sev•er•al**
sevveral : **sev•er•al**
sew•age
sewige : **sew•age**
sex•tant

sextent : **sex·tant**
sextint : **sex·tant**
sex·u·al
sexuel : **sex·u·al**
seyance : **sé·ance**
Seylon : **Cey·lon**
shaddoe : **shad·ow**
shaddow : **shad·ow**
shadoe : **shad·ow**
shad·ow
shaffeur : **chauf·feur**
shaffure : **chauf·feur**
shampagne : **cham·pagne**
shampaign : **cham·pagne**
shampaine : **cham·pagne**
shampane : **cham·pagne**
sham·poo
shampu : **sham·poo**
shantie : **shan·ty**
shan·ty
shaparon : **chap·er·on**
shaperone : **chap·er·on**
sharade : **cha·rade**
shareff : **sher·iff**
shariff : **sher·iff**
sharlatan : **char·la·tan**
sharlaten : **char·la·tan**
sharletan : **char·la·tan**
shartreuse : **char·treuse**
shartroose : **char·treuse**
shartruese : **char·treuse**
shartruse : **char·treuse**
shateau : **cha·teau**
shatieu : **cha·teau**
shatoe : **cha·teau**
shatoue : **cha·teau**
shauffer : **chauf·feur**
shauvenism : **chau·vin·ism**
shauvinism : **chau·vin·ism**
sheaf
sheafs : **sheaves**
sheald : **shield**

shealf : **shelf**
sheaves
shedule : **sched·ule**
sheef : **sheaf**
sheeld : **shield**
sheepherd : **shep·herd**
sheeves : **sheaves**
sheif : **sheaf**
sheild : **shield**
shelac : **shel·lac**
shelf (*noun*); **shelve** (*verb*)
shel·lac
shellaced : **shel·lacked**
shellack : **shel·lac**
shel·lacked
shellter : **shel·ter**
shel·ter
sheltor : **shel·ter**
shelve (*verb*); **shelf** (*sing.*)
shelves (*plur.*)
shemise : **che·mise**
shepard : **shep·herd**
shephard : **shep·herd**
shep·herd
sher·bet
sherbit : **sher·bet**
shereff : **sher·iff**
sher·iff
Sheyenne : **Chey·enne**
shield
shillac : **shel·lac**
shillacked : **shel·lacked**
shingal : **shin·gle**
shingel : **shin·gle**
shin·gle
shirbet : **sher·bet**
shism : **schism**
shivalry : **chiv·al·ry**
shivelry : **chiv·al·ry**
shoalder : **shoul·der**
shoartage : **short·age**
shoffeur : **chauf·feur**

sholder : **shoul·der**
short·age
shortege : **short·age**
shortige : **short·age**
should·er
shov·el
shov·eled
shovelled : **shov·eled**
shovil : **shov·el**
shovilled : **shov·eled**
shovinism : **chau·vin·ism**
shrapnal : **shrap·nel**
shrap·nel
shrapnle : **shrap·nel**
shread : **shred**
shreak : **shriek**
shred
shreek : **shriek**
shreik : **shriek**
shrewd
shriek
shrival : **shriv·el**
shrivaled : **shriv·eled**
shriv·el
shriv·eled *or* **shriv·elled**
shriv·elled *or* **shriv·eled**
shrivil : **shriv·el**
shrivle : **shriv·el**
shrude : **shrewd**
shugar : **sug·ar**
shuger : **sug·ar**
shurbet : **sher·bet**
shute : **chute**
shutle : **shut·tle**
shuttal : **shut·tle**
shuttel : **shut·tle**
shut·tle
Siameese : **Si·a·mese**
Si·a·mese
Siameze : **Si·a·mese**
sianide : **cy·a·nide**
Siattle : **Se·at·tle**

Sibeeria : **Si·be·ria**
Si·be·ria
sibernetics : **cy·ber·net·ics**
Sibirea : **Si·be·ria**
Sicaly : **Sic·i·ly**
sicamore : **syc·a·more**
Sicely : **Sic·i·ly**
Sicili : **Sic·i·ly**
Sicilly : **Sic·i·ly**
Sic·i·ly
sickal : **cy·cle** (rotation) *or*
    sick·le (knife)
sickel : **cy·cle** (rotation) *or*
    sick·le (knife)
sick·le (knife); **cy·cle** (rotation)
siclone : **cy·clone**
sicomore : **syc·a·more**
sicophant : **sy·co·phant**
sidal : **si·dle**
sidan : **se·dan**
sid·le
siege
sience : **sci·ence**
siesmic : **seis·mic**
siesmology : **seis·mol·o·gy**
sieve
sieze : **seize**
sigar : **ci·gar**
sigh (deep breath); **scythe**
    (blade)
signafy : **sig·ni·fy**
sig·nal
signall : **sig·nal**
sig·na·ture
signefy : **sig·ni·fy**
signel : **sig·nal**
sig·net (ring); **cyg·net** (swan)
signeture : **sig·na·ture**
signifacant : **sig·nif·i·cant**
signifficant : **sig·nif·i·cant**
signiffy : **sig·ni·fy**
sig·nif·i·cant

sig·ni·fy
signiture : sig·na·ture
silacon : sil·i·con
silance : si·lence
si·lence
silense : si·lence
sil·hou·ette
sil·i·con
silince : si·lence
silinder : cyl·in·der
siliva : sa·li·va
sillable : syl·la·ble
sillabus : syl·la·bus
sillence : si·lence
sillhoette : sil·hou·ette
sillicon : sil·i·con
silloette : sil·hou·ette
silute : sa·lute
simalar : sim·i·lar
simblance : sem·blance
simbol : cym·bal (brass plate)
    or sym·bol (meaningful
    image)
Simese : Si·a·mese
simester : se·mes·ter
sim·i·lar
sim·i·le
similer : sim·i·lar
similiar : sim·i·lar
similie : sim·i·le
simitar : scim·i·tar
simmetry : sym·me·try
simmilar : sim·i·lar
simmulate : sim·u·late
simpathize : sym·pa·thize
simphony : sym·pho·ny
simplafy : sim·pli·fy
simplefy : sim·pli·fy
simpliffy : sim·pli·fy
sim·pli·fy
simposium : sym·po·sium
simptem : symp·tom

simptom : symp·tom
simtem : symp·tom
simtom : symp·tom
sim·u·late
sinagogue : syn·a·gogue
sinario : sce·nar·io
since (from that time); sense
    (intelligence)
sinceer : sin·cere
sinceir : sin·cere
sin·cere
sincerety : sin·cer·i·ty
sin·cer·i·ty
sinchronize : syn·chro·nize
Sincinnati : Cin·cin·nati
sindicate : syn·di·cate
sinema : cin·e·ma
sinemon : cin·na·mon
Singapoor : Sin·ga·pore
Sin·ga·pore
Singapour : Sin·ga·pore
singe·ing (burning); sing·ing
    (music)
sing·ing (music); singe·ing
    (burning)
Singopore : Sin·ga·pore
sing·u·lar
singuler : sing·u·lar
sinicism : cyn·i·cism
sinile : se·nile
sinility : se·nil·i·ty
sin·is·ter
sinnamon : cin·na·mon
sinnister : sin·is·ter
sinonym : syn·o·nym
sinphony : sym·pho·ny
sinsere : sin·cere
sinserity : sin·cer·i·ty
sinsual : sen·su·al
sinted : scent·ed
sintenal : sen·ti·nel
sinthesize : syn·the·size

sipher : **ci·pher**
sipress : **cy·press**
Siracuse : **Syr·a·cuse**
sirca : **cir·ca**
sircus : **cir·cus**
sirfeit : **sur·feit**
sirfiet : **sur·feit**
sirgeon : **sur·geon**
sirgery : **sur·gery**
sirgion : **sur·geon**
sir·loin
sirmount : **sur·mount**
sirname : **sur·name**
sirpent : **ser·pent**
sirplus : **sur·plice** (vestment) *or*
　　sur·plus (excess)
sirrhosis : **cir·rho·sis**
sirum : **se·rum**
sirup *or* **syr·up**
Sisily : **Sic·i·ly**
sism : **schism**
sissors : **scis·sors**
sistem : **sys·tem**
sistern : **cis·tern**
sithe : **scythe**
sitrus : **cit·rus**
siv : **sieve**
sive : **sieve**
siz·able *or* **size·able**
size·able *or* **siz·able**
sizeble : **siz·able**
sizible : **siz·able**
sizmic : **seis·mic**
sizzel : **siz·zle**
siz·zle
skaffold : **scaf·fold**
skalpel : **scal·pel**
Skandinavia : **Scan·di·na·via**
skarlet : **scar·let**
skech : **sketch**
skedule : **sched·ule**
skelaton : **skel·e·ton**

skeletan : **skel·e·ton**
skeletin : **skel·e·ton**
skel·e·ton
skeliton : **skel·e·ton**
skelleton : **skel·e·ton**
skeme : **scheme**
skep·tic *or* **scep·tic**
skep·ti·cism *or* **scep·ti·cism**
skepticizm : **skep·ti·cism**
skermish : **skir·mish**
sketch
ski
skie : **ski**
skied
skiied : **skied**
ski·ing
skiis : **skis**
skilet : **skil·let**
skil·let
skillit : **skil·let**
sking : **ski·ing**
skirmesh : **skir·mish**
skir·mish
skirmush : **skir·mish**
skis
skolar : **schol·ar**
skool : **school**
skorpion : **scor·pi·on**
skulptor : **sculp·tor** (artist)
skulpture : **sculp·ture** (work of
　　art)
skurmish : **skir·mish**
skurry : **scur·ry**
slagh : **sleigh**
slaghter : **slaugh·ter**
slaigh : **sleigh**
slaugh·ter
slauter : **slaugh·ter**
slavary : **slav·ery**
Slavec : **Slav·ic**
slaverry : **slav·ery**
slav·ery

Slav•ic
Slavick : **Slav•ic**
Slavvic : **Slav•ic**
slawter : **slaugh•ter**
slay (to kill); **sleigh** (sled)
sleak : **sleek**
sleap : **sleep**
sleapily : **sleep•i•ly**
sleasy : **slea•zy**
sleat : **sleet**
sleave : **sleeve**
slea•zy
sledge
sleek
sleep
sleep•i•ly
sleepyly : **sleep•i•ly**
sleesy : **slea•zy**
sleet
sleeve
slege : **sledge**
sleigh (sled); **slay** (to kill)
sleih : **sleigh**
sleive : **sleeve**
sleizy : **slea•zy**
slepe : **sleep**
slete : **sleet**
sleuth
slewth : **sleuth**
slice
sliceing : **slic•ing**
slic•ing
sliegh : **sleigh**
slimey : **slimy**
slimmy : **slimy**
slimy
slipery : **slip•pery**
slippary : **slip•pery**
slip•pery
slise : **slice**
slive : **sleeve**
slobenly : **slov•en•ly**

slo•gan
slogen : **slo•gan**
slogin : **slo•gan**
sloped (at an angle); **slopped** (spilled)
slopped (spilled); **sloped** (at an angle)
slouch
slov•en•ly
slovinly : **slov•en•ly**
slowch : **slouch**
sluce : **sluice**
slueth : **sleuth**
slugard : **slug•gard**
slug•gard
sluggerd : **slug•gard**
sluggird : **slug•gard**
sluice
sluise : **sluice**
sluth : **sleuth**
smear
smeer : **smear**
smithareens : **smith•er•eens**
smith•er•eens
smitherenes : **smith•er•eens**
smitherines : **smith•er•eens**
smoak : **smoke**
smoalder : **smol•der**
smoke
Smo•key (the Bear); **smoky** (filled with smoke)
smoky (filled with smoke); **Smo•key** (the Bear)
smol•der or **smoul•der**
smorgasboard : **smor•gas•bord**
smor•gas•bord
smorgesbord : **smor•gas•bord**
smorgisbord : **smor•gas•bord**
smoul•der or **smol•der**
smudge
smuge : **smudge**
smuggel : **smug•gle**

smugglar : **smug·gler**
smug·gle
smug·gler
smugle : **smug·gle**
snach : **snatch**
snatch
sneak
sneak·er
sneaky
snease : **sneeze**
sneaze : **sneeze**
sneek : **sneak**
sneeker : **sneak·er**
sneeky : **sneaky**
sneeze
sneke : **sneak**
snipet : **snip·pet**
snip·pet
snippit : **snip·pet**
sniv·el
sniv·el·ing *or* **sniv·el·ling**
sniv·el·ling *or* **sniv·el·ing**
snivil : **sniv·el**
snoarkel : **snor·kel**
snobbary : **snob·bery**
snob·bery
snobery : **snob·bery**
snobry : **snob·bery**
snorkal : **snor·kel**
snor·kel
snorkle : **snor·kel**
snuggal : **snug·gle**
snuggel : **snug·gle**
snug·gle
soak·ing
soap
soap·i·er
soapyer : **soap·i·er**
soarcerer : **sor·cer·er**
soarcery : **sor·cery**
soard : **sword**
soberiety : **so·bri·ety**

sobrietty : **so·bri·ety**
so·bri·ety
soccar : **soc·cer**
soc·cer
socciology : **so·ci·ol·o·gy**
soceable : **so·cia·ble**
soceology : **so·ci·ol·o·gy**
sociabal : **so·cia·ble**
sociabilety : **so·cia·bil·i·ty**
so·cia·bil·i·ty
so·cia·ble
socialibility : **so·cia·bil·i·ty**
socible : **so·cia·ble**
societty : **so·ci·ety**
so·ci·ety
sociollogy : **so·ci·ol·o·gy**
so·ci·ol·o·gy
sodder : **sol·der**
soddium : **so·di·um**
sodeum : **so·di·um**
sodiem : **so·di·um**
so·di·um
soffen : **soft·en**
sofisticated : **so·phis·ti·cat·ed**
sofmore : **soph·o·more**
sofomore : **soph·o·more**
soft·en
sojern : **so·journ**
sojorn : **so·journ**
so·journ
sojurn : **so·journ**
soking : **soak·ing**
so·lace
so·lar
solataire : **sol·i·taire**
solatary : **sol·i·tary**
solatude : **sol·i·tude**
sol·der (metal); **sol·dier**
  (fighter)
soldiar : **sol·dier**
sol·dier (fighter); **sol·der**
  (metal)

sole (only; fish; part of foot or shoe); **soul** (inner essence)
soled (having a sole); **sol•id** (not gas or liquid)
soledarity : **sol•i•dar•i•ty**
sole•ly
solem : **sol•emn**
sol•emn
soler : **so•lar**
solice : **so•lace**
solicet : **so•lic•it**
solicetor : **so•lic•i•tor**
solicetous : **so•lic•i•tous**
so•lic•it
so•lic•i•tor
so•lic•i•tous
solicitus : **so•lic•i•tous**
sol•id (not gas or liquid); **soled** (having a sole)
solidarety : **sol•i•dar•i•ty**
sol•i•dar•i•ty
solidefy : **so•lid•i•fy**
soliderity : **sol•i•dar•i•ty**
so•lid•i•fy
solilaquy : **so•lil•o•quy**
solilloquy : **so•lil•o•quy**
so•lil•o•quy
soliloqy : **so•lil•o•quy**
solise : **so•lace**
soliset : **so•lic•it**
solisetor : **so•lic•i•tor**
solisetous : **so•lic•i•tous**
soliss : **so•lace**
solissit : **so•lic•it**
solissitor : **so•lic•i•tor**
solissitous : **so•lic•i•tous**
sol•i•taire
solitare : **sol•i•taire**
sol•i•tary
solitery : **sol•i•tary**
sol•i•tude
sollace : **so•lace**

sollatude : **sol•i•tude**
sollemn : **sol•emn**
sollicit : **so•lic•it**
sollicitor : **so•lic•i•tor**
sollicitous : **so•lic•i•tous**
sollid : **sol•id**
sollidarity : **sol•i•dar•i•ty**
sollidify : **so•lid•i•fy**
solliloquy : **so•lil•o•quy**
sollitaire : **sol•i•taire**
sollitary : **sol•i•tary**
sollitude : **sol•i•tude**
solluble : **sol•u•ble**
sollvency : **sol•ven•cy**
sollvent : **sol•vent**
solstace : **sol•stice**
sol•stice
solstiss : **sol•stice**
soluable : **sol•u•ble**
sol•u•ble
soluible : **sol•u•ble**
solumn : **sol•emn**
solv•able
solve (to find a solution); **salve** (ointment)
sol•ven•cy
solvensy : **sol•ven•cy**
sol•vent
solvible : **solv•able**
solvincy : **sol•ven•cy**
solvint : **sol•vent**
soly : **sole•ly**
som•er•sault *or* **sum•mer•sault**
sommersault : **som•er•sault**
sonada : **so•na•ta**
so•na•ta
sonatta : **so•na•ta**
sonet : **son•net**
son•ic
son•net
sonnic : **son•ic**
sonnick : **son•ic**

sonnit : **son·net**
sonter : **saun·ter**
soparific : **so·po·rif·ic**
sope : **soap**
sophistacated : **so·phis·ti·cat·ed**
sophistecated : **so·phis·ti·cat·ed**
so·phis·ti·cat·ed
sophmoar : **soph·o·more**
sophmore : **soph·o·more**
soph·o·more
sopier : **soap·i·er**
soporiffic : **so·po·rif·ic**
so·po·rif·ic
sopranno : **so·pra·no**
so·pra·no
sor·cer·er
sorceror : **sor·cer·er**
sor·cery
sord : **sword**
sorded : **sor·did**
sor·did
soroarity : **so·ror·i·ty**
sororety : **so·ror·i·ty**
sororitty : **so·ror·i·ty**
so·ror·i·ty
sororrity : **so·ror·i·ty**
sorrority : **so·ror·i·ty**
sorserer : **sor·cer·er**
sorsery : **sor·cery**
sosiety : **so·ci·e·ty**
sosiology : **so·ci·ol·o·gy**
sosser : **sau·cer**
sossialibility : **so·cia·bil·i·ty**
sothern : **south·ern**
soufflay : **souf·flé**
souf·flé
souffley : **souf·flé**
soufle : **souf·flé**
soul (inner essence); **sole** (only; fish; part of foot or shoe)
sourcerer : **sor·cer·er**
sourcery : **sor·cery**

South Caralina : **South Car·o·li·na**
South Carlina : **South Car·o·li·na**
South Car·o·li·na
South Carrolina : **South Car·o·li·na**
South Dahkota : **South Da·ko·ta**
South Da·ko·ta
South Dakotah : **South Da·ko·ta**
south·ern
souveneer : **sou·ve·nir**
sou·ve·nir
souvineer : **sou·ve·nir**
souvineir : **sou·ve·nir**
soveregn : **sov·er·eign**
sov·er·eign
soveriegn : **sov·er·eign**
soviat : **so·vi·et**
so·vi·et
sovrin : **sov·er·eign**
spaceious : **spa·cious**
spacial : **spa·tial**
spa·cious
spacius : **spa·cious**
spagetti : **spa·ghet·ti**
spa·ghet·ti
spaghetty : **spa·ghet·ti**
Span·iard
span·iel
Spanierd : **Span·iard**
Span·ish
Spanniard : **Span·iard**
spanniel : **span·iel**
Spannish : **Span·ish**
sparce : **sparse**
sparcety : **spar·si·ty**
sparcity : **spar·si·ty**
sparow : **spar·row**
spar·row

sparse
sparsety : **spar·si·ty**
sparsitty : **spar·si·ty**
spar·si·ty
spasial : **spa·tial**
spasim : **spasm**
spasm
spatela : **spat·u·la**
spa·tial
spatiel : **spa·tial**
spattula : **spat·u·la**
spat·u·la
spatulla : **spat·u·la**
spaun : **spawn**
spawn
spazm : **spasm**
speach : **speech**
speak
spear
specafy : **spec·i·fy**
specamen : **spec·i·men**
specamin : **spec·i·men**
spechial : **spe·cial**
spe·cial
specifec : **spe·cif·ic**
speciffic : **spe·cif·ic**
speciffy : **spec·i·fy**
spe·cif·ic
specifick : **spe·cif·ic**
spec·i·fy
spec·i·men
specimin : **spec·i·men**
speckter : **spec·ter**
spectackular : **spec·tac·u·lar**
spec·ta·cle
spec·tac·u·lar
spectaculer : **spec·tac·u·lar**
spectater : **spec·ta·tor**
spec·ta·tor
spectecle : **spec·ta·cle**
spec·ter
spectical : **spec·ta·cle**

specticle : **spec·ta·cle**
spector : **spec·ter**
spectre (*Brit.*) : **spec·ter**
spedometer : **speed·om·e·ter**
speech
speedameter : **speed·om·e·ter**
speed·om·e·ter
speedomiter : **speed·om·e·ter**
speek : **speak**
speer : **spear**
speghetti : **spa·ghet·ti**
speir : **spear**
sperit : **spir·it**
speritual : **spir·i·tu·al**
spern : **spurn**
sperrow : **spar·row**
spert : **spurt**
spesafy : **spec·i·fy**
spesamen : **spec·i·men**
spesial : **spe·cial**
spesific : **spe·cif·ic**
spesify : **spec·i·fy**
spesimin : **spec·i·men**
spessify : **spec·i·fy**
spheer : **sphere**
spheir : **sphere**
sphenx : **sphinx**
sphere
sphinks : **sphinx**
sphinx
spicket : **spig·ot**
spicy
spigget : **spig·ot**
spiggit : **spig·ot**
spiggot : **spig·ot**
spighetti : **spa·ghet·ti**
spig·ot
spilled
spilt : **spilled**
spin·ach
spinaker : **spin·na·ker**
spi·nal

spindal : **spin·dle**
spindel : **spin·dle**
spin·dle
spinel : **spi·nal**
spinich : **spin·ach**
spinnacer : **spin·na·ker**
spinnach : **spin·ach**
spin·na·ker
spinnal : **spi·nal**
spinneker : **spin·na·ker**
spinnet : **spin·et**
spinnich : **spin·ach**
spinx : **sphinx**
spi·ral
spirel : **spi·ral**
spiret : **spir·it**
spiretual : **spir·i·tu·al**
spir·it
spir·i·tu·al
spirituel : **spir·i·tu·al**
spirrit : **spir·it**
spirritual : **spir·i·tu·al**
spirt : **spurt**
spisy : **spicy**
splean : **spleen**
spleen
splended : **splen·did**
splender : **splen·dor**
splen·did
splen·dor
splerge : **splurge**
splindid : **splen·did**
splindor : **splen·dor**
splirge : **splurge**
splurge
spoiled or **spoilt**
spoilt or **spoiled**
Spokan : **Spo·kane**
Spo·kane
sponser : **spon·sor**
spon·sor
spontaineous : **spon·ta·ne·ous**

spontainious : **spon·ta·ne·ous**
spon·ta·ne·ous
spread
spred : **spread**
spright·ly
sprily : **spry·ly**
spritely : **spright·ly**
sprock·et
sprockit : **sprock·et**
sproose : **spruce**
spruce
spruse : **spruce**
spry·ly
spu·mo·ne or **spu·mo·ni**
spu·mo·ni or **spu·mo·ne**
spumonie : **spu·mo·ni**
spureous : **spu·ri·ous**
spu·ri·ous
spurn
spurrious : **spu·ri·ous**
spurt
squadren : **squad·ron**
squadrin : **squad·ron**
squad·ron
squak : **squawk**
squaled : **squal·id** (filthy) or
  squalled (cried)
squal·id (filthy); **squalled**
  (cried)
squalled (cried); **squal·id**
  (filthy)
squall·er (one that cries);
  squal·or (filthiness)
squallid : **squal·id** (filthy) or
  squalled (cried)
squallor : **squall·er** (one that
  cries) or **squal·or** (filthiness)
squal·or (filthiness); **squall·er**
  (one that cries)
squawk
squeak
squeal

squeam·ish
squeaze : squeeze
squeek : squeak
squeel : squeal
squeemesh : squeam·ish
squeemish : squeam·ish
squeese : squeeze
squeeze
squerrel : squir·rel
squiar : squire
squier : squire
squire
squirl : squir·rel
squirral : squir·rel
squir·rel
squirrl : squir·rel
squirt
squize : squeeze
stabelize : sta·bi·lize
stabilety : sta·bil·i·ty
sta·bil·i·ty
sta·bi·lize
stabillity : sta·bil·i·ty
stableize : sta·bi·lize
stablize : sta·bi·lize
stacado : stac·ca·to
stacato : stac·ca·to
stacatto : stac·ca·to
stac·ca·to
stackato : stac·ca·to
stacotto : stac·ca·to
staddium : sta·di·um
stadiem : sta·di·um
sta·di·um
stag·nant
stagnent : stag·nant
stagnint : stag·nant
staid (set in one's ways);
   stayed (remained)
stair (step); stare (look)
stake (pointed piece of wood;
   to bet); steak (meat)

sta·lac·tite
sta·lag·mite
stalion : stal·lion
stallactite : sta·lac·tite
stallagmite : sta·lag·mite
stallian : stal·lion
stal·lion
stallwart : stal·wart
stal·wart
stalwert : stal·wart
stalwirt : stal·wart
sta·men
stamena : stam·i·na
stamin : sta·men
stam·i·na
staminna : stam·i·na
stammina : stam·i·na
stam·pede
stampeed : stam·pede
stampide : stam·pede
stan·dard
standerd : stan·dard
stapel : sta·ple
sta·ple
stapple : sta·ple
stare (look); stair (step)
stareotype : ste·reo·type
starile : ster·ile
statec : stat·ic
stat·ic
sta·tion·ary (fixed);
   sta·tion·ery (paper)
sta·tion·ery (paper);
   sta·tion·ary (fixed)
statisstic : sta·tis·tic
sta·tis·tic
statium : sta·di·um
stattic : stat·ic
stattistic : sta·tis·tic
stattue : stat·ue
statture : stat·ure
stattus : sta·tus

stattute : **sta·tute**
stat·ue
stat·ure
sta·tus
stat·ute
stayed (remained); **staid** (set in one's ways)
stead·fast
steady
steak (meat); **stake** (pointed piece of wood; to bet)
steal (to rob); **steel** (metal)
steaple : **stee·ple**
stear : **steer**
steddy : **steady**
stedfast : **stead·fast**
stedy : **steady**
steel (metal); **steal** (to rob)
steepal : **stee·ple**
steepel : **stee·ple**
stee·ple
steer
stelactite : **sta·lac·tite**
stel·lar
steller : **stel·lar**
stencel : **sten·cil**
sten·cil
stensel : **sten·cil**
stensil : **sten·cil**
steralize : **ster·il·ize**
ste·reo·type
stergeon : **stur·geon**
steril : **ster·ile**
ster·ile
sterilety : **ste·ril·i·ty**
sterilise (*Brit.*) : **ster·il·ize**
ste·ril·i·ty
ster·il·ize
sterillity : **ste·ril·i·ty**
sterillize : **ster·il·ize**
sternam : **ster·num**
ster·num

sterrile : **ster·ile**
stethascope : **steth·o·scope**
steth·o·scope
stew·ard
stew·ard·ess
stewardiss : **stew·ard·ess**
stewerd : **stew·ard**
stewerdess : **stew·ard·ess**
stewird : **stew·ard**
stifel : **sti·fle**
stiffle : **sti·fle**
sti·fle
stilactite : **sta·lac·tite**
stilagmite : **sta·lag·mite**
stileto : **sti·let·to**
sti·let·to
stilleto : **sti·let·to**
stimied : **sty·mied**
stimmulate : **stim·u·late**
stimmulus : **stim·u·lus**
stim·u·late
stimulis : **stim·u·lus**
stimulous : **stim·u·lus**
stim·u·lus
stincil : **sten·cil**
stipand : **sti·pend**
sti·pend
stippulate : **stip·u·late**
stip·u·late
stirep : **stir·rup**
stirrep : **stir·rup**
stir·rup
stirup : **stir·rup**
stoalen : **sto·len**
Stock·holm
Stockhome : **Stock·holm**
sto·len
stol·id
stollid : **stol·id**
stom·ach
stomache : **stom·ach**
stomack : **stom·ach**

stomich : **stom•ach**
stomick : **stom•ach**
stopige : **stop•page**
stop•page
stoppige : **stop•page**
straddel : **strad•dle**
strad•dle
straight (not crooked); **strait** (isthmus)
straight•laced *or* **strait•laced**
strait (isthmus); **straight** (not crooked)
strait•laced *or* **straight•laced**
straitlased : **strait•laced**
stratafy : **strat•i•fy**
strat•a•gem
stratajem : **strat•a•gem**
stratajy : **strat•e•gy**
stratasphere : **strat•o•sphere**
stratefy : **strat•i•fy**
strategem : **strat•a•gem**
strat•e•gy
strategy : **strat•e•gy**
stratiffy : **strat•i•fy**
strat•i•fy
stratosfere : **strat•o•sphere**
stratospheer : **strat•o•sphere**
strat•o•sphere
strattify : **strat•i•fy**
strattigem : **strat•a•gem**
strattigy : **strat•e•gy**
strattle : **strad•dle**
strattosphere : **strat•o•sphere**
streak
stream
streat : **street**
strech : **stretch**
streek : **streak**
streem : **stream**
street
strenghthen : **strength•en**
strength•en

stretch
strichnine : **strych•nine**
stricknine : **strych•nine**
stridant : **stri•dent**
stri•dent
strin•gent
stringient : **strin•gent**
stringint : **strin•gent**
striped (with stripes); **stripped** (pealed)
stripped (pealed); **striped** (with stripes)
stroake : **stroke**
stroaler : **stroll•er**
stroke
stroler : **stroll•er**
stroll•er
struggel : **strug•gle**
strug•gle
strugle : **strug•gle**
strych•nine
stubbern : **stub•born**
stub•born
stuborn : **stub•born**
stuc•co
stucko : **stuc•co**
stuco : **stuc•co**
studant : **stu•dent**
studdio : **stu•dio**
stu•dent
studeo : **stu•dio**
studeous : **stu•di•ous**
stu•dio
stu•di•ous
stultafy : **stul•ti•fy**
stultefy : **stul•ti•fy**
stul•ti•fy
stupafy : **stu•pe•fy**
stuped : **stu•pid**
stupeffy : **stu•pe•fy**
stu•pe•fy
stuper : **stu•por**

stu•pid
stupify : stu•pe•fy
stu•por
stuppid : stu•pid
stur•geon
sturgion : stur•geon
sturgon : stur•geon
sty•mied
suacidal : sui•cid•al
suade : suede
suami : swa•mi
suarthy : swar•thy
suave
suavety : sua•vi•ty
sua•vi•ty
subblety : sub•tle•ty
subbtle : sub•tle
subcidize : sub•si•dize
suberb : sub•urb
suberban : sub•ur•ban
subgigate : sub•ju•gate
subjagate : sub•ju•gate
subjigate : sub•ju•gate
sub•ju•gate
sublamate : sub•li•mate
sub•li•mate
sub•merge
sub•merse
submirge : sub•merge
submirse : sub•merse
submishion : sub•mis•sion
submissian : sub•mis•sion
sub•mis•sion
submurge : sub•merge
submurse : sub•merse
subpena : sub•poe•na
subpina : sub•poe•na
sub•poe•na
subsadize : sub•si•dize
subsedize : sub•si•dize
sub•se•quent
subsequint : sub•se•quent

subservant : sub•ser•vi•ent
subservent : sub•ser•vi•ent
subserviant : sub•ser•vi•ent
sub•ser•vi•ent
subsiddy : sub•sid•iary
    (auxilliary) or sub•si•dy
    (assistance)
sub•side
sub•sid•iary (auxilliary);
    sub•si•dy (assistance)
sub•si•dize
sub•si•dy (assistance);
    sub•sid•iary (auxilliary)
subsiquent : sub•se•quent
sub•stance
substanse : sub•stance
substatute : sub•sti•tute
substence : sub•stance
substetute : sub•sti•tute
substince : sub•stance
sub•sti•tute
subtel : sub•tle
subteranean : sub•ter•ra•nean
sub•ter•ra•nean
sub•tle
sub•tle•ty (noun); sub•tly (adv.)
subturrainian : sub•ter•ra•nean
sub•urb (city outskirts);
    su•perb (superior)
sub•ur•ban
suburben : sub•ur•ban
succede : suc•ceed
suc•ceed
succeptible : sus•cep•ti•ble
suc•cess
suc•cinct
succulant : suc•cu•lent
suc•cu•lent
succulint : suc•cu•lent
suc•cumb
sucede : suc•ceed
sucess : suc•cess

470

sucidal : **sui·cid·al**
sucint : **suc·cinct**
suckulent : **suc·cu·lent**
sucsede : **suc·ceed**
sucum : **suc·cumb**
sucumb : **suc·cumb**
suecidal : **sui·cid·al**
suede
suffacate : **suf·fo·cate**
sufficate : **suf·fo·cate**
suf·fice
suffise : **suf·fice**
suffle : **souf·flé**
suf·fo·cate
sufice : **suf·fice**
sug·ar
suger : **sug·ar**
sugest : **sug·gest**
sug·gest
suggestable : **sug·gest·ible**
sug·gest·ible
sui·cid·al
sui·cide
suisidal : **sui·cid·al**
suiside : **sui·cide**
suit·able
suiter : **suit·or**
suitible : **suit·a·ble**
suit·or
sulfer : **sul·phur**
sullphur : **sul·phur**
sulltan : **sul·tan**
sulpher : **sul·phur**
sul·phur
sul·tan
sulten : **sul·tan**
sultin : **sul·tan**
su·mac
sumack : **su·mac**
sumary : **sum·ma·ry**
sumersalt : **som·er·sault**
sumit : **sum·mit**

sumlemate : **sub·li·mate**
summac : **su·mac**
sum·ma·ry
summen : **sum·mon**
summersalt : **som·er·sault**
summersault : **som·er·sault**
sum·mer·y (like summer);
    sum·ma·ry (synopsis)
summet : **sum·mit**
sum·mit
sum·mon
sumon : **sum·mon**
sun·dae (confection); **Sun·day**
    (day of week)
Sun·day (day of week);
    sun·dae (confection)
supeerior : **su·pe·ri·or**
supeeriority : **su·pe·ri·or·i·ty**
supeirior : **su·pe·ri·or**
supeiriority : **su·pe·ri·or·i·ty**
su·perb (superior); **sub·urb**
    (city outskirts)
su·per·cede *or* **su·per·sede**
superceed : **su·per·sede**
supercileous : **su·per·cil·ious**
su·per·cil·ious
supercillious : **su·per·cil·ious**
superentendent :
    su·per·in·ten·dent
su·per·fi·cial
superfishial : **su·per·fi·cial**
superfisial : **su·per·fi·cial**
superfissial : **su·per·fi·cial**
superier : **su·pe·ri·or**
superierity : **su·pe·ri·or·i·ty**
superintendant :
    su·per·in·ten·dent
su·per·in·ten·dent
su·pe·ri·or
superiorety : **su·pe·ri·or·i·ty**
su·pe·ri·or·i·ty
superiorrity : **su·pe·ri·or·i·ty**

su·per·sede
superseed : su·per·sede
supersilious : su·per·cil·ious
supersillious : su·per·cil·ious
su·per·vise
superviser : su·per·vi·sor
su·per·vi·sor
supervize : su·per·vise
supervizor : su·per·vi·sor
supirior : su·pe·ri·or
supiriority : su·pe·ri·or·i·ty
suplament : sup·ple·ment
suplant : sup·plant
suplement : sup·ple·ment
suplicate : sup·pli·cate
suply : sup·ply
suport : sup·port
suppena : sub·poe·na
suppina : sub·poe·na
supplacate : sup·pli·cate
supplament : sup·ple·ment
sup·plant
supplecate : sup·pli·cate
sup·ple·ment
sup·pli·cate
suppliment : sup·ple·ment
sup·ply
sup·port
sup·press
supreem : su·preme
su·prem·a·cy
supremasy : su·prem·a·cy
su·preme
supremicy : su·prem·a·cy
supremissy : su·prem·a·cy
supress : sup·press
suprimacy : su·prem·a·cy
suprime : su·preme
suprise : sur·prise
suprize : sur·prise
surch : search

sure·ly (with certainty); sur·ly (sullen)
surf (waves); serf (peasant)
sur·face
sur·feit
surfet : sur·feit
surfice : sur·face
surfiet : sur·feit
surfise : sur·face
surfiss : sur·face
surfit : sur·feit
surge (to rise up); serge (cloth)
sur·geon
sur·gery
surgion : sur·geon
surgirgy : sur·gery
surloin : sir·loin
sur·ly (sullen); sure·ly (with certainty)
sur·mise
surmize : sur·mise
sur·mount
sur·name
surogate : sur·ro·gate
surpent : ser·pent
sur·plice (vestment); sur·plus (excess)
sur·plus (excess); sur·plice (vestment)
surpreme : su·preme
surpress : sup·press
sur·prise
surprize : sur·prise
surragate : sur·ro·gate
surregate : sur·ro·gate
sur·ro·gate
surroget : sur·ro·gate
survaillance : sur·veil·lance
survallence : sur·veil·lance
survay : sur·vey
survayer : sur·vey·or
survayor : sur·vey·or

surveilance : **sur·veil·lance**
sur·veil·lance
survellance : **sur·veil·lance**
sur·vey
surveyer : **sur·vey·or**
sur·vey·or
surviellance : **sur·veil·lance**
sur·viv·al
survivel : **sur·viv·al**
surviver : **sur·viv·or**
survivil : **sur·viv·al**
sur·viv·or
susceptable : **sus·cep·ti·ble**
sus·cep·ti·ble
suscinct : **suc·cinct**
suspence : **sus·pense**
sus·pense
suspician : **sus·pi·cion**
sus·pi·cion
sus·pi·cious
suspince : **sus·pense**
suspinse : **sus·pense**
suspishious : **sus·pi·cious**
suspission : **sus·pi·cion**
suspissious : **sus·pi·cious**
suspition : **sus·pi·cion**
suspitious : **sus·pi·cious**
susseptible : **sus·cep·ti·ble**
sussinct : **suc·cinct**
sustainance : **sus·te·nance**
sustanence : **sus·te·nance**
sus·te·nance
sustenanse : **sus·te·nance**
sustinance : **sus·te·nance**
sutable : **suit·able**
suthern : **south·ern**
suttle : **sub·tle**
suvenir : **sou·ve·nir**
swade : **suede**
swammi : **swa·mi**
swamy : **swa·mi**
swar·thy

swasstika : **swas·ti·ka**
swastica : **swas·ti·ka**
swasticka : **swas·ti·ka**
swas·ti·ka
swave : **suave**
swealter : **swel·ter**
sweap : **sweep**
sweapstakes : **sweep·stakes**
sweat·er
Swedan : **Swe·den**
Swe·den
Swed·ish
Sweeden : **Swe·den**
Sweedish : **Swed·ish**
sweep
sweep·stakes
sweepsteaks : **sweep·stakes**
swel·ter
swerve
sweter : **sweat·er**
swetter : **sweat·er**
swindlar : **swin·dler**
swin·dler
Swisserland : **Switz·er·land**
Switzarland : **Switz·er·land**
Switz·er·land
swival : **swiv·el**
swiv·el
swiv·eled
swivelled : **swiv·eled**
Switzzerland : **Switz·er·land**
swoallem : **swol·len**
swolen : **swol·len**
swol·len
sword
sworthy : **swarthy**
swove : **suave**
swurve : **swerve**
syanide : **cy·a·nide**
sybernetics : **cy·ber·net·ics**
sycamoor : **syc·a·more**
syc·a·more

sycaphant : **sy·co·phant**
sycaphent : **sy·co·phant**
syckle : **cy·cle** (rotation) *or*
  sick·le (knife)
sycle : **cy·cle** (rotation) *or*
  sick·le (knife)
sycofant : **sy·co·phant**
sycomore : **syc·a·more**
sy·co·phant
sykamore : **syc·a·more**
sykophant : **sy·co·phant**
sylabus : **syl·la·bus**
sylalble : **syl·la·ble**
sylinder : **cyl·in·der**
syl·la·ble
syl·la·bus
sylleble : **syl·la·ble**
syllebus : **syl·la·bus**
symbal : **cym·bal** (brass plate)
  or **sym·bol** (meaningful
  image)
sym·bol (meaningful image);
  cym·bal (brass plate)
symetry : **sym·me·try**
symmatry : **sym·me·try**
sym·me·try
sym·pa·thize
sympethize : **sym·pa·thize**
sym·pho·ny
symposiem : **sym·po·sium**
sym·po·sium

symptam : **symp·tom**
symptem : **symp·tom**
symp·tom
symtom : **symp·tom**
syn·a·gogue
synanym : **syn·o·nym**
synchrinize : **syn·chro·nize**
syn·chro·nize
syncronize : **syn·chro·nize**
syndacate : **syn·di·cate**
syndecate : **syn·di·cate**
syndicat : **syn·di·cate**
syn·di·cate
synegogue : **syn·a·gogue**
synicism : **cyn·i·cism**
synonim : **syn·o·nym**
syn·o·nym
synpathize : **sym·pa·thize**
synphony : **sym·pho·ny**
synthasize : **syn·the·size**
synthesise : **syn·the·size**
syn·the·size
sypress : **cy·press**
Syr·a·cuse
syrep : **syr·up**
syrrup : **syr·up**
syr·up *or* **sirup**
systam : **sys·tem**
sys·tem
systum : **sys·tem**
sythe : **scythe**

T

tabarnacle : **tab·er·na·cle**
tabbernacle : **tab·er·na·cle**
tabbleau : **tab·leau**
tabblet : **tab·let**
tabbloe : **tab·leau**
tabboo : **ta·boo**
tabelware : **ta·ble·ware**
tabernacal : **tab·er·na·cle**
tabernackle : **tab·er·na·cle**
tab·er·na·cle
tab·leau
tab·let
ta·ble·ware
tablewear : **ta·ble·ware**
tablieu : **tab·leau**
tablit : **tab·let**
ta·boo
tabu : **ta·boo**
tacet : **tac·it**
taceturn : **tac·i·turn**
tac·it
tacitern : **tac·i·turn**
tac·i·turn
tackal : **tack·le**
tackel : **tack·le**
tack·le
tacktics : **tac·tics**
tactecs : **tac·tics**
tact·ful
tactfull : **tact·ful**
tac·ti·cal
tacticks : **tac·tics**
tacticle : **tac·ti·cal**
tac·tics
tactikal : **tac·ti·cal**
tafeta : **taf·fe·ta**
taf·fe·ta
taffita : **taf·fe·ta**
tafita : **taf·fe·ta**
Taheti : **Ta·hi·ti**

Ta·hi·ti
Tahitti : **Ta·hi·ti**
Tahity : **Ta·hi·ti**
Tailand : **Thai·land**
tailer : **tai·lor**
tai·lor
Talahassee : **Tal·la·has·see**
talant : **tal·ent**
talcem : **tal·cum**
tal·cum
talen : **tal·on**
tal·ent
tal·is·man
talissman : **tal·is·man**
talk·ative
talkitive : **talk·ative**
Tallahasee : **Tal·la·has·see**
Tal·la·has·see
tallant : **tal·ent**
tallcum : **tal·cum**
tallent : **tal·ent**
tallisman : **tal·is·man**
tallon : **tal·on**
Talmed : **Tal·mud**
Talmid : **Tal·mud**
Tal·mud
tal·on
talor : **tai·lor**
ta·ma·le
tamaly : **ta·ma·le**
tamborine : **tam·bou·rine**
tambourene : **tam·bou·rine**
tam·bou·rine
tamburine : **tam·bou·rine**
tamole : **ta·ma·le**
tamolle : **ta·ma·le**
tan·dem
tandim : **tan·dem**
tandum : **tan·dem**
tangarine : **tan·ger·ine**

tangeble : **tan•gi•ble**
tan•gent
tangerene : **tan•ger•ine**
tan•ger•ine
tangibal : **tan•gi•ble**
tan•gi•ble
tangient : **tan•gent**
tangierine : **tan•ger•ine**
tangint : **tan•gent**
tangirine : **tan•ger•ine**
tanjerine : **tan•ger•ine**
tannary : **tan•nery**
tan•nery
tantalise (*Brit.*) : **tan•ta•lize**
tan•ta•lize
tantallize : **tan•ta•lize**
tantelize : **tan•ta•lize**
tantilize : **tan•ta•lize**
tantrem : **tan•trum**
tantrim : **tan•trum**
tan•trum
tapeoca : **tap•i•o•ca**
tapestery : **tap•es•try**
tap•es•try
tap•i•o•ca
tapioka : **tap•i•o•ca**
tapistry : **tap•es•try**
tappestry : **tap•es•try**
tappioca : **tap•i•o•ca**
tappistry : **tap•es•try**
taranchula : **ta•ran•tu•la**
tarantoola : **ta•ran•tu•la**
ta•ran•tu•la
tareff : **tar•iff**
tar•get
targit : **tar•get**
tar•iff
tarnesh : **tar•nish**
tar•nish
tarpalin : **tar•pau•lin**
tarpaulen : **tar•pau•lin**
tar•pau•lin

tarpolin : **tar•pau•lin**
tarriff : **tar•iff**
tar•tan
tar•tar
tarten : **tar•tan**
tarter : **tar•tar**
tasel : **tas•sel**
taseturn : **tac•i•turn**
tasit : **tac•it**
tasiturn : **tac•i•turn**
tas•sel
tassit : **tac•it**
tassiturn : **tac•i•turn**
tassle : **tas•sel**
tatle : **tat•tle**
tatoo : **tat•too**
tattel : **tat•tle**
tat•tle
tat•too
tav•ern
tavurn : **tav•ern**
tavvern : **tav•ern**
tax•able
taxadermy : **taxi•der•my**
taxedermy : **taxi•der•my**
taxible : **tax•able**
taxi•der•my
taxidurmy : **taxi•der•my**
tea (drink); **tee** (golf)
teach
teadious : **te•dious**
tear•ful
tearfull : **tear•ful**
tease
technecal : **tech•ni•cal**
tech•ni•cal
technicle : **tech•ni•cal**
tech•nique
tecnical : **tech•ni•cal**
tecnique : **tech•nique**
tedeum : **te•di•um**
te•dious

te·di·um
tedius : te·dious
tee (golf); tea (drink)
teech : teach
teerful : tear·ful
teese : tease
teeth (*noun*); teethe (*verb*)
teethe (*verb*); teeth (*noun*)
Te·he·ran *or* Teh·ran
Teh·ran *or* Te·he·ran
telacast : tele·cast
telagram : tele·gram
telaphone : tele·phone
telascope : tele·scope
telavise : tele·vise
telavision : tele·vi·sion
tele·cast
tele·gram
tele·phone
tele·scope
tele·vise
tele·vi·sion
televize : tele·vise
tellecast : tele·cast
tellegram : tele·gram
tellephone : tele·phone
tellescope : tele·scope
tellevise : tele·vise
tellevision : tele·vi·sion
temblar : tem·blor
tembler : tem·blor
tem·blor
te·mer·i·ty
temmeritty : te·mer·i·ty
temmerity : te·mer·i·ty
tempachure : tem·per·a·ture
temparary : tem·po·rary
tempature : tem·per·a·ture
tem·per·ance
temperanse : tem·per·ance
tem·per·a·ture
temperence : tem·per·ance

temperince : tem·per·ance
temperment : tem·per·a·ment
temperture : tem·per·a·ture
tem·pest
tempirary : tem·po·rary
tempist : tem·pest
tem·po·rary
temporery : tem·po·rary
temprature : tem·per·a·ture
ten·a·ble
te·na·cious
tenacle : ten·ta·cle
tenament : ten·e·ment
tenamint : ten·e·ment
ten·ant
Tenasee : Ten·nes·see
tenat : te·net
tenatious : ten·a·ble
tenative : ten·ta·tive
tendan : ten·don
tendancy : ten·den·cy
tendansy : ten·den·cy
ten·den·cy
tendensy : ten·den·cy
tenderhook : ten·ter·hook
tendin : ten·don
tendincy : ten·den·cy
ten·don
tendrel : ten·dril
ten·dril
tendrill : ten·dril
ten·e·ment
tenent : ten·ant
tener : ten·or
Tenesee : Ten·nes·see
te·net
tenint : ten·ant
tenir : ten·or
tenis : ten·nis
Tenisee : Ten·nes·see
tenit : te·net
tennable : ten·a·ble

477

tennacious : **te•na•cious**
tennament : **ten•e•ment**
tennant : **ten•ant**
tennement : **ten•e•ment**
tennent : **ten•ant**
tennes : **ten•nis**
Tennesee : **Ten•nes•see**
Ten•nes•see
tennet : **te•net**
ten•nis
tennor : **ten•or**
tennuous : **ten•u•ous**
tennure : **ten•ure**
ten•or
ten•ta•cle
ten•ta•tive
ten•ter•hook
tentetive : **ten•ta•tive**
tentical : **ten•ta•cle**
tenticle : **ten•ta•cle**
tentitive : **ten•ta•tive**
ten•u•ous
ten•ure
teped : **tep•id**
tep•id
teppid : **tep•id**
terace : **ter•race**
teradactyl : **ptero•dac•tyl**
terain : **ter•rain**
terantula : **ta•ran•tu•la**
terban : **tur•ban** (headdress) *or*
    tur•bine (engine)
terbine : **tur•ban** (headdress) *or*
    tur•bine (engine)
terestrial : **ter•res•tri•al**
terible : **ter•ri•ble**
teridactyl : **ptero•dac•tyl**
terier : **ter•ri•er**
teriffy : **ter•ri•fy**
terific : **ter•rif•ic**
terify : **ter•ri•fy**
teritory : **ter•ri•to•ry**

terkey : **tur•key**
termenal : **ter•mi•nal**
ter•mi•nal
terminel : **ter•mi•nal**
terminnal : **ter•mi•nal**
ter•mite
termmite : **ter•mite**
ternip : **tur•nip**
terodactile : **ptero•dac•tyl**
terodactill : **ptero•dac•tyl**
terpentine : **tur•pen•tine**
terquoise : **tur•quoise**
terrable : **ter•ri•ble**
ter•race
terrafy : **ter•ri•fy**
ter•rain
terrane : **ter•rain**
terratory : **ter•ri•to•ry**
terrestial : **ter•res•tri•al**
ter•res•tri•al
terretory : **ter•ri•to•ry**
terribal : **ter•ri•ble**
ter•ri•ble
terrice : **ter•race**
ter•ri•er
terriffic : **ter•rif•ic**
ter•rif•ic
ter•ri•fy
terriss : **ter•race**
territorey : **ter•ri•to•ry**
ter•ri•to•ry
tesstify : **tes•ti•fy**
testafy : **tes•ti•fy**
tes•ta•ment
testamony : **tes•ti•mo•ny**
testement : **tes•ta•ment**
testemony : **tes•ti•mo•ny**
testiffy : **tes•ti•fy**
tes•ti•fy
testiment : **tes•ta•ment**
tes•ti•mo•ny
tetanis : **tet•a•nus**

tet·a·nus
tetnis : **tet·a·nus**
tetnus : **tet·a·nus**
tettanus : **tet·a·nus**
Teusday : **Tues·day**
Tex·as
textil : **tex·tile**
tex·tile
textill : **tex·tile**
Texus : **Tex·as**
thach : **thatch**
Thai·land
than (rather than); **then** (not now)
thatch
theaf : **thief**
thealogy : **the·ol·o·gy**
thearem : **the·o·rem**
theary : **the·o·ry**
theasaurus : **the·sau·rus**
the·a·ter *or* the·a·tre
the·a·tre *or* the·a·ter
theavery : **thiev·ery**
theaves : **thieves**
theef : **thief**
theevery : **thiev·ery**
theeves : **thieves**
theif : **thief**
their (belonging to them); **there** (not here); **they're** (they are)
theirem : **the·o·rem**
theirfore : **there·fore**
theirs (belonging to them); **there's** (there is)
theiry : **the·o·ry**
theiter : **the·a·ter**
theivery : **thiev·ery**
theives : **thieves**
then (not now); **than** (rather than)
theoligy : **the·ol·o·gy**

theollogy : **the·ol·o·gy**
the·ol·o·gy
the·o·rem
theorum : **the·o·rem**
the·o·ry
ther·a·peu·tic
therapuetic : **ther·a·peu·tic**
theraputic : **ther·a·peu·tic**
ther·a·py
there (not here); **their** (belonging to them); **they're** (they are)
therefor : **there·fore**
there·fore
therem : **the·o·rem**
therepeutic : **ther·a·peu·tic**
there's (there is); **theirs** (belonging to them)
theripy : **ther·a·py**
ther·mal
thermel : **ther·mal**
thermiss : **ther·mos**
ther·mos
thermus : **ther·mos**
therrapy : **ther·a·py**
Thersday : **Thurs·day**
thery : **the·o·ry**
the·sau·rus
thesoris : **the·sau·rus**
thesorrus : **the·sau·rus**
thesorus : **the·sau·rus**
theter : **the·a·ter**
thevery : **thiev·ery**
theves : **thieves**
they're (they are); **their** (belonging to them); **there** (not here)
Thialand : **Thai·land**
thief
thiefery : **thiev·ery**
thiefs : **thieves**
thievary : **thiev·ery**

thiev·ery
thieves
thievry : **thiev·ery**
thirmos : **ther·mos**
thiroid : **thy·roid**
Thirsday : **Thurs·day**
thirtean : **thir·teen**
thir·teen
thir·ti·eth
thirtine : **thir·teen**
thirtyeth : **thir·ti·eth**
thisel : **this·tle**
thissle : **this·tle**
this·tle
thoarax : **tho·rax**
tho·rax
thorogh : **thor·ough**
 (painstaking) *or* **through**
 (into and out of)
thor·ough (painstaking);
 through (into and out of)
thorow : **thor·ough**
 (painstaking) *or* **through**
 (into and out of)
thou·sand
thousend : **thou·sand**
thousind : **thou·sand**
thowsand : **thou·sand**
thread
thread·bare
thred : **thread**
thredbare : **thread·bare**
threshhold : **thresh·old**
thresh·old
through (into and out of);
 thor·ough (painstaking)
thru : **through**
thrugh : **thor·ough**
 (painstaking) *or* **through**
 (into and out of)
thum : **thumb**
thumb

thurmal : **ther·mal**
thurmos : **ther·mos**
Thurs·day
thy·roid
ti·ara
tiarra : **ti·ara**
tibbia : **tib·ia**
tibea : **tib·ia**
tib·ia
tickal : **tick·le**
tickel : **tick·le**
tick·le
tiera : **ti·ara**
tigar : **ti·ger**
ti·ger
tigeress : **ti·gress**
tigger : **ti·ger**
ti·gress
tigriss : **ti·gress**
tim·ber (wood); **tim·bre**
 (quality of sound)
tim·bre (quality of sound);
 tim·ber (wood)
Timbucktu : **Tim·buk·tu**
Timbuktoo : **Tim·buk·tu**
Tim·buk·tu
timerity : **te·mer·i·ty**
tim·id
timmid : **tim·id**
timpature : **tem·per·a·ture**
timperament : **tem·per·a·ment**
timperature : **tem·per·a·ture**
timperment : **tem·per·a·ment**
timperture : **tem·per·a·ture**
tinant : **ten·ant**
tinc·ture
Tinnessee : **Ten·nes·see**
tin·sel
tinsell : **tin·sel**
tinsill : **tin·sel**
tinsle : **tin·sel**
tinture : **tinc·ture**

tinuous : **ten·u·ous**
tipest : **typ·ist**
tipewriter : **type·writ·er**
tiphoid : **ty·phoid**
tiphoon : **ty·phoon**
tipical : **typ·i·cal**
ti·rade
tiraid : **ti·rade**
tiranny : **tyr·an·ny**
tirban : **tur·ban** (headdress) *or*
   tur·bine (engine)
tirmite : **ter·mite**
tirnip : **tur·nip**
tirrade : **ti·rade**
ti·tan
ti·tan·ic
titannic : **ti·tan·ic**
titen : **ti·tan**
tittan : **ti·tan**
toaken : **to·ken**
toast
to·bac·co
tobacko : **to·bac·co**
tobaco : **to·bac·co**
tobbacco : **to·bac·co**
tobogan : **to·bog·gan**
to·bog·gan
toboggen : **to·bog·gan**
toboggin : **to·bog·gan**
tobogin : **to·bog·gan**
tocan : **tou·can**
tocksic : **tox·ic**
tofee : **tof·fee**
tof·fee
toffy : **tof·fee**
toi·let
toilit : **toi·let**
to·ken
tokin : **to·ken**
tol·er·a·ble
tol·er·ance
toleranse : **tol·er·ance**

tol·er·ate
tolerence : **tol·er·ance**
tolerent : **tol·er·ance**
tolerible : **tol·er·a·ble**
tolirable : **tol·er·a·ble**
tollarance : **tol·er·ance**
tollerable : **tol·er·a·ble**
tollerance : **tol·er·ance**
tollerate : **tol·er·ate**
tollerense : **tol·er·ance**
tollerent : **tol·er·ant**
tollerint : **tol·er·ant**
tom·a·hawk
tomain : **pto·maine**
tomane : **pto·maine**
to·ma·to
tomatoe : **to·ma·to**
to·ma·toes
tomatos : **to·ma·toes**
tomb·stone
tommahawk : **tom·a·hawk**
tommorow : **to·mor·row**
tommorrow : **to·mor·row**
tomohawk : **tom·a·hawk**
tomorow : **to·mor·row**
to·mor·row
tonage : **ton·nage**
tonge : **tongue**
tongue
ton·ic
tonick : **ton·ic**
to·night
tonite : **to·night**
ton·nage
tonnege : **ton·nage**
tonnic : **ton·ic**
tonnige : **ton·nage**
tonsal : **ton·sil**
tonsel : **ton·sil**
tonsell : **ton·sil**
ton·sil
top·ic

topick : **top•ic**
toppic : **top•ic**
Toranto : **To•ron•to**
torchure : **tor•ture**
torent : **tor•rent**
torid : **tor•rid**
tornaddo : **tor•na•do**
tor•na•do
tornaido : **tor•na•do**
tornato : **tor•na•do**
To•ron•to
torpeado : **tor•pe•do**
tor•pe•do
torpeto : **tor•pe•do**
torpido : **tor•pe•do**
torrant : **tor•rent**
torrea : **tor•ti•lla**
torred : **tor•rid**
tor•rent
tor•rid
Torronto : **To•ron•to**
tort (civil wrong); **torte** (pastry)
torte (pastry); **tort** (civil wrong)
tortia : **tor•ti•lla**
tortice : **tor•toise**
tortila : **tor•ti•lla**
tor•ti•lla
tortise : **tor•toise**
tortiss : **tor•toise**
tor•toise
tor•tu•ous
tor•ture
torturous : **tor•tu•ous**
tost : **toast**
toste : **toast**
to•tal
totam : **to•tem**
totel : **to•tal**
to•tem
totil : **to•tal**
totim : **to•tem**
tottal : **to•tal**

totum : **to•tem**
tou•can
tough
tounge : **tongue**
toupay : **tou•pee**
tou•pee
toupey : **tou•pee**
tour•ist
tournakette : **tour•ni•quet**
tour•na•ment
tournamint : **tour•na•ment**
tournaquet : **tour•ni•quet**
tournement : **tour•na•ment**
tournequet : **tour•ni•quet**
tour•ney
tourniment : **tour•na•ment**
tour•ni•quet
tousalled : **tou•sled**
touselled : **tou•sled**
tou•sled
towal : **tow•el**
to•ward
tow•el
towerd : **to•ward**
towl : **tow•el**
towselled : **tou•sled**
toxec : **tox•ic**
tox•ic
toxick : **tox•ic**
tra•chea
trachia : **tra•chea**
trackia : **tra•chea**
trackter : **trac•tor**
tracktor : **trac•tor**
tracer : **trac•tor**
trac•tor
trad•er (one who trades);
    trai•tor (one who betrays)
traffec : **traf•fic**
traffecked : **traf•ficked**
traf•fic
trafficed : **traf•ficked**

traffick : **traf•fic**
traf•ficked
trafic : **traf•fic**
traficked : **traf•ficked**
tragectory : **tra•jec•to•ry**
trageddy : **trag•e•dy**
trag•e•dy
tragety : **trag•e•dy**
tragidy : **trag•e•dy**
traichea : **tra•chea**
traitor (one who betrays);
　trad•er (one who trades)
trajactary : **tra•jec•to•ry**
trajectery : **tra•jec•to•ry**
tra•jec•to•ry
trama : **trau•ma**
tramel : **tram•mel**
trammal : **tram•mel**
tram•mel
trancend : **tran•scend**
trancient : **tran•sient**
trancit : **tran•sit**
tranquel : **tran•quil**
tran•quil
tranquill : **tran•quil**
transam : **tran•som**
tran•scend
transcet : **tran•sit**
transcind : **tran•scend**
transem : **tran•som**
transferance : **trans•fer•ence**
trans•fer•ence
transferense : **trans•fer•ence**
transferrence : **trans•fer•ence**
transiant : **tran•sient**
tran•sient
tran•sit
tran•som
transsend : **tran•scend**
transum : **tran•som**
trapazoid : **trap•e•zoid**
trapeeze : **tra•peze**

trapese : **tra•peze**
tra•peze
trap•e•zoid
trappeze : **tra•peze**
trappezoid : **trap•e•zoid**
trau•ma
travasty : **trav•es•ty**
trav•el
travessty : **trav•es•ty**
trav•es•ty
travil : **trav•el**
travisty : **trav•es•ty**
travvel : **trav•el**
treacal : **trea•cle**
treachary : **treach•ery**
treacherry : **treach•ery**
treach•ery
trea•cle
tread
treakle : **trea•cle**
treashure : **trea•sure**
trea•son
trea•sure
treat
treatace : **trea•tise**
treatase : **trea•tise**
treatice : **trea•tise**
trea•tise
trebal : **tre•ble**
trebble : **tre•ble**
trebel : **tre•ble**
trebile : **tre•ble**
tre•ble
trechery : **treach•ery**
treck : **trek**
tred : **tread**
treecle : **trea•cle**
treeson : **trea•son**
treet : **treat**
treetise : **trea•tise**
trek
trekea : **tra•chea**

tremer : **trem•or**
trem•or
trenket : **trin•ket**
tres•pass
tresspass : **tres•pass**
tressure : **trea•sure**
tresure : **trea•sure**
trib•al
tribbutary : **trib•u•tary**
tribel : **trib•al**
tributarry : **trib•u•tary**
trib•u•tary
tributery : **trib•u•tary**
trilegy : **tril•o•gy**
triligy : **tril•o•gy**
trilligy : **tril•o•gy**
trillogy : **tril•o•gy**
tril•o•gy
trimor : **trem•or**
Trinadad : **Trin•i•dad**
Trin•i•dad
trin•ket
trinkit : **trin•ket**
Trinnidad : **Trin•i•dad**
tripal : **tri•ple**
tripel : **tri•ple**
tri•ple
trip•let
triplit : **trip•let**
tripple : **tri•ple**
tripplet : **trip•let**
triumf : **tri•umph**
tri•umph
trivea : **triv•ia**
triv•ia
trivvia : **triv•ia**
troley : **trol•ley**
trol•ley
trolly : **trol•ley**
troma : **trau•ma**
troop (organized group);
    troupe (group of actors)

tropec : **trop•ic**
trop•ic
trop•i•cal
tropicle : **trop•i•cal**
troppic : **trop•ic**
troppical : **trop•i•cal**
troubador : **trou•ba•dour**
trou•ba•dour
troubidor : **trou•ba•dour**
trou•ble
troul : **trow•el**
troupe (group of actors);
    troop (organized group)
trou•sers
trouzers : **trou•sers**
trow•el
trowl : **trow•el**
trowsers : **trou•sers**
tru•ant
trubadour : **trou•ba•dour**
trubble : **trou•ble**
truely : **tru•ly**
truent : **tru•ant**
trully : **tru•ly**
tru•ly
trum•pet
trumpit : **trum•pet**
trust•ee (*noun*); **trusty** (*adj.*)
trusty (*adj.*); **trust•ee** (*noun*)
tsar *or* **czar**
tucan : **tou•can**
Tues•day
tuff : **tough**
tulep : **tu•lip**
tu•lip
tullip : **tu•lip**
tumbstone : **tomb•stone**
tumer : **tu•mor**
tumestone : **tomb•stone**
tummor : **tu•mor**
tummult : **tu•mult**
tu•mor

tu•mult

tunec : tu•nic

tungue : tongue

tu•nic

tunnal : tun•nel

tun•nel

tunnic : tu•nic

tunnle : tun•nel

tupee : tou•pee

tur•ban (headdress); tur•bine
    (engine)

turbelant : tur•bu•lent

turben : tur•ban (headdress) or
    tur•bine (engine)

turbin : tur•ban (headdress) or
    tur•bine (engine)

tur•bine (engine); tur•ban
    (headdress)

tur•bu•lent

turet : tur•ret

turist : tour•ist

tur•key

turkoise : tur•quoise

turky : tur•key

turmite : ter•mite

turnament : tour•na•ment

turnep : tur•nip

turney : tour•ney

tur•nip

turniquet : tour•ni•quet

tur•pen•tine

turpintine : tur•pen•tine

turquoice : tur•quoise

turquois : tur•quoise

tur•quoise

tur•ret

turrit : tur•ret

Tusday : Tues•day

tuter : tu•tor

tu•tor

tux•e•do

tuxeto : tux•e•do

tuxido : tux•e•do

tweazers : twee•zers

tweesers : twee•zers

twee•zers

twelfth

twelth : twelfth

twelvth : twelfth

twen•ti•eth

twentyith : twen•ti•eth

tyfoid : ty•phoid

tyfoon : ty•phoon

typeriter : type•writ•er

type•writ•er

ty•phoid

ty•phoon

typhune : ty•phoon

typ•i•cal

typicle : typ•i•cal

typ•ist

typpical : typ•i•cal

typpist : typ•ist

tyr•an•ny

ty•rant

tyrenny : tyr•an•ny

tyrent : ty•rant

tzar : czar

U

ubiguitous : **ubiq·ui·tous**
ubiquitiss : **ubiq·ui·tous**
ubiq·ui·tous
ubiquitus : **ubiq·ui·tous**
Ucharist : **Eu·cha·rist**
ufemism : **eu·phe·mism**
Ugan·da
Ugganda : **Ugan·da**
ug·li·ness
uglyness : **ug·li·ness**
Ugonda : **Ugan·da**
ukalele : **uku·le·le**
ukelale : **uku·le·le**
ukelayle : **uku·le·le**
ukelele : **uku·le·le**
ukeley : **uku·le·le**
ukilele : **uku·le·le**
Ukrain : **Ukraine**
Ukraine
Ukrane : **Ukraine**
uku·le·le
ul·cer
ulogy : **eu·lo·gy**
ulser : **ul·cer**
ultearior : **ul·te·ri·or**
ulteerior : **ul·te·ri·or**
ultereor : **ul·te·ri·or**
ulterier : **ul·te·ri·or**
ul·te·ri·or
ul·ti·mate
ultimet : **ul·ti·mate**
ultimite : **ul·ti·mate**
ultirior : **ul·te·ri·or**
ultravilet : **ul·tra·vi·o·let**
ultravilot : **ul·tra·vi·o·let**
ul·tra·vi·o·let
ultraviolit : **ul·tra·vi·o·let**
ultreviolet : **ul·tra·vi·o·let**
umbrela : **um·brel·la**
um·brel·la

umpior : **um·pire**
um·pire
unabal : **un·able**
unabel : **un·able**
un·able
unacorn : **uni·corn**
unafy : **uni·fy**
unalatiral : **uni·lat·er·al**
unanamous : **unan·i·mous**
unanemous : **unan·i·mous**
unan·i·mous
unanimus : **unan·i·mous**
unannimous : **unan·i·mous**
unarring : **un·er·ring**
unason : **uni·son**
unatural : **un·nat·u·ral**
unaverse : **uni·verse**
unaversity : **uni·ver·si·ty**
unbeleavable : **un·be·liev·able**
unbeleevable : **un·be·liev·able**
unbeleivable : **un·be·liev·able**
unbelievabel : **un·be·liev·able**
un·be·liev·able
unbelieveble : **un·be·liev·able**
uncal : **un·cle**
un·can·ny
uncany : **un·can·ny**
un·cle
uncooth : **un·couth**
un·couth
uncuth : **un·couth**
undalate : **un·du·late**
undelate : **un·du·late**
un·de·ni·able
undenyable : **un·de·ni·able**
un·der·neath
underneeth : **un·der·neath**
underneith : **un·der·neath**
undertoe : **un·der·tow**
un·der·tow

underware : **un·der·wear**
un·der·wear
undulait : **un·du·late**
un·du·late
undully : **un·du·ly**
un·du·ly
unecorn : **uni·corn**
uneeke : **unique**
uneeque : **unique**
unefy : **uni·fy**
uneqivocal : **un·equiv·o·cal**
unequivacal : **un·equiv·o·cal**
unequivecal : **un·equiv·o·cal**
un·equiv·o·cal
unering : **un·err·ing**
un·err·ing
uneson : **uni·son**
unet : **unit**
unety : **uni·ty**
uneversal : **uni·ver·sal**
unfaigned : **un·feigned**
unfained : **un·feigned**
un·feigned
unfeined : **un·feigned**
unferl : **un·furl**
un·furl
unholesome : **un·whole·some**
uni·corn
uniffy : **uni·fy**
uni·fy
unike : **unique**
uni·lat·er·al
unilaterel : **uni·lat·er·al**
unilatiral : **uni·lat·er·al**
unilatteral : **uni·lat·er·al**
unint : **unite**
unique
unisen : **uni·son**
uni·son
unit (*noun*); unite (*verb*)
unite (*verb*); unit (*noun*)
uni·ty

univercity : **uni·ver·si·ty**
uni·ver·sal
universel : **uni·ver·sal**
universety : **uni·ver·si·ty**
universitty : **uni·ver·si·ty**
uni·ver·si·ty
univursal : **uni·ver·sal**
univurse : **uni·verse**
univursity : **uni·ver·si·ty**
unkanny : **un·can·ny**
un·kempt
unkimpt : **un·kempt**
unkle : **un·cle**
unkouth : **un·couth**
unkuth : **un·couth**
un·law·ful
unlawfull : **un·law·ful**
un·leav·ened
unlevened : **un·leav·ened**
un·mer·ci·ful
unmercifull : **un·mer·ci·ful**
unmersiful : **un·mer·ci·ful**
unmurciful : **un·mer·ci·ful**
unnateral : **un·nat·u·ral**
un·nat·u·ral
unnaturel : **un·nat·u·ral**
unnicorn : **uni·corn**
unnify : **uni·fy**
unnit : **unit**
unnite : **unite**
unnity : **uni·ty**
unniversal : **uni·ver·sal**
unniverse : **uni·verse**
unniversity : **uni·ver·si·ty**
un·pal·at·able
unpaletable : **un·pal·at·able**
unpalitable : **un·pal·at·able**
unpallatable : **un·pal·at·able**
un·prec·e·dent·ed
unprecidented :
    un·prec·e·dent·ed

unpresedented :
  un·prec·e·dent·ed
unpressidented :
  un·prec·e·dent·ed
unraval : **un·rav·el**
un·rav·el
unravil : **un·rav·el**
unravvel : **un·rav·el**
un·ready
unreddy : **un·ready**
un·re·li·able
unrelible : **un·re·li·able**
unrelieble : **un·re·li·able**
unrelyable : **un·re·li·able**
un·ri·valed *or* **un·ri·valled**
un·ri·valled *or* **un·ri·valed**
unriveled : **un·ri·valed**
unrivelled : **un·ri·valed**
unrivilled : **un·ri·valed**
unruley : **un·ruly**
unrully : **un·ruly**
un·ruly
unsanatary : **un·san·i·tary**
unsanetary : **un·san·i·tary**
unsanitarry : **un·san·i·tary**
un·san·i·tary
unsaniterry : **un·san·i·tary**
unsanitery : **un·san·i·tary**
unsavarry : **un·sa·vory**
unsaverry : **un·sa·vory**
unsavery : **un·sa·vory**
unsavorry : **un·sa·vory**
un·sa·vory
unscaithed : **un·scathed**
un·scathed
unseamly : **un·seem·ly**
unseemely : **un·seem·ly**
unseemily : **un·seem·ly**
un·seem·ly
unsheath : **un·sheathe**
un·sheathe
unsheeth : **un·sheathe**

unsheethe : **un·sheathe**
unsheith : **un·sheathe**
unsheithe : **un·sheathe**
unsoceable : **un·so·cia·ble**
unsochable : **un·so·cia·ble**
un·so·cia·ble
unspeakabel : **un·speak·able**
un·speak·able
unspeakible : **un·speak·able**
unspeekable : **un·speak·able**
un·steady
unsteddy : **un·steady**
un·til
untill : **un·til**
un·time·ly
untimly : **un·time·ly**
untootered : **un·tu·tored**
untudored : **un·tu·tored**
untutered : **un·tu·tored**
un·tu·tored
unuch : **eu·nuch**
unussual : **un·usu·al**
un·usu·al
unusuel : **un·usu·al**
unuzual : **un·usu·al**
unvail : **un·veil**
unvale : **un·veil**
un·veil
unviel : **un·veil**
unwealdy : **un·wieldy**
unweeldy : **un·wieldy**
unweildy : **un·wieldy**
un·whole·some
unwholesum : **un·whole·some**
unwhollsome : **un·whole·some**
unwholsome : **un·whole·some**
un·wieldy
upbrade : **up·braid**
up·braid
up·heav·al
upheavel : **up·heav·al**
upheeval : **up·heav·al**

upheevel : **up·heav·al**
upheival : **up·heav·al**
uphemism : **eu·phem·ism**
uphevel : **up·heav·al**
upholstary : **up·hol·stery**
upholsterry : **up·hol·stery**
up·hol·stery
upholstry : **up·hol·stery**
uphoria : **eu·pho·ria**
uppraid : **up·braid**
uproareous : **up·roar·i·ous**
up·roar·i·ous
uprorious : **up·roar·i·ous**
up·stream
upstreem : **up·stream**
Uraguay : **Uru·guay**
urainium : **ura·ni·um**
Urainus : **Ura·nus**
uraneum : **ura·ni·um**
uraniem : **ura·ni·um**
Uranis : **Ura·nus**
ura·ni·um
Ura·nus
urbain : **ur·ban**
ur·ban (of a city); **ur·bane**
  (witty)
ur·bane (witty); **ur·ban** (of a
  city)
urbanitty : **ur·ban·i·ty**
ur·ban·i·ty
urbannety : **ur·ban·i·ty**
urbannity : **ur·ban·i·ty**
urben : **ur·ban**
urchen : **ur·chin**
ur·chin
Ureguay : **Uru·guay**
urene : **urine**
ur·gen·cy
urgensy : **ur·gen·cy**
urgincy : **ur·gen·cy**
urginsy : **ur·gen·cy**
urine

urinn : **urine**
urn (vase); **earn** (work for gain)
Uroguay : **Uru·guay**
Urope : **Eu·rope**
urranium : **ura·ni·um**
Urranus : **Ura·nus**
Uru·guay
Urugway : **Uru·guay**
usabal : **us·able**
usabel : **us·able**
us·able *or* **us·eble**
usadge : **us·age**
us·age
usally : **usu·al·ly**
useable : **us·able**
us·eble *or* **us·able**
use·ful
usefull : **use·ful**
usege : **us·age**
useing : **us·ing**
userp : **usurp**
usery : **usu·ry**
usful : **use·ful**
usible : **us·able**
usidge : **us·age**
usige : **us·age**
us·ing
usirp : **usurp**
usserp : **usurp**
ussurp : **usurp**
ussury : **usu·ry**
usuage : **us·age**
usu·al·ly
usully : **usu·al·ly**
usuly : **usu·al·ly**
usurp
usury
Uta : **Utah**
Utah
utalize : **uti·lize**
utelize : **uti·lize**
utencil : **uten·sil**

utensel : **uten·sil**
uten·sil
uterice : **uter·us**
uteris : **uter·us**
uteriss : **uter·us**
uter·us
uthanasia : **eu·tha·na·sia**
utilatarian : **util·i·tar·i·an**
utiletarian : **util·i·tar·i·an**
utilety : **util·i·ty**
utilise (*Brit.*) : **uti·lize**
util·i·tar·i·an
utiliterian : **util·i·tar·i·an**
utilitty : **util·i·ty**
util·i·ty
uti·lize
utillety : **util·i·ty**
utillitarian : **util·i·tar·i·an**

utillity : **util·i·ty**
utillize : **uti·lize**
utilyze : **uti·lize**
utincil : **uten·sil**
utinsel : **uten·sil**
utinsil : **uten·sil**
utirus : **uter·us**
utopea : **uto·pia**
uto·pia
utoppia : **uto·pia**
Utta : **Utah**
ut·ter·ance
utteranse : **ut·ter·ance**
utterence : **ut·ter·ance**
utterense : **ut·ter·ance**
uttopia : **uto·pia**
utturance : **ut·ter·ance**
uturus : **uter·us**

V

vacacion : **va·ca·tion**
va·can·cy
vacansy : **va·can·cy**
vacasion : **va·ca·tion**
va·ca·tion
vaccancy : **va·can·cy**
vaccant : **va·cant**
vaccate : **va·cate**
vaccation : **va·ca·tion**
vaccene : **vac·cine**
vac·cine
vaccume : **vac·u·um**
vaccuous : **vac·u·ous**
vaccuum : **vac·u·um**
vacellate : **vac·il·late**
vacency : **va·can·cy**
vacilate : **vac·il·late**
vacillait : **vac·il·late**
vac·il·late
vacine : **vac·cine**
vacissitude : **vi·cis·si·tude**
vacseen : **vac·cine**
vacsene : **vac·cine**
vacsillate : **vac·il·late**
vacsine : **vac·cine**
vacuim : **vac·u·um**
vacuiss : **vac·u·ous**
vacume : **vac·u·um**
vac·u·ous
vac·u·um
vacuus : **vac·u·ous**
vadeville : **vaude·ville**
vag·a·bond
vagarry : **va·ga·ry**
va·ga·ry
vagebond : **vag·a·bond**
vagery : **va·ga·ry**
vaggabond : **vag·a·bond**
vaggery : **va·ga·ry**
va·grant

vagrent : **va·grant**
vagrint : **va·grant**
vagury : **va·ga·ry**
vaiporize : **va·por·ize**
vakcume : **vac·u·um**
valadictorian : **val·e·dic·to·ri·an**
va·lance (drapery); **va·lence** (in
    atoms)
valantine : **val·en·tine**
valece : **va·lise**
valed : **val·id**
valedictorean :
    val·e·dic·to·ri·an
val·e·dic·to·ri·an
valeece : **va·lise**
va·lence (in atoms); **va·lance**
    (drapery)
val·en·tine
valese : **va·lise**
valey : **val·ley**
val·iant
valice : **va·lise**
val·id
validdity : **va·lid·i·ty**
validety : **va·lid·i·ty**
validitty : **va·lid·i·ty**
va·lid·i·ty
valient : **val·iant**
va·lise
valladictorian :
    val·e·dic·to·ri·an
vallant : **val·iant**
vallantine : **val·en·tine**
valled : **val·id**
valledictorian :
    val·e·dic·to·ri·an
vallentine : **val·en·tine**
valler : **val·or**
val·ley
vallid : **val·id**

vallidity : **va·lid·i·ty**
vallient : **val·iant**
vallise : **va·lise**
vallor : **val·or**
valluable : **valu·able**
vally : **val·ley**
val·or
valour (*Brit.*) : **val·or**
valting : **vault·ing**
valuabel : **valu·able**
valu·able
valubel : **valu·able**
valuble : **valu·able**
valueble : **valu·able**
valuible : **valu·able**
valure : **val·or**
vampiar : **vam·pire**
vam·pire
vampyre : **vam·pire**
Vancoover : **Van·cou·ver**
Van·cou·ver
Vancuover : **Van·cou·ver**
Vancuver : **Van·cou·ver**
van·dal
vandel : **van·dal**
vandle : **van·dal**
vanella : **va·nil·la**
vanety : **van·i·ty**
vangard : **van·guard**
vangarde : **van·guard**
vangaurd : **van·guard**
van·guard
vanguish : **van·quish**
vanila : **va·nil·la**
va·nil·la
van·ish
vanitty : **van·i·ty**
van·i·ty
vannilla : **va·nil·la**
vannish : **van·ish**
vannity : **van·i·ty**
vanqish : **van·quish**

vanquesh : **van·quish**
van·quish
vantadge : **van·tage**
van·tage
vantege : **van·tage**
vantige : **van·tage**
vaperize : **va·por·ize**
va·pid
vaporise (*Brit.*) : **va·por·ize**
va·por·ize
vappid : **va·pid**
vapporize : **va·por·ize**
vaquous : **vac·u·ous**
varafy : **ver·i·fy**
varanda : **ve·ran·da**
varatious : **ve·ra·cious**
varcety : **var·si·ty**
varcitty : **var·si·ty**
varcity : **var·si·ty**
vareable : **vari·able**
vareance : **vari·ance**
vareation : **vari·a·tion**
varecose : **var·i·cose**
vareous : **var·i·ous**
variabal : **vari·able**
variabel : **vari·able**
vari·able
vari·ance
varianse : **vari·ance**
variasion : **vari·a·tion**
variatian : **vari·a·tion**
vari·a·tion
variatty : **va·ri·ety**
variaty : **va·ri·ety**
varible : **vari·able**
var·i·cose
varience : **vari·ance**
variense : **vari·ance**
varietty : **va·ri·ety**
va·ri·ety
varify : **ver·i·fy**
varily : **ver·i·ly**

var·i·ous
varnesh : var·nish
var·nish
varrecose : var·i·cose
varriable : vari·able
varriance : vari·ance
varriation : vari·a·tion
varricose : var·i·cose
varriety : va·ri·ety
varrious : var·i·ous
varsetty : var·si·ty
varsety : var·si·ty
varsitty : var·si·ty
var·si·ty
varyable : vari·able
varyation : vari·a·tion
varyis : var·i·ous
varyous : var·i·ous
vasal : vas·sal
vasel : vas·sal
vasillate : vac·il·late
vas·sal
vassel : vas·sal
Vatecan : Vat·i·can
Vat·i·can
Vatikan : Vat·i·can
Vattican : Vat·i·can
vaudaville : vaude·ville
vaudevile : vaude·ville
vaude·ville
vaudville : vaude·ville
vault·ing
vecinity : vi·cin·i·ty
veehicle : ve·hi·cle
Veetnam : Viet·nam
vegatable : veg·e·ta·ble
vegetabal : veg·e·ta·ble
veg·e·ta·ble
vegeteble : veg·e·ta·ble
vegetible : veg·e·ta·ble
veggetable : veg·e·ta·ble
vegitable : veg·e·ta·ble

vegtable : veg·e·ta·ble
vehamence : ve·he·mence
vehemance : ve·he·mence
vehemanse : ve·he·mence
ve·he·mence
vehemense : ve·he·mence
vehical : ve·hi·cle
vehicel : ve·hi·cle
vehickal : ve·hi·cle
vehickel : ve·hi·cle
ve·hi·cle
vehimence : ve·he·mence
Veinna : Vi·en·na
veinous : ve·nous
Veitnam : Viet·nam
veiw : view
vejetable : veg·e·ta·ble
veksatious : vex·a·tious
vellocity : ve·loc·i·ty
vellosity : ve·loc·i·ty
vellvet : vel·vet
velocety : ve·loc·i·ty
velocitty : ve·loc·i·ty
ve·loc·i·ty
velosity : ve·loc·i·ty
velvat : vel·vet
vel·vet
velvette : vel·vet
velvit : vel·vet
vemence : ve·he·mence
Venace : Ven·ice
venareal : ve·ne·re·al
venarial : ve·ne·re·al
venason : ven·i·son
Venazuela : Ven·e·zu·e·la
vendebta : ven·det·ta
vend·er or vend·or
vendeta : ven·det·ta
ven·det·ta
vendette : ven·det·ta
ven·dor or vend·er
venear : ve·neer

Venece : **Ven·ice**
ve·neer
veneir : **ve·neer**
ven·er·a·ble
ve·ne·re·al
venerial : **ve·ne·re·al**
venerible : **ven·er·a·ble**
veneson : **ven·i·son**
Venesuela : **Ven·e·zu·e·la**
Venezeula : **Ven·e·zu·e·la**
Venezuala : **Ven·e·zu·e·la**
Ven·e·zu·e·la
vengance : **ven·geance**
ven·geance
vengeanse : **ven·geance**
venge·ful
vengefull : **venge·ful**
vengence : **ven·geance**
vengense : **ven·geance**
vengful : **venge·ful**
vengiance : **ven·geance**
vengince : **ven·geance**
Ven·ice (city); **Ve·nus** (planet)
venicen : **ven·i·son**
venier : **ve·neer**
venigar : **vin·e·gar**
venim : **ven·om**
venimous : **ven·om·ous**
venirable : **ven·er·a·ble**
Venis : **Ven·ice** (city) *or* **Ve·nus**
  (planet)
Venise : **Ven·ice**
ven·i·son
Veniss : **Ven·ice** (city) *or*
  Ve·nus (planet)
Venizuela : **Ven·e·zu·e·la**
vennareal : **ve·ne·re·al**
Vennazuela : **Ven·e·zu·e·la**
venndetta : **ven·det·ta**
vennerable : **ven·er·a·ble**
vennereal : **ve·ne·re·al**
Vennezuela : **Ven·e·zu·e·la**

Vennice : **Ven·ice**
Vennis : **Ven·ice** (city) *or*
  Ve·nus (planet)
vennison : **ven·i·son**
vennom : **ven·om**
vennomous : **ven·om·ous**
vennum : **ven·om**
vennumous : **ven·om·ous**
Vennus : **Ven·ice** (city) *or*
  Ve·nus (planet)
ven·om
venomiss : **ven·om·ous**
ven·om·ous
venomus : **ven·om·ous**
venoo : **ven·ue**
ve·nous (having veins); **Ve·nus**
  (planet)
ventalate : **ven·ti·late**
ventelate : **ven·ti·late**
ven·ti·late
ventrilloquist : **ven·tril·o·quist**
ventriloquest: **ven·tril·o·quist**
ven·tril·o·quist
venue
venum : **ven·om**
venumous : **ven·om·ous**
Ve·nus (planet); **Ven·ice** (city);
  ve·nous (having veins)
veracety : **ve·rac·i·ty**
ve·ra·cious (truthful);
  vo·ra·cious (hungry)
veracitty : **ve·rac·i·ty**
ve·rac·i·ty
veracose : **var·i·cose**
verafiable : **ver·i·fi·able**
veraly : **ver·i·ly**
ve·ran·da *or* **ve·ran·dah**
ve·ran·dah *or* **ve·ran·da**
veranduh : **ve·ran·da**
verashious : **ve·ra·cious**
verasious : **ve·ra·cious**
verasitty : **ve·rac·i·ty**

verasity : **ve·rac·i·ty**
veratious : **ve·ra·cious**
verbage : **ver·biage**
verbaitim : **ver·ba·tim**
verbatem : **ver·ba·tim**
ver·ba·tim
verbatum : **ver·ba·tim**
verbeage : **ver·biage**
verbege : **ver·biage**
ver·biage
verbige : **ver·biage**
verboce : **ver·bose**
verbocity : **ver·bos·i·ty**
ver·bose
verbosety : **ver·bos·i·ty**
verbositty : **ver·bos·i·ty**
ver·bos·i·ty
verbossity : **ver·bos·i·ty**
verces : **ver·sus**
vercify : **ver·si·fy**
vercis : **ver·sus**
ver·dant
verdect : **ver·dict**
verdent : **ver·dant**
verdick : **ver·dict**
ver·dict
verdint : **ver·dant**
verefiable : **ver·i·fi·able**
verefy : **ver·i·fy**
verely : **ver·i·ly**
vergen : **vir·gin**
vergin : **vir·gin**
Verginia : **Vir·gin·ia**
vericose : **var·i·cose**
ver·i·fi·able
ver·i·fy
verifyable : **ver·i·fi·able**
verile : **vir·ile**
verillity : **vi·ril·i·ty**
ver·i·ly
verious : **var·i·ous**
verman : **ver·min**

vermen : **ver·min**
vermilian : **ver·mil·ion**
ver·mil·ion
vermillion : **ver·mil·ion**
ver·min
Ver·mont
vermooth : **ver·mouth**
Vermount : **Ver·mont**
ver·mouth
vermuth : **ver·mouth**
vernackular : **ver·nac·u·lar**
ver·nac·u·lar
vernaculer : **ver·nac·u·lar**
vernakular : **ver·nac·u·lar**
ver·nal
vernel : **ver·nal**
verracious : **ve·ra·cious**
verracity : **ve·rac·i·ty**
verraly : **ver·i·ly**
verranda : **ve·ran·da**
verrifiable : **ver·i·fi·able**
verrify : **ver·i·fy**
verrily : **ver·i·ly**
versafy : **ver·si·fy**
Ver·sailles
Versalles : **Ver·sailles**
ver·sa·tile
versatle : **ver·sa·tile**
versefy : **ver·si·fy**
versetile : **ver·sa·tile**
ver·si·fy
Versigh : **Ver·sailles**
Versilles : **Ver·sailles**
versis : **ver·sus**
versitile : **ver·sa·tile**
versitle : **ver·sa·tile**
versittle : **ver·sa·tile**
ver·sus
Versye : **Ver·sailles**
vertabra : **ver·te·bra** (*sing.*)
vertabrae : **ver·te·brae** (*plur.*)
vertacle : **ver·ti·cal**

vertago : **ver•ti•go**
ver•te•bra (*sing.*); **ver•te•brae** (*plur.*)
ver•te•brae (*plur.*); **ver•te•bra** (*sing.*)
vertebray : **ver•te•brae** (*plur.*)
vertecle : **ver•ti•cal**
vertego : **ver•ti•go**
vertibra : **ver•te•bra** (*sing.*)
vertibrae : **ver•te•brae** (*plur.*)
ver•ti•cal
verticel : **ver•ti•cal**
verticle : **ver•ti•cal**
vertiggo : **ver•ti•go**
ver•ti•go
vertikal : **ver•ti•cal**
vertue : **vir•tue**
vesel : **ves•sel**
vessal : **ves•sel**
ves•sel
vessle : **ves•sel**
vestabule : **ves•ti•bule**
vestage : **ves•tige**
vestebule : **ves•ti•bule**
vestege : **ves•tige**
vestiboole : **ves•ti•bule**
ves•ti•bule
vestidge : **ves•tige**
ves•tige
vestigeal : **ves•ti•gial**
ves•ti•gial
vetaran : **vet•er•an**
vetarinarian : **vet•er•i•nar•i•an**
vet•er•an
veteren : **vet•er•an**
veterenarian : **vet•er•i•nar•i•an**
veterin : **vet•er•an**
veterinarean : **vet•er•i•nar•i•an**
vet•er•i•nar•i•an
veterinerian : **vet•er•i•nar•i•an**
veternarian : **vet•er•i•nar•i•an**
veterran : **vet•er•an**

veterrinarian : **vet•er•i•nar•i•an**
vetiran : **vet•er•an**
ve•to
vetoe : **ve•to**
ve•toes
vetos : **ve•toes**
vettaran : **vet•er•an**
vetteran : **vet•er•an**
vetterinarian : **vet•er•i•nar•i•an**
vexacious : **vex•a•tious**
vexasious : **vex•a•tious**
vex•a•tious
vexatius : **vex•a•tious**
viabal : **vi•a•ble**
viabel : **vi•a•ble**
viabilety : **vi•a•bil•i•ty**
viabilitty : **vi•a•bil•i•ty**
vi•a•bil•i•ty
viabillity : **vi•a•bil•i•ty**
vi•a•ble
viablety : **vi•a•bil•i•ty**
viaduck : **via•duct**
via•duct
vi•al (container); **vile** (filthy)
vibility : **vi•a•bil•i•ty**
vible : **vi•a•ble**
vi•brant
vibrater : **vi•bra•tor**
vi•bra•tor
vibrent : **vi•brant**
vic•ar
vicareous : **vi•car•i•ous**
vi•car•i•ous
vicarrious : **vi•car•i•ous**
vicenity : **vi•cin•i•ty**
vicerious : **vi•car•i•ous**
vicinetty : **vi•cin•i•ty**
vicinety : **vi•cin•i•ty**
vicinitty : **vi•cin•i•ty**
vi•cin•i•ty
vicinnity : **vi•cin•i•ty**

vi•cious (immoral); vis•cous
  (thick liquid)
vicisitude : vi•cis•si•tude
vicissatude : vi•cis•si•tude
vi•cis•si•tude
vicker : vic•ar
victary : vic•to•ry
victem : vic•tim
victer : vic•tor
victery : vic•to•ry
vic•tim
vic•tor
victorry : vic•to•ry
vic•to•ry
victum : vic•tim
viddeo : vid•eo
viddio : vid•eo
vid•eo
vidio : vid•eo
viduct : via•duct
viel : vi•al (container) *or* vile
  (filthy)
Viena : Vi•en•na
Vienese : Vi•en•nese
Vi•en•na
Viennease : Vi•en•nese
Vi•en•nese
Vienneze : Vi•en•nese
Viet•nam
Vietnom : Viet•nam
view
vigalant : vig•i•lant
vigel : vig•il
vigelant : vig•i•lant
viger : vig•or
vigger : vig•or
vig•il
vig•i•lant
vigilent : vig•i•lant
vigill : vig•il
vignet : vi•gnette
vi•gnette

vig•or
vijil : vig•il
viker : vic•ar
vilafication : vil•i•fi•ca•tion
vilafy : vil•i•fy
vilage : vil•lage
vilain : vil•lain
vilan : vil•lain
vilate : vi•o•late
vile (filthy); vi•al (container)
vilefy : vil•i•fy
vile•ly
vilent : vi•o•lent
vilet : vi•o•let
vilifacation : vil•i•fi•ca•tion
vil•i•fi•ca•tion
vil•i•fy
vilin : vi•o•lin
villadge : vil•lage
vil•lage
vil•lain (evil one); vil•lein
  (peasant)
villan : vil•lain (evil one) *or*
  vil•lein (peasant)
villege : vil•lage
vil•lein (peasant); vil•lain (evil
  one)
villen : vil•lain (evil one) *or*
  vil•lein (peasant)
villidge : vil•lage
villification : vil•i•fi•ca•tion
villify : vil•i•fy
villige : vil•lage
villin : vil•lain (evil one) *or*
  vil•lein (peasant)
vily : vile•ly
vinagar : vin•e•gar
vinager : vin•e•gar
vindacate : vin•di•cate
vindecate : vin•di•cate
vineer : ve•neer
vin•e•gar

vineger : **vin•e•gar**
vineir : **ve•neer**
vinel : **vi•nyl**
vinell : **vi•nyl**
vinette : **vi•gnette**
vine•yard
viniette : **vi•gnette**
vinigar : **vin•e•gar**
vinil : **vi•nyl**
vinill : **vi•nyl**
vin•tage
vintedge : **vin•tage**
vintege : **vin•tage**
vintelate : **ven•ti•late**
vintidge : **vin•tage**
vintige : **vin•tage**
vintilate : **ven•ti•late**
Vinus : **Ven•ice** (city) *or*
   Ve•nus (planet)
vinyard : **vine•yard**
vinyette : **vi•gnette**
vi•nyl
violant : **vi•o•lent**
vi•o•late
violen : **vi•o•lin**
vi•o•lent
vi•o•let
vi•o•lin
violint : **vi•o•lent**
virgen : **vir•gin**
Virgenia : **Vir•gin•ia**
vir•gin
Vir•gin•ia
Virginnia : **Vir•gin•ia**
vir•ile
virilitty : **vi•ril•i•ty**
vi•ril•i•ty
virill : **vir•ile**
virillity : **vi•ril•i•ty**
viris : **vi•rus**
virmooth : **ver•mouth**
virmouth : **ver•mouth**

virmuth : **ver•mouth**
virrus : **vi•rus**
vir•tue
vi•rus
visability : **vis•i•bil•i•ty**
visable : **vis•i•ble**
vis•age
viscious : **vi•cious** (immoral) *or*
   vis•cous (thick liquid)
viscositty : **vis•cos•i•ty**
vis•cos•i•ty
viscossity : **vis•cos•i•ty**
vis•cous (thick liquid); **vi•cious**
   (immoral)
viseble : **vis•i•ble**
visege : **vis•age**
viser : **vi•sor**
visibal : **vis•i•ble**
visibel : **vis•i•ble**
visibilety : **vis•i•bil•i•ty**
visibilitty : **vis•i•bil•i•ty**
vis•i•bil•i•ty
visibillity : **vis•i•bil•i•ty**
vis•i•ble
visige : **vis•age**
visinity : **vi•cin•i•ty**
visious : **vi•cious**
visissitude : **vi•cis•si•tude**
visiter : **vis•i•tor**
vis•i•tor
vi•sor
vissage : **vis•age**
vissitor : **vis•i•tor**
vis•u•al
visualise : **vis•u•al•ize**
vis•u•al•ize
visuel : **vis•u•al**
visule : **vis•u•al**
visulize : **vis•u•al•ize**
vi•tal
vitalitty : **vi•tal•i•ty**
vi•tal•i•ty

vitallity : **vi·tal·i·ty**
vitamen : **vi·ta·min**
vi·ta·min
vitel : **vi·tal**
vitemin : **vi·ta·min**
vit·re·ous
vitrious : **vit·re·ous**
vivacety : **vi·vac·i·ty**
vi·va·cious
vivacitty : **vi·vac·i·ty**
vi·vac·i·ty
vivasity : **vi·vac·i·ty**
vivassity : **vi·vac·i·ty**
vivatious : **vi·va·cious**
vix·en
vixin : **vix·en**
vizage : **vis·age**
vizer : **vi·sor**
vizitor : **vis·i·tor**
vocabularry : **vo·cab·u·lary**
vo·cab·u·lary
vocabulerry : **vo·cab·u·lary**
vocabulery : **vo·cab·u·lary**
vocal chords : **vo·cal cords**
vo·cal cords
vodca : **vod·ka**
voddville : **vaude·ville**
vod·ka
voiage : **voy·age**
vol·a·tile
volatle : **vol·a·tile**
volcanno : **vol·ca·no**
vol·ca·no
volentary : **vol·un·tary**
volenteer : **vol·un·teer**
voletile : **vol·a·tile**
voletle : **vol·a·tile**
volkano : **vol·ca·no**
vollatile : **vol·a·tile**

vol·ley·ball
vollume : **vol·ume**
vollyball : **vol·ley·ball**
volt·age
voltege : **volt·age**
voltige : **volt·age**
vol·ume
voluntarry : **vol·un·tary**
vol·un·tary
vol·un·teer
volunteir : **vol·un·teer**
voluntery : **vol·un·tary**
voluntier : **vol·un·teer**
vom·it
vommit : **vom·it**
vo·ra·cious (hungry);
  ve·ra·cious (truthful)
votarry : **vo·ta·ry**
vo·ta·ry
votery : **vo·ta·ry**
voudeville : **vaude·ville**
vow·el
vowl : **vow·el**
voy·age
voyege : **voy·age**
voyige : **voy·age**
vulcano : **vol·ca·no**
vul·gar
vulger : **vul·gar**
vulnerabal : **vul·ner·a·ble**
vul·ner·a·ble
vulnerble : **vul·ner·a·ble**
vulnerible : **vul·ner·a·ble**
vurbatim : **ver·ba·tim**
vurbose : **ver·bose**
vurbosity : **ver·bos·i·ty**
vurnacular : **ver·nac·u·lar**
vynel : **vi·nyl**
vynil : **vi·nyl**

W

wachful : **watch·ful**

wad (small mass); **wade** (to walk in water)

waddel : **wad·dle** (to move clumsily) or **wat·tle** (hut)

wad·dle (to move clumsily); **wat·tle** (hut)

wade (to walk in water); **wad** (small mass)

wadle : **wad·dle** (to move clumsily) or **wat·tle** (hut)

wafe : **waif**

waf·er (disk); **waiv·er** (relinquishment); **wav·er** (to hesitate)

waffer : **wa·fer** (disk) or **waiv·er** (relinquishment) or **wav·er** (to hesitate)

waf·fle

wafle : **waf·fle**

wagen : **wag·on**

wa·ger

waggon (*Brit.*) : **wag·on**

waght : **weight**

wag·on

wagur : **wa·ger**

waif

waifer : **wa·fer** (disk) or **waiv·er** (relinquishment) or **wav·er** (to hesitate)

Wai·ki·ki

wail (to cry); **whale** (mammal)

wain (cart); **wane** (to diminish)

wainscoat : **wain·scot**

wain·scot

wainscote : **wain·scot**

wairily : **wari·ly**

waist (part of body); **waste** (unused)

waistbasket : **waste·bas·ket**

waistbassket : **waste·bas·ket**

waistful : **waste·ful**

waistrel : **wast·rel**

wait (to stay for); **weight** (heaviness)

waiteress : **wait·ress**

wait·ress

waive (to forgo); **wave** (ridge of water; gesture)

waiv·er (relinquishment); **waf·er** (disk); **wav·er** (to hesitate)

wake·ful

wakefull : **wake·ful**

walet : **wal·let**

walit : **wal·let**

wallep : **wal·lop**

wal·let

wallip : **wal·lop**

wallit : **wal·let**

wallnut : **wal·nut**

walloe : **wal·low**

wal·lop

wal·low

wallris : **wal·rus**

wallrus : **wal·rus**

wal·nut

walow : **wal·low**

walris : **wal·rus**

walriss : **wal·rus**

wal·rus

walts : **waltz**

waltz

wane (to diminish); **wain** (cart)

wanescot : **wain·scot**

want (desire); **wont** (custom); **won't** (will not)

wanten : **wan·ton**

wan·ton

warant : **war·rant**

warbal : **war·ble**
war·ble
war·den
wardon : **war·den**
ware·house
warely : **wari·ly**
warent : **war·rant**
warf : **wharf**
wari·ly
warior : **war·rior**
war·rant
war·ran·tee (one who receives warranty); **war·ran·ty** (guarantee)
war·ran·ty (guarantee); **war·ran·tee** (one who receives warranty)
warrent : **war·rant**
warrentee : **war·ran·tee** (one who receives warranty) *or* **war·ran·ty** (guarantee)
warrier : **war·rior**
warrint : **war·rant**
warrintee : **war·ran·tee** (one who receives warranty) *or* **war·ran·ty** (guarantee)
war·rior
warsh : **wash**
Warshington : **Wash·ing·ton**
wash
washabel : **wash·able**
wash·able
washeble : **wash·able**
washible : **wash·able**
Washingten : **Wash·ing·ton**
Washingtin : **Wash·ing·ton**
Wash·ing·ton
Washinton : **Wash·ing·ton**
was·sail
wassal : **was·sail**
wassel : **was·sail**
wassell : **was·sail**

wasstrel : **wast·rel**
wastbasket : **waste·bas·ket**
waste (loss of use); **waist** (part of body)
waste·bas·ket
wastebaskit : **waste·bas·ket**
waste·ful
wastefull : **waste·ful**
wastful : **waste·ful**
wastral : **wast·rel**
wast·rel
wastrell : **wast·rel**
wastrill : **wast·rel**
watch·ful
watchfull : **watch·ful**
wa·ter
wateress : **wait·ress**
watermelan : **wa·ter·mel·on**
watermelin : **wa·ter·mel·on**
watermellin : **wa·ter·mel·on**
watermellon : **wa·ter·mel·on**
wa·ter·mel·on
waterry : **wa·tery**
watershead : **wa·ter·shed**
wa·ter·shed
wa·tery
watter : **wa·ter**
wattermelon : **wa·ter·mel·on**
wattershed : **wa·ter·shed**
wattery : **wa·tery**
wave (ridge of water; gesture); **waive** (to forgo)
wav·er (to hesitate); **waf·er** (disk); **waiv·er** (relinquishment)
wayfairer : **way·far·er**
way·far·er
waylade : **way·laid**
way·laid
waylayed : **way·laid**
way·ward
waywerd : **way·ward**

wayword : **way·ward**
weadle : **whee·dle**
weak·en
weakleng : **weak·ling**
weak·ling
weald : **wield**
wealp : **whelp**
wealterweight : **wel·ter·weight**
wealthy
weapen : **weap·on**
weap·on
wearas : **where·as**
wearhouse : **ware·house**
wearisom : **wea·ri·some**
wea·ri·some
weary
wearysome : **wea·ri·some**
wearysum : **wea·ri·some**
weasal : **wea·sel**
wea·sel
weasil : **wea·sel**
weath·er (atmospheric condition); **weth·er** (sheep); **wheth·er** (if)
weave
weavel : **wee·vil**
weavil : **wee·vil**
Weddnesday : **Wednes·day**
Wednes·day
weedal : **whee·dle**
weedle : **whee·dle**
weeken : **weak·en**
weekling : **weak·ling**
weel : **wheel**
weeld : **wield**
weerd : **weird**
weerisome : **wea·ri·some**
weerwolf : **were·wolf**
weerwulf : **were·wolf**
weery : **weary**
weerysome : **wea·ri·some**
weesel : **wea·sel**

weeval : **wee·vil**
weeve : **weave**
weevel : **wee·vil**
wee·vil
weght : **weight**
weight (heaviness); **wait** (to stay for)
weiken : **weak·en**
weild : **wield**
weird
weirwolf : **were·wolf**
weiry : **weary**
weirysome : **wea·ri·some**
weisel : **wea·sel**
weive : **weave**
weivil : **wee·vil**
welch (to cheat); **Welsh** (from Wales)
wel·come
welcume : **wel·come**
welfair : **wel·fare**
wel·fare
wellcome : **wel·come**
wellfair : **wel·fare**
wellfare : **wel·fare**
wellterweight : **wel·ter·weight**
wellthy : **wealthy**
welp : **whelp**
Welsh (from Wales); **welch** (to cheat)
wel·ter·weight
welterwieght : **wel·ter·weight**
welthy : **wealthy**
weman : **wom·en**
wemman : **wom·en**
wence : **whence** (from where) *or* **wince** (to flinch)
wendlass : **wind·lass**
Wendnisday : **Wednes·day**
Wendsday : **Wednes·day**
wendward : **wind·ward**
Wensday : **Wednes·day**

wepen : **weap·on**
wepon : **weap·on**
weppen : **weap·on**
weppin : **weap·on**
weppon : **weap·on**
were (*past of* to be); **we're** (we are)
we're (we are); **were** (*past of* to be)
were·wolf
werewulf : **were·wolf**
werl : **whirl**
wership : **wor·ship**
wersted : **wor·sted**
werthy : **wor·thy**
werwolf : **were·wolf**
Wesconsin : **Wis·con·sin**
West Verginia : **West Vir·gin·ia**
West Vir·gin·ia
west·ward
westwerd : **west·ward**
westword : **west·ward**
wet (moist); **whet** (to sharpen)
weth·er (sheep); **weath·er** (atmospheric condition); **wheth·er** (if)
wetstone : **whet·stone**
whale (mammal); **wail** (to cry)
wharf
wharfs : **wharves**
wharves
wheadle : **whee·dle**
wheal : **wheel**
whealp : **whelp**
wheaze : **wheeze**
whee·dle
wheel
wheeze : **wheeze**
wheil : **wheel**
whelp
whemsical : **whim·si·cal**

whence (from where); **wince** (to flinch)
wheras : **where·as**
where as : **where·as**
where·as
wherehouse : **ware·house**
wherewolf : **were·wolf**
whet (to sharpen); **wet** (moist)
wheth·er (if); **weath·er** (atmospheric condition); **weth·er** (sheep)
whetstoan : **whet·stone**
whet·stone
which (what one); **witch** (sorceress)
whicked : **wick·ed** (evil) *or* **wick·et** (gate)
whicket : **wick·ed** (evil) *or* **wick·et** (gate)
whickit : **wick·ed** (evil) *or* **wick·et** (gate)
whim·per
whimsecal : **whim·si·cal**
whim·si·cal
whimsickal : **whim·si·cal**
whim·sy
whimzy : **whim·sy**
whince : **whence** (from where) *or* **wince** (to flinch)
whine (sound); **wine** (beverage)
whin·ny (neigh); **whiny** (given to whining)
whiny (given to whining); **whin·ny** (neigh)
whip
whipet : **whip·pet**
whipit : **whip·pet**
whipoorwill : **whip·poor·will**
whipperwill : **whip·poor·will**
whip·pet
whippit : **whip·pet**
whip·poor·will

whipporwill : **whip•poor•will**
whirl
whis•ker
whis•key *or* **whis•ky**
whis•ky *or* **whis•key**
whis•per
whissle : **whis•tle**
whisstel : **whis•tle**
whisteria : **wis•te•ria**
whistful : **wist•ful**
whis•tle
whith•er (to where); **with•er** (to
 shrivel)
whittal : **whit•tle**
whittel : **whit•tle**
whit•tle
whol•ly (completely); **hol•ly**
 (tree); **ho•ly** (sacred)
wholy : **ho•ly** (sacred) *or*
 whol•ly (completely)
who's (who is); **whose**
 (belonging to whom)
whose (belonging to whom);
 who's (who is)
wich : **which** (what one) *or*
 witch (sorceress)
wick•ed (evil); **wick•et** (gate)
wick•et (gate); **wick•ed** (evil)
wickit : **wick•ed** (evil) *or*
 wick•et (gate)
wieght : **weight**
wield
wierd : **weird**
wierwolf : **were•wolf**
wiery : **weary**
wiesel : **wea•sel**
wieve : **weave**
wievil : **wee•vil**
Wikeekee : **Wai•ki•ki**
wikked : **wick•ed** (evil) *or*
 wick•et (gate)
wildernes : **wil•der•ness**

wil•der•ness
wilderniss : **wil•der•ness**
wildurness : **wil•der•ness**
wil•ful *or* **will•ful**
wilfull : **will•ful**
wil•i•ness
willderness : **wil•der•ness**
will•ful *or* **wil•ful**
willfull : **will•ful**
wilyness : **wil•i•ness**
wiman : **wom•en**
wimen : **wom•en**
wimman : **wom•en**
wimmen : **wom•en**
wimper : **whim•per**
wimsical : **whim•si•cal**
wimsy : **whim•sy**
winary : **win•ery**
wince (to flinch); **whence** (from
 where)
windlas : **wind•lass**
wind•lass
windles : **wind•lass**
Windsday : **Wednes•day**
windsheald : **wind•shield**
windsheeld : **wind•shield**
windsheild : **wind•shield**
wind•shield
wind•ward
windwerd : **wind•ward**
windword : **wind•ward**
wine (beverage); **whine** (sound)
winerry : **win•ery**
win•ery
wintery : **win•try**
win•try
Wioming : **Wy•o•ming**
wip : **whip**
wippet : **whip•pet**
wippoorwill : **whip•poor•will**
wird : **weird**
wirl : **whirl**

Wisconsen : **Wis•con•sin**
Wis•con•sin
wis•dom
wisdum : **wis•dom**
wish•ful
wishfull : **wish•ful**
wisker : **whis•ker**
wiskey : **whis•key**
Wiskonsin : **Wis•con•sin**
wisky : **whis•key**
wisper : **whis•per**
wissel : **whis•tle**
wis•ta•ria *or* **wis•te•ria**
wis•te•ria *or* **wis•ta•ria**
wistfull : **wist•ful**
wistle : **whis•tle**
witch (sorceress); **which** (what
    one)
with•al
withall : **with•al**
with•draw•al
withdrawel : **with•draw•al**
withdrawl : **with•draw•al**
with•er (to shrivel); **whith•er** (to
    where)
with•hold
withold : **with•hold**
wit•ness
witniss : **wit•ness**
wit•ti•cism
wittisism : **wit•ti•cism**
wittle : **whit•tle**
wittness : **wit•ness**
wittycism : **wit•ti•cism**
wiz•ard
wiz•ard•ry
wizerd : **wiz•ard**
wizerdry : **wiz•ard•ry**
wizzard : **wiz•ard**
wizzardry : **wiz•ard•ry**
wizzerd : **wiz•ard**
wizzerdry : **wiz•ard•ry**

wod : **wad**
woddle : **wad•dle** (to move
    clumsily) *or* **wat•tle** (hut)
wofel : **waf•fle**
woffle : **waf•fle**
wofle : **waf•fle**
wolf (animal); **woof** (weaving)
wolfs : **wolves**
wollow : **wal•low**
woltz : **waltz**
wolves
wom•an (*sing.*); **wom•en** (*plur.*)
wom•en (*plur.*); **wom•an** (*sing.*)
womman : **wom•an**
wommen : **wom•en**
won•der•ful
wonderfull : **won•der•ful**
wonderous : **won•drous**
won•drous
wont (custom); **want** (desire);
    won't (will not)
won't (will not); **want** (desire);
    wont (custom)
woof (weaving); **wolf** (animal)
wool•en *or* **wool•len**
wool•len *or* **wool•en**
wool•ly
wooly : **wool•ly**
worbal : **war•ble**
worble : **war•ble**
word•age
wordege : **word•age**
wordige : **word•age**
world•li•ness
worldlyness : **world•li•ness**
wor•ri•some
worrysome : **wor•ri•some**
worrysum : **wor•ri•some**
wor•ship
wor•ship•ing *or* **wor•ship•ping**
wor•ship•ping *or* **wor•ship•ing**
worstead : **wor•sted**

wor·sted
wor·thy
worysome : wor·ri·some
wranglar : wran·gler
wran·gler
wrastle : wres·tle
wraught : wrought
wreak (to inflict); reek (to stink); wreck (to destroy)
wreath (*noun*); wreathe (*verb*)
wreathe (*verb*); wreath (*noun*)
wrech : wreak (to inflict) *or* wreck (to destroy) *or* wretch (miserable one)
wreck (to destroy); wreak (to inflict)
wreck·age
wreckege : wreck·age
wreckige : wreck·age
wreek : wreak (to inflict) *or* wreck (to destroy)
wreeth : wreath (*noun*)
wreethe : wreathe (*verb*)
wreith : wreath (*noun*)
wreithe : wreathe (*verb*)
wrekage : wreck·age
wrench
wressel : wres·tle
wrestal : wres·tle
wrestel : wres·tle
wres·tle
wretch (miserable one); retch (to vomit)

wriggal : wrig·gle
wriggel : wrig·gle
wrig·gle
wrigle : wrig·gle
wrily : wry·ly
wrinch : wrench
wrinkal : wrin·kle
wrinkel : wrin·kle
wrin·kle
wrist
writen : writ·ten
writ·er
writh : writhe
writhe
writ·ing
writ·ten
writter : writ·er
writting : writ·ing
wrought
wry (ironic); rye (grain)
wry·ly
wrythe : writhe
wufe : wolf (animal) *or* woof (weaving)
wulf : wolf (animal) *or* woof (weaving)
wunderful : won·der·ful
wundrous : won·drous
wursted : wor·sted
wurthy : wor·thy
wyerd : weird
Wykiki : Wai·ki·ki
Wy·o·ming
wyrd : weird

X

xe•non
xe•no•pho•bia
Xe•rox
xilophone : **xy•lo•phone**

xylaphone : **xy•lo•phone**
xylephone : **xy•lo•phone**
xy•lo•phone

Y

yacht
yack : **yak**
yaht : **yacht**
yak
yall : **yawl** (sailboat) *or* **yowl** (howl)
yamaka : **yar·mul·ke**
Yanckee : **Yan·kee**
Yan·kee
Yankey : **Yan·kee**
Yankie : **Yan·kee**
Yanky : **Yan·kee**
yard·age
yardege : **yard·age**
yardidge : **yard·age**
yardige : **yard·age**
yar·mul·ke
yat : **yacht**
yaught : **yacht**
yaun : **yawn**
yawl (sailboat); **yowl** (howl)
yawn
yeald : **yield**
year
yearn·ing
yeast
yeer : **year**
yeest : **yeast**
yeild : **yield**
yello : **yel·low**
yelloe : **yel·low**
yel·low
yelow : **yel·low**
Yeman : **Ye·men**
Ye·men
yeo·man
yerning : **yearn·ing**
yerself : **your·self**
yestday : **yes·ter·day**
yes·ter·day

yestoday : **yes·ter·day**
yesturday : **yes·ter·day**
yew (tree); **ewe** (female sheep); **you** (*pron.*)
Yid·dish
Yidish : **Yid·dish**
yield
yo·del
yodell : **yo·del**
yo·ga (Hindu philosophy); **yo·gi** (follower of yoga)
yogah : **yo·ga**
yogart : **yo·gurt**
yogert : **yo·gurt**
yogha : **yo·ga**
yoghi : **yo·gi**
yoghourt : **yo·gurt**
yoghurt : **yo·gurt**
yo·gi (follower of yoga); **yo·ga** (Hindu philosophy)
yo·gurt
yoke (harness); **yolk** (egg yellow)
yo·kel
yokle : **yo·kel**
yolk (egg yellow); **yoke** (harness)
yoman : **yeo·man**
Yoming : **Wy·o·ming**
yondur : **yon·der**
yool : **yule**
yor : **yore** (time past) *or* **your** (belonging to you) *or* **you're** (you are)
yore (time past); **your** (belonging to you); **you're** (you are)
Yosemety : **Yo·sem·i·te**
Yo·sem·i·te
Yosemitty : **Yo·sem·i·te**

Yosimete : **Yo·sem·i·te**
yot : **yacht**
you (*pron.*); **ewe** (female
    sheep); **yew** (tree)
young
youngstor : **young·ster**
your (belonging to you); **yore**
    (time past); **you're** (you are)
you're (you are); **yore** (time
    past); **your** (belonging to
    you)
yours
your's : **yours**
your·self
yoursself : **your·self**
youth
Yu·ca·tán
yuc·ca

Yuccatan : **Yu·ca·tán**
yucka : **yuc·ca**
Yucon : **Yu·kon**
yuel : **yule**
Yugaslavia : **Yu·go·sla·via**
Yu·go·sla·via *or* **Ju·go·sla·via**
Yugoslovia : **Yu·go·sla·via**
Yu·kon
yule
yull : **yule**
yung : **young**
yur : **yore** (time past) *or* **your**
    (*pron.*) *or* **you're** (you are)
yurning : **yearn·ing**
yurself : **your·self**
Yutah : **Utah**
yuth : **youth**

Z

Zambeezi : **Zam·be·zi**
Zam·be·si *or* **Zam·be·zi**
Zam·be·zi *or* **Zam·be·si**
Zambezy : **Zam·be·zi**
zaney : **za·ny**
Zansibar : **Zan·zi·bar**
za·ny
Zan·zi·bar
zar : **czar**
zeabra : **ze·bra**
zeal
zeal·ot
zeal·ous
zealus : **zeal·ous**
zearo : **ze·ro**
ze·bra
zeel : **zeal**
zeenith : **ze·nith**
zefer : **zeph·yr**
zeffer : **zeph·yr**
zefir : **zeph·yr**
zellot : **zeal·ot**
zellous : **zeal·ous**
zelot : **zeal·ot**
zeneth : **ze·nith**
zenia : **zin·nia**
ze·nith
zennith : **ze·nith**
zenon : **xe·non**
zenophobia : **xe·no·pho·bia**
zepelin : **zep·pe·lin**
zepher : **zeph·yr**
zephir : **zeph·yr**
zeph·yr
zep·pe·lin
zeppilen : **zep·pe·lin**
zercon : **zir·con**
ze·ro

Zerox : **Xe·rox**
zigote : **zy·gote**
zinc
zinck : **zinc**
zin·fan·del
zinfendel : **zin·fan·del**
zinfundel : **zin·fan·del**
zinia : **zin·nia**
zink : **zinc**
zin·nia
zinya : **zin·nia**
zippur : **zip·per**
zir·con
zirkon : **zir·con**
ziro : **ze·ro**
zoan : **zone**
zodeac : **zo·di·ac**
zo·di·ac
zodiac : **zo·di·ac**
zodiack : **zo·di·ac**
zodiak : **zo·di·ac**
zology : **zo·ol·o·gy**
zom·bie
zomby : **zom·bie**
zoolegy : **zo·ol·o·gy**
zo·ol·o·gy
Zooloo : **Zu·lu**
zuc·chi·ni
zuccini : **zuc·chi·ni**
zucheni : **zuc·chi·ni**
zukeeni : **zuc·chi·ni**
Zu·lu
zuology : **zo·ol·o·gy**
Zu·rich
Zurick : **Zu·rich**
zurkon : **zir·con**
Zurrich : **Zu·rich**
zy·gote
zylophone : **xy·lo·phone**

Guidelines for American English Spelling

1. *I* BEFORE *E*...

The most well-known spelling rule is

> *i* before *e*
> except after *c*
> or when sounded like *ay*
> as in *neighbor* and *weigh*.

This one works for many common words like *field, niece, receive*, and *ceiling*. The rule even works for some more unusual words like *sleigh* and *chow mein*. But there are a number of qualifications and exceptions.

a. The rule applies only when the *c* is sounded like *see*. *Science* is spelled *ie*, because the *c* is not sounded *see*. When the *c* is sounded as *sh*, the spelling also remains "*i* before *e*," as in *efficient, proficient*, and *ancient*.

b. The "*i* before *e*" rule applies after a *see* sound, even when the letter *c* is not actually present, as in *seize* and *seizure*.

c. The following words are spelled *ei* even though they do not come after a *see* sound and are not sounded *ay*:

caffeine	*height*
codeine	*leisure*
counterfeit	*neither*
either	*protein*
forfeit	*sovereign*
heifer	*weird*

d. The following words follow a *see* sound, yet are spelled *ie*:

    fancier   *financier*   *siege*

2. *-CEDE/-CEED/-SEDE*

There are scores of verbs that end with the sound *-seed*. All of these are spelled *-cede* except for four:

    succeed   *exceed*   *proceed*

Only one *-seed* verb ends *-sede*:

    supersede

3. *-IFY/-EFY*

There are likewise a great number of verbs ending *-ify*. Only five end *-efy*:

    liquefy   *stupefy*
    putrefy   *tumefy*
    rarefy

4. *-ND* BECOMES *-NSE*

When a verb ends *-nd*, some of the words derived from it will substitute *s* for *d*:

    defend   →   *defense*
    expand   →   *expansive*
    offend   →   *offense*
    pretend →   *pretense*
    suspend →   *suspenseful*

5. *-DGE* ENDINGS

Words ending *-dge* drop the *e* before adding *-ment*:

    abridge   →   *abridgment*
    acknowledge →   *acknowledgment*
    judge   →   *judgment*

6. -ABLE/-IBLE

There are more words ending *-able* than *-ible*, so if it comes to a coin toss, choose *-able*. Generally, *-able* is added to words that could stand alone without a suffix:

agree	→	*agreeable*
break	→	*breakable*
depend	→	*dependable*
predict	→	*predictable*

-able also follows word stems ending *i*: *appreciable, reliable, sociable*.

The ending *-ible* is usually added to word parts that could not stand alone without the suffix:

aud	+	*ible*	=	*audible*
cred	+	*ible*	=	*credible*
feas	+	*ible*	=	*feasible*
vis	+	*ible*	=	*visible*

7. HARD *C*/SOFT *C*

The letter *c* can be sounded like a *k* (as in *cash*) or like an *s* (as in *city*). These are called "hard *c*" and "soft *c*," respectively.

Normally, when adding *-able* to a word ending in *-e*, drop the *e*:

desire	→	*desirable*
pleasure	→	*pleasurable*
use	→	*usable*

However, if a word ends soft *c* + *e*, retain the *e* befor *-able* (to retain the soft *c* sound):

notice	→	*noticeable*
peace	→	*peaceable*
service	→	*serviceable*

Word stems ending with a hard *c* sound take the *-able* suffix:

applicable
despicable
implacable

8. HARD *G*/SOFT *G*

Like the letter *c*, *g* can be sounded as a "hard *g*" (as in *gate*) or "soft *g*" (as in *gentle*). The spelling rules regarding hard *g* and soft *g* are similar to those concerning hard *c* and soft *c*.

Words ending soft *g* + *e* retain the *e* before adding *-able* or *-ous* (to retain the soft *g* sound):

change	→	*changeable*
knowledge	→	*knowledgeable*
manage	→	*manageable*
advantage	→	*advantageous*
courage	→	*courageous*
outrage	→	*outrageous*

Word stems ending hard *g* add *-able*:

indefatigable   *navigable*

Soft *g* may also be followed by *-ible* endings (see Rule 6 above):

eligible   *negligible*
intelligible   *tangible*

9. *C* ENDINGS

Words ending in *c* add a *k* (to retain the hard *c* sound) before adding a suffix:

bivouac	→	*bivouacked*
frolic	→	*frolicking*
panic	→	*panicking*
shellac	→	*shellacked*

10. *-Y/-EY*

In forming plurals, a final *-y* preceded by a consonant is usually replaced by *ie* before adding *s*:

baby	→	*babies*
caddy	→	*caddies*
poppy	→	*poppies*

But if the word ends *-ey*, simply add *s*:

alley	→	*alleys*
attorney	→	*attorneys*
chimney	→	*chimneys*
valley	→	*valleys*

(One exception here is *money* → *monies.*)

11. *PRIZE/-PRISE*

Prize ends *-ze*. But when part of another word, the ending is spelled *-prise*:

comprise	*enterprise*	*surprise*

12. *-N + -NESS*

When adding *-ness* to a word already ending with an *n*, retain both *n*'s:

drunkenness	*greenness*
evenness	*thinness*

13. ADDING *-LY*

Most words ending in *e* retain the *e* when the ending *-ly* is added.

love	→	*lovely*
base	→	*basely*

There are three common exceptions, words in which the *e* is dropped when *-ly* is added:

true	→	*truly*
due	→	*duly*
whole	→	*wholly*

When adding *-ly* to words ending in *l,* retain the *l:*

brutal	→	*brutally*
cynical	→	*cynically*

14. WORDS ENDING IN SILENT *E*

Most words drop a silent final *e* before adding a suffix beginning with a vowel. The *e* is usually not dropped if the suffix begins with a consonant:

suffix begins with vowel			suffix begins with consonant		
forgive	→	*forgiving*	*forgive*	→	*forgiveness*
confine	→	*confining*	*confine*	→	*confinement*

15. DOUBLING CONSONANTS

When adding *-ed* or *-ing* to words ending in *t* or *l* preceded by a single vowel, double the *t* or *l* if the last syllable of the word is accented. Use only one *t* or *l* if the last syllable is not accented:

last syllable accented			last syllable unaccented		
commit	→	*committed*	*limit*	→	*limited*
control	→	*controlling*	*cancel*	→	*canceled*

Words ending in a single accented vowel and consonant usually double the consonant when a suffix that begins with a vowel is added. The consonant is usually not doubled if the suffix begins with a consonant:

suffix begins with vowel			suffix begins with consonant		
fit	→	*fitting*	*fit*	→	*fitful*
regret	→	*regretting*	*regret*	→	*regretful*

16. *-ISE/-IZE*

In American spelling, there are hundreds of verbs ending in *-ize*. There are only ten common verbs ending in *-ise*:

advertise	*exercise*
advise	*improvise*
chastise	*revise*
despise	*supervise*
devise	*surprise*